ALWAYS ON THE OFFENSE

ALWAYS ON THE OFFENSE

BY MIKE SCHMIDT
WITH BARBARA WALDER

NEW YORK   1982   ATHENEUM

Photographs by Daniel Kron

Library of Congress Cataloging in Publication Data
Schmidt, Mike, 1949–
    Always on the offense.

        1. Baseball—Offense.   2. Schmidt, Mike,
1949–   .   3. Baseball players—United States—
Biography.   I. Walder, Barbara.   II. Title.
GV867.7.S35   796.357'2   80–69764
ISBN 0–689–11165–7   AACR2

Picture design by Robert Michaels
Composition by American-Stratford Graphic Services, Inc.
Brattleboro, Vermont
Printed and bound by Halliday Lithograph Corporation,
West Hanover and Plympton, Massachusetts
First Printing May 1982
Second Printing September 1982

For Jack, Lois, Donna, Jessica Rae, and Jonathan

INTRODUCTION

I DIDN'T have to come to Philadelphia to find out what kind of player Mike Schmidt is. When I was a Red and the Phillies came to Cincinnati, Mike was always the Reds-killer. He seemed to hit two or three home runs in every series. In fact he has more home runs in Riverfront Stadium than any other opposing player.

But then as now, Mike helped to win games with more than home runs. He's one of the premier players in the game today because he understands there's more to offense than just swinging for the fences. Joe Morgan got two MVP awards for winning games by getting base hits, turning double plays, and running the bases—for all the ways he could help his team win. And Mike has won his two League MVPs and his World Series MVP for the same reason. He wins games by being Mike Schmidt the feared home run hitter, the Gold Glove third baseman, and Mike Schmidt the knowledgeable baserunner.

Mike and I may have different styles at the plate, but we share many of the same ideas about how to play the game and how to use our ability to do it. We also share a love for the game. He plays with just as much intensity as I do, and I know the pride he takes in his game. I respect and admire him for the way he's used his ability to become the player he is today. And knowing what makes him tick, I know he will become an even better player. The fans are clapping for him now and they should. This man can play—this man plays to win. He can help you learn to play, too, with *Always on the Offense*.

PETE ROSE

CONTENTS

ALWAYS ON THE OFFENSE

ALWAYS ON THE OFFENSE

HOME RUNS ARE an exciting part of baseball. I think the average fan, hearing my name, thinks of home runs, because of the consistency I've shown in leading the majors in 1974, 1975, 1976, 1980, and 1981 and in hitting more home runs than any other major leaguer over the last eight years.

But in that time I've also averaged 100 walks, 100 runs batted in, and 100 runs scored a year. Those statistics are just as important to me as my home runs.

I've learned that always being on the offense in baseball means playing situational baseball. The question I always ask myself is, What can I do in this situation that will help my team score runs? It could be a home run or a bunt, a sacrifice fly or hitting behind the runner, a stolen base or a smart slide—whatever helps my team score runs.

That's why runs batted in is the most important statistic for me as a hitter. Home runs in key situations are important, but that kind of hitting really takes discipline. Any batter strong enough can swing as hard as he can all year long and hit 20 home runs—but he'll probably also hit .200. The key is to be able to hit .280 or .290, drive in 120 runs, and still hit 30–35 home runs a year.

In offensive baseball, hitting adapted to the game situation—hitting to help score runs—is ideal. Even young players should be aware of game situations. They should be aware, for instance, when it is essential to try to make contact with the ball. Late in the game, with a man on first and the tying run on third, there's no way you should overswing, because you have to put the ball into play. Even if it means hitting into a double play, you have to make contact. Don't strike out swinging for a home run.

At the plate and on the bases then, and even defensing offensively in the field, you should have a plan in mind. And that plan should be dictated by the game situation. That's the way a player has to think to always be on the offense in baseball.

I'd like to be remembered as a player who could do just that: adapt to a game situation by doing a little bit of everything—run, field, drive in runs, hit with power, and hit for average. Only a select few in baseball have been able to do these things, but those are the players I've always admired. I didn't have one particular idol growing up, but those players who could play all phases of the game well—Roberto Clemente, Mickey Mantle, Hank Aaron—did influence me.

This ideal of "doing it all" may not seem to fit too well with

my .263 lifetime batting average, and many times I've been criticized for trying to be an all-around offensive player. It's been said
that I overthink, try to do too much by going outside my limitations and therefore interfere with my natural ability. Some have
argued that I'd be better off if I just swung from the heels at every
pitch, rather than searching constantly for that smooth, sweet
stroke.

There's some validity to that theory. Polished styles of hitting
and concern for pitch selection usually are for players who don't
have the natural ability to go up there and hit whatever's pitched.
But with the 1980 and '81 seasons under my belt, I know that if I
can team my natural ability with a solid theory on the way I want
to hit, I'll be on my way.

I'm not ready to say that all my theories and concepts haven't
hindered my performance at times in the past. They might have.
Many times I went through periods when I wanted to get rid of
all my so-called ideas about hitting and get up there and turn it
on, swing hard at everything. But for the last seven years, except
for an off-year in 1978, I've played as well as anybody in baseball.

My use of the bunt in the 1980 World Series supports my
theories about hitting and the game situation. Without the bunt
as one of my tools, I couldn't have set up the sequence of at-bats
that resulted in a crucial infield hit in Game Five. Earlier in the
Series I had attempted to bunt, then bunted successfully. So
when I led off the ninth inning of Game Five, the Royals infielders were so concerned about a bunt that the third baseman was
not in position to handle my smash to third. That was pure situational hitting, a "power hitter" using the bunt as effectively as the
home run.

All my experiences in nine years with the Phillies have taught me that it's best to be an all-around player, one who can make things happen with his bat and is aware of and understands situational hitting.

Not that I mind being known as a home run hitter. Fans love home runs more than any other part of the game, and home runs are an important part of baseball. One swing of the bat can turn a game around, spark the team, ease the pressure of a game, or make the pitcher mad enough to get him off his game. A home run hitter can also intimidate the pitcher enough to get good pitches for the man in front of him, because the pitcher doesn't want *two* more runs on the scoreboard.

Home runs are fun to hit, too. It's gratifying to hit the ball right on the "meat" of the bat and see how far out of the ball park it can go. I've felt this way about home runs ever since childhood, when I was the only batter who could pull the ball to leftfield and out of the playground, into the parking lot and down the street.

I had to pull the ball to left in those days—without enough kids to cover the outfield, any ball hit to right was an automatic out. But I still have the same instinct when I go to the plate today. It's so tempting to swing for home runs—but it's a temptation I have to fight, like not having dessert after dinner. I have to fight it not only because I'll hit more home runs if I do, but because I've also learned that day-in, day-out consistency—not striking out as often, putting the ball into play, moving the runner from second to third, bunting for a single—is what's important in offensive baseball.

I feel that it was in 1980 that I started to become the kind of hitter I want to be. By making adjustments in my style of hitting, I've begun to eliminate the constant temptation to pull the ball and hit home runs. Standing farther away from home plate, as I do now, makes it easier for me to get hits to rightfield, to move runners over—to get *hits*, period. I get more hits because I use more of the field. I'm more of the straightaway hitter I've always thought I could be.

My teammates used to kid me a little—a pull hitter all of a sudden wanting to become a Roberto Clemente? Well, there *is* glory in home run hitting, and I guess in my early years in Philadelphia I was on a bit of an ego trip. But there are so many facets to the game that a player is totally wrong to concentrate exclusively on being a home run hitter, or even just a hitter.

My role on the Phillies is bigger than that. As a six-time Gold Glove third baseman and an integral part of the team's defense, I'm not just in the game to hit home runs. If you believe that is your role—as does Dave Kingman of the Mets, for example—I think that in trying to fulfill that role, in trying to just hit home runs, you'll fail more often than you'll succeed.

What I have to do as a player to be always on the offense is use all my abilities out on the field—to play third base as well as I can, steal bases now and then, score runs, and, occasionally, hit home runs that break up ball games. That's the kind of player I was in the 1980 World Series. I didn't do anything unbelievably spectacular or have an awesome Series, but in every game, I did something to help the team—a bunt, a home run, a good fielding play. I had a workmanlike Series and so did the whole team. I don't think there was one stand-out performer, just the Phillies as a *team* doing all the little things well. We were a team of fundamentally sound players, and players like that make a winning lineup on any ball club—high school, college, or professional.

*   *   *

As you can see, I have some very definite feelings about offensive baseball—feelings that other players may not share. Still, I believe strongly that a team made up of nine guys who are tuned in to being situational players—who are aware of what's needed at the time to score runs—has a better chance of winning.

The Los Angeles Dodger teams of 1977 and 1978 and the Kansas City Royals of 1980 stand out in my mind as having the greatest number of multifaceted players in the lineup. Rather than just having one or two guys who hit home runs, they put eight players in the lineup who complemented each other by doing what the situation called for. To me, they approached the game offensively, which was why they were tough to beat.

Prior to our 1980 pennant drive, I think the Phillies used to get into ruts. Many times we'd look so much for the big hit or the big inning that we'd end up losing games because we didn't take advantage of our unique abilities to bunt, to hit-and-run, and to run the bases. I think we sat back and played cozy because we knew that Greg Luzinski was going to hit 30, that I was going to hit 30—that with four guys capable of hitting over 25 home runs it should all come out in the wash anyway, right?

That's why our team was still inconsistent through most of 1980. We would win four and then lose four, win five and lose five. Until the pennant drive, we could never put together several months of consistently good offensive baseball—and that's what it takes to win it all. A championship team must win close ball games by knowing how to play sound, fundamental, offensive baseball. Players who are used to thinking about that kind of ball and who have the ability to play it are more apt to use it when the game calls for it. And a team made up of such players will win most of its games.

On the other hand, you'll be a .500 team, at best, if you lay back and look to explode with the wham-bam, "two-run homer or we lose" type of baseball. Sure, you may wipe out some team in a three-game series, but before you know it, you'll have lost three in a row to another team because you found yourself in close ball games and didn't know how to execute fundamentally to beat them.

Think back to the Phillies in the last month of the 1980 season. We had to come from behind as much as any team I've ever heard of, and most of those wins came without home runs. We won with *rallies*—a walk, a walk, an error, a sacrifice fly, a double, a bunt—not with base hit–base hit–home run. In the World Series, except for the last game, we came from behind in every game we won. And we did it with a lot of "little stuff"—fundamental baseball in response to the game situation. We won by doing small things right during our drive to the championship, and we gained confidence that we could consistently come from behind by playing basic baseball. A team with a multidimensional attack is successful because there are simply more ways to win—and fewer ways the other team can defense you. Always remember that the big home runs are icing on the cake and a direct result of doing the little things well.

It's tough to win when you won't run and steal because the next guy up might hit a three-run homer and you want to let him do his thing. If you have to let the next batter stand up there and hack, hoping he gets a home run, you'll be putting much more pressure on him to perform. That very home run will come more often if the team doesn't depend on it exclusively to win. And it will probably come from more than just one or two power hitters—the game situation will allow home runs more easily if there's already been a double steal or a bunt for a base hit. I think all the home runs we hit in the World Series resulted from *not* trying to hit them. Nobody was *expected* to produce one for the team to win.

With the exception of Larry Bowa, who's going to hit ground-balls and line drives and singles in just about any situation, the entire 1980 Phillies lineup, myself included, could hit the ball out of the park, bunt for a single, hit a line drive to right with a man on second, or draw a base on balls if the pitcher was slightly wild.

Not that any of us can do this every day. I can't hit a home run every time the situation calls for one, or guarantee a line drive to rightfield—but I have the knowledge and have developed the ability to adapt my offensive game to situations that come up in the nine innings of a ball game. The more hitters you have in your lineup with the ability to play situational, offensive baseball, the better team you'll have.

THE MENTAL GAME

BEFORE YOU CAN EXECUTE good offensive baseball, you must be able to *think* good offensive baseball. There will be periods during the season when I will apply this type of thinking, and there will be periods when I may be struggling a bit mentally. When the game starts and the adrenaline starts to flow, it takes a great deal of mental discipline to apply good offensive-baseball ideas to a game situation. In a very important ball game, or a game in which you don't know what the pitcher throws, it takes real professional ability and concentration to play good offensive baseball.

Concentration is the key. You've got to concentrate on that white ball. You see in your mind what you want to do, but the pitcher has the ball and a game plan of his own. He may throw a curve, a slider, or who knows what when he lets the ball go.

It's tough to analyze a situation, adapt your hitting to it, and concentrate. Until recently, I was normally just a right-handed pull hitter who hit home runs, and it was difficult for me to hit a line drive to rightfield to move a man over to third. It was a lot easier for me to stand up at the plate in the bottom of the ninth with no one on—as I did in a game against the Mets at the end of the '78 season—and hit a home run to win it. That was easier because it doesn't take intense concentration or really fine, fundamentally sound, "good-pitch-to-hit-to-rightfield" hitting. It fit my style then and was right in the situation. I could just stand in there, drop the head of the bat on the ball, and hope it would go out of the park—the "hack and hope" method of hitting for power hitters or one-dimensional players I talked about before.

But in another game in '78, in Montreal, I was faced with a different situation. I walked up to the plate against Scott Sanderson in the second inning, after he had struck out our first three hitters and Richie Hebner had hit a double. With no outs, on the first pitch I hit a line drive to the right of the first baseman Tony Perez that moved the runner to third and put me on first with a single. So the same player who hit a home run to win a game could also execute a less dramatic but fundamentally sound brand of baseball to help decide a game. It's all part of knowing the game situation, having a plan, and then concentrating while you try to carry it out.

It's important to realize that you'll more often fail than succeed in carrying out your plan, and how that affects you is crucial to your game. Baseball is very different from all other sports. For even the best players on offense, it's a game of learning to adapt to and cope with what appears to be failure. Think of it this way: if you're a .300 hitter, you get only three hits every ten times you walk up to home plate. Seven times you fail—or so it seems. In failing, you actually could be succeeding, at least in carrying out your plan. You could hit a line drive right at someone, or you could hit a groundball to second base and move the runner from second to third. In either case, your statistics will say "at-bat, no hit, you failed"—to someone reading the box score the next day. But success and failure are impossible to define by statistics alone. Sometimes the hitter actually did succeed, did do what was called for.

That was true for me in the 1980 play-offs. People said that I had a bad series at the plate. But if three or four of the balls I hit with men in scoring position had gone through the infield rather than being caught . . . well, five feet one way or the other and they would have been RBI singles. I hit the ball on the nose and put it into play, but it just wasn't in the cards for me to get base hits. And the box score showed the next day that I failed each of those times.

Statistics (which I'll discuss more fully later) *are* important. Baseball is a game of record books—past performances, famous names, famous games. You don't usually hear people talk about a great individual performance when a man has gone oh-for-four. But young players—and even major leaguers—have to understand that statistics aren't everything, that individual performance isn't everything. Your ability to handle the negative aspects of the game and the example you set by the way you handle game situations and the game environment are important for you and your teammates. It's not only how you think about the game, it's how you think about yourself.

Learn to respect the game of baseball. Learn that the game requires dealing with adversity. Your ability to handle real failure
(not just the failure of a plan that *was* carried out)—making an
error, striking out—will have a direct effect on your ability to
succeed as the game progresses.

I think too many players—and in the past, I was one—let previous incidents affect their concentration and ability for the rest
of the game.

Let's say you strike out the first time up and get angry, not believing you missed the pitch. You think, "How can that guy get
me out? I'm swinging too hard—I'm swinging too easy—I'm
pulling off the ball—I'm doing something fundamentally
wrong." Then you go back to the dugout, your teammates see
that you're thinking negatively, and you spend the whole game
trying to adjust your swing or your stance.

Ideally, you should write that at-bat off and keep the confident
feeling that you're better than the other guy, that you'll get your
hits before the game is over. You shouldn't let one at-bat affect
your baserunning, your defensive game, your game attitude or
that of your teammates. *Positive, positive, positive*—think that
way all the time. Especially during the toughest times, when a
display of positive thinking will do the most for you as an individual and the most for your teammates.

I've come a long way in this respect as a ballplayer. In the fifth
game of the 1980 play-offs, Houston's Ken Forsch struck me out
with the tying run on third, in what was probably the most de-
feating at-bat I had the whole year. I knew that my teammates, as
well as a huge television audience, were watching my reaction.
And I knew that a display of positive emotion or of confidence in
rooting for the next hitter would do nothing but good for myself

and my teammates in the long run. So I went back to the dugout with my head held high. As it turned out, Del Unser got a hit to tie the score, and I've since gotten many compliments about the way I carried myself. But I haven't mastered that ability completely yet. Not too many ballplayers have. It's a touchy, touchy area. I can count on one hand the number of players who have mastered the mental approach to baseball.

Pittsburgh first baseman Willie Stargell, in the years that I've seen him, comes as close as anyone to letting nothing bother him. He'll strike out four times, then go down to first and pat you on the rear and say, "It's great to be alive." Another master of the mental game is Johnny Bench, who reflects the attitude that he's always thinking positively, that he's always got the upper hand. You never really know what players like Bench or Stargell are thinking on the inside, but the waves they throw off make the people around them think that they're always confident, always in charge.

On the Phillies, I've been very impressed in the last few years with the approach to the game of our former catcher, Bob Boone. He always seems to have a positive frame of mind, never flying off the handle, always in control of himself. And that's especially important for a catcher, who must also control the game.

Greg Luzinski was well known for being even-tempered and for staying on the same emotional level during a game in his years with the Phillies. There's a natural tendency to talk when you come back to the dugout after an at-bat and Greg always had positive things to say about his performance: "I just missed that pitch—he made a great pitch on me. There's nothing I can do about it, but he can't make those good pitches all night." You don't want to exude overconfidence or false confidence, but if you have to talk—as most players do—comments like Greg's are good. His thoughts are positive; negative ones would only hamper his performance for the rest of the game.

Perhaps the ultimate example of self-control on the baseball field was provided by Steve Carlton all the way through the 1980 season. Opposing pitchers are in awe of his ability not to let anything bother him. He never does anything out of the ordinary on the pitcher's mound, never overreacts to an umpire's call or to any adversity the game may present.

He gets the ball, looks at the sign, throws the ball; gets the ball, looks at the sign, throws the ball. Then he goes into the dugout, sits down, gets his bat, does his job at the plate—and then repeats that mound routine all over again. Steve never lets opposing players feel that they've gotten to him, and he doesn't ever show up opposing players, either. He just does his thing. Steve's powers of concentration are probably the best of all the pitchers in baseball.

Other players express a positive attitude through a different kind of game personality. Former teammate Tim McCarver was a unique personality on the Phillies who had a great deal of influence on me. Tim had a lot of the old-time, get dirty, street-fighting baseball player in him. He did a lot of yelling and screaming at people from the dugout. Unlike Steve Carlton, he believed in being boisterous and in expressing himself all the time. But like the other players I've mentioned, he was always under control. I never saw him throw a bat or break things in the dugout.

I think you see a personality like Tim's in older, more experienced ballplayers who came up 10–15 years ago or more, when a rookie was still called a rookie and was supposed to look up to the veterans. Most of the time, this rah-rah, old-time attitude has its place—it most definitely did on the Phillies.

I counted on Tim for more than just an upbeat attitude, however. He also gave me, personally, positive reinforcement. I could always count on Tim being in my corner, as Dave Cash was when he was with the team. Both Tim and Dave played important positive roles at a time in my career when I particularly needed it.

It was Dave Cash who first told me that not only was I good, but I had a chance to be a great ballplayer. He constantly reinforced my ego with the remarks he made about my playing ability, always referring to great plays that I made and balls that I hit hard. Dave never said anything negative about any of his teammates, in fact. And being the perhaps too-sensitive person that I was (not always good in life or in baseball), I needed as much positive reinforcement as I could get.

Pete Rose has given me this kind of respect and reinforcement in the years he's been with the Phillies. We've developed a tremendous professional rapport, and I've grown as a ballplayer through this relationship. We understand each other well, and I know Pete has a great respect for my ability to play the game. He always shows me how much he wants me to succeed. I also know he enjoys watching me play, because he always tells me so. That's great positive reinforcement coming from a living legend like Pete, and I try to return the respect he shows me.

It feels good to have someone like Dave Cash or Tim McCarver or Garry Maddox constantly referring to the positive things you do, and if they talk about the negative things at all, to do so in jest. Players at any age need that kind of help in building their confidence. For instance, every September the team calls up about ten players from the minor leagues for the balance of the season. They're just up to watch, and they need positive reinforcement whenever possible. If I see a young player hit eight or ten line drives in practice and notice that he's improved since I saw him in spring training, I'll tell him so. I'll let him know that an older, more experienced player has been watching and taking an interest. So let some of that positive reinforcement flow out to your own teammates. You may find out that some of them have the same sensitive feelings and needs that you do.

I also feel that a highly confident mental approach can overcome physical limitations. For example, I could have the worst fundamentals in the world and still tell myself over and over that I'm better than that pitcher and I'm going to get a hit. I *know* I'm going to get a hit—I can see line drives in my mind. And, by concentrating so much on succeeding, I find a way to get a hit—a chopper over first base, a broken bat single, or a cue shot off the end of the bat. But a hit, no matter what.

Many times my mind will be channeled in such a way, positive vibrations flowing so well, that even if I do something drastically wrong at the plate I get a hit. This is what happens to players who get in grooves. If they're hitting .310 and they drop down to .305, they just believe so strongly that they're going to hit over .300 that the next time up, *bang*—a hit. Then they chink one in somewhere and two line drives later they're four-for-four and back in the groove.

There are many .300 hitters who don't have consistently good fundamentals. Willie Mays was never really a fundamentally sound hitter; he took some of the ugliest swings at a baseball you'll ever see. But when a guy whose fundamentals always seem to be out of whack hits .300 year after year, you can't tell him he's not going to do it again. He *knows* he is and has a constant positive feeling about his hitting.

A lot of hitters around the .240–.250 level have a tendency to lose that aggressive, confident attitude. Rather than going up to home plate believing that no matter how they swing at the ball they're going to get a hit, their minds are clouded with fundamentals. Such a hitter goes up to the plate thinking, "I'm going to hold my hands here, I'm hitching my swing, I'm going to hit down on the ball and hit it on the ground, I'm going to take a pitch and work on my stride." The .300 hitter simply finds a way to get one more hit a week than the .250 hitter. And that's the difference between them—26 hits a year. Therefore a hitter should try to keep out of his mind the only thing that may be holding him back—negative thoughts.

Eliminate those thoughts that detract from that ability to make happen what you see in your mind. If you visualize getting a hit, and believe it, you can make it happen. But if you go up to the plate thinking about the finer points of technique, you just won't have your concentration where it should be. You can think too much at the plate—about your own game, but not the game situation.

There's a balance, of course. You have to be confident and aggressive enough to let things happen, not to force them to happen. That's a Mike Schmidt theory I've tried to live by. It can be brutal trying to control your mind while standing at home plate with the winning run on second and fifty thousand people in the stands, two thousand of them yelling, "Go ahead and strike out again" or "Start earning your money."

You get so channeled into the fact that you have to succeed, that a fear of failure takes over. At that point, you have a much better chance of getting a base hit if you can just block out everything but the ball and concentrate on what you want to do when the pitch comes in. Standing at home plate with ten different things buzzing through your mind about your chances of proving your ability can prevent you from just letting it happen.

I've experienced that many times in the past at Veteran's Stadium. I would appear cool and calm, but at times I would react so much internally to my environment that I was ready to explode. It was hard for me to perform as a hitter and fielder because I was trying so hard to prove something to the people in the stands. My reaction prevented me from just letting my physical talents flow.

I feel fortunate to have had such experiences early in my career. Now, I feel I've matured enough to look past this kind of pressure, which affects me much less than it used to. I can't remember too many times in the past few years when I was overcome by the fear of failure as a hitter. It was in 1980, more so than at any other time in my career, that I found I was able to focus my thoughts and concentrate on the ball and what I wanted to do with it. This approach, along with a physical change in my batting style, has helped me become the kind of player I always felt I could be.

I was able to alleviate outside pressures in part because I learned not to derive approval from fan or media reaction, or from any group reaction. A player who performs to satisfy his own standards, rather than those of fifty thousand people in the stands, has a much better chance of succeeding. Fans can't help but expect too much. If they're booing you and you're completely plugged into them, responding to them and not to the situation, your motor reactions will be the same as those of any person who is subjected to pressure: your hands and arms will get tighter, and you won't perceive things the way you want to. Only a hitter who can stay within himself, can define his audience and his standards, will relieve that kind of pressure and be able to go up to home plate loose and relaxed in the most difficult game situations.

A relaxed attitude toward life in general will also help things to flow professionally. To achieve that, you must have your priorities in life in line. When one phase of your life—in my case, professional baseball—goes wrong, if you have your priorities straight you realize it's an important, but not the most important, part of your existence. And that takes the pressure out of your professional life.

You'll also do better in your down times if you realize they can make you stronger, help develop the "character" written and talked about so much in sports. If there's one thing I learned early as a ballplayer, it's that a low period in your professional or family life gives you a chance to grow as a person—you have a chance to build character, you learn to live with those times and be the same person during them. That, in turn, teaches you to come to grips with the concept of patience. And, tempered by your experiences, you will be better able to face whatever comes in the future.

Pitcher and ex-teammate Jim Kaat is a great example of a ballplayer with character. He is also one of the finest men I know. Jim has played baseball in four decades, and his ability to cope with the highs and lows throughout his career in the major leagues had much to do with making him the man he is today. He has his priorities in line: his professional life is not of number-one importance, but Jim always believes in his ability to perform well.

A big part of coming out of bad periods as a hitter is constantly believing in yourself, as Jim does, in his pitching. You must believe that you're better than the man on the mound. A pitcher can recognize when a hitter is in a pressing period and when he's in a confident period. The pitcher knows when you're 0-for-15 and pulling off the ball—opening up the front shoulder and trying to pull everything—and if he's good, he'll be able to keep you that way. He'll throw the ball inside, because he knows you'll keep swinging at it, and keep opening up trying to hit it. Other pitchers haven't found that edge yet. If a hitter is pulling off the ball and opening up they'll think. "Here's my chance to throw breaking balls away." But that only makes the hitter close back up to hit, which brings his shoulder back to where it's supposed to be.

A pitcher also knows when you're swinging level and hitting .350. He's aware that you seem to be hitting everything—hard! He knows he'll have to make good pitches to get you out, and in trying to do so he'll tend to make bad ones. He ends up pressing, and he won't have that loose, relaxed delivery. He'll hang curveballs because he knows he has to throw really good curveballs; or, trying to be so fine, he'll bounce a pitch in the dirt in front of the plate.

This competition between pitcher and hitter makes the game of baseball what it is. No other one-on-one competition in sports involves so many variables. And players can watch it happening. Nine times out of ten, we can determine who's feeling the pressure. We can sit in the dugout and see when a pitcher is overly concerned about a hitter—often the three, four, or five batter in the lineup—or when the hitter is worried at the plate.

I was a late bloomer when it came to confidence and aggressiveness. I don't think I was really willing to fight for myself, to stand up for my rights, until I got to college. Not that I wasn't cocky in high school about my athletic ability. I knew I had as much talent for sports as anyone—I felt that whatever the season, I'd be the best athlete.

Then I met Steve Yeager (now a catcher for the Dodgers), who played for a rival high school. He was the only guy I'd seen up to that point who had all the physical qualities I had and something else besides: he was meaner than I was, tougher mentally, and that was the difference between us.

That kind of toughness has much to do with upbringing and environment. When you come from the type of background I did—not having to fight for anything, or get out and scuffle—you grow up differently from kids like Steve, who came from a rougher environment. In my experience, when those two types confront each other on the athletic field, the kid with a background like Steve's has the upper hand. Both might be aggressive, but one kid will have a certain confidence to go with it, because he's more used to displaying aggressiveness and taking hard knocks.

In high school, opposing pitchers would really take advantage of me if they could throw curveballs. Yeager used to catch Jim Sherman, one of his good pitchers, who would throw me curveballs that would make me flinch. Then they'd break over the plate and Yeager would look up at me and say, "You looking for this?" and throw the ball back out to the pitcher. At times I'd get so frustrated I'd go home and cry.

I never did like Steve in high school, because I was jealous. He was such a good hitter and a good all-around athlete, I *knew* he was going to get to play professional ball. I was so far from any kind of stardom then that I left for college with a portfolio and a

T-square, thinking I was going to be an architect, while Steve left for the minor leagues. I had no idea whatsoever I'd end up in professional ball.

It was in college that I started to gain the maturity, and insight into life generally, that I needed to make it to where I am today. That's when I started to get my confidence in order. I realized that teammates appreciated my ability and looked up to me, and that I had the qualities necessary to become one of the respected players of whatever team I was on—to become a leader. It looked like I might have a shot at the dream I'd once had, although I also realized I needed the right breaks and had to take advantage of them. But it did seem like I might play pro ball after all. And as I started to feel that way, I started to become a good player.

Until college I'd never really been tested. Many young athletes have to struggle to develop the maturity needed to achieve success. And a large part of that maturity lies simply in answering the question, Do I have the guts, do I have what it takes to play this game?

As you come up through the baseball ranks, from Little League and high school through college and the minors, at some point you start to feel that you've got to stand up for yourself. For me, it started in college. I realized I was no longer playing with the boys back home, on the Little League or high school team, where I was the best. I was now out on my own and playing with *men*, with guys who were as good as I was and who came from all over the *country* to play at this level. I was playing with the best athletes from every high school, not with a bunch of guys I *knew* I was better than—and who knew it, too. In college, I was playing with a whole league of guys who were the same as me.

Then I moved into professional ball, where I was playing

against the best players out of the group I'd just come from. And then I graduated to the higher minors, where the survivors were again the best out of the group I'd just come from. Finally, I got to the major leagues, with the cream of the crop of all players everywhere. Now I'm in the process of trying to get through this league the same way I got through college and the minors.

It was only once I was through college and into professional baseball that I gained the confidence and maturity to view myself as a total man. I became self-confident—not cocky—and no longer felt that I was merely fooling people with an air of self-confidence. Finally, I felt that I could back it up.

Through experience, I've come to realize that intimidation is part of the game, especially at the major league level, and I've learned to stick up for myself when I feel that someone is taking liberties they shouldn't. I believe in talking first, but sometimes a little scuffle can't be avoided. Up to this point in my career, I've caused two big brawls on the field.

At times, it gets down to that kind of fighting for yourself. I don't want to drum into youngsters that fighting is the only way to handle these situations, but occasionally it is unavoidable. There comes a point in all our lives when we have to fight for what we know is right. For Yeager, it came earlier than it did for me, but the end result was the same.

Players as well as parents should understand that some athletes are late bloomers, not only physically but in their mental readiness to play as well. A young player may have the physical skills early, as I did, but the mental maturity needed to apply them may only come later in life.

Along with ability, of course, it is this mature self-confidence that you have to have to make it. Some people are born with it, some have to learn it, and some have to foster it through many experiences, as I did. I can't put my finger on the exact things that gave me self-confidence—probably anything and everything from being jealous of Steve Yeager in high school to getting my point across to a pitcher in front of a major league crowd. Maybe I didn't gain it until I got into a fight on the field. You don't know when it happens; you just realize it has, and from that point on you know you'll be able to stand up for yourself.

The other cause of lack of mental toughness at a young age is rooted in attitude. When I was sixteen, nothing but personal achievement, getting ahead individually, mattered to me. In a game, I'd just be hoping to hit a couple of home runs; if I did that, I'd usually go home feeling good, even if the team lost.

I'd also go home and cry sometimes, not only if I couldn't hit one of Jim Sherman's curveballs, but also if I'd struck out three or four times. I'd get frustrated with my schoolwork—with life in general. My daily attitude was simply based on my individual performance in whatever athletic event was taking place—football, basketball, or baseball. And that seemed to run my life.

I think what motivated me then was peer pressure and the ego inflation that went along with being the best athlete on the high school team—a motivation carried over somewhat to my professional career. Today I'd be very happy if I could walk down the streets of Philadelphia and not be recognized, but early in my career I'd have been disappointed if that had happened. After the great season I had in 1974, for instance, I would walk down the street and occasionally be recognized. That really boosted my ego, because I knew I was just starting to get to where I wanted to be, to become a "star."

I passed out of that phase a long time ago. What motivates me now is team performance and my contribution to it, along with an inner drive to perform to the best of my ability.

I no longer worry about being popular or unpopular. Whether the fans and the media like me or dislike me as a ballplayer, they have no basis to come to a conclusion about me personally, since they don't know me. Of course, some ego is involved, but only to a small degree now, because I've been through so many stages of ego inflation and deflation in my ten years of professional ball. I've gone from hitting .196 my first full year up and wondering if I'd ever play another game in the major leagues to being the leading home run hitter in baseball since my career began and the only player to twice hit four home runs in a row—all while playing on a division-winning team four times and in 1980 winning the National League pennant, the World Series, and two Most Valuable Player awards, with another MVP in 1981. I've been at the top and I've been at the bottom in my career, but at this particular point I'm at the top in life and that's what's important to me.

Now, at the end of a game, if I can come back to the locker room and look in the mirror and say I gave as much of myself as I could, I can feel like and call myself a winner. I'm a winner on that particular day, whatever the scoreboard says about my team's or my individual performance. I think that the desire to be this type of winner, along with personal pride and gamesmanship— the desire to excel—is enough motivation for an athlete at any level. Whether you're the highest-paid athlete in the majors or on the grade school basketball team, an inner desire to perform well and to contribute to your team will make you a winner.

*   *   *

My ideas about attitude and winning and losing have helped me to control my emotions on the field. Some people feel that this kind of control is bad, because the emotions will build up inside of you and without an outlet, will affect your play. I've been criticized for this, as I have for "overthinking." *Show more emotion on the field*, I've been told. But to me there's a difference between temper and emotion, and I feel that for my game it's important to control the kinds of emotion that temper unleashes.

That kind of control is important in the play and the mental approach of players I admire. But everybody has different emotional levels in baseball, of course. On the Phillies in recent years, the extremes were represented by me and by Larry Bowa, who is known for having a temper. We're both very successful in what we do in the major leagues, so I can't say one is wrong and the other is right. I do know that temper should not be confused with desire. I play the game of baseball just as hard and apply myself and care as much as Larry Bowa, but I'm not going to let baseball run my life. Baseball isn't necessarily Larry's whole life, either— but you might think it is from his personality on the field and in the clubhouse. Larry's more open displays of emotion can be good for a team, and at times had a positive effect on the Phillies. I wouldn't try to change Larry—I just have a different way of carrying myself that I know works for me and has worked for other successful players.

Temper or lack of it really comes from your attitude toward the game. Young players should know that showing a quick temper doesn't necessarily mean a feisty, effective player. In fact, it can mean the opposite, if it's not part of your personality, a natural part of your game. Out-of-character displays of temper can disrupt your concentration, and your game, and you won't be as productive. Igniting a quick temper with an incident here and there often throws your game out of whack. Everyone has a boiling point, but staying within yourself, responding with a certain evenness to the ups and downs of a game, like a Johnny Bench or a Willie Stargell, usually makes you more of a productive player. So if you tend to get thrown out of games or break bats, you shouldn't get high on the fact that you're known as a guy with one of the hottest tempers around. That kind of a reputation can lead the opposition to believe that they can get to you and your game.

Of course, it's very rare to see someone come into the game completely mild-mannered, with a total lack of temper. I had a temper when I first started to play, and I was known to kick in a few water coolers and knock out a few light bulbs. But I also knew then that that wasn't the way I wanted to be. I still have a temper today, but I've learned to control it. And further, in 1980 I learned for the first time that you can show emotion in a positive rather than a negative way, and that that ability can help your game. It can give you, instead of the opposition, an edge.

I found that I had a great deal of fun playing in the 1980 World Series, because I was letting myself enjoy the fact I was in the Series. I let myself relax—something that's now become part of my game. I began to show more of the fun I have in a game, to have a smile on my face more often, to establish some rapport with the people in the stands. If you have more of Pete Rose's and Tug McGraw's openness in your game, you don't let anyone know playing baseball seems like work, no matter how tough it gets out there. And that's what scouts want to see in a young athlete—fire and competitiveness in someone who has a lot of fun playing the game.

No one should—or really could—teach you any of these approaches. Don't try to model yourself after a particular player. Do what comes naturally to you, but be aware of this facet of your game. I appreciate the different on-the-field attitudes of many of the players in the major leagues today, but I don't try to pattern myself after them. You have to find your own way—you have to discover what works for *you*.

A lot of work, both mental and physical, goes into improving your game, but playing baseball is just plain fun, too. There have been periods in my career when I couldn't think of anything I'd rather be doing than playing baseball, because it's so much fun. At those times the idea that someone is *paying* me to do this seems absurd. But there have also been periods when I've really been tested; then I wonder whether there isn't something else I could be doing that I'd enjoy more, in which I didn't have the pressure that baseball offers. It really depends on the time of the year, the league situation, and where the team stands. But the players who think baseball is just work and do it for the money or the fame or as an ego trip, just don't do as well. It's guys who love to play the game and have a good time doing it who will do the best and be best rewarded in the end.

There's one final thing to know about the way you should think about the game: high school and college athletes should remember that for most the dream of becoming a professional ballplayer will remain just a dream. Any boy who feels he has a chance to play pro ball must realize that whatever his talents, making it to the pro ranks takes a lot of luck. Often, it comes down to simply being in the right place at the right time.

My roommate in college, for example, was a much better prospect in high school than I was. He could have signed a contract then but decided to go to college instead. A left-handed hitter and a good athlete, he had a reasonably good college career but just didn't get all the attention I did. He was a great professional prospect who didn't make it to pro ball. You can have good talent, but you have to have the breaks too—it has to be in the cards for you.

If it's not, a young player should be ready for the end of his dream. He should accept the fact that he must take other directions in life, and he should meet the challenges there as he would have in baseball. My roommate couldn't do that because he had put all his eggs in one basket. The emotional strain of not playing in the major leagues and of not coming along with me really held him back as a person. I think he lost a great deal of enjoyment in life because of his lack of success in athletics.

Realize that there are other things in life, and realize that the odds of making it in pro ball are against you. There are just too many variables involved that you can't control. Look at a baseball career as sort of icing on the cake—I could be this or that, but if I make it, I'll stay with baseball.

I had the talent and luck to stay with it. In high school I never did anything when a scout was in the stands; I guess that just wasn't my time to shine. But in college it was different—it seemed I always did well. When Paul Owens, the Phillies general manager, came to see me play in one college game, I hit a home run, took an extra base, and threw a man out from the hole while playing shortstop. He had come to see me do four or five things, and I did them all! I was in the right place, doing the right thing, at the right time—so it must have been in the cards for me.

Always remember that no matter how much confidence and

ability you have, there are some things you can do nothing about other than go out on the field and try to apply yourself with your best effort, at whatever level. Then just let the chips fall where they may. If you have that attitude daily, in the long run things will work out for the best.

THE PHYSICAL GAME

ONE OF THE THINGS you as an athlete do have power over is the physical condition of your body. And this much is sure: only if you're willing to do what you can to succeed, while not worrying unnecessarily about what you can't, are you going to make it in baseball. If you do everything you can to get your body as physically fit as possible, you'll have done everything you can to *prevent* an injury that could hold you back.

This approach to physical fitness is part of letting it happen, not trying to force it to happen, in baseball. As in your mental game, you want to remove what obstacles you can in your physical game that could block the development and display of your talent.

Fitness is a part of baseball that isn't always a whole lot of fun, but it's something you have to make a commitment to in order to get the most out of your game. I'm not talking here about all-around physical conditioning—that's ideal, of course. But realistically, what's important is to be fit to play. In baseball, that means prevention of injury—and particularly, prevention of muscle pulls, which cause so many of those nagging little injuries that impair performance, or cause major ones that can sit you down for a month or more. Physical conditioning in baseball can include a whole spectrum of activities from pumping Nautilus machines to running—whatever you've got to do to prevent injuries.

Baseball is different from other team sports. It's not constantly rough and taxing on your body, and it's a game you can play (though it's definitely not to your advantage to) when you're not in top physical condition.

Guards in the NBA and running backs in the NFL need a different kind of strength and stamina. They make their money by being in the kind of top shape that allows them to endure the punishment they must constantly take.

To me, a baseball player in good condition means a player who can endure the length of a season. For 162 games over 180 days, he has to be able to withstand not only breaking up double plays, crashing into walls and catchers, falling into dugouts, and being hit by pitches, but also running full speed, stopping and starting, diving and sliding. Baseball is a game of pulled muscles and hamstrings, because it's stop-and-go, stop-and-go. You stand still much of the time, and then must make quick movements one way or the other. At the most basic level, players must be able to perform all the short, quick movements they go through every day without becoming seriously injured.

Basketball and football players must have a lot more *awareness* of conditioning just to be able to play, but I think you should have that awareness in baseball, too. In the last few years, baseball has improved quite a bit in this respect—partly because the whole country has been swept up in a new wave of concern with the body. Players will spend more time and management more money because "thin is in" for everyone now. You see more players reporting to spring training in shape from off-season workouts and more players extending their careers. But for the most part, physical conditioning of all kinds still is taken too lightly in baseball.

As a result, the majority of players just aren't in the kind of shape they should be. Just listen to the announcers on NBC-TV's *Game of the Week* talk about injuries. Hearing about sore feet, ankles, and shoulders would be understandable if the game were football. In baseball, all those nagging little injuries occur mainly because players don't take care of themselves during the season and don't prepare themselves enough in the off-season.

On a physical-fitness scale of 1 to 10, most players are a 5 or 6. So if you've ever looked out on the field and said to yourself, "I'm in as good shape as that guy," you might have been right. A major leaguer in the worst shape is probably in about the same condition as the average man in the street, and it goes up from there. There are some great physical specimens in baseball, but there also are a lot of overweight men making a lot of money in the game, because you don't have to be in great all-around shape to play.

I can go through two or three games, or even a week of baseball, and maybe, at the most, have to run 90 or 180 or 270 feet as hard as I can. First-to-third, second-to-home, or first-to-home is often as far as I'll have to run full speed in a given week. Then there will be other weeks of playing six or seven really hard games in a row, when I'm running the bases, stealing and sliding, and it seems like they're hitting everything at me. At those times, I really wish I was in the best possible shape.

Personally, I think I'm in average, or a bit above-average shape. When I say that, though, I'm talking about wind. My level of conditioning for injury prevention is much higher. I couldn't get on a track in the middle of the season and run a mile in a reasonably good time; it would even be tough for me to run hard around our field twice. But I would have worked hard to protect those parts of my body prone to pulls.

The lack of overall conditioning shown by baseball players results in part from the nature of the game. Baseball makes it harder for players to be in top shape, because of the schedule. Individual games are not usually hard or taxing, as those in other sports, but the demand is constant. We play almost every day for seven months. It's not like basketball, in which there will be three or four days without a game, or football, in which there's one game on Sunday and the players are able to spend much of their time during the rest of the week on conditioning. In baseball, the length of the season and the day-in, day-out strain prevents an everyday player like me from remaining in top shape.

That's why year-round conditioning has become so important in baseball. You build to your peak physical condition in the off-season and then work to maintain it through the 162-game grind. The Phillies have been very successful doing this. We're one of the best-conditioned teams in the game because of management's willingness to invest in equipment and in our excellent, year-round strength-and-flexibility teacher, Gus Hoefling. Without Gus, I wouldn't have had a program that's not only kept me feeling good at a time when most guys are beginning to feel their age, but also has kept me progressing physically. I've been working with Gus and the machines for several years—for three months straight from November through January, as well as during the season—and I've been getting stronger and more flexible every year.

Bob Boone and Steve Carlton are the best-conditioned players I know personally. Both work all winter, and they're in great shape, conditioned as well as possible for the jobs they do. I don't know whether Bob, for example, could run a mile in a good time, but he has what he needs—very strong forearms, hands, upper body, and legs—and it's very hard to hurt him. He's in the shape he needs to be to play at the top of his game.

Not many players are that well prepared. Whatever shape a player is in, I would recommend that he at least find a way to loosen up and stretch his body, to prevent those pulls that are so much a part of baseball. From the beginning of the season, players should have a daily routine that increases flexibility. Whatever basic program a team has is fine. I think each player can pretty well figure out what will do the most for him before a game. The key is to make yourself go through your routine regularly.

As much as you'd rather take batting practice or do other things that are fun before a game, the most important thing is to first do your exercises. I know how hard it is to make yourself do that all the time. But I've also thought, when I've worked my body just enough to get through the ball game that particular day, that if I could just take better care of myself during the year—if I spent more time prior to batting practice, for instance, strengthening or stretching—I'd be more fit.

Major leaguers generally, though, have a tendency to do just

STRETCHING A POINT

Here are three simple pregame exercises to help prevent those pulls that are so much a part of baseball. With full extension, work on stretching your:

hamstrings,

groin area and
hamstrings,

upper body
and shoulders.

enough preparation to get them through a game. For example, if I get four hits in a game without having taken batting practice, I might skip batting practice the next day, too. Trying that with conditioning can really hurt you. Just because I didn't have to make a difficult, quick move one way or the other in one game, doesn't mean I can take a chance and play without loosening up the next day. Who's to say I won't top a ball down the first-base line and pull a muscle trying to beat it out, because my legs weren't loose? All it takes is one pulled hamstring to miss the next 25 games.

Along with the basic stretching-and-loosening conditioning, it's important to develop strength in the areas you need it most. Sometimes that strength comes naturally, from just playing the game; but you may have to do special work in areas especially vulnerable to injury.

My arms, which are as strong as any in the league, are in great shape from just doing my job. And by throwing the ball and swinging the bat every day, I've built up enough strength in my wrists and fingers. What I need to work on are my knees, the part of my body most vulnerable to injury during those quick movements that baseball requires. I've had two operations on my right knee and one on my left, so I spend a great deal of time, especially during the off-season, strengthening my hamstrings and quadricep (front of the thigh) muscles. How well I do that will determine how long I play. If I can keep my legs strong, I'll be able to play at least ten more years in the major leagues.

As for weight training, I do it in the winter and I recommend it. You want to be toned and strong, as well as stretched and flexible, in the areas of the body you use constantly. But you don't want to become a Mr. Universe. If your living depends on your ability to hit, you'll hit best when your forearms and hands are strong. The stronger your forearms and hands, the harder you can swing the bat with less effort, and the better hitter you become. But you don't want to bulk up, with pectoral muscles so big you can't get the bat through the strike zone.

The same holds true for running. Obviously, the stronger the muscles in your legs, the faster you can run. Again, by "stronger," I mean more powerful without great bulk, great muscle mass. The stronger *and* lighter you are, the better off you are.

Flexibility exercises and conditioning awareness become much more important as you get older. I find that now it's tougher for me to get loose. Older players find that it takes longer for an injury to heal and that susceptibility to injury increases.

When I was young, you'd never find me staying in on a sunny day and lifting weights or putting on some shorts and running a mile. I was always the first one at the playground with a basketball or football, getting up a game. I didn't care anything about weightlifting or stretching, because I didn't get injured. At a young age you're just not subject to muscle pulls and strains.

And that's how it should be. When you're young, the most important thing is having a desire to go out and participate in all sports. Up to college age, too much emphasis on conditioning can turn a player off to the point that he thinks being a major leaguer or a professional football player is not for him.

A young player doing all the physical work he can by playing all the sports he can, will develop naturally. He shouldn't do this or that or strengthen this or that specifically. Once again—let it happen, don't try to make it happen. Stay in the kind of shape that lets your talent come through. As a player grows up and his game progresses, he'll know what kind of conditioning he needs to compete at each level.

You get out of baseball what you put into it. I hope to dedicate myself to the game for 20 years, and I hope to get the most out of it in that time by playing physically sound. You can't have a banner career if you're injured for long periods of time each year. You have to prepare your body for the daily test baseball will give it.

THE FINE ART OF HITTING I:
BEFORE THE AT-BAT

HITTING A ROUND BALL "square" with a round bat is said to be the toughest act in all of sports. That's what makes hitting not only a science, but when done correctly, a beautiful art form. So while you can prepare physically and mentally to hit, and you can learn the science of hitting—the when and how in what situation, and the physical setup—as with every art form, there are certain intangibles that make it all come together differently for each player.

You can look at a successful hitter and take his game apart, noting that he swings like *this* or strides like *that* or is able to generate bat speed *there*. But that doesn't mean his style will work the same way for you. There are certain fundamentals in hitting, basic *dos* and *don'ts*, but in the end, hitting is very individualized, very personal. You have to know yourself and what will work for you as a hitter—what complements your ability and everything else you bring to the game.

That's why I talk so much about doing what comes naturally. In hitting, as in other parts of the game, you shouldn't copy anyone. I can't point to a picture in this book and tell you to stand a particular way because I do. What I want to do in this section is to examine the art of hitting by breaking down my style into the basics and showing how one part relates to another. Even more important, I'll examine the mental side of hitting. What I think about while I'm hitting seems to me to be a very valuable part of this book. Because each hitter has to find his own style and mechanics, how I think, not how I play, can help you the most. After all, how you think about the game determines how you play it—how you'll use your talent, whatever it is.

That's why this is really a book that teaches you how to *think* about the game. I'll give you the basics of conditioning, hitting, baserunning, defense, the batting order, and statistics, but I'll emphasize how to think about these parts of the game, as well as about yourself and baseball as it's played today. In addition, I want to show how the game is all of a piece, how all areas of the game should be connected by your mental approach. There are many ways to play the game physically, but I feel there is one way to approach the game properly. This is what I've had to learn to be a successful player, and what I can best pass on to you.

I'm not a great hitter yet, but someday I hope to be, using the theories in this book. Some of the ideas I'll discuss contradict certain theories, while others are common knowledge. Overall, I've tried to give you what I feel are physical fundamentals common to all successful major league hitters, along with a simple, logical, and proven mental approach to hitting.

You have to *think* in baseball to play well. You have to understand the game to be able to control what you can in it—luck and raw talent only carry you so far. A way is needed to apply your talent—a plan with which to approach the game in general and hitting in particular. You can get the basics from others, but I can give you a way to think about the game that will help you understand what will work best for you.

I've also tried to show that it takes courage to find your own game, which means sometimes going against what the experts say. It also takes patience. For instance, some thought that I didn't have the ability to try for the ideal combination that makes an all-around hitter. But I knew myself and what I could do, and over the last few years I've had real success working toward my goal. At what some would call the height of my career, I've changed my game for the better.

This change has allowed me better to fulfill the hitter's one responsibility—hitting according to the game situation. Keep in mind that this is what you're aiming for as a hitter, and remember that the various ways of carrying out this responsibility are all centered around the idea of scoring runs. You have to get to the point where there's nothing more important to you as a hitter and offensive player than driving a run across the plate or scoring one yourself. You do whatever it takes, from a base hit to getting hit with a pitch with the bases loaded, to get a man across the plate. And once on base, you do whatever it takes to get to home plate. That's how you help your team win.

BAT SELECTION

Hitting begins with bat selection, and bats are as important as you want to make them. Some players are real sticklers about bats; they have bats designed to their liking and stick with them. Others, including myself in the last couple of years, change models a lot. I try other bats because they feel good on a given day. The bat will seldom weigh more or less—it's just that when a bat feels good, I like to try it.

I don't recommend this kind of experimentation for young players. I'm not really a fan of changing bats, even though I've had success at times doing it. One time I grabbed a Tony Taylor model, simply because I needed a change, and I hit four straight home runs. Another time I had seven hits in a row using Johnny Oates's bat, when he was with the Phillies. His bat was basically the same shape as mine, but an inch shorter and two ounces lighter. It felt as if I had the same bat in my hand, but it seemed light as a feather.

Most good hitters, those in the top ten in hitting every year, have the same bat in their hands every time up. If I go up to the plate 600 times a year, I go up with my own bat probably 500 times.

Young kids are apt to choose a bat because of the name on it, rather than the way it feels in their hands. That's fine for really young players, because for them, an interest in baseball is all that's important. But once a player is old enough to know about the feel of a bat and whether or not it will cover the plate, he'll have an idea of the type of hitter he's going to be, and he can pick a bat that will help him do what he wants to with the ball.

DIFFERENT STROKES

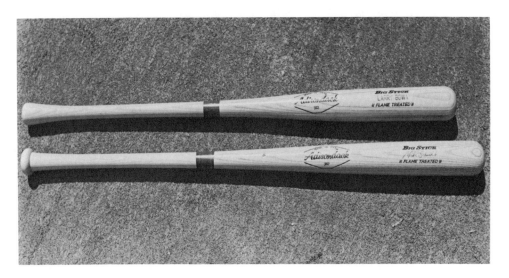

If he's small and doesn't hit the ball a long way, and so isn't going to be a power hitter, he should get a bat he's able to choke up on. His bat would taper more in the barrel and wouldn't be as long as one of my bats, or have a knob at the end. That kind of hitter needs a bat like the one Larry Bowa uses.

Larry's bat is small and light, because he's not as interested as I am in creating bat speed through the ball. With my hitting style, I want as much bat speed and leverage as I can get, and the thinner the handle in comparison with the head, the more bat speed and leverage I create. My bat weighs 33½ ounces and is 35½ inches long, with a head bigger than that found in most bats but tapering down into a thin handle. This top-heavy bat fits me, because I don't hit the ball on the handle very often—I like to extend my arms when swinging. My bat is not designed for a player who likes to choke up and hit singles.

My bat feels comfortable to me, just as it would to a young player who has a strong swing, the ability to control a big bat, and no need to choke up. A smaller bat probably wouldn't feel right to such a hitter.

You have to pick a bat that feels good to you, not one that has "Mike Schmidt" or "Pete Rose" on it. Use a Marv Throneberry bat if it feels good to you. Cross out his name and put yours there, if you want to. In college, I used a Hank Aaron model because I felt comfortable with it, not because of the name on it.

Use a bat that in addition to feeling good—balanced in your hands and well-matched to the type of swing you have—has enough length to cover the outside corner of the plate when your arms are extended. Don't use a 34-inch bat unless, like Garry Maddox, you hang out over the plate when you hit. Since Garry's upper body is out over home plate, he can cover the outside corner with a shorter bat. I position myself farther off the plate and swing standing up a little straighter, so I need more length on my bat to reach some pitches. Using a bat like Garry's would throw off my style.

As they become more consistent in their play, high school and college players start to get a feel for the kind of stance and swing they have, and they begin to define their style of hitting. Then they are able to stay with one type of bat—the one best suited to them as hitters.

Whatever bat you use, it's important that you grip it with your fingers, so it's not sitting back in your palm. If I gave you a bat and asked you to throw it as far as you could with one hand, you'd hold it with your fingers, because that's where the strength in your hand is. Controlling the bat with your fingers gives you more power out of the top hand, too.

UNDER CONTROL

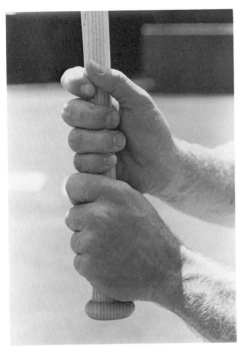

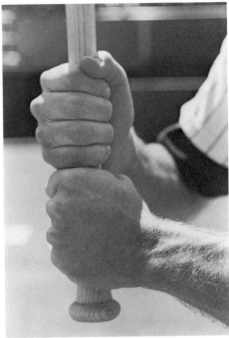

Grip your bat with your fingers, because that's where the strength is in your hands.

Don't hold your bat back in your palm.

As for taking care of your bat—first of all, try to get bats with as little grain as possible. Fifteen to twenty lines of grain are too much. A bat with five lines, as I once had, is about as good as you'll find. With a bat like that, players generally take all the precautions they can, boning or sanding it so the bat won't split.

There are many things you can do to care for bats, and each hitter has his own routine. I don't do much of anything except mark the bats I'll use in a game, the ones I rely on. But then, I don't break many bats anyway—something that's disappointed me at times about my hitting.

A good hitter breaks a lot of bats, because he hits a lot of pitches that are in on the hands. If a hitter is approaching the ball properly and keeping his shoulder in, he'll sometimes fight off inside pitches, breaking the bat but maybe getting a single to the opposite field. Bill Madlock of the Pirates often does that; so does Steve Garvey of the Dodgers. They rarely open up on an inside pitch, trying to pull it. Instead, they'll just go ahead and try to fight off the pitch for a base hit.

When I see the ball inside, I sometimes have a tendency to open up and try to get the head of the bat on the ball. That can be good—you can hit home runs like that—but most of the time when you try to get the head of the bat on an inside pitch, you foul it off or pop up. You don't break as many bats, but you don't get as many hits, either.

You'll find that .300 hitters break a lot of bats by fighting off inside pitches. Well, I may not be tempted to go downtown with pitches as often (especially since I changed my hitting style), but I still have lots of bats; I only break eight or nine a year. I wouldn't mind starting to break them more often and having a few less.

THE ON-DECK CIRCLE

The on-deck circle is the place where your at-bat actually starts. Players have a tendency to overlook the time spent on-deck, as I myself have at times. But if used properly, the on-deck circle can be an important part of your at-bat.

Once you leave the dugout, you should begin concentrating on your at-bat. The first thing to do is to go over in your mind, as you have been throughout the game, what the pitcher normally throws to you. You may also want to go over what he's throwing to the player hitting before you, depending on your place in the lineup. For example, when I was hitting fifth behind Greg Luzinski, I would watch every move the pitcher made throwing to Greg, because he and I were known as similar hitters. I knew that if the pitcher had success with particular pitches against Greg, he'd try the same pitches with me. I also knew that if Greg had success hitting a certain pitch, the pitcher would be less apt to try to get me out with it.

But since I usually hit third, in front of Greg, when we played together, he was able to take advantage of this situation more often than I was. It was a big advantage for Greg over the years, to come on-deck and watch exactly how the other teams pitched me. I guarantee it added 20 points to his average. Certain pitchers did pitch us differently, but eight out of ten times, if a pitcher was successful with a certain pattern against me, Greg could expect to see it, too.

Here's how it worked. I'd get a high, inside pitch and take it. Maybe the next pitch would be a good slider, low and away, which I'd miss. Then, after another strike, I'd strike out on a slider low and away. That's basically a standard way of pitching hitters, but Greg can see that the pitcher is confident in his slider at that point.

On the other hand, maybe I'd hit that slider after getting moved off the plate, driving it to rightfield. Then the pitcher would think that he doesn't have his slider where he wants it or that I hit a good pitch. Either way, he'd be less apt to try the same pattern on the man behind me.

Anticipation, then, is one way to use the on-deck circle to get ready for an at-bat. You can anticipate pitches by watching the pitcher's pattern to the man in front of you, if he's a similar hitter; or you can anticipate pitches by refreshing your memory as to how you were pitched the last time up or in the last game you faced this particular pitcher. Part of this thinking is done prior to the game, of course. But when it's time to hit, you should review it. You may want to stand in the on-deck circle and actually time the pitcher's windup, or pretend he's throwing to you, seeing the pitches in your mind and practicing swinging at them.

You also should be anticipating what can happen in the game and what your at-bat might call for. Again, you have to be aware of the game situation. If it's the eighth inning of a close game and the man in front of you hits a double, you should get him over any way you can. With no one on in the late innings of a one-run game, your job is to get on base any way you can.

Finally, you have to anticipate what can happen *before* your at-bat. If there's a man in scoring position, you must be ready to run to home plate in order to tell him whether or not to slide, and if so, how—away from or inside the catcher. You may also have to clear away the catcher's mask, the bat, or anything else that can get in the runner's way. Baserunners get hurt because the on-deck hitter isn't paying attention to the game. He's looking at the stands, swinging his bat, or maybe even still at the bat rack while his teammate is coming around third, unsure whether to slide. As the next hitter, you must coach the batter coming home.

Every hitter has his own on-deck style, but I believe it's a big waste of energy to stand there and pump a lot of iron (lead doughnuts and bats) while waiting to hit. I also think that a hitter who kneels quietly in the on-deck circle, as Hank Aaron always did, gives the impression that he's planning his strategy—that he's in control, on top of his game. Aaron used to walk up there, lay his helmet down, and kneel quietly, watching every move the pitcher made. Former teammate Dick Allen did the same thing. I knew both of them well, and both men were students of the game—especially Dick, who learned from teammate Tony Taylor always to look for a pitcher to give away something in his windup or delivery.

I often take the same approach in the on-deck circle, but there are times when I'm too fidgety. Kneeling calmly is something I'd like to learn to do consistently. When this kind of approach becomes second-nature, your mind is free to concentrate on important things.

I also like to take to the circle a weighted bat so that my own bat will feel slightly light at the plate. I don't swing the bat much, but I work it in my hands. If I can get my wrists used to pumping that slightly heavier weight, I should have just a bit more pop in my wrists when I go to hit. (Be careful if you do this, however. The adrenaline you generate each time you go up to hit can be enough to make the bat as fast as you want it. If you add that extra-light feeling, you might be too quick, as I am sometimes.)

When it's my turn to hit, I walk around the back of the batter's box and take a couple of slow, smooth practice swings. I'll up the tempo a bit when I actually get in the box, because those practice swings aren't real rips, just cuts I think are picture-perfect. Then I get into the batter's box relaxed and ready to hit, without a lot of fidgeting.

What I've just described is the on-deck routine that is ideal for me as a hitter. If I go to the on-deck circle 600 times a year, maybe 400 times I use it for the right purpose. The other 200 times, the pine tar on my bat doesn't feel good, or I'm practicing my swing because my bat felt heavy the previous at-bat—my concentration is disturbed. You can't help that sometimes. The important thing is to set up and attempt to follow an on-deck routine that suits you as a hitter.

THE FINE ART OF HITTING II:
STANCE AND SWING

THE STANCE

A hitter's stance in the batter's box is personal, like his bat. If I gave you a bat and asked you to stand at home plate, you'd pick a spot in relation to the plate where you'd instinctively stand if someone was going to throw you a pitch. That's the first thing a player should do: walk into the batter's box and stand where his instincts tell him to. From that point, he should adjust his stance based on the kind of hitter he is or feels he can be. I made a major, and successful, adjustment in my stance before the 1979 All-Star Game. Essentially, the adjustment made me more of a gap-type, straightaway hitter, which allowed me to hit for a higher average without taking away from my home run production.

My stance used to be perfectly average. By "average" I mean it

IN THE BOX

Roberto Clemente's stance

my stance

an average stance

was slightly closed (my front foot a bit closer to the plate than my back foot), with my back foot positioned in roughly the same place in the batter's box as that of most hitters.

That particular position in the box felt natural to me, because I'd been using it ever since I was young and all I wanted to do was pull the ball out of the playground. By 1979, however, I'd begun thinking about changing my position, as well as other parts of my batting style. I felt I could not only improve one facet of my game—hitting for average—without taking anything away from my power hitting, but even benefit my hitting in general. I wanted a stance that combined the one used by the late Roberto Clemente—who positioned himself as far off the plate as anyone I've ever seen—and the stance used by Pete Rose. I wanted a stance that gave me a strike zone like Pete Rose's and that produced balls hit in Clemente-fashion—with power to all fields. Clemente stood off the plate because he liked the ball out and away, on the outside corner. Having to force his upper body to go

ROSE AT BAT
Note Pete Rose's stance, and approach to the ball.

1

2

3

4

out after the ball was what felt right to him. The same is true for Rose, and I thought it would suit me best as a hitter, too.

That's why I adopted a stance in which I backed up about eight inches off the plate and moved a bit deeper in the box. From that position, I could stride into the plate instead of striding toward the pitcher. That forced me to take my left shoulder into the ball, rather than to open up (that is, to throw my left shoulder away from the plate), and so I hit the ball more to center and to the right- and left-centerfield gaps than down the left side. When I hit now, I can see the centerfielder lined up directly behind the pitcher; before, when I was a pull hitter, he would play in left-center. This adjustment opened up all kinds of new hitting areas for me.

By moving off the plate, I've also become less vulnerable to the inside pitch. Pitchers don't like to let me (or any other power hitter) extend my arms, so they jam me. In my old stance, the only way I could get to the inside strikes I see so much was by opening up to hit. I wanted to stride into the ball, but I couldn't because I was so close to the plate.

Backing off the plate made it more comfortable for me to hit that pitch. It also made it possible for me to wait longer on the ball. I still have spells, though, when I pull off the ball a bit and don't keep my left shoulder closed all the way through the swing. I feel I can hit for an even higher average if I limit my vulnerability to these spells of inconsistency by controlling the temptation to open up and go for home runs that I'll hit anyway. Still, I've made improvements with this new approach—and made them at a time when everyone around me (except for fans who didn't like my strikeouts) seemed satisfied with my performance, because I hit home runs.

STRIDE RIGHT

If you stand close to the plate when you hit, stride straight to cover the hitting zone.

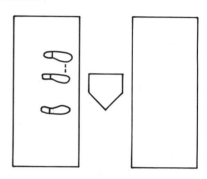

If you stand very deep in the box, as Roberto Clemente did, you must stride into the plate to cover the hitting zone.

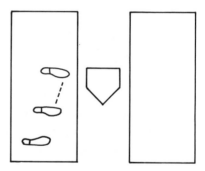

Here is my stance and the stride I use to cover the hitting zone. Using this stance—somewhat deep and off the plate—and this stride produces balls hit straightaway.

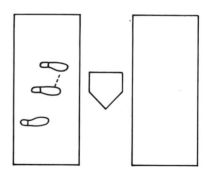

Changing my position in the batter's box is more complicated than experimenting with different bats. Where and how you stand affects your whole style of hitting. I made a conscious change in my style that was as much mental as physical, one that helped me become the kind of hitter I knew I could be. It's worked so far, making me a better all-around hitter who still hits home runs—and maybe even more of them. My new position feels so normal and good to me that now I couldn't even walk in the batter's box and show you where I used to stand.

But let's say you're a young player who just wants to make contact. What good would it do for you to stand back in the box, like Clemente? If you're going to be a contact hitter like Larry Bowa, you might not even cover the inside—much less the outside—corner from deep in the batter's box. You have to stand tight at the plate and take a shorter stride or just shift your weight to hit the ball.

Some hitters stand so close that their stride carries the front foot in front of home plate. Lonnie Smith of the Cardinals does that. It's a natural position for some contact hitters.

Whatever type of hitter you are, there are two main things to remember about positioning yourself to hit: assume a stance that's comfortable and find a location in the box that fits your style of hitting. You have to stand where your stride and swing allow you to cover the strike zone with your bat. To cover the strike zone, the meat of the bat should pass through the imaginary cylinder over the plate in which the pitch is a strike.

But as you progress in baseball and discover more about what kind of a hitter you are, you will begin to find your own strike zone, as well as the one set by baseball. Your location in the batter's box dictates how much of home plate you can cover—or how much you want to cover. Nobody ever said that to be a great hitter you have to stand in a spot where you can hit only strikes, or that you have to learn to take pitches that are inside, or that you have to hit pitches that come in at the knees or at the letters. Simply not true: you can give away the whole plate, or any amount you want, and still hit well.

The plate is for the pitcher, the catcher, and the umpire. The hitting area is for the hitter. The batter must determine for himself what his hitting area is. He has to be aware of the legal strike zone but not confined by it.

The strike zone and the hitting zone can be two different areas, depending on a player's style of hitting. Larry Bowa's contact style, for instance, tends to make the strike zone and his hitting zone the same. With Johnny Bench's style, there are two different zones. Throw Bench inside and he's going to hurt you; pitch him on the outside corner and he's vulnerable.

Players like Bench don't care if they cover the outside quarter or so of the plate. They'd rather have the hitting surface of the bat cover the other three-quarters of the plate and a quarter off the inside corner. With their hitting technique—where and how they swing—they'd prefer to hit the pitch that's three inches inside.

Bench-type hitters might not care whether or not a pitch hits the outside corner. Not many pitchers can consistently throw strikes there, and these hitters know that they're going to smoke a ball that's five to six inches off the inside of the plate. Rather than wanting to hit everything the pitchers throw, including his best slider on the outside corner, they really want to get a pitch they can pull, and the inside pitch lends itself better to that. They can hit that pitch with more authority and often drive it out of the ball park.

A hitter will set up for the inside pitch by mentally moving the plate; it's as if he picks it up and pulls it toward him. A player who likes the outside pitch will mentally move the plate *outside,* conceding the inside quarter of the strike zone to the pitcher. What the hitter gives up depends on how he defines his hitting zone.

At this stage of my career, my hitting zone is inconsistent, because I still have a tendency to try to do too much at the plate. For instance, at times I'll want to smoke an inside pitch and at other times I'll want to take it. I'll do the same thing with certain outside pitches. I try to do *everything* within my ability as a hitter, but that can be self-defeating. If you try to do too much, you won't have the consistency you should have. You must know yourself and decide what kind of hitter you are or can be.

Instead of trying to do everything against every pitcher, I like to hit based on the style of the man I'm facing. When Don Sutton of the Astros pitches to me, his approach is to tie me up inside, to prevent me from extending my arms. He's had success pitching me that way, so I know that in every at-bat he's going to try to tie me up with something hard. Against him, then, I'll be more apt to lay off pitches on the outside of the plate. I'll be better prepared to hit the inside pitch that day, because I'll be concentrating on it.

That's my thinking going into the at-bat. Once I'm at the plate, I may reach out and hit a ball low and away—that's instinct taking over. But basically, against a pitcher like Sutton I'll mentally pick up home plate and move it inside. That's *my* hitting zone for that game.

Against Tommy John (when he was in the NL), I'd be more likely to look for every pitch to be low and away. With John ready to release the ball, I'd get into position to make contact on the outside corner.

Some people may say that in doing this, I'm giving in to the pitcher. Their argument is that John, for instance, will keep throwing the ball outside a little farther and a little farther each time, and before I know it, I'll be swinging at pitches a foot off the plate. John will be making me hit *his* pitch, and so have a better chance of getting me out.

I don't agree. My theory with Tommy John is that I can hit his pitch. I feel that I can position myself so that against a sinkerball pitcher like John or the Mets' Randy Jones, I can add about six inches to the outside of the plate. I'm not worried about anything they throw inside. So I don't have one best pitch to hit; I can hit the pitcher's pitch.

In a few instances, a player may want to change his hitting zone by moving up (but never back) in the batter's box, especially against someone with a trick pitch—like a knuckleball, spitter, or what Bruce Sutter of the Cardinals calls his split-finger fastball. There's not much you can do with those pitches except try to counteract the break or movement by cutting down the distance the pitch travels. If you see a pitch that travels 60 feet and then drops, why not move up in the box and hit it before it makes its break?

Sutter has the perfect pitch to try this with. If I move up a foot and a half from my normal stance in the batter's box, his pitch is less apt to drop before I have a chance to make contact. Either I'll hit it or it will drop after I swing. I've had some success against Sutter because I'm willing to adjust my stance.

Against a knuckleball pitcher, you can also try moving up in the batter's box. But every knuckleball breaks differently. I feel that the key to hitting the knuckleball is to try to hit it back even with your body. Of course, I've seen Phil Niekro's knuckleball break from behind my head down into the dirt on the outside corner, and there's not much anyone can do about that.

Many players won't make adjustments in their game. They'll position themselves the same way in the batter's box whether Don Sutton or Tom Seaver is burning them inside with fastballs or Randy Jones is throwing little sinkers outside.

Some people would say that a player like that is doing the right thing by staying within himself. I would never argue with anyone else's success, but I do feel that to be a great hitter you occasionally have to be able to adjust your style to the game situation. Not major adjustments, just small things that make sense when certain pitchers are out there. In the same game, I may start out facing a finesse pitcher and then have to hit later against a reliever who comes at me with hard stuff. Sooner or later, a good hitter will figure out how to hit with any kind of pitcher. I have several different plans I use against "special" pitchers. To me, that's offensive baseball.

Much of what I've just been discussing is very advanced and not for young players. You can get the most out of a young player just by letting him go out and play. In the batter's box he shouldn't think about strike zones and stances and adjusting to pitchers. He should just step in and stand wherever it feels natural, then relax and look for the ball. If it's in the cards for him to learn the more technical material, he will when he gets to the big leagues someday.

Players should be aware, though, that the hitting/strike zone distinction I've been discussing actually describes what happens naturally to players at all levels of the game. A young player may actually have a hitting zone, an area where he likes to hit the ball—say, every time the pitcher throws it two inches in off the plate. He may not know his hitting zone is different from the strike zone, and he may have no idea the pitch he's hitting is a ball. But every time the pitcher throws it in there, he smokes it; and he'll probably go right to the big leagues doing that.

BETWEEN STANCE AND SWING

The transition from stance to swing is a crucial part of the at-bat. First of all, you have to learn to pick up the ball as soon as possible after the pitcher releases it. To do that, you have to watch the *slot* the pitcher throws out of, the point at which he releases the ball. I don't watch the ball go around the pitcher's body and up over his head; I just look at the slot. And each pitcher has his own slot. As with a pitching machine, you know the ball is going to come out of the same place every time. That's why if Tom Seaver, who always throws over the top, ever came at me sidearm, I guarantee you I'd be surprised and, with fewer than two strikes, take the pitch.

As the pitcher is winding up and getting ready to deliver the ball, you should keep in mind three points I talked about in the opening chapter: concentration, relaxation, and controlled aggressiveness.

By "concentration," I mean complete concentration on the ball. Not on the sign in centerfield or the pitcher's neckchain or the umpire in your line of sight. Those are the kinds of things you see when you're not hitting well. When you are hitting well, you have complete concentration on the ball. In golf, if you're playing well and someone coughs or makes noise while you're standing over the ball, you just block it out of mind. But if you're having a bad day and nothing feels good, those distractions sharpen and you notice everything. It works the same way at the plate.

"Relaxation" means that you're not trying too hard. You're not squeezing the bat and grinding the sawdust out of it; you're not pressing and rushing to hit the ball. In order to do what you want as a hitter, to create maximum bat speed, you have to be relaxed. At times I've been so relaxed at home plate, with such a light grip on the bat, that when I take an inside pitch the bat will fall out of my hands. But there also have been times when I've squeezed the bat as hard as I can. So I know what it's like to be completely relaxed and I know what it's like to be tense and pressing. And relaxed, I get the best results.

Being relaxed *doesn't* mean you lose the feeling of controlled aggressiveness as a hitter. Not overaggressiveness—which I've experienced many times, when the fans are booing, the game is on the line, and I'm thinking, "Now's my chance to win this game; I'm going to win this game with a home run." Then, I want to do everything so badly my movements become tense and tight and quick—not relaxed and smooth, as they should be when hitting.

If you can do these three things and remain under control, staying within yourself and taking a short, relaxed stride with your hands back, you'll create a certain rhythm, a groove, at the plate.

Part of this rhythm is a trigger—a physical mannerism that relaxes you but gets you moving and ready to swing the bat. A trigger can be an important part of a good groove at the plate. There are famous triggers—Joe Morgan flapping his elbow, Willie Stargell windmilling his bat, Sadahra Oh lifting his front leg off the ground—but each player has his own unique motion, even if it doesn't stand out. Usually a trigger serves to move the hands back or turn the wrist away. Turning away in order to turn it back in starts movement—like cocking a trigger. If you watch golf, you'll see Jack Nicklaus turn his head a certain way before he hits; that's his trigger.

Sometimes hitters aren't aware of the trigger they use. I had to think hard about what I do. If I'm relaxed, my hands will move back and my elbow will go up easily. If I'm tense, my elbow will go up tight and fast, and from that position it's hard to get my bat back to a level swing. There are hitters who hit with the elbow up—George Foster of the Mets, for example—but they don't start with it down and take it up.

The movement that the trigger starts is important. There are very few hitters who stand completely still before approaching the ball. Dave Kingman is the only hitter I can think of who's been successful hitting from a stationary position; to me, it looks as if every muscle in Dave's body is tense before he swings. That may work for him, but a trigger helps most people relax and concentrate. A deep breath will do the same thing. Let all the air out of your body, and you become relaxed. Many times it's helped me to take a breath as the pitcher is getting ready to come to the plate. You'll see pitchers, and free-throw shooters in basketball do it, too. It helps us all relax.

Now that you've got your trigger, you have to think about your stride. The pitcher has released the ball, you're getting ready to swing the bat, and you begin your stride—into the ball, toward the mound, just shifting your weight, whatever. That stride is very important. It gives you movement through the ball, allowing you to transfer your weight. If you don't shift your weight from back to front, you'll have no power. You must generate forward movement, even if, like Garry Maddox, you only pick up your front foot and put it down. You have to come off your back leg.

The stride is part of that rhythm you're trying to create at the plate. A player who has a smooth and easy movement in his stride usually has good rhythm. The stride, along with the trigger, comprise the first stages of execution for all good hitters.

THE SWING

Over the years I've learned a lot about myself as a hitter, and I'm just now beginning to develop a consistently smooth swing. Steve Garvey has the kind of swing I'm talking about—a smooth cut that's the same all the time. He has the ability, as I said before, to stay the same from at-bat to at-bat. That ability has its merits, especially in comparison with a player who wants to change but isn't successful doing so; when the comparison is made with a player who adjusts and is making the right changes, staying the same doesn't seem so advisable.

Whatever kind of adjustments you make in your swing and whatever age you are, I recommend that you hit with a level swing, trying to drive through the ball. If you hold the bat perpendicular to the ground, as I do, think *down* to end up with a level cut. To swing as you should, anticipate hitting six balls lined up in a row, and start your bat from whatever point will bring it

IN THE SWING
I recommend that you hit with a level swing, trying to drive through the ball. To swing as you should, anticipate hitting six balls lined up in a row, and start your bat from whatever point will bring it in a level plane through the balls.

in a level plane through the balls. Dave Parker and Steve Garvey have high batting averages because they hit like that—always keeping the bat head level through the ball.

Ted Williams advises swinging up through the ball. His theory is that the pitcher is throwing slightly downhill, so if you have a slight upswing, you'll hit level with the ball. I disagree. Hitting up through the ball leaves only one point over the plate at which the bat can make contact for a base hit. If you hit too early, it's a little topper; too late, it's a foul ball; and right on top, it's a flyball. You've got to hit the ball perfectly in order to hit a duck-hooking line drive for a single. That's the kind of hit Dave Kingman or Reggie Smith get when they hit the ball. But Smith, unlike Kingman, has an uncanny ability to hit for a high average swinging up through the ball. The same is true for the Royals' Amos Otis. It was awesome the way he hit in the 1980 World Series—I couldn't figure out how a guy could hit that well with an upper-cut.

One theory sums up the upswing-downswing idea: try to prevent pop-ups. The fewer flyballs you hit, the better hitter you are. I'll bet Pete Rose hasn't popped up more than five times a year since I've played with him. I'll bet I popped up 125 times.

Pete's ball is always on a line or on the ground. That's why it's so tough to get him out. He doesn't hit long flys against the fence or pop up in the infield. Any hitter—home run hitters included—will hit more home runs by trying to drive the ball on a line. Graig Nettles of the Yankees, for example, has a slight upswing. So he hits a lot of flyballs—many of them home runs to right and right-center in Yankee Stadium, but many more of them flyball outs. He could do even better with a level swing. Always remember how easy it is to catch a flyball or a pop-up.

There are exceptions to every rule, and there are a select few players in the majors today—some of whom I've mentioned—who can get by with that type of uppercut. It's their natural swing—not a home run swing—and they've had success with it. What I'm saying is, don't swing up trying to hit the ball out of the park. Home runs don't happen that way. And they're not an either/or proposition. If you're a good hitter with the ability to hit home runs, you'll hit them. If you're a hitter with bad habits but the ability to hit home runs, you'll be a bad hitter who hits some homers. In any case, you'll hit more home runs with a proper swing and game approach. You don't have to settle for being either a home run hitter or a good hitter—you can be both, if you have the talent.

Hank Aaron had the classic line-drive, home run swing. He stands out in my mind as the player who had the best idea about hitting down through the ball with a level swing, and he got the best results. The balls he hit took off out of the infield on a line and started to rise. That's the kind of swing you should aim for.

For me, still, it's natural to uppercut a little. Because my natural swing has a tendency to be up, the ball is in the air more often and my average is down. So I have to think about hitting down through the ball to compensate, to end up with a level swing. Believe me, that's not easy to do through 162 games, but I know it's a key fundamental if I'm going to hit .300 consistently.

Swinging up also puts you in the wrong position to get a good start to first if you do get a hit. That's why you never want to see a hitter falling back, with his weight on his back leg, like you see sometimes in pictures of Mickey Mantle and Johnny Bench. It may make a nice picture, but it's all wrong and they'd say so, too.

You just don't get many hits that way. Most often you get a pop-up; or if you're lucky, a long flyball for a home run.

You don't want to be known as a back-leg hitter (weight on the back side during the swing). Most times a player hits a good crisp line drive, his front leg will be bent and his weight will be over the plate, or at least perpendicular to it. Bake McBride, a great hitter, leans way forward over the plate. That works for him and is a better extreme than falling back.

I can pretty well tell from pictures of me hitting what the result of a particular swing has been. In one game picture, for instance, I'm almost erect over my front leg. I'd be in a perfect position to hit, except I'm falling back just a bit and my top hand is under the bat. I guarantee that the contact that resulted from that swing ended in either a topped groundball or a flyball, because I had to swing up on the ball to get into that position. When (as a right-handed hitter) my right hand is underneath, I'm swinging up at the ball instead of driving the head level *through* the ball, as I would with my right hand on top. In a level swing, your left hand is doing nothing but pulling the bat through the swing. The left hand actually determines whether you're going to go down level through the ball or loop your swing.

Even though I have definite theories about my swing and what's good for me, I still have that old, high school urge to hit the ball in the air. If I'm guessing for the pitch and guess right, I sometimes want to take a big, uncontrolled, playground swing and go for the seats.

The toughest thing for me to do is look for a fastball, get it right where I want it, and just try to hit it with authority. Having the ability to just wrist the ball into the upper deck is the problem. If I couldn't do that, I wouldn't be subject to those periods when I want to get a run for the team with one swing and so open up, trying to hit the ball out of the park. That's what makes me different from a hitter like Pete Rose. It's tough for Pete ever to get away from his game, because he knows he isn't a home run hitter. For him to think about home runs would be like me thinking that to hit a home run, I'd have to put the ball out of Veteran's Stadium—I'd probably never try to do it, because it isn't possible.

More hitters would have the temptations that helped get me my .263 lifetime average if they had my particular home run ability. And those temptations are strongest when I haven't hit a homer for a while. The more time that passes, and the more I have "home run" on my mind, the less likely I am to keep my shoulder closed and the less likely I am to hit the line drives I want, or even the home runs. Learning to handle that temptation will make me a better hitter with a higher average and fewer strikeouts, and I'll still get my homers.

I have the ability to do that if I can get more control, more consistency in my game. I'm a natural home run hitter—when my swing is in a groove, it produces home runs—but I'm also a natural athlete and I think I've shown that I can use my ability to hit .300, as I did for the first time in the shortened 1981 season, while not sacrificing my homers. I want to maximize my role as a major league player, not just settle for home runs.

Critics say if I worry about my strikeouts and try to cut them down by making more contact, I'll be less aggressive as a hitter and hit fewer home runs. They think I'm trying to go beyond my limits as a player. But in fact, I think that my way, I hit more home runs. Knock 80 strikeouts off my sometimes league-leading

BETWEEN THE LINES

Balls hit between the A lines are hit by standing off the plate and going into the pitch. This is a straightaway hitter, like myself and George Brett.

Balls hit between the B lines are produced by a dead-pull hitter. This area is easier to defense, so the percentage of hits is lower. This kind of hitting is usually the result of being close to the plate and opening up to get to the ball.

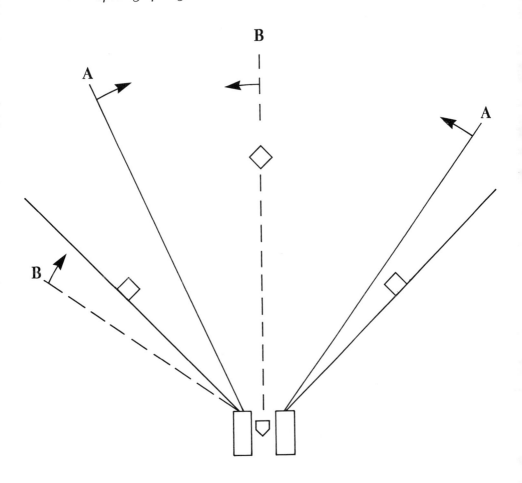

total and I have to hit at least 10 more home runs. I've been moving in that direction over the last few years. Even though I'm much more of a straightaway hitter now, using the whole field far more than ever before, I hit just as many, if not more home runs. The difference is that most of my home runs now are hit from right-center to left-center. I don't hit many down the leftfield line anymore.

But when you're not taking the healthy kind of swing at home plate that the fans want to see, they get angry, because you don't seem to be the aggressive hitter you're supposed to be. They like to see you spin around in the batter's box, with your helmet flying off.

Home runs aren't hit like that. I can't emphasize enough that home runs result from *technique*. Summing up the home run philosophy, you could say that homers come from a combination of perfect hitting execution, strength, pitch location, and bat speed.

It's not just a question, then, of muscling the ball out of the park. I'm a strong man, but Dave Parker, for instance, is probably a lot stronger (in terms of lifting weight)—and Reggie Jackson might be, too. I know Bob Boone is much stronger. I hit all the home runs I do because I have the almost ideal combination of the strength and body proportions to produce leverage; and it's leverage that enables me to create as much if not more bat speed through the ball than anyone else in baseball. Just about every major-league player can hit a home run, but very few can hit them as often or as far as I can.

Larry Bowa's home runs—at most, two or three a year—occur when he has a perfect, fundamentally sound swing at a pitch in the location he needs to hit a home run. As for me and other home run hitters, we need the same good swing, but we can combine it with pitches in many more locations. We hit 25 home runs a year on talent—a combination of strength and coordination—and we hit 10–15 on sheer strength, by reaching out and pulling the ball, or by getting under the ball and using our strength to put enough on it to drop it just over the fence.

With the right execution, I can make home runs out of more pitches than Larry or most other players can. But I don't have to take a big, uncontrolled swing to do that. Swinging from the heels is easier than swinging under control, but since I want to be as successful a hitter as I can be, I steadily fight to stay relaxed and under control.

I've already had good results with home runs this way. In recent seasons I very seldom hit wall-scraping home runs. All but four or five of the 48 and 31 home runs that I hit in 1980 and 1981, respectively, were long ones, hit with authority. You knew they were gone when they were hit. Cutting down on flyball home runs means I'm consistently hitting the ball on the nose. I'm hitting line drives to straightaway center rather than the ones that arc up and lob into the bullpen. This way, if I don't connect in just the right way to get a home run, I'm much more likely to get a base hit than a flyball out.

The key is to be able to hit the ball with authority. If it goes out in pressure situations, fine. If a young kid who was big for his age and strong, with some athletic ability, wanted to know about hitting home runs, I wouldn't tell him to *try* to hit home runs. I'd tell him to hit line drives, because the home runs will come.

THE BATTING TEE

Once you have the basics of stride and swing, practice is important. How you practice is, again, an individual matter. It depends on the flow you're in as a hitter. Practice can be used to work on mechanics, reinforcing the good habits and eliminating the bad, or as a time of discovery, to find out what might be causing a bad spell.

To my mind, the foremost technique for practicing hitting a baseball is hitting off a batting tee. Along with other major leaguers, I use the tee constantly in spring training and during the season to work on that smooth, controlled, level swing through the ball.

The key to using the tee is knowing where to place it in relation to home plate and at what height to place the ball on it to get the practice you need. If you were going to practice hitting an inside pitch off the tee, you wouldn't just put the tee down on home plate and hit baseballs off it. Contact with the baseball occurs along many points—think of the contact plane as a diagonal line intersecting the plate—and you have to set the tee where you want to make contact to hit a particular pitch. In order to hit an inside pitch—the first contact point on the line—to leftfield, I have to make contact with the ball almost a foot in front of home plate. So that's where the batting tee has to be—for me, that is. You have to hit an inside pitch in front of the plate so that your arms will be extended through the pitch when you make contact, but where you place the tee to do that depends on where you stand in the batter's box. For a player who stands farther up in the box, the tee should be placed even farther out. For someone who stands where Clemente used to stand, the tee may be back even with home plate. But to Clemente, that would have been like hitting the ball out in front of home plate.

Once you get the tee placed properly for an inside pitch, imagine a pitcher winding up and getting ready to throw the ball. Then, as you swing at the ball sitting on the tee, drive the bat head down level through the ball and strike a crisp line drive.

Now, if you move the "pitches" out a bit more on that diagonal line, almost even with the middle of the plate, you don't have to make contact as far out in front; instead, you make contact just in front of the plate. If you're going to hit a ball on the outside corner, you should try to hit it even farther back, more even with the plate. Remember, use the same "line-drive" swing on all pitches.

The theory is that you can wait longer to hit balls on the outside corner than balls on the inside corner. Keep that in mind when placing your batting tee. The best hitters hit the outside pitch back even with the plate. The only way to hit that pitch in front of the plate is to pull it, which is what a lot of dead-pull hitters do. You have to be a special kind of hitter to be successful pulling outside pitches consistently. Not many dead-pull hitters hit .300.

That's why pitches thrown to the inside corner that break to the outside corner are so tough. You try to hit those pitches in front of the plate, then they break low and away and you end up hitting a little dribbler to third or shortstop. You're fooled thinking it's a fastball and you end up grounding out, at best.

You can see what a good practice tool the batting tee is, how representative it can be of the basic ways of hitting and of the choices you can make. That's why you don't just put the tee

TEEING OFF

To use the batting tee as an effective practice tool, you must understand how to position it, and adjust the height to simulate the pitch you want to hit.

An inside pitch must be hit out in front of the plate, so I place the tee where my swing and stance allow me to do that.

1

2

3

4

5

I place the tee even with the plate to practice hitting a pitch low and outside.

1

2

3

4

down and move your body around. You adjust the tee for the kind of pitch you want to hit, moving it along that hypothetical diagonal line, depending on where you stand in the batter's box.

You can also adjust the height of the tee to simulate pitches in different parts of the strike zone. Since I'm known as a good low-ball hitter who doesn't hit the high pitch consistently, I'll often hoist the tee up as high as I can, setting the ball just above the strike zone. Technically, such a pitch would be a ball; but it's a good pitch to hit if you use the proper fundamentals, and learning to hit it consistently would expand my hitting zone.

By using the batting tee the way I do, I'm also practicing keeping my bat back and hitting everything with my hands above the ball. You should always keep your hands above the ball, as Steve Garvey does. You never see him drop his hands and end up underneath the pitch, below the plane of the ball. High ball, he's over the top; low ball, he's down through it.

If I practice with the tee at the highest possible level, I feel that eventually I can develop good enough habits to hit high pitches, especially hanging breaking balls. Good hitters generally lay off high fastballs, but there are several good high-ball hitters in the league. The Cubs' Jerry Morales is one; Houston's Jose Cruz is another. Latin players, as a rule, are good high-ball hitters. If you watch them in the on-deck circle, you'll see that they all practice swinging down on the ball.

Reggie Smith, as I've said before, is just the opposite. Reggie is a *great* low-ball hitter. He swing starts with his bat high, but he ends up looping his swing—and has a lot of success doing it. However, even though you can loop your bat into low pitches all day, there's no way you can loop it into a high pitch.

Here the tee is set for a high inside pitch. Note the extension of my arms as I hit down and level through the ball.

1

2

3

4

5

*   *   *

I also practice hitting the high pitch without the tee. In batting practice when I throw the ball up to hit fungos to one of the infielders, I throw it up high to practice hitting it high. I'll also practice my swing that way.

I feel that the more I practice what's proper as a hitter, the sooner in my career it's going to come naturally. I do know that uncontrolled feeling I get at times as a hitter lessens each year.

I'm not saying that every year I've had more success statistically, but even in an off-year such as 1978, when my batting average and output were way down, I thought throughout the year that I was a much more controlled hitter who consistently hit the ball with greater authority than in the previous three years. I hit .250 and didn't hit too many home runs, but I always had the fielders moving somewhere. I hit the ball back to the pitcher or to the second baseman, lined out to center or down the right-field line. I did a lot of things I hadn't done in my better years—things I thought I should be doing. I did much more in that year than people really gave me credit for. Using that experience to build on my progress as a hitter, I came back for a very good year in 1979, and even better ones in 1980 and 1981.

Throughout my career the batting tee has been a tremendous practice tool. Billy DeMars, the Phillies' former hitting coach, swears by the tee. He has a very sound knowledge of the dynamics of hitting and we practiced a great deal together. Billy has played a big role in my development as a hitter, and so has his batting tee.

THE FINE ART OF HITTING III:
HITTER VS. PITCHER

AS I'VE SAID, I consider hitting to be an art. Part of the art lies in combining the physical process—standing in the box, striding, and swinging—with the mental process of choosing which pitch to hit, and then adapting your style to your team's ultimate goal of scoring runs.

What I especially have to offer you in hitting is how to think about the game in the batter's box. There you should think about how to work the pitcher, not about your swing. In the batter's box, you can think too much about mechanics, but not about how to compete with the pitcher. You need a general mental approach to hitting to get the kind of pitches you want, but one that you can adapt to specific situations.

FEAR OF THE BALL

Pitch selection is part of the mental game of hitting; in fact, it's a major weapon in your one-on-one competition with the pitcher. But before you can make this or any other part of your game work, you must master another facet of hitting's mental game. Fear of the ball must be erased from your mind if you're ever to become a good hitter.

I know how tough that is to do. At a young age I was deadly afraid of a ball hitting me in the head, and I was very open to intimidation by pitchers who, like Steve Yeager's batterymate, could throw a curveball. I still had some fear when I first got to pro ball (my years as a switch-hitter in high school and college could have contributed to this, by delaying my development as a right-handed hitter), and pitchers used to throw me only breaking balls or sliders. Just as in high school, I'd flinch and the ball would curve over the plate. I didn't stop reacting physically until the last half of my Triple A season, and it wasn't until 1974 or so that I had no fear whatsoever of a baseball coming at my head. It's no coincidence that this is when my really strong years in the game began. I know that my ability to hit, and hit well, in the major leagues has been directly related to my totally losing all fear of the ball.

The key to eliminating that fear is experience: first, just seeing pitches over and over again; and then experiencing balls coming at your head and recognizing that they almost always break over the plate. Occasionally one doesn't, and you have to get out of the way. But that becomes routine. You also have to recognize that past a certain point, you have to leave that part of the game up to chance and hope you're protected. My attitude about getting hit with the ball is, if it's going to happen, it's going to happen.

I've also been gifted with good enough reflexes to be able to follow the ball right to the plate and get out of the way if it doesn't break. If balls coming at you below the shoulder, down on your body, hit you, it will hurt for a bit—or even for a long time, if you're hit in the right place—but that's an occupational hazard you must learn to live with.

I've learned to do that. At this point in my career, I'm in just the position I want to be. I'm not afraid of the ball, and if anything, I'm going to be a better hitter if I do get hit. I'm respected enough by pitchers around the league that they know one way *not* to get me out is to knock me down or hit me. If they do, I'll get right back into the batter's box. I may not hit a home run, or even a double or a single, on the next pitch or in the next at-bat; but I won't be afraid, and they know it. I'll just dive into the pitch all the more. Being thrown at makes me more aggressive. Getting hit by a pitch does the same thing: it can wake me up with an "all right, I needed that" kind of feeling.

That's the attitude I had one night when I went four-for-four against the Dodgers. After I had gone two-for-two against Rick Rhoden, he hit me in the back. I was then driven in, and as I was coming around third base on the way to the plate, Rhoden asked me if I was okay. I told him, "Yes—and thanks, I needed that to wake me up." I got two more hits later in that game, including one more off Rhoden.

I do need to get hit every now and then, just to keep me aware that it doesn't hurt so much and to remind me that when I do get hit, I'm still not going to be afraid of the ball. In the same way, I need to have balls thrown at my head every once in a while, to keep the feeling that I can get out of the way. But I don't ever want to have to do that twice in a row. With the respect I've gained, I don't think any pitcher would try to hit me twice; but if he does, it becomes an issue. You can often tell if a pitcher tried to hit you the first time, depending on who the pitcher is and what he throws. If he hits you a second time, you have to confront him with it—as I've had to do at times in my career.

You can't let pitchers take advantage of you. You have to stand up for yourself, especially if you're hit by the same pitcher more than once. By the same token, you also have to realize that you can't fight everybody who hits you with a baseball. If you do, pretty soon everybody will know you can be intimidated. Whether you challenge every pitcher who throws at you or always back off the plate, the result will be the same: you'll be off your game.

Intimidation is a big part of major league baseball. To get the edge in the one-on-one competition, the cat-and-mouse game between pitcher and hitter, pitchers will use direct physical intimidation if they feel they have to. One way to get someone out, if you can't do it with ability alone, is to drill him and see how he likes that. It's part of every game, part of every series played in baseball. If a player goes four-for-four one night and he's two-for-two or three-for-three the next night, he can expect a try at intimidation. Players are fighting for their professional lives, and if protecting their livelihood means hitting someone with a pitch, most of them will do it.

Think back to the fourth game of the 1980 World Series, when George Brett was the hitter and Dickie Noles had an 0–2 count on him. Noles threw high and inside at George's chin, and George went down on his back. I believe that pitch had a great deal of purpose behind it—it was a pitch meant to intimidate.

Sometimes it's important for a pitcher, whether he's trying to win a regular-season game or a World Series title, to let a hitter—especially a great hitter—know that every pitch isn't going to be right down the middle of the plate, like it's been set on a batting tee for him to hit. Noles didn't want to continually fire the ball and let George rope it somewhere, while he's standing out there saying to himself, "This guy's just a good hitter." Not that Noles really thought he could intimidate George. One reason a great hitter is great is because he's not afraid of the ball. The idea at that point was to change the status quo. Noles had to make Brett mad enough or disturb his concentration enough to change his game.

That seems to be exactly what happened to George and to the whole Royals team. They didn't get a good swing at the ball the rest of that game—and, in fact, didn't hit well against our pitchers in the rest of the Series. Possibly they were intimidated by one pitch; whatever, I do feel that it made their hitters try too hard. It made them so mad that they wanted to hit a ball back up the middle. They were swinging too hard and it threw them out of their flow, and they got away from their game.

As that Series incident shows, the higher you go up the ladder in baseball, the more necessary it becomes to eliminate the fear of the ball if you hope to become a good hitter. The higher you go, the better the pitchers are, not only at the physical game, but at the mental game, too. And so not only must you not be afraid of the ball, you must also learn not to overreact to a pitcher's challenge. If a pitcher can get you off your game by making you mad enough to lose your concentration, he'll be just as effective.

PITCH SELECTION

The other part of the mental game of hitting—selecting a pitch—is as important as any part of your at-bat. You have to be able to adjust to the pitcher and feel you can hit his pitch, but there's no reason to do that until you have to. You want to make him throw what you want to hit.

I want my approach to bring me into a position to hit the best fastball—the pitch I can do the most with—if that's what I get. If not, with my hands and bat back I'm in a position to hit the best curveball, because it will be moving slower than the pitch I'm geared for. But if I'm looking for a curve and get a fastball, I'll probably have to rush my swing and open up my shoulder to hit it. A hitter should only look for a curveball when it's a good time to anticipate one—early in the count with a curveball pitcher, but not with two strikes. To do that you have to be on the offense as a hitter, with the count in your favor.

The best way for me to hit, then, is off the fastball—and off a fastball in the toughest location. As a hitter, I anticipate and position myself on every pitch for a fastball low and away—the toughest fastball for me to hit. If I can hit it, if it's right there, I'll be able to hit it hard.

There are times when I'm positioned for a fastball and can let the curves go by, and there are times I can't. It depends on the count. What pitches do you look for, based on the count, as an offensive rather than a defensive hitter? You become a defensive hitter only when you have two strikes on you; that's when you give in to the pitcher.

You anticipate or guess a fastball where you want it when you're an offensive hitter. But when you're a defensive hitter, with two strikes, you've got to hit what you see. You can't stand there and guess fastball when the count is 0–2. If the pitcher throws a curve and you take it, obviously you're out. When you're in an offensive position as a hitter, on the other hand, you can do what you feel makes you successful. If you guess wrong it's just a strike or a foul ball. When it's 2–0 or 3–1, you're not out if it's a strike.

When you're on the offense as a hitter, you have the freedom to do whatever you want to. When you're on the defense, you have to give in to the pitcher and hit whatever he's throwing. That's why, even with my power, with two strikes I choke up enough to have more control of the bat. I give in to the pitcher and just try to make contact. And I probably hit more home runs doing that than I have not choking up with two strikes.

Get one idea in your mind with two strikes: "I'm not going to get strike three." Not striking out is an obsession with me, simply because I've struck out so much in my career and have heard so much talk about it. I've heard, too, that it's good for me to strike out, it means I'm aggressive. But as I've shown, *controlled* aggression is what you want. Striking out doesn't help a player with his hitting or with his team responsibilities in a game situation. You've got three swings at least, and I think a hitter should be able to put the bat on the ball with that many opportunities.

To be on the offense as often as possible, then, use *all* the advantages you have as a hitter. Also, use what the pitcher gives you. You want to make the pitcher throw what you want to hit in a particular situation. Never swing at a pitcher's best pitch until you have to. After all, baseball gives you three strikes, and there's no reason you have to use them right away. Why not take a chance and try to put some pressure on the pitcher? Most of the time you can get ahead in the count simply by not swinging.

I've been using this technique successfully since the last half of 1979, and it's widely used by other players today, too. Not that this is a new idea—Pete Rose has been taking the first pitch for years, and Ted Williams did it his whole career—but you could say it's fashionable now. Keith Hernandez of the Cardinals takes the first pitch almost every time, and so do the Royals' George Brett and Hal McRae.

Taking the first pitch is one of the reasons everybody thought Ted Williams had such a good eye. He guessed the pitch he wanted to swing at, and if he didn't get that pitch, he wouldn't swing. Sometimes he'd take a breaking ball just off the plate, and people would be amazed at his uncanny ability to know to lay off the pitch. And then, of course, he was more likely to get the pitch he wanted and nail it.

I remember when I couldn't believe that Pete took the first pitch. I couldn't understand how he had the hitting ability to stand there and take the pitch like he did. But hitters today are finding out that it's smart, and doing it. Taking the first pitch is popular now because it makes sense. Other hitters probably started doing it, as I did, because it looked like something different to try. I wanted to see what players like Pete were getting out of it. What I found were several good reasons for making it part of my game, especially the first time up.

Number one, by taking the first pitch you get to see it. If it's a curveball, you see how it breaks; if it's a fastball, you get to see how hard it is. And you get a good look at it, because you're not jumping at it. You don't have anything else on your mind but standing there and striding, timing the guy and seeing what the pitch looks like. That gives you a better idea about the pitch later in the at-bat or in the game, when you see it under pressure.

I think you should see as many pitches as you can in the first at-bat. I go three-and-two many times now, not so much to see what pitchers have—I pretty much know by now—but because with my hitting success and home runs, pitchers are more apt to try and trick me. Or throw harder against me, as they do against Parker and Garvey. They don't want to work the middle of the plate, so they end up throwing a lot of balls.

Number two, by taking the first pitch you may get a ball. And if that happens, the odds are even greater that the next pitch will be the one you want. The pitcher is thinking, "I better get a strike on this guy now. If I don't, it will be two-and-oh and I'll *have* to throw a strike."

Number three, by taking the pitch I can sometimes set the *pitcher* up. The next time I go up to home plate, I take it again. Now the pitcher doesn't know. I may have him thinking I'm going to do it again. Who knows? But the third time up, maybe I'm looking for a fastball and hitting away. So I go to the plate like I'm not going for the first pitch, and then all of a sudden I'm up there swinging, taking a shot that the pitcher will be throwing a strike.

I may or may not do this, but the point is I'm opening up the possibility of setting him up for a first pitch later in the game, when I know he wants to get ahead of me and it might be an important at-bat.

By taking the first pitch, then, you've seen what the pitcher is throwing, you may have gotten ball one, and you may have set up the pitcher. You've also rehearsed your swing—taken a fundamentally sound stride into the ball, keeping your hands back, your shoulder in, and your eye on the ball, and reinforced your feeling of relaxation. So it's worth the chance of taking strike one, especially the first time up in a game.

But there are times when you may not want to spot strike one to anyone. With pitchers like Houston's J. R. Richard and Nolan Ryan on the mound, you know you're going to get a fastball and you know you better be swinging, because they're just too tough. But there are only five or six guys in the league like that. With the other 120, you're not giving up too much taking the first pitch.

In pressure situations this theory can be even more effective, because there's more temptation under pressure to swing at the first pitch, whatever it is. You're anxious, and you're concerned the pitcher will get ahead of you. What you have to realize is that the guy on the mound is pressing a bit, also. With no outs and the bases loaded in the ninth, the last thing he wants to do is stick a fastball down the middle. He'd like to throw a good, hard breaking ball low and away and hope you try to pull it, grounding out to short. Or, if he does throw a pitch as hard as he can, he's hoping you'll pop up. The pitch will probably be high in the strike zone, but even if it's strike one, you've definitely told the pitcher, "I'm not afraid, you can have that strike."

I remember in our first play-off series, in 1976, the Reds blew us away in the first two games in Philadelphia. I know that was because everyone was overanxious. We couldn't wait to get up there and get that bat moving. First pitch, a high fastball—and a pop-up. Then a groundball to short, another out, and suddenly the inning is over and we're on the field.

When we went to Cincinnati we had a meeting, and I said, "Why don't we show some poise and stop swinging at the first pitch?" I took my own advice and in the next game went three-for-four. I stood right there at home plate and took the first pitch every time. And in three of four of those at-bats, they threw ball one.

But even though this theory works many times in pressure situations, people watching can really second-guess you, and you can even second-guess yourself. In the 1980 World Series, I took the first pitch I saw, and it was right down the middle. Then I waved at two sliders, striking out on four pitches. At that point I couldn't believe I'd taken the first pitch. But I went on to have a good game and a good Series, and there's really nothing I'd have done differently.

Still, the first-pitch theory doesn't fit everyone's style. For instance, Garry Maddox agrees with me about the advantages of taking the first pitch, but first-ball hitting is so much a part of his game that my approach just doesn't work for him. He'll go out there and try it, taking the first pitch each time up, and we'll keep count. He'll get strike one twice and ball one twice and go oh-for-four, and before you know it, that will be that. Garry, like many other big leaguers, is an overaggressive hitter. Someday he may change, but he's been very successful with his style.

But working the count that way, especially the first time up, and then getting a pitch that I hit well, gives me a great advantage. If I can hit the pitcher's fastball on the nose the first time up, it puts me on the offense the rest of the game. Then I know

I'm right on a guy who has a good fastball, and I don't have to make any kind of mental or physical adjustment to hit his bread-and-butter pitch. All I have to do is try to hit his other stuff—and he knows it, too. If I work the count to the point where he gives me his best fastball, and I hit a line drive or a flyball that just misses being a home run, he knows that's not a pitch he can go to later on in the game, under pressure.

That's an important edge, because as a ball game builds up, so should your confidence as a hitter. You start from scratch in a game and build up to the late innings, when the hitting often really counts and you really want to feel confident. So it's important to have hit the ball solidly a couple of times going into the last innings of a game. It's what I call "being in the flow." You don't want to be still searching for the pitcher's fastball in your fourth or fifth at-bat. It's best to be a confident hitter in the waning moments of a ball game.

Hitting off the fastball and according to the count isn't for kids at the grade school or Little League level. Like the hitting zone/strike zone distinction, it's too complicated. I think kids at that age should just walk into the batter's box and say, "Hey, c'mon, throw the ball. I'm going to hit it." Nobody at that level can hit the curveball anyway. If a pitcher can throw it, he just strikes everyone out. Not many pitchers at the college level can throw curveballs for strikes consistently enough to make hitters swing at them, but you can talk about the count and hitting off the fastball to players at that age. You can also talk about sliders and curveballs and maybe single out certain kids to talk to about location of pitches—in or out, up or down. For others it would be too complicated. At the high school level, I'd talk about the fastball versus the curveball, but not about location. At the Little League level, I wouldn't even get into the discussion.

While many of my theories are too complicated for kids, I want them to be aware of the higher levels I've been talking about. On the other hand, I wouldn't want them to be thinking constantly about my theories while they're trying to hit a baseball.

There are times when hitters at any age can be thinking too much. When you're hitting, at a certain point, your mind should go blank, usually when the ball is out of the pitcher's hand and on the way to home plate. In that one-tenth of a second you have to decide whether or not to swing. Your mind is blank, and your ability to hit is turned over to your instincts and habits.

In that fraction of a second, ideally what comes to your mind is a good habit. If that's the case, you're more apt to be a good hitter. If you're forced into a bad habit, you have less chance of hitting well, because you have to think through those bad instincts. You have to think *longer*. Every hitter has periods of good and bad habits, but the best hitters at the end of the year will be those who have the fewest periods of falling into bad habits or those who have the ability to adjust to get out of them quickly. There is a group of hitters who can make the adjustment without realizing it, another group with just bad habits, and yet another group with only good habits. In the past few years, I've changed to a batting style that can hold good habits for a longer period of time.

One side of the coin is to be able to walk into the batter's box and not think at all, because in all your previous at-bats you did everything right, à la Steve Garvey. There are only a select few hitters like that, of course. But those are the hitters that very seldom get themselves out. It takes good pitching that can set them up along with good defense, to get them out consistently. It's much easier to get out hitters who have bad habits and are concerned about their stride and their swing, thinking, "I'll never get a hit unless I think all the way through the ball coming to home plate and I'm relaxed," and so on. A hitter who does that has no chance. You have to find a happy medium, some workable combination between your mental preparation and your instincts—at the major league level, anyway.

THE FINE ART OF HITTING IV: BUNTING

YOU CAN'T FORGET the art of bunting when discussing hitting, but it's a separate skill that should be given separate consideration. Bunting has its own mechanics and pitch selection—you use a different type of physical and mental approach at the plate. Bunting and swinging away do complement each other, however, each making the other more effective.

VALUE OF THE BUNT

The bunt is a very significant offensive weapon, but one that's not used as well today as it could be. In fact, bunting is getting to be a lost art. Very few players in baseball now can be labeled good bunters. That wasn't the case 15 or 20 years ago. Then, many players could drop a ball down the third-base line like Rod Carew can now, putting a little backspin on it and just setting it down. How many of today's players can do that, besides Carew?

One reason there aren't too many is artificial turf, which has almost wiped out the art of bunting. It's very tough to make a good bunt on turf—especially a sacrifice bunt—unless you get a high chopper. You simply can't get away with bunting the ball a little too hard, like you can on grass.

Bunting also isn't practiced enough. Players who are called on to bunt should practice even more now, because conditions dictate that they have to be even *better* bunters than before. It's just harder to gain the skill, not less important. And in fact, bunting for a base hit can be even more important to a hitter's game today.

Baseball may lend itself to less bunting generally, with the designated hitter in the American League and all the turf fields in the National League, but the less bunting there is, the less the defense looks for it and the bigger the element of surprise. So you can do more with the bunt, even if you have to work harder at it.

One reason Larry Bowa was definitely the best bunter on our team in his years with the Phillies is that he works very hard at it. I do too, and, as a result, I'm a *very* good bunter who usually gets seven to ten bunt base hits a year. Very seldom do I bunt for a base hit and not get one when I bunt the ball fair. I take pride in my ability to bunt for a base hit, and I've worked at it ever since I learned its value, along with so much else about the game, in college.

I think bunting had value for me in college in part because I was known as a home run hitter. I thought it was neat to be able to stand at home plate, drop a little ground ball down the third-base line, and get a base hit anytime I wanted to. I still feel that way now, but the ability to bunt for a base hit also gives me more of a complete game. Bunting for a base hit by anybody other than the leadoff man or the eighth-hole hitter may sometimes be laughed at today, but it does give you real advantages.

In the first place, the bunt can be very valuable for a hitter's personal momentum. It can get you a base hit to start you rolling again when you're oh-for-seven, or even oh-for-three. That's why Steve Garvey sometimes will bunt in a game—to get that one hit. It's important for hitters to be able to do that. One hit a game equals 162 hits a season. Do that and play every day, and you'll hit .280 for sure.

A bunt can also keep a batting streak alive. Ask Pete Rose how valuable that can be. During his record-breaking hitting streak in 1978, he bunted twice against the Phillies to keep the streak alive, once reaching back for a bunt base hit his fifth time up in the thirty-eighth game.

The bunt is also very valuable when it comes to game momentum. Nothing changes the momentum of a game like a hitter dropping a bunt down the third-base line, so it's something that all the hitters in your lineup should be able to do.

Even though we don't use it enough, the Phillies are good bunters as a team. Among the regulars, only Garry Maddox isn't adept at dropping the base-hit bunt. Garry did work very, very hard to learn how in spring training in 1980, but during that season I believe he only tried to bunt one time. I think Garry felt that of all the possible results of bunting, the last thing he'd end up with would be a base hit. He seemed to be afraid that the ball would go foul or back to the pitcher, or that he'd pop it up, miss it, or get hit with it. He just didn't have the confidence to try for it. I feel that Garry could add at least ten points to his batting average if he got five base-hit bunts a year.

Greg Luzinski, like Garry, couldn't bunt for a base hit; but unlike Garry, Greg wouldn't bunt because he'd decided that he didn't want to. Greg worked constantly on his hitting, but not on his bunting. Although he'd bunt two balls every day in batting practice, he wouldn't work on the art of bunting for a base hit.

But maybe that's taking credit away from Greg. Maybe I should be saying that he has learned to stay within himself. Put it this way: when he was with the Phillies, I couldn't imagine the situation where he'd want to bunt for a base hit. But I could with the Dodgers' Steve Garvey, who also bats fourth. When Garvey leads off the bottom of the ninth with his team down two or three runs, he can bunt for a base hit if he catches the third baseman back.

As a third baseman I have to be aware of that and play in a bit. But by moving up because he *might* bunt, I'm giving him more of an opportunity to get a base hit by me. In that situation, you'd play Greg normally, because you know he's not going to change his style.

The bunt can act just like the drop shot in tennis. The idea in both sports is to keep the defense off-balance. In tennis, if you have a guy laying back, you just drop a little shot over the net. It's probably one of the most effective shots in the game (though it also seems to be a dying art) if you're good at it. The guy on the other side of the net always has the feeling you're going to drop the ball on him any time he gives you a chance. It's the same in baseball. So if the game situation warrants getting a man on base or the advancement of baserunners, the *idea* of a bunt can be as important as that of a home run at other times.

Because of my ability to bunt, I got an important hit in just this way in the 1980 World Series. In the top of the ninth in the third game, we had two outs and the winning run on third. All we needed to do was get that run across and get the Royals out in the bottom of the inning. So while hitting against Dan Quisenberry, I dropped what I thought was a perfect bunt down the third-base line. But the ball trickled about six inches foul and, luckily, I ended up flying out to centerfield.

I say "luckily" because with so much at stake in that at-bat, there was no way I could pop up or let the pitcher have any chance to get his hands on the ball and throw me out. If I had, the whole *idea* of the third-hole hitter in the lineup bunting with a man on third looks bad. A hitter in my position can't afford to make an out bunting in that situation. In this case, since the bunt went foul, I had a chance to drive in the run by swinging away. So even though I eventually flied out, I had played the game situation as well as I could.

Although I didn't get what could have been one of the biggest bunts of the 1980 season, I had told the Kansas City Royals that I was a potential bunter in a bunting situation. I showed them I definitely had the confidence and the ability to drop a bunt. That impression was reinforced when I bunted successfully in the very next game, against Dennis Leonard, at a time when we were down, 3–0. That bunt got a runner to first base and kept my hitting streak alive in the World Series—it did nothing but good for my team and for me individually at that point. I was glad then— as I had been the night before—that I had done all that practice bunting.

I was even happier in the fifth game of the Series. We were down one run and I was leading off the ninth. There's no way that the best home run hitter in baseball is going to drop a bunt in that situation, but the Royals had a fear of me bunting and getting to first base. Third baseman George Brett moved up even with the bag, and I hit a hard groundball to his left that he had to dive for and couldn't come up with. I ended up with a base hit and we went on to win the ball game—the pivotal game of the Series. And it was all set up because of the ability of the third-hole hitter to bunt.

MECHANICS

The first thing to learn in bunting is to make contact with the ball as if you're catching it with your bat. When I bunt, all I'm really doing is standing at the plate with my right hand held out in front of me—just as if someone is throwing the ball to me and I'm reaching out to catch it. But instead of catching it with my bare hand, I catch it with the bat, which is cradled in that outstretched hand and steadied by my left hand.

To hold the bat correctly when bunting, pinch it between the thumb and index finger of your right hand (if you're right-handed), so it's not wedged back into your palm. By doing that, you absorb the shock of the ball hitting the bat. That, in turn, deadens the ball coming off the bat and you don't get a great deal of speed or topspin. Also, you have a greater chance of injuring your hand if you wrap your fingers around the bat.

Secondly, you should not try to bunt high pitches. Square around (up through college, anyway; only professionals should try

GETTING A GRIP

When bunting, pinch the bat between the thumb and index finger of your right hand, if you're right-handed.

If you hold the bat back in your palm, you can't absorb the shock of the ball coming off the bat, and your fingers are easily injured.

other stances) and hold the bat at the top of your own personal strike zone. *Never* bunt any pitch that comes in higher than you hold your bat. If the pitch is that high, take it. If it's even with or below the bat, you should be able to bunt it. You never want to be in a position where you have to come up with the bat to bunt the ball.

Thirdly, you must be sure to step up in front of the batter's box when you bunt. My heels are almost even with or just above the top of home plate. That way, I give myself the most advantageous angle from which to execute a fair bunt.

Picture the two front corners of home plate and the foul lines. If the ball is outside (to a right-handed hitter) and you're standing even with the plate, a perfect bunt down the first-base line will be foul. If you execute the same bunt standing up front in the box, it will be fair. By standing up as far in the batter's box as you can, you're taking advantage of all the fair territory you're given. Always keep in mind that a bunt that would be foul from one part of the batter's box will be fair from another. You must give yourself as much margin for success as possible.

My actual stance in the batter's box can differ, depending on whether I'm bunting for a sacrifice or a base hit.

With a sacrifice, everyone knows what you're going to do. So as a sacrifice bunter, I just lean forward, shifting my weight up to the front of the batter's box on my left foot, to get the bat two or two-and-a-half feet in front of the plate. I feel I can bunt anything from that position.

Even though the defense knows what you're going to do in a sacrifice situation, on artificial turf you have to be a bit more careful just how soon you give it away. Players used to be told

PLAYING THE ANGLES

Keep in mind that a bunt hit fair from one part of the batter's box will be foul from another. Here are the proper positions—in the front of the batter's box—for bunt attempts down the third- and first-base lines, respectively.

there's no problem with squaring around too early on sacrifices. But if the cornermen come right at you on artificial turf, they can have an easy play at second base. Because of turf, we throw out more runners at second on sacrifice bunts than we ever have before.

Bunting for a base hit is different, because of the element of surprise. Right-handed hitters have various ways of positioning themselves, but I think the best bunters are those who drop the back foot and take a stride, as if they're going to hit. In that position, you're in a dead line toward first base, and you're also out in front of home plate. When I bunt that way, I feel relaxed, my weight is balanced on both feet, and the bat is in the right position to absorb the shock of contact. As I get ready to hit, my legs straighten to keep the head of the bat above the ball, so I don't pop up. Again, however, remember that bunting technique is personal. You should do whatever is necessary to get the bat out in front of home plate.

The best pitch to bunt is a slow curveball, or a ball that's breaking out over the plate. On a pitch like that, you can be moving toward first when you make contact. An inside pitch doesn't allow that, because it pushes you the opposite way.

Bunting from the left side gives you a two-step advantage and allows you to do more with the ball. For instance, I don't believe in a right-handed hitter trying to push the ball by the pitcher. Some guys are good at it—the A's Davey Lopes, for one, is *very* good at it—but it's not something I'd recommend. A left-hander, however, can drag an inside pitch with him, bunting it by the pitcher, and be two steps ahead of everyone else. He can also stay back in the box and drop the ball down on the third baseman, or

LAYING ONE DOWN
When you bunt, reach out with your bat to "catch" the ball.

Bunting for a base hit, I drop my back foot and take a stride, as if I'm going to swing away.

run up in the batter's box and bunt the ball down the third-base line, and still get to first.

Left-handers have another advantage as bunters: to bunt successfully, they're forced to watch the ball all the way through the bat. Though both hitters are on the way to first when they hit the ball, the left-hander normally is moving away from the ball. Because of this, he knows he has to take extra care not to take his eye off the ball too soon. If he pulls out too quickly, he knows he has no chance to bunt successfully.

Right-handers are just the opposite. They're moving through the ball to get to first, so they have a tendency to lose concentration and take their eyes off the ball because everything happens right in front of them.

The key to bunting from either side of the plate is watching the ball through the bat, just as you should when you're swinging away.

The Phillies have great hitting pitchers, so we use the sacrifice less than other teams. But we do use the squeeze play all the time. When I say "squeeze play," I mean suicide squeeze. The safety squeeze—in which, with runners on first and third, the runner on third waits to see the ball on the ground, and possibly a play being made to another base, before trying to score—is very seldom used, especially on artificial turf. It's an old-time play, really, and limited. It's not a very good percentage play, either.

But the suicide squeeze is a great tool at all levels of baseball and can be used in a number of situations. In this play, the runner at third leaves for home expecting the batter to make a fair bunt that can't be handled by the pitcher or any of the infielders. There's no turning back, no matter what the batter does. The runner leaves when the pitcher's arm is at the top of his arc and he can't change what he's going to do. It's exactly like a sacrifice bunt, except the hitter can't take the pitch. He has to make contact with the ball as a bunter, no matter where it is.

The squeeze play is one of the reasons the bunt is a useful and versatile offensive weapon available to everyone in the lineup, not just to pitchers moving a man over. Hitters should have the confidence and ability to execute it, just as they should other bunt plays.

Remember, the bunt not only gives you added dimension as a player, allowing you to respond to various game situations, but it also makes you more effective as a hitter, if only because the offense knows you have the bunt as a working part of your game. I learned to value the bunt early enough in my career for it to have a real effect on my game. After all, there's no physical reason a home run hitter shouldn't be able to bunt—and no "image" reasons, either. I've tried to show that bunting for a base hit can be as important as hitting a home run. It should be every player's goal to do as much as he can in a game, and a player who can bunt demonstrates to everyone that he has the knowledge of the game and the ability to use it to be always on the offense.

SWITCH HITTING

A final note on hitting: now that you have the mechanics and approach, think what you could do as a hitter from *both* sides of the plate.

I'd like to suggest that players at the Little League and high school levels try switch hitting. My manager in Little League let me hit left-handed occasionally and by the end of my freshman year in college, I was switch hitting all the time.

It turned out that I spent four or five years hitting left-handed against right-handed pitching to no avail (I stopped in my second year in college), but the experience was fun and I realized the advantage it can give you. There's nothing like having all the breaking pitches coming into your hitting zone instead of going away from it. Even today I like to take a few left-handed swings in batting practice to experience that. Switch hitting can be so valuable I believe it should be taught to anyone who looks like he has natural talent, especially small, fast, singles hitters who don't use a great deal of leverage when they hit.

CIRCLING THE BASES I:
AGGRESSIVE BASERUNNING

YOUR DUTIES as an offensive player start in the on-deck circle and don't end until you score at home plate or make an out. Baserunning is a major part of those responsibilities and an important facet of offensive baseball that doesn't get enough attention. It's more than just stealing bases and sliding, speed and running. It's how you get from the plate to first and back home again, and all the things you have to do in between.

But many players just take baserunning for granted. The major leagues are filled with players who take one base at a time, who won't take any chances. Good, aggressive, "take the extra base, take chances at the right time" baserunning will win ball games by changing the momentum of a game and putting pressure on the defense. It creates a winning baseball environment.

Think about the difference in a close ball game if after getting a broken-bat hit to left-center and making an outfielder go that way to catch the ball, a runner just keeps going to second. Think about the difference in the game situation with a man on second and no outs versus a man on first and no outs. Think how much easier it is to score that man and how much the momentum changes when a man forces himself to take the extra base.

Pete Rose is the best example of why baserunners must use strategy and situation as well as speed and sliding. He's not the fastest baserunner around, but he's made baserunning such an identifiable part of his game, such a part of his baseball personality, because he takes advantage of so many things that nobody else does. Pete creates opportunities on the basepath because the fielders know that he's always going hard on the bases. He's gotten that reputation with a hard, aggressive style that makes him a very intimidating baserunner. More young players in college and the major leagues should try to adopt that style, if it's within their ability. But Pete has his aggressiveness under control. He knows when to take that chance—he knows the game situation.

However important baserunning is, it's something that nobody wants to read about or be taught, because compared to other parts of baseball it's hard to practice, and boring. It doesn't involve a bat and contact with the ball, or a glove and catching the ball. It doesn't involve the special talents you use hitting the ball or making a pinpoint throw, and it's something you may not do for two or three games in a row. And even if you're good at it, the label of "good baserunner" doesn't come for years.

Only one or two players have made it to pro ball because of their baserunning, and they were basestealers, period. But there are many players making a great deal of money because baserunning is one of their fortes. Baserunning is certainly one of the strong points of my game, and it's one I'm proud of. There are an awful lot of good hitters. There are fewer power hitters. But there are even fewer good baserunners who also are power hitters.

If you're noted for your ability to run the bases, you're in a minority. Most teams in the league have only two or three guys who are known as their good baserunners. We were lucky in Philadelphia to have more than that on our 1980 championship team. Along with Pete Rose, we had Larry Bowa, Garry Maddox, Bake McBride, and Lonnie Smith—four runners who are as fast as anyone in baseball. It was tough being labeled a good baserunner in that crowd—that's why I'm so proud of that part of my game.

Every player should learn to take pride in that part of his game, even if he doesn't feel he has the kind of abilities needed to run the bases. You should put stock in becoming as complete a ballplayer as *you* can become. A 240-pound freshman in college obviously isn't going to break any of Lou Brock's records. But that same kid could show he's not going to throw in the towel when he becomes a baserunner. By losing weight or working extra hard to learn technique, he can become an *adequate* baserunner.

The same is true for major leaguers. Willie Aikens of the Royals is the type of player who could go either way as far as baserunning is concerned. A big man and not a gifted athlete in terms of running speed, he needs to put a lot of consideration into this area of his game. He may already have—I don't know—but he still can become more than the below-average baserunner I saw in the 1980 World Series by practicing the techniques I'll discuss later.

Players who don't have at least average speed sometimes don't have the incentive to develop the techniques they need. They forget about everything else that makes a good baserunner, because they feel they're not going to get any better and it won't be an important part of their game. They should remember what Pete Rose has done as a baserunner. Not everyone can be like him, of course, but technique, knowledge, and desire can make Aikens and others like him at least average baserunners.

Showing a keen interest in baserunning may help a player to get to the major leagues. The other parts of the game may come naturally to him, but if he's not concerned about baserunning, he might not become a major league player.

Baserunning was one reason I got to the big leagues and one of the reasons why, in college, I was told for the first time that I was a complete ballplayer and a professional prospect. This was true not just because I was a great hitter for average then, or had a great arm, or hit home runs, or had a good glove—I had several scouts tell me I had all those things. But one thing they were especially impressed with was my knowledge of baserunning—my ability to slide in a variety of ways, to take the extra base, to steal a base. There aren't many guys 6'2", 200 pounds who have the ability to steal 25 bases a year. Generally, the strength to hit home runs doesn't go along with the instincts and speed needed to steal bases. It takes a good athlete to do both, a Mickey Mantle or Willie Mays or Bobby Bonds—and a lot of steal signs, of course.

I worked hard at that part of the game in college, and I liked doing it once I found out that people watched me on the bases and that I was being called a good baserunner. I said to myself, "Hey, people sometimes are going to watch what I do when I get on first. The announcers are going to say, 'We have Mike

Schmidt on first, an excellent baserunner.' " When they do that, you're flattered and you have something to live up to.

As much pride as I take in my knowledge of hitting, I feel that I'll always want to learn more about and do what I can with my baserunning, too. That's why my baserunning reputation has stayed with me so far in my career.

Back in 1975, people were telling me I could be in the 30/30 club—30 home runs and 30 stolen bases in one season—something that very few players have accomplished. It was said that all I had to do was stay healthy, maintain the good stolen-base percentage I had shown in the past, and hit 30 home runs again. Well, I made it—but not officially, since I was credited with only 29 stolen bases that year. My 30th had come in a game against the Mets. John Matlack was pitching to Greg Luzinski, and I was on second. Since Dave Kingman was playing third almost in the outfield, I easily took my 30th base. But Greg was called out for interfering with the catcher, and that was that.

Thinking about my almost-30/30 year now, it doesn't seem to have been that tough a goal. That year, at least, it came together easily for me. But the longer I play in the big leagues, the less effective I'm going to be running the bases. Even with the right conditioning program, I'll lose some of my speed. And as I get a bit older, it seems wise to forego some of my recklessness on the basepaths. With my history of torn hamstrings, pulled groins, and knee operations, I find that at times I'm a bit more apprehensive about letting it all happen on certain artificial-turf fields.

Still, I'm just as concerned about my running now as I was in college, and I've learned more about it. I know that pitchers are concerned, too, when I get on base. They generally know I'll run—though some will forget at times, since I'm a big man who hits home runs. You don't have to remind pitchers that a player like Maddox will run. But when I'm on, the catcher often has to come out to the pitcher and say, "Hey, he'll run." To me, that's the same as saying, as the scouts once did, that I'm a good baserunner. And I'm still flattered by it.

When I walk into the batter's box, I don't have the slightest doubt whatsoever about what I'm going to do when I get a hit. As soon as I make contact with the ball, it's time for me to put on a baserunning show. Not just get on base and hope I get around, but start exploiting that part of my game.

The same is true when I'm out on the field on defense—I'm exploiting my talents as a third baseman. When you have the reputation that comes with six Gold Gloves, you're at third to put on a defensive show. I'm not out there because it's between at-bats and the manager has to find a place for me. People will be coming to the ball park that day expecting me to make plays in the field.

It's the same with hitting. Once I get in there to hit, it's time for me to put on a hitting show—I hope. I try my best because people come to the park to see me hit.

It's all of a piece—hitting, baserunning, and defense—part of how I play and part of the pride I take in what I do on the field.

CIRCLING THE BASES II:
MECHANICS

NOW WE'RE READY to talk about how you should actually run the bases, and what you should think about when you do it. The first thing to know about baserunning—and it's something I only learned a few years ago—is to run relaxed. When I hit the ball in the infield, the harder I try to run to first base, the slower I go in comparison to running there on a ball that I know is a single. With sure base hits, I seem to glide along, running relaxed and smooth.

You can see the difference by comparing players who can really run with those who can't. One type glides along, the other labors as hard as he can, pumping with all his might and going nowhere. Every muscle in his body is going. His arms and legs are tight (and more susceptible to muscle pulls), his fists are clenched, he's trying to get every ounce of speed he can from his body. But the best make it look easy. Think how Willie Mays ran—or Dick Allen, a good example of a guy who could really run without anyone knowing it, because he didn't seem to grind it out. Rod Carew is the same today. They all look like they're not trying to run—they're gliding, their bodies moving smoothly.

It's that kind of relaxed running that lets you cover ground so much better from first to second when you sense a triple. You get to second faster than you do when you know you have a single and you're trying to stretch it into a double. Stretching for a triple, you glide from first to second and then pour on the speed, but through that glide you're running relaxed and looking at the ball, not concentrating on getting to second as fast as you can. So you actually end up covering the ground faster.

I learned this stealing bases in spring training in 1978. I had decided I would try a new method of running—going relaxed and confident. I told myself, "Go ahead and take it three-quarter speed one time. Don't think you want to get there as fast as you can, because you'll end up running slower than you would using a smooth, relaxed glide." And thinking that, I went five-for-five stealing.

It's the same as thinking you've got to hit the ball as far as you can versus thinking about hitting the ball with authority. A tense, tight, nonrelaxed body accomplishes less than a loose, relaxed, smooth-flowing body. Your muscles are freer to work when you're relaxed, so running relaxed as well as hitting relaxed is a good thing to think about and practice. Again, it's all part of letting your talent flow. Being relaxed is important in all phases of your offensive game.

The second thing to remember about baserunning is that it's

part of offensive, not defensive, baseball. You should always be on the offense on the basepaths. You're running to the next base all the time. You should be thinking, How do I get to the next base, and the next base after that?

Generally, if you hit the ball on the ground in the infield, your target is first—as fast as you can get there, head down and straight-on running. But if you hit the ball out of the infield, your target should be second base. So when you hit a line drive or fly-ball, or a groundball that you can see is going to go through the infield, aim for second.

Good baserunners know this, and act on it. Mediocre or bad baserunners are satisfied with a single. The status quo is fine with them. The line drive they hit to the rightfielder looks like a single, so why try for a double? These players just make their little three-quarter-speed turn and stop. Some players in the big leagues even stop right on the bag!

But then there is the ultimate—a player like Pete Rose, who will run as hard as he can until the outfielder makes him stop. Pete provides an example of great baserunning in the way he intimidates outfielders. They always want to throw behind Pete, because they know he'll take that big turn at first. Pete himself knows as he's taking that turn that 99 times out of 100 he's not going on to second unless the outfielder misplays the ball. But because he knows that Pete is going to put out that extra effort, will take the big turn no matter what, the outfielder may be forced into a defensive mistake. It makes him think, "He's going to make *me* stop him. I'm going to have to get the ball in quickly."

Whenever an outfielder thinks he has to do that—get to the ball and make an unusual play—there's a chance he might bobble the ball. If you put any kind of pressure at all on him, you increase the chance of an error that will enable you to take the next base.

However, the outfielder will rarely make an error if he knows that he can just go down on one knee, pick up the ball nice and slow, and lob it into second, because the players on this particular team don't put on any kind of running pressure. He won't bobble the ball or let it go through his legs or try for a difficult play.

To create as many scoring opportunities as possible, runners at whatever level—Little League, high school, or college—should work to give the opposing outfielders the feeling that they'll have to be stopped. When you hit a single, round the bag as hard as you can until you see the outfielder come up cleanly with the ball. Then put on the brakes and come back to first. But you'll already have gone almost halfway to second, and in doing so, let the outfielders know that with your team, or at least in your at-bat, they have to make the hitter stop. And you'll also have taken away the feeling of order, routine, and predictability in their play. The outfielders then will become either apprehensive, and try to do things too fast, or overcautious about doing anything out of the ordinary. All in all, they will be more likely to make an error and you will have a better chance to take an extra base.

As a baserunner, you must make this approach become a habit. When you're always on the offense, you not only force mistakes but also are ready to take advantage of unforced defensive lapses. Applying that kind of pressure, your thoughts are focused on the idea of getting to second until you're stopped from doing so. When you hit a single, the box score is going to say "single" but in your mind it was a double until they made you go back to first. You're not slowing down before you get to the first-base bag, you're running by first as hard as you would run by second when going from first to third.

The same theory applies to hitting a double or triple. When you hit a double, in your mind you've really hit a triple until you're stopped at second base. You don't just pull up and coast into second when the outfielder has the ball. If he makes a bad throw or it gets away from the cutoff man, you'll have missed the chance to take the extra base you could have had if you'd aggressively gone through second base on your way to third.

You may win the doubles title in your league that way—that's how many players in the National League (with the exception of Pete Rose, of course) pad their doubles numbers. But if you had gotten to third those times when most guys would have stopped at second, you probably would have won four or five more ball games for your team.

In the 1980 World Series, the Royals proved how easy it is to take an extra base on a questionable ball, by running more than once on our outfielders. If you hit a ball in the gap and run hard from home to first, as the game situation warrants, what you're doing is taking a chance that the outfielder won't make the perfect throw necessary to get you out. And it has to be perfect. The outfielder has to reverse-pivot and fire a perfect strike to the second baseman, who has to catch the ball and make the tag. And then the umpire has to call you out. All those things have to happen, and nine times out of ten, they won't. But baserunners often act as if nine times out of ten, they will.

There are times, however, when a hitter *does* want to stop at first on a potential double, depending on the game situation. Let's say I'm hitting third in the batting order, and Trillo is on first with one out in the bottom of the ninth of a tie ball game. I hit a ball right at the centerfielder, and Trillo goes from first to third. Although the ball is thrown to third to try to get Trillo out, I stay at first base because we're facing a left-handed pitcher and a right-handed hitter, Gary Matthews, is the next batter.

At times, I've been called back from the on-deck circle and told to stay on first if I hit a double; that way, the first baseman will have to stay on the bag to hold me close, and the next hitter can bat with the hole open between first and second. But that's a bit more advanced baserunning and probably won't be used until players get into the big leagues.

FOOTWORK

It's natural for you to want to watch the ball when you make contact. Whether you should or not depends on where the ball is hit. It's easy to look at the ball if it goes to centerfield or right-field. If it goes down the third-base line, it's a little tougher to follow, because you have to look over your shoulder and touch first base at the same time.

That's why someone who is feeling confident in his footwork as he leaves home plate has a better chance of flying by first and touching the bag without looking down to make sure he hits it right. I can hit the ball, get my running angle, look out into the outfield to see what's happening to the ball, and then, maybe ten feet from first, get a bead on the bag and be able to round it without looking down.

I think that at the high school and early college level, the approach to first base on a ball hit for a single or a double should be

practiced and practiced, to the point where the batter knows exactly how many steps he wants to take between home plate and
the first-base bag. Whenever we'd practice rounding first base, I'd
take off, counting my steps, and every time they would add up to
15. I'm sure that hasn't changed, but now I don't have to know.
The point is that I can run to first without looking at the ground
or having to think about what I'm doing. It's so grooved, so sure,
that I could look out toward the field and count "1" as soon as I
hit the ball, and when I hit "15" my foot would be coming down
on first base. I can keep my mind and eye on the ball.

The number of steps I take comes naturally from the way I run
to first base, moving outside the foul line about halfway down the
line. Each person has his own method of rounding the bag—what
he feels will get him to second most efficiently.

But whatever that method is, however sharply he makes his
turn, a player who hits the ball out of the infield should never run
in a straight line from home to first base. You want to prevent
that as a baserunner, because the centrifugal force you create will
throw you out into rightfield as you're trying to get to second.
What you want to try for is a straight line to *second* base, not to
first. Many times you'll see players sliding into second with their
legs almost pointing to third, rather than sliding in straight. That
kind of slide shows how far out into rightfield they were forced by
the momentum generated running straight at first. You want to
hit first at an angle that will make it possible for you to go straight
to second.

How you do that—the kind of approach you use—is personal
and usually depends on your size and agility. Some players take
off outside the foul line immediately after leaving the plate.
Others will go down the chalk almost to the break in the line by

the coach's box and then cut out sharply and come back. Light players can do that. Larry Bowa, for instance, can run almost straight down the line and make a 90-degree turn to second. That's impossible to do for someone like me who weighs 200 pounds, because my momentum would end up carrying me out to rightfield.

Sometimes, though, you can't help being thrown out into rightfield when you round first. It depends on how you hit the ball. With a grounder between short and third, you take off not knowing whether it's going through or whether the shortstop might backhand it, and you have to run right at the bag, planning to run through it. Then, if the first-base coach, who's watching the play, suddenly yells at you to round the bag, you have to snap out of that hard-and-straight run as best you can to get down to second.

You always look at the bag and never at the ball when you're trying to beat out an infield hit. As I said earlier, when you hit the ball in the infield, run straight at first base. And with one exception, always run through first—never slide into the bag. If you're running as hard as you can to first base, you'll get to the bag faster by staying on your feet than you would by sliding. Use slides only to avoid getting hurt or to keep from overrunning the bag. You slide into second and third on close plays because you can't come in hard and expect to stop right on the bag.

At first base, you're given the advantage of running over the bag. If sliding meant getting there faster, a 100-yard-dash man would slide into the finish line, wouldn't he? If he could get to the tape faster that way, he'd just get up to the tape and dive. Some baseball players think they can get to first faster that

way, though. I've seen a lot of players slide into first. The crowd
thinks they're hustling more, too. But Pete Rose is the ultimate
hustler in baseball in the crowd's eyes, and I've never seen him
slide into first.

The only time Pete would slide into first—and the only time
I've ever had to—is to avoid a tag by the first baseman. You slide
if you see him coming off the bag and reaching to catch the ball
to tag you before you get to the base. You can sense that happening as a runner. Then you slide away from or underneath the tag.

When you hit the first-base bag as you're running through it,
you always want to come down with the ball of your foot on the
front of the bag—preferably on the foul side away from the first
baseman's foot, which is usually on the fair side of the bag. You
never want to end up with your whole foot or your heel on the
bag, which can lead to an injury. You can avoid doing this—or
having to shuffle your feet at the last minute to touch the bag because you don't know which foot will hit it—by not taking your
eyes off the front part of the bag on your way to first. If you get to
the bag with your last step coming down right in front of it, your
next step will be over it, and you'll have to shuffle your feet to hit
it. But if you pick up first as soon as the ball is hit, knowing you're
going to have to run through the base, you'll never shuffle-step.

For some reason, if I stare directly at the front of the bag I
never come out wrong. But if, when I'm running down to first, I
look to see if a fielder caught the ball, I get out of synch and have
to shuffle. And when you have to do that on a play in the infield,
generally you'll be out—you just won't get to first safely if there's
a split-second difference. Also, you might get hurt. (In the 1980
NL play-offs, Houston's Cesar Cedeno lost his concentration

RUNNING IT OUT

*When you're running to first
on a ball hit in the infield,
make sure you hit the front of
the bag with the ball of your
foot*

*instead of landing
squarely on top of it.*

running to first and ended up having either to shuffle his feet or to step on the wrong part of the bag—and broke his ankle.) Players should work on picking up the front of the bag, until it comes naturally to them in a game.

One final point about running to first on a groundball to the infield: Listen to the first-base coach! If he sees the ball go through to the outfield, he'll yell at you to round the bag. Your eyes should be trained on first base, not on the coach. If you know the ball is in the hole, you should still concentrate mainly on the bag, while being aware that the coach may tell you to round first.

Once you get to first or safely past, how you round second or third is really an individual matter, at any level of the game. Do it in the most economical way you can and still maintain good control over your body.

Many coaches and players endorse catching the bag with the inside foot when rounding a base. I can't understand why. I say hit the bag with whatever foot is available when you get there, because you don't want to come around second thinking you have to touch the bag with one foot *or* the other. The runner shouldn't have to break stride—that's like shuffling to touch the bag at first. You want a long, loping stride—that "glide" I talked about before—and you can't have that if you have to think about how to hit the bag.

But if you're more comfortable with a set way to hit the bag, you're better off trying to make contact with the outside foot. I think your body is forced out farther into the outfield if you try to touch second with your inside foot; to me, it seems that if I hit second with my outside foot, my weight will be pushed back toward the infield and my centrifugal force will be cut down. So when in doubt, use the outside foot—even if that goes against most theories.

STEALING

I believe that every player who reaches first base, from the slowest guy on the team to the fastest, is a potential basestealer. The same is true for every player who reaches second base, and third base is sometimes easier to steal than second.

The first decision you have to make about stealing is whether you're a diver or a stand-up man when you have to get back to first. When the pitcher throws over to first to bring you back to the bag, are you going to cover the ground back to first with a step and a dive or a step and a hop? This is important, because if you're a diver, you can take a longer lead off first. And with that lead you're more apt to be going either way, so you have to concentrate on going back to first as much as you do on going to second. From that far off the bag, you can't be thinking 90 percent about getting to second. You're in a 50–50 position. When you're back a stride or so, in a stand-up lead, it's more like 90–10. You can even start for second and still get back.

I'm basically a stand-up man, because I'm afraid diving will be too hard on the shoulder I dislocated some years ago. So although I still dive occasionally, depending on the pitcher, I steal bases now with a little less of a lead than I'd like. The best way for a stand-up man to come back to first is to hit the outside of the bag with his left foot, falling away from the tag. When you can't do that, you just get back any way you can.

There's been some talk about leading off from the front of the bag, but I don't endorse that. I come off the back corner of the bag because that's where I'll be aiming if I have to come back, and where I'll be going into second if I think there's going to be a bad throw. I very seldom head for the inside of second base. I'll go either straight into second or off the back side. That way, I'm also going to be in a better position to round second base.

Another thing I endorse and try to do as a baserunner is to get a walking lead. That gets my body moving toward second base, which automatically gives me a great jump. The walking lead I take is what's bothering catchers when they yell, "Make him stop, make him stop!" They don't want me to be able do that, because even the slightest forward movement gives you momentum toward second, and a real edge. The catcher wants the pitcher to make me come to a dead stop. Often the pitcher will stand and hold the ball until I do. If he doesn't, and he gives me the feeling that he's not worrying about me, I'll come off the bag with a walking lead and suddenly take off. I'll also do that if we're down by a lot—say, 7–0. I just walk off the bag and keep going, because I know the pitcher is giving me second base.

There's no sense to the old theory that when down by a lot, the offense should play it cozy and not run. The Phillies have scored several runs in one inning before, and there's no way I'll automatically give the defense a groundball double play. In the first game of the 1980 World Series, for example, we were down 4–0, but Larry Bowa stole second base anyway. Not only did that prevent the possibility of a double play, but it also seemed to change the momentum of the game. We ended up scoring five runs and winning the game.

When you're taking a stationary lead, make sure your right

Taking a stationary lead, make sure your right toe is slightly open and you're ready to throw your right shoulder and elbow toward second base.

Try to stay low as your crossover step is made.

Exaggerate your arm drive, like a sprinter coming out of the blocks, to get the best break you can.

Here is the same sequence, as seen from second base.

toe—your lead toe—is slightly open (slightly pointed toward second base), so that your hips can pivot and you can clear your right hip out of the way when you take off. If your right foot is closed, you have to take an extra step, picking up your foot and then putting it down in order to cross over and go.

As for what you do with the rest of your body when leading off, that's individual. Some guys like to put their hands on their knees, others like their arms wide out. The key is to be relaxed and in a position that you can spring out of like a cat.

You should be as relaxed standing on the bases as you are running them. If you're thinking about stealing and get tight, you won't have the fluid and easy movement you should. If you're nice and relaxed, thinking, "I'm ready to go, I'm ready to go" when the pitcher makes his move to home plate, you're more apt to respond by taking off for second quickly and smoothly—and more likely to be successful doing it.

That kind of initial movement allows me to steal my bases. I don't steal them with speed, I don't steal them with sliding— I steal them off my first two or three steps making my break. I'll cover the first few feet down the line faster than almost anyone else, even Lou Brock. After that, though, Lou would catch me and get there faster. Also, someone like Brock, Garry Maddox, Larry Bowa, Cesar Cedeno, or Omar Moreno can steal bases against good pitchers and good catchers on good pitches. I have to pick my spots to steal.

If I don't get that good jump and come out slowly, if I don't beat Brock or Cedeno in those first few steps, then I'll be out at second. Those guys have the ability almost to outrun the ball. Great speed demons don't need an excellent jump. I must have one to be able to steal, and that's why a walking lead is vital to a basestealer like me.

* * *

Stealing third is easier than stealing second: first, because of the element of surprise; and second, because when you steal third, you're stealing on the pitcher, period. Once on second, I'll walk toward third on each pitch, and if the pitcher continues to just let me walk away and maintains the same rhythm with each pitch, I have a chance. If he does that three times in a row, he's going to do it a fourth time, so I'll walk off and I'll be gone.

Stealing second, you're still stealing on the pitcher, but you have to be good enough on the bases so that when you've taken second on the pitcher, you won't be thrown out by the catcher. There are two or three catchers in the league good enough to throw you out even if you've stolen on the pitcher. Steve Yeager is one; Bench was, but he's tailing off some. Ex-Met Jerry Grote was another who could throw you out, and Bob Boone, I feel, has become that kind of catcher, too. So at times when going from first to second, you should be more apprehensive about stealing.

Stealing third is easier, but you should only do it with one out. There are so many different ways to score a runner from third in that situation that the advantage of being at third instead of second with one out is worth the risk of the steal. If you don't make it, there are two outs, but the hitter still has a chance to come up.

A baserunner never wants to make the first or last out at third on a steal attempt. With no outs, you want to give the hitter a chance to get you in, or at least to third. And with two outs, you want to give the hitter a chance to bat. Even if you get to third on a steal, with two outs a sacrifice fly won't score you, and neither will a groundball to the infield. So the risk won't get you much in return.

The only time you'll see an attempt to steal third with two outs is if it will move two men into scoring position. With men on first and second and two outs, a double steal could move the runners to second and third and is sometimes worth the risk.

Stealing home is an aggressive play that takes an exceptional jump at third base. You must also think you have an exceptional chance to make it, since so many things have to come together for it to be successful.

I stole home once in the minor leagues, against a left-hander in the Giants' organization named Skip Pitlock, who had an incredibly convoluted motion. His eyes were dead on the guy at first, and I thought, "I'm going to try it." The minute he started that motion again, I broke for the plate. By the time he got his hands over his head, he knew I was going home and threw there, but I was safe. That won a ball game.

I remember that steal so well because it was one of my two attempts to steal home in pro ball, and it was successful. (When I tried it once in a 0–0 game against Montreal's Scott Sanderson in Veteran's Stadium, I was out—just out, but out.) Stealing home is not something I'd do often, obviously, and it's not something many major leaguers would try. If you see as good a runner as Garry Maddox try it and get thrown out by a mile to end a ball game, it becomes pretty clear why. But although stealing home shouldn't be and isn't tried often, it can be one of the most exciting plays in baseball.

STEALING SIGNS

Stealing signs is another of the baserunner's responsibilities. It's something always done at first base for yourself (to help you steal); and something done by some runners at second for the batter (to help him hit).

As a runner at first base, I can take my lead and see the catcher's signs almost any time I want to, as long as the pitcher has the ball in his glove. It's tougher to do this against a pitcher who takes his signs or makes his stretch with the ball in his hand, because you have to be ready for him to snap around and throw it to first. But generally, it's not too difficult to get out to see the catcher giving the signs for the pitch or the location, and so get a better idea of when to steal. A low-and-away location more than likely means a breaking ball coming, and therefore a good time to steal. A fastball sign—usually, one finger down—means the opposite.

Even against a pitcher who holds runners close to the bag, some basestealers can still get an idea about the next pitch. Lou Brock told me that on warm days, if he couldn't see the actual signs flashed, he could still see whether or not the veins were moving in the catcher's arm as he gave the signs. And that gave him information, since the veins move whenever the catcher wiggles his fingers or gives location or changes signs. But if he just puts one finger down and holds it there, there's no movement. In that case, he's probably called for a fastball and it's not a good time to go.

Stealing signs at second base also is an integral part of the game today. Most teams have a policy of trying to get the pitches with a runner on second, in order to pass them on to the hitter. On the Phillies, though, most of the players don't want to know what's coming, so we don't. The San Francisco Giants used to be the best at sign stealing, and all the players coming out of that organization are still aware of the importance of learning how to steal signs and relay them. There are several ways of relaying the signs, but whatever method is used, I think it's very important for the hitters in the lineup to have good signals with each other.

What you have to do first is learn about signs by talking to some of the catchers and finding out what some of the pumps and indicators are. There are a whole series of complex ways to give signs, but in most cases, teams use very simple systems. The first baserunner to reach second has to look in and try to figure out what system the other team is using that day. If you see what sign is given and what pitch is thrown, you can figure out what the next pitch will be.

It's obviously easier to steal signs against pitchers who have two pitches than it is against guys who have four. But whoever the pitcher is, if your team likes to know what's coming, you should put out that bit of extra effort to go for the signs, because it can be very valuable in a clutch situation to be able to relay the pitch to the hitter. Let him know what's coming; let him get that edge. Sign stealing is something a player should always be willing to learn and use.

SLIDING

Sliding is a skill you should have at all levels of baseball. You slide to avoid overrunning a base when you're running hard and don't have the luxury of running through the bag. It's also necessary for avoiding a tag in a close play, the kind you might get at home when you want to slide away or underneath a catcher's tag. As a basic part of baserunning, sliding is a tool you should learn to feel comfortable with, so that you can use it and not get hurt.

Every player should learn the four basic types of slides—diving, straight-in, pop-up and hook. I recommend a diving slide, if you can do it, because it's the quickest way to get to the bag and the easiest way of avoiding a tag: you can give one arm or take it away, and then hit the base with the other one.

I don't dive much now, as I've said, because of my old shoulder injury. If I do dive, I have to concentrate so much on not getting hurt again that some of the effectiveness is taken away. Also, when you dive it's easier to get cut or spiked.

But I think it's something kids should learn to do. On some Little League fields and playgrounds, I wouldn't recommend diving, but running and sliding are things that come naturally to young kids, because that's what they do anyway. Sliding is fun for kids to practice, and they can do it on dirt or grass.

Kids should also practice straight-in and pop-up slides. For a pop-up slide, you go straight into the bag with your left or right side tucked under. That way, when you hit the front of the bag you pop up to a standing position, because your forward momentum is translated into upward movement. You should also learn the hook slide, because it can take you to the left or right of the bag, away from whichever side the tag is coming from.

Since I know I might have to slide anytime I'm on the basepaths, I wear my batting gloves at all times for protection. Sometimes my hands get involved when I slide, and the gloves could help me to avoid injury.

Any injury from the tip of your fingers to your shoulder makes it tough to play baseball. You rip a fingernail and you can't play for a week. But if you slide normally and get a "strawberry" on your rear, that's not going to keep you from playing.

You should also practice starting your slide the right distance from the bag. You don't want to start sliding right on top of the bag, but you don't want to be so far away that you end up not reaching the bag. Where you should start varies with different fields, depending on how wet or dry the ground and how thick the dirt. That's why you hear every once in a while about field crews doctoring the basepaths to suit the runners on their team. Field conditions can even affect the kind of lead you take, as well as the kind of slide you make.

Whatever the condition of the field, sliding is sloppy in the big leagues. Only a few players are very good sliders. But then, fans don't notice slides much anyway—at least with out calls. They'll remember a slide for weeks, though, when a good one makes a runner safe.

An infielder, too, might remember a good slide for weeks, if it's part of a successful attempt to break up a double play. Even though you can intimidate the defense on the basepaths by letting them know you'll take more than one base at a time, the effect is a bit more direct when you break up a double play memorably. Not that you want to hurt anyone, but breaking up a double play is one of the most underrated plays in the game, and a good, hard slide alone won't accomplish that.

Contact has to be made with the guy who's turning the pivot, and it has to be made *while* he's in the process of releasing the ball. I do it several ways—with a football-type roll block into the guy's legs; with a stand-up slide underneath, trying to raise him up on my shoulder and back; or with a hook slide into his feet just as he touches the ground. With enough experience, you'll find the way that suits you best—but whatever that is, the important thing is to try to establish that you're one of the players in the league who comes into second base as hard as he can every time. What you want is one shortstop or second baseman to be a bit tentative at a pressure point in a game because he knows you're the runner. Many times that will be enough to keep him from completing the play.

So I try to go at the guy's legs and body with everything I've got, sometimes risking life and limb to do it. Flipping a second baseman or shortstop or making him throw the ball away is almost as satisfying as hitting a home run. It proves your desire to win. It shows your intestinal fortitude—you're not afraid to do anything (within the game) to win.

That's why, unlike other underrated parts of the game I've discussed, breaking up the double play is done well by many players. Teammate Gary Matthews does it as well as anyone, and the same is true of Pete Rose, Bill Madlock, and Hal McRae of the Royals. I'm very good at it, too.

Do be careful not to be called for interference. If you are, both runners are out. You have to make it clear that you're trying to make contact with the base, not going out of your way to hurt an infielder; or that you're not trying to break up the double play at all costs—by letting the ball hit you, for instance. But it has to be an obvious violation—the interference call isn't made often.

RUNNING IT OUT

To be on the offense in baserunning, you need the same combination of relaxation, concentration, and controlled aggression you use to hit. That's why you have to work at your baserunning. At the very least, it's important to run hard all the time, especially through first base. Even when you and everybody else in the ball park thinks it's a sure out, run out the play as hard as you can. The difference could mean a hit. I don't know why players don't run out balls hit in the infield. I'm not claiming to be an all-out hustler every minute of the game, but one thing I've always done is run hard on balls to first base.

Not running out balls is done mostly by players on lesser teams, those that are out of divisional races. Against these teams, I may be able to field a shot hit to me at third and throw it to first before the hitter is halfway there, and then he'll circle out.

In the 1971 World Series Roberto Clemente proved how wrong that lack of hustle can be. On a ball chopped back to the pitcher, Clemente started running as hard as he could from home to first. Just as the pitcher was about to throw Clemente out, he dropped the ball. He then picked it up and got it to first, but Clemente beat the throw. If Roberto had thought, "Well, the pitcher has it and he'll throw me out easily at first," the pitcher would have had the time to do just that. If you're not going hard all the time, if you're not always on the offense, you're not in a position to take advantage of the defense's mistakes.

The worst label you can get at any level of baseball is that of a player who has the attitude "If it doesn't mean anything, why should I care? Don't worry—if I'm supposed to be there, I'll be there." We had a player on the Phillies who was famous for thinking like that. He was a great hitter, but he used to create havoc and controversy on our team because of that attitude. On groundballs he considered sure outs, he'd be stopped dead by the time he got to first base, from just loafing down the line. He's a friend of mine and we talked at great length about this, but he always claimed, "Hey, don't worry. I'll be at first base if there's ever a questionable hit or if I smell a base hit. But I'm not going to go all out to get there if I know I'm definitely going to be out."

But how do you ever know *definitely* that you'll be out? Ninety-nine times out of 100 you will be out, but how do you know that the first baseman isn't going to get something in his eye or drop a a throw or not be able to find the bag with his foot? You can help force those mistakes by running hard all the time. Getting that split-second "safe" call because somebody dropped a ball that 99 out of 100 times he'd catch, can do so much for a team—and for your career. The whole world will label you a great hustler.

So don't take the attitude that it's never going to happen to you. Or that you don't care if you're in position anyway, because you get your glory from other parts of the game and hustling to first base should be left to the little guys who are supposed to run.

Finally, I don't agree with that attitude because whether you play in high school, college, or the pros, you're on the field only two to four hours a day. There's no reason you can't give all you've got in all phases of the game, from mental preparation and concentration during the game through all it demands physically. You've got 20 other hours to relax in. And in the big leagues, most of us are getting paid pretty good money to run out groundballs and do everything else the game requires.

ON THE OFFENSE ON DEFENSE

''ON THE OFFENSE ON DEFENSE'' may sound contradictory but by thinking offensively as a defensive player, you're defensing *aggressively*. What you're doing, in fact, is the opposite of what you do on offense—everything you can to *prevent* the other team from scoring runs. You play *against* the game situation.

You just don't go out there and play defense because it's your opponents' turn to hit. You go out there and do your best over a long period of time to shut down the other team's ability to score. To do this, you must understand the vulnerability of the defense during certain points of the game, and what that vulnerability can mean for momentum. And you must understand that the game of major league baseball is designed defensively around the double play, and that you as a defensive player must do what you can to keep that play in order.

You also have to accept that the results of defensing offensively won't show up just in one game or in a week, but, as with statistics, will make themselves felt over the course of a month or a year. You need patience and dedication to play this way.

Most players just spend time on the field. They go out there and move around a bit, because they've been taught over the years the best way to play certain guys—but that's it. There's a lack of desire to learn a great deal about defense and to respect defense. When starting out in baseball, everybody wants to be a hitter. Nobody wants to be a defensive wizard.

But caring about the defensive phase of the game is all part of being a winning ballplayer. It's part of being a *complete* ballplayer. I've always enjoyed making good plays, and I've always enjoyed being referred to as a good defensive player. I have six Gold Gloves and five home-run crowns, and I don't know which I'm most proud of. But I've probably won as many games making a play defensively that doesn't show up in the box score as I have hitting a home run that gets a lot of press. I respect that. It means I've put some time in, put some thought into playing defense.

It does take work, though. I was always flashy with the glove—always made great plays, but I didn't make the routine plays enough. I didn't put a whole lot of time into my defense, and I didn't have the consistency that makes a first-rate defensive player. It wasn't until I played more and more in the big leagues that I gave defense the kind of value it deserves in my game.

Starting, I guess, in the Dave Cash years in Philadelphia (1974–76), I realized that I was on a team that played good defense and valued defense. Dave Cash wasn't an outstanding defensive player, but he did all the little things right and he cared about it. We—the whole infield—talked all the time about defense, and Dave, Larry Bowa, and I took great pride in our play in the field. I think we led the league in double plays one year. We concerned ourselves with things like that. Most other teams never did.

What you do on defense helps determine what you can do on offense. It's important early in a ball game to establish momentum. When one team gets on top, it takes away much of the other's offense—their ability to take chances on the bases; the hit-and-run; the steal, on some teams. A team is limited in its ability to take chances when the other team gets ahead. So, early in the game you want at all costs to prevent the other team getting ahead.

To defense offensively in this situation—to keep the other team's chances of scoring a run at a minimum—Dick Allen, in those same middle years of the 1970s, taught me to shut down the double down the line early as well as late in the game. That's to be done at all times, really, when both teams are fighting for the upper hand. It's a unique type of defense, and a controversial one. Although the first and third baseman guarding the lines in the eighth and ninth innings of a close game is by-the-book baseball, there's even disagreement on that. There are a lot of hard-line anti–"guard the line" theorists around who don't ever like to give the batter a big hole to hit the ball into. But I believe the line should be guarded at those times throughout the game when the defense is particularly vulnerable. You may give up more hits this way—*a lot* of hits to the left of the third baseman that otherwise would be easy outs—but you won't give up runs. And that's what's important. At those times in the game, you guard more against situational hitting than against the style of individual hitters. You're still going by the book, just expanding it a bit to cover situations like those you face in the late innings of close games.

So with two outs and no one on in the first, second, or third innings, I'm not going to let a man get a double down the line. That would put him in scoring position immediately, and if the next hitter gets a single, it's a run. If the batter hits one in the hole that I might have gotten if I wasn't guarding the line, too bad. They get a single, but it still takes two more hits to knock the run in.

Once the personality of the game is established—usually by the middle innings—you know if it's going to be a close or a runaway ball game and can defense offensively according to the type of hitter at the plate. But not if the game is still o–o in the fifth. With two outs, I'm still going down to shut the double. I'm not going to give them the chance at one run.

There are exceptions. With a left-handed contact hitter in the sixth inning, it would be ridiculous for me as a third baseman to guard the line. The leftfielder can play shallower, right behind the bag, against that kind of hitter, so I don't have to worry about him getting a double down the line. Anything hit that way, the leftfielder can hold to a single.

What I can do is try to minimize that hitter's chances of getting any kind of hit at all, by playing off the line and in the hole—shutting down *everything* I can on the ground. And since that left-handed hitter is highly unlikely to get the ball over the bag anyway, the odds are that we can. By spreading the defense—not having the third baseman and leftfielder prevent the same thing—you increase the chance that the hitter will make an out.

When the fielders on the corners defense offensively by guarding the lines and shutting down the double, they keep the tying or winning run out of scoring position. They also keep the double play, the cornerstone of defense for major leaguers, in order.

A statement of this idea was drummed into me all through college by my coach, Bob Wren. He'd always end an explanation of how to defense somebody by saying, "That guy stays on first; next guy, groundball double play; inning over." It may be trite, but you can use your head on defense and back up everything you do as a manager or defensive player, from playing a bunt to making a throw, with that statement. Not that you're going to get a chance for a double play every time, but you should give your team an opportunity for one whenever there's a man on first. As often as you can, you want to put your team in a position to make a double play whenever a batter hits a groundball to third, short, or second.

The double play is not such a central play below the major league level, because it's not so automatic. Players in Little League and high school are just not as adept at turning the play, and the fields are tougher. There's more success with it in college, but in the big leagues it's for the most part a given, especially on artificial turf. Out of every 1000 chances to turn the double play, it will be turned 990 times. (That's why you have to work so hard as a baserunner to break it up—or help prevent it in the first place, by taking that extra base.)

Defensing offensively for outfielders also means keeping the double-play situation in order as much as possible. And that means outfielders trying their best never to overthrow the cutoff man. You have to get a set of outfielders who are 100 percent willing to do this, no matter how nice it is for them to hear about their strong arms after they make the long, perfect throws that every now and then get runners out.

Those long strikes don't outweigh the seven or eight imperfect throws that went over everybody and into the stands, allowing two guys to move up. A lot of games in the course of a season are won or lost because an outfielder tried to throw out a runner at third when he shouldn't have, or overthrew a cutoff man. Players with the best arms have to be the most careful about this: it's a temptation for them, like it is for me with home runs. They can be the easiest to run on because they dare you to. They always want to throw runners out.

The cost of this kind of play won't show up immediately. But when the score comes up 9–8, you can look back and see what might have happened if the fielder had hit the cutoff man. Maybe you catch a runner in a rundown. Maybe you prevent the hitter from going to second and set up the double play. Maybe one less run and a win.

To be on the offense on defense you have to think, "What can I do in this situation that will prevent the other team from scoring runs?" That means a player with an aggressive idea of his role in the field. I believe the Gold Glove is given to that type of player—to whomever is thought to be the best all-around defensive player at a position, not necessarily to the player with the best fielding percentage. I know that's been true with me. My fielding percentage may be lower than others, but I make plays that other guys don't dream of. I sometimes make errors on those plays, too, but I think there's respect for my ability to cover a great deal of ground. I've gained respect over the years for my defensive play generally, and by defensing offensively, I hope to keep it.

MY ULTIMATE TEAM

I WANTED TO choose my ultimate team of National Leaguers playing today to illustrate how a batting order should be balanced to win games in offensive baseball. By "ultimate" I mean a team made up of players who fit perfectly at every position. Keep in mind that I have no intention of slighting any player. What I'm outlining is the team that I feel blends together not only through the batting order, but on defense, too. I made up the team by first finding the best defense up the middle and then teaming those players with the best offensive players on the corners.

I feel that at this time, Keith Hernandez of the Cardinals has asserted himself as the best all-around (offensive-defensive) first baseman in the league. He's won four Gold Gloves and a batting title, and was in the top ten in RBIs in 1979 and '80 and runs scored in 1979 through 1981. Keith would be especially valuable in my batting order because he's left-handed, very selective at the plate, and can also handle left-handed pitching very well. His greatest attribute is his poise as a hitter and his ability to hit the ball straight away.

Pete Rose and Steve Garvey could also be chosen of course. Pete is one of the top five hitters of all time, and Steve was probably the best player in the 1970s. However, I feel that Keith Hernandez blends best with my other choices.

Manny Trillo of the Phillies is a magician with the glove at second base and has the strongest infield arm in the league from any angle. Because of his arm, he's the best I've seen going behind second base. He can turn the double play consistently on any type of throw from the left side, and he has an uncanny feel for the location of the baserunner while making the double-play pivot. Only once or twice have I seen him knocked off-balance.

Manny has a unique feel for his position, always realizing just how much time he has to throw out runners on tough plays. He's also got the good tempo you need to play second. I think his play in the 1980 NL championship and World Series showed his total command of his position.

He's also shown his command of hitting. Many times in his career Manny has been among the league leaders in hitting. However, he is prone to tiring over the course of 162 games, because of his build and what is required of him on defense. He is also prone to injury because of his vulnerability to contact on double plays and in his style of hitting. But one of his most impressive qualities is that he never lets his hitting affect his fielding. Any way you look at it, Manny Trillo is my second baseman.

Joe Morgan was considered, too. He's had a great career and

blends with his teams perfectly. But I chose Manny because defensively he's second to none.

You could probably second-guess my choice for shortstop, because I've said that I want the best defense I could find up the middle. But Garry Templeton of the Padres might be the best natural athlete in the game today. He covers more ground than any other shortstop, and that, combined with his super-strong arm, enables him to make more great plays. One reason he can cover more ground is his relaxed, loosey-goosey style. Garry gets more done by not playing tight. He just glides up the middle and into the hole when he's charging the ball. He has a tension-free style.

I feel Garry will learn to play the hitters better as he gains more experience; and with this experience, he will learn to concentrate more on the routine plays. That's what separates the good from the great. Good shortstops make all the routine plays and, every now and then, a spectacular play. Great shortstops make all the routine plays, too, but have the natural ability to pull off the unbelievable once or twice a game. Garry has a chance to be the best ever, but only time will tell.

I also choose Garry because I feel that teaming him with Manny Trillo gives my ultimate team the best double-play combination possible. Garry can also lead the league in hitting any year and is always a cinch to get 200 hits.

As All-Star shortstops year after year, Larry Bowa and Dave Concepcion have both had outstanding careers. After playing next to Larry for nine years, I marvel at his concentration day in and day out. Larry has made me a better third baseman and also owns most of the league fielding records, but I choose Garry Templeton because of his youth and potential.

*   *   *

Third baseman Bob Horner of the Braves has more offensive potential than any other player I know. He's been able to amass some unbelievable statistics while only playing parts of his first three baseball seasons. Once he gets off to a good start and plays a full year, he'll be certain to lead the league in home runs and RBIs. He does have a long way to go to become a polished defensive player, but in time he will realize the importance of defense. Already he has led the Braves out of the cellar and made them a contender.

Ray Knight of the Astros and Ron Cey of the Dodgers both deserve consideration at the hot corner. Cey is a very consistent fielder and annually hits 25–30 home runs and drives in 80–90 runs. Knight is one of the toughest outs in the National League. He's a line-drive hitter who's always in the .290s with 80–90 RBIs, and is possibly the most underrated fielder at his position. But I choose Bob Horner because of his power, which will help him produce 35–40 more runs per year than Cey or Knight.

On any team, the leftfielder is probably the least effective defensive outfielder, but a key to the team's offense. Despite two subpar years recently, George Foster of the Mets is my choice in left, because he's the most complete hitter in the game today. He hits for power and average consistently. In his off-years he still hit between .250 and .300 and drove in 100 runs. And when George is right, he is far and away the best hitter in the game.

I also considered my teammate, Gary Matthews, who is probably the most underrated player in baseball. Now as a member of a contending ball club, Gary has a chance to assert himself as one of the best players of the game. I considered the Dodgers' Dusty Baker, too, who had his best year ever in 1980; also Gene Richards of San Diego, who has amassed some excellent leadoff statistics and is improving other parts of his game. Probably the most consistent of all the NL leftfielders over the last few years has been Jose Cruz of Houston. There's obviously talent in leftfield all around the league, but I feel that George Foster would best complement my team.

My centerfielder is very easy to choose. Defense is the key here. I want the best defensive player I can find—someone who is willing to sacrifice everything for the sake of covering ground in center and is a student of opposing hitters. My centerfielder must catch singles—meaning he must play shallow and still be able to catch almost anything hit over his head. He has to be a "gamer"—a guy who will run through the wall to make a catch.

I've seen Garry Maddox do it all. In my estimation, he's the best defensive centerfielder ever to play the game. This may sound like a bold statement, but as his teammate for all these years, I'll stick by it.

I considered other great players, too. At the top of the list is Andre Dawson of the Expos, because of his all-around offensive ability, and Dale Murphy of Atlanta. Cincinnati's Cesar Cedeno and Pittsburgh's Omar Moreno, who helped lead the Pirates to the 1979 world Championship, were also considered. Centerfield, like leftfield, is a hotbed of talent, but for the ultimate team I'm creating, I need Maddox in center.

In most cases the rightfielder is the best athlete on the team. There is good reason for this. He must have the best arm; be as adept at covering ground as the centerfielder; and as a key hitter, must complement the team's offense. Many times a team's success in a given year is dependent upon the rightfielder's performance.

For example, in order for the Giants, Cardinals and Dodgers to in a given year is dependent upon the rightfielder's performance.

For example, in order for the Giants and Cardinals to be successful, Jack Clark and George Hendrick must have good years. Notice that I left out my best example—Dave Parker. As he goes, so go the Pirates.

I believe that Parker is the most intimidating player in the game today, and possibly the guy under the most pressure to perform well. Because of his salary, his size, and his ability, people expect perfection. He led the Pirates to the World Championship in 1979 and has won two batting titles. Add in his Gold Gloves and his love for the game, and you can see why the Pirates need Dave to play well to win. You can also see why he's my choice for rightfield, with Clark running close behind.

The catcher is as important in baseball as the quarterback is in football. A team cannot win over the long run without a good defensive catcher. There are four of five top catchers in the National League now who stand out for different reasons.

The Mets' John Stearns stands out for his hardnosed play and leadership on a less talented team. In past years I would have had to choose between Johnny Bench and Steve Yeager. But injuries have been slowing John down recently, and he only wants to catch part-time, while Yeager has never put it together offensively. So all things considered—defense, knowledge and experience, offense, and durability—my choice behind the plate is Gary Carter of the Expos. He had his best year so far in 1980 driving in 100 runs, winning his first Gold Glove, and nearly leading his team to a divisional title. Gary has a great attitude for a guy playing in the Montreal weather—I really admire that—and he's a leader. He comes to play and he's only going to get better.

* * *

I want to mention pitchers not only because they affect the strategy of the batting order, but because my choice is not only a great pitcher, but a fine offensive player, too. That's Steve Carlton, of course—in my opinion, the model starting pitcher in baseball. Steve has the best concentration, he's in the best physical condition, and pitch for pitch he has the best "stuff" in baseball.

Steve also has the best move to first base—possibly the best move ever—and it has offset his at-times shaky defense. He's a "money" pitcher who always gives you a good game when you need one. As I've said many times, Steve Carlton on his worst day will keep you in the ball game for seven innings.

IMPORTANCE OF THE BATTING ORDER

I can think of no better way to demonstrate why a batting order is so important than to take my ultimate-team lineup and set up my ultimate batting order.

Ideally, the leadoff hitter should show the personality of the team to follow, and the ideal personality would be that of Pete Rose. You want the opposing pitcher to hope that the rest of the team isn't that scrappy. But while Pete is probably the best leadoff hitter of all time, he's not on my roster. Garry Templeton is, though, and with his base hits, speed, and switch-hitting, and ability to handle the bat, he more than satisfies the requirements of hitting first. Garry is perfect for the leadoff hitter's role of igniting the offense. The first hitter should be among the league leaders in on-base percentage, using whatever combination of hits, walks, and being hit by pitches it takes to do that. He must have no fear of hitting with two strikes, since very often he will take strike one. Speed and baserunning ability, as well as a sound knowledge of the game, are musts.

Keith Hernandez is the George Brett of the National League and my man to hit second. He makes contact with the ball as much if not more than anybody else in the league, and when he does, he can pretty much do what he wants to with it. That's important for the second-hole hitter—as key a spot as the third-hole man—who has to keep rallies going. That's why the second hitter should have a high average, as Keith does. Any power is icing on the cake. Also, like the first hitter, he has to be willing to spot the pitcher a strike. He must, as Keith does, subscribe to the theory of taking the first pitch. He has to be willing to make the pitcher pitch.

The number-two hitter should also be a fast man who won't hit into double plays. A left-hander like Keith will have a better chance to avoid double plays, because of the extra jump to first. A left-handed second hitter also makes it easier for the first man to steal, since it's tougher for the catcher to throw with a left-hander up. It's also easier for a left-hander to move a man into scoring position from first—if he has the discipline to look for a pitch to pull—or to move a man up from second into sacrifice-fly position.

All of these conditions would be met with Garry and Keith as the one-two men in the order, since both hit a lot of doubles (Hernandez is among the league leaders every year). They complement each other well. Hitting second, Keith wouldn't drive in the 100 runs a year he does hitting third with the Cardinals, but his normal offensive style fits perfectly with this team. He can do what the second man must—keep rallies going by working the pitcher and controlling him, not only when he's two-for-two and it's easy, but when he's oh-for-three in his fourth at-bat.

The third hitter often is the best athlete in the lineup and, along with the fourth hitter, the RBI man on the team. A great deal of respect goes along with being the acknowledged third-hole hitter—most of the best hitters in the game today bat third. They should be able to do a little bit of everything, winning ball games in different ways from one day to the next—with a steal, a home run, a clutch hit, or a pinpoint throw. The best all-around players, period.

Dave Parker fills this role perfectly on my team. I also like the fact that Dave is left-handed, which gives me three left-handers in a row in front of my right-handed fourth hitter, George Foster. Against right-handed pitching I can picture those three running around the bases all day. Against lefties, I've got a switch-hitter (Templeton) and two left-handers who have no fear whatsoever of left-handed pitching.

The only drawback to Parker hitting third is his home-run production—at present, about 20 a year. I'd like both the third and fourth men on my team to hit 30–40 home runs a year. But it's tough for any player to do everything—to perform at the highest level in all phases of the game—even with the kind of ability Dave has. (As a third-hole hitter, I understand the situation: people were always saying they would like me to hit for a higher average.) Parker is definitely the ideal third-place hitter and someday could win the Triple Crown.

The third and fourth hitters should complement each other, and despite his off-years, no one in baseball complements Parker better than George Foster, the finest all-around hitter in the game. When he's on, Foster has as good a chance as Parker of winning the Triple Crown. He's proven he can control his desire to hit the ball out of the park enough to hit .330 while still hitting

52 home runs and driving in 140-plus runs. That's why I want him behind all of those left-handed hitters—he'll get the RBIs that are the bread and butter of the fourth-hole man.

Good third and fourth hitters should have distinct traits. Just as the number-three hitter must always keep rallies going, the cleanup man has to focus on RBIs at all times. That means he has to be a good situation hitter. He'll try to get a run in if there's nobody on base and two outs—and sometimes with no outs. But the ability to score runners from second with two outs is a must for a great cleanup man. He has to be a man whom everyone knows will be a tough out with men in scoring position.

It's a plus for a team, of course, if the number-three and -four men each drive in 100 runs, as Greg Luzinski and I did when we were both having good years. But that's an unusual situation, and on this ultimate team, Foster would get many more RBIs than Parker, because Parker wouldn't hit as many home runs. Parker gives the number-four man more opportunities to drive in runs, because he hits fewer home runs but gets on base more of the time and thus sets the table for the cleanup hitter. These two men complement each other and the rest of the team very well.

The fifth hitter is very important in making the lineup work. Like the two men in front of him, he has to be respected by the opposition. He should hit 20–25 home runs and drive in 80 or 90. Also, he should either hit from the side opposite that of the fourth man or be respected for his ability to hit any kind of pitching. You don't want to have the cleanup man walked because the fifth hitter can't hit left-handers.

Dick Allen in his waning days was an ideal fifth hitter. Even if he never got a hit, I guarantee nobody wanted to face him. Bob Horner is the man to do that on my team. Right now he can strike as much fear into a pitcher as anyone in baseball. He would be the man in this lineup who would get the pitcher to come right at Foster with men in scoring position. He's also a legitimate .280, 35-home-run man who on this team could easily drive in 110 runs, because he's got four .300 hitters in front of him.

I could flip Horner and Foster in the order—or Horner and Gary Carter, the man I have hitting sixth—depending on who's swinging the hottest bat at the time. But I like Horner fifth because he hits for a little higher average than Carter and he'd command the right amount of respect on my club. Horner is a solid, play-every-day hitter who's feared enough to get Foster those three-and-one, three-and-two, and two-and-oh fastballs, and that's very important to a team.

I don't think any good team has a weak number-six hitter. In that spot, you need a hitter who can break up a game. Garry Maddox does that well for the Phillies with his speed and 10–15 home runs a year. Gary Carter, a game-breaker, would do the same for my ultimate team. I'm hitting Carter sixth only because there's nowhere else to put him on a team this good. The sixth and seventh hitters on good teams often would be hitting third and fourth on other teams. The bottom of the order is where your strength shows up, as it definitely would with Carter hitting sixth and Maddox seventh.

The sixth and seventh spots are good places to hit players you don't want to put a lot of extra pressure on. A catcher who plays every day already has the pressure of calling the game and handling the pitchers, and a centerfielder has the pressure of anchoring the outfield. You don't want either of these players to have the double burden of their defensive work and of driving in 100 runs. Johnny Bench at his peak was an exception, but you won't often find a catcher or a centerfielder with both responsibilities. And as good as my ultimate team is, I can take the pressure off the two guys who are the keys to my defense.

The eighth-place hitter is in basically the toughest position in the order, because he's always being pitched around. The other team isn't usually worried about what the pitcher can do (though with Carlton, they would be) so the number-eight man often is walked intentionally. You need a man, then, who has patience and control of himself as a hitter, and who can hit the bad pitches he's forced to chase.

You also need a man content with hitting in the eighth spot, one who believes that last is not necessarily least—and it's not, on some teams anyway. It could be the seventh man who's the lesser hitter. For instance, when Bob Boone and Larry Bowa were on the Phillies, Boone hit eighth and Bowa seventh because Bowa isn't as patient as Boone. Bowa will swing at everything and not take walks that are given to him, and so become more frustrated in the eighth spot. Hitting seventh gets Bowa more of the pitches that frustrated hitters need, because pitchers don't want to walk him to get to Boone.

On some teams, the eighth hitter can be underrated. The eighth hitter on my ultimate team, Manny Trillo, certainly proves that. He'll fill the role well, because he's patient, can handle the bat, and will take what the pitcher gives him.

The designated hitter in the American League changes the role of the eighth hitter, of course. But using the DH changes more than just the offensive responsibilities of the hitters in the lineup. The DH affects everything from beanballs to managing. Not only are more hitters thrown at because pitchers don't have to suffer the consequences, but the DH eliminates the all-important role the pitcher plays in the strategy of your offensive attack. The fact that the pitcher usually plays the smallest role in your offense does present a big problem, but one that good baseball fans enjoy. I think that the game of baseball was designed so that a team not only needs the big-gun offense you get in the top of the order, but also must execute the fundamentals required of those hitting near the pitcher. So while the DH may provide more offensive punch, with fewer bunts and pitching changes, it also takes a lot of managing out of the game—and with it, a lot of second-guessing by the fans. I suppose it's just a matter of defining whom you want to please, but I think traditional baseball, with the pleasure of the second-guess, is what most fans want to see.

With or without the DH, I think you can see why the batting order is an important part of offensive strategy and situational baseball. But the batting order has to be made up not only according to the particular abilities of the players on your team—as with the one, two, and three hitters being the most important in the order in terms of total offensive baseball—hitting and base-running—but also according to the players' willingness to adjust to certain roles. Since the batting order is important to you as well as to your team, how you feel about it depends on how you see your role. Certain guys say, "I don't care where I hit as long as I get an opportunity to play." I've said that at times in my career, and meant it—as I did in the last half of the '78 season, when I was moved around from third to first to sixth in the order.

But most times in my career I've fought as hard as I could for the right to hit in a particular spot in the order—for me, the third spot—because it *does* matter where you hit. Since each spot in the order has its own requirements and responsibilities, where you hit, depending on your ability, can affect your hitting style and your statistics. It can also affect your confidence. I think its clear that certain spots in the order can confer pressure and the status that goes with handling that pressure. This is important at any point in your career, but especially when you're young.

At the beginning of my sophomore year at Ohio University, I was still just sort of a throw-in at shortstop who hit seventh or eighth. Then I started really hitting the ball, and I can vividly remember my coach, Bob Wren, telling me after lunch at Western Michigan, "You're going to hit third for me tonight." That was his way of telling me that I had gained his respect, that he wanted me in a key spot in the batting order. That gave me a real shot of confidence. Knowing that people around you respect you, you respect yourself more, especially at that age.

But moving to an important spot can also have the opposite effect, if a hitter isn't ready for that position in the order. Putting hitters into roles they aren't used to can make them press, make them think they've got to do too much. Guys will say, "Well, you couldn't hold the four-hole. You hit there a couple of days and went oh-for-eight." You might feel it, too, and some damage might be done.

But moving an established player away from his normal role in the order can sometimes help him get back to form if he's struggling a bit. Hitting third is a responsibility I've accepted as well as anybody could most of the time, but I've also occasionally fallen victim to what it demands. To some extent, that's what happened to me in 1978 when I was moved around in the order after the first 100 games. Since I was having difficulty putting it together enough to be the third-place hitter, that was one time I would have said I didn't mind where I was hitting in the lineup, and pretty much meant it. In fact, the further I was moved down or up in the order, the less pressure I felt.

The same was true for the manager. Not only was Garry Maddox a hotter hitter then, but the manager also was sitting there thinking, "Do I want the key man in my lineup to get a standing round of boos every time he goes to the plate?" You have to think about that, because you don't want your key man to have to deal with all the problems I had to as a hitter then. You're putting a lot of money on that third-place hitter, and he shouldn't be a guy hitting .250 and getting booed out of the stadium for striking out.

I had lost the right to hit third then, so it was legitimate to move me. It was better for me as a hitter and for the team as a whole. I had all the requirements to hit sixth or first—the game-breaker punch for sixth and the on-base percentage and bat-handling and running ability for first. What I didn't have command of that year was the complete offensive game that you need as a third hitter.

Trying me in the leadoff spot suited what I could do then as a hitter, so I could accept that role for a while—and even like being the sparkplug of the offense instead of the big bomber and the feared guy in the batting order. It also had the desired effect on my hitting: I went 40-plus at-bats without striking out and I scored a lot of runs.

So no matter how important the batting order may be to a team and to situational baseball, I think you can see why sometimes the manager feels he wants to pull the order out of a hat. Making up a lineup card can be complicated and delicate at times, with all that ability and ego coming into play—especially on good teams.

STATISTICS — BASEBALL'S
NECESSARY EVIL

STATISTICS MAY tell the fans how much to cheer you and the owner how much to pay you, but to me statistics are baseball's necessary evil. "Necessary" because these numbers are the backbone of the sport; "evil" because some statistics are totally misleading. Too often these numbers are not used correctly to evaluate a player, and the wrong ones are emphasized.

What's a good year, and for whom? How do you compare top players with a whole range of ability? How do you compare players with different but average baseball talent? And how do you compare players in one group with players in another? Judging a player is a bit more complicated than looking up at the numbers flashed every night on the stadium scoreboard.

That's why, in fact, I'd change some of those numbers up

there—at least for some of the players. The batting-order discussion should give you an idea why. Statistics are not only determined by your ability but by your place in the batting order—your job and who's in front of and behind you. That's how players evaluate each other when looking at the morning box score—not just from the numbers but from what they mean for a particular player and his place in the order. Individual stats are important only when they're applied to certain players on a team. They should be used to evaluate in relative, not absolute terms. For instance, for the first, second, and third men in the lineup and the sixth and seventh men, too, I'd put on-base percentage (OBP) on the scoreboard. But there's no such number as far as most people are concerned. It's an unknown stat, really, until you discuss players whose job it is to get on base.

To me, it seems very logical that on-base percentage be one of the league-leading statistics. Then you'd have a category with clout for all those players whose main job at the plate is to get on base. Those players should be judged by how many times they get to first base versus how many times they go up to hit. And they should be paid on how well they do that job over a long period of time.

On-base percentage is also important for other players. In talking about the team concept of offensive baseball and what stats over a long period of time determine what players are doing for their teammates, there's no bigger statistic than OBP—and no smaller team stat than slugging percentage or total bases. After all, what counts is how many times you get around the bases or drive somebody else around the bases, because that's what wins and loses ball games. On-base percentage tells it all: how many

times a hitter goes to home plate and how many times he walks
back to the dugout.

Still, OBP is especially significant for a leadoff hitter. Maybe
leadoff hitters should be judged by OBP instead of batting average. Although Pete Rose may not quite agree with that, he always
talks about his on-base percentage. If he averages 200 hits and
100 walks, and gets hit by five pitches annually, in many of those
years he's probably gotten to first base more than any one else in
baseball. And he'd be right to let you know about that, because
that's his job. All other stats concerning Rose are secondary.

You also need OBP to be able to take credit away. If a player
like Omar Moreno used OBP to measure his performance, he
would find out that he's not doing his job. As a leadoff hitter for
the Pirates, Moreno should be, but isn't, among the league leaders in on-base percentage. OBP as a statistic would also give
Moreno something to shoot for—a particular percentage that,
like 100 RBIs or 30 home runs, signifies top performance. He
can't really expect to do that with home runs or RBIs, but he
could improve what's within his ability and better fulfill his role if
a stat like on-base percentage were given the right emphasis.

The same is true for Larry Bowa. He'll never be able to challenge me for the home run title, but he could be a top OBP
player. If he were paid by the number of times he got on base, he
might find himself a better player and making even more money.

Getting on base is all that Rodney Scott did when he was with
the Expos. He was a .220 or .230 hitter who went up to home
plate hoping they'd walk him. He wouldn't swing unless he
got a strike. All he cared about was getting on base. Even if the
winning runs were on second and third, if he could get down
to first base, and let the next guy knock them in, he'd

be satisfied. And percentage-wise, the other guy would have a better chance of doing just that.

Rodney Scott knew his capabilities as an offensive player. He needed to improve as a hitter, but he walked a lot, stole a lot, and got on the nerves of the teams he played. He produced runs in his own way.

I'm a player with a very good on-base percentage: I get 150 hits a year, walk 100 times, and get hit by ten pitches. But as a third-place hitter, I'm not judged on my OBP. People don't care whether or not I get to first base (or about my batting average) because, like the four and five hitters, my job is to knock in the on-base guys, to hit home runs.

When I'm judging my year, I do look at my RBIs first, but then I look at my runs scored and my batting average. I don't even look at my home run total. That's just a number that, taken alone, doesn't tell me much about my role as an offensive player. Home runs are important only as they contribute to my RBIs and runs scored. That's why when I hear people talking about the "home run king," I'm not impressed. I may have more home runs over the last eight years than anyone else in baseball, but I guarantee that I'm also right up there in runs scored, bases on balls, RBIs. And it's the 100 RBIs I've averaged in that time that I feel should be considered my most important career stat.

Runs scored is a very important stat, too. I think the number of runs scored should be the pivotal statistic used to judge the best players in the game. Almost all the best players have high RBI and home run totals, high total bases, and high slugging percentages. You get one of those stats and you pretty much get the others. But you have to earn runs scored in a different way—you have to stretch your ability as an offensive player.

To score 100 runs a year, you can't just go up to home plate swinging away. You have to walk, you have to know the strike zone, you have to be able to steal a base and know how to run the bases. There will be 10 to 12 times a year when good baserunning will get a run scored. Think how that stat will be reflected in a team's won–lost record, which is the bottom line.

I think runs scored should be an important statistic when considering the MVP award. On the Expos in 1980, for instance, no player scored 100 runs. Andre Dawson and Ron Leflore came close, but with their natural ability and speed they should have found a way. Granted, scoring 100 runs depends a great deal on someone else knocking you in; however, the ability to be selective at the plate—which produces a good on-base percentage—makes it possible. Remember, an MVP is a player who contributes to his team's success daily. He can't hit everyday, but he can get on base and score runs when he's not driving in a run.

A player who ranks among the leaders in runs scored as well as in the other stats has outstanding all-around offensive ability. Keith Hernandez, for example, is such a valuable player because he'll hit .320, walk 110 times, *and* score 115 runs.

I've been a big runs-scored person ever since I understood what it meant for my game. The same is true for walks. Probably 50 of the 100 runs I score a year start with walks. But like OBP, which it helps determine, the base on balls is a very underrated statistic. Fans may not think much of walks—many may see them as kind of ho-hum—but managers, or pitchers who give them up, know the value of the walk as an offensive weapon.

They understand there's an art to getting a pitcher to throw four balls and thus getting to first base without a hit. It's one of the rewards of being selective at the plate. You have to have the eye and the patience—the controlled aggressiveness—to get a pitch you can hit and hit it, or to take the pitches you can't hit and walk to first. It's not often you get an RBI or move up a runner with a walk, but otherwise the base on balls is the same as a single—and many times, as hard to get. Runs you score while on base count the same whether you got to first by a hit or a walk.

I get walks when I'm hitting well because I have a good eye and the book on me is to pitch me—often with high fastballs—in spots that are tough for pitchers to get strikes in. You need perfect fundamentals to hit those pitches; otherwise, you lay off them and take a ball. I also get walks when I'm not hitting well and I'm fouling off my pitch. If I foul off enough pitches, eventually I'll get a ball. So in off-periods, if I can't connect with a good pitch, I can lay off balls out of the strike zone and still contribute to the offense. Thus my 100 walks a year.

It's the 100 RBIs, runs scored, and walks I average a year that show I'm fulfilling my role in the batting order and my role as an offensive player—to drive in a run and score one myself. That's why I don't care who's leading the league in stats like slugging percentage or total bases, even when it's me. They're just numbers, manufactured statistics that, right off, I couldn't even tell you how to figure out. These stats are no barometer whatsoever for my game.

Game-winning RBIs is another statistic I've lead the league in that doesn't work at all as far as I can see. With that connotation of "character" and clutch hitting that everyone likes, it has become an *important* statistic in baseball—one that's kept track of on a day-to-day basis. You get a game-winning RBI for knocking in the run that gives your team a lead it never relinquishes. But the way it's set up is so misleading. For instance, you can hit a sacrifice fly in the first inning to put your team ahead, 1–0, and get the game-winning RBI even though in the second your team scores 15 runs, the other team scores 10, and you go on to win, 16–10.

What game did that RBI win? For a game-winning RBI to mean anything, you have to have been up in a critical situation. That wasn't always the case for me in 1979, for instance, when I led the league with 20 supposed game-winners. Probably 15 of them were "cribs" in the first or second inning of games in which we later went ahead to kill somebody. I think the game-winning RBI should be awarded only after the seventh inning, unless all the scoring is done before that. A game-winner should be counted only in the important or final periods of a game, because great stock should be put in a stat that has "game-winning" in front of it. It should be something you've got to earn.

But you don't necessarily want to earn that game-winner with a sacrifice fly. Although a sacrifice fly is an important way to get a runner across the plate, it's often a misunderstood statistic because of its name. "RBI fly" would better describe *one* of the results of trying to drive in a man from third with fewer than two outs.

What you want to do in that situation is score a run by making contact for a hit, not a flyball out. Unlike a sacrifice bunt, you don't want to give yourself up at the plate. You want to score a run, but also, if you can, get on base in the process—with a triple, say, so the next hitter can drive *you* in with a sac fly. To do that, you have to hit the ball with authority—whether it's in the air or on the ground. But you have to make contact no matter how you hit the ball. As many runners are scored from third on ground-balls to shortstop or second base as on flyballs.

A sac fly, then, is one of the possible outcomes when you just go ahead and hit the ball with good fundamentals with a man on third. Like home runs, sacrifice flys are executed most often by hitters not trying to hit them. You don't change your style to hit either one, but in trying to hit the ball with authority, long fly-balls *and* home runs result. In fact, I've found that often the easiest time to hit a home run is with a man on third, because then I'm trying to get him home by just making good contact. You can learn a lot about yourself as a hitter, as I did, when you try to put the ball into play in that situation. Once you get the feeling it's easy to hit then (because you're only trying to make contact), you realize you should be the same kind of hitter—have the same feeling at the plate—with no one on.

Knowing a sacrifice fly would be useful in a situation only means that, understanding situational baseball, you know that this is one of the times you have to put the ball into play. A good sacrifice-fly hitter is a player who, with a man on third, tries to do this by *driving* the ball and ends up with a lot of flyball RBIs. Leading the league in sacrifice flys means you're a good situational hitter, and it can give you confidence in your ability to score a runner, but it's not a goal you should aim for as a hitter.

What I've been giving you is the ideal, some ways I think stats could be better used to show what a player contributes to his team. But it isn't realistic to think that even part of this approach will be adopted. Or that baseball will accept new stats like sportswriter Tom Boswell's "total average," which shows total offensive ability in terms of team contribution rather than individual accomplishments. Baseball is a team sport, but one held up completely by individual accomplishment (which seems to be more important today, with the big contracts). On-base percentage just doesn't have that home run glamor.

I may want people to take notice of the whole range of my ability as a player—to look at my game and the different ways I help the team—but it would be ridiculous for me to say I'm making my living as an offensive player because of anything else but my home runs and RBIs. To most people, I'm a home run hitter and an RBI man: they could care less about anything else. They'll give me credit if I have a high batting average but won't say anything if I don't. To them, as long as I have 45-plus homers and 100-plus runs batted in, I've done my job. But that doesn't do me any good. I know what I'm capable of.

If you can't get satisfaction from statistics as they're set up now, you should remember what these numbers can or cannot tell you about your game or what you should aim for as a player. Whatever they may mean to others, I know that statistics more often measure your failures than the different abilities you bring to the game. I also know that statistics are tools used to judge an individual's performance over a long period of time. Consistency, and the patience and evenness you need to achieve it, is what counts in baseball even if the fans and the media only care about what you did for them last night.

But you can't expect the attitude of the fans and the media to change toward statistics any more than you can hope to perfect the numbers themselves. It's one of the frustrations you accept when you play the game. Statistics are baseball's necessary evil.

BASEBALL IN OCTOBER

NO ONE CAN really say what makes a successful player. That fragile combination of skill, attitude, and circumstances is different for each one. But there are certain qualities that successful players share—qualities that make it possible for them to be there in the end, that let their talent come through in clutch situations, when the most is demanded of a player. That's what it means to play baseball in October.

Superior skill alone doesn't make a successful player. It's using what skills you have and getting the most out of them—performing to your capacity and then some when it counts the most. As I said with statistics and the batting order, it's doing the job you are asked to as part of your team (as Del Unser did perfectly for the 1980 Phillies from the pennant drive through the World Series) that makes the difference. But for those players with *exceptional* ability, how well they use it when it counts the most will determine if they move into the ranks of the all-time great players.

World Series baseball for me, as for many others, seemed to be the missing ingredient for top-player status. October baseball in 1980 seemed to move me over the line. Sometimes you'll hear one player saying about another, "He's good, but he's never been on a winner." You have to play to *win*. That's the one thing successful players share, and that quality rubs off on the people around them—they reinforce each other. That's essential, because to be a *complete* success as a major league ballplayer at the end of your career, you have to have played on a "winner," as well as be one yourself. You have to have been a winner as part of a team that's a winner.

That's why no matter how you perform individually—no matter how many home run titles you win—it means little if you're not part of a winning team. Baseball is a team game, and it's team, not individual stats that should count for you. Stats are for the fans. It takes a total team—a team of winning players—to get to the World Series. You need a team of guys who will get the big hit for you, who will come through in the clutch more often than not. And in Philadelphia—and in my case individually—I didn't get that label until the 1980 World Series.

Being part of a team of players that knows what it takes to win and uses it, allows each player, not just one or two, to make a contribution. The Phillies were such a good team in 1980 that when I or another player didn't come through, the guy that pinch-hit behind us did. And then, still alive in a game or the World Series, we'd get a chance to redeem ourselves by getting

the big hit in the next at-bat or game. As a result of different players coming through when necessary, each of us, as we went along,
got a chance to come through, and we all got that intangible label
of "winner" that all major league ballplayers want and only a very
few end their careers with.

That's why in my eyes, as in others', I wasn't the success I feel
I am now as a player. I knew I had a lot of ground to cover before
I could give myself that label. There's too much that goes into
getting over that hump—both my teammates and myself had
failed too many times in crucial situations, crucial games. We'd
get to a certain point, but couldn't go any further. It was a part of
my career that kept me from being able to say I was a total success.

The last few weeks of baseball in 1980—what I did and what
my teammates helped me to do from the last week of the season
when we had to win four straight from the Cubs, through the
World Series—allowed me to make the transition from an impressive to a truly successful ballplayer. And that was because the
team was successful. Down through every player on the team we
were just so good when we had to be, that the team came together. People executed when they were asked to, and we came
together as a situational team. It's that simple. It had nothing to
do with intangibles (character or heart) or anything else other
than individual players having the talent and using it at the right
time. And when we looked at each other and shook hands and
embraced in the dugout, there was the feeling—momentum or
whatever it is that along with fate makes a team come together—
that this was our year. It just engulfed us, took hold of us, and we
rode it right on out to the world championship.

I think the catalyst for the Phillies' magic in October was our come-from-behind, extra-inning win over Chicago. It was there, in the first of many must-win situations we faced in that period, that we came through as a team, picking ourselves up after the potential low point of the season—two defeats in weekend games just before with the Expos. And it was in that game that I experienced my first of two real failures during that crucial time—popping up with one out and the tying run on third.

In other years, it seemed I wouldn't get picked up by my teammates at that point, and the burden of failure would seemingly be even greater for me than for others in the same situation. But Garry Maddox came off the bench to tie the game, and then Manny Trillo won it. Those guys picking me up the way they did made it possible for me to do some of the things I did against the Cubs in the other three games of that series—including two game-winning home runs—and during the rest of the week against the Expos. In Montreal, I remember feeling so gratified because I ended what became my first MVP year with probably my two biggest hits—two more home runs that were credited with helping clinch the division title.

But it was the play-offs with the Astros that year that really showed we had become the kind of team that finds a way to win instead of lose. After our previous play-off losses, we had to get over this hurdle—it was the hex we had to get off our team. And we did, overcoming everything from the umpiring to left-on-base records to win as a team, in one of the most exciting play-offs ever. It was in the midst of this triumph I had my second humbling experience in this period. With the tying run on third in the fifth game, I struck out—the biggest strikeout of my career to that point. But I was picked up again, this time by Del Unser, and we went on to a win and a pennant.

I don't think we could have survived another play-off loss as a team. We were on the edge individually and as a team, and the organization and certainly some of the players would have taken another direction had we lost. But we got over a hurdle that possibly no other team in baseball had a tougher time overcoming. All the negatives of that year and the years before, which would have become central issues with a loss, were wiped out by that win. And having had so much at stake in the five-game series with Houston and in the earlier games at Montreal, the World Series seemed like a real breather.

I don't think there was anywhere near the same level of pressure in the World Series as there was to get there. I know I felt relaxed and easy (letting things happen, not forcing them) and I found my concentration superior. Not that every at-bat wasn't pressure-filled—but I felt really good as a hitter, and I believe that feeling was shared by our whole team.

After all, we were in the World Series and the worst we could do was to be the second-best in baseball. Besides, we felt unbeatable. We knew that while the Kansas City Royals may have been a consistently better team through the season, from opening day until they clinched their division, we also knew, from October 1 on, that there was no team in baseball better than the Phillies. And with the help of the DH, which made us an even better team, and the superiority of our pitching, we proved it. We fulfilled our roles as well as anyone could—as situational players using all facets of the game—and emerged as successful ballplayers.

We were playing to win. There's no substitute for the feeling of being on a winner, the feeling that "we are going to find a way to win in each and every ball game." And that's what I've been trying to describe in this book: how to win by always being on the offense in every phase of the game.

To be able to do that and get the most out of his talent, a player has to know himself. Even if you never get a chance to play in a World Series, you can be successful by being the best player you can be—the individual winner I talked about earlier in the book—no matter what your talent. Just as with holding a bat or dealing with your temper, you have to do what comes naturally. You can't try to pattern yourself after anyone. I had to find my own way, and you will, too. The value of a book like this is to show what has worked most often for other players and, more important, to show you how I found my own way to a satisfying and successful game—a game I'm still trying to improve. It's not what I do, but what I can tell you about how to *think* about what you do.

But you have to know baseball as well as yourself. I don't know of any other every-day player who has played this game mentally as deeply as I have. I wanted to use *all* my ability to take advantage of game situations, and to do that consistently, I had to study the game as well as myself. I've always wanted to know *why*.

Because of that, I think I have more of a real grasp of why I succeed and fail. And that can't do anything but improve my game. By thinking about and trying to better understand myself and baseball, I haven't tampered with something you can damage by examining it too closely. In fact, you have to examine the game in order to enjoy it the way you should and be the player you can be. But you have to do it with respect. You have to understand you're never going to master the game, that you can't get four hits every 10 times up. There are intangibles in baseball—that's why hitting at it's best is an art—but what you can do is understand and analyze the parts of the game open to you. Learn what you *can* control and what you *can't* in the game.

In examining the game closely, I know that no matter what I do, I'm still going to hit my slumps, make errors, and have hot spells as well as mental lapses, because the season is so long and the game is so unpredictable. Something new happens every night—that's part of the attraction of baseball for everyone. But while I say constantly, "Well, that's baseball, it's a crazy game," that doesn't mean I can't affect my game.

What I'm trying for is improvement, not perfection, and in studying the game I'm just trying to come as close as possible to finding out what's going to make me as successful as I can be. That way, when I retire, I can look back and say I gave everything I had and, I hope, even leave something with the game.

To be this kind of player, you have to have the confidence in yourself to *know* you can improve your game. You can't be afraid to admit you don't do it perfectly all the time. Most players won't talk about or associate themselves with improper fundamentals, however. If they're statistically successful, they aren't willing to face the fact that they have some bad habits, so they'll play at the same level, never getting any better. Most players are just sold on the bottom line, and they don't care how they get there. It may be a .300 hitter, a .260 hitter, a Gold Glove shortstop, or a guy who drives in 100 runs. Someone told them what they do is good, and they've left it at that.

Which brings to mind Milwaukee's Gorman Thomas. It seems to me that Gorman is a great athlete. He runs well and must have great hand–eye coordination, because he hits 40–45 home runs a year and is an excellent golfer. Yet Gorman has settled in the role of just being a home run hitter, which seems to be all he cares about. But he's not getting the most out of his God-given ability. If Gorman studied the game and understood what he could do as a player and applied himself more, he could improve not only his home run totals but also his RBIs, his batting average, and even his basestealing. By doing that, he could produce more runs on a yearly basis for his team, and therefore become a better player for his team.

I don't mean to single out Gorman, but I identify with him because he has some of the same bad habits I did—and some of the same talent, too. He's just one example of the many players in the big leagues who are making a lot of money and may not be getting the most out of their talent.

Remember, I'm not talking here about a utility man who hits .240. Not every player can or should change his game. I'm talking about very good players who could do better, who could be "successful" players. There are some players who could legitimately say, "I don't have your natural ability, and if I try to make adjustments, I might lose the game I have." But not the ones with the kind of talent I've been talking about. They might tell you it's too late in their career to change, or that (in the case of home run hitters) they're up there to yank the ball out and put a run on the board. Well, it's never too late—but thinking that way, they'll never hit more than .250 or .260. They'll enjoy success in one area, and that may be enough for them—and for others. I think many players aren't forced to become better hitters because their teams, as well, are satisfied with what they are doing. Also, there are just not enough knowledgeable coaches.

So it's not always easy to improve your game, even if you want to. It can be difficult to overcome criticism when you want to do

184 Baseball in October

things your way, especially when there's general satisfaction with your level of performance. Teams, like players, feel that if a player tries to change what they consider to be a good game, he might lose it. The Phillies were totally satisfied with my 100 RBIs, 30 home runs, and .250 average, and they thought I should be, too. "That's all we want out of you" is what I heard over and over again when I said I thought I could drive in 140 runs, hit 40 home runs, and bat .330. They saw me as only having one-dimensional home run ability, while I felt that my talent was multidimensional. As easy as it would have been for me to settle for that, I wanted to get rid of some bad habits, to let *all* my ability flow.

Well, I've come to realize that .330 isn't possible with my hitting style—you need to hit more groundballs than you get with 48 home runs—but I've made great strides as a hitter. I've gone from a dead-pull .250 hitter to a straightaway .316 hitter with power, and people just can't believe the change. And I feel I'm just scratching the surface! As I see it now, I haven't reached the point at which I feel I've realized my potential, because I don't know what that is. And with my natural ability and desire to learn the game, I don't think I ever will.

Until I take off my uniform, I'll continually be looking to improve in all phases of the game, but especially in hitting. Although I can accomplish some great things if I hit .280 the rest of my career, I believe strongly I can be a consistent .300 hitter. Because I can analyze my style better than most players in the game today, I can enjoy more success as I go along. I feel I can make the right adjustment, and I'm not afraid to try.

If you approach the game with respect, there's no way you can "overthink" (except, of course, with the ball coming at you, when you shouldn't think at all, but respond with instincts formed by good habits). Hitting, like the whole game, is mental as well as physical. Remember, after a certain point attitude can be as important as ability.

But not too many players have the desire to give themselves that extra-percentage chance of getting a hit by using their heads. You can get eaten up with thinking about the game if you're not willing to accept the down times that are inevitable in baseball. Throughout my career it's been said that I think too much about the game—and there were times in the very early going when I *was* held back because I didn't understand why I couldn't hit a line drive every time up—but now people want to know what I've been thinking about all these years! More and more people are telling me they can't believe what a smart hitter I am now, when I'm thinking basically the same things I thought about five years ago. It's just that five years ago I didn't have proper fundamentals to go along with my approach. I'd have loved to hit the ball to right-center then, but I didn't have the stance, the stride, or the swing to do that. Now when I think "right-center," I have the mechanics to accomplish what I want to.

That's why by understanding yourself and the game you have a better chance of doing the right thing for your team when hitting under pressure. You have to learn what you're capable of and what you have to think about in order to come through. It took me a long time to realize what I needed—everything from getting the burden of thinking "I've got to do this, I've got to do this" off my back to the physical act of moving off the plate. Understanding how to handle everything from mental anxiety to my batting stance has helped me become the player I am today. And I've done it by analyzing what I can do and deciding what would be best for me, as well as learning to respect the game.

I used to be just lucky as a player. By that I mean that a player with great God-given ability who doesn't study it and examine what the game is about mentally will be just lucky to stay at a good level as a player. Sooner or later the game is going to catch up with you if you don't take advantage of what there is to know about how to play it. That's what you have to do to become a successful player—or a top player, if you have that kind of talent—how you turn luck and fate into greatness.

To be as successful a player as you can be individually, then—one who gets the most out of his talent—you have to be willing to make changes in your game. You can't stay at one level. But for top players, there are other requirements as well.

Talent is the first. I feel I'm special in the sense I was given a great gift. I was chosen to be a gifted athlete, and that gives me a special feeling. All major leaguers, really, have been given this gift, but in my case I feel I was given something extra. Many times it's been a burden as well as a blessing for me in my life and career, because of the potential I'm supposed to have. But it's something I've learned to deal with. And you do have to have extraordinary skill to be a top player.

Bake McBride, for instance, is a different type of ballplayer from me. In 1980 we both had our best years up to that point in our careers—we performed at the top of our games—but I was a better performer for our team. My style of play enables me to some special things few others, including Bake, can do. What I have that he doesn't is the ability to hit home runs consistently, to put a run on the scoreboard immediately. You have to have a special gift to amass special stats, but you have to play every day to do it. Hitting 48 home runs is special. Hitting .350 is special. So is averaging 100 RBIs a year. And the more years a player displays that kind of performance, the more important it becomes.

That's why Pete Rose, of all the special players, is in a class by himself. He does everything that everyone else does, but he's done it until other guys are blue in the face watching him. And then he does it again. It's his *consistency*, that quality I've talked about throughout this book, that is so important. It's going to be a long time, if ever, before there will again be someone as consistently excellent as Pete.

So there are players, and there are special players. Major leaguers know the special players in the game and would come up with most of the same names if asked. There are probably 20 players at any one time in contention for the top 10—players teams can't win without, players with unique abilities who can't be replaced from the bench or a trade. You have to have a special talent to get on this exclusive list, and you have to use it.

My list includes Pete Rose, Steve Garvey, Reggie Jackson, George Brett, Steve Carlton, Rod Carew, Rollie Fingers, Dave Parker, George Foster, Tommy John, Tom Seaver, Bruce Sutter, Johnny Bench, Goose Gossage, Cecil Cooper, and Keith Hernandez. These are my top players, successful players with the best talent who can get that talent out when it counts and who can withstand all the pressures of baseball today. They consistently put together great years.

And the pressures are greater today, with the high prices and high expectations and power of the press. Not that these pressures are unfair—it's what the top players bargain for. When you get the most credit you also get the most blame. You should expect a lot of the blame if your team doesn't win, and it shouldn't make me or any other player miserable to have fingers pointing at us. It's always been part of the game, but it's intensified today because of the entertainment and business value of baseball now.

But if off-the-field pressures in professional baseball are tougher today, I know from talking to former ballplayers and old-time baseball men that the competition on the field is as tough, if not tougher, than it was, too. Players run faster, the fields are faster, and more pitchers throw the ball harder than ever before. Knowledge of the game is better overall, and so are the techniques the players learn.

But older baseball men say that if players today had the love of the game they did, there's no telling how good we could be. Well, much more is expected from players today to show their love of the game—to show they're playing as much for love as money— but I think you still have to love the game if you're going to be a successful, winning player. More than talent and the confidence and guts to use it go into making a top player.

You have to enjoy the sound of the ball hitting the bat. You have to enjoy keeping your shoulder in and cracking a line drive. You even have to enjoy putting on your uniform with everything just so. You need that kind of feeling for the game, along with everything else, to be a special athlete.

So whether it's true or not that more players today love the game less, I think it is true that not enough of the good players today feel about the game the way they should. I know that some players won't go the whole route—they just don't love the game enough, for instance, to be with me in the end in a home run or RBI race. Other guys will. I *know* they will. When George Foster is healthy, I know he will be my main competitor for the home run and RBI titles. It's the same for AL hitters with high batting averages when George Brett is on his game, or for NL pitchers when Steve Carlton is having one of his years. They all have that necessary love for the game as well as a special talent. Just because Steve doesn't talk to the press, doesn't mean he lacks that deep feeling for the game. I know how much he loves baseball from our personal relationship—but I'd know it anyway by the way he performs.

Other very good players haven't been made to realize exactly where they are and the gift they've been given. I think some players take it for granted that they're playing in the big leagues, in the *major leagues,* and that they've got a chance to be the best. They don't really appreciate where they are or the number of people who'd like to be in their shoes.

Other players, with less talent, do. Not everyone can be a top player, but you can be a successful player—a player who helps his team win—by using all the talent you do have. Phil Garner comes to mind immediately as the best example of this kind of winning player. He does everything to win with everything he has. He's always on the offense.

But it's not easy for anyone to get his talent out. I've emphasized throughout this book how important it is to have the patience and confidence to let things happen, not force them to happen. You can't force yourself to hit a home run, you have to let yourself hit a home run. You can't force yourself to have a good year, you have to let yourself have a good year. And that's why you work to remove whatever blocks your talent. You try to prevent yourself from getting injured or from copying someone else's game personality—or even from talking to the press, if that's what you need to do to play. Staying within yourself in baseball means knowing yourself and using the talent you have. That's why situational baseball is as important to you as it is to your team. It gives you a variety of ways to use your talent.

You also need the courage and will to back it up. You have to conquer fear of the ball and face the fact that you sometimes will fail. You need an approach to the game, too, a certain gamemanship that's part of the competition. Intimidation in all its forms, from the on-deck circle to taking the first pitch to breaking up a double play, is a part of your game that's just as important and one you have to learn to use to your advantage.

I realize it may be difficult to identify with major league players who write books. We seem to have gotten where we are by some predetermined course and to be all of a piece, finished. The gap between you and me seems wide, and you may think, "How could he have started like me and gotten where he is today?" But what I've wanted to show in this book is that you're never really finished forming yourself as a player—or never should be, anyway. Nobody is a "natural," no matter how much talent he has. You may have a superior athletic gift, as I do, but you still have to try to master it. Major leaguers faced some of the same frustrations, failures and vulnerabilities you experience now when we were young—and we still do today.

Remember, I haven't had what you could call a smooth-sailing career. I certainly wasn't a "phenom" out of high school. When I left for college it didn't even seem that playing professional baseball was a possibility. Once in college, even though I did begin to learn about myself and the game, it was still a big deal when I moved from seventh to third in the batting order. And I was far from being any kind of rookie sensation once in the majors. I hit .196 my first year.

So it took a lot of luck to go with my raw talent—that luck I said everyone needs—for instance, that good college game for Paul Owens that got me into professional ball. And it was luck that kept me there, at least in the beginning, playing with a team that needed to fill my spot in the lineup. But I wouldn't have been in a position to take advantage of my luck if I hadn't been working at my game.

I got my confidence and understanding of the game later than some. It took me time to see that I had what it takes mentally and physically to play, and to understand what's important in baseball. I had to learn the value of my game through other people's eyes first, to see the different kinds of things I could do with my talent. For instance, remember I first learned to take pride in my baserunning and bunting for what they meant to others, not to my game. I needed a great deal of work to get my talent out and to make it mean something at the major league level. Home runs were the easy part. The rest I had to fight for.

You have to love the game to work that hard. And a player who loves the game has a better chance of maximizing his ability, whatever it is, and becoming the best player he can be. This is what I've been trying to become my whole career, and what I hope this book has shown you you can be, too.

MIKE SCHMIDT'S MAJOR LEAGUE STATISTICS

YEAR	CLUB	AVG	G	AB	R	H	2B	3B	HR	RBI	BB	SO	SB
1973	Phillies	.196	132	367	43	72	11	0	18	52	62	136	8
1974	Phillies	.282	162	568	*106	160	28	7	*36	116	106	*138	23
1975	Phillies	.249	158	562	93	140	34	3	*38	95	101	*180	29
1976	Phillies	.262	160	584	112	153	31	4	*38	107	100	*149	14
1977	Phillies	.274	154	544	114	149	27	11	38	101	104	122	15
1978	Phillies	.251	145	513	93	129	27	2	21	78	91	103	16
1979	Phillies	.253	160	541	109	137	25	4	45	114	*120	115	9
1980	Phillies	.286	150	548	*104	157	25	8	*48	*121	89	119	12
1981	Phillies	.316	102	354	*78	112	19	2	*31	*91	*73	71	12
M.L. Totals		.263	1336	4615	856	1216	227	41	314	878	851	1148	141

GWRBI—1980-17; 1981-10

* Led League

MIKE SCHMIDT *was born in Dayton, Ohio and is a graduate of Ohio University. He has spent his entire professional baseball career with the Philadelphia Phillies organization and lives year-round in the Philadelphia area with his wife, Donna, and their children, Jessica and Jonathan. He is active in fund raising for the Philadelphia Children's Guidance clinic and other area charities.*

BARBARA WALDER *has written about baseball and other sports for eight years, and has worked for* Sport *and the Associated Press. She is a graduate of Mount Holyoke College and lives in New York City.*

la guardia secreta imperial empezaron a impregnar el parque del Castillo de Miramar, donde había vivido desde hacía dos años con apenas una discreta escolta.

Cuando el avión aterrizó en el Aeropuerto Internacional Agustín II, a las tres treinta de la madrugada, a Fernando Carlos le quedó totalmente clara su responsabilidad a cargo del imperio al ver que lo recibía una numerosa comitiva rodeada por una fuerza de caballería del tamaño de una brigada y al mando del ministro de la guerra, el general Alfonso Peña-Bazaine. De pie, aún en el avión, mirando hacia abajo, supo que ya desde ese momento, pese a su nerviosismo y cansancio, tenía que caminar y actuar como emperador. Aquéllos que lo esperaban y que no le quitaban la mirada de encima, incluida su tía, la duquesa Carlota, todos sin duda con más carácter que él, y con experiencia en situaciones complejas, todos ellos estaban a las absolutas órdenes de Su Majestad Imperial, que era él, y eso lo ayudó para bajar del avión con más confianza en sí mismo, mientras se escuchaban las salvas de artillería, que saludaban al emperador. Carlota, que conocía a su sobrino, no lo creyó aún preparado para desenvolverse entre los ministros, así que apenas ocurrieron los saludos de rigor, y dirigiéndose a él como Majestad -ya no como Fer o *Tesoro*, ya nunca más así-, lo subió a un helicóptero que se elevó por los aires y tomó el rumbo del castillo de Chapultepec. Desde las alturas el joven emperador vio la enorme e iluminada estatua ecuestre de su antepasado Maximiliano I *el Grande*, situada al inicio del Paseo de Juárez, la avenida más bella e importante de la capital.

Fernando Carlos señaló la estatua y dijo a su tía:

—¿Cómo lograré ser tan buen gobernante como lo fue él?

—Tiene usted que ser todavía más que él, Majestad, mucho más— fue la respuesta casi imperativa de la duquesa.

Palacio de Schönbrunn, enero de 1917

El joven emperador Carlos I, recién coronado y bajo una presión sin precedentes, se sintió en confianza frente el embajador Maximiliano Mejía, el representante del Imperio Mexicano ante Austria desde hacía una década. Era un hombre de tez morena y aspecto serio, que aparentaba los cincuenta años que estaba por cumplir. Aunque no ostentaba título nobiliario alguno, dado que su padre rechazó el de conde que alguna vez le fue ofrecido por sus servicios al imperio, en la corte de Viena se le veía con simpatías, incluso como un hombre de confianza del gobierno, dado que a fin de cuentas era un súbdito leal de la casa de Habsburgo, hijo de un bravo general que había contribuido en gran medida para la consolidación de la dinastía en América. El viejo emperador Francisco José, que apenas llevaba poco más de dos meses como huésped en la Cripta Imperial de los Capuchinos, a menudo lo invitaba a desayunar con él y le pedía su opinión sobre asuntos políticos.

Así pues, frente a aquel mexicano de llamativos ojos color café que dominaba perfectamente el alemán, Carlos casi sintió estar hablando con uno de sus súbditos, aquella fría mañana en su despacho de Schönbrunn.

—¿Cómo se encuentra la salud de mi querido primo, el emperador Agustín?

—Su Majestad, el emperador Agustín II, goza de buena salud — respondió el embajador.

—Me alegro mucho, aunque creo que si él le pregunta lo mismo al embajador de Austria la respuesta no será tan satisfactoria.

—¿Sufre Su Majestad Imperial?

Carlos tardó en responder.

—Ésta es sin duda la guerra más terrible a la que nuestro imperio se ha enfrentado jamás.

—Comprendo, pero Su Majestad debe de hacer acopio de todas sus fuerzas. No puede permitir que lo abatan los acontecimientos. Austria lo necesita fuerte.

—Embajador, me sentiría bastante bien si usted me trajera buenas noticias. El sangriento y devastador desastre de Verdún fue una clara muestra de que estamos en franco declive. El poderío de Alemania ha llegado a su límite, en tanto que su resistencia pronto se agotará, y si mi primo no ataca a los yanquis para evitar que se metan en esto, no habrá esperanza alguna. Pero si ellos no vienen, si ustedes evitan que vengan, tengo aún fe en que equilibremos la guerra y así podamos pactar una paz honrosa para Austria.

—Majestad, tengo noticias de que el emperador Agustín ha leído ya su carta y ha sometido la situación al consejo de todos sus ministros.

—¿Y bien...? –dijo Carlos, visiblemente excitado.

—México no participará en la guerra. No es el momento adecuado para una guerra con Estados Unidos, que sería terrible y larga.

—Tampoco lo es para Austria –dijo Carlos, devastado.

—Precisamente, Majestad, si Austria ya cometió el error de enfrascarse en una sangrienta lucha de magnitudes aún impredecibles, lo más sensato es que México no cometa el mismo error. ¿No lo considera usted así?

—Señor embajador, cuando el Imperio Mexicano luchaba desesperadamente por cimentarse, el emperador Francisco José apoyó a su querido hermano todo cuanto le fue posible. Si bien es cierto que no pudo ayudarlo como quería, por la amenaza de los Estados Unidos y la compleja situación de Austria en aquella época, que acababa de perder la guerra ante Prusia, nunca lo abandonó. Las relaciones comerciales de ustedes en Europa, que les han acarreado tanta riqueza, fueron negociadas y abaladas por Austria, y no olvide que la conformación de su ejército, que hoy se ha ganado el respeto de las potencias, también se debió a que de aquí se enviaron legiones de oficiales durante años que les disciplinaron y adiestraron a sus guerrilleros, que entonces apenas tenían instrucción militar. Incluso parte de su aristocracia la exportaron de aquí. No es justo que el emperador Agustín me abandone así, México le debe mucho a Austria.

—Con el debido respeto y humildad, Su Majestad, creo que no está usted midiendo bien las cosas ni analizándolas correctamente. La situación de Austria de momento es en extremo crítica, tanto económica como militarmente, e incluso si hoy terminara la guerra, el imperio no tendría muchas facilidades de maniobra. ¿Acaso se considera usted capaz de enviar tropas a América en cantidad suficiente como para ayudarnos en una guerra contra los yanquis? Yo, sinceramente, lo veo imposible, pero digamos que Alemania sí podría, porque sabrá usted que el emperador Guillermo también ha querido tentarnos, mas si Francia e Inglaterra ganan esta contienda, no recibiremos ninguna ayuda, y tendremos que enfrentar solos un conflicto al que no estamos obligados a entrar. ¿Comprende usted la posición de mi soberano?

—México ganaría mucho si derrota a los yanquis, podría recuperar…

—Sí, Majestad, pero también perdería mucho si no tiene éxito en la guerra. Además, hay otros factores. El imperio está lleno de agitación, las nuevas tendencias culturales son, en muchos casos, contrarias a la monarquía. El pueblo no se siente representado por el Senado Imperial, y exige la creación de una cámara de diputados donde los cargos sean consecuencia de la votación popular y no adquiridos por herencia o por decisión exclusiva de Su Majestad. Ante un clima social tan complejo, el emperador ha accedido a crearla y en adelante las reformas importantes pasaran por la aprobación de ambas cámaras, lo que desatará el inicio de una era difícil ya que muchos representantes del pueblo no son partidarios de la monarquía. Pero es preferible oír a los que piden una cámara de diputados que a los que claman por echar de México al extranjero austriaco, como llaman ellos a su augusto primo, e instaurar una república.

En ese escenario, Su Majestad, no basta la propensión históricamente mexicana de sentir desprecio por los yanquis para llamar al pueblo a una guerra. Tan sólo imagine usted una derrota en la primera batalla, los enemigos de la monarquía aprovecharían para hacerle al emperador Agustín lo mismo que en su momento los franceses le hicieron a Napoleón III. En el peor de los casos, imagine que la guerra los echara a usted y a su primo de sus tronos al mismo tiempo. Sería terrible para la familia Habsburgo después de tantos siglos participando en las decisiones del mundo pasar a ser ciudadanos ordinarios de un día para otro.

—¿Quiere decir con eso, señor embajador, que yo ya estoy perdido y mi primo aún no gracias a que su imperio no está en guerra?

—La situación de Su Majestad es desesperada, tiene que maniobrar muy hábilmente para salvar el imperio de los Habsburgo en Europa.

—Embajador, ¿acaso no entiende que ustedes están desperdiciando una gran oportunidad para colocarse militarmente por encima de los yanquis? Si ellos vienen y somos derrotados, cobrarán más fuerza ante el mundo, y recuerde usted que nunca les ha gustado que su vecino sea una monarquía. Se sentirían listos para invadirlos y cambiarles la forma de gobierno si vuelven de aquí triunfantes. Cuando el emperador Agustín vino a Austria después de los funerales de nuestro mutuamente amado Francisco José, tenía muy clara esa realidad, y me dijo estar haciendo una evaluación exhaustiva de su capacidad militar para tomar pronto una decisión. ¿Cómo es que ahora ha cambiado de parecer tan repentinamente, si apenas hace dos meses casi me aseguró su entrada en la guerra?

—Los ministros sin duda han dado su opinión...

—¿Los ministros o la emperatriz viuda? ¿Acaso, embajador, piensa que yo ignoro que esa mujer manda en México desde que murió el emperador Maximiliano I?

—Vuestra Majestad se equivoca —dijo el embajador, sin que se viera ninguna emoción de incomodidad en su rostro pétreo—, se equivoca básicamente en las fechas, porque nuestra amada Mamá Carlota manda en México desde que abandonó el país el mariscal Bazaine. Desde entonces la máxima autoridad es ella y sus sabias decisiones nos han sido muy provechosas.

—Ha dirigido la voluntad de su esposo, de su hijo y ahora también lo hace con su nieto. ¿Cuándo piensa morirse esa mujer?, ¿acaso es eterna?

—La emperatriz Carlota tiene setenta y seis años, y por fortuna todavía goza de muy buena salud. La tenemos rodeada de nuestros mejores médicos y esperamos que Dios todopoderoso nos la conserve muchos años más.

—Apenas puedo creer que ustedes los mexicanos, con la fama que los caracteriza, permitan que los mande una mujer.

—Ah, pero los discursos públicos y la firma de leyes corren a cargo de nuestro soberano. Mamá Carlota toma las decisiones en la comodidad de sus aposentos y se las informa a su nieto para que él las haga públicas. Así las cosas tienen un matiz diferente. Aunque, en honor a la verdad, nadie ni en el más remoto rincón de México ignora cómo funciona el gobierno en realidad. Desde que se consolidó el imperio, se hizo popular una cancioncilla que decía: *Con su augusta esposa nos vino de Europa un hombre rubio y barbado, aunque los testículos venían en el cuerpo de al lado.*

—Entonces la emperatriz viuda ha decidido no participar en la guerra —dijo Carlos, impaciente.

—Mamá Carlota ha decidido esperar. Una mujer con su inteligencia y su edad sin duda ya está muy ejercitada en las artes de la paciencia. Sin embargo, Majestad, tengo instrucciones de manifestarle abiertamente que México no está abandonando a Austria a su suerte. Si usted se inclina por una paz por separado, pondremos toda nuestra capacidad diplomática ante Francia e Inglaterra para que tenga éxito.

—¿Y abandonar a Alemania, que entró en la guerra para apoyarnos?, ¿dónde quedaría el honor de los Habsburgo si tomo ese camino?

—Majestad, Alemania no entró en la guerra para apoyar a Austria. Ese supuesto respaldo fue en realidad un pretexto del emperador Guillermo para poner en práctica su potencial militar. Austria es una sufrida víctima de la megalomanía y vanidad del emperador alemán.

—Puede que así sean las cosas, embajador, pero así no las ve el mundo.

—Quizás Guillermo monte en uno de sus acostumbrados ataques de cólera por la decisión de Vuestra Majestad, pero en diez años Austria y Alemania volverán a tener relaciones diplomáticas. De momento, sálvese usted, es lo que México le recomienda. Tome en cuenta que Austria no está preparada militarmente para una guerra de esta magnitud, sus soldados están siendo masacrados como corderos y lo seguirán siendo si usted no toma una decisión drástica.

—Créame que lo pensaré.

—Sería bueno, Majestad, que recomendara al emperador Guillermo no seguir insistiendo tan furiosamente para que nosotros entremos en guerra. Si Estados Unidos no nos agrede nosotros tampoco lo haremos, y lo que puede ocasionar su aliado es que los yanquis se enteren de sus pretensiones. Entonces su entrada en la guerra sería inevitable.

—Comprendo —dijo Carlos, poniéndose de pie—, ustedes no quieren ningún problema. Informe al emperador Agustín que procuraré ya no molestarlo.

—Majestad, su amado primo me ha ordenado que lo informe de que, si llega a suceder que esta terrible guerra lleve a Austria a cambiar de gobierno, en México usted será bienvenido y tendrá un palacio donde vivir con su augusta familia.

—Dígale al emperador Agustín, o más bien a la emperatriz viuda, que si me llegan a echar de aquí, México será el último lugar a donde vaya. Es todo, embajador, se puede usted retirar.

—A las órdenes de Vuestra Majestad.

Maximiliano tenía en su escritorio las cartas de Napoleón III. Las había leído varias veces esa noche, esperando que las letras cambiaran de orden y dieran otro mensaje menos desalentador. Pero sabía que eso no iba a ocurrir, la realidad ya estaba escrita por más que él se negara a aceptarla. Al siguiente día acompañaría a Charlotte en el inicio de su viaje a Europa, en una desesperada intentona de último momento para lograr que el emperador de los franceses cambiara de opinión y no lo abandonara a su suerte de una forma tan egoísta, pero realmente se alegraba de enviar a su esposa lejos del peligro que pronto se cerraría como niebla entorno al imperio. Con la retirada de los franceses y el apoyo de los yanquis a Juárez, lo más sensato era que Charlotte ya no estuviera en México.

De pronto en su rostro demacrado se dibujó una sonrisa amarga, al recordar que cuando aceptó la corona de México dijo que sólo sería provisionalmente, mientras el país se montaba en las vías del progreso y la paz. En aquellas palabras estaba un mensaje oculto, él quería dar a entender que una vez probado en México como un extraordinario monarca, le arrebataría el milenario trono de los Habsburgo a su hermano Francisco José, orillándolo por mal gobernante a abdicar, como él había hecho con su tío Fernando. Qué estúpidamente vanidoso había sido, qué ingenuo y confiado por prestarse al juego de Napoleón. Ahora si bien parado salía de la empresa, regresaría derrotado a Austria para someterse a humillaciones y burlas, y en el peor de los casos Juárez lo pondría frente a un pelotón de fusilamiento, lo que tal vez sería mejor que las burlas.

—¿Lloras, Max?

—¡Charlotte! Debiste anunciarte. No oí tus pasos.

—Quizás te distraía el ruido de tus lágrimas al caer al piso. Las gotas de una tormenta son más discretas.

—¿Qué quieres?

—He venido a limpiarte las lágrimas, Max. Un mensajero ha traído una noticia que lo cambia todo: Juárez murió en Chihuahua, hace cuatro días, de una angina de pecho.

—¿Es verdad eso?

—¿Tú crees que bromearía en esta situación?

—Qué lamentable la pérdida de un hombre tan brillante. De verdad lo lamento, pero debido a su muerte aún hay esperanza. Quizás ahora sí puedas convencer a Napoleón de que no nos retire su apoyo.

—Olvídate ya de Napoleón, no iré a Francia.

—¿Qué dices?

—Que no es a Francia a donde debo ir.

—Charlotte, no te entiendo.

—Max, tú has dicho más de una vez que admiras mi inteligencia y sensatez en cuestiones políticas, que soy digna hija de mi recién fallecido padre, el gobernante más hábil de la Europa de su tiempo. Y yo reconozco que siento el mismo amor por gobernar que tú sientes por impulsar las bellas artes y la jardinería. Si confías en mí, Max, ¿Por qué no dejas que de ahora en adelante las cosas se hagan a mi manera? Si tenemos éxito, a fin de cuentas el crédito será tuyo, tú eres el emperador y yo sólo soy una mujer.

—¿Y qué propones? —dijo Maximiliano, ya más serenado.

—¿Confiarás en mí? Te conviene, así podrás descansar y dedicarte a ver los planos de tus arquitectos.

—¡Está bien! Según tú, ¿cuál es el siguiente paso a dar?

—Sí tendré que hacer un viaje, Max. Pero no a Francia, sino a los Estados Unidos. El presidente Andrew Johnson no ha querido saber nada de ti, pero si voy yo a verlo será diferente. Los yanquis, aunque no lo son, tratan de parecer caballeros. Johnson no le cerrará la puerta en la cara a una princesa europea, hija y hermana de los reyes de Bélgica. Le explicaré que muerto Juárez, un hombre de leyes, culto y liberal, el gobierno republicano caerá en manos de Porfirio Díaz, un militar que podría sumir al país en el mismo caos de los tiempos de Santa Anna. En cambio nosotros representamos un gobierno con un proyecto real de pacificación del país, que podría serle muy provechoso al comercio de Estados Unidos dentro de pocos años. Lo convenceré para que deje de apoyar a los republicanos con armas.

—Por favor, Charlotte, eso que dices es insensato. Tú podrías desenvolverte como embajadora en una monarquía, pero la republica de los Estados Unidos es otra cosa bien diferente. En un lugar así hasta a mí me daría temor ir a meterme.

—A ti, Max, pero a mí no. Toma la sabía decisión de confiar en mí. Recuerda cuántas cuestiones de vital importancia se han resuelto en la historia de la humanidad con un correcto uso de la diplomacia. La grandeza que Napoleón le dio a Francia con sus cañones duró poco, en cambio la que después le dio Talleyrand defendiéndola tan sólo con sus palabras le ha durado más.

—Y si logras convencer a Johnson, ¿qué haremos después sin el dinero de Francia?

—Max, ¿acaso no entiendes que la actitud cobarde de Napoleón nos da un pretexto estupendo para no pagarle a Francia lo que le debemos? Sin el apoyo francés ya no hay más subsidio, cierto, pero tampoco tendremos una descomunal deuda.

—Quieres jugar con fuego, Charlotte.

—En las cuestiones de gobierno, querido Max, no se juega con otra cosa. Pero volviendo al tema de este momento, si logro convencer al presidente Johnson de que ya no apoye a tus admirados liberales, estaremos en las mismas condiciones que ellos, como al principio de la guerra que desató la constitución de 1857. Ellos tienen a Porfirio Díaz, nosotros ordenaremos que regrese de Europa el general Miramón. Lo dejaremos todo a una sola batalla. Por lo pronto es prudente ordenar el repliegue de nuestras tropas, sin importar cuánto territorio podamos perder. Pero seguir enfrascados en esa guerra de guerrillas que planeó muy hábilmente Juárez, en esas batallas anónimas de las que nadie se entera, sólo nos hará perder recursos y hombres y no nos llevará a nada bueno. Mejor reunámosle al general Miramón un ejército considerable que lo espere a su regreso. Díaz es vanidoso, quiere ser un héroe y quiere ser presidente, además de que tiene mucha confianza en sí mismo. Seguro también reunirá las tropas republicanas para una sola batalla que habrá de decidirlo todo.

Castillo de Chapultepec, enero de 2017

Fernando Carlos despertó como era su costumbre anteriormente en el Castillo de Miramar, entre las nueve y las diez de la mañana. La duquesa Carlota ordenó que no lo despertaran antes para que pudiera descansar del largo viaje desde Italia a México. Ya despierto, el emperador recordó que era habitual en los monarcas Habsburgo levantarse muy temprano, aún de madrugada, entre las tres treinta y las cinco cuando más tarde, y él estaba aún en su cama a las nueve con cuarenta. Decidió que habría de ser ésa la última vez por el resto de su vida, a excepción de cuando se hallara enfermo o tomando unos días de descanso. Tendría que volver a actuar como en su niñez, bajo una rigurosa disciplina que tanto detestó y de la que tanto se alegró de liberarse, cuando terminó su etapa de estudios, a los diecisiete años.

Aunque los miembros mexicanos de la casa de Habsburgo no habían llevado nunca el título de archiduques de Austria, debido a un *Pacto de Familia* que habían firmado Maximiliano *el Grande* y su hermano Francisco José, precisamente en el Castillo de Miramar, la anterior morada de Fernando Carlos, se había creado para ellos el título de archiduques de México, desde que nació el primer Habsburgo en tierras mexicanas, Moctezuma, a mediados de 1868. El cambio en el título, sin embargo, no varió en absoluto la típica educación de los archiduques mexicanos con respecto a la de sus primos austriacos. Se les sometía a una rígida disciplina que iniciaba de madrugada, desde los cinco hasta los diecisiete años, tiempo en el cual se les metía en la cabeza: historia, matemáticas, física, filosofía, literatura, apreciación del arte, geometría, dibujo, administración del Estado, oratoria, diplomacia y tácticas militares, acompañado de una gama de idiomas que iban desde el griego y el latín, las lenguas clásicas, pasando por el francés, el alemán y el inglés, las lenguas dominantes en el mundo, así como las características del imperio Austrohúngaro: italiano, húngaro, checo y polaco. Maximiliano *el Grande* creyó necesario que sus descendientes aprendieran tales idiomas porque tenía la seguridad de que algún día regresarían a Austria a gobernar en sustitución de los descendientes de su hermano. Así que mandó diseñar un plan de estudios muy similar al que habían usado para educarlo a él cuando era niño. Con el tiempo, sin embargo, después de la muerte de Maximiliano *el Grande*, la emperatriz Carlota decidió que los archiduques mexicanos ya no deberían aprender las lenguas del Imperio Austrohúngaro y las sustituyó por otras tres que consideró más necesarias para ellos: el náhuatl, el maya y el purépecha.

Algo que diferenciaba a los archiduques de México de los miembros de la realeza europea, era el hecho de que ya entrado el siglo XXI el protocolo de su comportamiento les impedía estudiar en escuelas por más prestigiadas que éstas fueran y por consiguiente no acudían a la universidad. Todo se derivaba de una antigua máxima de la emperatriz Carlota, quien afirmaba que si bien el monarca estaba obligado a amar y a darlo todo por su pueblo, tenía al mismo tiempo que mantener distancias con éste para poder gobernarlo bien. Así que toda la educación que los archiduques recibían en la vida era dentro de alguna de las residencias imperiales y concluía a los diecisiete años, justo la edad en la que millones de mexicanos hacían sus trámites para estudiar una carrera universitaria. Mas no por eso se les podía tachar jamás de ignorantes o faltos de conocimientos. Durante esos doce años en los que estudiaban todo el día bajo la mirada de rígidos preceptores se edificaban como verdaderas bibliotecas parlantes.

Cuando a Fernando Carlos terminó de vestirlo un ayuda de cámara -otro aspecto en que la monarquía conservaba costumbres muy antiguas-, recibió aún en sus aposentos la visita de su tía Carlota.

—¿Cómo se siente, Majestad?

—¿Ni cuando estamos solos me puedes llamar Fer?

—No, Majestad, imposible.

—¿Eso quiere decir acaso que al convertirme en emperador he perdido a mi familia?

—Majestad, si la familia Habsburgo lleva siete siglos luciendo coronas en la cabeza se debe a nuestra disciplina, y a que nos apegamos rigurosamente al protocolo.

—¿Por qué decidiste para mí el nombre de Fernando Carlos I? ¿No habría sido mejor sólo Fernando o Carlos?

—Habría sido mejor Maximiliano V.

—Ése era el nombre que llevaría mi hermano.

—Sí, pero le hubiera dado más jerarquía a usted, ahora que le ha tocado ceñirse la corona. De hecho, cuando usted nació, recomendé a su padre llamarlo Fernando Carlos Maximiliano, y de haber sido así, usted podría gobernar como Maximiliano V, pero su padre decidió llamarlo Fernando Carlos José, debido a que su hermano mayor ya llevaba el nombre de Maximiliano y él sería el emperador. Por ello he creído que le sienta bien el nombre de Fernando Carlos I, ya que es la unión de los nombres de dos grandes monarcas de quienes descendemos: Carlos V del Sacro Imperio Romano Germánico, el primer emperador Habsburgo en llamarse Carlos, en honor a su abuelo, el temerario duque de Valois, y Fernando el Católico, el gran rey en cuyo honor el nombre de Fernando se hizo bastante común en nuestra familia.

—Pues a mí no me habría gustado llamarme Maximiliano V, me sentiría como si estuviera robándole algo a mi hermano.

—No es robar, Majestad, en este caso usted está entrando al relevo, ya que la Providencia tenía decidido que su hermano no llegara a ser emperador.

—Debió ser él. Yo no estoy preparado, ni tengo la edad para serlo ni quiero serlo.

—Sí, está preparado, sí tiene la edad para ser emperador y sí quiere serlo. Despréndase por favor de esos estúpidos momentos de debilidad tan reprobables en nuestra familia. Doscientos sesenta millones de mexicanos esperamos mucho de usted. No tiene permitido fallarnos, Majestad.

—Puede pasar, también soy humano.

—Puede pasar, pero no debe pasar. Y ya tiene que ir a su despacho, en media hora recibirá al príncipe Bonaparte, el canciller del imperio. Cuando esté con él, no olvide algo muy importante: usted es el emperador, Majestad, y él es su súbdito. Ponga mirada de león, no de cordero. Por fortuna tengo la seguridad de que si comete alguna falta no tendrá consecuencias. Luis es uno de nuestros hombres de mayor confianza. Nada que ver con el príncipe Iturbide y su hipócrita hermana. Esos dos sí que son un par de hienas.

Cuando Fernando Carlos entró a su despacho, su moral decayó más aún. El valor que había sentido la noche anterior, al ver desde el avión el iluminado y hermoso suelo mexicano, se había esfumado por completo. Ahora no tenía la más remota idea de qué hacer con una responsabilidad tan grande. No se sintió con la fuerza suficiente para ser emperador, y por el contrario en ese momento se sintió un farsante que tenía que reconocer su debilidad al estar dentro de aquella legendaria habitación, no como un miembro de la familia que entraba a pedirle algo al emperador, sino como el mismísimo emperador. En aquel lugar se habían tomado cruciales decisiones para la supervivencia del imperio. ¿Qué hacía él allí, sintiéndose como un conejo al que habían obligado a ponerse la piel de un león? Conforme más observaba el lugar, más se debilitaba su carácter. Decían que la decoración no había cambiado más que en algunos pocos detalles desde tiempos de Maximiliano *el Grande*. Detrás de su escritorio, donde habría de sentarse a partir de ese día y hasta su muerte, se hallaba una pintura precisamente del gran emperador, salida del pincel de Franz Xaver Winterhalter, uno de los últimos trabajos del maestro. En una esquina sobresalía un busto idealizado de Rodolfo I de Habsburgo, en otra el busto era de Maximiliano I, no de México, sino del Sacro Imperio. La tercera esquina tenía un busto del duque Francisco III de Lorena, el afortunado que pudo unir el nombre de su dinastía con la casa de Habsburgo. La cuarta esquina del despacho estaba decorada con el busto del primer duque de Miramón, como un homenaje por parte de Maximiliano *el Grande* al valiente general que fue crucial para la consolidación del Imperio Mexicano.

Fernando Carlos dudó en sentare por primera vez en aquella antigua silla, un regalo del emperador Francisco José I de Austria a su sobrino Moctezuma III. Sabía que de hacerlo ya no podría eludir de ninguna forma la gran carga que trataba de acoplarse a sus espaldas. Y cuando por fin lo hizo sintió estar haciendo la travesura que jamás se atrevió a hacer de niño incluso instado y defendido por su hermano: sentarse en la silla del emperador.

El príncipe Bonaparte le recordaba enormemente a su antepasado, Napoleón III. Desde que había llegado el abatido y destronado monarca a México, junto con su esposa Eugenia y el joven heredero de apenas quince años, para resguardarse en la bondad de Maximiliano *el Grande,* ya habían nacido cinco generaciones de Bonapartes, suficientes como para que los genes de Napoleón III ya se hubieran diseminado entre muchos otros, pero el canciller del Imperio Mexicano hacía pensar que la reencarnación dentro de una misma familia estaba permitida. Tenía un rostro delgado y sus ojos eran aguileños, su nariz era un poco larga y huesuda y debajo de ésta llevaba un bigote y una barba de candado negros y tupidos, casi árabe. Cuando alguien le decía que era un auténtico Bonaparte, debido a su similitud con su antepasado, él respondía "No. Soy todo un Beauharnais. De eso sí hay seguridad", haciendo referencia a la leyenda según la cual la reina Hortensia le fue infiel a Luis Bonaparte y el producto de esa infidelidad había sido Napoleón III, lo que, de ser cierto, lo desvinculaba de Napoleón I, pero no de su esposa, la emperatriz Josefina de Beauharnais, de quien era descendiente en línea directa.

Sentado, frente al joven e inexperto emperador, los ojos aguileños del príncipe Luis Bonaparte no escudriñaban a un hombre débil llamado a un trono que le quedaba bastante grande. Lo veía como un súbdito dispuesto a cooperar en todo. Y esa mirada inteligente pero fiel y benévola a Fernando Carlos le daba confianza.

—Gracias por venir, canciller.

—A las órdenes de Vuestra Majestad.

—Desde hace dos años que me marché a Trieste no he sabido gran cosa de la política mexicana —dijo el emperador—, e incluso cuando estaba aquí no puse nunca mucha atención a esos asuntos. Pero estoy dispuesto a aprender.

—Y yo a ayudarlo en todo lo que haga falta, Majestad.

—Su mirada me dice que es usted un hombre sincero, así que voy a aprovechar para hacerle una pregunta importante. ¿Cree que tengo futuro como emperador?

—Francamente, Majestad, no.

—¿Y qué hace aquí, canciller, formando parte de un gobierno en el que no cree?

—La fidelidad, Majestad, no tiene nada que ver con lo que la lógica invita a pensar y a creer —dijo Bonaparte—. No interprete mis palabras como pesimistas, sino como un examen sincero de la realidad. Tome en cuenta que yo como canciller no puedo salvar solo al imperio, ésa tarea le toca a usted como emperador. Esta monarquía ha hecho mucho por mi familia durante casi siglo y medio. Si usted hace las cosas bien, yo daré lo mejor de mí, y si las hace mal, también daré lo mejor de mí. Seré uno de los últimos ladrillos del imperio en caer al suelo, y si no quiero ser exactamente el último, es porque deseo caer antes que usted, Majestad, para que caiga en mí y yo pueda aminorar su caída. El día que las cosas vayan mal, el día que el pueblo pida su renuncia en las calles, cúlpeme de todo a mí y yo aceptaré sus palabras. Eso es lo que quiero darle a entender.

—Canciller, si yo me creyera capaz de ser tan cobarde con la actitud de un hombre leal y honorable, renunciaría hoy mismo. Maximiliano *el Grande* decía que era necesario tener un hombre en quien confiar ciegamente. Él confió en el duque de Miramón y fue recompensado por ello. Yo confiaré en usted y espero lo mismo, pero no por mí, sino por el pueblo mexicano.

—Yo estoy, por convicción y por patriotismo —dijo el canciller—, a las absolutas órdenes de Vuestra Majestad. Si usted se digna a ordenarme algo y a pedirme consejo al respecto, le daré mi sincera opinión, pero si sólo me da órdenes y no me pide consejo alguno, de cualquier forma sus órdenes serán cumplidas en el acto, por contrarias que sean a mi forma de pensar.

—Por su cargo, su experiencia y su inteligencia, canciller, creo que usted es el hombre más indicado para decirme cuál es mi mayor problema en este momento.

—Pues, Majestad —respondió Bonaparte, tocándose la barba—, aunque problemas tenemos muchos, creo que el más grande es Donald Trump. Desde hace meses ha despotricado contra nosotros los mexicanos, contra nuestra forma de gobierno y contra nuestras relaciones comerciales con Estados Unidos. Su augusto padre dejó pasar sus comentarios porque sólo era un ciudadano que daba su opinión, y como tal consideramos que tenía derecho, por más que nos calentara la sangre su palabrería. Pero dentro de pocos días tomará posesión como presidente. Entonces, si vuelve a insultarnos, tendremos que recibir sus palabras como "algo oficial" y tomar medidas drásticas al respecto.

—¿Qué tan drásticas, canciller?

—Primero que nada, retirar a nuestro embajador, el príncipe Ángel de Iturbide y Green. Después nos adaptaremos de acuerdo a cómo vengan los acontecimientos.

—¿Tan graves son las cosas?

—Majestad, usted no puede permitir que un yanqui vulgar inflado de poder insulte a los mexicanos. Como ciudadano se lo permitimos, pero como presidente tendrá que respondernos por sus palabras, que son, desde luego, sólo estupideces.

—El problema, canciller, es que las estupideces suelen ser lo que más ofende. Y el embajador, ¿es confiable?

—Digamos que no me preocupa el hecho de que tenga sangre yanqui o que sea hermano menor del hombre que quiere que usted abdique para que la casa de Iturbide sustituya a la casa de Habsburgo al mando del imperio. Es un hombre dueño de su forma de pensar, y no tengo motivos para sospechar que sea un títere de su hermano. Es más realista que fantasioso y de esa madera se hacen buenos diplomáticos. Pero si Su Majestad lo desea, lo removeré de su cargo en seguida.

—No, canciller. Yo también creo que él debe de permanecer en su cargo. Que Trump considere como una deferencia de mi parte el hecho de tener ante su país a un embajador, como dice usted, con sangre yanqui. Además, si ese tipo vuelve a insultarnos, al embajador Iturbide le quedan pocos días en Washington. De nada sirve precipitarnos. Por lo pronto, quiere que me hagan una biografía de Trump, sin detalles innecesarios, sólo necesito tener una de idea de cómo piensa y qué tan inteligente es.

—Ah, Majestad, ya la tengo hecha y ya la analicé. No olvide que soy el canciller. En breve tendrá una copia y después, si usted lo considera pertinente, unificaremos criterios. Si vamos a lidiar con un toro bravo, es bueno que los dos sepamos el tamaño de sus cuernos.

—Alguna vez escuché a mi padre —dijo Fernando Carlos— comentar que la guardia secreta imperial tiene una red de espionaje por todo el mundo, con la posibilidad de infundir rumores creíbles, organizar destructivas campañas mediáticas y todo lo necesario para derribar a un gobierno débil y poner en jaque a uno fuerte.

—Es totalmente cierto, y esa red está a las absolutas órdenes de Vuestra Majestad.

—Bien, si Trump se modera y empieza a respetarnos, quizás lleve buenas relaciones con él. De lo contrario, me le echaré encima con todo lo que tengo.

Palacio Imperial de México, mayo de 1867

—Ahora que hemos desenterrado por completo la piedra de San Miguel Coatlinchán, Majestad —explicaba el arquitecto Julius Hoffman a Maximiliano, mientras observaban varios dibujos extendidos en una mesa—, nos damos cuenta de que sus piernas son mucho más estrechas de lo que habíamos pensado. En este dibujo usted puede ver cómo es ese dios gigante en realidad.

—Ah, vaya —dijo Maximiliano—, está bastante deteriorado. Además de que sus cualidades estéticas no existen, ya que sus detalles son grotescos y remontan a la barbarie. No obstante, tenemos que buscar la manera de trasladarlo hasta aquí. No cumple con las características necesarias para adornar una plaza pública, pero sí debe de ser estudiado por nuestros científicos y dar fe en el museo imperial de que los antiguos mexicanos, aunque con poco conocimiento de la estética en este caso, ya eran capaces de hacer esculturas monumentales. Siguen llamando más mi atención los dibujos de las cabezas gigantes halladas recientemente en las excavaciones que hemos realizado en el sureste del imperio. Si con esta piedra monumental se pretendió representar a una especie de ídolo de los sacrificios, con aquellas cabezas tal vez quisieron retratar a filósofos, gobernantes sabios o artistas. Es necesario trasladar la más bella hasta aquí, para colocarla en el parque de Chapultepec. Coordínese usted con el ministerio de fomento para que se financien los dos traslados.

—A propósito de fondos, Majestad —dijo el arquitecto—, no me han sido entregados los recursos para continuar la adecuación del Palacio de Cortés y el Jardín de Borda. Comprendo que el imperio pasa por momentos poco saludables en sus finanzas, porque he sabido que también el arquitecto Káiser ha tenido que detener las obras de ampliación en el Castillo de Miramar. Con el debido respeto, Majestad, creo que se despilfarra mucho dinero en las obras del imperio. Si se me diera la dirección de los sesenta y cuatro arquitectos que trabajan en las remodelaciones de la capital, tanto en los edificios públicos como en las plazas y parques, yo podría entregar mejores resultados en cuanto al aprovechamiento de los recursos.

—Analizaré su propuesta, señor Hoffman —dijo el emperador—, pero ahora la falta de recursos se debe no al despilfarro de los arquitectos, sino al hecho de que acaba de terminar la sangrienta guerra, que nos ha exigido en armas lo que tan buen provecho habría dejado al arte. No se desespere, ahora que la paz se ha cimentado, pronto tendremos los recursos que necesitamos. Por lo pronto, hágame el favor de diseñar el método por el cual habremos de trasladar las dos piedras.

—Así será, Majestad.

En ese instante entró el secretario José Luis Blasio para informar a Maximiliano de que se acercaba la hora en que habría de recibir a la Emperatriz. Hoffman se retiró junto con Blasio y apenas un par de minutos después entraba en el despacho de Maximiliano la emperatriz Carlota.

—Max —dijo ella—, acabo de ver salir al arquitecto Hoffman con planos suficientes como para reconstruir la Acrópolis de Atenas y la antigua Roma. ¿Por qué no dejas tu manía constructora por un tiempo? No le vendría mal al imperio un poco de escrupulosidad en los gastos.

—Te recuerdo, Charlotte, que no aceptó la corona de México un general analfabeto, sino un vástago de la casa de Habsburgo. Las artes y el buen gusto en cada una de ellas tienen que dar constancia de mi presencia aquí. La capital de mi imperio deberá ser, en pocos años, más admirada que París, Roma y Viena. Además, ahora que hemos dado fin a la guerra, no hay nada que me impida emprender mis grandes obras.

—La ruina quizás lo haga, Max, los ladrillos no se cortan ni se pegan solos. A pesar de que aceptas la superioridad de mi inteligencia en cuestiones políticas, desde que el general Díaz está encerrado esperando su juicio, ya no aceptas mi consejo. Sólo te valiste de mí cuando la debilidad de tu carácter te impedía hacer nada, Max.

—Soy el emperador, Charlotte.

—Pero dejarás de serlo si sigues comportándote de manera tan irresponsable. ¿Acaso no ves que estás sentado admirando pinturas, bustos y planos de edificios sobre dinamita, Max? En cualquier momento puede estallar una revolución que te costaría el imperio y la vida. La guerra fue desastrosa y la pobreza que asola a México no admite de momento a un emperador que dedica más tiempo a la belleza de las artes que a los problemas económicos del país. Y encima gastas lo que el tesoro público no tiene. En lugar de planear mover antiguas piedras de su lugar, porque no piensas qué hacer con el general Díaz. No acepta por ningún motivo unirse al imperio a cambio de un indulto.

—Voy a indultarlo de todas formas. El pueblo necesita saber la magnanimidad de su emperador, ya que durante muchos años sólo ha sabido de guerras y fusilamientos.

—Hay una frase muy usada por nuestros súbditos que ahora conviene usarla contigo: no seas pendejo, Max.

—¡Charlotte! ¡Cómo te atreves!

—Es mejor hacerte enojar llamándote pendejo que dejar que tires el imperio a la basura cuando ahora sí es posible que tengamos éxito.

—Yo no tiraré nada a la basura. Concluida la guerra, el imperio está totalmente consolidado. Ya no tenemos enemigos.

—El enemigo será el pueblo si te sigues negando a usar la sensatez en tus actos. Pero ya que hablas de que el imperio está consolidado, dime, Max, ¿cómo resolveremos el problema sucesorio? Se trata de algo serio y de eso no me puedes culpar a mí. No he visto ningún niño con el labio o el mentón de los Habsburgo y vaya que tus correrías con las damas mexicanas han sido muy abundantes. En cambio yo no he tenido más opciones de poner a prueba mi fertilidad. Es innegable que el problema es tuyo. Ahora bien, regalarle el trono al nieto de Agustín de Iturbide sería una noble labor pero haría breve la estancia de los Habsburgo en México. Se diría que sólo estuvieron de paso y tú no quieres eso, Max.

—El problema está resulto, Charlotte, porque sólo tengo una salida. Mi heredero será el archiduque Otto, el hijo de mi hermano Francisco Carlos. Él será el árbol que yo plante en México para que asegure la permanencia de mi estirpe aquí por siglos.

—Querido Max, lamento decirte que tu inteligencia no se compara con la mía. Indultar a Díaz y traer a México a un niño nacido en el extranjero para que gobierne a estos problemáticos mexicanos es lo mismo que cavar la tumba del imperio. ¿Acaso no entiendes que Díaz no se va a conmover si lo liberas, y que una vez libre formará un nuevo ejército?

—¿Y acaso no entiendes tú, Charlotte, que si lo fusilamos seré muy criticado ya que muchos mexicanos lo quieren bien por sus proezas militares? En tanto que no veo ningún problema en que los mexicanos acepten a un emperador extranjero si ya aceptaron a uno.

—Max, eres el único hombre en este mundo tan ingenuo que cree que el mismo milagro puede ocurrir dos veces en el mismo país.

—¿Y qué más puedo hacer? Y no me refiero a la cuestión de Díaz, hablo del heredero al trono.

—Escúchame bien, Max, los mexicanos no tienen una identidad nacional completa, y si no se las damos, duraremos menos de lo que te imaginas en el trono de México. Y tú no deseas eso por nada del mundo. ¿O acaso quieres olvidarte de tus proyectos, y encerrarte a llorar en Chapultepec poco antes de que nos echen o nos fusilen?

—Bien —dijo el emperador, tras reflexionar—, ya que eres tan inteligente, Charlotte, dime, ¿qué estás planeando?

—El plan que voy a desglosarte, Max, no quiero que lo tomes a la ligera. Ya que es la puerta para que seas ante la historia el gran emperador que quieres ser, y no el aventurero austriaco, como todavía te llaman algunos.

—Te escucho.

—El general Díaz debe de ser fusilado, y después de eso indultados los demás liberales que ahora tenemos encarcelados. Principalmente el señor Lerdo de Tejada y Vicente Riva Palacio. Eso nos ayudará a apoderarnos de Juárez, empezando por honrarlo como un gran pensador. Glorificaremos su imagen. Fue un hombre inteligente y de voluntad inquebrantable, además de su admirable amor al imperio de la ley, la clase de héroe que necesitan los mexicanos. Al único que no podremos glorificar será a Díaz como un gran general, puesto que sería una hipocresía debido a que nosotros mismos vamos a fusilarlo. Pero eso no puede ocurrir ahora, sino dentro de dos o tres meses, cuando yo esté embarazada y que mis damas ya lo hayan notado, para que lo propaguen por toda la capital y al pueblo no le quepa duda de que nacerá un príncipe de sangre imperial, pero completamente mexicano, un príncipe tan suyo como la Virgen de Guadalupe. Si a ti, que llegaste como un príncipe extranjero que no hablaba bien el español, te recibieron con tan desmesurado amor, a mi hijo van a amarlo más que los franceses al rey de Roma. La emoción que ese nacimiento causará en nuestros súbditos hará que sea menor el efecto del fusilamiento de Díaz. Supongo que lo que más te desconcierta de esto es el cómo voy a embarazarme. Bien, querido Max, en ese sentido no me quedará otra más que devolverte una de las muchas que me has hecho.

—¡Estás loca, completamente loca, Charlotte!

—¿Y qué otra cosa podemos hacer, Max, tú no puedes?

—¿Crees que yo, el emperador de México, voy a permitir que me hagas un cornudo?

—Max, te pedí que no tomaras esto a la ligera. De tus cuernos nadie va a enterarse, en tanto que de tu impotencia, infertilidad o alguna desviación ya sospecha todo el mundo. Un hijo mío, Max, aunque lo niegues, haría mucho por ti. Te consolidaría en el imperio y probaría que eres un hombre completo. Yo a cambio pido el privilegio de ser madre. Si vemos el trato sin prejuicios, Max, es bastante justo. Además, lo casaremos tan pronto tenga la edad con una archiduquesa. Si quieres, aunque me disguste, puede ser incluso con una hija de la propia Sissi. Eso garantizaría que los herederos al trono de las futuras generaciones tuvieran sangre Habsburgo, y poca importancia tendría que dicha sangre les llegue por el lado de su padre o de su madre. Recuerda que, como la española, la rama austriaca de los Habsburgo también se extinguió, y se habría quedado para siempre en el pasado de no ser porque el emperador Carlos VI se las ingenió para que los descendientes de su hija María Teresa llevaran un nombre dinástico que ya no les correspondía. Pero sin irnos tan lejos, Max, en caso de que tu verdadero padre fuera, como se rumora, Napoleón II —cosa que dudo porque eres idéntico a tu padre Francisco Carlos—, tú no dejarías de ser un Habsburgo, porque él era hijo de María Luisa, una archiduquesa de Austria. ¿Comprendes? Casar a mi hijo con una archiduquesa sería la solución a todo. Eso traería a la dinastía que tú estás fundando de regreso la sangre de los Habsburgo.

—Sí, pero no olvides que mientras tanto, mi heredero inmediato sería un bastardo que no tendría nada que ver con mi familia.

—En eso tienes razón, aunque, si somos totalmente justos, entonces te equivocas, Max. ¿O acaso olvidas que los Orleans, la familia de mi madre, descienden de Ana de Austria, una autentica Habsburgo? Si bien mi hijo no sería tu sobrino como en el caso del archiduque Otto, sí sería tu pariente. Si la emperatriz María Teresa gozó del privilegio de que sus descendientes fueran considerados los legítimos herederos de la sangre de Rodolfo I de Habsburgo, Rey de los Romanos, ¿por qué la reina Ana no? Ambas fueron princesas de la casa de Austria. Ahora bien, si ese argumento no te sirve, si crees que sólo los herederos de María Teresa ostentan la sangra Habsburgo, entonces te recuerdo que es tatarabuela tuya tanto como mía. Afortunadamente, Max, esa costumbre que tienen los reyes de emparentar sólo entre ellos, consigue el milagro de que los bastardos no salgan de su familia. Mi hijo sería tan Habsburgo como tú. Y ya que será tu hijo ante todo el mundo, tú podrás elegir su primer nombre de entre dos: Agustín o Moctezuma. Gobernará ya sea como Agustín II o como Moctezuma III. Es necesario que su derecho a gobernar el imperio no sea desde que nosotros llegamos a México, sino desde tiempos más antiguos. Si te inclinas por el nombre de Moctezuma, entonces creo que sería más conveniente cambiarle el nombre a la capital del imperio y llamarla Aztlán. Y por supuesto después del primer nombre, que será, como ya te he dicho, con el que gobierne, podrás ponerle el largo rosario de nombres Habsburgo: Fernando, José, Carlos, Francisco, Leopoldo, Rodolfo, Maximiliano y cuántos más quieras.

—¿Y cómo piensas hacer las cosas? Si te descubren…

—Max, no subestimes mi inteligencia. Saldré una noche disfrazada y fijaré mis ojos sobre un soldado francés, belga o austriaco, o hasta en un mexicano de piel blanca. Él no sabrá quién soy yo y yo me cuidaré mucho de no saber su nombre, ya que el único padre de mi hijo serás tú y el secreto sólo lo sabremos tú y yo. También cuidaré que sea alguien sin importancia, nada conocido entre la sociedad. No se puede acusar a un niño de bastardo cuando no hay un padre célebre que todo el mundo conoce con quien comparar sus rasgos.

—¿Y si nace una niña?

—Le pondremos el nombre de Guadalupe, después el de tu madre, el de María Teresa y si quieres también al final el de Sissi. Será la archiduquesa Lupita de México y los mexicanos van a amarla. Después de su nacimiento, para conseguir al heredero, tendré que cobrarte otra de las muchas que me has hecho, querido Max. Pero confiemos en que sea niño, y creo que el nombre más apropiado para él sería Moctezuma. Así podremos hacerlo pasar como el heredero de un hombre que gobernó este país hace ya varios siglos. De esa manera, no importa cuántos grupos de facinerosos e inconformes surjan, ya no podrán echarnos de México, Max.

—Y sí resulta que no eres tan fértil como piensas, Charlotte, ¿saldrás todas las noches hasta que consigas tu objetivo? Eso te acarreará mucha fama, además de que algún día podrían descubrirte.

—No seas tan pesimista, Max. Mejor reza tanto como yo para que sólo sea necesario salir una noche y el producto de esa noche sea un varón.

—¿Quieres que le pida a Dios que me hagas un cornudo, para que luego yo me haga pasar por el padre de un niño que será hijo de un hombre inferior a mí y a mi dinastía, y que con ello engañe a los míos metiéndoles a un bastardo como si fuera uno de sus miembros?

—No, Max, pídele a Dios que yo tenga un hijo para que gracias a él pases a la historia como un gran emperador y como el primero de muchos de tu dinastía aquí en México, y no como un archiduque sin importancia o, peor aún, como un simple aventurero fracasado, infértil, impotente o invertido.

Castillo de Chapultepec, noviembre de 2016

El archiduque Fernando Carlos tembló al hallarse sólo con su imperial padre, dentro de su despacho. Le había tenido miedo desde que era niño. El emperador Maximiliano IV había sido siempre severo con él, a la vez que elogiaba al primogénito. Fernando Carlos no era un estadista, como no lo podía ser cualquier persona emocionalmente inestable. Le gustaba el arte, los viajes y la soledad tan armoniosa con el océano dentro del Castillo de Miramar, donde vivía. Su hermano Maximiliano había sido siempre su escudo contra su padre, en él se refugiaba cuando lo llamaba "débil", "soñador", "estorbo". Pero Maximiliano había muerto, y quizás a eso lo llevó su actuar temerario, su convencimiento de que al ser un Habsburgo y futuro emperador de México era invulnerable. Una especie de consentido de Dios. Su afición a los deportes lo había llevado a jugar diez partidos amistosos con la Selección Imperial Mexicana, y en cada uno de ellos anotó gol, también hizo una destacada actuación en tres ediciones de los Juegos Olímpicos participando en Pentatlón Moderno. En tiro su puntería era extraordinaria y en esgrima no tenía un solo punto débil. Su afición más riesgosa era la de pilotear aeronaves. Le gustaba hacerlo en días poco recomendables para volar debido al clima. Una tarde emprendió un vuelo desde Aztlán con rumbo a un palacio de descanso de la familia en Veracruz, acompañado de su esposa, Luisa de Orleans, y de sus dos hijos pequeños, los archiduques Maximiliano, de siete años, y Rodolfo, de cinco. Los cuatro murieron cuando la avioneta se estrelló en la sierra, poco antes de llegar a su destino. Fernando Carlos recibió la aterradora noticia en Miramar. Devastado y sin poder siquiera hablar con nadie voló a México para participar en los funerales. De acuerdo a la tradición familiar, su hermano, su cuñada y los niños recibieron cristiana sepultura en la Cripta Imperial de Guadalupe. Se trataba de un edificio neogótico que Maximiliano *el Grande* había ordenado edificar en un rancho cercano al Castillo de Chapultepec, denominado entonces La Hormiga. El proyecto estuvo a cargo de Heinrich von Ferstel, y era bastante similar a la Iglesia Votiva de Viena, diseñada años atrás por el mismo arquitecto y también por iniciativa de Maximiliano *el Grande*, cuando sólo era un archiduque austriaco.

Concluido el entierro dentro de la Cripta Imperial, la duquesa Carlota informó a su sobrino que su padre lo esperaba en su despacho. Fernando Carlos tembló al oír aquellas palabras. Ya no estaba su hermano mayor, Maximiliano, para defenderlo. El emperador era un hombre en extremo severo, dominado por la razón de Estado y en quien jamás vislumbraban los sentimentalismos. Algunos decían que su carácter era bastante similar al de Francisco José I de Austria. De pie, con un puño apoyado en su escritorio, el monarca vio entrar a su hijo al antiguo despacho, y le hizo una señal de que se acercara.

—A las órdenes de Vuestra Majestad.

—Hace dos años —comenzó Maximiliano IV— al notar que no te interesaban en absoluto los asuntos de gobierno, y que no tenías tampoco talento para ello, permití que te alejaras de Aztlán, que te fueras a donde te diera la gana, con tal de que no hicieras escándalos que perjudicaran la imagen del imperio. Creo que te fuiste a encerrar al Castillo de Miramar, pero eso no tiene importancia ahora. Lo que importa es que eres el último archiduque que queda en México, puesto que, como ya sabes, mi único hermano varón, Fernando José, se dio un tiro por accidente a los catorce años, y ahora tu hermano Maximiliano ha muerto. Así las cosas, te pido que te quedes a mi lado, que participes en los asuntos de gobierno, que aprendas a ser el emperador que el pueblo mexicano necesita y exige, y que dejes para siempre en el olvido tus estúpidos sentimentalismos, tu pereza y tus trivialidades. Para mí es un sacrificio rebajarme a pedirte tal cosa, pero como ya te he dicho y bien lo sabes, eres el último archiduque de México que queda con vida. Lo que te pido lo hago en nombre del imperio. ¿Aceptas?

—¿Tengo opción de negarme? —se atrevió a decir Fernando Carlos.

—Claro, gobernar al Imperio Mexicano debe de ser algo que un archiduque desee, no una obligación. Los mexicanos quieren a un emperador de verdad, no suplican la atención de un malagradecido, a quien tanto le han dado y que en cambio no se interesa en ellos. Si tú no quieres a los mexicanos, ellos no te van a querer a ti. Te conviertes ante sus ojos en lo que muchos dicen que somos los Habsburgo en México: un extranjero indeseable. Pero te lo preguntaré una vez más, ¿aceptas ser emperador, quedarte a mi lado y aprender?

—No.

—Bien —dijo Maximiliano IV, sentándose y totalmente calmado—. No sé si ya lo sabes, pero te informo que llevo buenas relaciones con Elena de Grecia. No había pensado casarme, no obstante, la muerte de tu hermano lo hace necesario. Ella es soltera y tiene treinta y cinco años, y yo cincuenta y uno y soy viudo. Tengo la seguridad de que aún podemos tener dos o tres hijos. Confío en morir después de los setenta y cinco años, cuando ya tenga a un heredero perfectamente preparado para ser emperador. Te confieso que ése era mi plan desde que murió tu hermano, de ninguna manera permitiría que un inútil y débil metal como tú herede una responsabilidad tan grande. Pero no quise ser injusto contigo, decidí dejar que te negaras a gobernar el imperio por decisión propia. En cuanto nazca mi primer hijo, producto de mi próximo matrimonio, renunciaras legalmente a tus derechos al trono de México, ¿está claro?

—Sí, Majestad.

—Bien, ya puedes irte a Miramar, o a donde te dé la gana, pero fuera de México. Sigue llevando una existencia discreta y no hace falta que vengas a mi boda ni al bautizo de tus hermanos.

—Como usted disponga, Majestad.

—Después de todo, me evita un desgaste innecesario el hecho de que seas tan sumiso. Ahora lárgate de aquí y déjame trabajar.

Castillo de Chapultepec, enero de 1917

El emperador Agustín II tenía un porte regio impecable. No ostentaba ninguna de las características de los Habsburgo austriacos, ni la mirada débil ni el labio deforme, ni mucho menos el ya muy lejano genéticamente mentón pronunciado. En el aspecto físico se parecía mucho a su padre, Moctezuma III, y en menor medida a su madre, la archiduquesa María Valeria de Austria, pero en su carácter no tenía nada en común con ninguno de los dos, esclavos y víctimas hasta su muerte de la emperatriz viuda Carlota. Su personalidad era fuerte, sus ojos parecían de tigre y sus gesticulaciones eran sobradamente severas. En comparación con su primo Carlos I, de quien se decía en la corte mexicana que parecía un santo más que un emperador, Agustín II era una especie de ogro con encanto.

Sentado en la silla bellamente labrada y de impecable buen gusto que Francisco José I de Austria había mandado hacer como regalo para su padre Moctezuma III, tenía enfrente al duque de Miramón, el canciller del imperio, y al general Ángel de Iturbide, segundo príncipe de Iturbide y Green y ministro de la guerra.

—Señores —dijo el emperador—, ¿debo dar instrucciones a nuestro embajador en Viena de que informe a mi primo, Carlos I, que entramos en guerra o que no entramos en guerra?

El príncipe de Iturbide se dispuso a tomar la palabra. Era un hombre dotado en las artes de la oratoria y además desde su niñez se sentía autorizado para tratar con familiaridad a los Habsburgo, al ser una especie de nieto adoptivo de Maximiliano *el Grande* por el lado de su padre, en tanto que por el lado de su madre era bisnieto del famoso príncipe Klemens von Metternich, debido a un matrimonio que arreglaron Carlota y la ex emperatriz Eugenia de Montijo, una vez que ésta se exilió en México.

—Majestad —dijo—, esa guerra es una moneda al aire. Si cae de lado que usted quiere, le espera una gloria inimaginable, pero si cae del lado adverso, le esperan consecuencias terribles, en tanto que no está obligado a lanzar dicha moneda.

—¿Y qué posibilidades tenemos que caiga del lado que nos conviene?

—Si me lo permite Vuestra Majestad —dijo el príncipe y extendió un mapa en el escritorio del emperador, que contenía a México y a los Estados Unidos—, esta enorme frontera es indefendible tanto para ellos como para nosotros. Pero ellos nos llevan una gran ventaja. Es cierto que nuestro ejército es poderoso, tenemos disciplinados y adiestrados a más de un millón de hombres, y posibilidades de aumentarlos en poco tiempo. Además, nuestro armamento es de primer nivel, el mismo con el que combate ahora Alemania. Pero la flota de ellos es mejor. Eso significa que tendrían el dominio absoluto del mar. Así las cosas, nuestro avance tendría que ser por tierra, en un territorio enorme, descomunal, y para llegar a Washington, porque ningún país se rinde si no se toma su capital, tendríamos que recorrer miles de kilómetros. Sería un milagro que las líneas de aprovisionamiento no fueran rotas en ningún momento de la guerra por el enemigo, y, de ser así, de incomunicar a nuestras tropas, tan sólo con eso nos estarían derrotando.

—Desolador su diagnóstico, príncipe —dijo el emperador—, ¿Y usted qué opina, duque?

El aún joven canciller Miramón, del otro lado del despacho y a unos metros del busto de su legendario abuelo, parecía incrédulo ante la posición de Iturbide.

—Majestad —dijo—, nuestro ministro de la guerra ve las cosas desde una posición muy tradicional. No tenemos que llegar hasta Washington, primero causémosles tales derrotas cerca de nuestra frontera que sean capaces de desmoralizarlos muy hondamente. Una guerra relámpago en extremo destructiva y humillante para ellos, los obligará a negociar a nuestro favor, así jamás estemos cerca de su capital y tengan una mejor flota que la nuestra.

—Señor duque —intervino Iturbide—, usted, desde la hazaña heroica de su abuelo, creerá que todo se resuelve con una sola batalla o con pocas. Pero si así fuera, si todo dependiera de la guerra relámpago que usted sugiere, nada nos asegura el éxito. Los yanquis también van a defenderse con todo lo que tienen. Si la guerra se alarga, que es lo más probable, estaríamos perdidos.

—Es cierto —dijo el emperador—. Wilson parece un pacífico profesor jubilado, pero esa clase de hombres son los que se defienden como fieras al sentirse agredidos. Sospecho que tiene una voluntad de acero debajo de su pasividad. No se conformaría con nuestra rendición, querría obligarme a abdicar.

—Majestad —intervino Miramón—, tenemos un millón de hombres listos para el combate. Napoleón tenía menos, hambrientos y mal armados cuando llegó a Italia, y ése fue su inicio para poner a toda Europa a sus pies. Las guerras no son cuestiones matemáticas, como cree el general Iturbide, mucho tiene que ver la inteligencia y el arrojo de los generales, que pueden hacer que cien mil hombres parezcan un millón. El príncipe Khevenhüller-Rivas es nuestro mejor estratega, y lo considero tan brillante como el propio Napoleón o César. En calidad de agregado militar en varias embajadas, tan solo con verter su opinión, lo han descrito como un general terrible. Se ha dicho que para ganarle una guerra a México habría que envenenarlo antes de que esa guerra inicie. El príncipe Iturbide acaba de señalarnos que tenemos la desventaja de la inferioridad de nuestra flota, pero ha olvidado que tenemos la ventaja de decidir dónde y cómo empieza la guerra. Si invadimos una ciudad fronteriza donde nuestro ejército tenga mejor posicionamiento, Wilson, enfurecido, querrá vengar la afrenta sin medir el terreno. Nos atacará precipitadamente y ésa será la oportunidad de ganarles una primera gran batalla que sería demoledora para su moral.

—Planea usted la guerra muy a su gusto, duque —dijo Iturbide—, pero quizás le convenga consultar antes con Wilson para ver si él está dispuesto a adaptarse a sus planes. Porque yo pienso que tiene otros. Creo, sin ánimo de ser irrespetuoso, que el odio a los yanquis se hereda, y que usted trae consigo todo el que llevaba su honorable abuelo. No digo que ese resentimiento sea injustificado, yo también llevo una parte, como todo mexicano, aunque algunos digan que soy medio yanqui por mi abuela, pero está usted tratando de empujar al emperador a un conflicto que podría ser terrible para treinta millones de mexicanos. Es cierto que el príncipe Khevenhüller-Rivas ha hecho simulacros brillantes, en los que ha movilizado cuerpos de ejército en tiempo admirable, pero aún no ha entrado en batalla, y allí las cosas pueden ser totalmente diferentes a cómo las podemos imaginar. Por mi parte, analizando detenidamente las cosas, no me queda más que recomendar a Vuestra Majestad voltear a ver a la prudencia.

—Majestad —volvió a tomar la palabra Miramón—, los yanquis no quieren una guerra larga en su territorio, como no la querrá nunca ningún país tan dado al comercio. Si no logramos derrotarlos por completo, al menos podemos demostrarles de lo que somos capaces. El honor de México exige al menos unas cuantas victorias, en una guerra breve y finalizada con una firma de paz honrosa.

—Quizás Guillermo II pensó lo mismo —dijo Iturbide—, que tendría una guerra breve y de la que podría salir con apenas unos trámites burocráticos. Pero, a fin de cuentas, Majestad, yo soy su ministro de la guerra, y no soy un cobarde. Cumplo con prefigurarle el escenario al que podríamos enfrentarnos, mas como soldado estoy a vuestras imperiales órdenes.

Agustín II se puso de pie, vio los cuatro bustos que decoraban su despacho, después se dio la vuelta para ver a los ojos a Maximiliano *el Grande*. Cuando volteó nuevamente a ver a sus ministros, dijo:

—Que el general Khevenhüller-Rivas movilicé las tropas. Entraremos en guerra, señores.

—Cabe una pregunta más —dijo Iturbide—, ¿con qué argumento atacaremos?

—Príncipe, por cómo nos han tratado los yanquis desde los tiempos de su antepasado, Agustín I, tenemos el derecho de estar en pie de guerra con ellos siempre. Quizás si van a meterse a la contienda de Europa y vuelven triunfantes, tomen una distancia considerable de nosotros y ya no podamos devolverles nunca el mal trato que nos han dado. Ésta puede ser nuestra última oportunidad. Enviaré un telegrama a mi acobardado primo, para informarle que no se preocupe más por los yanquis, que nosotros vamos a ocuparnos de ellos. Ahora veremos quién le debe favores a quién.

De pronto las puertas del despacho se abrieron. Cuando Iturbide y Miramón voltearon, vieron de pie en la entrada a la anciana emperatriz Carlota. Conservaba su porte arrogante, y se veía enhiesta y digna, irradiaba autoridad y, pese a su avanzada edad y a que su cuerpo había empequeñecido con los años, causaba miedo enfrentársele. Los dos ministros del imperio fueron a inclinarse ante ella.

—Caballeros —dijo Carlota—, me es penoso interrumpir de forma tan inapropiada al emperador. Mas sabiendo que aquí se decide justo ahora la paz o la guerra, me he visto obligada a hacerlo. Les ruego que nos dejen a solas, y que no acaten ninguna de sus órdenes por ahora.

—Señora, a los pies de usted —dijeron a coro los ministros, y salieron del despacho, dejando a Carlota y a su nieto atrás.

—Conociéndolo, Majestad —dijo Carlota, acercándose al emperador—, creo que se había inclinado usted por la guerra de forma precipitada e irresponsable.

—Mi decisión no ha sido ni precipitada ni irresponsable, señora.

—¿Ah, no? Señáleme en ese mapa por qué punto nos han invadido ya los yanquis, y yo misma iré a cerciorarme de que las tropas del príncipe Khevenhüller-Rivas los cuelguen a todos.

—Si bien es cierto que los yanquis aún no nos atacan, señora, mi decisión ha sido adoptada por estrategia.

—Me permito el atrevimiento de informarle, Majestad, que su estrategia es bastante estúpida —dijo Carlota—. ¿Por qué no piensa en regalar a su pueblo leyes justas, prosperidad, bienestar, y no una guerra?, ¿acaso ya olvidó que es nieto de Maximiliano *el Grande*, ese gran emperador que nos trajo el comercio en abundancia, que hizo de México el paraíso de los emigrantes europeos, que embelleció las ciudades, que llenó el país de monumentos más hermosos que los hay en Europa, que tanto detestó la guerra, y cuya sabiduría lo llevó a su sufrir cuando tuvo que enfrentarla?, ¿acaso ignora que él pudo anexionarse por la fuerza de las armas a Guatemala, pero que prefirió respetar la decisión de ese noble pueblo de ser independiente y tener relaciones armoniosas con él, para que tan sólo cinco años después los propios habitantes desde Guatemala hasta Costa Rica se anexaran voluntaria y jubilosamente al gran imperio que tenía el poder para darles seguridad? Majestad, compórtese como un digno descendiente de Maximiliano *el Grande*, y gobierne con sabiduría, no con instinto.

—Lo lamento, señora, lo lamento de verdad, pero casi he dado mi palabra a mi primo, el emperador Carlos I, de entrar en guerra contra los yanquis, y no puedo traicionarlo.

—¡Claro que puede, Majestad! —Alzó la voz Carlota—. Usted puede traicionar a todos, menos a los mexicanos. ¿Cómo se ha atrevido a comprometer la paz de México sugiriendo promesas absurdas? Si los europeos se han metido en una guerra sin precedentes es problema de ellos, que no quieran que nosotros los mexicanos actuemos con su misma estupidez.

—¿Se da cuenta, señora, de que ésta es una gran oportunidad para México?

—Me doy cuenta de que usted piensa y decide como niño, Majestad, pero gracias a la Providencia estoy yo aquí para enseñarlo a comportarse como hombre. ¿Acaso no ve que la guerra heroica de los tiempos de Napoleón I ha llegado a su fin? Esta guerra tan extremadamente cruel y destructiva es nueva, Majestad, y nosotros representamos una forma de gobierno muy vieja. Quizás no seamos compatibles. Cualquier emperador medianamente inteligente esperaría a ver qué pasa con este conflicto del que no tiene memoria el mundo y con las monarquías que se metieron en él estúpidamente. Prepare al ejército, sí, en eso procure siempre estar a la altura de los yanquis, pero no cometa la estupidez de ir a meterse a una guerra como si fuera un carnaval. La nueva guerra nos es totalmente desconocida, y por fortuna otros idiotas la están experimentando en nuestro lugar, así podremos aprender de ella sin sufrirla. Aprenda, Majestad, aprenda, para un emperador siempre es pequeña toda sabiduría. Y olvídese por lo pronto de esa estupidez romántica de ir a vencer a los yanquis y coronarse como amo de todo el mundo. Preocúpese por los mexicanos que sufren por hambre, por enfermedades o por injusticias. Yo entretanto me ocuparé de enviarle un telegrama a nuestro embajador en Viena para que le diga a su primo que resuelva sus problemas solo, que para eso es emperador, y si no puede, entonces que mejor renuncie a su cargo y se venga a vivir a México. Aquí nos ocuparemos de él como nos hemos ocupado de tantos desdichados que tras su desgracia ha venido a lamernos la mano.

—¿Entonces México sencillamente no sacará ningún provecho de esta guerra?

—Claro que sí, tampoco somos santos —dijo Carlota—. Los ingleses piensan que en cualquier momento atacaremos a los yanquis, y es bueno que lo piensen. Yo misma, gracias a las buenas relaciones que llevo con el rey Jorge, miembro de mi familia aunque tanto lo niegue ahora por distanciarse de su origen alemán, me he encargado de hacerle ver que estamos decididos a entrar en el conflicto.

—¿Y qué ganamos con engañar a los ingleses? —preguntó el emperador—. Eso puede propiciar que ellos mismos insten a los yanquis a atacarnos primero.

—En realidad ya tengo redactara una carta para el rey Jorge en la que le garantizo que debido al cariño que le tengo, en recuerdo a mi querida prima Victoria, lo he convencido a usted de mantenerse neutral, pero que esa neutralidad no será del todo gratis. Inglaterra tiene que pagarnos con algo. Él debe de entender que Belice es un territorio incrustado en el Imperio Mexicano, cuya naturaleza geográfica lo convierte en parte de éste. Nuestra neutralidad, a ojos de los ingleses, tendrá que ser a cambio de que las buenas relaciones que tenemos con ellos, tan importantes para nuestro comercio, no se rompan cuando la bandera del águila y la serpiente se pose en Belice y lo convierta en un departamento más del imperio. Es el último territorio que nos falta para que toda Centroamérica sea mexicana. Su anexión tenía que pasar tarde o temprano y es bueno aprovechar esta oportunidad, para que todo sea pacíficamente. Debemos recordar que la anexión de Panamá hace quince años estuvo a un solo tiro de costarnos una guerra contra los yanquis, y si es que no se nos vinieron encima fue porque ya desde entonces respetaban nuestro poderío militar. Roosevelt sabía bien que no era lo mismo desmembrar a España, una antigua potencia moribunda y tan lejana, que meterse con el Imperio Mexicano, tan joven, lleno de buenas ideas, en pleno crecimiento militar y pegado a su frontera. Su abstención me ayudó mucho para conocer la mentalidad de los yanquis. En fin, ¿qué le parece mi plan, Majestad?

—Está bien —dijo Agustín II—, acataré su consejo. Pero, señora, no deseo que me vuelva a contradecir delante de los ministros, eso pone en tela de juicio mi autoridad, ni tampoco que vuelva a emprender un proyecto tan importante como la anexión de Belice sin consultármelo. Recuerde que yo soy el emperador, y que usted legalmente no goza de facultad alguna.

—Lo trataré como el emperador que es, Majestad, mientras se comporte como tal. Pero si se empeña en tomar decisiones estúpidas en perjuicio de los mexicanos, soy capaz de envenenarlo para elevar al trono a mi bisnieto, el archiduque Maximiliano. Y le recomiendo que no me rete

—dijo Carlota, cuando ya se retiraba—, porque quizás salga mejor librado de una guerra con los yanquis que de una guerra conmigo. Usted, sí, es el emperador, pero los hilos del imperio los tengo yo, y pese a mi avanzada edad, no me he sentido tan débil como para soltar uno solo... A las órdenes de Vuestra Majestad —añadió inclinándose.

Desde la muerte del archiduque Maximiliano y su familia, la duquesa Carlota vivía en el Castillo de Chapultepec. Y no se debía a que su hermano el emperador se lo hubiera pedido para no sentirse solo, sino que ella tomó la decisión y él no objetó nada al respecto, dando a entender que comprendía la actitud de su hermana como una especie de responsabilidad familiar, pese a que Carlota había renunciado a pertenecer a la casa de Habsburgo en su juventud, cuando se enamoró de un talentoso pianista y decidió casarse con él, aunque antes se había planeado para ella un matrimonio con un archiduque austriaco, de aquellos que sólo eran tales ante ellos mismos, ya que perdieron sus privilegios aristocráticos con el desastre de la primera guerra mundial. Pero Carlota se reveló y, heredera del carácter de la primera Carlota, se casó con su pianista y adoptó su apellido, González, bastante mexicano, como decía ella. Su hermano, el emperador Maximiliano IV, con quien estaba muy unida desde la niñez, menos de un año después de su boda la perdonó y le dio a ella y a su esposo el título de duques de Cuernavaca, en tanto que para sus sobrinos, una mujer y dos hombres —ninguno de ellos con los nombres tradicionales de los Habsburgo, debido a que no lo eran—, otorgó títulos condales y ordenó que fueran adiestrados para tareas de administración del Estado. Les dio un trato mucho mejor que a sus cuatro bastardos, a quienes les negó un título y la posibilidad de que formaran parte del gobierno, aunque los dotó de una buena preparación universitaria y de algunas propiedades, e incluso con el hijo de su amante favorita, al que llamó Juan —nombre común en los bastardos de los Habsburgo, según le dijo la propia Carlota—, solía convivir algunas veces, pasar sus días de descanso o cenar con él en Chapultepec, cuando el archiduque Maximiliano estaba de viaje. Nunca quiso que se reunieran bajo ninguna circunstancia. Sus hijos legítimos eran una cosa y sus bastardos otra, y eso por cuestiones de Estado tenía que estar bastante claro.

—Le traje un té, Majestad —dijo Carlota, entrando al despacho del emperador, poco después de la media noche.

—Gracias, no te hubieras molestado. Tampoco me gusta que tomes atribuciones de servidumbre. No lo eres.

—¿Y quién le prepara el té mejor que yo?

—Basta, Carlota, puedes traerme lo que sea. Para un emperador con tantas responsabilidades y que ha perdido a su heredero, ya nada tiene buen sabor.

—No se ve bien —dijo la duquesa, preocupada—. Ya debe ir a descansar, el médico de palacio ha dicho que su corazón no está en óptimas condiciones.

—¿Y cómo podría estar bien? Mi heredero ha muerto junto con sus dos pequeños hijos que pudieron ser la salvación del imperio, y el único hijo que me queda es un imbécil del que avergüenzo.

—No me gusta que sea tan injusto con Fer. Es su hijo y se siente solo y abandonado. Siempre se ha sentido así a causa del trato que le da.

—Un Habsburgo mexicano no tiene derecho a padecer por emociones ordinarias. Ha olvidado quién es, por eso sufre.

—Él no es como su hermano, y usted no lo ha sabido entender, por eso su relación es tan difícil. Con Fer usted no supo ser buen padre.

—No tengo que ser buen padre de un solo hombre, cuando mi prioridad es ser un buen emperador para doscientos sesenta millones de personas. Aunque voy a ser criticado por el luto que tendría que guardar, me veo obligado a adelantar mi boda. Tengo que casarme cuanto antes y engendrar herederos. Tiemblo de sólo pensar que algo me pase y el único Habsburgo que quede nacido en México sea Fernando Carlos. Sería el fin del imperio.

—Aunque decirlo no me agrada —respondió Carlota—, reconozco que tiene razón. Fer no nació para gobernar. Tiene el corazón de un soñador y sus emociones son muy inestables. Es un genuino representante de la rama Habsburgo-Wittelsbach. El imperio no sobreviviría con él.

—Ya que me comprendes, ayúdame a organizar cuanto antes mi boda. Quiero algo lo más discreto posible, sólo se trata de un requisito para poder tener hijos legítimos, facultados para heredar el imperio, ¿comprendes?

—Sí, Majestad, lo comprendo, pero lo ayudaré con una condición.

—¿Ahora me pones condiciones a mí, al emperador?

—Y si no cumple, ya no voy a ayudarlo en nada —dijo Carlota, en tono serio.

—Sabes que eres mi punto débil, que en todo el imperio sólo tú me puedes exigir algo. Dime, ¿qué quieres?

—Que ya se vaya a descansar, que cuide su salud, que le haga caso al médico.

El emperador cambió su rostro severo para dedicarle una discreta pero dulce sonrisa a su hermana.

—Te prometo que en una hora me voy a dormir y que me despertaré hasta las seis. Sólo reviso unos cuantos despachos más.

—Si no cumple, olvídese de mi ayuda. Y tómese ese té antes de que se enfríe.

—Ve tú a descansar, también te noto fatigada.

—Sí, lo estoy —reconoció la duquesa—. Estos días han sido difíciles y no he podido dormir bien. Buenas noches, Majestad —añadió y se dio la vuelta.

—Por cierto, Carlota, ¿quién era la dama vestida de blanco, que por la mañana vi caminando en los jardines del castillo?

La duquesa se detuvo y meditó un instante, después volteó, extrañada, hacia su hermano, y todavía alcanzó a ver cómo el emperador caía precipitadamente hacia el suelo, oprimiéndose con ambas manos el corazón.

—¡Max! —gritó con todas sus fuerzas y corrió hacia él.

Diez minutos más tarde, el médico de palacio declaraba muerto al emperador de México. La duquesa, dueña de sí misma y sin permitirse llorar, tomó las manos del príncipe Bonaparte, cuando éste llego a toda prisa.

—¡Qué desgracia, señora, qué terrible desgracia!

—Tenemos que informar a Fer en seguida, príncipe. En este momento él ya es el emperador, y todos nosotros, las instituciones civiles y el ejército, estamos obligados a obedecer sus órdenes sin titubear.

—Señora, pero ese joven...

—Su Majestad Imperial, príncipe —lo reprendió Carlota—. Así tenemos que llamarlo desde ahora, no lo olvide, por favor. En usted confío más que en nadie, y por ello quiero contar con toda su ayuda.

—Sabe que estoy incondicionalmente a la disposición del imperio, señora. Su confianza no será nunca mal correspondida.

—Gracias, de verdad, Luis. Tiene que ir alguien a Trieste cuanto antes, para empezar a adiestrar al emperador y aconsejarlo bien. Pero no podemos ir ni usted ni yo. El imperio nos necesita aquí.

—¿No sería mejor pedirle al emperador que venga de inmediato? —dijo Bonaparte—. Es lo más prudente. El pueblo necesita saber que tiene un gobernante.

—No creo que el emperador quede con fuerzas para volver pronto a México, después de recibir la noticia —dijo la duquesa—. La muerte de su hermano lo dejó devastado, apenas pudo venir. Esta vez no se trata tanto del dolor que él pueda sentir como del peso de la losa que le echaremos encima, al decirle quién es ahora. Lo mejor es que alguien de confianza y adicto al imperio vaya por él, lo aconseje, le dé ánimos y lo acompañe en todo momento. La reacción que va a tener el emperador es a lo que más temo ahora, Luis. Si logra asimilar pronto su responsabilidad, habremos dado un gran paso.

—¿Qué le parece entonces si enviamos al duque de Miramón? Es un hombre de nuestras confianzas.

—Sí —dijo Carlota—. Me parece una buena opción. Pobre de mi sobrino, tan frágil que ha sido siempre, y tiene que volverse de acero de un día para otro.

Castillo de Chapultepec, junio de 1962

Jack Kennedy sonrió amablemente al descender de su limosina descapotable. Era un hombre carismático y en extremo agradable, y como político era aún joven. Su conquistadora personalidad era muy evidente, sus gestos y sus maneras inspiraban confianza, y la suma de estos detalles minimizaban el efecto de su gigantesca y fea sonrisa. El emperador Maximiliano III, más joven que él y con una melena más rubia todavía, lo recibió con la misma sonrisa y vestido de civil, contrario a la tradición vigente hasta entonces de recibir a un líder extranjero con el uniforme de general de división del ejército imperial mexicano. Pese a que era la primera vez que se veían las caras, su saludo fue el de dos amigos jóvenes que se reencuentran, contrastando enormemente con el que se habían dado apenas seis años atrás Maximiliano II y el presidente Eisenhower en la Casa Blanca, muy frío y completamente formal; el saludo de dos hombres físicamente desgastados que se veían obligados por el protocolo a darse la mano. En ese entonces aún andaban en el aire las secuelas de que México se hubiera negado rotundamente a declararle la guerra a Alemania, y de una provocadora carta que Roosevelt le había enviado al emperador, en la que le decía que si no estaba dispuesto a luchar contra el totalitarismo descendiera al rango de rey. Se contaba que en aquella visita de Maximiliano II a Washington el presidente Eisenhower le había preguntado qué le parecía la Casa Blanca, a lo que el arrogante Habsburgo respondió, después de mirar a ambos lados, "es blanca". No se entendieron en lo más mínimo, y cuando Maximiliano II regresó a México las relaciones entre ambos países eran, si cabe, más tensas todavía.

Al concluir su efusivo saludo con el emperador, Kennedy extendió su mano hacia la hermosa emperatriz María Victoria de Saboya, al tiempo que le dedicaba una sonrisa coqueta. Quién sabe qué estaría pasando por su cabeza. Maximiliano III mientras tanto recibió a Jacqueline besándole la mano. Quizás estaba pensando lo mismo que el presidente, a juzgar por su mirada. Ella le habló en español con una voz dulce y un acento extraño, y el Habsburgo se sintió halagado y agradecido por la deferencia.

Después de posar para los fotógrafos, mientras la emperatriz y la primera dama recorrían Chapultepec admirado las obras de arte que adornaban el edificio desde tiempos de Maximiliano *el Grande*, el presidente y el emperador se encerraron en el despacho a tratar los temas que tenían en su agenda. Kennedy quería un aliado contra la Unión Soviética y que a la vez lo ayudara a erradicar el comunismo en la zona. Sabía que el Imperio Mexicano también deseaba una alianza de ese tipo con los Estados Unidos. Los regímenes comunistas eran contrarios a la monarquía, tanto que se empeñaban en influenciar a los comunistas mexicanos para que organizaran una revolución capaz de derribar a los Habsburgo del trono, tan odiados por los seguidores de Marx en todas partes del mundo por pertenecer a las "raza de dominadores" que siglos atrás habían tenido el control de la humanidad en manos de unas pocas familias.

Cada que Kennedy hablaba, Maximiliano III sonreía con discreción porque, al ser un extraordinario poliglota, como tantos de los gobernantes Habsburgo a lo largo de la historia, entendía todo perfectamente pero tenía que esperar a que el traductor terminara de pasar las palabras del presidente al español, ya que los emperadores de México, cuando las relaciones diplomáticas eran inmejorables, podían hablar francés de visita en Francia, inglés en la corte del Reino Unido o italiano en Roma con el Papa, pero en México hablaban siempre en español cuando recibían la visita de un líder extranjero, y jamás, bajo ninguna circunstancia, hacían una excepción. En tanto que con el presidente de los Estados Unidos, debido a las tensas relaciones de siempre, nunca hablaban en inglés fuera cual fuera el escenario donde se reunían. En ese clima político, cuando se ajustaban los detalles de la visita de Maximiliano II a Washington, el embajador yanqui quiso saber si el emperador estaba dispuesto a hablar en inglés con Eisenhower para que la charla fuera más fluida, evitando las intervenciones siempre molestas de los traductores, a lo que el emperador respondió tajante: "Si quiere evitar los traductores, el presidente tiene todavía un mes para aprender español, tiempo más que suficiente".

—¿Qué le parece si yo lo llamo Max y usted me llama Jack? —dijo Kennedy—. Somos buenos vecinos y tenemos que tratarnos amigablemente.

Sólo por tratarse del presidente de los Estados Unidos, el emperador estuvo a punto de tomar aquello como una buena idea. Pero recapacitó en que Kennedy posiblemente en menos de tres años ya no sería presidente, en tanto que él sería emperador hasta su muerte. Así las cosas, no quería ser saludado tan familiarmente dentro de diez años por un tipo ya sin importancia. No obstante, buscó una salida que no ofendiera a su huésped.

—Comprenderá que habiendo sido educado en protocolos monárquicos tan rígidos, no deseo faltarle el respeto al presidente de los Estados Unidos, ni que me lo falten a mí. Si yo lo llamo presidente y usted me llama emperador estará bien. De cualquier forma, le agradezco ese gesto de confianza que tiene conmigo. Le doy mi palabra de que no lo olvidaré, y en adelante puede considerarme su amigo.

—Gracias —dijo Kennedy, sonriendo—. Emperador, quisiera tener la seguridad de que nosotros dos, al ser gobernantes de países con un profundo amor a la libertad y los derechos humanos, tenemos claro que nuestro enemigo común es el comunismo y el deseo de la Unión Soviética de extenderlo a todo el mundo.

—Señor presidente, no creo que usted dude que en mí puede tener un aliado por naturaleza contra las ambiciones de Jrushchov. Tan sólo de pensar que esa revolución hubiera ocurrido aquí en mi patria, mi familia habría muerto masacrada. Pero no entiendo cómo es que me quiere de aliado y al mismo tiempo cuestiona nuestros experimentos nucleares.

—Emperador —dijo Kennedy, ocultando completamente su sonrisa—, dado el papel que ahora lleva mi país en el mundo, tengo que preocuparme por todos los países que se interesan por hacerse de un arsenal nuclear, por pequeño que pueda ser. ¿Acaso usted no sabe el peligro que eso significa para toda la humanidad?

—¿Usted usaría bombas nucleares contra pueblos pacíficos y sin motivo alguno? —preguntó el emperador.

—¡Claro que no!

—Yo tampoco. En mi opinión, señor presidente, las bombas nucleares son una especie de garantía de la paz. Cuando todos tememos sus efectos, nadie osará usarlas, y así ya no habrá guerras.

—Usted sabe que puede haber líderes locos que son capaces de usarlas, sin medir el daño que causan.

—Supongo que hace referencia al señor Truman, porque no he sabido de otro que haga lo mismo.

—¿Se le reprochará toda la eternidad a América el hecho de resumir los muertos de varios años en unos pocos días? —preguntó Kennedy—. Porque eso fue exactamente lo que hizo el presidente Truman. Ahora bien, nosotros tememos por el peligro que significa la Unión Soviética para el mundo, pero ¿ustedes?, ¿de quién se quieren defender ustedes?

—Naturalmente también de la Unión Soviética. Usted lo acaba de decir, es un peligro para todo el mundo.

—¿Y qué tan adelantado va su programa nuclear? —dijo Kennedy.

—Supongo que no quiere hacer pruebas.

Kennedy sonrió.

—Señor presidente, me alegra que lo tome con buen humor. Comprenda que si donde usted vive hay otros que tienen una pistola y a veces se vuelven locos, su instinto de supervivencia lo llevará a comprarse una pistola, por si las moscas. Además, usted sabe bien que México sólo obedece órdenes de México. Si alguna potencia pretende cuestionar nuestro armamento, derivado de proyectos estrictamente defensivos, tendrá que obligarnos por la fuerza. Creo que mi padre se lo dijo al presidente Eisenhower, pero con gusto se lo repetiré a usted: a México ya no lo humilla nadie, esos tiempos quedaron en el pasado. Y si bien es cierto que ustedes han logrado muchos éxitos enviando tropas a Europa, no les recomiendo meterse con un vecino que se sabe defender. Por las buenas somos piadosos y buenos católicos, pero si nos hacen enojar, le aseguro que hasta el Diablo se esconderá hasta que no sepa que nos hemos calmado.

—No sólo soy yo, emperador, las armas nucleares son la antítesis de la paz mundial. Desprender a las potencias de algo tan peligroso es necesario para que el mundo viva tranquilo. La ONU...

—La ONU es como la iglesia, allí todos prometen muchas cosas —dijo el emperador—, pero volviendo a casa nadie las cumple. Señor presidente, México no se va a poner de rodillas ante nadie. Comprenda nuestro derecho a estar listos para defendernos. Además, de qué se preocupa, si esta reunión es para que acordemos ser en adelante buenos vecinos. ¿Acaso no nos abrazamos hace apenas una hora?

—Respetaré su programa nuclear, emperador, si nos deja supervisarlo, junto con inspectores de la ONU, claro.

—¿Qué le parece si empezamos primero con el suyo? —dijo Maximiliano III.

—Emperador, comprenda usted que América ha invertido muchas vidas en lograr la paz para el mundo, entre ellas la de mi propio hermano, y México ni una sola. Eso nos da ciertos privilegios.

—Lo lamento, señor presidente, mi postura no va a cambiar, y si eso perjudica los buenos deseos que teníamos para este encuentro, lo lamentaré más todavía.

—De ninguna manera, emperador —dijo Kennedy—. Habría sido un logro demasiado grande para mí imponer mis intenciones a un hombre cuya familia lleva casi siete siglos tomando decisiones de Estado, mientras que yo apenas llevo poco más de un año en esto. Dígame, con tanta experiencia que usted lleva en sus genes, ¿hay algún consejo que pueda darme y que me sea de utilidad?

Maximiliano III se sintió complacido con aquellas palabras de Kennedy. Ese yanqui de ascendencia irlandesa católica le agradaba.

—Trate con respeto a México y México será su amigo. Es el mejor consejo que puedo darle. Somos un pueblo noble y católico, como usted. Quizás ése sea el punto de partida para el inicio de una duradera amistad.

—Emperador, los focos comunistas que los soviéticos impulsan por toda Latinoamérica son más peligrosos para usted que para mí. Nosotros somos una república, la forma de gobierno de moda, podría decirse. Nuestra institucionalidad está a salvo. En cambio usted, al representar a una monarquía, corre el peligro de que el comunismo latinoamericano contamine a México más de la cuenta, y eso representaría un grave peligro para su gobierno. Usted sabe bastante bien lo que las masas sin control son capaces de hacer a los aristócratas, a quienes consideran sus enemigos por antonomasia. Pero siendo que ese peligro existe, y que usted no lo ignora, sólo América gasta millones de dólares para combatir al comunismo en la región, mientras que ustedes no han tomado medidas que podamos llamar significativas.

—Señor presidente —dijo Maximiliano III—, créame que los comunistas en mi país están bien vigilados, y casi me atrevería a decir que controlados. Incluso de los extranjeros que llegan nos hemos ocupado de forma exitosa. Hace algunos años, precisamente cuando mi advenimiento al trono, llegó de Cuba un tal... Castro, si mal no recuerdo, y lo metimos a prisión junto con todos sus hombres, a purgar condenas de treinta años, para que a otros comunistas no se les ocurra venir a aquí a alborotar a mi pueblo.

—Comprendo y celebro esos éxitos, emperador —respondió Kennedy—, pero vivimos en una zona demasiado frágil que necesita invertir recursos fuera de nuestras fronteras.

—Y yo comprendo lo que quiere, señor presidente, pero los mexicanos no pagan impuestos para que ayudemos a gobiernos inestables que durarán, de cualquier forma, muy poco tiempo y no nos agradecerán nunca la ayuda que les demos.

—Emperador, yo también valoro los impuestos de mis compatriotas, pero creo que es necesario hacer esfuerzos, aunque sean mal agradecidos, para propiciar una región donde las personas puedan vivir con dignidad y libremente. Somos un gran pueblo desde que Colón, entonces tan joven como usted y yo ahora, sembró la semilla de la civilización tan solo con su descubrimiento. A nosotros, sus herederos, nos corresponde terminar la tarea inconclusa. Toda el continente americano debe de estar unido bajo los mismos ideales, y si a fin de cuentas todos tenemos ideas diferentes, al menos que ésta sea una región libre para expresarnos.

—Ahora yo celebro que tenga tan buenas intenciones, señor presidente —dijo el emperador—, pero creo sinceramente que en algunos países del continente se puede gastar mucho, mas aun así se logrará poco.

—¿Entonces no me va ayudar?

—Dígame en qué exactamente quiere que lo ayude.

—Sé que usted posee una red de espionaje distribuida en todo el continente, incluido mi país. No lo cuestiono, nosotros hacemos lo mismo. ¿Podría compartirnos su información? Recuerde que a la emperatriz Elisabeth de Austria, su tatarabuela si no me equivoco, la asesinó un anarquista. Es probable que en toda Latinoamérica existan muchos que quieran imitar a Luigi Lucheni con usted o con alguien de su familia. Si usted nos comparte su información quizás podamos detener a alguien que por ahora está destinado a causarle daño. Piénselo.

—¿Y ustedes también compartirían sus expedientes con nosotros?

—Claro, emperador, el trato debe de ser reciproco.

—De acuerdo, pero no recibirá información ninguna sobre mexicanos, aunque los consideremos comunistas peligrosos.

—¿Por qué? —dijo Kennedy.

—Porque sean como sean, siguen siendo mexicanos. Pueden odiarme o incluso desear mi muerte, pero de ellos me ocupo yo. No daré información sobre mis compatriotas a un gobierno extranjero, ni mucho menos autorizaré su extradición, eso sería traicionarlos, y los mexicanos no nos traicionamos entre nosotros.

—Está bien, lo comprendo. Y créame que desearía mayor colaboración de su gobierno para fortalecer a toda la región. A fin de cuentas, todos somos americanos. Vale la pena el esfuerzo. Yo tengo grandes esperanzas, y eso que mi gobierno será cuando mucho de ocho años, en cambio usted tiene demasiados años más por delante. Debería de compartir mis anhelos en ese sentido.

—¿Qué le parece —dijo el emperador—, si esperamos un año para ver cómo funciona la recién nacida OEA? Entonces nos volveremos a reunir y de acuerdo a los resultamos es posible que pueda comprometerme mayormente con usted. No obstante, le anticipo que yo guardo pocas esperanzas. Aunque nosotros también somos hispanohablantes, nos odian por nuestro gobierno monárquico, como si los de otros países de la región funcionaran muy bien.

—A nosotros también nos desprecian por no ser ni latinos ni hispanohablantes, entre otras cosas más —dijo Kennedy—, y sin embargo yo tengo deseos de que, pese a nuestras diferencias culturales, podamos ser todos buenos amigos.

—Bien, en mis próximas reuniones con presidentes latinoamericanos, procuraré dar garantía de sus buenas intenciones, argumentando que yo confío en usted. La palabra del emperador de México, señor presidente, créame, vale mucho.

—Se lo agradeceré como no se imagina, emperador —dijo Kennedy— ¿Ahora ve cómo esta reunión sí ha sido exitosa? Me dará gusto recibirlo dentro de un año en la Casa Blanca.

Kennedy se quedó como huésped en Chapultepec durante dos días. Salió a montar a caballo por el bosque con el emperador y tuvieron más charlas prolongadas pero ya más personales. Un año después, Maximiliano III visitó la Casa Blanca con su esposa, la emperatriz María Victoria de Saboya. Charló con Jacqueline en su perfecto inglés, en agradecimiento a que ella le había hablado en español en México, y la felicitó sinceramente por su exitosa decoración de la residencia presidencial. Con Kennedy el emperador analizó un programa de cooperación militar que no gustaba en absoluto en el Kremlin. Aunque no se trataban entre ellos como Max y Jack, algo que el presidente hubiera querido, se podía decir que eran buenos amigos, unión que nunca antes se había logrado entre un presidente yanqui y un gobernante mexicano en toda la historia. Las relaciones entre los jóvenes mandatarios eran en realidad bastante buenas, y parecía que serían aún mejores después de que Kennedy, gracias a su carisma y al de su esposa, logró reelegirse. Pero la salida a la luz no de uno sino de varios escándalos sexuales lo obligaron a renunciar y a dejar el poder en manos de su vicepresidente, Lyndon Johnson, quien por alguna razón nunca explicada no sentía simpatías por la monarquía mexicana. Algunos llegaron a afirmar que esa animadversión era producto de las buenas relaciones de Maximiliano III con su antecesor, ya que se acusó a Johnson de ser quien sacó secretamente a la luz los escándalos sexuales y de odiar a Kennedy. Así las cosas, las relaciones entre ambos países se volvieron a enfriar, y los programas de cooperación quedaron al poco tiempo en el total olvido, para ser sustituidos por la anterior política de desconfianza y vigilancia mutua.

Puerto de Veracruz, agosto de 1884

Rodeados por una vistosa comitiva militar, José Luis Blasio y el archiduque Moctezuma miraban a lo lejos a un barco que en pocos minutos estaría delante de ellos. El día era soleado y el mar estaba bastante tranquilo, ideal para desembarcar. Con sus ojos fijos en la nave, el archiduque parecía bastante emocionado.

—Barón —dijo—, usted que ha estado de visita en la corte de Viena, dígame, ¿es guapa la archiduquesa María Valeria?

—Tan guapa como en las fotografías que ya ha tenido oportunidad de ver Su Alteza —respondió Blasio.

—Pero las fotografías pueden engañar, barón. Usted, personalmente, ¿la encuentra guapa?

—Mucho, Alteza.

—¿Y pasarán pronto los días que faltan para la boda?

—Los días suelen durar lo mismo, Alteza, aunque en algunos oscurece más temprano que en otros, todos tienen el mismo número de horas.

—¿Y cree que yo le guste a la archiduquesa, barón?

—Su Alteza es un caballero muy apuesto. Sin duda le resultará atractivo a ella.

—¿Y debo hablarle en alemán?

—Tengo entendido que el emperador Francisco José ha oblig... ha instado a la archiduquesa a aprender perfectamente el español, para que sea una buena emperatriz de los mexicanos. Debe de hablarlo ya con bastante fluidez.

—¿Y si le hablo en francés para impresionarla?

—Su francés no es muy bueno, Alteza, y el de ella es perfecto. Además, es regla que sea ella quien le hable en su idioma a usted, puesto que es el futuro emperador.

—¿Cuál idioma hablo mejor yo, barón?

—Eh, sin duda, el español, Alteza. Ya casi lo habla bien.

—Lo he practicado mucho.

—Tomando en cuenta que empezó a hablar a los cuatro años, lo ha practicado durante doce, todos los días y en abundancia.

—Y una vez que ella esté aquí, ¿ya podremos, barón?

—¿Poder qué, Alteza? —dijo Blasio.

—Eso...

—Ah, pues de que se puede, se puede, Alteza, pero lo correcto es esperar a que pase la boda.

—¿Cuántos días dice que faltan para la boda, barón?

—Una semana, Alteza. Todas las semanas suelen tener siete días.

—¿Y cuántos días tengo que esperar después de la boda?

—Ninguno, Alteza, ese mismo día se puede.

—Ya está más cerca el barco. ¡Ya casi llega!

—Lo he notado, Alteza, y también he notado que usted debe de tapar ese bulto que tiene allí, con su abrigo, de lo contrario asustará a la archiduquesa y se echará nadando al mar la pobrecilla.

Ligeramente sonrojado, el archiduque se cubrió.

—Con la mano no, Alteza, le he dicho que con su abrigo, de forma discreta, que ni siquiera se note.

—¿Qué debo decirle, barón? ¡Ya se me olvidó!

—Lo que hemos ensayado tanto: "Bienvenida a México, Alteza. Su pueblo, del que será emperatriz, la esperaba con ansias".

—¿Y la boca se la beso después o antes de decirle eso?

—La mano, Alteza, la mano. De momento sólo le puede besar la mano.

—Y ella, ¿qué va a besarme, barón? Yo quiero que me bese...

—Por ahora, nada, se limitará a decirle unas palabras de cortesía en español. Y cúbrase, por favor, que ya se le recorrió el abrigo.

—¿Y por qué el emperador Francisco José sólo me envía una silla como regalo de bodas? —dijo el archiduque, mientras recorría su abrigo—. Siendo un hombre tan poderoso, debería de mandarme construir un palacio, barón. Yo soy su sobrino y seré su yerno.

—Alteza, el regalo de una silla que lleva labrados los escudos de los Habsburgo a lo largo de la historia, incluyendo el del Imperio Mexicano, es algo enormemente simbólico. Recuerde que algún día usted será emperador, y el trono de un monarca no es otra cosa que un sillón.

—¿Entonces debo escribirle una carta a mi tío, dándole las gracias por la silla?

—No es necesario, Alteza, —dijo Blasio—. Vuestra madre, la emperatriz Carlota, ya la escribió imitando su letra, como todas sus demás cartas, y será enviada mañana mismo a Viena.

—Ah —dijo el archiduque—, mi buena madre todo lo quiere hacer por mí.

—Empezando por gobernar, Alteza.

—Mi padre sigue muy enfermo, barón. Si se muere antes de mi boda, ¿de cualquier formar voy a casarme?

—No, Alteza, tendría que guardar un año de riguroso luto.

—¿Y la archiduquesa María Valeria regresaría a Viena?

—Lo más probable es que no, Alteza. Se quedaría aquí como su prometida, hasta que pase el año de luto necesario.

—¿Y durante ese año...?

—No, Alteza, no se podría, puesto que ella aún no sería su esposa.

—¡Barón, no quiero que mi padre, el emperador, se muera!

—Nadie lo quiere, Alteza, su pueblo lo ama y todos rogamos a Dios que nos lo conserve muchos años más.

—Y si mi padre muere después de la boda, Barón, ¿tampoco podré?

—Sí, Alteza —dijo Blasio, sin dar ninguna muestra del fastidio que ya habría dado para entonces cualquier otro ser viviente—. Las bodas no se anulan por la muerte de un miembro de la familia, sólo se cancelan cuando aún no se han efectuado. Además, con los deseos que tiene la emperatriz de que el país esté impregnado de archiduques que tomen parte en las funciones del gobierno, no se preocupe usted por poder hacer eso que tanto quiere, si no por lograr hacerlo en la medida que ella lo desea.

—No le entendí nada, barón.

—Eso me imaginé, Alteza.

—¿Usted cree que a la archiduquesa le guste mi nombre? Quizás debí llamarme Francisco José, como mi tío.

—O Carlos Fernando, Alteza, en honor a Carlos II de España y a Fernando I de Austria.

—¿Ellos fueron dos grandes soberanos, barón?

—Algo así, Alteza.

—Se lo preguntaré a mi madre cuando vuelva a verla.

—Lo dudo mucho. Para mi fortuna, Alteza, usted ya habrá olvidado eso que le dije cuando estemos de regreso en Aztlán.

—Barón, ¿es cierto que soy muy joven para casarme?

—Desde mi punto de vista, un poco, Alteza, pero vuestra madre, la emperatriz, muere de deseos por saber si para engendrar hijos sí sirve.

—Qué buena es mi madre, barón. Ojalá que cuando mi padre ya no esté con nosotros, ella siga siendo tan buena y me ayude a gobernar. Se lo voy a pedir como un gran favor.

—Ay, Alteza, ¡para su pobre madre será un sacrificio!

—¡Barón, el barco por fin se ha detenido! ¿Puedo ir a ayudar a bajar a la archiduquesa?

—Su bulto, Alteza, cúbralo discretamente ahora que ya se hizo más grande. Y no, no puede ir. Usted debe de permanecer aquí, sin moverse siquiera, para esperar a que ella y su comitiva lleguen hasta nosotros.

Veinte minutos más tarde, María Valeria de Austria estuvo frente a su flamante prometido. El archiduque, de tan feliz que se hallaba, olvidó por completo las palabras de Blasio y no impidió que el aire moviera su elegante abrigo. Él estaba más emocionado que nunca y la archiduquesa quería que se la tragara la tierra. Definitivamente Cupido no andaba cerca de Veracruz ese día. No obstante, juntos formaban la esperanza de la dinastía Habsburgo en México.

Castillo de Miramar, diciembre del 2016

Quizás la duquesa Carlota se equivocó al decirle a su sobrino Fernando Carlos, en cuanto éste respondió el teléfono: "Tu padre ha muerto, Fer, ahora tú eres el emperador", porque, aquellas palabras que habrían hecho feliz a un ambicioso con sueños de grandeza, a aquel joven soñador lo demolieron por dentro. Llevaba dos años recluido en el paradisiaco Castillo de Miramar, con apenas vida social y sin responsabilidad alguna más que pagar a su servidumbre, y ahora su tía lo llamaba para decirle que el porvenir de doscientos sesenta millones de personas dependía de él. Como para tirarse al mar. Posiblemente, si la duquesa hubiera buscado palabras más suaves, el joven no habría entrado en una crisis nerviosa que llevó a sus sirvientes a dudar de su salud mental. Cuando el duque de Miramón llegó, apenas un día después de la terrible noticia, Fernando Carlos estaba postrado, sin querer hablar ni comer; parecía un niño huérfano, y en realidad huérfano sí era, pero niño ya no tanto. Legalmente era un hombre y también legalmente era el emperador de México.

Cuando Miramón informó a la duquesa del estado de la salud de su sobrino, ésta envió a Trieste no a una legión de psicólogos y psiquiatras como hubiera podido imaginarse, sino a los curas de su mayor confianza, a quienes hizo jurar ante un crucifijo y ante la Virgen de Guadalupe llevarse a la tumba sin revelar cualquier cosa que vieran u oyeran en los días que pasaran como guías espirituales del emperador. Los curas llevaban una consigna bastante clara: procurar por todos los medios posibles que Fernando Carlos alejara de su mente cualquier idea de abdicar al trono, por más que eso fuera lo más recomendable para su estabilidad emocional.

Carlota y el príncipe Bonaparte, mientras tanto, iniciaron una campaña mediática en la cual se hizo saber al pueblo mexicano que el emperador, tanto de día como de noche, tenía un teléfono en cada oído para dar órdenes a sus ministros sobre el funcionamiento del imperio, pero que desgraciadamente, aunque se hallaba lleno de energías, una caída en la que sufrió lesiones menores lo tenía postrado en cama. Su vida no corría peligro en lo más mínimo y desde la cama atendía los asuntos de Estado, pero los médicos le habían recomendado guardar reposo durante dos semanas, y el emperador había decidido atender ese consejo por mucho que le doliera no asistir a los funerales de su padre, ya que lo más importante para él era su responsabilidad al mando del imperio, y ésta requería que su salud estuviera totalmente restablecida pronto.

A la par de esa información difundida, Bonaparte también se encargó de hacer hablar ante los medios a los que fueron maestros del emperador en su etapa de preparación, con la consigna de que, fuera o no cierto, tenían que dejar claro que Fernando Carlos había sido un extraordinario estudiante, con una facilidad enorme para el aprendizaje de cualquier materia, desde los idiomas hasta el cálculo, la oratoria y la diplomacia. En realidad los maestros no tuvieron que mentir mucho, ya que el emperador había sido un estudiante bastante bueno, su problema no radicaba en su inteligencia, que era mucha, si no en su carácter, que era bastante poco.

Mientras la duquesa hacía todo lo posible para que no se corrieran por todo el imperio el pánico y los rumores nocivos, las noticias que llegaban de Miramar no eran nada buenas. El emperador seguía sin salir de su recamara siquiera, y pese a los esfuerzos de los curas, hablaba bastante poco, solo monosílabos, cuando mucho. Así las cosas, otra de las intentonas desesperadas de Carlota y Bonaparte para ayudar al emperador a llenarse de ánimos, y de lucidez, fue pedirle al Papa, por medio del embajador de México ante El Vaticano, que le enviara una carta a Fernando Carlos capaz de guiarlo en su camino, una tarea tal vez sencilla para el Santo Padre. Después de todo, no había un gobierno sobre la tierra tan ligado históricamente al Papa como la última monarquía de los Habsburgo, y una relación de tanto peso tenía que llevar al heredero de Pedro a procurar por todos los medios posibles la supervivencia del Imperio Mexicano.

Después de que fuera sepultado el emperador Maximiliano IV, la duquesa recibió una llamada de Miramón que le devolvió un poco las esperanzas: ese día Fernando Carlos había salido de su recamara, luego charló un poco con los curas y fue solo a caminar por los jardines. No se había alterado, como días atrás, cuando hicieron el experimento de llamarlo "Majestad". Al siguiente día las noticias que llegaron a México fueron todavía mejores. El duque de Miramón le había dicho a Fernando

Carlos: "Majestad, vuestro amado padre había indultado a una mujer que mató a su esposo mientras éste golpeaba cruelmente a su pequeño hijo, pero la muerte le impidió firmar ese indulto y la mujer sigue en prisión, mientras que el pequeño está muy triste al cuidado de las autoridades". Ante aquellas palabras, el emperador había solicitado que le llevaran los documentos que tenía que firmar, y después ordenó que fueran enviados a México sin la menor demora. Cuando Carlota le relató esa historia a Bonaparte, el canciller lloró de alegría. Fernando Carlos estaba actuando como emperador.

Pero aun cuando debido a sus frágiles emociones había firmado aquellos documentos y cuando ya no temblaba como una hoja con el viento cuando lo llamaban "Majestad", el emperador seguía dudando mucho, despertaba por las noches sobresaltado, miraba por la ventana y sentía deseos de escapar. Si bien tenía claro que él era el emperador, no creía que ya estuviera preparado para serlo. Por más que buscaba no hallaba dentro de sí el carácter necesario. Debido a una noticia en la televisión –se estaba interesando un poco por la política, lo que nunca antes había hecho-, supo que quien sería el nuevo presidente de los Estados Unidos llevaba ya tres matrimonios, y en cambio él, el emperador de México, seguía siendo virgen. En realidad nunca había besado siquiera a una mujer, y no era debido a que no se sintiera atraído por ellas, sino que su timidez le había impedido acercárseles, y, aunque su aspecto no era desagradable en absoluto, pese a que no era tan elegante y apuesto como su fallecido hermano, quizás ellas se habían reprimido al momento de interactuar con el hijo menor de Maximiliano IV, esperando que él fuera quien tomara la iniciativa.

Después de cinco días de haber vuelto poco a poco a la normalidad, e inclusive de enviar a sus ministros, por medio de la duquesa Carlota, algunas acertadas instrucciones, el emperador recibió una tarde un sobre con el sello de El Vaticano. Era la tan ansiada carta que su tía había pedido encarecidamente al Papa, documento que se esperaba aliviara más los temores del emperador. Éste quitó el sello, extrajo la carta y empezó a leer.

Estimado Fernando Carlos de Habsburgo

Se me ha rogado que ayude a aliviar el alma de un católico, lo que acepto hacer con gusto porque ésa es una de mis misiones en este mundo, pero a la vez se me ha pedido que con mis rezos y mis consejos le dé energías a un hombre para que acepte gobernar a doscientos sesenta millones de personas sin elecciones previas, sólo por el hecho de que los ha heredado, como si fueran simples objetos que se pueden clasificar en un testamento. Y a eso yo me niego rotundamente. Vos no podés gobernar a un pueblo sin que ese pueblo te lo autorice. Vos no sos un elegido de Dios para desempeñar un alto puesto, sos sólo un hombre como los demás, con los mismos derechos de todos los mexicanos. De ceñirte vos esa corona, estarás formando parte de una dictadura que le fue impuesta a un pueblo por la fuerza de las armas hace siglo y medio.

Si es verdad que vos querés aliviar las penas de tu alma, si en verdad querés paz para ti mismo, sólo hay una cosa que podés hacer: renuncia, renuncia a tu egoísmo y renuncia a tu trono. Dale al pueblo mexicano la posibilidad de experimentar la democracia por primera vez en muchos años.

Que Dios te ilumine, jovencito

Francisco

Al terminar la lectura, Fernando Carlos estaba convencido de que el Papa tenía razón. Aceptar el papel de emperador no era más que integrarse a una dictadura envuelta en milenarios protocolos, pero dictadura al fin. Dejó caer la carta y fue a su habitación, pensando cómo le diría a su tía, de forma que le quedara bastante claro, que él no sería el emperador de México. Pero tampoco tenía el valor para hacerlo. Su mayor problema era que renunciar le resultaba tan difícil como aceptar definitivamente gobernar.

Quizás si aquella carta en el suelo la hubiera encontrado uno de los curas enviados por Carlota a Miramar, la habría roto por creerlo lo más conveniente. Pero la encontró un miembro de la guardia secreta imperial, y al leerla decidió hacérsela llegar cuanto antes al duque de Miramón. En segundos una copia cruzo el Atlántico gracias a las tecnologías. Diez minutos después de que la carta fuera leída por Miramón, ya la estaba leyendo el canciller Bonaparte.

—Parece que cometimos un error terrible al solicitar su ayuda, señora —dijo el canciller, cuando le entregó la carta a la duquesa—. A este tipo se le pegó el rojo más de la cuenta durante el tiempo que fue cardenal.

—¡Viejo cabrón!, ¡ésta me la paga! —dijo la duquesa, furiosa, y rompió la carta.

Castillo de Chapultepec, enero de 1979

La llegada de Juan Pablo II a México fue un acontecimiento sin precedentes. Las calles de la capital estaban llenas de alegría, como si Wojtyła fuera un viejo conocido que volvía después de una larga espera. El cincuenta por ciento de la población era católica, y le organizó tal recibimiento al papa polaco que éste quedó verdaderamente conmovido. Al Aeropuerto Internacional Agustín II fueron a darle la bienvenida la emperatriz María Victoria de Saboya y el canciller Carlos Khevenhuller-Rivas. Las órdenes del emperador Maximiliano III a sus ministros, a los cardenales y al prefecto de Aztlán eran bastante claras, Wojtyła tenía que recibir el mejor trato posible, todas las condecoraciones eran pocas y toda hospitalidad insignificante. Prohibió el pase de revista reservado por el ministro de la guerra a los líderes extranjeros, por considerarlo algo totalmente impropio para la persona del Papa. Al siguiente día de su arribo lo recibió en Chapultepec para tratar asuntos de Estado. Wojtyła no sólo llegaba a México a visitar a los fieles, era un convencido luchador contra el totalitarismo impuesto por los comunistas en muchos países del mundo, incluido el suyo, y sabía bien que un gran aliado en esa lucha, a la que pensaba dedicarle el resto de su vida, podía ser Maximiliano III, el heredero del pagano emperador Moctezuma.

—Aunque jamás lo he hecho por respeto a mi pueblo, Santo Padre, si no se siente cómodo con el español, debido a que es un idioma que aprendió recientemente —dijo el emperador, una vez que se hallaron solos en el despacho de los cuatro bustos—, yo puedo hacer una excepción por tratarse de usted, sólo por tratarse de usted. Creo, modestamente, que mi polaco es bastante bueno, ya que he procurado aprender todos los idiomas que alguna vez fueron muy útiles a los gobernantes mi familia en Europa.

—No se preocupe, Majestad —respondió Wojtyła, en tono amable—, aunque me hable rápido en español, lo entenderé perfectamente, y creo que puedo lograr sin problemas que usted me entienda.

—En ese caso hablaremos en español, Santo Padre. Quiero empezar por agradecerle que haya tenido la bondad de aceptar mi petición de celebrar una misma en la Cripta Imperial de Guadalupe, en honor a los miembros de mi familia que allí descansan.

—Majestad, si usted no me lo hubiera pedido, yo se lo habría pedido a usted –dijo Wojtyła–. La relación del Papa con el emperador Habsburgo es la tradición de Estado aún vigente más antigua en la historia de la humanidad. Nos debemos respeto y afecto mutuo. Somos, institucionalmente, dos viejos que se niegan a morir.

—Sí, y esa antigüedad que nos caracteriza es la espada con la que quieren hacernos daño nuestros detractores –dijo el emperador.

—Yo no quiero minimizar los abundantes pecados de la propia Iglesia, Majestad, ni mucho menos andar por el mundo como si no hubieran existido. Y siendo que usted es un hombre sabio e ilustrado, me imagino que tampoco ignora que las monarquías Habsburgo no han estado exentas de errores en su larguísima historia. Pero estoy convencido que pese a nuestras equivocaciones, lo peor que podemos hacer es claudicar en nuestra tarea, porque veo claramente que aquello que nuestros detractores ofrecen al mundo no es mejor que lo que nosotros podemos dar. Es necesario, Majestad –continuó el Papa, después de una pausa–, que hagamos profundas reformas a nuestras instituciones.

—Santo Padre, usted sabe que aquello que es tan antiguo cuando alguien lo cambia lo desfigura y termina por destruirlo. Si con esas reformas que usted sugiere está hablándome de democratizar mi gobierno, de manera que yo pase a ser sólo un emperador de adorno, como lo son los reyes de Europa, le confieso sinceramente que preferiría que el último imperio de los Habsburgo en el mundo se extinguiera para siempre. No nos hacen levantarnos de madrugada desde que somos niños para llenarnos la cabeza de conocimientos, con el fin de aprender a posar perfectamente en las fotografías al lado de un presidente o de un primer ministro, y no tener más función que ésa.

—Majestad, con el debido respeto, su imperio es muy rígido, conserva una estructura que ya ningún país tiene en la cultura occidental –dijo el Papa.

—Por supuesto que sí, Santo Padre, ya que es el único imperio que queda con vida.

—El problema es que los pilares más fuertes de su imperio están muy asociados a la ausencia de libertades, a ojos de muchos. Yo lo sigo viendo como lo que realmente es, Majestad, el gobierno más perfecto que existe en una época tan difícil, donde los países son devorados por el comunismo totalitario con tanta frecuencia. Pero me preocupa que su pueblo no tenga mi misma perspectiva, debido a esos rasgos tan anacrónicos que caracterizan a su imperio, empezando, claro, por el nombre.

—Creo que estamos al límite de las libertades a que un imperio puede llegar. En México hay democracia en abundancia: el pueblo vota a los diputados, a los prefectos de provincias y a los gobernadores de los cincuenta y siete departamentos. Mas yo me reservo el derecho, ante probados actos de corrupción de cualquier género, de destituir a quien sea, no sólo a gobernadores o a prefectos, si no a obispos, cardenales, rectores universitarios, jueces, senadores y diputados, sin tener que buscar la aprobación de las cámaras. Y la historia ha comprobado que los servidores públicos son menos corruptos cuando saben que su destitución depende de un solo hombre, y no es un trámite burocrático interminable que hace las veces de indulto. México es el país menos corrupto de Latinoamérica, Santo Padre, y le puedo asegurar que si soltara la rienda a los burócratas, en pocos años estaríamos peleando por el primer lugar. Ahora bien, no soy un vulgar generalillo que ha llegado al poder gracias a un golpe de Estado y que ahora usa su poder para destituir o encarcelar por venganzas o por simples antipatías. Jamás, Santo Padre, jamás he usado mi poder para satisfacer emociones vulgares. La cámara de los diputados está llena de personas que me critican abiertamente, y nunca, ni en mis peores pesadillas, he pensado en destituirlos si no se ven implicados en actos de corrupción que puedan ser probados, sino tan sólo porque no son de mi agrado, y si mi hijo Maximiliano llegara a hacerlo cuando sea emperador, lo repudiaría y me avergonzaría de él desde donde me encuentre, ya sea el cielo o el infierno. Mención aparte merece el hecho de que dejo a todos hacer su trabajo, ganarse su sueldo. Los gobernadores y los prefectos realmente hacen funciones de gobierno, y los diputados y los senadores elaboran leyes y las aprueban con completa libertad, tanta que algunas no merecen siquiera mi censura, y no monto en cólera cuando me modifican o descartan una ley que yo les he enviado. Tengo un gran poder, es cierto, pero me cuido mucho de usarlo con la mayor sabiduría que puedo.

—Es cierto todo lo que me dice, Majestad, pero un gobierno tan centralizado, donde el trabajo de todos depende de usted, formado en la médula siempre por descendentes de los fieles súbditos que ustedes se trajeron de Europa, más los descendientes de aquéllos que aquí les prestaron fiel adhesión a su llegada, es una completa insensatez en una época en que los pueblos reclaman protagonismo. Comprenda que hay mexicanos que pueden sentirse menospreciados por su soberano, al ver que los ministerios prácticamente también se heredan, igual que el cargo de emperador. Y no crea que lo estoy reprendiendo, Majestad, sino que me preocupa mucho que en estos tiempos en que el mundo corre tanto peligro, el milenario imperio de los Habsburgo, que ahora se halla en México, se debilite o deje de existir. Tome mis palabras tan sólo como el consejo de un amigo.

—Así las estoy tomando, Santo Padre —dijo el emperador—, y por eso me esmero tanto en explicarle las razones que me han llevado a actuar como lo hago, y que me impiden contemplar reformas. Mis actos no son producto del egoísmo, pero quiero que entienda que nací destinado a ser emperador, no presidente. Y si bien mi gobierno tiene rasgos dictatoriales como los tuvo cualquier monarquía verdadera en la historia, tanto yo como mis antepasados hemos cuidado de que los mexicanos sean totalmente libres de hacer de su vida lo que les dicte su conciencia, y de que tengan la seguridad de que hay un Estado que se encarga de garantizar su integridad. México, Santo Padre, desde la última batalla que libró hace tantos años el primer duque de Miramón, no ha vuelto a padecer ni revoluciones ni guerras. Hemos sido lo bastante sensatos como para no meter a nuestro pueblo en sufrimientos tan indescriptibles, y para eso mucho ha ayudado el poder ilimitado con que cuenta la figura del emperador en este país.

—Lo entiendo perfectamente, Majestad —dijo Wojtyła—, mas me he tomado el atrevimiento de pretender aconsejarlo porque estoy seguro de que es en beneficio de su imperio. Por mi parte, yo sí pienso reformar a la Iglesia. Ya no es tiempo de que sea juez de los católicos, sino que ha llegado la época de que camine a su lado como consejera. Si el comunismo da a cambio de la confianza que pide ceguera e inflexibilidad, nosotros debemos de ofrecer a los fieles todo lo contrario.

—Le deseo la mayor de las suertes, Santo Padre. Pero recuerde que un monumento antiguo cuando se le restaura puede perder su esencia, dejar de ser lo que era para convertirse en algo desconocido y sin valor alguno.

—Majestad —continuó el Papa—, hace unos instantes corrí el riesgo de llevarlo al límite de su paciencia con mis intromisiones en su forma de gobernar, algo en lo que ustedes los mexicanos suelen ser muy celosos, según tengo entendido. Pero ahora le voy a revelar el porqué de mi actitud. La Unión Soviética tiene bien claro que no puede de ninguna manera dañar institucionalmente a los Estados Unidos, por ello intenta derribar a los gobiernos que, en un eventual conflicto, podrían tomar partida del lado de los yanquis. Y se han dado cuenta de que el Imperio Mexicano ofrece un blanco ideal para destruir su gobierno.

—Santo Padre, eso yo ya lo sabía. No sólo los soviéticos sino todos los gobiernos comunistas del mundo quieren que a mi familia le pase lo mismo que a los Romanov. México en ciertos momentos ha estado lleno de espías rusos que se unen a los comunistas locales, y hemos logrado minimizar el peligro que representan.

—¿Y también sabía que hay un plan para derribarlo de su trono, que será llevado a cabo el próximo dieciséis de septiembre?

—¿Cómo dice? Santo Padre, un golpe de Estado en México es imposible, el ejército le es totalmente fiel a la figura del emperador.

—No hablo de un golpe de Estado usando al ejército —dijo Wojtyła—, hablo de acabar con su gobierno, acusándolo de decadente, anacrónico y asesino, encabezado por un extranjero austriaco. Los comunistas mexicanos piensan sustentar sus actos en los poderes casi dictatoriales que ostenta usted. Por eso le he sugerido tan encarecidamente reformas, Majestad. Escúcheme bien: el próximo dieciséis de septiembre, durante el desfile militar, habrá una gran manifestación, a propósito de que los soldados estarán en las calles. Los manifestantes, entre los que se hallarán mujeres y niños, tendrán en sus filas a hombres discretamente armados que van a disparar a los militares, y si éstos no responden al fuego, habrá quienes sí lo hagan, quizás extranjeros, pero de manera que todo parezca como que los militares fueron los que respondieron a los disparos. Todo lo anterior con la intención de forzar su renuncia o de que se aferre al poder de manera intransigente, lo que sus adversarios aprovecharían para levantar a todo el pueblo contra usted. Le tienen preparado un destino bastante similar al de Nicolás II, de principio a fin.

—¿Es verdad todo eso, Santo Padre?

—Le he traído un regalo, Majestad —dijo el Papa, y sacó varias hojas de una carpeta que tenía en sus manos—. Tome, es la lista de los mexicanos que formarían el nuevo gobierno, según los planes rusos. Todos ellos han viajado al extranjero últimamente, pero nunca a la Unión Soviética. Han sido adiestrados en otros países para que su guardia secreta no desconfíe de ellos.

—Me sé los nombres de los cincuenta y siete diputados que representan a los cincuenta y siete departamentos —dijo el emperador—. La mayoría de las personas que figuran en esta lista son diputados.

—También tiene en sus manos, Majestad, los detalles del complot y el proyecto del nuevo gobierno para México, incluyendo qué parte saben los mexicanos y qué parte los rusos se han reservado para conocimiento exclusivo de ellos. Como podrá ver, respecto a los tiradores que simularían ser el ejército, así como los que irían ocultos entre los manifestantes, los rusos no han querido revelar a sus patrocinados todos los detalles. Ellos piensan llegar a los extremos que sean necesarios, en tanto que los mexicanos creen que sólo habrá unos cuantos muertos.

—¿Cómo obtuvo usted esta información, Santo Padre? —preguntó el emperador, afectado seguramente, pero imperturbable y natural en sus maneras.

—Me llegó directamente de Rusia.

—¿Es posible eso?

—La Iglesia, Majestad, tiene sus recursos. Usted lo sabe. Y ahora también sabe el peligro que corre. Confío que tomará las medidas necesarias para evitar la catástrofe. Tiene aún muchos meses para prepararse. No quiero, por ningún motivo, que la monarquía Habsburgo deje de existir. Sin ella la lucha contra el comunismo será más difícil. Y discúlpeme por no haberle hecho llegar esta información por otros medios, pero temía que fuera a caer en manos de espías y es conveniente que sus enemigos no sepan que usted sabe de sus planes. Por eso decidí traérsela personalmente.

—Santo Padre, el servicio que usted le ha hecho a México es invaluable. Gracias a la información que me ha traído, resolveré esto de la mejor manera posible y cuanto antes, hoy mismo si es posible. Y en reconocimiento a su valiosa ayuda, tenga plena seguridad de que mi imperio seguirá siendo su principal aliado. A todos los refugiados de países con gobiernos ligados al comunismo que usted considere necesario que debo darles asilo, México los recibirá amistosamente, y aquellos que corran peligro, tendrán la protección directa del Estado.

—Gracias, Majestad —dijo Wojtyła, con su sonrisa más amable de las muchas que tenía a su disposición—. No sabe usted cómo le agradezco a Dios que exista un país a donde pueden llegar los infelices a quienes la maldad ha dejado sin patria. Y, por lo que más quiera, haga todo lo posible para que esta hermosa monarquía no desaparezca ni pierda su esplendor. También quiero pedirle que no subestime todo lo que le he dicho sobre las necesarias reformas. La estructura actual de su imperio sólo es funcional si se dispone de un gobernante con grandes cualidades en tantos aspectos, como lo es usted, pero no olvide que es posible que alguno de sus herederos no nazca apto para dominar tanto poder. Y entonces su imperio se irá directo al precipicio.

—No se preocupe por ello, Santo Padre, mis herederos serán miembros de la casa de Habsburgo. Sabrán comportarse a la altura de las circunstancias, siempre anteponiendo el bienestar de los mexicanos.

—Ruego a Dios que así sea, Majestad —dijo Wojtyła.

Maximiliano observaba complacido el aspecto que daban a su despacho dos nuevos bustos en mármol que le acababan de llegar de Europa, uno era del general Miramón, fallecido apenas un año atrás, a quien hizo duque después de la consolidación del imperio, y otro de su antepasado Francisco III de Lorena. Ambos habían sido realizados por el escultor francés Auguste Rodin, por quien sentía una profunda admiración y que se hallaba en esos momentos realizando otro de sus encargos, una estatua ecuestre de su suegro, el rey Leopoldo I de Bélgica. Los bustos hacían perfecto juego con otros dos que Maximiliano ya tenía en su despacho desde algunos años atrás, ambos obras del escultor mexicano Felipe Sojo. Los arquitectos, los escultores y los pintores mexicanos dotados de talento sobresaliente, con la consolidación del imperio se habían sentado en la gloria. La ciudad de Aztlán era una total desconocida para aquellos que se habían ausentado del país antes de la llegada de Maximiliano, y que repentinamente volvían del extranjero. El emperador la había modificado ya bastante, y las obras no paraban nunca. No sentía ningún respeto por los edificios que aunque fueran antiguos no estuvieran dotados de estética desde su muy refinado y exigente criterio, o que simplemente estorbaran a sus nuevos proyectos megalómanos. Ciertamente, su buen gusto estaba dejando huella, tanto que la prensa Europea afirmaba que las capitales del viejo continente ya eran muy inferiores en belleza a Aztlán, la capital del imperio mexicano, y al mismo tiempo llamaban al emperador, por su descomunal manía constructora y por haber consolidado un gobierno sólido y respetado donde todos le auguraban un negro desenlace, Maximiliano *el Grande*.

Enfrascado en el placer que le propiciaba ver la ciudad desde la ventana de su despacho, con sus grandes obras levantándose por doquier, fue interrumpido por su secretario para informarle que había llegado la hora de su reunión con la emperatriz.

—¿Soñando como siempre, Max? —dijo Carlota en cuanto lo vio, de pie frente a la ventana—. Está bien, no te preocupes. Mientras tú sueñas yo gobierno. Así cada quien hace lo que mejor se le da. Además, debo reconocer que la ciudad ha cobrado una belleza extraordinaria. Eres un excelente decorador.

—Blasio me ha entregado un informe sobre los avances de tu hijo en sus estudios —dijo el emperador, ya sentado frente a su escritorio.

—¡Nuestro hijo, Max! Es el archiduque Moctezuma, tu heredero al trono de México.

—Creo que en privado la hipocresía es innecesaria, Charlotte.

—La servidumbre tiene oídos muy agudos. No seas impertinente. Si la verdad saliera a la luz, quedarías en ridículo y el imperio correría grave peligro. El heredero es necesario para que tú sigas soñando con tus obras de arte, Max. Las sumas exorbitantes de dinero que gastas salen del pueblo mexicano. Si te echan, tendrás que conformarte tan sólo con decorar tu barba.

—Créeme, Charlotte, me satisface enormemente no ser el padre de ese idiota —dijo el emperador—. Sus avances en los estudios son mediocres. Me dijiste que buscarías a alguien nada conocido, totalmente insignificante para que fuera el padre de tu hijo. Pero creo que se te pasó la mano. Al menos te hubieras cerciorado de que sabía hablar.

Carlota tenía su aspecto arrogante de toda la vida, no parecía furiosa por las palabras de Maximiliano.

—Vino el señor Altamirano —dijo, cambiando completamente el tema—. Su biografía de Juárez ya está casi terminada. Tan sólo le marqué unas cuantas correcciones. Altamirano es un hombre bastante feo, pero su presencia es muy agradable. Es un gran conversador.

—Sigues empeñada con glorificar la imagen de Juárez, después de que fuimos nosotros quienes le causamos las graves preocupaciones que sin duda le provocaron la muerte. Qué grande es tu hipocresía.

—Juárez fue un mexicano ejemplar. Si otro gobierno existiera en lugar de nosotros, también se apropiaría de su imagen para lucrar políticamente con él. Además, su inteligencia merece todos los homenajes que me he propuesto hacerle. He leído todo lo que dejó escrito. Su mente era brillante, Max, tanto que si su piel hubiera sido blanca, me habría gustado que fuera el padre de mi hijo. Un niño con la inteligencia de Juárez y la mía hubiera sido el mejor gobernante de todos los tiempos.

—Qué lástima, Charlotte, el hijo de tus sueños no se parece nada al que tienes.

—Por lo menos tengo uno, Max. Pero, ¿no crees que estas tontas peleas son infantiles, innecesarias y peligrosas? —preguntó la emperatriz—. Lo digo porque, después de todo, siempre terminas sintiéndote peor tú que yo. Mejor dime, ¿qué asunto quieres que tratemos?

—El ministro de colonias me he enviado un informe —dijo Maximiliano, cediendo ante la aplastante superioridad—, según el cual has interferido más de una vez para evitar el asentamiento en el norte del país de colonos españoles. ¿Acaso te has vuelto loca? Si el imperio ha crecido y va camino a volverse una potencia del comercio, mucho de ello se debe a la emigración.

—No estoy en contra de la emigración, Max —respondió la emperatriz—, sé muy bien lo provechosa que resulta a México. Pero aún no se me olvida que Pío Nono fue muy insensible con nosotros. Enfrascado en proteger sólo sus intereses, nos causó muchos problemas en lugar de ayudarnos siquiera un poco. Así que primero lleno el imperio de protestantes, judíos y musulmanes, antes que permitir un asentamiento de católicos españoles, de los que ya en el pasado llegaron más de la cuenta.

—Charlotte, lo que dices no tiene sentido. El Imperio Mexicano es oficialmente católico.

—Únicamente por cuestiones políticas, Max. Sería mal vista una monarquía Habsburgo laica. Pero eso no indica que tiene que estar poblada sólo por católicos.

—Tu colección de razas puede traer problemas más adelante —dijo el emperador—. A los mexicanos les gustan sus apellidos peninsulares.

—Ah, querido Max, yo no lanzo una piedra sin estar segura de dónde va a caer. Lo de la colección de razas me tiene sin cuidado, ya que tu hermano mayor tiene una más grande aún que la nuestra y los hace convivir a todos pacíficamente. En cuanto a los apellidos de los mexicanos, estoy preparando una ley para que los hijos de emigrantes y mexicanos hereden a sus descendientes un apellido compuesto. Por ejemplo, los descendientes del valiente príncipe Khevenhüller, que tantas pruebas de lealtad nos ha dado, se llamaran Khevenhüller-Rivas. Los apellidos compuestos dan más elegancia a un nombre, Max.

—Tus ideas absurdas me dan risa, Charlotte. ¿Cómo se te ocurre unir nombres de familias que son aristócratas desde hace siglos, con los de mexicanos sin títulos nobiliarios, que apenas y saben cómo se llamaban sus abuelos? En ese sentido, hasta Napoleón I hizo cosas menos ridículas que tú.

—Max, me enternece la cortedad de tu inteligencia —dijo la emperatriz—. ¿Qué no te das cuenta que tenemos que arraigar a como dé lugar este imperio a los mexicanos y a México, un lugar en el que durante medio siglo no hubo gobierno estable? Además, toma en cuenta que aquí todo inicia de nuevo. No importa lo antiguo que sea un apellido, sino que todo debe amoldarse a mis... a nuestros propósitos. El Imperio Alemán ha convertido a tu hermano en una completa nulidad en Europa, lo tiene contra la pared e indefenso. Para nadie es un secreto que el futuro de la monarquía Habsburgo está en México, esperanzada en los descendientes de mi hijo. Deberías de agradecerme, Max, todo lo que hago por tu familia. La grandeza que alcancen en México me la deberán a mí, mientras que los míos, los Sajonia-Coburgo-Gotha, de la grandeza que aquí se logre no recibirán nada. Qué triste es ser mujer, y que bendición ser hombre, ustedes son capaces de tener hijos falsos sin la penosa necesidad de fingir un embarazo.

—Como si eso fuera un orgullo —dijo el emperador, molesto.

—Ah, Max, cuando no es posible alcanzar algo, agradécele siempre a quien estire la mano por ti, en lugar de sentirte humillado. El padre de mi hijo quizás ya duerme en una tumba anónima, muerto de alcoholismo o de hambre, sin que nunca hayas pensado darle las gracias por el gran favor que te hizo. Qué malagradecida es la raza humana, que antepone el orgullo por encima de todo.

—¿No fuiste tú la que propuso hace unos momentos que dejáramos eso en paz?

—Francamente, me molesta que no reconozcas todos los esfuerzos que hago por la grandeza del imperio, algo que hará más grande aún a tu familia, mientras que a mí me olvidarán en cuanto muera.

—Ya te puedes retirar, Charlotte.

—Sí, Max, te dejo para que recibas a tus arquitectos, pintores y escultores —dijo la emperatriz—, yo en tanto me ocuparé de dar instrucciones a los ministros. Ah, Max, lo olvidaba, como bien recuerdas, los mexicanos se acostumbraron pronto al nombre de Aztlán que ahora lleva la capital, pero a este edificio lo siguen llamando Chapultepec. Así que olvídate de esa fantasía infantil de Miravalle. Volverá a llamarse como antes. Haré que lo publiquen mañana mismo en el diario del imperio.

El príncipe Ángel de Iturbide y Green era un joven elegante y cosmopolita, viajero incansable y con un innegable don de gentes, además de poseedor de un refinamiento exquisito. Graduado en Harvard, había pasado muchos años de su vida en los Estados Unidos, conviviendo con unos parientes suyos. Las relaciones cordiales que habían mantenido Maximiliano IV y Obama propiciaron que el emperador optara por poner a cargo de su embajada a un mexicano casi yanqui. De visita en México con motivo de los funerales del archiduque Maximiliano, el heredero al trono, Iturbide fue llamado por el emperador a su despacho de Chapultepec, pocos días después de que el archiduque fuera sepultado en la Cripta Imperial de Guadalupe. El joven embajador de treinta y tres años no pudo menos que sentirse admirado de la naturalidad con que se comportaba Maximiliano IV. Después de haber recibido un golpe tan terrible no había dejado de ocuparse de los asuntos de Estado ni un solo día. El luto tan sólo se le notaba en su atuendo negro que hacia resaltar su piel blanca, casi pálida.

—A las órdenes de Vuestra Majestad.

—Buen día, príncipe. ¿Cuándo tiene pensado volver a los Estados Unidos?

—La próxima semana, Majestad.

—No, necesito que regrese mañana mismo a ocuparse de sus funciones. El presidente electo de ese país es un tipo demasiado desconcertante. Ya me está colmando la paciencia, y eso que aún no toma posesión de la Casa Blanca. Quiere que regrese a su puesto cuanto antes para que sea mis oídos cerca de él.

—Lo haré como usted disponga, Majestad —dijo el príncipe—. Y tiene razón en sentir desconfianza, Trump ha dicho que no es amigo de México, y si él mismo lo dice tenemos que creerle.

—Supe que cenó con él hace unos días, en su mansión de Florida. Dígame, ¿qué impresión le dio?

—Horrible, infame. Pasto para un incendio. Los ingleses sembraron en los Estados Unidos muchas de sus virtudes, pero su buen gusto no fue una de ellas.

—Me refería a Trump, no a su mansión. ¿Qué le pareció ese hombre?

—Ah, Majestad, pues es un poco más desagradable que el edificio —respondió el príncipe—. Le dije que ahora que es presidente electo, un insulto hacia nosotros no lo pasaremos por alto sino que lo habremos de tomar como algo muy enserio.

—¿Y cómo reaccionó?

—Se me quedó viendo a los ojos, simulando una risa idiota que él piensa que es desafiante. Después rompió el silencio para enviarle saludos a usted, y añadió que espera recibirlo en la Casa Blanca en cuanto tome posesión de la presidencia. Quizás antes de que termine el mes de enero. Le dije que usted ya tiene una agenda y que no suele modificarla, y él volvió a simular la risa idiota.

—Dígame, príncipe, ¿usted cómo piensa que debemos proceder?

—Yo creo, Majestad —respondió Iturbide—, que tenemos que esperar a que se debilite. Ahora es fuerte porque hace poco tiempo que ganó las elecciones, pero los medios yanquis que querían su derrota sólo creen que han perdido una batalla, más no la guerra. Le darán con todo. Además, él dice mucho, pero las leyes estadounidenses no le permiten ni siquiera la mitad de las facultades que tiene usted como jefe de Estado. Trump es un toro bravo que se lanza incluso contra las piedras. Dejemos que gaste sus energías.

—¿Lo considera inteligente?

—Como empresario se puede decir que es bueno, más no brillante, puesto que inició su trayectoria desde el peldaño de un heredero y no como alguien que se hace así mismo de pies a cabeza. Pero como político es bastante idiota, se sorprendería usted de lo ignorante que es en algunas cuestiones de vital importancia para la economía de los yanquis. Aquéllos que ven la cortedad de su intelecto, se consuelan pensando que la institucionalidad de los Estados Unidos le mantendrá las manos bien atadas.

—De acuerdo, príncipe, confiaré en la sensatez de su buen juicio —dijo el emperador—. ¿Y qué me puede decir del presidente Obama? —añadió.

—También cené con él hace unos días. Está devastado, tanto como lo estaría cualquier hombre tan extremadamente vanidoso que ve que su sucesor ya tiene en sus manos la pala para echarle tierra encima a su legado. Me dio pena por él.

—Dele mis saludos si lo vuelve a ver.

—Así lo haré. Me dijo que también se siente afligido porque Trump arruinará la buena relación que él había logrado entablar con México. Tomé la precaución de decirle que usted lo seguirá considerando su amigo, y que nunca lo culparemos a él de lo que haga Trump.

—Él, ciertamente, no es el culpable de lo que vaya a hacer Trump, príncipe, pero sí es el culpable de que Trump esté donde está. En fin, eso es todo. Apresúrese a regresar a ocuparse de su puesto. Tiene mi autorización para responder de la manera que crea pertinente a los comentarios de ese tipo. Denueste de todo, menos cobardía. México no le tiene miedo a nadie, ni siquiera a los Estados Unidos. Si ese cabrón vuelve a insultar a los míos, ya como presidente, voy a tener que enseñarle que el Diablo es mexicano.

—A las órdenes de Vuestra Majestad.

Castillo de Miramar, enero de 2017

Después de leer la carta del Papa, Fernando Carlos pasó toda la noche sin dormir. En algunos instantes se sentía convencido de abdicar al trono y minutos después sentía deseos de trasladarse a México para dedicarse de lleno a sus funciones. Pero lo aterraba tan sólo la idea de ocupar la misma silla que había usado apenas días atrás su padre, Maximiliano IV. Él había sido un hombre imperturbable, dueño de sí mismo siempre, incapaz salvo raras ocasiones de permitir que su rostro dejara que se asomaran sus sentimientos, un auténtico emperador Habsburgo en la línea más clásica, a quien no podría igualar nunca.

Por la mañana, uno de los curas que estaban en Miramar le entregó, aún en su cama, una carta. Pero esta vez no era del Papa. La duquesa Carlota había decidido contratacar la influencia de Francisco enviándole a su sobrino otra carta, pero no reciente, sino que llevaba en poder de la familia mucho tiempo. En los primeros días de enero de 1927, poco antes de morir a los 86 años, la anciana emperatriz Carlota había escrito una larga carta para su bisnieto, Maximiliano II, recientemente ascendido al trono de México. Carlota no dudaba de la inteligencia y las capacidades del joven emperador, pero como ya había influido en la voluntad de tres, decidió que tenía derecho a hacerlo con uno más. Añadiendo a ello que sentía temores de que el joven monarca cometiera errores producto de su falta de experiencia durante su primer año en el trono, pese a que lo había educado, como a su hijo y a su nieto, debajo de sus faldas y a un lado de su escritorio para enseñarlo a gobernar. Conmovido por tratarse de una carta de su antepasada, Fernando Carlos abrió el sobre y empezó a leer.

Majestad

Le escribo esta carta con las últimas fuerzas que le quedan a mi cansado cuerpo y a mi cansada mente. Créame que no dudo que usted tiene claro cuál es el deber que le ha asignado la Providencia, pero albergo el temor de que las agitaciones que han envuelto al imperio lo hagan dudar respecto a si sus facultades son verdaderamente legitimas. Son muchos los que lo llaman austriaco y dictador, y que claman porque México, a imagen y semejanza de toda América, se vuelva una república. Majestad, si acaso usted llega a dudar, recuerde siempre que nadie tiene la verdad absoluta en sus manos. No es la imperfecta democracia el mejor gobierno para los pueblos, sino aquél que les dé paz, prosperidad y justicia. De nada sirve un gobierno del pueblo cuando no ayuda en absoluto para aliviar las penas de ese pueblo.

Es necesario que tenga muy claro, Majestad, que usted no es un dictador. Jamás fue detrás del poder, nació para que el poder fuera detrás de usted, y no tuvo la oportunidad de escoger otro nacimiento. Muchos le dirán que el tiempo de las monarquías ha quedado en el pasado, que la Gran Guerra ha dejado bien demostrada esa verdad. No obstante, Majestad, yo me atrevo a jurar, incluso arriesgándome a condenar mi alma, que aquellos que van a criticarlo a usted y a su gobierno, no lo harán tanto porque vean un mal desempeño sino por el hecho de que querrán el poder para sí mismos. Pero usted tendrá siempre una razón muy poderosa para no dejarse influenciar: con el destino de los mexicanos no se juega. Si los ambiciosos hambrientos de poder quieren derrocarlo para hacer experimentos con el gobierno de México, que destruyan la paz y la estabilidad de todo el pueblo, que hagan pelear a unos con otros, usted manténgase firme, recuerde siempre que no por darles gusto a unos cuantos que se creerán iluminados podrá traicionar a tantos millones de inocentes.

No importa qué tan antigua es la institución que usted representa, Majestad, mientras existan mexicanos que vivan felices con los suyos, que tengan un trabajo, paz en su tierra y un entorno seguro, mientras los niños puedan salir a jugar a la calle, mientras las ancianas puedan ir seguras de su casa a la iglesia, mientras los campesinos puedan sembrar sus parcelas, mientras el ejército tenga el poder para defender a México de quien sea, y mientras el pueblo se alegre con el nacimiento del heredero al imperio, usted nunca dude de la legitimidad de sus funciones, porque seguramente estará haciendo bien las cosas. Porque las tiene que hacer bien, Majestad. Nunca tome decisiones apresuradas, ni por vanidad, resentimiento o egoísmo. Siempre tómelas por el bienestar de los mexicanos. Y cuando dude, cuando su carácter flaquee, recuerde que es descendiente directo de Rodolfo I, el hombre que puso la primera piedra para la grandeza de la casa de Habsburgo; recuerde que desciende de Fernando el Católico, quien liberó a España de los moros y puso los cimientos para la construcción de un gran imperio, que humildemente heredó a la familia de usted; recuerde que desciende de Carlos V, el hombre que gobernó el imperio más grande que ha existido en la historia de la humanidad; recuerde que desciende de María Teresa, la gran emperatriz que impidió que se perdiera para siempre la casa de Habsburgo.

Pero si en algún momento de angustia ya no le dicen nada los nombres de soberanos tan antiguos, recuerde, Majestad, que desciende de Maximiliano el Grande, ese gran emperador dotado de una inteligencia sin precedentes, que la Providencia destinó sabiamente para que reviviera al sufrido pueblo mexicano. Si en algún momento se le terminan las fuerzas, si en algún momento flaquea su carácter, si en algún momento está a punto de rendirse, recuerde esta gran verdad que es tan grande con el mundo mismo: Maximiliano el Grande no se habría dejado vencer por el cansancio, no se habría dejado amedrentar ni se habría rendido. Tal era su amor por los mexicanos, por este pueblo que lo recibió con amor y lo hizo suyo, que si México hubiera enfrentado una invasión él habría sido el último soldado en morir en el campo de batalla, su espada habría sido la última en caer al suelo, pero jamás la habría tirado ni entregado al enemigo. Se lo juro yo en estos momentos previos a mi muerte, que lo conocí perfectamente bien. Si en algún momento deja de sentir orgullo por todos sus grandes antepasados, jamás deje de sentirlo por Maximiliano el Grande. Él no se lo merece. Si en algún momento están a punto de derribarlo, recuerde que es un legítimo descendiente de ese gran hombre para que pueda recobrar el equilibrio, y si llega a tocar el suelo, recuerde que desciende de él para que tenga las fuerzas necesarias para poder levantarse.

Y si su angustia llegará a ser mucha, Majestad, si el peso de sus problemas llegara a ser superior a la voluntad del mejor de los hombres, si todas las salidas se cierran ante usted, entonces traicione a sus antepasados si lo requiere, incluido al glorioso Maximiliano el Grande, olvídese de su ancestral estirpe, olvide todo el invaluable pasado de su familia, pero nunca olvide que es mexicano, y nunca jamás, bajo ninguna circunstancia, traicione a los mexicanos. Porque entonces no lo perdonará nadie, ni los grandes monarcas de la casa de Habsburgo, ni la Providencia, ni yo.

Carlota de México

Cuando Fernando Carlos terminó la lectura, estaba llorando. La carta de Francisco había sido la arenga de un loco comparada con este monumento. La duquesa Carlota había sido muy acertada al enviársela, y era posible que la antigua emperatriz la hubiera escrito no sólo pensando en su bisnieto Maximiliano II, sino en sus demás descendientes a lo largo de la historia que le quedaba al imperio, porque Fernando Carlos llegó a sentir que la carta había sido escrita exclusivamente para él. Cuando se repuso de la enorme impresión de la lectura, fijó su mirada en un cuadro al que días atrás no le había querido poner atención, y que decoraba aquella recamara donde él dormía, que había sido la que ocupara Maximiliano *el Grande* antes de partir hacia México, hacia su destino. Se trataba de una copia de una pintura que decoraba uno de los salones del palacio Imperial en Aztlán, y era conocido sólo por algunos pocos como *La coronación*, aunque en dicha pintura no se coronaba a nadie, pero de allí había salido la idea principal para el acto protocolario que significaba la ascensión de un nuevo Habsburgo al trono del Imperio Mexicano. La obra, como todas las demás que decorabas la estancia, también databa de tiempos de Maximiliano *el Grande*. Una vez que éste logró consolidar su gobierno, y ante el regreso del general Santa Anna al país, se sintió atraído como tantos otros por la idea de conocer al legendario caudillo. Sólo se reunieron una vez y no trascendió de qué hablaron en ese encuentro, ni tampoco llegó a constar que Santa Anna le regalara nada al emperador. Pero Maximiliano encargó al pintor Santiago Rebull un cuadro en el que el viejo general le obsequiaba a él una espada, con la intención de que fuera interpretado como la cesión de la responsabilidad de cuidar a los mexicanos en adelante, algo que Santa Anna jamás logró hacer en realidad. El cuadro cobró tal fama que la emperatriz Carlota mandó hacer una hermosa espada con las insignias del imperio mexicano, que ella misma puso en manos de su hijo el día en que fue coronado. La tradición empezó a llamar al objeto como "la espada de Santa Anna", aunque éste jamás la tuvo entre sus manos. Pero en adelante todos los emperadores de México, al ascender al trono, recibieron en sus manos la espada, la misma que en pocos días habría de tomar con las suyas Fernando Carlos, como un acto meramente protocolario, ya que desde el momento mismo de la muerte de su padre, él era el emperador de México.

Con una determinación que sorprendió a los curas que lo rodeaban, el joven Habsburgo empezó a dar instrucciones para que se preparara lo necesario, porque habría de partir para México ese mismo día. Recorrió el castillo de Miramar, habitación por habitación, fue a contemplar la belleza del parque, observó embelesado las estatuas, después fue al muelle, a ver como un primerizo el azul del Adriático, puso su mano sobre la milenaria esfinge y permaneció allí varios minutos. Sintió que estaba experimentando las mismas emociones que había sentido siglo y medio atrás Maximiliano *el Grande*. Se trataba de renunciar para siempre a la hermosa paz, belleza y tranquilidad que ofrecía el castillo de Miramar. Quizás él sí podría volver, pero ya sólo de visita, y siempre saturado de los problemas del imperio, incapacitado para entregarse al descanso y a la paz. Para el joven soñador que había sido hasta entonces, esa partida de Miramar, de lo que representaba el hermoso castillo blanco en sus emociones, era para siempre.

No sólo quería despedirse de cada rincón, sino que quería verlos por última vez con los ojos del archiduque que había llegado dos años atrás. Sabía que al volver, varios años después, su mirada y su sensibilidad habrían cambiado para siempre, ya verían el castillo como un todo, y no como un edificio lleno de detalles que trasmitía tantas emociones. El que volvería algún día sería el emperador, rodeado de ministros y militares, como hacían los emperadores de México durante sus "días de descanso". Sus ojos serían los mismos, pero ya no verían lo mismo.

Después del desayuno, el emperador recibió una visita que no esperaba. Aunque su vida social era discreta y a veces inexistente, había apoyado económicamente a un joven escultor triestino, Luigi Venosta, de quien se podía decir que era un buen amigo. Aunque no le había hecho encargo alguno, su decisión de apoyar a Venosta fue para que tuviera posibilidades de desarrollar su arte, ya que el emperador había juzgado que tenía un talento poco común. El artista llevaba una pequeña caja en sus manos, a la que Fernando Carlos, sumido como estaba en sus meditaciones, no le prestó mucha atención.

—Me voy, amigo Venosta.

—Lo suponía, Majestad, por eso me apresuré a venir a verlo.

—Ya también tú me llamas así.

—No me es posible llamarlo de otra manera. Nos separan distancias muy grandes. Usted es el emperador de uno de los países más poderosos del mundo.

—No hay distancias para la amistad, incluso en un campo de batalla.

—Quiero darle las gracias por todo, y principalmente por confiar en mí —dijo el artista—. Cuando uno empieza a adentrarse en algo desconocido, vale oro una persona que le dice "tú puedes". Y más valor tienen esas palabras cuando vienen de un emperador.

—A veces también los emperadores son sinceros, Venosta. Dime, ¿qué trae allí?

—Un regalo para Su Majestad. Cuando murió su padre, supe que usted se marcharía pronto de aquí y me di prisa en hacerlo.

Con una señal, el emperador indicó a Venosta que pusiera el contenido de su caja en una mesa. Se trataba de un busto en mármol de Fernando Carlos, una obra soberbia, admirable, cercana a la perfección. Era el rostro del emperador, pero el retratado era un hombre fuerte de ánimos, decidido, con un valor ilimitado. Parecía un soldado que sabe que la batalla estará ganada siempre y cuando él no se rinda, pero que al final perderá la vida, o el de un marinero que ve cómo se hunde su barco y no hace nada porque piensa que abajo del mar estará mejor. Venosta había logrado hacer el rostro de un emperador autentico, apropiándose de las facciones de Fernando Carlos.

—Se parece a mí, pero no soy yo.

—¿No le gusta, Majestad?

—Venosta, ése del busto es un héroe, y yo no lo soy.

—Pero lo será. Dígame, Majestad, ¿le habían hecho un busto antes?

—No. Ni siquiera se me había ocurrido esa idea.

—Pues me alegra ser el primero que lo hace, tomando en cuenta que usted será un gran emperador. Llévelo al bello México como un recuerdo de Trieste, si es que mi regalo le gusta.

—Me gusta más de lo que te imaginas. Es extraordinario, una verdadera obra maestra. El arte sólo nos conmueve a unos pocos y allí radica su belleza, si les gustara a todos habría que destruirlo por vulgar. ¿Cómo es que lograste terminarlo en tan poco tiempo?

—Trabajando mucho, Majestad.

—Gracias por el regalo, mi buen amigo. Procura ser feliz.

—Usted también, Majestad.

—Yo no puedo, Venosta. Los emperadores no son felices.

—Majestad, yo creo que la felicidad depende de cada persona, y cada persona depende de sí misma.

—Eso es cierto, pero los emperadores no dependen de sí mismos. Ellos dependen de su pueblo.

Cuando Fernando Carlos se interesó por el duque de Miramón, le informaron que antes del amanecer había partido hacia Roma. Aunque no se le dieron más detalles, el emperador entendió perfectamente que la duquesa, su tía, seguramente ya estaba al tanto de la carta del Papa y de su contenido, y había enviado a Miramón, uno de los aristócratas más simbólicos del imperio, a que tomara el lugar del embajador de México ante El Vaticano en una discusión digna de ver, con gritos y en español, y quizás con amenazas. Consciente de que Miramón había ido a Roma a pelearse y no a negociar algo, comprendió que su misión sería breve, así que dio instrucciones de que se reuniera con él en el Aeropuerto de Trieste horas más tarde, para partir hacia México. Esta vez no fue el pueblo ni las autoridades a despedirlo, como siglo y medio atrás a su antepasado. La historia a fin de cuentas no se repetía, tan sólo el pasado tenía algunas similitudes con el presente. Cuando Fernando Carlos subía al avión, dos oficiales del ejército imperial mexicano le hicieron el saludo militar a ambos lados de la escalera con un respeto admirable. Ya empezaba a comprender lo que era ser el emperador.

Castillo de Chapultepec, agosto de 1942

El archiduque Francisco José suspendió sus vacaciones veraniegas en Acapulco porque su hermano, el emperador Maximiliano II, le había ordenado que volviera inmediatamente a Aztlán. Con la guerra a gran escala desarrollándose en otras latitudes, por un momento el archiduque llegó a temer lo peor, y se apresuró a volver a la capital del imperio, ya que él desempeñaba el cargo de canciller. Media hora después de que le llegó la orden de su hermano, se tranquilizó un poco. De haber recibido México una declaración de guerra, su hermano se lo habría dicho para que se fuera preparando. Así las cosas, dejó a su esposa y a sus hijos en Acapulco y él se apresuró a volver a Aztlán acompañado de su chofer y varios escoltas, sabiendo que algo serio ocurría, pero no de extremada gravedad. Aunque tenía una esposa a la que amaba y tres hijos varones, ninguno de éstos era Habsburgo, y no podían, eventualmente, heredar la corona. El archiduque Francisco José se había casado con una hermosa e inteligente mexicana del montón, desdeñando a princesas europeas que después de la pérdida de sus privilegios a consecuencia de la Gran Guerra, habrían estado felices de casarse con él. Sabedor de las reglas de la familia, supo desde antes de casarse que sus hijos quedarían automáticamente fuera de la casa de Habsburgo. Su hermano, el emperador, aunque decepcionado porque deseaba inundar los ministerios de archiduques —y debido a que su esposa sólo había tenido un hijo y después quedó estéril al sufrir un aborto—, se molestó con él, pero al final accedió a autorizar su matrimonio y prometió títulos nobiliarios para sus sobrinos.

Cuando el archiduque llegó por fin al castillo de Chapultepec, se encontró con que ya lo estaban esperando su hermano y el conde Kodolich, ministro de la guerra.

—¿Qué pasa, Majestad?, ¿cuál es la urgencia?

—Lee esta carta, en voz alta —le pidió el emperador—, me la envió Roosevelt.

El archiduque tomó el documento y empezó a leer.

Emperador Maximiliano II de México

Estimado señor, le he pedido repetidas veces por vía telefónica, por medio de su embajador y del nuestro en Aztlán, que tome una posición respecto a la guerra. Usted me ha asegurado que no comulga con el totalitarismo y el fascismo de nuestros enemigos, sin embargo, no ha roto relaciones diplomáticas con Alemania, y eso me lleva a pensar que las mismas esperanzas que tengo yo de que entre en la guerra de nuestro lado, las tiene Hitler de que entre del suyo.

Se supone, señor, que usted es el jefe de Estado de un imperio que posee los recursos necesarios para luchar por la libertad. En estos momentos hombres muy valientes de varias potencias luchan en diversas partes del mundo por una sola razón: que el mañana que disfruten nuestros hijos y nietos sea mejor del que nos ha tocado vivir a nosotros. Y yo me pregunto todos los días, ¿dónde están los soldados de México?, también ellos llevan una responsabilidad para lograr la paz del mundo, ¿o acaso quiere usted, emperador, que el fascismo desaparezca de la faz de la tierra, pero que quien ponga los sacrificios y los muertos sea América? Eso no sería junto, señor.

Le pido, emperador, fijar pronto una posición. Si acaso decide entrar en guerra de nuestro lado, América será su mejor amigo y entre nuestras dos naciones se tenderán lazos inquebrantables de fraternidad duradera. Si, por el contrario, usted decide apoyar a los alemanes, tan sólo le agradeceré no cometer el error de los japoneses de atacarnos sin declaración de guerra. Eso nos haría enfurecer mucho. Y si ignorando su deber usted opta por seguir impasible ante la guerra, sin tomar parte de ningún lado, tan sólo le pido que nos lo haga saber de una vez. Y también le sugeriría, en ese caso, que descienda al rango de rey, porque la palabra emperador me recuerda a Napoleón y a gobernantes del imperio romano, no a un jefe de Estado que espera que otros le regalen la paz mundial.

Espero tener su respuesta a la brevedad

Franklin D. Roosevelt

—¡Tullido hijo de la chingada! —dijo Maximiliano II, cuando su hermano terminó la lectura—. ¿Quién se cree este cabrón que es? A nosotros no nos han bombardeado, no estamos obligados a entrar en guerra con nadie.

—Creo, Majestad —dijo Kodolich—, que esa insultante carta es un buen pretexto para entrar en guerra. Francia e Inglaterra están prácticamente en el suelo, la Unión Soviética sin duda será aplastada por el poderío de los nazis, y los yanquis tienen abiertos dos frentes. Es un buen momento para atacar. No nos podrán detener si los atacamos con todo.

—No estoy pensando en la guerra, conde —dijo el emperador—, aún falta mucho para que me decida a entrar en el conflicto. La emperatriz Carlota me repetía constantemente cuando era niño que antes de la guerra hay que agotar todos los recursos diplomáticos posibles, y que se debe atacar por motivos verdaderamente graves. Sus palabras todavía resuenan en mi cabeza, de tantas veces que la escuché.

—Entonces al menos redactémosle una carta para ponerlo en su sitio —dijo Kodolich—. Que sepa que México no está obligado a nada porque no ha sido agredido por nadie y que debe disculparse cuanto antes por sus palabras.

—Por supuesto que le enviaremos una respuesta —dijo el emperador—. Jamás me quedaría con los insultos de ese yanqui advenedizo que seguro no sabe hablar otro idioma más que el inglés.

—Hacer eso sería hacer lo que Roosevelt quiere, Majestad —dijo el archiduque Francisco José—. Y aquí se trata de no darle gusto.

—Explícate —pidió el emperador.

—Primero que nada, conviene que tengamos claro que de ninguna manera podemos entrar en guerra del lado de los alemanes. Apoyar a una forma de gobierno tan agresiva nos traería serios problemas tarde o temprano. Lo más sensato habría sido entrar en apoyo de los yanquis, pero al no haber sido agredidos, nos estaríamos portando como si estuviéramos a su disposición. Así que lo que más conviene para México a estas alturas es mantenerse totalmente al margen, mientras no nos agredan. Y eso es exactamente lo que quiere Roosevelt, pero no se lo vamos a decir.

—Roosevelt quiere que entremos en guerra de su lado —dijo Kodolich.

—No, no nos equivoquemos. Creo, Majestad —continuó el archiduque Francisco José—, que es necesario leer esa carta no sólo en lo que dice, sino en el mensaje que está oculto en ella. Roosevelt está desesperado, por lo que puede verse. Con dos frentes abiertos y con nosotros haciendo maniobras militares y con un programa de producción de armamento, lo que él quiere saber es qué es lo que tenemos en mente. Ya no espera que México le declare la guerra a Alemania, sabe que las últimas líneas de su carta eliminan por completo esa posibilidad. Pero él quiere estar seguro de que no los atacaremos por ahora.

—Es cierto eso —dijo el emperador—. Roosevelt sabe que por sus insultos jamás voy a ayudarlo, pero le urge que le digamos que nos mantendremos quietos.

—Y no se lo diremos —dijo el archiduque—. Vamos a mantener en la incertidumbre al viejo tullido. Primero que nada, el emperador debe cortar todo contacto con él. No le va a responder la carta. La respuesta la dará nuestro embajador en Washington y de su relación aquí con ellos me ocuparé yo, nunca el emperador.

—¿Y qué respuesta va a dar el embajador? —preguntó Kodolich.

—Sencillo, va a presentar una queja, argumentando que el emperador está furioso por la carta de Roosevelt.

—Eso no es mentira, estoy realmente furioso.

—Sí, pero no lo dirá usted, Majestad. Si le dejamos la tarea al embajador, Roosevelt pensará que las relaciones quedaron bastante fracturadas por su estupidez. Mientras tanto nosotros seguiremos con nuestras maniobras y nuestra producción de armamento, algo que los yanquis sabrán por sus espías. Así pensarán que estamos a punto de entrar en guerra, y le causaremos a Roosevelt más preocupaciones de las que ya tiene, al pensar que vamos sobre ellos. Quizás en una de esas se muere.

—Pero también podemos propiciar que los yanquis nos ataquen repentinamente —dijo Kodolich.

—Lo dudo —respondió el archiduque—. Roosevelt no es idiota. Tres frentes abiertos al mismo tiempo es algo extremadamente riesgoso hasta para los Estados Unidos. No entrarían en un conflicto con un país militarmente mediocre del otro lado del mundo, sino con el Imperio Mexicano, que está pegado a su frontera. Roosevelt tendría que estar muy drogado por las pastillas que toma, para pensar en atacarnos.

—Y si nos atacan —dijo Maximiliano II—, nos darán el pretexto para iniciar un conflicto que se ha pospuesto durante muchos años. Después de todo, en algún momento hay que escribir la parte que falta de la historia entre México y los yanquis.

Castillo de Chapultepec, despacho del canciller Bonaparte, enero del 2017

—¿Qué impresión le dio el emperador, Luis? —dijo la duquesa Carlota—. Por favor, sea totalmente sincero conmigo.

—Señora, me complace saber que Su Majestad Imperial es un hombre consiente de su misión —dijo Bonaparte—. Es un patriota mexicano y fue educado como un archiduque, lo cual le ayuda mucho a desenvolverse. Está dispuesto a aprender y creo que también a atender nuestros consejos. El problema es su edad, es bastante joven, y no se ve un león detrás de su mirada, sino un muchacho inofensivo. No lo quiero imaginar discutiendo con cocodrilos del tamaño de Ángel Miguel Morador, el líder del partido socialista que tanto añora derribar la monarquía y establecer una república en México, o el príncipe Agustín de Iturbide y Green, que sueña con ser emperador y cree que éste es su momento, o al propio Donald Trump. Se lo van a comer con la mirada, lo van a amedrentar y quizás salga corriendo de la entrevista.

—Eso jamás va a pasar, Luis. El emperador tiene claro que es un Habsburgo. No lo subestime. Lleva dentro de sí los genes de personas que han tomado las riendas de diferentes gobiernos a lo largo de siete siglos. Algo bueno habrá heredado.

—Como no sean las tendencias suicidas del archiduque Rodolfo.

—Por favor, Luis, no sea pesimista.

—Discúlpeme, señora —respondió Bonaparte—. Es que estaba acostumbrado a ver en esa silla al hombre que irradiaba tanto poder, que fue su hermano, y el joven emperador dista mucho de parecerse a su padre. Incluso cuando trata de mostrar firmeza con sus palabras, sus ojos dejan ver su timidez.

—Tengámosle un poco de paciencia, Luis. Es nuestro deber.

—Señora, yo estoy dispuesto a todo por él. Pero me temo que hay cosas que no podemos posponer. A Morador no está obligado a recibirlo, el encuentro con Trump aún no tiene fecha, pero a Iturbide tiene que recibirlo pronto. Es su ministro de Hacienda. Justo esta mañana me llamó para preguntarme si hoy mismo lo podía recibir el emperador. Le dije que Su Majestad de momento sólo me recibirá a mí, mientras se empapa de todos los asuntos pendientes, y que los ministros por órdenes empresas del emperador, al menos durante una o dos semanas, tendrán que darme a mí cuentas. Pero no creo que una semana o dos sean suficientes para que Su Majestad esté listo.

—Lo estará, Luis. Yo hablaré con él cuántas veces haga falta. Dígame, ¿ha tenido oportunidad de ver con detalle qué dijo la prensa internacional y la mexicana sobre su llegada a México?

—Sí, señora, y temo decirle que casi nada bueno, a excepción de los diarios que nos son afines, claro. Su juventud es su peor enemigo. Sólo algunos diarios ligeramente imparciales han hecho hincapié en que está arropado por los mismos ministros de su padre, personas probadas en las cuestiones de gobierno. Pero la mayoría siguen repitiendo malintencionadamente que los últimos Habsburgo en gobernar España y Austria también llevaban el nombre de Carlos. Y no es para enfurecernos, señora, después de todo, algunos señalaban que el imperio tenía los días contados cuando gobernaba su hermano, un estadista de pies a cabeza. Es normal que ahora que está al mando un jovencito tímido se den más vuelo.

—El fin del imperio lo han predicho desde los tiempos de Maximiliano *el Grande*, y desde él no ha habido emperador de México a quien no le garanticen que tendrá que abdicar. Mas sin embargo aquí seguimos.

—Si me permite, señora —dijo Bonaparte—, creo que tenemos que darle cuanto antes la espada de Santa Anna, y prepararle un discurso extraordinario para esa ocasión. Si lo pronuncia adecuadamente, el pueblo tendrá confianza en su emperador y en el extranjero sabrán que México tiene un jefe de Estado capaz. Ése sería un gran triunfo, o al menos un buen inicio.

—El discurso ya lo tengo escrito —dijo la duquesa—. Hoy mismos pensaba dárselo al emperador para que empiece a practicarlo. Sería genial que lo pronunciara de memoria. También le haré llegar una copia a usted, para que me dé sus impresiones y haga las sugerencias que considere oportunas. En cuanto al día de la coronación, estoy de acuerdo con usted en que tiene que ser cuanto antes. Creo que no hay que invitar a ningún miembro de la realeza europea, ni siquiera a los Habsburgo austriacos, ni a jefes de Estado de otros países. Porque estando aquí, el emperador se vería obligado por cortesía a concederles audiencia, y quizás se lleven una mala impresión de lo poco preparado que está. Y no podemos permitir de ninguna manera que se difunda en el extranjero que el emperador de México es un hombre débil.

—Señora, ¿y si pasadas las semanas el emperador no reacciona? A mí me ha dicho cosas extraordinarias, sobre todo cuando tocamos el tema de Trump. Hablaba como hablaría un emperador inexperto, pero emperador al fin. Mas el problema es que si yo hubiera sido el príncipe de Iturbide me habría reído de cómo me lo decía.

—No hay más opción que ponerle una difícil prueba, Luis —dijo la duquesa—. Ahora que tiene claro que es emperador hay que llevar sus nervios al límite. Que tenga que tomar él solo una determinación de vida o muerte.

—Señora, algo así es muy extremo. ¿Y si se nos echa en cama otra vez como en Miramar? Ya no es seguro que nos crean otra caída accidental.

—Luis, ahora que mi sobrino ha aceptado ser emperador, hay que enseñarle a serlo.

—¿Tiene algo concreto ya en mente? —dijo Bonaparte.

—Sí, creo que sí. ¿Qué hay de la misión en Egipto?

—Ya casi ubicamos el lugar donde posiblemente los tienen, no muy lejos del mar, por fortuna. Es posible un rescate sin llamar la atención —respondió Bonaparte.

—Bien —dijo la duquesa—, cuando eso sea un hecho, que lo decida el emperador.

—Pero habíamos acordado no informarlo de esta misión, por lo delicada que es y porque todo sucedió cuando él se hallaba tan indispuesto. Si se entera, quizás se enfurezca con nosotros y cancele todo.

—Si hace una cosa u otra, Luis, tendríamos que aceptarlo, porque él es el emperador.

Castillo de Chapultepec, al día siguiente

Cuando Fernando Carlos fue informado de que el canciller quería verlo en seguida, dio la instrucción de que éste se reuniera con él en su despacho. Se puso un poco nervioso, ya que una urgencia de verlo por parte de un hombre que al parecer lo tenía todo bajo control no significaba nada bueno.

—Me urgía que me recibiera, Majestad —dijo Bonaparte, no muy dueño de sí, en cuanto estuvo enfrente del emperador—. Tenemos una emergencia, algo muy grave.

—Dígame, príncipe, de qué se trata. ¡Pronto! —dijo el emperador, ya un poco contagiado del nerviosismo del canciller.

—No pensaba decírselo, pero yo no puedo tomar esta decisión solo.

—Hizo bien en venir, príncipe. Si es algo tan grave, yo debo estar enterado. Hable, por favor.

—Hace varios días, Majestad, una pareja de mexicanos que estaba de luna de miel en Egipto desapareció repentinamente. Nuestra inteligencia logró seguirles el rastro poco después. Hemos confirmado que fueron secuestrados por un grupo extremista y también hemos ubicado en dónde los tienen.

—¡Maldición! —dijo el emperador—. Esos extremistas no lo piensan dos veces antes degollar a alguien para difundir su terrorismo, y menos tratándose de extranjeros con fachas de occidentales. ¿Podemos pedir apoyo al gobierno egipcio?

—Majestad, los gobiernos de la zona no pueden hacer nada contra los terroristas. Algunos también lo son. La tarea del rescate será absolutamente nuestra.

—De acuerdo, príncipe, ¿y qué opciones tenemos?

—Majestad, quizás me destituya por lo que voy a confesarle —dijo Bonaparte—. Pero créame que lo hice porque tenía conocimiento de que usted no se sentía muy bien emocionalmente, por ello actué solo. Al saber la grave noticia, aprovechando que algunos de nuestros buques militares se encuentran realizando un recorrido por la zona, ordené un despliegue de nuestros marines en suelo egipcio. Un grupo de elite de no más de treinta elementos. Mi urgencia, Majestad, se debe a que en este momento, aprovechando que allá es de noche, nuestros marines están a pocos metros de la aldea donde están los mexicanos secuestrados, y tienen en la mira a varios terroristas. Lamentablemente no a todos. Esperan la orden para disparar a los que tienen a su alcance, después entrarían a la aldea, disparándole a todo lo que se mueva. El problema es que además de terroristas hay mujeres, niños y ancianos. Es una aldea a fin de cuentas, y aunque las víctimas inocentes no están en el objetivo de nuestros marines, usted sabe, el fuego cruzado.

—¡Maldita sea, Bonaparte!

—Majestad, acepto que me extralimité, y mi renuncia está a sus órdenes.

—No, no diga tonterías —respondió Fernando Carlos—. Usted hizo lo correcto. No podía consultar de algo tan grave a un emperador que estaba temblando entre las cobijas en su alcoba de Miramar, y se movilizó para salvar vidas mexicanas. Estoy orgulloso de usted. Ahora, dígame, ¿cuál sería el mejor escenario posible?

—Lo mejor que podría pasarnos, Majestad, es que nuestros marines den en el blanco, que entrando a la aldea puedan liquidar pronto al resto de los terroristas, y que para ese entonces la pareja de mexicanos aún sigan con vida. Después todavía rogamos a la fortuna que puedan llegar hasta donde los recogerán nuestros helicópteros.

—Así que necesitamos no de uno, sino de varios milagros. Y dígame, los mexicanos secuestrados, ¿qué tan probable es que aún se encuentren con vida?

—Sospechamos que siguen vivos, Majestad —respondió el canciller—. Es lo más probable. Pero en caso de que ya no podamos rescatarlos, ¿no cree que es nuestro deber vengarlos?

—¿Y qué garantías tengo de que no morirán inocentes?

—Majestad, lo que casi puedo asegurarle es que morirán algunos inocentes. Por otro lado, me preocupa más que los terroristas sean más de los que pensamos y se defiendan mejor de lo que pensamos. O que aun teniendo éxito nuestros marines, el ejército egipcio los intercepte. La crisis diplomática sería grave, México será acusado de enviar tropas a un país violando su soberbia. Nuestros marines incluso pueden ser pasados por las armas, si llegan a caer heridos, ya que tienen la orden de no rendirse por nada del mundo.

—¿Me está diciendo que debo ordenar el asesinato de muchas personas, que aun así varios mexicanos podrían perder la vida, y que el imperio tendría un grave problema diplomático?

—Perfecta su síntesis, Majestad.

—Canciller, yo no soy un asesino. Jamás en mi vida pensé en serlo. Pero nunca voy a dejar a mexicanos abandonados a su suerte. Dígame, en caso de que las cosas se compliquen, ¿qué posibilidades tenemos de enviar ayuda a nuestros marines?

—De momento, ninguna, Majestad. Los helicópteros de combate que están listos para llevarlos al mar no podrían brindar apoyo significativo ante un ejército. Si bien es cierto que Egipto no es un rival para el Imperio Mexicano, nuestras posibilidades de ayuda inmediata son pocas. Además, no estamos buscando una guerra. Sólo se trata de un rescate. Lo mejor que puede pasarnos es que la misión sea breve y exitosa. Pero si usted lo considera muy riesgoso, Majestad, puedo ordenar la retirada. Que nuestros marines se vayan sin disparar un solo tiro y regresen al mar.

—Antes seré yo quien se meta un tiro, príncipe —dijo el emperador, en tono resuelto—, si llego a traicionar a los míos. Si esos mexicanos están vivos, haremos todo lo necesario para salvarlos. O en el peor de los casos morirán sabiendo que no los abandonamos. Si las cosas se complican, quiero que me pongan en la línea con el presidente de Egipto. Me disculparé y ofreceré una indemnización económica. En parte la culpa de esto es de ellos por no poner orden en su país. Y si se porta intransigente, nos consideramos en guerra. Quizás nuestros marines mueran luchando, pero que antes de eso tengan bien claro que ya vamos en camino. Supongo que el ministro Peña-Bazaine está esterado de esto.

—Está enterado del rescate. De hecho, solo lo sabíamos la duquesa, él y yo. Pero lo que usted ha resuelto, eso de llegar a la guerra, tendríamos que informárselo. Majestad, con el debido respeto, ¿usted cree que dos mexicanos justifican una guerra en la que morirían muchas personas?

—Príncipe, aún si fuera un mexicano desahuciado por una enfermedad, entraría en guerra para que viniera a morir a su país, con su familia, con los suyos, y para que tuviera claro que para mi gobierno era una persona importante. No sé cómo habrían hecho las cosas mi padre, mi abuelo o los demás emperadores, pero yo las haré como creo que es lo correcto.

—¿Entonces, Majestad?

—Dé la orden. Que nuestros marines ejecuten la misión.

—La tiene que firmar usted —dijo Bonaparte, mostrándole un documento—, ya que se trata de que miembros del ejército imperial mexicano habrán fuego en suelo extranjero.

Completamente dueño de sí, Fernando Carlos firmó el documento y se lo devolvió al canciller. Éste marcó un número desde su teléfono móvil.

—Su Majestad Imperial autoriza la misión —dijo y cortó la llamada—. Me retiro a mi oficina, tengo que hablar con el ministro de la guerra, para informarle lo que usted ha decidido en caso de que las cosas se compliquen.

—Está bien, pero infórmeme todo lo que pase al instante.

—Justo ahora, Majestad, quizás nuestros marines ya están disparando. Pase lo que pase, bueno o malo, lo sabremos en seguida.

Fernando Carlos fue hacia su ventana. Extrañamente, los nervios se habían ido. Sentía como si hubiera dado una orden cotidiana. Vio a través de la ventana, hacia el Paseo de Juárez, primero contempló la estatua ecuestre de Leopoldo I de Bélgica, aquel rey que supo ser grande y ser considerado un extraordinario estadista pese a que su reino era bastante pequeño. Después recorrió su mirada hasta la gigantesca estatua ecuestre de Maximiliano *el Grande*, que marcaba la división entre el bosque y la ciudad. Fernando Carlos pensó que quizás no se parecía a ninguno de los grandes gobernantes de quienes descendía directamente, pero aun así tenía una misión que cumplir y la cumpliría. En ese momento tuvo la seguridad de que los grandes gobernantes del pasado con los que él tenía parentesco, admirados por la humanidad gracias a sus hazañas extraordinarias, al igual que él, también habían tenido miedo. Quizás Rodolfo I, Carlos *el Temerario* o Fernando *el Católico* habían pasado días de dudas y nerviosismo antes de cumplir su misión en la historia. No era un pecado ni una falta grave tener miedo, creyó, sino sucumbir a él. Ignoraba si se debía a la excitación del momento, pero tenía la certeza de que el miedo a ser emperador por fin se había ido. Cuando Bonaparte se anunció, dio la instrucción de que entrara al despacho, pero lejos de ir a tomarlo de la solapa para que dijera cuánto antes qué había pasado, el emperador se sentó completamente recto en la silla que Francisco José I de Austria le había regalado a su sobrino Moctezuma III.

Bonaparte hasta se sorprendió de la compostura que exhibía su soberano.

—Buenas noticias, Majestad —dijo el canciller—. En este momento, nuestros marines y la pareja de mexicanos van en los helicópteros, rumbo al mar. La misión fue todo un éxito gracias a la rapidez de nuestros extraordinarios soldados. No tuvimos bajas —añadió el canciller lleno de júbilo—, tan sólo un elemento fue herido en un brazo. Pero su vida no corre peligro.

—¿Aún es posible que nuestros helicópteros sean detectados por radares egipcios? —preguntó el emperador.

—Es muy poco probable, Majestad, ya que hemos tomado todas las precauciones debidas. Además, en una zona tan conflictiva ese tipo de vuelos no encenderán las alarmas. Es Egipto, no los Estados Unidos.

—Me alegro. Los Habsburgo hemos sido durante siglos amantes del arte, me habría apenado mucho tener que hacer volar por los aires esfinges, obeliscos y pirámides. ¿Y qué me puede decir de las bajas civiles?

—Majestad, entienda que es muy pronto para interrogar a nuestros marines al respecto. Pero no dude que pudo haberlas. Ellos tenían órdenes de hacer lo posible por salvar a sus compatriotas. Le tiraban a lo que se movía...

—Comprendo, canciller. Fueran cuales fueran sus actos, ellos no han hecho nada malo. Son héroes mexicanos. ¿Es posible que me puedan poner en la línea al hombre que estaba al mando, y a la pareja rescatada?

—De momento no lo creo, Majestad —dijo el canciller—. Esperemos a que estén todos a salvo, a bordo de uno de nuestros buques y en aguas internacionales.

—Deseo recibirlos aquí a todos, cuando esto pase. Y por ahora quiero que los mexicanos que fueron rescatados se enteren de que al saber de su situación, nada en este mundo fue más importante para mí que salvar sus vidas, y que nuestros marines tengan claro que me siento orgulloso de ellos, y si es que hubo bajas civiles, que aparten eso de su conciencia. La única conciencia en la que deberán caer los crímenes que mi gobierno se vea obligado a cometer por situaciones como ésta, será la mía. Que eso quede bien claro, príncipe.

—A las órdenes de Vuestra Majestad —dijo Bonaparte, inclinándose.

Minutos más tarde, cuando el canciller salió del despacho del emperador, lo primero que hizo fue llamar por teléfono a la duquesa.

—Señora —dijo emocionado—, las cosas salieron a las mil maravillas. El emperador ahora sí parecía lo que es. Lo hubiera visto, señora, con qué seguridad hablaba. Por un momento me intimidó más que su padre.

—¡Gracias a Dios, Luis! —respondió la duquesa—. Ya hacía mucha falta que reaccionara. A fin de cuentas, es él quien debe de tomar las decisiones. Nos estábamos tomando muchas atribuciones que no nos corresponden, debido a su incapacidad.

—Ya no más, señora. México ahora sí tiene un emperador.

—Supongo, duque —dijo Francisco—, que viene a hacerme una reclamación en nombre del Imperio Mexicano. Pero antes de que empiece a hablar, le aclaro que ustedes me pidieron que escribiera una carta para ayudar moralmente a un católico, no que mintiera sobre mi forma de pensar, lo que jamás haría.

—Señor Bergoglio…

—Vaya, veo que sí están enojados en México. Todavía ayer me llamaban "Santo Padre". Aunque puede llamarme como guste. Le confieso que no me incomoda en absoluto mi apellido.

—Le rendiremos honores sólo a un Papa que se muestre amigo del Imperio Mexicano —dijo Miramón.

—¿Y eso de ser *amigos* significa que haga lo que ustedes quieren, para que pueda seguir existiendo su dictadura, que exhibe en cada acto un capitalismo salvaje?

—Cómo iba decirle, señor Bergoglio, si no estaba dispuesto a ayudarnos, tan sólo se hubiera negado a escribir la carta. Confiamos en usted, le dimos acceso a un documento suyo hasta los aposentos de Su Majestad sin revisarlo antes, y cuál fue nuestra sorpresa al constatar que esa carta era un intento para asesinar a nuestro imperio.

—¡No exagere! Yo sólo le expresé mi opinión a ese joven…

—¿Querrá decir Su Majestad Imperial?

—Como sea. Y en todo caso, no me hubieran pedido que escribiera carta alguna —dijo Francisco, ya muy molesto—, al contrario, les habría agradecido que me dejaran tranquilo. Apenas puedo creer que pretendieran que yo contribuyera a perpetuar una dictadura a todas luces caduca en esta época del mundo. ¡Faltaba más!

—¿Y el Papado qué es? No me diga que los mil doscientos millones de católicos en el mundo votaron por usted para elevarlo a Papa. Los cardenales son designados libremente por el Papa, y después, cuando hace falta, ellos se encierran como viles mafiosos y se ponen de acuerdo para elegir a quien los gobierne, sin explicar nunca su criterio. ¿Eso no es una dictadura peor que la nuestra? Nosotros al menos procuramos la seguridad en todos los sentidos de doscientos sesenta millones de seres humanos, en cambio ustedes sólo almacenan dinero.

—¿Pero qué estás diciendo, pelotudo egoísta? Yo he renunciado a muchos privilegios...

—¡Mas no ha renunciado a ser Papa, lo que a todas luces es una institución caduca en esta época del mundo! ¿Por qué no reforma la Iglesia Católica?, ¿por qué no ordena cardenal a una mujer?, ¿por qué siguen encerrando a las mujeres en los conventos, o las ponen únicamente a cuidar enfermos o a hacer dulces, y ustedes los hombres se reservan todos los privilegios?

—¿Cómo vos te atreves a venir y decirme semejantes estupideces aquí? —dijo Francisco, al borde del infarto—, ¿Quién te crees que eres para faltarme el respeto de esa manera?

—Escúcheme bien, Bergoglio, tanto el Imperio Mexicano como el Papado son, ciertamente, dos instituciones que conservan inocultables anacronismos, pero nosotros no hemos desaparecido nuestro imperio porque consideramos que es difícil que algo mejor pueda suplantarlo, porque todavía es capaz de hacer de México un lugar donde millones de personas puedan ser felices. Y hemos supuesto durante muchos años que ustedes no habían desaparecido el Papado porque también lo consideraban útil para el cristianismo y para la paz del mundo. En ese entendimiento, nuestras relaciones se habían desarrollado muy bien y el respeto mutuo proliferaba, ya que una institución valoraba la existencia de la otra y existía un gran apoyo. Tanto Juan Pablo II como Benedicto XVI estuvieron conscientes de ello y siempre apreciaron con honestidad la existencia del Imperio Mexicano. Nuestras relaciones con ellos fueron extraordinarias. Pero ciertamente le hablo de dos grandes intelectuales con los que usted no se puede comparar de ninguna manera, porque es sólo un viejo comunista, necio y resentido.

—¡Hijo de... Lárgate inmediatamente de aquí!

—No me quedaría ni aunque me rogara. Y por supuesto que su visita a México de febrero próximo queda tajantemente cancelada, sólo nos desquiciaría el tráfico y no serviría para nada útil. También le aclaro una cosa, Bergoglio, el emperador de México ha dejado de ser amigo del Papa. Aténgase a las consecuencias de su estupidez.

—¡Fuera, te he dicho!

Palacio Imperial, junio de 1910

El emperador Agustín II se agachó un poco para tomar la mano del popular caudillo Francisco I. Madero, el ya tan famoso en todo México agitador de las masas, que tantos dolores de cabeza le estaba dando. Le pareció, a simple vista, un hombre inteligente, sensato y de voluntad enérgica. Su amplia frente, su grueso bigote y su tupida barba, le daban cierto señorío y grandeza intelectual, a pesar de sus ojillos tímidos. Sabía que no podía de ningún modo subestimarlo, puesto que ese hombre tenía al imperio en jaque.

—Señor Madero, sea usted bienvenido.

—Señor de Habsburgo, gracias por aceptar dialogar conmigo. Soy el último de los mexicanos que quisiera usar las armas para lograr nuestra libertad, y por ello he venido hasta aquí, para apelar a su sensatez y propiciar así que todo ocurra pacíficamente.

—Estimado señor —dijo Agustín II—, me parece que hace usted un uso indebido de la palabra libertad. Los mexicanos, todos, somos libres y hay instituciones que lo garantizan.

—No, no creo que esté usando la palabra de manera incorrecta, señor de Habsburgo. Usted sabe bien que los mexicanos disfrutábamos de la democracia hace medio siglo, pero su abuelo, apoyado por un ejército invasor, vino a arrebatárnosla. En ese entonces, el pueblo mexicano tenía un presidente, no un emperador, podía elegir a su gobernante, la República garantizaba la posibilidad de suprimir un mal gobierno mediante el voto. Y ustedes nos han quitado esa posibilidad, sometiéndonos a una dictadura que pretenden disfrazar con una corona.

—No conozco tan bien la historia de ningún país como conozco la del mío, señor Madero —dijo el emperador, sin alterarse en lo más mínimo—, y en esa época de la que usted me habla, cuando llegó mi abuelo a nuestra patria, los mexicanos no tenían paz y no había manera alguna de garantizarles su añorada seguridad. El ejército no podía procurar la seguridad de nuestras fronteras y las instituciones no tenían la capacidad de hacer nada por la paz y la tranquilidad diaria de nuestros compatriotas. Pero desde que la forma de gobierno cambió, hay una policía y unas instituciones que protegen a todos, incluso a los perezosos que no quieren trabajar, y un ejército capaz de hacer ver a cualquier otro, incluido el de los Estados Unidos, que éste es suelo mexicano y que quien lo profana lo pagará con la vida. Si usted, como mexicano, quiere que vuelvan aquellos tiempos, francamente me resulta difícil de entender, porque yo como mexicano, señor mío, daría mi vida antes de ver a mi patria débil, incapaz de proteger a sus hijos.

Madero dejó pasar un rayo de debilidad en su mirada. Aunque se creía dueño de la razón y la verdad absolutas, comprendió que no las tenía todas consigo al momento de discutir con aquel Habsburgo. Finalmente era el nieto de Carlota, y era de esperarse que lo hubiera preparado bastante bien, aprovechado que éste, a diferencia de su hijo, sí había nacido con inteligencia. Pero don Pacho había acudido a aquella cita con bastante seguridad en sí mismo, y no pensaba darse por vencido a la primera estocada que lo tomara con la guardia baja.

—Dice usted que conoce bastante bien la historia de su país, señor de Habsburgo, y no pienso cuestionar que sea un experto en la historia de Austria, en tanto que la historia de mi país, México, no la conoce usted mucho. Dice que cuando su abuelo, escoltado por las tropas de Napoleón III, llegó a estas tierras, México era débil. Eso se lo reconozco, pero la otra parte de la historia la oculta o la omite. Porque justo en ese entonces, un grupo de hombres capaces y dotados de una elevada inteligencia, dirigidos por el licenciado Benito Juárez, acababan de triunfar en una feroz revolución, y ya sin enemigos, apoyados en una constitución liberal, se disponían a hacer de México un lugar seguro y próspero, pero en eso llegó su abuelo a perseguirlos, como si ellos hubieran sido los extranjeros. Su abuelo lo que hizo fue robar la oportunidad que otros ya habían ganado, verdaderos mexicanos, dueños de estas tierras, y capaces de hacerlas prosperar.

—Señor Madero —dijo Agustín II, aún sin alterarse—, no muy lejos de aquí, en el castillo de Chapultepec, vine a este mundo, y también en el idioma español aprendí a comunicarme con mis semejantes, aunque luego aprendí otros once. Creo que el simple antecedente de mi nacimiento me hace tan mexicano como usted. Y si usted argumenta que mi apellido es extranjero, yo tendría que argumentar que los apellidos Madero González no me recuerdan a nada que tenga que ver con el antiguo imperio Azteca, del que he procurado aprender cuanta historia se conoce. Francamente, señor Madero, para que usted pueda acusarme a mí de ser un extranjero austriaco, tendría usted que tener un nombre mexica y hablar náhuatl. Yo, como usted bien lo sabe, no llevo en el nombre nada que me relacione con los antiguos mexicanos, pero el náhuatl lo hablo bastante bien, y usted, ¿lo habla? No se preocupe, no lo cuestiono, ya que no es su obligación. En mi caso sí lo es ya que hay muchos mexicanos que conservan ese idioma, que sólo ése conocen, y yo como su soberano también tengo que hablarlo. Pero creo que es justo reconocer, señor, que la mayoría de los mexicanos actuales somos importados. Usted probablemente de España, yo de Austria, con sangre española, pero como usted, completamente patriota mexicano. Lo que quiero lograr con este alegato tan extenso, es que no me acuse de ser un extranjero, porque francamente me ofende. En lo que respecta a la guerra de aquel entonces –añadió el emperador–, creo que ahora es usted, señor Madero, quien desconoce u omite la historia, porque los principales generales del bando conservador, Miramón, Márquez y Mejía, estaban vivos, incluso los últimos dos seguían luchando. ¿Usted realmente cree que Juárez había ganado la guerra, o que tan sólo gozaba de un agitado receso? Yo más bien creo que la inestabilidad habría continuado durante muchos años, debilitando completamente al país, para que los yanquis escogieran la parte que más les gustara, ya fuera en el norte, cerca de sus fronteras, o en el sur, para hacer un canal. También me permito resumirle otra parte de la historia que omite o que desconoce: mi abuelo, el emperador Maximiliano I, no fue un dictador. Un amplio sector de la población pidió su presencia en México, y eso quedó totalmente probado cuando él llegó, el pueblo lo recibió con enormes muestras de júbilo, con arcos triunfales y flores a su paso. México se inclinó por la monarquía, señor Madero, y yo que nací siendo parte de ella, no estoy aquí robándole nada a nadie, sino cumpliendo con mi deber.

Madero estaba empezando a sudar. Agustín II, aunque aún joven, era un adversario terrible. Sin duda se trataba de la mejor obra de Carlota, quien quizás por allí estaba detrás de unas cortinas, escuchando, y sintiéndose orgullosa de la paliza que su nieto le estaba dando. Sin embargo, había ensayado mucho en su cabeza aquel encuentro como para darse por vencido tan pronto.

–La supuesta elección de los mexicanos de aquel entonces –respondió Madero–, fue un completo engaño de los franceses, seños de Habsburgo. Sin embargo, no niego que es muy cierto que un sector de la población realmente apoyaba la creación de la monarquía al mando de un príncipe extranjero. Saber si se trató de una minoría o de una gran mayoría nos es imposible a estas alturas, aunque está probado que los franceses influyeron a favor de su abuelo todo cuanto les fue posible. Pero digamos que acepto que se trató de una mayoría, y que fueron los mexicanos y no Napoleón III quienes colocaron aquí a su abuelo. Le aclaro que no es algo en lo que creo, aunque ustedes se empeñen tanto en difundirlo como verdad, pero dejemos así las cosas. No pelearemos por una historia difícil de desenmarañar a estas alturas. Mas aquel acontecimiento sólo legitimaría a su abuelo, no a usted. Los mexicanos de aquella época decidieron, nosotros aún no lo hemos hecho. Somos otras personas y tenemos el libre derecho de elegir. Queremos unas elecciones en las que usted realmente sea elegido por el pueblo como nuestro mandatario, puesto que de momento nadie lo ha elegido, por lo tanto está usurpando funciones. Y no me vaya a decir aquello del derecho divino que tienes ustedes los monarcas, porque usted bien sabe que desde la revolución francesa Dios perdió la costumbre de meterse en política. Queremos elecciones, señor de Habsburgo, demuestre que tiene el derecho de estar donde está.

Don Pacho sonrió satisfecho de su alegato, estaba claro que había sabido atacar, puesto el emperador se había quedado de piedra.

—¿En qué año nació usted, señor Madero? —preguntó Agustín II.

—En 1873. ¿Por qué?

—Yo nací a finales de 1885. Cuando ambos vinimos a este mundo, México ya era una monarquía. Ni usted ni yo hemos vivido como ciudadanos de una república. En Imperio ha dado estabilidad al país, ha vuelto indispensable ante el mundo su comercio y posee el poder para dar seguridad a los mexicanos. Siendo así las cosas, dígame, ¿Por qué quiere hacer una república de un país que funciona bien como una monarquía?

—Eso es sencillo, señor de Habsburgo, porque en una república democrática todo el pueblo posee el poder, en tanto que con una monarquía el único poderoso aquí es usted… y su abuela. Me olvidaba de ella.

—Está usted muy equivocado, señor Madero —respondió el emperador—, en una república el pueblo no posee más poder que en una monarquía. La única diferencia es que posee la facultad de decidir a quién dárselo, pero el pueblo no posee ese poder y no tiene manera de usarlo. Tan sólo lo pone en las manos del mejor mentiroso, del mejor comediante, o del mejor orador. Pero no precisamente del mejor gobernante. No hace falta saber gobernar para ser presidente, y usted lo sabe. No me he enterado nunca que a un presidente de los Estados Unidos lo hayan levantado de madrugada cuando tenía seis años echándole agua helada en su espalda, para después encerrarlo en una habitación oscura, asegurándole que allí había un león. A quien no se le tiene predestinada una gran responsabilidad desde la niñez, no se le capacita para desempeñarla. Por eso Santa Anna y los demás presidentes que mandaron en México durante más de cuarenta años cometieron tantos errores. No tenían, realmente, la más remota idea de lo que era gobernar a un país. No es por ser presuntuoso, señor Madero, pero creo que los conocimientos de política, economía, diplomacia y táctica militar que tenía Santa Anna a los sesenta años, yo ya los tenía a los doce.

—Dígame una cosa, señor de Habsburgo, ¿cuántos mexicanos adultos, en edad de tomar sus propias decisiones, viven en México?

—Once millones de hombres, y trece de mujeres. También ellas tienen derecho a tomar sus decisiones. ¿No lo cree usted?

—Lo creo, por supuesto que sí —dijo Madero—. Y ya que somos tantos, ¿por qué se reserva el derecho de decidir la forma de gobierno del país usted solo?

—Es que yo no la elegí. Le vuelvo a recordar que la monarquía ya existía cuando usted y yo vinimos al mundo.

—Pero al estar empeñado en continuarla, les arrebata a los demás mexicanos la posibilidad de elegir su forma de gobierno —respondió Madero.

—Señor Madero, a los reyes o a los emperadores no se les elige. No es así como funciona una monarquía. Mucho del sufrimiento que ha soportado Polonia en su historia se debió a ese terrible error de querer elegir a los reyes. La estabilidad y al mismo tiempo la fortaleza de la monarquía radican en el nacimiento de un príncipe imperial, no en votación alguna. No es que yo odie la democracia, sino que en la forma de gobierno en que me tocó nacer no está contemplada para elegir al jefe de Estado.

—Y no podemos negar que eso a usted lo favorece mucho.

—Dígame usted, antes de su nacimiento, ¿le preguntaron si quería ser el hijo de un rico hacendado? Sospecho que no, porque a mí no se me preguntó si quería ser el hijo de un emperador. Es cierto que mi nacimiento significó para mí una gran fortuna, pero también una gran responsabilidad, y lo que hago día a día es portarme en reciprocidad con ambas. Trabajo para que aquéllos que no nacieron con mi suerte tengan una mejor vida, y para que nunca tengan una carga como la que yo llevo encima.

—Pues permítame decirle, señor de Habsburgo, que ambas tareas las ha hecho mal. Hay miles y miles de mexicanos por todas partes que no se han beneficiado de esa gran responsabilidad que usted llevar encima, y que le podrían contar lo que es el hambre, ya que usted visto está que no la conoce. Por ello me he vuelto el guía de los desheredados, de aquéllos que tienen el justo derecho de impulsar una nueva forma de gobierno, ya que la existente, que ellos no pidieron, los ha ignorado siempre.

—No existe, señor Madero, en toda la historia registro alguno de un gobierno formado por los hombres en el que no haya habido hambre, injusticias y corrupción —dijo Agustín II—. No es una justificaron para las omisiones de mi parte que hayan podido afectar a nuestros compatriotas. Tan sólo puedo decir que una economía tan revolucionaria como la nuestra, tan ligada a las enormes oleadas de emigrantes que nos llegan de Europa, es muy propensa a dejar olvidados por doquier. Pero tiene usted mi palabra de que haré todo lo que esté en mis manos para remediar cuántos pueda de esos males que usted menciona, y más aún, le ofrezco que sea mi ministro, y así usted podrá cerciorarse personalmente de que la situación sea atendida y dirigir recursos a donde los crea convenientes.

—Tan sólo le faltó ofrecerme el título de conde, señor de Habsburgo, pero le advierto que yo no cedo a sobornos. Los mexicanos debemos gozar del derecho de elegir libremente a nuestro gobierno. Usted no puede albergar tanto poder sin que el pueblo se lo haya dado. Y si se niega a darnos nuestra libertad, lucharemos por ella.

—Escúcheme bien, señor Madero —dijo el emperador, poniéndose de pie—, si hay alguna alteración del orden público que ponga en peligro la seguridad de los mexicanos, lo haré a usted responsable.

—Señor de Habsburgo, si los mexicanos alcanzan su sueño de vivir en una país libre, donde puedan gozar de las bondades de la democracia, será un honor para mí ser aunque sea un poco el responsable de ello. Con su permiso.

Palacio Imperial, al día siguiente

Pueblo de México

Ayer he hablado con el señor Agustín Fernando Francisco Carlos José de Habsburgo y Lorena, con la finalidad de convencerlo de que México no puede estar controlado por una forma de gobierno obsoleta y ajena a nuestro continente, en la que el pueblo no tiene la posibilidad de elegir a su gobernante, como debiera de ser un derecho por naturaleza. He encontrado en el mencionado señor una total necedad y cerrazón para aceptar la verdad y para renunciar a unos privilegios que no le ha dado nadie y que no debería tener.

Agotada la vía del dialogo, imposibilitados como estamos de convencer a este señor de que renuncie a un cargo que nos hace ver a los mexicanos como simples animales que le fueron heredados, hago un llamado para que el pueblo se levante en armas y conquiste de una vez por todas su tan negada libertad.

Francisco I. Madero

Terminando la lectura, la emperatriz Carlota dejó caer el documento en el escritorio del emperador.

—Ese tal Panchito no sabe la bomba que ha lanzado al aire con esta proclama —dijo—. Me temo que puede haber levantamientos en el norte y en el sur, incluso en la propia capital. ¿Qué piensa hacer al respecto, Majestad?

—Señora, si Madero es tan intransigente, no me queda otra opción más que demostrar mano dura. Ordenaré al general Khevenhüller-Rivas y al príncipe Iturbide que movilicen al ejército y disparen contra los seguidores de Madero si éstos llegan a alterar el orden.

—¿Y qué más?

—A Madero lo declararé fuera de la ley. Será capturado y pasado por las armas si hay tan solo un muerto a causa de la agitación que él ha causado.

—No sabe usted, Majestad, cuánto agradezco a Dios seguir viva para evitar que usted cometa errores tan absurdos, totalmente ajenos a la inteligencia —dijo Carlota.

—Pero, Señora, ¿qué otra opción tengo? Si me muestro débil, Madero y los suyos me arrastrarían por las calles de Aztlán, amarrado como un perro rabioso.

—Es verdad eso, pero proceder como usted se lo propone sería una completa estupidez.

—¿Y cómo se supone que debo actuar, señora, ya que usted parece que todo lo sabe?

—Lea esto en voz alta, por favor —dijo Carlota, extendiéndole un documento al emperador. Él lo tomó en sus manos y empezó a leer.

Pueblo de México

Es mi voluntad que a partir del día de hoy, a lo largo y ancho del Imperio Mexicano, las siguientes disposiciones sean tomadas por leyes inviolables por los gobernadores de todos los departamentos y aplicadas sin ninguna excepción bajo ninguna circunstancia:

1-. La jornada laboral diaria de los trabajadores mexicanos será de tan sólo ocho horas.

2-. Los mexicanos empleados en cualquier tipo de trabajo deberán descansar el domingo.

3-. Ninguna deuda puede ser heredada, ningún hijo estará obligado a pagar los adeudos que haya dejado su difunto padre.

4-. Todo patrón a quien se le compruebe que después de la publicación de las actuales disposiciones se valga de la esclavitud para proveerse de mano de obra, será pasado por las armas.

5-. Todo patrón que en adelante trate de estimular a los peones por medio de golpes, será sancionado con veinte años de prisión.

6-. El salario por las jornadas de trabajo, en ningún caso podrá ser en especie. Los mexicanos tienen el derecho de recibir su pago en dinero y disponer de éste con total libertad.

7-. El hacendado que posea tierras cuya propiedad no pueda comprobar con documentos válidos, y que no corrija sus cercas en el plazo de un mes, será pasado por las armas.

Agustín II

Emperador de México

—Pero, Señora —dijo el emperador, cuando terminó la lectura—, ¿qué significa esto? Hay más radicalismo aquí que en todas las proclamas que ha publicado Madero en el último año.

—Eso, Majestad, es precisamente el arma más poderosa con la que podemos tratar de detener a Madero. Y es menester que la usemos en seguida. Que el telégrafo la envíe a cada rincón del imperio y que los soldados del ejército imperial la distribuyan y la lean en voz alta en las plazas públicas. Si la proclama de Madero ya prendió fuego en todas partes, esas siete disposiciones serán el agua que se ocupa para apagarlo.

—¿Tiene usted idea, Señora, del daño que esto puede causar a la economía del imperio? Por no mencionar los enemigos que me echaré encima —dijo Agustín II.

—Majestad, ¿acaso no ve que si los soldados disparan contra los campesinos que va a levantar en armas Madero, el pueblo lo odiaría y ya jamás podría recuperarse de ese duro golpe? Si el emperador mata a mexicanos pobres que están dispuestos a pelear por los derechos más básicos, será ése el inicio de un conflicto de magnitudes incalculables todavía, pero que podría poner fin al imperio. En cambio, por fusilar a unos cuantos hacendados, dudo mucho que el pueblo se moleste con usted. Hasta es probable que lo vean como un héroe por ello.

—Esto es precisamente la revolución que quiere hacer Madero, incluso la de él la veo mucho menos drástica —dijo el emperador.

—Así es, Majestad. Ya que es inevitable una revolución, lo más conveniente es que la haga usted. En realidad muchas leyes enfocadas a proteger a los mexicanos más humildes fueron publicadas por ese extraordinario gobernante que fue vuestro ilustre abuelo, Maximiliano I, a quien el pueblo en agradecimiento a su determinación y sabiduría llama *el Grande*, pero como era necesario rehacer la economía de un país devastado, tuvieron que quedar relegadas, sin aplicarse nunca. Y ahora lo correcto con ellas no es recordarle al pueblo que existen y que nunca las hemos aplicado, sino hacer como si no existieran, para que los mexicanos tengan bien claro que usted se preocupa por ellos.

—¿Y ya pensó, Señora, en los negocios que irán a la quiebra si esto lo aplicamos rigurosamente?

—No creo que tantos. Las ganancias de muchos poderosos disminuirán, eso sería todo. Pero por más que se enojen en un principio, tendrán que asimilarlo después. Les haremos ver que era eso o aceptar que Madero y los suyos demolieran todo lo que se ha logrado desde la fundación del imperio. Porque no harían otra cosa si es que llevan a cabo su revolución.

—La economía del Estado puede resultar gravemente afectada.

—Deje de preocuparse por eso, Majestad. Lo que importa es salvar al imperio, y mantener la estabilidad al mismo tiempo que nos adaptamos a los cambios sociales.

—¿Y si resulta que un empresario yanqui se vale de mano de obra de esclavos?

—Lo pasamos por las armas y ya, sin dudarlo siquiera. No creo que ese gordo de Taft quiera una guerra con nosotros por uno de sus mezquinos y avaros empresarios. Y en caso de que ocurra, prefiero mil veces una guerra contra los yanquis que una guerra entre mexicanos.

Ahora, Majestad, le ruego que no pierda el tiempo, haga que ese documento sea divulgado por todo el imperio cuanto antes.

—Como usted disponga, Señora —dijo Agustín II, resignado.

—Y no tiene que darme las gracias por nada, Majestad —dijo Carlota—. Estoy enteramente a vuestras órdenes, siempre dispuesta a salvarlo de sus errores.

Cuernavaca, residencia campestre del príncipe Iturbide, enero del 2017

El príncipe Agustín de Iturbide y Green poseía unas maneras extremadamente elegantes de levantar su copa, beber apenas un pequeño sorbo y devolverla a la mesa. Mientras él analizaba diversos documentos tanto de sus empresas como del ministerio de Hacienda que tenía a su cargo, su hermana, la princesa Ana María, cabalgaba a lo lejos a un hermoso caballo que parecía tener perfectamente dominado y al que manipulaba con una facilidad casi infantil. A sus treinta y nueve años, el príncipe Agustín era considerado el ministro más inteligente del gabinete imperial y el hombre más rico de México. Su presencia o de miembros de su familia en los diarios cotidianamente era un suceso inalterable. Cuando él no aparecía, figuraba alguna noticia sobre su hermano menor, Ángel, quien estaba a cargo de la embajada de México ante los Estados Unidos, o de su hermana, hija única del segundo matrimonio de su fallecido padre, quien a sus veinte años ya era considerada por los medios como la mujer más hermosa del imperio. Agustín no ocultaba un deseo que quizás en el pasado habían atesorado con discreción los demás príncipes de Iturbide. Él creía firmemente que el gobierno de México tenía que seguir siendo monárquico, pero que la familia con más derechos para encabezar la monarquía era la suya y no los Habsburgo, puesto que el primer emperador del México moderno había sido a fin de cuentas un Iturbide. Sin embargo, aunque en banquetes y demás reuniones defendía esa teoría, no tenía pensado de ninguna manera alterar el orden establecido. Aceptaba el lugar secundario de su familia por el bienestar del imperio, e incluso del tema había llegado a hablar infinidad de veces con el emperador Maximiliano IV, de manera informal y amistosa, y éste jamás llegó a considerarlo un peligro ni pensó en sustituirlo del ministerio, ya que tenía claro que Iturbide sabía separar sus deseos más intensos de la necesaria estabilidad que debía tener el Imperio Mexicano.

Pero con las muertes del archiduque Maximiliano en un accidente aéreo y después del emperador, Iturbide entendió que había llegado la oportunidad histórica de que su fantasioso deseo se hiciera realidad, por una razón bastante valida: a su juicio, el único Habsburgo mexicano que quedaba con vida era un completo imbécil, mientras que los miembros de la rama austriaca de la familia no tenían legalmente ningún derecho de acceder al trono de México y eso lo sabía todo el mundo. Creía que el imperio solo tenía una posibilidad de sobrevivir: con él al mando, y que no generaría ninguna alteración social el hecho de que Fernando Carlos renunciara a sus derechos en favor de él, puesto que a fin de cuentas los Iturbide siempre habían caminado junto a la monarquía, desempeñando diversos cargos de gran importancia. Eran la otra familia imperial de México, así eran conocidos en todo el imperio y así los llamaba la prensa incluso en otros países. Y si bien era cierto que en linaje los Iturbide no tenían nada que hacer contra los Habsburgo, durante siglo y medio los suyos habían procurado inmejorables parentescos. Su fallecida madre había sido miembro de los borbones carlistas, en tanto que su abuela nació como una Mountbatten, o Battenberg, nombre de la familia hasta la Primera Guerra Mundial. Y él, para no ser menos que sus antepasados, se había procurado una esposa Hohenzollern. Con tales antecedentes, solía decir que los miembros de su familia eran los únicos en México que podían hacerle una donación de sangre al emperador.

Cuando Murió Maximiliano IV, el príncipe Agustín llegó a pensar que su advenimiento al trono tan sólo dependía de estar unos minutos a solas con aquel joven tan débil de carácter, para pedirle que dejara cuanto antes de estorbar en su camino y permitiera ocuparse de los problemas de México a un verdadero emperador. El único obstáculo que vio para que eso pasara era la duquesa Carlota, a su juicio, una completa serpiente venenosa, siempre apoyada por el canciller Bonaparte en todo lo que se propusiera, su eterno enamorado. Él consideraba que la duquesa se tomaba atribuciones para las que no tenía ningún derecho. Legalmente no era Habsburgo ni archiduquesa de México, había firmado su renuncia para casarse con un pianista, y no siendo en realidad nadie, era inaceptable que fuera ella, por medio de Bonaparte, quien gobernara el imperio, mientras su cobarde sobrino se le escondía a la corona debajo de la cama, encerrado en su alcoba de Miramar.

—¿De qué te ríes? —preguntó su hermana, quien acababa de entregarle su caballo a un sirviente y se aproximaba para sentarse a su lado.

—La víbora de Carlota llamaba a su fallecido hermano "Majestad" —dijo el príncipe—. Tú deberás seguir su ejemplo y dejar de tutearme.

—Ah, vaya. Ahora sé de qué te reías tan placenteramente. Aunque desglosas tus planes como la cosa más sencilla de hacer en este mundo, no olvides que los emperadores en México son los Habsburgo, no nosotros. Y recuerda que ya uno de ellos, Moctezuma III, gobernó siendo un completo idiota y no fue obligado a abdicar porque una mujer muy inteligente, también llamada Carlota, lo sostuvo en el trono valiéndose de mil maniobras. Y ésta no parece menos inteligente ni menos decidida que aquélla.

—Son otros tiempos.

—¿Y eso qué? Dime una cosa, hermano, ¿qué te asegura que Fernando Carlos va abdicar y va a señalarte como su sucesor? Es tímido, me consta. Cuando teníamos quince años lo miraba directamente a los ojos y lo hacía voltearse para otro lado. Me divertía tener ese poder sobre el hijo del emperador. Pero una cosa es que sea tímido y débil de carácter y otra que no se vaya a aferrar a su trono con uñas y dientes. Además, Bonaparte, tu jefe, estará siempre de su lado.

—Tal parece que no me quieres ver convertido en emperador —dijo el príncipe.

—Yo también puedo tener mis planes.

—¿Tú? Si te refieres a planes que tengan que ver con el futuro de México, te aclaro que aquello de que en la política hay mucho maquillaje es sólo una analogía. Tú no sabes nada. Deja de opinar tonterías.

—Es que... ¿no te parece que es muy peligroso eso de derribar a una familia del trono para colocar en su puesto a otra? Tal cosa puede desestabilizar a México, porque no es otra cosa que un golpe de Estado. Yo estaba pensando en algo menos peligroso para que nuestra familia forme parte de la monarquía.

—¿De qué hablas, loca caprichosa?

—De que soy la única mexicana que se puede casar con Fernando Carlos, sin que él altere la ley y sin que sus hijos dejen de ser Habsburgo. La Constitución dice claramente —añadió la princesa— que el heredero al trono deberá de ser el primer varón concebido dentro del matrimonio del emperador con una mujer no inferior. Como bien sabes, princesas de antiguos linajes sólo hay en Europa y nuestro tímido gobernante es capaz de morir soltero si ellas no vienen a buscarlo. Hace unos días, mientras cenaba con la duquesa Carlota, le hice ese comentario en broma, y ¿qué crees que me respondió, totalmente seria y meditabunda?

—No tengo la más remota idea —dijo el príncipe, visiblemente furioso.

—Sus palabras, sin alteración alguna, fueron éstas: "¿Y estarías dispuesta a casarte con él cuanto antes y a embarazarte no una sino varias veces, de manera que a los veinticinco años ya seas madre de tres hijos?"

—¡Maldita víbora! —dijo el príncipe.

-¿Quién, ella o yo?

—¡Las dos!, y dime, ¿qué le respondiste?

—Me reí de la forma más elegante que pude. Eso de los múltiples embarazos a capricho de Carlota no suena nada agradable. Además, sospecho que a Fernando Carlos hay que violarlo. No me lo imagino tomando la iniciativa, y la idea de forzarlo no me atrae tampoco, aunque quizás sea divertido, nunca se sabe. Pero sólo quería que supieras, querido hermano, que es más fácil que yo sea emperatriz a que tú seas emperador. Siempre va a ser menos costoso un matrimonio que un golpe de Estado, ¿no crees?

—Entiendo perfectamente lo que esa víbora quiere —dijo Iturbide—. Si su sobrino llega a abdicar, y ya para entonces tiene un hijo reconocido legalmente como un Habsburgo, así se trate de un bebé recién nacido, la constitución ordena que se forme una regencia presidida por el canciller del imperio, o por un hermano menor del emperador, que en este caso no existe, hasta que el niño tenga la mayoría de edad. Carlota pretende que si cae su sobrino, lo que indudablemente va a pasar, la familia Habsburgo no sea apartada del Imperio Mexicano. Quiere gobernar ella junto con Bonaparte, escudados en un niño durante dieciocho años. Qué mujer tan ambiciosa, pero ingenua. Se necesita ser muy idiota para creer que el débil mental de su sobrino va durar siquiera algunas semanas al mando del imperio. Yo no se lo pienso permitir.

—Yo no lo veo así —dijo la princesa—, estoy segura de que ella quiere que su sobrino gobierne. No es nada tonta, sabe que una regencia escudada en un niño no soportaría dieciocho años a los comunistas disfrazados de socialistas de Morador, que tanto anhelan adueñarse del poder. El pueblo quiere a un emperador, no a un regente. Eso está claro. Si Carlota está interesada en que Fernando Carlos se case cuanto antes y tenga hijos, es porque evidentemente quiere asegurar pronto la sucesión, y lograr que su sobrino deje de ser el único Habsburgo mexicano que queda con vida. Pero se nota claramente que ella quiere que él gobierne.

—Te equivocas. Lo que se nota es que no conoces a esa víbora. Además, tú no sabes nada de política.

—El que se equivoca eres tú. Estás subestimando demasiado a Fernando Carlos. Pretendes ir a humillarlo y a darle órdenes para que deje su cargo, cuando sabes muy bien que lo que estás obligado a decirle, en cuanto estés frente a él, es: "A las órdenes de Vuestra Majestad". No lo olvides, hermano, porque quizás él no tenga ningún reparo en recordarte que si nuestra familia ha gozado de tantos privilegios durante siglo y medio es gracias a los Habsburgo. Ya éramos unos exiliados sin fortuna en los Estados Unidos, y ellos nos trajeron de regreso, nos llenaron de títulos y de inmensas riquezas. Fernando Carlos tiene muchos motivos para reclamar nuestro agradecimiento. Ten eso bien claro cuando te reciba en el famoso despacho de los cuatro bustos.

Cripta Imperial de Guadalupe, enero de 2017

Fernando Carlos sintió una extraña sensación aquella fría noche, parecida a la nostalgia, al penetrar en la semioscuridad de la cripta neogótica, quizás porque, a fin de cuentas, estaba en familia. El ruido de sus zapatos rompía de forma irrespetuosa el silencio, tan asociado al justo reposo que merecían los emperadores que ya habían cumplido con su misión. Al centro había una fila formada por pares de tumbas, empezaba con las tumbas gemelas de Maximiliano *el Grande* y Carlota de Bélgica, y concluía con las que pertenecían a su recién fallecido padre y a su madre, Olga Romanov, muerta después del parto que lo había llevado a él a conocer la luz del sol. En medio se hallaban las tumbas de Moctezuma III y María Valeria de Austria, Agustín II y Josefina de Suecia, Maximiliano II y Guillermina de Prusia, y Maximiliano III y María Victoria de Saboya. Su expresión adoptó un aspecto extraño al notar que estaba de pie junto a la tumba de su padre, porque ese lugar precisamente era el que se hallaba destinado para él. Lo que no tenía idea era quién llegaría a ocupar el lugar inmediato a la tumba de su madre. No había pensado en casarse, pero como emperador estaba obligado a hacerlo, y como último Habsburgo mexicano con vida, su obligación era mayor todavía. Vio en un extremo la tumba de su tío bisabuelo, el archiduque Francisco José, hermano del emperador Maximiliano II, tumba totalmente sola, pese a que él había tenido esposa e hijos. Pero al haberse casado morganáticamente, sus descendientes y su esposa no fueron elevados a la categoría de archiduques de México, y perdieron el derecho a ser sepultados allí. Fernando Carlos sintió tristeza al recapacitar en que su querida tía, la duquesa Carlota, no compartiría esa cripta con su tan amado hermano, Maximiliano IV, ya que también se había casado morganáticamente y, al ser mujer, había dejado de ser archiduquesa; recibió un peor castigo que Francisco José solamente por su género. El emperador pensó que las leyes de la monarquía eran en muchos aspectos anticuadas e injustas, y que haría las reformas necesarias para que su tía, en caso de así desearlo, fuera sepultada en la cripta. Aunque quizás ella tenía en mente tomar el descanso eterno junto a su amado pianista, quien definitivamente no podía entrar allí.

Aquella era la noche que sucedió al día en que había tenido que tomar la difícil decisión del rescate en Egipto. A las diez, cuando su ayuda de cámara le había dejado un té junto a su cama, le ordenó con una voz ausente: "despiérteme a las tres y media", una orden habitual de los emperadores de México a sus ayudas de cámara, pero ésa era la primera vez que Fernando Carlos la daba en su vida. No obstante, aunque estaba a punto de acostarse a la hora ordinaria en un emperador, él no tenía sueño en ese momento. Lo que quería era salir a pasear por Aztlán, completamente solo.

Media hora más tarde, visiblemente preocupado llegó al castillo de Chapultepec el conde Andrássy, el jefe de la guardia secreta imperial, quien tenía la misión de impedir que cerca del emperador de México volaran incluso las moscas. Ya introducido en su habitación, el conde se dirigió a Fernando Carlos.

—Me informan que Su Majestad Imperial ha pedido una motocicleta, y que pretende bajar a la ciudad completamente solo.

—Así es, conde.

—No deseo de ninguna manera contradecir la órdenes de Su Majestad —dijo Andrássy—, pero, señor, mi misión es protegerlo, y sus deseos ponen en serio peligro el correcto desempeño de mis funciones.

—No se preocupe, conde, mi hermano alguna vez me enseñó a conducir una motocicleta. Recuerdo que no es tan difícil. Confío en no matarme.

—Majestad, le ruego que recapacite, si se empeña en la loca idea de la motocicleta, al menos permita que la guardia lo acompañe.

—Conde, me quedan claras sus buenas intenciones y se las agradezco, pero no tolero que mis órdenes sean desobedecidas. Y no lo tome como prepotencia de mi parte, sino que sería un pésimo emperador si lo hiciera. Así que en caso de que no me obedezca, tendré que buscar a alguien más para su puesto.

—Sus órdenes serán cumplidas, Majestad —dijo Andrássy—. Pero, por el amor de Dios, lleve un teléfono, y no dude en llamarme por cualquier cosa.

—Gracias, conde. En verdad estimo la lealtad con que hace su trabajo. Creo que usted será un buen confidente.

—Si Vuestra Majestad me honra con su confianza.

—Por favor, que no se enteren la duquesa o el canciller que he salido solo —dijo el emperador—. No quiero causar las mismas preocupaciones que causaría un niño.

—Como usted lo ordene, Majestad.

En cuanto la motocicleta de Fernando Carlos empezó a alejarse del Castillo, Andrássy llamó a uno de sus hombres.

—Que lo sigan a la distancia —ordenó—. Quizás me destituya si lo descubre, pero no puedo permitir de ninguna manera que el emperador corra el más mínimo peligro.

El primer informe que sus hombres le dieron al conde fue que Su Majestad se había detenido afuera de la Cripta Imperial de Guadalupe, y que había entrado a hacerles una visita a sus antepasados.

Fernando Carlos contempló por varios minutos la ya larga fila de seis emperadores que habían gobernado México desde la llegada de Maximiliano *el Grande*. Seis emperadores en siglo y medio evidenciaban el peso de la corona, puesto que ninguno había muerto ya siendo anciano. Algo más que le parecía muy extraño, y que volvió a su memoria en ese momento, era el hecho de que los Habsburgo habían llegado a un país donde los matrimonios se reproducían con una extraordinaria fertilidad que derivaba en abundancia de hijos y, cosa bastante rara, había llegado uno y después de siglo y medio solo quedaba uno. Ciertamente él no ignoraba que sus antepasados habían dejado bastardos repartidos en México que quizás en algunos casos incluso desconocían que eran descendientes por línea directa del emperador Carlos V, y que podían ser numerosos. Pero los emperadores mexicanos con sus esposas se habían reproducido bastante poco. Quizás se debía simplemente a la ausencia de amor. La monarquía mexicana conservaba aquella vieja tradición de la aristocracia de casarse para obtener un heredero legítimo e incuestionable, sin que importaran los sentimientos o la atracción. Fernando Carlos tenía bastante claro que sus padres no se habían amado, y él no quería un matrimonio así. Pero tampoco podía escaparse de su destino tan fácilmente.

—Quiero hablar con ustedes —dijo, e imaginó que seis emperadores habrían los ojos—. Quiero decirles que acepto quién soy. Ahora tengo bastante claro que soy Fernando Carlos José de Habsburgo y Lorena, miembro de la familia imperial más antigua del mundo y emperador de México. Toda mi vida, hasta hace apenas unos días, quise desentenderme de mi identidad. Yo no quería ser emperador, ni siquiera ministro, archiduque o general del ejército mexicano. Pensaba que serlo implicaba perder mi libertad, y no quería renunciar a ella por nada del mundo. Pero ahora entiendo perfectamente que en nuestra familia no existe la libertad, sólo existen las obligaciones. Al aceptar quién soy, acepto también que ya nunca en mi vida seré un hombre libre, que la paz de mi alma se ha marchado para siempre. No reniego de mi destino, y me gusten o no mis circunstancias, les juro que pondré lo mejor de mí para procurar el bienestar de nuestro pueblo, y que nunca tomaré una decisión sin antes pensar en las consecuencias que ésta tendrá sobre el destino de los mexicanos. Pero también les advierto que haré las cosas a mi manera, de tal forma que quizás algunas no les gusten. No es culpa mía, ustedes debieron tener más hijos, y entonces tal vez yo no me habría visto obligado a ponerme la corona. Si soy el último Habsburgo mexicano que queda con vida, los culpables son ustedes. Pero lo cierto es que ya no caben las lamentaciones, las cosas son como son, y ahora yo estoy al mando. No me critiquen, haga lo que haga, porque yo soy el emperador y ustedes son sólo miembros de mi familia. Cuando a ustedes les tocó gobernar, exigieron de la familia total sumisión, y ahora yo se las exijo a ustedes. Si no quisieron hacer ninguna clase de reformas, está bien, lo acepto como cualquier miembro de la familia acepta las decisiones del emperador. Pero ahora yo soy el emperador, y si considero que la monarquía tiene que actualizarse, acéptelo, puesto que se trata de una decisión del emperador. Los demás mexicanos tienen el derecho de cuestionarme, pero ustedes no. Tan sólo pueden, si es que les está permitido, rogar a Dios por mí. Y el día que venga a reunirme con ustedes para siempre, no les aceptaré ningún reproche, porque habré puesto lo mejor de mí para cumplir con la responsabilidad que tiene nuestra familia al mando del imperio, y sin duda, como ustedes, me habré equivocado, pero también habré dado todo de mí por los mexicanos, y eso y sólo eso es lo que se le exige a un emperador.

Dio varios pasos a un lado de las tumbas de los emperadores, mirándolas de una en una hasta llegar a la de Maximiliano *el Grande*. Luego se giró para ver la tumba de su hermano, la contempló por un par de minutos, mientras impedía con todas sus fuerzas que dos lágrimas huyeran de sus ojos. Cuando caminaba hacia la salida, habría jurado que los seis emperadores se habían puesto de pie para darle su bendición. Era tanta la seguridad que tenía de que eso estaba pasando realmente, que decidió no darse la vuelta, para no faltarles al respeto.

Varios minutos después estaba llegando al centro histórico de Aztlán. Pese a ser una de las capitales más pobladas del mundo, aquel martes por la noche el tráfico le permitía transitar libremente. Cuando llegó a la hermosa plaza Moctezuma III, se detuvo para contemplar un poco aquel entorno del que se decía que Maximiliano *el Grande* se había ocupado de cada detalle. Lo único que no había modificado habían sido las torres y la fachada de la Catedral, pero a un edificio anexo, el llamado Sagrario, lo mandó demoler para que la plaza estuviera dividida por dos ejes que le dieran más amplitud y modernidad. Respecto al palacio Imperial, había visto en fotografías su fachada anterior al imperio, alargada, monótona y de poca jerarquía. Maximiliano *el Grande* la había mandado modificar drásticamente, dotándola de un eclecticismo neogótico poco armonioso pero imponente. Desde allí despachaban los ministros, y comúnmente el emperador sólo bajaba de Chapultepec para eventos importantes. Tanto le había gustado el castillo ya terminado al primer emperador, que los otros cinco habían gobernado desde Chapultepec y el palacio Imperial lo destinaron para que albergara funciones más administrativas que protocolarias. Los líderes extranjeros eran comúnmente recibidos en el castillo, salvo en ocasiones en que había alguna disputa diplomática, entonces eran recibidos en el palacio Imperial, debido a que los Habsburgo consideraban que Chapultepec era su hogar, y no permitían la visita allí de alguien que les resultara desagradable o que consideraran que no era amigo de México.

Cuando Fernando Carlos se quitó el casco, al centro de la plaza, en ningún momento pensó que alguien pudiera reconocerlo. Las personas pasaban a su lado sin siquiera verle la cara, y él desde niño había aprendido a honrar la discreción con cada uno de sus movimientos. No era la clase de hombre que otras personas quisieran ver, y menos de noche. Volvió a subir a su motocicleta y se puso en marcha nuevamente. A espaldas de la catedral dio vuelta en la calle General Mejía, y al llegar a la calle Félix Eloin la maniobra fue precipitada, debido a que decidió dar vuelta allí en el último momento. La motocicleta derrapó y el ilustre tripulante salió rodando encima de los adoquines. Por fortuna, ningún vehículo le paso las ruedas en la cabeza porque esa parte del centro estaba poco transitada, pero tampoco nadie fue en su auxilio porque los miembros de la guardia secreta imperial se habían quedado atrás debido a la distancia que guardaban para que no descubriera su presencia. Cuando Fernando Carlos empezó a recobrar el conocimiento, apenas un minuto después, vio que una joven morena de ojos extrañamente hermosos le levantaba la cabeza.

–¡Oye, amigo!, ¿estás, bien?

–Sí –dijo, él, recordando incluso quién era–. Creo que sí.

–¿No te rompiste nada?

–Me duelen varias partes del cuerpo, pero creo que son sólo golpes superficiales.

–¿Te quieres levantar? Te ayudo.

El emperador tomó los hombros de la joven, y ella rodeó su espalda con sus brazos para ayudarlo. A él le hubiera gustado que aquel momento durara al menos una hora. Era ése el contacto más cercano que había tenido con una mujer en su vida adulta.

–¿Te puedes sostener solo? –dijo ella.

–¡No!

–Yo creo que sí. ¿Qué te parece si me sueltas?

–Tienes razón, sí pude sostenerme solo.

–Ya ves. ¿Te ayudo a levantar tu moto?

–No te molestes, yo lo hago.

–No es molestia –dijo ella, mientras la levantaba–. Es bonita, y sospecho que muy cara.

–Es una herencia de mi hermano –dijo el emperador.

–¿Tu hermano murió? –Preguntó ella, girándose para verlo.

Fernando Carlos se quitó el caso, pero quizás debido a que la iluminación allí era escasa, ella no dio muestras de reconocerlo, y como aún no había dado ningún discurso por televisión, era normal que tampoco le dijera nada su timbre de voz.

—Sí —dijo el emperador, visiblemente triste—, mi hermano murió hace un par de meses.

—Lo siento mucho.

—Gracias. ¿Cómo te llamas?

—Tengo el nombre femenino más popular en México —dijo la joven.

—Ah, mucho gusto, Guadalupe.

—No, Carlota. No hay una familia mexicana que no le rinda homenaje a la antigua emperatriz. Aunque yo no tengo ningún rasgo europeo, mi abuelo era haitiano y llevo su única herencia en la piel. Y tú, ¿cómo te llamas?

—Me llamo…, puedes llamarme Fer.

—¿Fernando? —dijo Carlota.

—Sí.

—Vaya, tú también llevas un nombre imperial.

—Cierto…

—¿Y en tu familia te llaman Fer?

—Me llamaban —reconoció el emperador—. ¿Y a qué te dedicas?

—Trabajo de mesera en un restaurante, en la tarde y noche, y en el día doy clases de baile. Tengo dos empleos.

—Qué bien. ¿Y a dónde te dirigías?

—A mi casa —dijo ella, sin mucho ánimo—. Acabo de salir de mi segundo trabajo, hace apenas unos minutos.

—¿Y en qué viajas?

—Caminando. A esta hora solo hay taxis, y como sólo hago media hora caminando a mi casa, prefiero ahorrarme el costo, de lo contrario no tendría sentido este empleo. La capital, como bien sabes, es muy segura. Se puede caminar sola por las noches, incluso siendo mujer.

—Si mi motocicleta arranca nuevamente, ¿me permites llevarte a tu casa? —dijo el emperador.

—No tengo muchas ganas de llegar a mi casa justo ahora. ¿Qué te parece si vamos a un parque, y nos sentamos a platicar? Tu charla me agrada, Fer.

—¿Por qué?

—Porque estás triste, como yo. Supongo que tu tristeza es por tu hermano, la mía es por mi papá.

—Lo lamento mucho —dijo el emperador—. ¿Cuándo murió?

—Ya pasó un año, pero a veces me siento como si sólo hubiera pasado un día.

—Nos vamos —dijo él, tendiéndole la mano.

La motocicleta arrancó y fueron a un parque cercano, mientras los miembros de la guardia imperial, multiplicados, daban vueltas como locos por todo Aztlán y el conde Andrássy ladraba órdenes con un teléfono en cada oído. Fernando Carlos eligió la banca donde la iluminación era más escasa, le gustaba que ella no lo hubiera reconocido.

—¿No te da miedo estar sola conmigo? —dijo el emperador—. Soy un desconocido.

—Aparte de baile he practicado judo y kick boxing —dijo ella—, y soy casi tan alta como tú. Mejor cuéntame a qué te dedicas.

—Tengo un trabajo de oficina —dijo el emperador—, y no quiero aburrirte explicándote detalladamente lo que hago todos los días.

—¿Trabajo de oficina? Te ves muy joven para ya haber estudiado una carrera. ¿Cuántos años tienes?

—Casi veintiuno.

—Yo ya los cumplí. Razón de más para que me tú me tengas miedo a mí, soy mayor que tú. ¿Y cómo es que tienes ese trabajo siendo tan joven? Por tu ropa, sospecho que tu familia no se preocupa por el fin de mes.

—¿Y eso te incomoda?

—No, ¿y a ti te incomoda hablar conmigo?

—Me gusta hablar contigo.

Ella sonrió.

—¿Y por qué no estudias?, ¿acaso la posición de tus padres te garantizará un trabajo siempre?

—Sí —dijo el emperador—, ya tengo el trabajo asegurado de por vida. Pero no tengo padres, ellos murieron.

—Vaya, qué triste. Tus padres y tu hermano…

—Sí, es triste. ¿Y tú dejaste de estudiar?

—Interrumpí mis estudios un año —respondió Carlota—, para tener dos empleos y ahorrar, así cuando vuelva a la universidad, podre arreglármelas con un solo empleo y mis ahorros.

—¿Y qué estudias? —dijo el emperador.

—Historia del arte. ¿Y tú no crees que debes estudiar algo? Aún eres muy joven.

—Pues ya he aprendido algunas cosas, y para las que me faltan por aprender no hay universidad.

—¿Y con quién vives?

—Con… mi tía.

—¿Y te llevas bien con ella?

—Es la mejor tía del mundo.

—Qué bueno que la tengas —dijo la joven, sonriendo—. ¿Y cómo se llama?

El emperador también sonrió.

—Hace poco tú dijiste algo así como que en todas las familias mexicanas hay una Carlota.

—Ah, qué casualidad.

Fernando Carlos estaba preocupándose un poco. La joven no era idiota, y ya con tantos datos que le había dicho sobre él, en cualquier momento descubriría quién era.

—¿Y tú con quién vives? —le preguntó.

—Con mi mamá y mis dos hermanos. Ellos son menores que yo. Ahora comprenderás porque me preocupo tanto por el dinero.

—Sí, te entiendo —dijo el emperador, algo incómodo porque él jamás se había preocupado por eso—. ¿Y cómo se llaman?

—Mi mamá se llama Alma, y mis hermanos David y el más pequeño Maximiliano. También allí mi familia le rinde homenaje a la monarquía.

—Vaya —dijo él, sonrojado.

—Apuesto que tú también tienes un pariente que se llama Maximiliano.

—Eh…, sí.

—¿De veras?, ¿y cuál es el parentesco?

El emperador dudó unos segundos, después se apresuró a decir:

—Mi papá y mi hermano, ambos llevaban ese nombre.

—Tu papá… Un momento, tienes una tía llamada Carlota, tu papá se llamaba Maximiliano, y está muerto, igual que tu hermano, quien murió hace dos meses, y además trabajas en una oficina haciendo cosas que no me quieres decir. ¿Tú eres…? —y al decir estas palabras, ella le iluminó el rostro con su teléfono—. ¡Dios! Pero…, Majestad, ¿qué hace usted aquí?

—Es un país libre, y sígueme tuteando, por favor.

—¡No! ¿Cómo cree que lo voy a tutear? Estoy segura que ni siquiera su tía lo hace. Majestad, tengo que irme…, ya es tarde y tengo que llegar a mi casa.

—Quedamos en que yo te llevaría.

—Majestad, por favor, esto es muy incómodo.

—No te dejaré ir sola a tu casa.

—No se preocupe, Majestad, de verdad —dijo ella, nerviosa—, como usted sabe, la ciudad es muy segura.

—Te preocupaste por mí cuando estaba en el suelo, llevarte a tu casa es lo menos que puedo hacer.

—Majestad, cualquiera se preocuparía por alguien que se ha caído de una moto. Se hace por instinto. Por favor, no insista, yo me puedo ir sola a mi casa.

—Dejaré de insistir si me tuteas otra vez.

—Está bien —dijo Carlota, más nerviosa aún—. Fer, me tengo que ir a mi casa. Ya es tarde. Cuídate.

—Si ya me tuteaste —dijo el emperador—, eso quiere decir que aceptas que soy el mismo hombre con el que estabas platicando, el que te llevaría a tu casa.

—Majestad, ¿acaso los emperadores no tienen palabra?

—Tengo palabra, y por ello te prometo que pase lo que pase te llevaré a tu casa. No corres peligro conmigo, sabes judo y kick boxing, y yo apenas estoy aprendiendo a gobernar.

—Majestad, el lugar donde yo vivo no creo que le vaya a agradar, además de que no puedo tomarlo a usted por la espalda. Me resulta imposible. Creo que la Constitución reserva una declaración de guerra en caso de que un presidente extranjero se atreva a darle una palmadita en el hombro, y supongo que a mí me encerrarían veinte años.

—Es probable que haya un artículo en ese sentido —dijo él, sonriendo—, pero si me vuelves a tutear, te garantizo un indulto.

—No lo voy a convencer, ¿verdad?

—Vengo de una familia de necios.

—Vamos pues.

—Ponte mi casco —le pidió el emperador—. La noche ya está más fría.

Ella pensó en negarse, argumentando que si se accidentaban y él moría ya no habría quien gobernara, pero se sentía tan incómoda que prefirió no decir nada para que la dejara cuanto antes en su casa. Cuando por fin llegaron, Carlota se quitó el casco y se bajó lo más pronto posible, con la intención de meterse a su casa.

—Gracias, Majestad —dijo despacio, para que su madre no la oyera y pensara que se había vuelto loca.

—¿Te puedo pedir un favor? —dijo el emperador.

—Sí —dijo ella, dudando.

—Me puedes tutear otra vez.

—¿Y me promete irse?

—Palabra de emperador —dijo él en voz baja.

—Gracias por traerme, Fer. Eres buena persona...

—¿De verdad lo crees?

—Prometió que se iría.

—Vamos a hacer un trato.

—¿Qué clase de trato?

—Si de aquí en adelante me tuteas siempre, prometo dejar de ser tan necio contigo.

—¡Majestad, pero si no hay motivo para que nos volvamos a ver! Seguramente yo a usted sí, en las noticias, pero usted a mí no.

—¿No te gustaría que nos volviéramos a ver? —dio el emperador, mirándola a los ojos.

—Quizás sí, Majestad, pero no es correcto. Y cumpla lo que me dijo, ya váyase.

—Si me tuteas otra vez, te prometo que me iré en seguida.

—Ya vete, Fer, por favor.

—Nos vemos —dijo él, y arrancó antes de que ella dijera algo. Cuando Carlota vio desaparecer la motocicleta, notó que tenía el casco del emperador en sus manos.

—Ojalá que no se vuelva a caer. Sin el casco seguro se mata.

Mientras conducía, el emperador pensaba que a fin de cuentas el hecho de que una mujer lo tratara de igual a igual, sin que se notara su rango, había resultado ser el antídoto para su timidez. O era eso o sencillamente Carlota lo había curado. Deseaba volver a verla cuanto antes, de ser posible, al siguiente día, o ese mismo día, puesto que ya había pasado desde hacía mucho la media noche. Cuando ya iba en el Paseo de Juárez, a tan sólo unos minutos de Chapultepec, un oficial de tránsito, también en una motocicleta, lo alcanzó y le marcó el alto. Cuando el emperador se detuvo, el oficial hizo lo mismo detrás de él, bajó de su motocicleta y empezó a hablarle.

—Buenas noches, caballero, soy el oficial Benito Rueda, oficial del departamento de conducta vial. Puede corroborar mi nombre en la placa que llevo en el pecho. Le he marcado el alto porque no lleva un casco puesto. Y como no veo ninguno en su motocicleta, no puedo dejarlo continuar. Tendrá que irse en un taxi, si no dispone de dinero yo lo llevaré a su casa, pero el costo del traslado se sumará al costo de la infracción que va a pagar por no traer casco. En tanto que su motocicleta, podrá pasar mañana desde las ocho por ella a un centro de detención de vehículos que yo le indicaré. ¿Tiene alguna duda?

—No oficial, ninguna. Olvidé mi casco hace unos minutos. No era mi intención cometer esta falta. Le aseguro que no había notado que no lo traía hasta que usted me detuvo.

—Sí, suele pasar. ¿Me puede permitir su permiso para conducir motocicletas?

—Francamente, oficial, no tengo. Es la primera vez que manejo una motocicleta en mucho tiempo.

—De acuerdo. Serán dos infracciones las que pague. ¿Enterado?

—Sí, oficial.

—Me puede permitir cualquier otra identificación.

—No llevo ninguna identificación, oficial.

—Entonces dícteme su nombre, y usaremos el número de matrícula de su motocicleta como referencia —dijo el oficial—. ¿Su nombre es...?

—Fernando Carlos José.

—¿Y su apellido? —preguntó el oficial, cuando terminó de anotar el nombre.

—De Habsburgo y Lorena o de México. Puede poner cualquiera de los dos.

—Mira, cabrón, no estoy de humor...

El oficial por primera vez puso atención al rostro del motociclista que había detenido.

—¡Mama Majestad..., perdone mi torpeza, Majestad, juro por mi madre muerta que no lo había reconocido, y como aún no nos es familiar su voz!

—No se preocupe, oficial, está usted haciendo su trabajo —dijo el emperador—, y lo hace muy bien, lo felicito, estoy orgulloso de usted. Le decía que puede poner de Habsburgo y Lorena o de México, ambos funcionan como mi apellido.

—Su Majestad me honra no enojándose conmigo, y disculpando tan amablemente mi torpeza. Pero de ninguna manera voy a infraccionar a nuestro emperador.

—Por favor, oficial, sólo cumpla con su trabajo. Lo hace usted muy bien.

—Majestad, por favor, todos sabemos que se levanta diariamente a las tres treinta de la madrugada para quebrarse la cabeza todo el día y hacer de éste un mejor país. De ninguna manera voy a venir yo a complicarle la vida con una infracción. Esto podría salir en los diarios, puede haber en el departamento algún perro malagradecido que lo divulgue, y yo no me lo perdonaría nunca.

—Si eso pasa, bien ganado me lo tengo. Usted no sería culpable —dijo el emperador.

—Le suplico que no insista, Majestad. Es bien sabido que los oficiales del departamento de conducta vial de Aztlán jamás se corrompen ni dejan de cumplir con su deber, puesto que cada infracción que levantan es en beneficio de la ciudadanía, pero por una vez que yo falte a la tradición del gremio al que pertenezco, no creo que se nos caiga el cielo encima.

—Está bien, oficial, es usted tan buen mexicano que no me atrevo a seguir contradiciéndolo.

—Su Majestad me honra hasta con el privilegio de platicar conmigo. Si usted me lo permite, le confieso que tenía mucho miedo por pensar que usted no iba a venir y se quedaría en Miramar. Fui el mexicano más feliz al leer en los diarios que usted ya estaba en Chapultepec, en el despacho de los cuatro bustos, dando las órdenes que hacían falta para que aquí todo marche bien. Ya con usted son tres emperadores a los que sirvo, Majestad. Cuando entré a este trabajo, gobernaba su ilustre abuelo, Maximiliano III. Qué gran señor. Y siempre que he tenido un problema, me ha levantado el ánimo el hecho de saber que el emperador, ya fuera su abuelo, su padre y ahora usted, se preocupa diariamente por nosotros. Eso me hace pensar que mi problema realmente no es tan grande, porque pase lo pase, estoy siempre protegido por mi emperador.

Fernando Carlos estaba tan conmovido que no sabía qué decir.

—Majestad —continuó el oficial—, perdone usted la pregunta, pero ¿dónde están los miembros de la guardia secreta imperial que deben protegerlo?

—Me imagino que dormidos, decidí salir solo.

—¡Pero cómo! Eso es inconcebible, el emperador tiene que estar protegido. Majestad, usted sabe que los miembros del departamento de conducta vial no estamos armados, ya que Aztlán es una de las ciudades más seguras del mundo, pero aun sin estar armado, permítame escoltarlo hasta Chapultepec, y si acaso un perro extranjero atentara contra mi emperador, yo sería el hombre más feliz del mundo rompiéndole todos los huesos.

—Acepto la compañía de tan honorable escolta —dijo el emperador.

—Majestad, mi casco, úselo, por favor. Si yo muero, mi mujer tendrá una pensión segura, pero si a usted le pasa algo, México ya no tendrá quien lo gobierne y muchos moriremos de pena.

Cuando el emperador se puso el casco de aquel hombre, sintió que estaba recibiendo la más codiciada de las condecoraciones militares.

Minutos después ya estaban en el patio del castillo de Chapultepec, rodeados por miembros de la guardia imperial y ante la sorpresa del conde Andrássy, quien parecía que acababa de resucitar.

—Le devuelvo su casco —dijo Fernando Carlos al oficial.

—Majestad, puedo pedirle un favor.

—El que usted quiera. Será un honor darle gusto.

—Verá usted, Majestad, violé el código de ética al no infraccionarlo, y además no usé mi casco en el trayecto hasta acá, cuando los oficiales debemos dar el ejemplo a la ciudadanía. Por tan graves faltas, yo debería renunciar. A menos que... que Su Majestad Imperial me indulte.

—De acuerdo —dijo el emperador, sonriendo—. Oficial Benito Rueda, yo le concedo el perdón. ¿Quiere que lo protocolicemos en documentos oficiales con el sello imperial y mi firma, o que quede entre nosotros?

—Que quede entre nosotros, Majestad. Será un honor para mí tener un secreto en común con mi emperador. He notado que ha dicho mi nombre sin leer nada en mi pecho, mirándome a los ojos. ¿Acaso Su Majestad se memorizó mi nombre?

—No podría ser emperador si olvidara el nombre de un buen mexicano.

—Su Majestad Imperial me ha indultado, ha memorizado mi nombre, y ahora pone su mano en mi hombro. Mis nietos no me lo van a creer nunca.

—Si no le creen —dijo el emperador—, tráigalos aquí de visita, yo con gusto les afirmaré que todo es cierto.

Cuando el viejo oficial se alejó de Chapultepec, estaba llorando, y justo cuando pasaba junto a la estatua ecuestre de Maximiliano *el Grande*, gritó con todas sus fuerzas:

—¡Dios salve al emperador!

Algunos minutos más tarde, Fernando Carlos estuvo de regreso en su recamara. Fue a su ventana, a ver las luces de la ciudad. Creía que podía ubicar desde allí el punto exacto donde vivía Carlota. Sus deseos de volverla a ver y de que ella lo tuteara ya se habían vuelto más intensos. En ese instante se encendieron las luces de su recamara.

—Ya es hora de levantarse, Maje…

—Sí, lo sé —dijo el emperador a su ayuda de cámara.

—Majestad, está usted despierto, y vestido.

—Prepáreme el baño, por favor, tengo mucho trabajo que hacer el día de hoy, y quiero empezar cuanto antes.

—A las órdenes de Vuestra Majestad.

Diario de la emperatriz Carlota de México, 20 de diciembre de 1871

Últimamente he tenido poco tiempo ya no sólo para escribir en mi diario, sino incluso para mantener activa mi correspondencia con mis seres queridos en Europa. Son tantas las obligaciones que ha puesto en mis manos la Providencia en bien de todos los mexicanos, que tengo que sacrificar a ellas incluso los más pequeños placeres de que una emperatriz puede disponer. Sin embargo, hoy he decidido robarle unos minutos a mis obligaciones porque ocurrió un suceso digno de hacerle mención: llegó a Aztlán el exemperador Napoleón III, junto con su esposa y su hijo. Aunque ahora sólo se trata de un pobre hombre que al verle me ha causado lástima, el emperador le dio un trato de igual a igual, envió a Veracruz al bravo mariscal del imperio Tomás Mejía junto con una numerosa comitiva, para que Napoleón fuera recibido como si aún se hallara al mando del imperio francés. Incluso pudo ir a recibirlo él personalmente sino fuera porque me empeñé en convencerlo de que ese mismo hombre nos abandonó a nuestra suerte hace apenas cinco años, sin importarle si los juaristas nos fusilaban a ambos.

Cuando por fin estuvieron los tres ante nuestra presencia aquí en el castillo, debo decir que tanto Napoleón como Eugenia me causaron una triste sorpresa. Parecen fantasmas de lo que fueron, están tan desfigurados que yo me pregunté: "¿dónde quedaron esos emperadores que prestaron su belleza al gran Winterhalter para hacerles tan hermosas pinturas?, ¿acaso estas dos personillas tan insignificantes fueron las que apenas ayer dominaron el imperio que alguna vez perteneció a Napoleón *el Grande*?".

Al ver frente al emperador a ese hombrecillo triste y lloroso, el contraste era tan radical que juro que Su Majestad no opaca tanto al más enfermizo de sus jardineros, con los que tanto disfruta hablar por horas. Napoleón está totalmente envejecido, incluso pareciera que en cualquier momento se puede caer al suelo muerto. Mientras que el emperador, a pesar de todas las preocupaciones que tuvo que soportar antes de la consolidación del imperio, está mejor que nunca. Si bien es cierto que su calvicie ya es bastante visible, conserva la apariencia de un redentor, su juventud no ha desaparecido por completo, y por el contrario se une a los rasgos propios de su rango y su estirpe y todo ello lo engrandece. En tanto que Napoleón no tiene siquiera de dónde echar mano para exhibir una figura que al menos inspire un poco de respeto. Qué gran diferencia con aquel hombre poderoso y astuto que fuimos a visitar cuando aceptamos la corona de México, qué cruelmente castiga la Providencia la cobardía de aquéllos a quienes ha concedido enormes responsabilidades y las abandonan a causa de la debilidad de su carácter. El emperador lo llamo *Sire* y el hombrecillo negó con la cabeza y se echó a llorar. ¡Llorar como un niño el heredero de Napoleón *el Grande*! Juro que ni en mis peores pesadillas llegué a imaginar tal cosa.

A pesar de que cuenta con bastantes años menos que su esposo, Eugenia también ha perdido toda su juventud y con ello su gran belleza. Es una típica matrona de la decadente España que lo peor que podría hacer es engordar más, para dar el aspecto de una cocinera. Por la tarde la recibí en privado, y tuvo el atrevimiento de decirme que ellos esperan de nosotros el pago por habernos facilitado la corona de México. Me enfurecí tanto que tuve que recordarle su abandono tan ruin y mezquino, y fui muy clara al decirle que si ellos gozarán en delante de la hospitalidad del Imperio Mexicano se debe únicamente a la bondad con que se conduce el emperador, y no porque tengamos una deuda de gratitud con ellos, ya que si bien por ellos nos fue señalado el camino a nuestra actual posición, nosotros tuvimos que pelear para consolidarnos con las mismas desventajas que un náufrago trata de sobrevivir en una isla desierta. Enojada, con el típico carácter español, me dijo que conservan la invitación de mi querida prima la reina Victoria para vivir el tiempo que deseen bajo la protección de la corona británica.

Hasta este momento nuestra charla se había desarrollado en francés, y no por iniciativa mía, sino porque de ella fueron las primeras palabras. Pero fue tanta mi indignación que tuve que decirle en español: "Señora, usted es española, yo soy mexicana, y estamos en México. ¿No le parece ridículo que hablemos en francés, ya incluso como un homenaje al imperio del que a ustedes los han echado y que nunca van a recuperar? Por otro lado, si tienen la invitación de mi prima Victoria para residir de forma permanente en Inglaterra, le aclaro de una buena vez que el Imperio Mexicano nos los tiene en calidad de prisioneros. Ante mis palabras, la arrogancia española se esfumó de su rostro y la anciana se echó a llorar. Quizás me excedí un poco, pero ella fue la que se propuso llevarme al límite de mi paciencia.

También por la tarde el emperador firmó el reconocimiento por parte del Imperio Mexicano del título de príncipe de Bonaparte para ese bello joven que ya nunca será Napoleón IV. Parece estar dotado de una valentía extraordinaria y de una inteligencia por encima de lo común. Nos ha expresado su intención de entrar a formar parte del ejército imperial mexicano, para tener la oportunidad siquiera alguna vez de emular las proezas de su tío abuelo protegiendo nuestra hermosa bandera del águila y la serpiente coronadas. Quizás a él sí le saquemos en un futuro algún provecho, mientras que a los otros dos, a los ancianos, tendremos que mantenerlos hasta que se mueran sin esperar nada de ellos.

Castillo de Chapultepec, enero de 2017

—¿Te molesta que te llame Fer, y no te hable de usted o te diga Majestad…?

—No, al contrario. Me resulta reconfortante que por primera vez en varios días alguien que está frente a mí no empiece diciendo: "A las órdenes de Vuestra Majestad". Esas palabras tan solo me recuerdan lo sólo que estoy.

—Pues te agradezco que me recibas, tomando en cuenta lo ocupado que también estás —dijo Ana María de Iturbide—. Hace mucho que no entraba aquí, tu padre me intimidaba. Pero es una habitación agradable, muy agradable. Y dime, ya que eres un emperador algo fuera de lo común, ¿no piensas hacer algunos cambios? No sé, quizás quitar uno de esos cuatro bustos y poner el tuyo, por ejemplo, o añadir un toque más contemporáneo, que le dé un aire de juventud.

—No —dijo Fernando Carlos—, este despacho se quedará tal como está. Si mi hijo desea hacerle cambios, ya será decisión suya.

—¿Piensas tener un hijo? —dijo la princesa, sonriendo.

—Casi cualquier hombre en algún momento de su vida desea tener hijos. Además, es una de mis obligaciones como emperador. La continuidad del imperio depende de ello.

—Bueno, me imagino que estás hablando de un proyecto muy a futuro, porque aún estás muy joven para casarte y ser padre de una familia.

—Supongo que mi situación es diferente. En casos como el mío, no importa la juventud —respondió el emperador.

—Me vas a hacer pensar que ya tienes una novia —dijo la princesa—. ¿Acaso conociste a alguien de la realeza italiana en estos dos años?

—Ana María…

—Sólo Ana, por favor. No me gusta que me llamen María. Las vírgenes ya pasaron de moda.

—También los emperadores, y yo sigo aquí.

—Te ves muy seguro sentado en esa legendaria silla, te noto demasiado diferente a la última vez. Aunque físicamente no te pareces mucho a tu padre, sí pareces todo un emperador. —la princesa sonrió—. Cuando éramos niños fuimos buenos amigos, pero después te volviste muy tímido, más o menos a los trece años, incluso me dejaste de hablar. ¿Por qué lo hiciste, Fer?, ¿acaso me tenías miedo? Eso me parecía cuando desviabas la mirada.

—Es verdad, te tenía miedo —dijo el emperador.

—¿Y por qué? —dijo ella, sonriendo maliciosamente.

—Porque empezaste a gustarme.

Fernando Carlos hablaba sin poner mucha atención, como si su mente se hallara en ese momento en otro lado, y sus respuestas no contenían emociones de ningún tipo, tan sólo eran palabras sin el menor mensaje oculto.

—¿Y ya no te gusto?

—Les gustas a todos los hombres de México. ¿Qué más da si también me gustas a mí?

—Supongo que eso fue un sí —dijo la princesa.

—Supongo lo mismo.

—Es agradable gustarle a un emperador. Pero hace unos momentos evadiste mi pregunta, no me has dicho si...

—No, Ana, no tengo ninguna novia en Italia, ni en ninguna otra parte de Europa.

—Eso me indica que tengo el camino libre —dijo ella.

La princesa notó que la enorme timidez que había caracterizado a Fernando Carlos ya no estaba. Se había marchado, y quizás para siempre. Su rostro no reflejaba emociones, realmente parecía lo que era, y eso de alguna manera la molestaba, ya que le habría gustado tener más poder sobre él.

—No sé realmente qué decirte al respecto —fue su respuesta.

—Mi hermano se va a enojar cuando sepa que me recibiste primero que a él —dijo ella, cambiando el tema.

—Dile que me disculpe. Tengo que leer muchos documentos y reflexionar sobre todos ellos, antes de empezar a recibir a mis ministros. De lo contrario no sabría qué decirles. Pero ya casi termino, tan sólo demoraré un par de días más. Mientras tanto, el príncipe Bonaparte se está ocupando de atender todos los informes que vienen de los ministerios. Es un hombre de mi total confianza.

—De cualquier forma no te preocupes por hacer enojar a mi hermano, siempre lo está.

—No me preocupo por ello en lo más mínimo. ¿Y te llevas bien con él?

—En lo que cabe. Continuamente amenaza con recortarme los privilegios si no me porto como él quiere. Ignora que mi trabajo como modelo me da la posibilidad de vivir cómodamente sin su ayuda. Ése es su problema, cree que todos dependen o deben depender de él, y cuando no es así se enfurece.

—Deberías llevarlo con un psicólogo.

—La idea es buena, pero no creo que quiera. Te ves cansado, Fer —dijo la princesa—. Espero que no te vuelvas un adicto al trabajo, como tu padre. Pareciera que pasaste una pésima noche.

—En realidad pasé una noche extraordinaria —dijo el emperador.

—¿Dormiste bien?

—No dormí nada.

—Me estás haciendo que piense mal de ti.

—Tenías algo importante que decirme…

—Ah, sí. Vine a invitarte a salir. ¿Qué te parece si nos escapamos un fin de semana a nuestra casa en la sierra de Chihuahua? Te va a gustar, el paisaje es hermoso, y el frio de esta época es ideal para pasar veladas muy agradables. ¿Qué me dices?

—Acepto la invitación, pero debemos de posponer ese viaje. Tengo demasiado trabajo, y mis funciones acaban de empezar. Sería absurdo que ya tan pronto me tomara un fin de semana de descanso. Quizás dentro de unos meses.

—Eso fue un no muy largo, Fer —dijo la princesa—, y no me gusta que me desprecien.

—No lo tomes así. Envidio la libertad que tú disfrutas, y que para mí se ha ido para siempre.

—¿Y no puedes dejar a cargo a Bonaparte, y llevar contigo unas cuantas carpetas que podrás analizar mientras yo salgo a cabalgar?

—No, lo siento. Mis obligaciones no conceden ese tipo de libertades. Soy un emperador, no un presidente.

—De acurdo, Majestad, a vuestras órdenes.

—Me alegro que lo entiendas, Ana —dijo el emperador.

—¿No te molestó que hablara con apego al protocolo?

—Hazlo como te sientas más cómoda.

—Pues sí que has cambiado, Fer. Pronto será tu cumpleaños, ¿qué tienes pensado hacer?

—En lo íntimo nada, aún estoy de luto. Sólo participaré en el desfile militar.

—¿Qué te parece una cena, solos tú y yo? Porque me imagino que sí te alimentas.

—Está bien.

—Qué emocionado te has visto, Fer. Sabes, no estoy acostumbrada a invitar, sino a que me inviten, y también a ver que los hombres casi se mueran de alegría cuando acepto.

—Gracias por visitarme, Ana. Después definimos el lugar de la cena, ¿de acuerdo?

—Mejor de una vez ¿Qué te parece en mi departamento? –preguntó la princesa–. Supongo que, como tu padre, te inclinas por las cosas discretas.

—Está bien. Ahora, si no te molesta…

—Sí, lo entiendo. Tienes que arreglar la vida de doscientos sesenta millones de personas.

—Con no complicárselas me doy por bien servido.

—Hasta pronto, Fer. Y ve pensando qué me vas a pedir de regalo de cumpleaños –dijo la princesa, y se dirigió a la puerta, justo cuando el emperador ya tenía una carpeta abierta en sus manos.

Llevaba toda la mañana analizando documentos referentes a infinidad de problemas que aquejaban al imperio, relacionados con la situación de los internos en las cárceles, el estancamiento del sistema educativo, los altos impuestos que pagaba la población, las posibles irregularidades en la administración de los departamentos, los problemas en la frontera sur, siempre llena de emigrantes dispuestos a entrar a territorio mexicano, el gasto excesivo que significaba tener a uno de los ejércitos más grandes del mundo, lo costoso que salía el salario de todos los miembros del clero, que era pagado por el Estado, y una larga lista de etcéteras. El emperador trabajaba a la manera de sus antepasados, leía y leía documentos, y subrayaba párrafos con un color de acuerdo a la importancia que les consideraba. Su padre lo que hacía después era dictar las instrucciones que creía pertinentes, pero él aún no había llegado a esa etapa, primero quería comprender en su totalidad al enorme imperio, y después tomar decisiones, sin titubear.

Por la mañana, a las siete, después de tres horas de trabajo, apenas desayunó pan, un poco de fruta y café. La hora de la comida la omitió, tan sólo tomó varias rondas más de café y continuó encerrado trabajando. La duquesa, que estaba al tanto de sus movimientos, le comentó a Bonaparte que "Cada día parece más un Habsburgo". Ya entrada la noche, se trasladó a una sala del castillo, ya que en el despacho de los cuatro bustos no había televisión. De hecho no había allí más tecnología que unas lámparas y el teléfono, e incluso su padre y su abuelo habían tenido la costumbre de trabajar con velas en la oscuridad, prescindiendo en absoluto de las bondades de la electricidad. Fernando Carlos se trasladó para ver la televisión, acompañado de su tía y el canciller Bonaparte, pero no se trataba de algo recreativo, sino que daría una entrevista el líder de la izquierda mexicana, Ángel Miguel Morador, el principal enemigo del imperio.

La entrevista correría a cargo de Ramiro Milet, el comunicador de moda en México, de filiación conservadora pero imparcial en sus juicios, y famoso por poner en jaque a sus invitados cuando su biografía tenía alguna irregularidad. Justo a las nueve de la noche empezó el programa, y Milet dio la bienvenida a Morador con una sonrisa amigable. Era un hombre elegante, con cierta distinción. Parecía un casanova llegado a los cincuenta y tantos que se conservaba lo mejor que podía. El que no daba tan buen aspecto era Morador. Llevaba un traje gris y una corbata a cuadros, pero la elegancia le quedaba algo grande. Su pelo estaba totalmente blanco, mas eso no le daba aspecto de sabio ni mucho menos. Sus rasgos eran bastante simples, y al sonreír rayaban en la vulgaridad. Parecía más un contador inescrupuloso que un líder político, un hombre ajeno totalmente a cualquier manera de sofisticación.

–Ángel Miguel –comenzó Milet la entrevista–, tú has llamado a una marcha nacional para suprimir la monarquía, a la que llamas dictadura, e instaurar una república. Esto fue apenas dos días después de la muerte del emperador Maximiliano IV, por lo que recibiste muchas críticas y también apoyo en ciertos sectores. Hablamos al respecto, por favor.

–Gracias, Ramiro, muchas gracias por concedernos unos minutos en este espacio –dijo Morador, en tono lento y pausado–, y más por las circunstancias. Porque yo sé, yo sé bien que hay presiones, que cuando algunos queremos decir la verdad, desde la cancillería te llaman…

–No, no, a ver, Ángel Miguel, no nos confundamos –dijo Milet–, mi programa no está regulado y jamás hemos recibido ninguna advertencia desde la cancillería.

–Bueno, yo tengo otra información. Pero no nos vamos a pelear, eh, yo, sinceramente agradezco mucho este espacio en tu programa, Ramiro. Eres un hombre al que respeto por encima de las diferencias ideológicas que podamos tener. Y bien, volviendo al tema. Yo creo que esta es una oportunidad histórica para que México recupere su libertad de forma no violenta. Es… la hora, es el momento. Eh, tan sólo piensa que somos el único país de América con este tipo de gobierno, el único, no hay otro. Porque si contamos casos como el de Canadá, son situaciones totalmente diferentes, ellos son libres, nosotros no. Nosotros somos esclavos de una sola familia, fíjate bien, de una sola familia. Y creo que ya son muchos, muchísimos años, de estarlos manteniendo, ya es hora de que se regresen a Austria...

—Perdón que te interrumpa, Ángel Miguel —dijo Mllet—, pero el emperador es mexicano. Aún si no tuviera su rango, sería tan mexicano por nacimiento como tú y como yo. Es ilógico querer enviarlo a Austria, cuando él no tiene la nacionalidad de ese país. Nació aquí, en Aztlán, en el castillo de Chapultepec. Todo el mundo sabe eso.

—Lo que dices sobre su nacimiento es cierto, pero él no es mexicano. Fíjate bien, eh, Ramiro, cómo eran conocidos ellos en España; allí gobernaron más tiempo del que llevan aquí, gobernaron casi dos siglos, y hasta el final los llamaron los Austrias. Eran austriacos, y ellos lo tenían claro. Jamás se consideraron españoles.

—Perdóname, Ángel Miguel, pero Carlos II murió en 1700, si no me equivoco. ¿Qué tiene que ver él con nuestro emperador?

—Casi nada —dijo Morador, riéndose maliciosamente, lo que aumentaba la vulgaridad de su rostro—, se llaman igual y son de la misma familia. Ramiro, esto es muy importante, se trata de la libertad de México. Fernando Carlos es un extranjero, eso lo tenemos bien claro, quizás tú no, pero el movimiento que yo represento sí lo tiene claro, él pertenece a una familia de invasores, que durante siglos se han trasladado de un país a otro para vivir entre lujos, entre alhajas, oro y mármoles, a costillas del pueblo. Son una familia austriaca... alemana, podría decirse, y sin embargo han vivido, fíjate bien, han vivido de los españoles, de los húngaros, de los polacos, de los croatas, de los serbios, de los holandeses, de los belgas, de los italianos, y de todos esos lugares ya los han echado, desde hace siglos, pero nosotros no, nosotros somos los únicos tontos que los seguimos manteniendo. Nos explotan, y es injusto e inhumano que algunos hombres vivan entre lujos gracias a la explotación de otros hombres. Se trata de un crimen que no podemos seguir permitiendo. Es... es para avergonzarse, Ramiro, porque ya estamos en un tiempo diferente, la libertad ya no es un secreto ni un mito, la democracia tampoco. Este señor, Fernando Carlos, es el líder de una mafia integrada por pocas familias: los Iturbide, los Bonaparte, los Khevenhüller, los Miramón, eh, vamos, un pequeño grupo de privilegiados, que tienen en sus manos a México, que se han adueñado de toda la riqueza, por eso te digo que esto no es un juego. Mi movimiento es serio, y vamos a triunfar, le pese a quien le pese, porque México merece ser libre. Ni nuestras riquezas, ni mucho menos nuestro gobierno pueden estar en manos de extranjeros. Fíjate, fíjate, eh, Ramiro, el ministro de la guerra, Alfonso Peña-Bazaine, el hombre que manda a todos los soldados mexicanos, desciende de Aquiles Bazaine, el invasor, el enviado por Napoleón a oprimirnos, a matar mexicanos, y el canciller, el hombre más fuerte del imperio después del emperador, desciende del propio Napoleón III, hasta se parecen. Es imposible…, es imposible que continúe esta situación. Yo no llamo al pueblo a lincharlos, que no dudo que no lo merezcan, porque soy pacifico, mi movimiento es pacífico, pero sí hago un llamado a echarlos, no a lincharlos, a echarlos, a que regresen a sus países, a Austria y a Francia, a donde quieran, pero que se vayan de México. Merecemos libertad y merecemos democracia.

–Ángel Miguel, entiendo que tú tengas una postura hacia la monarquía. Eres libre de tenerla, pero los demás mexicanos también. Tú haces un llamado a derrocar el gobierno como si esa fuera la única salida posible y necesaria, y creo que no estás tomando en cuenta el sentir de todo el pueblo. Solo quieres hacer lo que tú consideras correcto.

–No, no, Ramiro, yo creo que no cabe… el espacio para defender lo indefendible. Hace unos momentos tú mencionaste la marcha que yo convoqué. Recibimos un gran apoyo, la marcha se llevó acabo en los cincuenta y siete departamentos. Ni uno sólo se quedó sin movilizarse, ni uno sólo, Ramiro. Eso ya dice mucho. Y si tú me preguntas por qué la convoqué justo cuando murió este señor, eh… Maximiliano IV, es muy fácil, Ramiro, con ello les dábamos una oportunidad a los Austrias para que regresaran a su país de forma pacífica, tranquila, vamos. Si se hubiera cambiado la forma de gobierno y se hubiera convocado a unas elecciones, este joven, que de hecho no quiere gobernar, eso yo lo sé bien, habría tomado el mando del país sólo por unos días, mientras se celebraban las elecciones para elegir presidente, y después él mismo, de la forma más pacífica y civilizada posible, le hubiera cedido el poder al ganador, así de sencillo. El país no hubiera tenido alteraciones de ningún tipo, todo habría seguido igual salvo con una gran diferencia: seriamos libres, seriamos por fin un pueblo libre. Y yo creo, eh, Ramiro, que aún estamos a tiempo. Le pido, civilizadamente, a este joven, Fernando Carlos, que coopere, así se iría con dignidad a su país. Porque de otra forma, de la única que nos estaría dejando, él se iría mal, en el mejor de los casos, y en el peor se quedaría en una cárcel, porque la cárcel es el destino de los dictadores.

—Ángel Miguel…

—Permíteme, permíteme, Ramiro, ya sé que te pueden regañar, pero esto es muy importante. Ellos, estas familias, ya silenciaron a los que como yo han querido interponerse en sus ambiciones. Porque, aunque murió de una angina de pecho, ellos mataron a don Benito Juárez. Lo obligaron a vagar por el norte del país, y a estar lejos de su esposa y de sus hijos, y eso lo mató. Ellos también, Ramiro, fusilaron al general Porfirio Díaz, a ese gran hombre, un valiente de raza india, un ejemplo de buen mexicano que, junto con el general Zaragoza, derrotó a los franceses en Puebla. También silenciaron a don Francisco I. Madero. Lo hicieron quedar en ridículo, y después lo encerraron en una prisión, donde murió de tristeza, por no lograr ver a su amado México libre. Yo sé bien lo peligrosa que es la mafia a la que me enfrento, Ramiro, pero no les tengo miedo, porque…

—Espera un momento, Ángel Miguel, sigo insistiendo que quieres conectar a como dé lugar todos los errores de los Habsburgo con el emperador Fernando Carlos, lo que es ilógico.

—No, no, Ramiro —dijo Morador, levantando la voz—, es él quien se atribuye esos crímenes inhumanos al no renunciar. Él les da su aval, y con ello los hace suyos.

—Comprendo, Ángel Miguel, que tu proyecto político es muy importante para ti —dijo Milet—. Pero dime una cosa, si comparamos a México con la mayoría de los países de América, estamos mejor en educación, en economía, en seguridad, en impartición de justicia, en respeto a los derechos humanos, en infraestructura, y partiendo de esa realidad, Ángel Miguel, yo te pregunto, ¿por qué quieres derribar un gobierno que si bien no funciona de maravilla, sí funciona medianamente bien, mejor que muchos?

—Porque México es de los mexicanos, no del joven austriaco. Y nuestros logros y nuestras riquezas son nuestros, no de él. México debe de ser gobernado por un mexicano, y ese gobernante debe de ser elegido por el pueblo. Así es en todos los países del mundo, o en la gran mayoría, no estoy pidiendo una extravagancia.

—¿Tú cambiarias la estabilidad de México por una república, incluso si a consecuencia de ello el país se impregnara de pobreza y corrupción?

—Es que eso no va a pasar. Yo no soy un hombre corrupto, porque sencillamente yo no voy detrás del dinero…

—A ver, Ángel Miguel —dijo Milet—, con eso me estás diciendo que tú quieres ser el presidente de la republica que añoras.

—Eh, Ramiro —respondió Morador, sonrojado—, creo que ése no es el punto por ahora. Ya lo decidirá en su momento el pueblo.

—Hay otro aspecto importante que me gustaría tocar, Ángel Miguel. A tu marcha se sumaron mexicanos en los cincuenta y siete departamentos. Eso es muy cierto. Pero tan sólo fueron unos miles en cada departamento. Si los sumamos a todos, no llegarían a un millón. El imperio tiene una población de doscientos sesenta millones de personas. De lo que piensan los otros doscientos cincuenta y nueve, que no te dieron su respaldo, ¿qué nos puedes decir?

—Como ya te dije, Ramiro, el gobierno de México es una dictadura, y a las dictaduras los pueblos les tienen miedo. Millones de mexicanos se preocupan por su trabajo, por sus hijos, por su seguridad. No quieren verse en la mira de la guardia secreta imperial, que es tan eficaz en desaparecer personas como la CIA o el FBI.

—O como la KGB…

—Eh, lo importante, Ramiro, es no desestimar lo que piensa la gente, lo que realmente desea. Porque al pueblo no se le puede ignorar. Si te contara sobre todos los que salen a encontrarme en la calle durante mis viajes, a darme la mano, a darme ánimos…

—Precisamente de tus viajes quería hablar, Ángel Miguel. Tú llevas diez años paseándote por México. Hoy estás en California, mañana estás en Veracruz y luego en Panamá. Pero también llevas muchos años sin que se te conozca un empleo, y al mismo tiempo pregonas que eres pobre. Siendo así, Ángel Miguel, ¿de dónde sale el dinero para tus viajes? A todos los mexicanos nos consta que viajar de un departamento a otro no es barato, y menos en un país tan grande.

—Ehhh, Ramiro —dijo Morador, algo molesto—, creo que ése no es el tema. Pero te puedo decir que para nadie es un secreto que hay muchos mexicanos comprometidos con el movimiento que yo represento.

—Ángel Miguel, te repito tus palabras de hace unos minutos: "Es inhumano que algunos hombres vivan de explotar a otros hombres".

—No te permito, Ramiro, que digas eso. Yo estoy muy lejos de ser tal cosa...

—Lo que no entiendo, Ángel Miguel, es cómo un hombre que lleva diez años sin trabajar, pero que vive sin carencias y viaja por todo el país, no puede ser considerado un explotador. ¿Entonces cómo se le debe llamar, según tú?

—Ya entendí, Ramiro, ya entendí. Créeme que fui un ingenuo al pensar que esa mafia que tiene en sus manos al país no llegaba tan lejos. Pero ya veo que gastan mucho más de lo que yo suponía semanalmente en su nómina —dijo Morador, riéndose.

—Sólo una última pregunta, Ángel Miguel, dime, ¿todo el que no te dé la razón va a ser un mafioso siempre?

—No voy a caer en tus provocaciones, Ramiro. Represento a un movimiento muy grande y muy importante para México, como para dejarme llevar por unas preguntas diseñadas en la cancillería o por la guardia secreta imperial. Te deseo que seas feliz, Ramiro, que goces de paz y de privilegios, aun siendo lo que eres.

—¿Qué soy, Ángel Miguel?

—Buenas noches, Ramiro. Gracias, de cualquier forma. Créeme, no te guardo rencor, yo no odio a nadie, soy un hombre pacifico. Y cuando mi movimiento triunfe, porque va a triunfar, no tengas miedo, yo no me dedicaré a venganzas personales. No es mi proyecto.

—Pues gracias, Ángel Miguel. Qué alivio.

—Así que ese hombre podría ser el presidente de México, si no me porto a la altura de las circunstancias —dijo Fernando Carlos, cuando concluyó el programa.

—¿Qué le parece su posible sucesor, Majestad? —preguntó la duquesa Carlota.

—Me ha dejado sin palabras. Y se supone que tengo una reunión pendiente con él —añadió el emperador.

—La reunión la tenía prevista su padre, Majestad, y ya estaba ahorrando paciencia mi pobre hermano. Usted la heredó, junto con el imperio.

—En su favor podemos argumentar —dijo Bonaparte— que tiene una carrera universitaria. Le llevó quince años, pero se rumora que sí logró graduarse.

—Si ese hombre en verdad llegó a graduarse de una universidad, y si el sistema educativo sigue siendo el mismo, está peor de lo que yo me imaginaba —dijo el emperador—. Creo que en ese caso voy a tener que remover a muchos rectores de sus puestos. Cuando menos.

Castillo de Chapultepec, febrero del 2003

—A las órdenes de Vuestra Majestad —dijo el niño, temblando.

—Nunca te autoricé a que te sentaras, Fernando Carlos.

—¡Perdón, señor!

—Tú sólo piensas en la comodidad.

El niño desvió su mirada para no hallarse la de su padre, y fijó sus ojos en una esquina, en el busto del emperador Rodolfo I. Decían que era su antepasado, y en ese momento deseó que lo defendiera de los regaños de su padre.

—Tu preceptor me dice que tiemblas como una lagartija cuando escuchas un cañonazo, que en las clases de esgrima tiras tu arma al suelo y sales corriendo, qué eres débil, tímido, que aun cuando memorizas todo y razonas muy bien en tus clases de matemáticas, no tienes una sola gota de carácter. Dime, ¿es eso cierto?

—No me gusta la violencia, Majestad —dijo el niño.

—Fernando Carlos, eres un Habsburgo, y eres el hijo del emperador, ser valiente no es una opción para ti, estás obligado a serlo. ¿Me entiendes?

—Majestad, yo...

—Te he dado desde que naciste el rango de coronel, tienes un regimiento que se avergüenza de ti porque eres un niño débil. ¿Acaso no entiendes que los archiduques hacen falta en el ejército imperial mexicano? Algún día, cuando tu hermano sea emperador, tú tendrás que ser su ministro de la guerra, y deberás tener el carácter de un león, para que el ejército te obedezca. ¿Te queda claro, Fernando Carlos? Apenas puedo creer que teniendo yo tantas ocupaciones, me obligues a perder el tiempo recordándote lo que ya sabes. Mi tiempo es de los mexicanos, no de un niño temeroso y mimado.

—Majestad, yo no quiero ser militar, yo quiero ser pintor —dijo el niño, temblando más todavía.

—¡Cómo te atreves! —bramó Maximiliano IV—. Has nacido con el privilegio de ser un archiduque de México, y todos los mexicanos esperamos grandes cosas de ti. Es tu obligación obedecer al emperador, incluso más que cualquier otra persona, porque eres un miembro de la casa de Habsburgo. En la familia, las órdenes del emperador no se cuestionan, sencillamente se obedecen, y yo he decidido que tú serás militar y que serás un gran estratega, para que tu hermano, el futuro emperador Maximiliano V, pueda confiar en ti como su ministro de la guerra. Ése, Fernando Carlos, es tu destino, y no permitiré que te escapes de él.

El emperador se giró para darle unos segundos al niño y que éste reflexionara, pero pronto volvió su mirada de nuevo a él, totalmente llena de furia, porque Fernando Carlos estaba llorando sin control.

—¡No te atrevas a llorar delante del emperador! ¡Esto es inconcebible! Juraría que no eres mi hijo, de no ser porque tu madre era una santa. ¡Límpiate esas lágrimas y mírame a los ojos! Tan sólo imagina que muriéramos tu hermano y yo de un día para otro, tú serias el emperador. Ruego a Dios que no castigue de esa forma tan cruel a mi amado México, dándole un emperador tan débil como tú. El pueblo no se lo merece.

—¿Qué pasa aquí? —dijo la duquesa Carlota, que en ese momento abrió la puerta sin siquiera llamar.

—¿Quién te autorizo a interrumpir, Carlota? Estoy hablando muy seriamente con el archiduque.

Fernando Carlos corrió desesperado hacia los brazos de su tía. La duquesa lo recibió con ternura.

—Tranquilo, Fer, tesoro mío, tu padre sólo quiere tu bien.

—No lo trates como si fuera una niña, de esa forma lo haces más débil —dijo el emperador.

—Ya no lo escuches, mi amor. Deja de llorar, por favor. Yo no permitiré que te siga gritando.

—Carlota, tan sólo me complicas las cosas, deja de intervenir en la educación de mi hijo.

—¡Majestad, precisamente es su hijo! ¡Trátelo como tal!

—¡Lo trataré como tal, cuando él se comporte como tal! —dijo el emperador—. Llévatelo, por ahora me avergüenzo de él. Afortunadamente mi heredero será Maximiliano, y no este niño tan débil.

—Ven conmigo, mi amor, ya no lo escuches. Tu tía te va a consentir.

—Hubieras nacido mujer, Fernando Carlos, así tendrías un pretexto para ser tan débil —dijo el emperador, cuando el niño y su tía atravesaban la puerta.

Majestad:

He tenido noticias de que el monumento para usted que tuve el honor de financiar en mi departamento natal le ha gustado mucho, y que alberga la noble intención de darme el título de barón en agradecimiento. Quiero aprovechar este medio para darle las gracias, y si lo vuelvo a ver pronto, también le daré las gracias en persona. No obstante, Majestad, no me siento la clase de hombre que pudiera ser honrado con un título nobiliario. Soy un empresario exitoso, es cierto, y tal vez también sea cierto que mi fortuna es de las más grandes de México. Pero nunca olvido que salí de la clase más humilde, que mis padres sufrían mil y una peripecias para alimentarnos a mis hermanos y a mí. No me sentiría cómodo siendo barón viniendo de dónde vengo. Además, el monumento que para mi satisfacción le ha gustado tanto no lo financié para obtener de Su Majestad favor alguno, sino que lo hice por gratitud.

Cuando recuerdo mi lejana juventud, Majestad, viene a mi memoria que yo era un hombre lleno de energías y de inquietudes, con un temperamento agresivo y a veces incontrolable. Igual sentía deseos de matar que de atravesar a golpes las montañas o de cruzar corriendo el mundo. A veces pienso que si mi país hubiera sido otro, un país sin respeto por los pobres ni oportunidades, yo habría tomado el peor de los caminos y quizás no se hablaría tan bien de mí. Pero la seguridad que otorga al pueblo nuestra amada monarquía, la seguridad de que para el emperador todo mexicano es importante, y de que aquí las oportunidades son para el que las busca con decisión y coraje, me hizo, sin saber leer siquiera, emigrar desde mi humilde pueblo a Aztlán, a esta gran capital cosmopolita, y el trabajo constante y la fe en mí y en mi país me hicieron lo que soy.

Así las cosas, Majestad, usted no tiene nada porque darme las gracias. Las gracias se las doy yo por hacer de este país un lugar donde prospera el que quiere trabajar y ha sido dotado por la naturaleza con una inteligencia siquiera un poco por encima de lo común. Deseo a sus herederos la misma sabiduría que tiene usted, para que puedan seguir haciendo de México un país donde la energía de los jóvenes violentos como lo fui yo no se vuelva resentimiento hacia los suyos sino una oportunidad para lograr grandes cosas en beneficio de todos. Porque una patria que desperdicia por sus defectos políticos el talento de sus hijos mejor dotados, no es otra cosa que una mala madre. Y México, gracias a Dios y a usted, ya no lo es.

A las órdenes de Vuestra Majestad

Doroteo Arango

Aquella noche ya tan cercana al amanecer, Porfirio Díaz daba un aspecto admirable a la luz de las velas, luciendo su uniforme de general del extinto ejército de la República. Esa había sido su única petición a Maximiliano, que se le permitiera ser fusilado vistiendo el uniforme propio de su rango en un México que ya había quedado extinto. En esos momentos, mientras miraba las flamas de aquellas dos velas que iluminaban su celda como si se hallaran en un lugar muy lejano, se sentía listo para morir. Había hecho cuanto había estado en sus manos para salvar a México. El presidente Juárez, si es que llegaba a verlo después de que disparara el pelotón, no tendría nada que reprocharle. Y en caso de que así fuera, le recordaría las palabras de don Santos Degollado: su obligación como general había sido pelear, no ganar la batalla. Y de pelear sí había peleado, con tanto coraje y bravura como el más valiente de los valientes, pero Miramón había sido más astuto que él, y vaya que a Díaz se le podía considerar el maestro de los astutos.

Cinco meses habían pasado ya desde la Batalla de San Luis, así era conocida porque el combate había ocurrido a unos cuantos kilómetros de la capital potosina. Miramón había llegado un día antes, al mando de un ejército de setenta mil hombres, en su mayoría mexicanos, pero había entre ellos franceses, austriacos y belgas que se habían negado a volver a Europa y se habían integrado al ejército imperial mexicano. Díaz, que disponía quince mil hombres más, también contaba en filas extranjeros, estadounidenses en su gran mayoría, negros y blancos, aventureros caza fortunas y ex combatientes de la guerra civil. Aquellos días tanto el Imperio como la Republica habían dejado desprotegidos todos sus frentes. Los imperialistas tan sólo contaban con cinco mil soldados más en la capital, que hacían las veces de guardias de Maximiliano y Carlota, por si Díaz llegaba a ganar, pudieran escoltarlos a un puerto seguro donde les fuera posible embarcarse rumbo a Europa.

Ambos generales, Díaz y Miramón, habían jugado al gato y al ratón durante un par de semanas. Díaz había bajado del norte, esperando encontrar a su adversario en un terreno donde su capacidad de maniobra estuviera limitada, porque sabía bien que Miramón era un genio para la guerra siempre y cuando pudiera desplegar su ejército a su libre antojo, mientras que su brillantez disminuía ante las sorpresas o ante obstáculos que entorpecieran la rapidez de sus tropas. Miramón, por su parte, quería alcanzar a Díaz de forma que al menos él tuviera la posibilidad de iniciar la batalla, y si ésta no había ocurrido en dos semanas se debía a que cada general era consciente de la peligrosidad del otro.

Al saber que su adversario se había posicionado de la capital potosina, Díaz avanzó con la intención de cañonear la ciudad. Sus planes no eran iniciar un largo sitio, sino someter a una prueba a Miramón. Quería saber si seguía siendo tan bueno después de estar varios años alejado de los campos de batalla, y al mismo tiempo tener la certeza de que la ciudad al servir como trinchera y fortaleza le daría la posibilidad de recorrer sus líneas a su antojo y así evitar un ataque relámpago, la especialidad del famoso general conservador. La noche previa a la ejecución de sus planes, Díaz acampó en los alrededores de la ciudad, y tenía planeado ordenar el ataque poco antes del amanecer. Era de esperarse que Miramón, al no saber a qué hora iniciarían los cañonazos, tendría a sus soldados toda la noche despiertos y exhaustos, a punto de caerse al suelo justo antes de iniciar la batalla. Poco después de que Díaz ordenó que sus líneas avanzaran, una lluvia inesperada lo hizo dudar y decidió posponer el ataque. El lodo no sería buen aliado de sus planes y eso lo tenía bastante claro. En medio de un repliegue que desconcertó a sus subordinados se perdieron minutos cruciales para la historia de México. Miramón, que con su retorcidísimo colmillo sospechaba lo que ocurría, sacó sus tropas de la ciudad y entre el fango y la lluvia avanzó dispuesto a jugarse el todo por el todo. Díaz retrocedió sin que apenas ocurrieran algunos combates aislados, pero en los alrededores de la hacienda de Peñasco comprendió que siendo él el comandante absoluto del ejército republicano y contando con más soldados que su adversario, quedaría en ridículo al retirarse y su liderazgo sería puesto en duda. La lluvia, las dudas y la vanidad lo hicieron en apenas una hora dar inicio a una batalla justo como la deseaba Miramón. Al comenzar la mañana cesó la lluvia y el sol salió dispuesto a bañar con su luz los rostros de la bravura. La batalla se prolongó todo el día y conforme pasaban las horas ambos generales llegaron a pensar que ya habían perdido y contemplaron varias veces retirarse o, si eso no era posible, rendirse.

Cuando la última carga de caballería republicana fue barrida por la artillería enemiga, Díaz, que contemplaba todo desde los lomos de su caballo, sintió deseos de llorar y no se contuvo. Media hora más tarde la bandera del imperio ondeaba donde antes había estado el grueso de las tropas republicanas y Díaz le entregaba su espada a Miramón. Éste lo trató con respeto, y ocultó magistralmente la satisfacción que le causaba su triunfo. Díaz pensó en decirle: "¡General, son muchos los mexicanos muertos por un sólo austriaco!", pero decidió ser un buen perdedor y guardó silencio.

Estuvo prisionero varios días en la ciudad que había visto su derrota. Cuando le informaron que sería sometido a un consejo de guerra por haberse levantado en armas contra un gobierno legítimo y elegido por la gran mayoría de los mexicanos, pensó que sería trasladado a la capital pero en realidad se lo llevaron a San Juan de Ulúa. No obstante, contrario a lo que pensaba, no fue encerrado en una prisión húmeda y maloliente, como todos quienes habían tenido la mala suerte de ser encerrados en aquel infierno indescriptible, sino que su celda fue hasta cierto punto cómoda y su alimentación digna de un general. Cuando apenas llevaba cinco días confinado allí, llegó desde la capital el conde Khevenhüller, a quien recordaba haber visto en la batalla de San Luis batiéndose a espada contra los republicanos. El joven conde traía una propuesta directa de Maximiliano: unirse al imperio con su rango de general o aceptar un destierro en Austria, bajo el cuidado de aquel gobierno, previamente habiendo firmado un compromiso para no volver a intentar jamás ningún tipo de rebelión ni instar a nadie a ella contra el Imperio Mexicano. Díaz se negó rotundamente, y le dijo a Khevenhüller que apenas lograra escaparse volvería a luchar por la libertad de su patria contra quien fuera, las potencias europeas o los Estados Unidos. Pese a la tajante negativa, los dos hombres simpatizaron y estuvieron charlando por más de dos horas.

Tres meses más tarde, a Díaz le llegó la noticia de que Carlota estaba embarazada y también fue informado que al día siguiente sería sometido a un consejo de guerra. Se negó rotundamente a asistir y defenderse alegando que era inaudito que siendo un patriota mexicano que siempre había peleado por su país y jamás contra él fuera sometido a semejante farsa. El consejo de guerra lo halló culpable de crímenes contra la estabilidad del imperio, de causar con sus acciones la muerte de mexicano, y lo sentenció a muerte. Pero la pena no fue aplicada al día siguiente, como él creyó en un momento, y así pasaron casi dos meses, sin que se le informara nada sobre su destino. Era claro que Maximiliano dudaba. Tenía fama, a pesar de todo, de no ser un asesino. Sin embargo, una noche, después de la cena, le dieron una noticia que no alteró en absoluto las facciones de su rostro: al día siguiente, antes del amanecer, sería pasado por las armas. Se sirvió una copa de vino y se limitó a decir: "Bueno, ya era tiempo".

Aquella noche ya moribunda, envuelto en la débil luz de las velas, se bañó, se afeitó y se puso su uniforme de general. Ya listo para lo que sus carceleros dispusieran, se negó a recibir confesor alguno, alegando que por sus acciones no tenía nada de qué arrepentirse. Cuando escuchó pasos de varios hombres acercarse, poco después de las seis, supo que había llegado la hora. Se mantuvo tranquilo, con la mirada ausente, como quien está distraído en un momento de total aburrimiento, y cuando un hombre envuelto en el uniforme de general de imperio se paró frente a él, apenas movió un poco la mirada.

—Déjenos solos —ordenó el recién llegado.

Los demás soldados se retiraron y los generales se quedaron solos en la celda. Ambos tenían insignias del águila y la serpiente en sus uniformes, ambos eran mexicanos y ambos de raza india.

—¿Es usted el general Tomás Mejía? —preguntó Díaz.

—El emperador no quiere fusilarlo —dijo Mejía, tras afirmar su identidad—. Se niega a quitarle la vida a un mexicano tan valiente.

—Hace mal —respondió Díaz—. Si yo estuviera en su lugar, no dudaría un solo momento.

—¿Por qué no se une al imperio, general? El gobierno necesita hombres como usted.

—Porque no soy un traidor a la patria, general, porque los mexicanos ya teníamos un país y vino Maximiliano a poner otro encima, pero ése no es el México de nosotros.

—Es cierto —dijo Mejía—, ya teníamos un país. Pero no supimos cuidarlo nunca, los yanquis nos lo estaban comiendo a pedazos. El imperio hará a México fuerte, podremos defendernos de quien sea de ahora en adelante. Usted es muy libre de considerarme a mí un traidor a la patria, pero yo sólo le digo que me incliné por un gobierno que le diera fuerza, paz y prosperidad a mi país. Porque aquí no hemos conocido nada de eso nunca.

—Pues le fue bien, general —respondió Díaz—, usted vivirá para disfrutar la patria que quiere, y yo moriré defendiendo la que quería. Creo que, a fin de cuentas, a mí tampoco me irá tan mal. Para los verdaderos mexicanos, los que nunca dejarán de existir haga lo que haga Maximiliano, yo seré siempre uno de los suyos.

—Créame que lo admiro, general —dijo Mejía—. La muerte que le espera es de las más dignas a que puede aspirar un hombre valiente.

—Gracias —respondió Díaz, con un tono de voz muy débil—. Y usted créame que me siento honrado de que haya venido este día el más honorable de todos nuestros enemigos. Entre los republicanos siempre hemos dicho que el único que vale como hombre de todos los conservadores e imperialistas, es el general Mejía. Usted no nos odia, no es un matón como Márquez, muchas veces nos dio un trató que, de caer prisionero, jamás le habríamos dado a usted.

—General, el emperador le da una última oportunidad. Sin que firme usted nada, sólo deme a mí su palabra de honor de que ya no nos hará la guerra, y se le conseguirá asilo político en Colombia o incluso en los Estados Unidos, para que viva usted cerca de México. Sólo deme su palabra —insistió Mejía—, y su salvación será un hecho.

—Le doy mi palabra, general —dijo Díaz, viendo a Mejía a los ojos—, de que si me veo libre, inmediatamente empezaré a pelear por mi patria, así tenga que hacerlo yo solo. Que no lo extrañe lo que ahora le digo, eso es lo que hacemos los patritas.

—¿Entonces…?

—Quiero pedirle un favor muy especial —dijo Díaz—. Verá, general, aquí hay muchos que me odian, y no quiero rencores al momento de mi muerte ni que alguien la disfrute como una venganza personal.

—Dígame qué quiere, lo que sea —respondió Mejía.

—Usted no me odia, y créame yo a estas alturas tampoco lo odio. Por eso quiero que sea usted quien dé las órdenes al pelotón. ¿Me haría ese favor?

Quizás si Mejía no hubiera tenido ese rostro tan difícil de escudriñar, Díaz habría notado lo conmovido que se encontraba.

—Así lo haré, general. Cumpliré su deseo. El comandante de la prisión me ha dicho que también quiere que su cuerpo sea trasladado a Oaxaca, para ser sepultado allí. Cuente también con ello.

—Gracias, me preocupaba que Maximiliano quisiera enviar mi cuerpo lejos de México, para que los republicanos que seguirán existiendo no tengan una tumba adonde ir a visitarme. Y eso sí que me habría dolido mucho. Figúrese usted lo triste que sería para un hombre que siempre ha peleado por su patria y nunca contra ella estar sepultado en el extranjero. Nunca podría descansar en paz.

—No se preocupe por eso, le doy mi palabra de honor de que será sepultado en Oaxaca, tal como usted lo desea.

—De verdad, muchas gracias, general Mejía. Me llevaré un buen recuerdo de usted a la tumba.

—¿Está listo?

—Para morir por la patria, siempre lo he estado.

—Sígame.

Los generales salieron de la celda y caminaron hasta el patio donde Díaz sería fusilado, éste pasó en medio del pelotón y siguió caminando, dejándolo atrás varios pasos después, para dirigirse solo al muro que ya lo esperaba.

—No deseo por ningún motivo que me tapen los ojos —dijo a Mejía, cuando se acercó para despedirse definitivamente—. Quiero saber si es cierto que uno puede ver las balas cuando se acercan.

—General, yo...

—No, no se conmueva, general Mejía. Los valientes son de plomo y usted, pese a pensar cómo piensa, no tiene fama de cobarde. ¿Puedo pedirle otro favor?

—Pídame... lo que quiera, general.

—¿Me daría un abrazo?

—Será un honor.

Los generales se abrazaron, ambos estaban muy conmovidos, pero Díaz, pese a que solía ser propenso a ello, evitó llorar.

—Ande, pues, ya no perdonamos el tiempo —dijo Díaz—. Esto tiene que acabar de una buena vez.

Mejía se retiró apenas unos cuantos pasos, y Díaz miró de frente al pelotón, dispuesto a morir dignamente como el último soldado fiel a la República.

La voz del bravo general Mejía al pelotón sonaba débil, quebrada por momentos. Estaba llorando. Cuando gritó "fuego", los soldados apenas pudieron escucharlo.

Díaz se dobló por un instante tras la estruendosa descarga, pero luego volvió a enderezar su cuerpo y cayó con la cara al cielo. La sangre que salía de su pecho pronto empezó a hacer una enorme mancha que alcanzó a llegar hasta una de sus manos, que había quedado extendida.

—Qué hermosa y triste resulta la muerte de un hombre valiente —dijo Mejía para sí.

Diario El Imperio, 21 de enero de 2017

Su Majestad Imperial, Fernando Carlos I de México, recibe la espada de Santa Anna

Ayer hizo frío en Aztlán, pero los capitalinos salieron animados de sus casas desde muy temprano, debido a que estaban enterados de que ocurriría un evento que sólo ha ocurrido seis veces durante siglo y medio y que esperamos que tarde muchos años en volver a ocurrir: Su Majestad imperial, Fernando Carlos I, que es nuestro emperador desde el instante mismo de la muerte de su padre Maximiliano IV, se presentó en el Parlamento ante senadores y diputados para recibir simbólicamente la espada del general Santa Anna, lo que lo convierte en el guardián de todos los mexicanos, en el hombre que se levantará toda su vida mucho antes de que amanezca para asegurarse de que todo marche bien en el imperio.

Su Majestad acudió al célebre acto poco antes de que se cumpla un mes de la muerte de su padre, lo que ocurrió con total normalidad, puesto que Moctezuma III lo hizo a las tres semanas del fallecimiento de Maximiliano *el Grande*, Agustín II dejó pasar el mes completo, Maximiliano II casi hizo lo mismo, a los veintiocho días, Maximiliano III a los veinticuatro, y Maximiliano IV, nuestro recientemente fallecido emperador, tomó con sus manos la espada de Santa Anna a los diecinueve días de la muerte de su padre. Así pues, Fernando Carlos I siguió el protocolo fielmente en ese sentido, pero en otros dos el evento fue poco usual. Aunque se esperaba que ocurriría en cualquier momento, la noticia tomó a los mexicanos por sorpresa, debido a que el anuncio se dio apenas un día antes. Si bien no es una falta grave puesto que el hecho de que el emperador tome con sus manos la legendaria espada no tiene ningún revestimiento legal, salvo que con ello informa a los mexicanos que él acepta hacerse cargo de la seguridad del imperio.

El hecho de que Su Majestad haya elegido el mismo día que Donald Trump tomaría posesión de la presidencia de los Estados Unidos ha sido interpretado como una clara intención por parte del emperador de quitarle al yanqui maleducado algunas portadas en los diarios internacionales. Si ésa ha sido verdaderamente su intención, ya era tiempo de que el gobierno mexicano reaccionara de alguna manera u otra a las provocaciones de ese tipo, pegándole en lo que más le duele: su enorme ego.

El otro aspecto inusual que caracterizó al evento fue el hecho de que no hubo jefes de Estado invitados de ninguna parte del mundo ni miembros de la defenestrada o decorativamente en vigencia realeza europea. Fue un asunto exclusivamente de mexicanos, a puerta cerrada. Esto se explica debido a que Su Majestad Imperial se halla de luto. Y si bien también se hallaban de luto los otros cinco emperadores que han acudido al mismo evento que él ahora, en este caso las circunstancias son más tristes puesto que el emperador no sólo ha perdido recientemente a su padre, sino que aún no ha pasado mucho tiempo desde la terrible tragedia donde perdieron la vida el archiduque Maximiliano, su esposa y sus dos pequeños hijos.

Fue a las ocho de la mañana cuando miembros de la guardia imperial montada se formaron a ambos lados del Paseo de Juárez, a las afueras del castillo de Chapultepec, y apenas diez minutos después apareció el emperador en un hermoso y encabritado caballo negro, que acentuaba el luto que lleva por dentro Su Majestad, vestido para la ocasión tan simbólica de general de división del ejército imperial, de color completamente negro, cuyo único contraste figuraba en las insignias y botones dorados. En medio de su guardia montada, que lo escoltó hasta el Parlamento, Su Majestad cabalgada recto, con la mirada del hombre que siempre tiene preocupaciones, pero su atención estaba fija en la gente que lo saludaba a su paso o que gritaba ¡Dios salve al emperador!, a quienes volteaba a ver con ternura y con desmesurada atención, pero sin alterar más que mínimamente las facciones de su rostro.

A las afueras del Parlamento, tras hacerlo Su Majestad, diez miembros de la guardia también desmontaron de sus caballos y entraron con él al edificio para escoltarlo hasta la tribuna. Mientras los senadores y la mitad de los diputados aplaudían la llegada del emperador. Algunos cuantos diputados conocidos como moradoristas chiflaban y decían improperios, demostrando en mayor medida que su postura política su poca cultura y su excesiva vulgaridad. Pero el emperador no les prestó la mayor atención, y ya posicionado en la tribuna se apresuró a pronunciar el juramento con una voz más grave que la que podría esperarse de un hombre tan joven y de rostro tan bondadoso:

Yo, Fernando Carlos I de México, juro ante Dios y ante mi pueblo gobernar siempre pensando en el bienestar de los míos y nunca por motivos egoístas, juro hacer aplicar con igualdad las leyes, respetarlas y hacer respetar con ellas la libertad y la paz de todos los mexicanos; acepto la espada que simboliza mi compromiso inquebrantable de velar por la seguridad de mi patria y juro no desprenderme de ella hasta el día de mi muerte.

Terminada el juramento por parte de Su Majestad, la duquesa Carlota de Cuernavaca se levantó de su asiento, caminó con elegancia hasta la tribuna y puso en manos del emperador la hermosa espada con empuñadura de oro que luce en bellos relieves las formas del águila y la serpiente, siguiendo la tradición de que la espada le sea entregada al emperador por un miembro de su familia. Cuando la duquesa se retiró a su asiento, todos los presentes y quienes seguían el evento por televisión o desde su teléfono, quizás esperaban que Su Majestad sacara un puñado de hojas para leer un enorme discurso, pero cual fue la sorpresa de todos al ver que el emperador, siempre impecable en cada uno de sus regios movimientos, se lanzaba a hablar sin guía alguna.

Aquí se transcribe palabra por palabra el contundente discurso que ha servido como presentación de Su Majestad hacia su pueblo, un pueblo que hasta ayer no conocía el timbre de su voz:

Mexicanas y mexicanos, hace apenas unos pocos meses yo creía que jamás tendría esta responsabilidad. Y repentinamente la historia de mi amado México llegó a un punto en el que tiene un emperador que no quiso ni pensó en serlo, y en el que al mismo tiempo hay tanto mexicanos como extranjeros que cuestionan mi posición, alegando que nuestra monarquía es un completo anacronismo que viola la evolución de los gobiernos en el mundo occidental. He escuchado que algunos opinan que un emperador en estos tiempos es peor que un barco de vapor y se asemeja a un barco con remos. He recibido cartas instándome a renunciar, a poner la primera piedra para la supuesta libertad de México.

En un principio esas cartas me hicieron dudar, llegué a pensar que era cierto que nuestro país merecía evolucionar en su forma de gobierno, y que yo era un obstáculo para ello. Fueron muchas mis dudas en el momento en que me fue revelada mi actual posición, justo cuando murió mi padre. Si les digo esto es porque no he venido aquí a ignorar las polémicas que envuelven a mi gobierno. En el mundo civilizado hay monarquías con reyes, no con emperadores, y donde la figura del monarca es totalmente anodina. México es, ciertamente, una enorme excepción. Pero si bien es cierto que tenemos un gobierno anclado en una historia ya muy antigua, también es cierto que no he llegado hasta aquí con las armas en la mano, dispuesto a apropiarme del gobierno por la fuerza. No estoy donde estoy ni con mentiras, ni con imposiciones de ningún tipo, incluso mi actual posición no le ha costado un solo peso al erario público. Estoy donde estoy simple y sencillamente por apegarme a lo que somos como pueblo. México es dueño de una antigua tradición que, pese a sus problemas, ha sido aceptada por varias generaciones de mexicanos. Incluso mis más acérrimos críticos deberían de tener el valor de aceptar que el imperio es parte de nuestra historia, y la parte más prospera de lo que hemos logrado construir.

Por mi parte, dudar de mi posición como emperador, sería negar esencialmente lo que como pueblo somos hoy en día. Y fue gracias a la emperatriz Carlota, la persona que diseñó el México en que vivimos, que comprendí que mi misión no es satisfacer aquellos a los que México no les gusta, sino asegurarme de que en el imperio sigan existiendo la justicia y la libertad necesarias para que todos los mexicanos sean libres de luchar por sus sueños, libres para expresarse, libres para señalar mis errores y libres hasta para odiarme cuando haga las cosas mal.

He comprendido que no importa lo popular que sea una forma de gobierno porque ningún gobierno que ofrezca libertad de expresión estará exento de las críticas. Pero lo importante, lo verdaderamente importante, es que un gobierno funcione. Y ahora, al comprender claramente que México, con su gobierno que se asemeja a un barco con remos, aún funciona, tengo claro que mi deber no es cuestionar lo que somos, sino defender lo que queremos ser como pueblo libre y civilizado y hacer la parte que me corresponde. Y tengan todos ustedes la seguridad de que lo haré.

A los países amigos de México, que tienen para con nosotros una relación de respeto y afecto mutuo, les aseguro que defenderé esa amistad tan valiosa de la mejor forma posible, porque un mexicano no olvida nunca el valor del respeto y la amistad. En tanto que a los países que nos puedan ser hostiles y alberguen para nosotros malas intenciones, les advierto que cualquier daño a mi patria y a los míos se los cobraré diez veces. Porque un mexicano nunca olvida una ofensa.

También quisiera disculparme con mi pueblo porque en algún momento dudé de mi deber y dudé de mí, y eso jamás debe hacerlo el emperador. Pero les aseguro que ahora tengo bastante claro qué clase país es México, cuál es la importancia de su forma de gobierno y cuál debe de ser su lugar en el mundo. A todos los mexicanos, mujeres, hombres, ancianos y niños, y a todos los extranjeros que viven aquí incluso de forma ilegal, y que esperan en lugar de hostilidad una mano amiga, a todos ustedes le digo que ya estoy al mando, y que tengo claro cuál será mi deber de todos los días, hasta el día de mi muerte.

Gracias a todos, que Dios los bendiga, y a mí que me perdone mis actos futuros, porque estoy dispuesto a fallarle a Dios con tal de no fallarle nunca a mi pueblo.

Cuando Su Majestad Imperial concluyó su tan enormemente simbólico discurso, los senadores y la mitad de los diputados se pusieron de pie para aplaudir, bastante conmovidos. En tanto que los moradoristas se veían entre sí molestos. No esperaban un discurso que sabían sería tan bien recibido por los mexicanos. Verdaderamente, las palabras de Su Majestad fueron más contundentes y enérgicas que las de su padre hace ya tres décadas. Fernando Carlos I supo enviarnos un mensaje que significó algo importante para todos. Los mexicanos tenemos claro que estamos protegidos por un hombre que no va a dudar para defendernos, los extranjeros que se han refugiado en México ahora saben que el emperador no les será hostil, muchos otros países del mundo han comprendido que sus relaciones comerciales con nosotros están seguras, y Donald Trump, si es que ya le tradujeron el discurso, ahora sabe que si se mete de nuevo con nosotros tendrá enfrente a un terrible enemigo.

Carta del emperador Maximiliano I a la archiduquesa Sofía, agosto de 1870

Querida mamá:

Me hace feliz que me digas que todos están relativamente bien, o al menos sin problemas mayores que los habituales en la familia. A veces vienen a mi memoria los recuerdos más entrañables de mi infancia, cuando la felicidad y la alegría parecían eternas, y es entonces cuando más me duele estar tan lejos de Austria. Es bien cierto que ahora soy mexicano, que este hermoso pueblo me ha adoptado como suyo, y que hacer su dicha es mi alegría, pero creo que la Providencia tiene prohibido a cualquier hombre de este mundo olvidar el lugar donde ha nacido y donde ha sido feliz. Y saber que mis obligaciones al mando de mi imperio me tienen alejado de mi patria para siempre, cuando aún ni siquiera cumplo cuarenta años, es un hecho cruel que alarga mi tristeza.

Pero no quiero que te preocupes por mí. Tan sólo de imaginarlos a ustedes dichosos, llenos de niños, algunos que han nacido después de mi partida y que espero algún día puedan venir a visitarme, me llena de la felicidad que necesito para levantarme a trabajar todos los días. En tu carta me reprochas que no te hable tanto como tú quisieras del archiduque Moctezuma, y que ni siquiera celebre que quieras enviar a un pintor desde Austria para que lo retrate a tu gusto. Créeme que te doy las gracias por el cariño que le profesas al heredero del Imperio Mexicano. Ya también en otra carta le doy las gracias a mi hermano por haberle dado el rango de mariscal de campo. En gratitud por ello, ayer mismo firmé el nombramiento como general de ejército imperial mexicano del archiduque Rodolfo, mi querido sobrino a quien le deseo el mejor porvenir de los emperadores de nuestra familia. Pero no quisiera ofenderte sino explicarte de la mejor manera posible porque no considero pertinentes tus planes para el archiduque Moctezuma. Tu idea de que lo envíe a educarse a Austria me parece noble, pero no la creo practicable. Él es... mexicano. Lo normal es que sea educado aquí, con los suyos, para que el pueblo no tenga la más remota duda de que su próximo emperador será más proclive a entender sus emociones.

Me dices que sospechas que yo no sé muchas cosas sobre él, que Franz, con el carácter que le conocemos, sabe mucho más de Rodolfo que yo de Moctezuma. Quizás no le ponga tanta atención como otros padres suelen hacerlo, pero si yo gobernara en Europa mi imperio empezaría en Portugal y terminaría en Prusia. Así de grandes son mis deberes diarios. Las distracciones tan hogareñas y a veces tan unidas a la pereza ya me son totalmente desconocidas. Mis innumerables obligaciones me absorben demasiado y ya en su momento quizás me disculpe con el archiduque por permanecer un poco alejado de él. Pero cuando él sea emperador me entenderá.

Espero que tú también entiendas que si yo tuviera más hijos no hallaría ningún problema por enviarte a uno de ellos a Austria, para que creciera en los mismos lugares donde crecí yo y fui tan feliz. Pero no es el caso. La Providencia no ha traído a mi matrimonio la fertilidad deseada. El archiduque Moctezuma es necesario aquí, como parte fundamental del imperio, y eso tú lo sabes mejor que nadie. Tendré en mente pedir que le tomen una nueva fotografía para enviártela.

Gracias por conservar en tus rezos al hijo ausente, mamá.

Te quiero.

Max

—Ya estaba pensando que hoy no pasarías por esta calle —dijo Fernando Carlos—. Creí que podría verte aquí a la misma hora de ayer.

Al escuchar aquella voz, Carlota volteó, bastante sorprendida. El emperador estaba justo en el lugar donde se había accidentado la noche anterior, y trepado en la misma motocicleta.

—Llevo dos horas aquí —añadió Fernando Carlos—, aunque no te reprocho la tardanza, puesto que no teníamos ninguna cita.

—¡Majestad!

—Fer…

—Salí tarde hoy. Hubo muchos clientes en el restaurante. Y estuve a punto de irme a mi casa en un taxi. Esta noche sí estoy muy cansada y ya no quiero caminar.

—Eso lo vamos a solucionar sin ningún problema —dijo el emperador, señalando la parte trasera de su motocicleta.

—Majestad, me apena que haya perdido dos horas de su tiempo esperándome a mí.

—Mi trabajo suele concluir a las nueve de la noche. De allí hasta las tres treinta de la madrugada yo decido si ceno, me duermo o salgo a pasear.

—Majestad, yo…

—Pude haber averiguado sin ningún problema datos tuyos, para saber a qué hora vendrías o si no vendrías, pero la infraestructura del gobierno no es para eso.

—Es que…

—Deberías darme tu teléfono para que mañana la espera sea de cuando mucho una hora…

—¡Déjeme hablar!

—Si me llamas Fer, prometo ya no te interrumpirte —dijo el emperador.

—Fer…, estoy cansada, y ahora también estoy nerviosa. Sólo quiero irme. Hace media hora un cliente se enfureció porque tarde diez minutos en llevarle su cuenta, y paso por aquí y resulta que Su Majestad Imperial me ha esperado durante dos horas. ¿No cree que es un buen motivo para que me sienta incomoda y nerviosa?

—¿Qué te parece si de momento sólo te llevo a tu casa, y dejamos la charla para otro día?

—¿Cuál charla? —dijo ella, sonriendo, por fin, y él le devolvió la sonrisa.

—¿Te subes?

—¿Cuántos años de prisión me esperan, si se hace público que te tuteo?

—Esa importantísima ley todavía no la reviso, pero creo que son como setenta —respondió Fernando Carlos, divertido—. De cualquier forma, no te preocupes. Firmaré el indulto antes de que pises la cárcel —añadió y volvió a invitarla a subir a la motocicleta.

Durante el trayecto a su casa, Carlota notó que el emperador conducía bastante despacio, como si no hubiera querido llegar nunca.

—Servida —dijo él, cuando por fin llegaron—. Ahora puedes ir a descansar.

—Gracias por traerme…, Fer —dijo ella y empezó a buscar sus llaves en su bolso.

—No me has dado el número de tu teléfono —dijo el emperador.

—Nunca dije que te lo daría.

—Está bien, no insistiré.

—¡Vaya, por fin te gano una!

—No insistiré, pero será a cambio de una promesa.

—Ya me lo imaginaba. ¿Qué promesa?

—Que mañana no cambiarás de ruta, y no importa cuán tarde pases. Te esperaré.

—Majestad...

—Fer...

—Está bien, no cambiaré de ruta. ¿Contento?

—¿Es una promesa?

—Es una promesa, Fer.

El emperador volvió a poner en marcha el motor mientras ella procuraba entrar rápidamente a su casa.

—Carlota —le dijo y la hizo voltear—, ¿Cuántos hijos te gustaría tener?

—¿Para qué quieres saber eso?

—Para corroborar si coincidimos en ello.

—Estás loco, Fer.

—Hoy logré que me tutearas. Ahora sé que nada es imposible —dijo y se puso en marcha.

Carta de Émile van der Foket a su hijo, 02 de diciembre de 1904

Querido Philippe

Habiendo cumplido mi sueño de regresar a México, estoy feliz porque en este sueño mis expectativas han sido mayores de las que esperaba. Así pues, mañana mismo salgo hacia Veracruz, para embarcarme de regreso a Bélgica. Sin embargo, aunque deseo contarte con detalle todas mis experiencias cuando vuelva a verte, deseo escribir esta carta justo ahora que mis emociones aún están frescas, en esta hermosa tarde, que es la última que paso en Aztlán.

Como bien sabes, hace cuatro largas décadas que vine por primera vez a este enorme país. Entonces tenía tan sólo veinte años y añoraba alcanzar fama y fortuna combatiendo por la dicha de nuestra amada princesa Carlota. Ella era muy especial para nosotros los belgas porque se trataba de la primera princesa nacida en nuestro país como reino independiente, y la queríamos como una joya muy preciada. Yo deseaba distinguirme como un gran militar y que ella, a quien amaba tiernamente, me condecorara en persona. México era para nosotros un lugar sacado de *Las mil y una noches*, lleno de riquezas y de exotismo.

Las cosas aquella vez no salieron del todo bien. El oro no estaba tan a la vista, los republicanos de Juárez no buscaban batallas frontales sino matarnos de a uno por día y hasta el clima nos era hostil a los extranjeros. Tan sólo una vez y de lejos pude ver a nuestra princesa, la emperatriz para los mexicanos, y mis proezas militares se limitaron a recibir un balazo cerca del corazón en el pueblo de Ixmiquilpan, y a estar dos semanas moribundo y salvar al fin la vida de milagro. Al irme de aquí me sentía vacío, y al saber ya en Europa que el emperador Maximiliano había logrado consolidar su imperio, no me sentí partícipe de ello en absoluto. El recuerdo que me llevé de México era el de un país salvaje, alejado de la mano de Dios y acosado por la pobreza y la ignorancia, donde los territorios más agrestes eran para los nativos caminos y los criminales más analfabetos eran los hombres que impartían la justicia. La capital era una combinación de una vieja y sucia cuidad medieval con una ciudad pobre del siglo antepasado. Yo había visitado París y Roma un año antes de llegar aquí, así que al ver la ciudad que los mexicanos llamaban su capital no pude menos que reírme. Es cierto que los españoles hicieron grandes edificios durante sus tres siglos de dominio, pero se olvidaron en todo momento de dotarlos de belleza. Trataron a México como lo que era, su colonia, y nunca pensaron en embellecer nada sino en explotar todo.

Sin embargo, aunque no me llevé los mejores recuerdos de México, al sentir que se alejaba mi juventud, mi mente buscó, quizás a manera de refugio, aquellos recuerdos donde yo había sido un soldado en medio de una guerra, cuando desfilaba en mi caballo vestido con mi hermoso uniforme y las jóvenes mexicanas detenían en mí su mirada. Fue entonces cuando me sentí dominado por el enorme deseo de regresar a México, para ver con mis propios ojos el ahora poderoso imperio que si bien yo no había ayudado a construir sí había sido testigo de su nacimiento.

Y, por fin, después de tantos años de meditar la idea y planear el viaje, y gracias también a tu ayuda, pude embarcarme para volver a pisar las huellas que aquí dejé en mi juventud. Desde que mi mirada alcanzo a ver Veracruz, quedé enormemente sorprendido por los cambios tan drásticos que propició esa guerra en la que yo participé. En cuarenta años pasan muchas cosas, Philippe, y más tratándose de un imperio que va siempre en busca del crecimiento. Mi primer viaje al interior del país fue un infierno inimaginable, pero en esta ocasión pude llegar desde Veracruz a Aztlán con una comodidad verdaderamente envidiable.

La capital, que ahora sí que lo parece, me dejó gratamente sorprendido. Ahora es verdad que podemos decir que hace sonrojarse a París. El emperador Maximiliano, al que aquí conocen como *El Grande*, mandó demoler suburbios enteros e hizo avenidas amplias, llenas de árboles y hermosas fuentes y esculturas. Las plazas son enormes, tanto que en Bruselas las podríamos confundir con bosques, de no ser por la hermosa simetría y el ornato, tan cuidados en cada detalle. Las mansiones de la aristocracia, en su mayoría austriacos o húngaros que cambiaron a un hermano por otro, sorprenden por sus enormes dimensiones, su belleza y su buen gusto. En Palacio Imperial, que entonces era una bodega gigante, ahora luce en su fachada un soberbio eclecticismo que corrobora albergar en su interior a un poderoso gobierno. El Parlamento es un gigantesco edificio estilo grecorromano. Su cúpula tiene un diámetro de cuarenta y cinco metros. Tiene tres salas, pero de momento sólo una es ocupada por los senadores, que se halla en el ala derecha, el ala izquierda está reservada para un proyecto a futuro en lo político, la creación de una cámara de diputados, y la sala que está debajo de la cúpula sólo es utilizada cuando está de visita en el recinto el emperador Agustín II.

Hoy por la mañana visité la Cripta Imperial de Guadalupe, una esbelta y oscura iglesia neogótica, que se puede ver desde muy lejos. Tan solo figuran dos tumbas en su interior, la de Maximiliano *el Grande,* muerto a los cincuenta y dos años, y la de su hijo Moctezuma, quien murió siendo aún más joven que su padre, hace apenas diez meses. Se dice que su salud nunca fue del todo buena y que su madre, a quien eternamente llamaré "nuestra princesa", tuvo que asistirlo siempre en sus decisiones.

El día de mi llegada tuve la oportunidad de cenar con un viejo conocido que me impresionó por lo cambiado que está, a causa más que de los años de su debilitada salud. Me refiero a Carl Khevenhüller, conde cuando yo lo conocí y príncipe ahora. Recuerdo que en aquellos lejanos años era un joven increíblemente apuesto, valiente y temerario, por quien se decía que el propio Maximiliano *el Grande* tenía mucha estima. Hoy una enfermedad casi lo ha consumido, pero su vida en México tanto en sus funciones de soldado como en lo personal es leyenda. De joven, mató en un duelo al marido de su actual esposa, habiéndola embarazado previamente. Su hijo ya es general en el ejército imperial mexicano, y se hablan de él muy buenas cosas.

Ayer fui testigo de un espectáculo admirable aquí, en Aztlán. Recuerdo que en mi primera visita había en los límites de la ciudad una hermosa estatua ecuestre del rey Carlos IV de España, obra del gran maestro Tolsá. La escultura guardaba unas proporciones y un juego de líneas verdaderamente admirables. El caballo era un logro escultórico tanto en su pose en marcha como en su perfección, digno de opacar a las obras romanas. Tan sólo en el rostro del rey noté algunos defectos algo indignos de tan bella obra. Y ayer, cuando me dispuse a visitar nuevamente a tan magnífica escultura, ya no la vi ni tampoco a aquel despoblado agreste. Lo que vi fue la más deslumbrante avenida que te puedas imaginar, de muy amplias dimensiones, poblada por los más hermosos árboles de México y por las obras de los maestros más notables de la Imperial Academia de San Carlos. Los pájaros y las ardillas saltan entre los árboles sin la menor desconfianza a los paseantes, como si de un bosque salvaje se tratara. Como te dije líneas atrás, ya no hallé en su lugar la hermosa estatua de Carlos IV, pero sí una mucho más grandes y, si cabe, más perfecta. Según tengo entendido, lleva apenas dos meses en ese sitio y es obra del escultor mexicano de moda en el imperio, pues al parecer nuestra princesa no quiso que tan admirable monumento fuera de factura extranjera. Se trata, como la anterior, de la estatua ecuestre de un soberano, y también de un soberano extranjero. Es nada menos que Maximiliano *el Grande*, quien pareciera que se dirige en su hermoso caballo a ponerse al mando de su ejército en una batalla. Su rostro exhibe una energía y una determinación que, cuando llegué a verlo en persona, nunca pensé que pudiera adoptar. Es como si nuestra princesa hubiera mandado a hacer el rostro del esposo que ella hubiera querido tener, no precisamente del que en realidad tuvo.

Caminar en las calles de Aztlán es como si caminaras en las calles de Viena. Se escuchan varios idiomas al mismo tiempo. Los Habsburgo tienen el don de reunir de forma armoniosa a cuantas culturas puedan bajo su capa imperial. Aunque la diferencia entre Aztlán y Viena radica en que aquí los extranjeros recién llegados, si bien son bienvenidos, tienen que aprender pronto el español. Nuestra princesa al parecer ha sido muy minuciosa al pretender que México no se vuelva una colección de idiomas y le da toda la importancia del mundo al español. En el imperio abundan los apellidos extranjeros, pero todos los portadores están obligados a mexicanizarse si quieren prosperar, incluidos los descendientes del otrora poderoso Napoleón III.

Hace tres días, a mi vuelta de Ixmiquilpan —tenía que volver al lugar donde casi pierdo la vida, y lloré allí no sé si de emoción, de nostalgia o de tristeza—, el príncipe Khevenhüller me informó que nuestra princesa, al haberse enterado gracias a él que estaba de visita en México un antiguo miembro del cuerpo de voluntarios belga, me invitaba a Chapultepec a tomar el té con ella. Hacía apenas unas horas que había llorado en Ixmiquilpan, y ahora volvía a llorar, pero esta vez tenía la seguridad de que la causante era la alegría.

La gran señora me recibió en un balcón del hermoso castillo al que tanto empeño puso en embellecerlo Maximiliano *el Grande* en cuanto llegó al país. Aunque en su rostro se ve el paso de los años y de los grandes esfuerzos a que está sometida constantemente su poderosa inteligencia, su mirada sigue siendo la de aquella princesita a la que tanto amamos.

—Es un honor volver a verla, Majestad —le dije verdaderamente conmovido—. Reciba los más cordiales saludos de este viejo compatriota suyo.

—No se equivoque, mi buen barón —me respondió la princesa en español—. Lleve usted de mi parte a los belgas un mensaje: los recuerdo con cariño y los sigo llevando en mi corazón. Pero yo soy totalmente mexicana.

Aunque es cierto que durante mi estancia en México hace cuatro décadas aprendí bastante de la lengua española. Nunca me he considerado que la domino a la perfección. Y yo francamente pensaba que mi querida princesa me hablaría en francés.

—Espero que no se ofenda —continuó ella en español—, ni que piense que no estimo su contribución para que este imperio fuera una realidad, hace ya tantos años. ¿Me entiende bien usted en mi idioma?

—¿Su idioma? Con un poco de dificultad, pero sí —le respondí en nuestra lengua.

—De acuerdo —dijo la princesa—. ¿Qué le parece si usted habla en francés y yo en español? Así cada quien hablará en la lengua que más ama.

Ante estas palabras de la gran señora, sentí que me apretaban el corazón con fuerza. Ella realmente ya no era belga ni era nuestra princesa. Era la emperatriz viuda de los mexicanos, y eso estaba bastante claro.

—Espero que mis palabras no lo ofendan, mi buen barón —dijo cuando vio la tristeza en mi rostro—, pero usted sabe perfectamente que Dios ha puesto en nosotros los soberanos una responsabilidad muy grande, y en ella está incluido el hecho de pertenecer al pueblo que gobernamos, aunque no sea éste en el que hemos nacido. ¿Me comprende usted?

—Sí, Majestad —le respondí.

—Dígame una cosa, barón —continuó ella—, ¿ya se ha difundido en Bélgica ese rumor de que mi hermano, el rey, ha sido el causante de la muerte de millones de seres humanos en África?

—Sí, señora, ya lo sabe todo el mundo —le dije.

—¿Y qué reacción ha tenido el pueblo? —preguntó la soberana, con vivo interés.

—En algunos sectores se le acusa de asesino —le dije, dudando.

El rostro de ella fue cubierto por una sombra amenazadora.

—Qué daño tan grande ha hecho mi hermano a nuestra familia —dijo—. Esa mancha no será fácil de quitar. Se habla de varios millones de víctimas inocentes. Él sabe bien que Dios nos ha puesto al cuidado de los pueblos para hacer su felicidad, no para asesinarlos. La Providencia ha de castigarlo, y se lo tiene bien merecido.

—No está aún probado que la culpa sea de nuestro rey, señora —le dije—, él se halla tan lejos del lugar de los hechos...

—No lo defienda —me respondió la emperatriz—. La posición de mi hermano no es defendible bajo ninguna circunstancia. Pero lo entiendo, barón, al ser usted un hijo de Bélgica, es lógico que esa horrorosa realidad le cause vergüenza. Y si esa vergüenza acaso es tan grande y quiere usted instar a su familia a emigrar a México, cuente con todo mi apoyo, en agradecimiento a su valiente esfuerzo de hace cuarenta años. El príncipe Khevenhüller me ha dicho que en Ixmiquilpan estuvo usted a punto de morir.

—Mi vida habría sido lo menos que podía yo dar por mi princesa, a la que tanto amaba —le dije llorando.

Su rostro, por un instante, pareció ser el mismo de aquellos años, incluso el cabello blanco pareció alejarse, y yo me sentí más joven. Cuando me dio su mano a que la besara, procuré que mis lágrimas no cayeran sobre su guante.

—Dígales a los belgas que aún los amo —me dijo al despedirse.

Sentado aquí, Philippe, en mi habitación del mejor hotel de la Avenida Lucas Alamán, puedo ver desde mi ventana casi por completo la hermosa ciudad de Aztlán, y también cómo se la traga poco a poco la romántica noche. Quisiera despedirme de ella como se despidió el Conde de Montecristo de París, pero creo que mi filosofía no llega tan lejos. Así que tan sólo puedo decir: adiós, Aztlán, se despide para siempre un testigo de tu miseria y también de tu grandeza. Sigue estrujando el corazón de cuanto extranjero llegue a tus muros como lo has hecho conmigo.

Por ahora, querido Philippe, es todo lo que puedo decirte de mi emotivo regreso a México. Cuando esté de nuevo contigo, aclararé todas tus dudas y será un gusto relatarte mi viaje con más detalle.

Te quiere siempre

Tu padre

Castillo de Chapultepec, enero de 2017

A las siete de la mañana justas, el emperador y su tía la duquesa se sentaron en el enorme comedor que no dejaba de ser la mejor prueba de que en México sólo quedaba un Habsburgo. El emperador, que llevaba ya tres horas trabajando, le dio un sorbo a su café, sin azúcar —hacía apenas dos días que lo tomaba así—, mientras no dejaba de leer un informe.

—Nunca había notado lo mucho que se parece usted a mi hermano —dijo la duquesa Carlota—. Él también leía sus informes mientras desayunaba. ¿Pero usted no podría dejar esos papeles por lo menos mientras desayuna, Majestad?

—Es que hay un gobernador, Quirarte, que me tiene muy preocupado —dijo Fernando Carlos.

—¿Pues qué ha hecho? —preguntó la duquesa.

—Casi nada. Veo aquí pruebas irrefutables de que ha robado tanto como si viviéramos en un país gobernado por un totalitarismo comunista. Se supone que somos el país menos corrupto de Latinoamérica, ¿cómo le voy a explicar el descaro de este tipo a mi pueblo? ¡Apenas puedo creer esto! —dijo el emperador, y dejo los documentos a un lado.

—Majestad, los mexicanos leemos en promedio veinte libros al año, lo que indudablemente nos ayuda a no dejarnos engañar por los políticos bribones que sólo usan sus cargos para enriquecerse. Pero se dan excepciones, incluso en los países más cultos del mundo ocurren casos de corrupción alarmantes algunas veces. Y bueno, dígame, ¿qué piensa hacer?

—Ya le pedí al príncipe Bonaparte que me lo traigan en seguida —respondió Fernando Carlos—, Quirarte no puede gobernar un día más. Enviaré hoy mismo a un gobernador interino, mientras su departamento elige a un nuevo gobernador y yo le doy mi aprobación.

—No sabe cuánto me alegra verlo reaccionar así. Dios escuchó mis súplicas y le mostró el camino hacia su destino ineludible. Su discurso fue arriesgado, pero hermoso. Como mexicana me sentí orgullosa de usted. Cuando desestimó el que yo le había escrito, pensé que podía equivocarse, pero ahora veo que la equivocada fui yo. Realmente me ha hecho usted muy feliz.

—Y yo sería feliz si me tutearas como antes —dijo el emperador—. ¿Acaso no ves lo solo que me siento?

—Majestad, ya hablamos de eso. Ni los miembros de la familia tutean al emperador, y yo, recuerde, me case con un pianista ajeno a la aristocracia. Ya no soy una Habsburgo. Estoy totalmente imposibilitada para tutearlo. Pero, si se siente tan solo, ¿por qué no se casa?

—Tal vez la idea no sea mala —dijo el emperador, mientras se llevaba un tenedor a la boca.

—¿De veras lo cree así?

—Sí, en mis planes está tener una familia. Y te juro que trataré de ser un buen padre.

—¿Lo dice por mi hermano? Entienda que él era el emperador, pensaba siempre en su deber y dejaba su paternidad en segundo plano.

—No lo cuestiono a estas alturas —dijo Fernando Carlos—, pero no quiero ser el tipo de padre que él fue conmigo.

—Lo comprendo, créame. Y respecto a casarse, aunque esa joven no me agrada, ¿qué le parece la princesa Iturbide? Cumple con los requisitos para ser emperatriz.

Fernando Carlos no respondió y dio un sorbo a su café.

—Está bien —dijo la duquesa—, ¿le parece entonces si organizo una reunión con los Habsburgo austriacos aquí, en Aztlán? Tal vez se enamore de una archiduquesa. No sería nada raro que un emperador de la familia se case con una prima suya, sino la cosa más común de la historia.

—¿Y qué te hace pensar que quiero casarme con una princesa? —dijo el emperador.

—Majestad, no haga bromas —respondió la duquesa—. Se supone que ya aceptó su destino y usted conoce bien el protocolo.

—Los reyes de Europa se casan con plebeyas.

—Los reyes de Europa son copas persas. No gobiernan, su función es decorativa. Y usted no es un simple rey, es un emperador con poderes ilimitados, y todos sus seis antecesores se han casado con princesas.

—Cuando me case, será con quien yo realmente ame —dijo el emperador—. Y puede darse el caso de que no llegue ni a baronesa.

—Creo entender qué hay detrás de todo esto, Majestad —dijo la duquesa—. A usted le gusta alguien. Bueno, eso es la cosa más normal en un joven de su edad. Tengo ubicados a cuarenta y tres Habsburgos mexicanos que no son tales legalmente, algunos ni siquiera saben que llevan la misma sangre que nosotros y son nuestros parientes desde los tiempos de Agustín II. Majestad, si una mujer le gusta, puede hacerla su amante. Incluso tenga hijos con ella, si así lo desea. Vamos, tener bastardos ha sido algo demasiado frecuente en los gobernantes de nuestra familia. Hasta la duquesa de Parma, María Luisa de Habsburgo, la mismísima madre de Napoleón II, tuvo sus hijos bastardos. Y vaya que eso es más difícil siendo una mujer. Pero, por el amor de Dios, Majestad, para tener al heredero al trono de México elija a una mujer tal cual manda la tradición y la ley. Cásese con Ana María de Iturbide, y si no le agrada, yo puedo ocuparme de mantenerla bien vigilada y sin permitirle que lo moleste después de que llegue a parir al menos dos archiduques.

—Hablas de forma bastante fría, para ser tú una mujer.

—No desdeño los derechos de mi género —dijo la duquesa—. Pero aquí se trata del futuro y la estabilidad de México. Antes que mujer, soy patriota.

—Nunca tendré hijos ocultos, como mi padre y mi abuelo. Jamás le haría eso a un hijo mío. Dime una cosa, tía, ¿cuántos hermanos tengo, por parte de mi padre?

—Cuatro —dijo la duquesa—. A tres los envió al extranjero, sin que supieran jamás quién es su padre. El otro, el hijo de su amante favorita, vive aquí, en México. Sabe quién es y llevaba buenas relaciones con su padre. Tiene veintitrés años.

—¿Cómo se llama?

—Su nombre es Juan.

—Juan de México, algo así como Juan de Austria. La historia de los Habsburgo da muchas vueltas en el mismo sentido.

—Sí —dijo la duquesa—, llegué a hacerle bromas al respecto a mi hermano.

—¿El emperador aceptaba bromas?

—Tenía una parte muy humana, Majestad, y por desgracia usted no se la conoció.

—Pero no fue mi culpa —dijo Fernando Carlos.

—Lo sé.

—¿Es verdad que mi padre vio a la Dama Blanca el día que murió?

—Sí, Majestad, me lo confesó justo antes de morir. Aunque, por lo que pude darme cuenta, él no supo que se trataba de ella.

—Vaya, los Habsburgo nos trajimos de Europa mucho más de lo que la gente piensa. Se dice que también la vieron mi abuelo y el propio Maximiliano *el Grande*. ¿Eso significa que también va a visitarme el día de mi muerte?

—La Dama Blanca es tan allegada a la familia que creo que ya tiene su habitación aquí, en Chapultepec.

—Y a mi hermano Juan, ¿lo conoces?

—Lo veo con frecuencia, y lo quiero tanto como a usted. Se parece mucho a mi hermano, sobre todo en la mirada cuando está de buen humor.

—Deseo conocerlo también —dijo el emperador.

—Eso no es correcto, Majestad. Si él llega a intimar con usted, y con la cantaleta ésa de los derechos y la igualdad que se traen Morador y sus socialistas, puede llegar a reclamar su apellido legalmente, y recuerde que es mayor que usted. Es cierto que la Constitución es bastante clara y deja especificado que el heredero al trono será el hijo mayor del emperador y de su esposa, pero no veo para qué buscarnos problemas. Los Habsburgos que no nacieron como tales, deben de quedarse como están.

—Te agradezco que te preocupes por mí, tía —dijo Fernando Carlos—. Créeme que tengo bastante claro que sin ti no podría estar aquí. Pero tú misma me has instado a ocupar el lugar que ahora ocupo, y sabes bien que las órdenes del emperador no se cuestionan en lo más mínimo por parte de los miembros de la familia. Sencillamente se llevan a cabo. Quiero conocer cuanto antes a mi hermano, y yo sabré qué dispongo sobre él cuando lo tenga frente a mí.

—A las órdenes de Vuestra Majestad —dijo la duquesa—. Admiro su determinación, pero le recuerdo que la mayor virtud de los emperadores de México ha sido siempre la prudencia. Tenga, por favor, mucho cuidado.

Hace apenas unas horas que regresé de mi viaje al norte de México. Desde que fui a Yucatán, éste ha sido mi quinto viaje al interior del imperio y debo confesar que también en éste, como en todos los demás, mi corazón se ha llenado de una dicha indescriptible gracias al afecto que el pueblo demuestra por mí. No obstante, tengo absolutamente claro que mis funciones no se limitan a recibir el cariño de mi pueblo y a sentirme dichosa por ello, sino a utilizar mi inteligencia y la educación que me dio mi padre, el mejor gobernante de Europa de su tiempo, para hacer de México lo que en el nombre ya es: un imperio. Pero si de algo estoy totalmente segura, ahora que conozco bien a los mexicanos, es que nos es imposible construir una potencia mundial con la mentalidad que domina a la mayoría de los habitantes de México, porque un imperio significa poder, grandeza, y los mexicanos, con su mentalidad tan rezagada en el tiempo, demuestran no ambicionar tales cosas. Si bien es cierto que la gente del norte me ha causado una mejor impresión que la que conocí en mis otros viajes, también tengo claro que España, aunque trajo civilización a estas tierras, todo lo demás lo hizo mal: tanto como construyó edificios carentes de simetría y proporciones, educó a los mexicanos en un catolicismo esclavista, entregado a la sumisión y ajeno a cualquier ejercicio de la inteligencia. España veía a México como una simple colonia a la que no tenía por qué dotar de ilustración ninguna sino que debía mantenerla en el oscurantismo para que fuera su eterno proveedor de riquezas. Qué pecado tan grande. Y pensar que fueron los propios Habsburgo, desde Carlos I hasta Carlos II, quienes durante casi dos siglos forjaron el carácter del mexicano actual. Pero si ellos arruinaron esta cultura, sus descendientes habrán de corregir ese error tan grave, y de eso me he de ocupar yo personalmente, no importa cuánto tiempo y esfuerzo me cueste.

Estoy convencida de que la vía más adecuada para cambiar la mentalidad de los mexicanos es la emigración de enormes grupos de colonos desde Europa. Haré venir europeos de varios países con ideas diferentes, ajenos ellos a este catolicismo tan descaradamente contaminado que no propaga más que sumisión y conformismo. Confío en que un equilibrio en la población propiciado por los emigrantes habrá de lograr un cambio drástico en la mentalidad mexicana, tanto que pasadas una o dos generaciones de España solo habremos de conservar el idioma. Ya que es éste lo único admirable que dejaron aquí.

No quisiera que a la posteridad mis acciones fueran mal juzgadas. Si me propongo llevar a cabo tan grande empresa no es porque no ame a los mexicanos, sino porque estoy totalmente entregada para lograr la dicha y la felicidad de este pueblo. Quiero cambiarlos para que puedan defenderse, para que sean capaces de labrarse su riqueza y su felicidad. Los mexicanos de ahora solo saben dar y los vecinos que tenemos en el norte sólo quieren quitar. Si dejo las cosas como están, en un futuro no muy lejano de México no quedará ni el recuerdo. Es necesario traer extranjeros ambiciosos, capaces de reírse del temor al castigo divino, y hacer de ellos patriotas mexicanos, para que se atrevan a los peores actos con tal de defender lo suyo o incluso para aumentar su patrimonio. La historia demuestra que así es como nacen los grandes imperios y los propios yanquis son una prueba de ello. ¿Cómo entonces lograría que el Imperio Mexicano fuera tal si conservo una población que atesora la ignorancia y la miseria y que defiende menos lo suyo que un cordero su vida ante un lobo? Tengo totalmente claro que los mexicanos no están hechos para lograr con ellos construir un imperio, no son ellos la clase de gente que se requiere para lograr tal hazaña. Por eso debo de cambiarlos todo cuanto pueda. No será un proceso rápido pero estoy dotada de mucha paciencia. Incluso es probable que yo no alcance a ver los grandes frutos de mi obra. Mas me sentiré dichosa si de aquí a cien años me entero en mi fría tumba que no existe un solo pueblo en el mundo que cause temor al Imperio Mexicano. Mi dicha será mayor si para ese entonces todavía los mexicanos se acuerdan de mí, pero si tal cosa no ocurre, no me sentiré en absoluto mal pagada, porque a fin de cuentas quien en ese entonces sea el emperador de México, será también mi descendientes por línea directa, llevará mi sangre y mis ideas, y ésa sería la mayor recompensa que yo, como soberana y madre, podría recibir.

—¿Estás despierto, Fer? —dijo el archiduque Maximiliano, encendiendo la luz.

—Sí, pasa —respondió Fernando Carlos, sentándose en su cama—. Cuéntame, ¿cómo te fue en Inglaterra?

—Bien, la corte inglesa tiene sus encantos. Ellos y nosotros somos las últimas dos monarquías auténticas que quedan en este mundo.

—Supongo que sí. ¿Y acabas de llegar?

—Así es. Hace media hora me bajé del avión, pero quería venir a verte cuanto antes. ¿Cómo es eso de que te vas mañana?

—El emperador por fin me dio el permiso —respondió Fernando Carlos—. Me dijo que soy un imbécil sin carácter, que nunca podré ser ni ministro ni militar, ni siquiera funcionario de correos o jardines, tales fueron sus palabras. Así que no precisamente me autoriza irme a vivir a Miramar, sino que más bien entendí que me dio la orden. ¿Te das cuenta, Max? Por fin soy libre. Diré adiós a las ceremonias matutitos y a los desfiles militares, y sobre todo a la mirada furiosa del emperador. Podré vivir en paz.

—Voy a extrañarte, Fer. Eres mi hermanito, y te quiero como no te imaginas.

—No me quieres más de los que yo te quiero a ti. Pero deja de preocuparte, en estos tiempos la distancia no es ausencia. Podremos comunicarnos y vernos en una pantalla todos los días. Y cuando el emperador esté de viaje, vendré a verte. También tú podrás ir a visitarme a Miramar.

—Supongo que tienes razón —dijo el archiduque Maximiliano—. Es lo mejor para ti, por fin vivirás como quieres, tomarás cursos de pintura y dejarás en el pasado este antiguo protocolo que tanto te hace sufrir. Sinceramente, no te veías ni bien ni cómodo vestido con el uniforme de mariscal de campo del imperio. También tengo la esperanza de que cuando vaya a visitarte, por fin me presentes una novia.

—Gracias por desear lo mejor para mí, Max —dijo Fernando Carlos—. Siempre vas a ser el mejor hermano del mundo.

—¿A qué hora te vas?

—Mi vuelo sale a las seis.

—Me despertaré a tiempo para ir a despedirme al aeropuerto. Pero solo si te pones de pie, perezoso, y me das un abrazo.

—¡Max...!

—Ven, Fer.

Fernando Carlos se fue a parar junto a su hermano, era más bajo de estatura y su cuerpo, a diferencia del de Maximiliano, no evidenciaba músculos aun con la ropa puesta. Se abrazó a él como un niño y, segundos después, ambos estaban llorando.

Castillo de Chapultepec, enero de 2017

—A las órdenes de Vuestra Majestad.

—No le autoricé a que se sentara, señor Quirarte.

—Perdón, Majestad...

—Notará que no le he dado el tratamiento de gobernador, eso se debe a que hace una hora firmé su destitución. ¿Tiene algo que objetar al respecto?

—Pues, Majestad, yo he sido un gran defensor en el sentido de que México no es una dictadura, pero ahora que se me enjuicia y se me destituye sin siquiera avisarme, ya no sé qué pensar.

—Si me he apresurado tanto a firmar su destitución, señor Quirarte, se debe a que considero que usted no puede dar una orden más en su departamento. Ya fue mucho el daño que hizo.

—Si Su Majestad tuviera a bien informarme del daño a que se refiere —dijo el exgobernador, nervioso, mientras gotas de sudor corrían por su amplia frente.

—Señor Quirarte, la independencia economía de que gozan los departamentos, sustentada en la honorabilidad de los gobernadores, hace difícil ver desde aquí irregularidades a menos que las finanzas de un departamento en concreto sean revisadas minuciosamente. No fue un descubrimiento mío todo lo que usted ha hecho, mi padre notó una modestia alarmante en la construcción de infraestructura durante una visita a su departamento, y al regresar a Aztlán pidió saber el presupuesto que usted había gastado: suficiente para construir varios rascacielos de los más altos que tenemos en la capital. Mucho dinero que, sin embargo, no se reflejaba en nada nuevo durante los casi seis años que usted había sido gobernador. Él fue quien pidió una revisión exhaustiva, sin que usted lo supiera, y la carpeta con los resultados llegó a este escritorio poco después de que yo lo ocupé. Tan sólo en la primera página uno se pregunta si acaso los materiales en su departamento valen cincuenta veces más que en el resto del imperio, o si usted construye una pequeña escuela con los mismos métodos que usaron los antiguos griegos para edificar el Partenón, lo que explicaría su alto costo. O dígame, ¿cómo es posible que el gobernador de Iturbide construya un puente de quinientos metros y con esa misma cantidad de dinero a usted solo le alcance para pintar los muros de un viejo hospital? Tampoco me explico cómo es que darle mantenimiento a una estatua del gran sabio Lucas Alamán sea tan costoso como si se construyera el pedestal con oro puro.

—Majestad, yo…

—¡Estoy furioso, Quirarte! —dijo Fernando Carlos, mirándolo a los ojos—. Los mexicanos pagan impuestos para que les demos a cambio un imperio seguro donde puedan vivir en paz y trabajar por su propio bien, no para que un miserable sin escrúpulos se haga millonario. Los impuestos de los ciudadanos en este imperio son intocables para fines ajenos a sus necesidades. ¿Cómo se atrevió a pensar que desfalcos tan descarados podrían permanecer ocultos por siempre?, ¿acaso cree que vivimos en una república populista del sur del continente? Sigue usted siendo mexicano —añadió el emperador, tras una pausa—, y mi obligación es preocuparme por todos los mexicanos, sin importar sus actos. Por ello le daré una oportunidad de que se explique, una sola, ¡así que no me mienta!

Quirarte se quitó los lentes para poder limpiarse el sudor de los ojos, y también para poder evitar por unos instantes la mirada del emperador. Tan solo lo había visto en televisión y su mirada en la pantalla parecía la de un santo, pero ahora que lo tenía enfrente veía en él los mismos ojos que se apreciaban en los cuadros y las fotografías de la antigua emperatriz Carlota.

—Yo, señor…

—Le recomiendo, Quirarte, que sea totalmente sincero. Tenga en cuenta que le espera el resto de su vida en prisión, porque poseo pruebas de todo lo que ha hecho. Ya de nada le serviría tratar de engañarme.

—Está bien, Majestad, le diré toda la verdad. Cuando yo era joven —comenzó Quirarte—, soñaba con ser un hombre muy rico. Supongo que no hay crimen en tal cosa, la comodidad derivada de la fortuna es algo a lo que aspira casi cualquier ser humano. Sin embargo, aunque intenté probar suerte con varios negocios, en todos ellos fracasé. Entonces culpaba a la suerte de tales fracasos, ahora reconozco que quizás todo se debió a la falta de talento. Mas, pese a todo, seguía soñando con ser un hombre rico y poderoso, con regalarle a mi esposa una mansión deslumbrante y joyas muy caras para que siempre me mirara con amor, para que nunca pasara por su mente la idea de estar con otro hombre, ya que conmigo lo tendría todo. Y creo, Majestad, que cuando un hombre reconoce su falta de talento y al mismo tiempo sigue soñando con ser rico, una tabla de salvación es la política. Es ésta la última esperanza de los mediocres para cambiar su suerte. Me olvidé de cualquier negocio y enfoqué todas mis energías en prosperar políticamente, primero como asistente de un prefecto, aguatando regaños por errores que no eran míos, luego como prefecto y así poco a poco hasta llegar a gobernador, donde había mucho dinero a mi disposición y tan sólo necesitaba facturas alteradas emitidas por empresarios amigos míos para sacarlo de las cuentas del gobierno departamental. Ésa es, señor, a grandes rasgos, toda la verdad. No me siento el peor hombre del mundo por ello, la corrupción es algo muy natural en cualquier gobierno, ha existido a lo largo de toda la historia. Yo soy, después de todo, tan sólo un político común. Quizás no tan común en el Imperio Mexicano, pero sí en este mundo. Por tal cosa, le pido que no me vea con tanto odio, tenga un poco de piedad de mí.

—Si su crimen fuera otro, Quirarte —respondió el emperador—, quizás pasaría por mi mente la piedad y usaría mis facultades para reducir su condena un poco. Pero no puedo tener piedad con un hombre que se apropia de los impuestos de los mexicanos para satisfacer sus ambiciones. Si el pueblo al conocer sus actos se negara en masa a pagar impuestos, yo no tendría cara para pedir a nadie que rectifique, puesto que los asistiría la razón. Ningún hombre trabajador querría pagar impuestos si sospecha que éstos irán a parar a las cuentas de un perezoso cobarde y sin escrúpulos que ostenta un cargo público. Debo de ser implacable con usted, para que sirva de escarmiento a otros. Si quiere el perdón, pídaselo a Dios, porque yo no podré perdonarlo nunca. Mas me veo obligado a tener una consideración con usted, una sola: si su esposa y sus hijos quieren cambiar de apellido para eludir la vergüenza, ordenaré que se les facilite todo cuanto sea posible el trámite. Pero no espere nada más de mí. ¿Está claro?

Aunque lo intentó, Quirarte no pudo responder, puesto que sus ojos no dejaban de llorar.

—Detrás de la puerta —continuó el emperador—, lo esperan agentes de la guardia imperial. Vaya con ellos, lo llevarán a un lugar donde dispondrá de lo mínimamente necesario mientras termina su juicio.

—A las órdenes de Vuestra Majestad —dijo Quirarte, todavía llorando.

—Gracias por venir, canciller —dijo la embajadora—, es un gusto charlar y tomar café con un caballero tan amable.

—Es usted muy gentil, embajadora —respondió el príncipe Bonaparte—, como casi todos los embajadores de su país.

—Gracias, me siento alagada. ¿Qué le parece si hablamos en inglés? Me consta que lo habla perfectamente. Mucho mejor que yo el español.

—Ah, me temo que no es posible. Mas si algún día nos vemos en los Estados Unidos quizás le dé gusto en ese sentido. Pero en México no puede ser. Los mexicanos en nuestro país sólo hablamos nuestro idioma, no somos sirvientes de nadie en nuestra propia casa. Espero me entienda.

—Creo, canciller, que ustedes guardan muchos prejuicios desde los tiempos en que las grandes potencias los trataban con la punta del pie. Siempre están a la defensiva. Me atrevería a decir que ven enemigos donde no los hay.

—El ser desconfiados y advertirles a los demás lo que no nos gusta —respondió Bonaparte—, nos ha traído buenos resultados.

—Sí, eso está claro —respondió la embajadora—. Pero esa brusquedad que acompaña siempre a su política puede herir a sus aliados algunas veces.

—¿Acaso lo dice por algo en particular?

—En mi país —respondió la embajadora—, no ha gustado mucho esa repentina decisión de Su Majestad, el emperador Fernando Carlos I, de inaugurar su gobierno el mismo día de la toma de posesión de nuestro presidente. Pareciera que fue acto deliberado, con la intención de molestar a un buen vecino. Además, Su Majestad no llamó al presidente Trump para facilitarlo, y cuando él lo hizo, el emperador no atendió la llamada.

—Embajadora, le confieso que sus palabras me desconciertan demasiado. El presidente de Trump ha dicho que no somos sus amigos, que gracias a nuestros tratados comerciales los robamos, y también que los mexicanos que viven allá son violadores y asesinos. Usted dice que Trump se siente ofendido por la actitud del emperador, y yo le confieso que si no le he devuelto a usted sus credenciales se debe sólo a que los comentarios de su presidente fueron cuando todavía no tomaba el cargo. ¿Cómo se le ocurre a ese hombre que Su Majestad Imperial va a tomarle la llamada?, ¿acaso, con el debido respeto, está loco? Con su actitud ha abierto una grieta en nuestras relaciones que quizás no pueda ser sellada en los cuatro años de su gobierno.

—Entiendo que ustedes estén... algo molestos —dijo la embajadora—. Pero comprendan que el presidente Trump ha sido un empresario toda su vida. En algunos aspectos, apenas está aprendiendo a gobernar.

—Eso está bastante claro —respondió Bonaparte—, pero sería bueno que le dijera que no intente aprender más con nosotros. Es probable que después no le guste lo que vamos a enseñarle.

—Si me lo permite, canciller, debo decirle que no se puede decir que su emperador sea un gran estadista, lleno de experiencia. De todos es conocido que no estuvo cerca de su padre aprendiendo nada sobre el gobierno del imperio, sino que se ha pasado los años refugiado en Trieste, alejando totalmente de la política. Además, su juventud es por sí sola una prueba de su inexperiencia.

—Algunas cosas, embajadora —dijo Bonaparte, sonriendo—, no se aprenden, se heredan.

—No subestimo la preparación que recibió el emperador desde niño —dijo la embajadora—, pero yo creo que México está en un momento en el que requiere de un aliado fuerte en la región, para disipar la zozobra que por ahora envuelve a su gobierno. No olvidemos tampoco que se trata de una monarquía en tiempos de libertades.

—Y suponiendo que tenga razón, embajadora, ¿usted sugiere que ese aliado fuerte serían los Estados Unidos?

—¿Quién más, canciller?, le aseguro que el presidente Trump no tiene malas intenciones para con México. Él sabe la importancia comercial de un imperio tan poderoso y grande. Entiendo que los haya ofendido por decir algunas verdades incomodas, pero...

—El presidente Trump no ha dicho verdades, tan sólo su visión egoísta y absurda de la realidad —dijo Bonaparte, dejando a un lado su taza de café—. Y si a esas vamos, nosotros también tenemos mucho qué decir.

—Canciller, por favor, tomen las palabras del presidente como simples comentarios informales de campaña. Él estima a México más de lo que ustedes suponen. Además, nuestros países tienen una economía tan compartida que creo que todo debemos analizarlo con la cabeza bien fría. ¿O acaso están pensando en cancelar la reunión que siempre ocurre cuando un presidente de mi país toma posesión o cuando un emperador mexicano sube al trono? En esta ocasión se han suscitado ambas cosas, así que la reunión es doblemente importante. No cerremos la puerta al dialogo, por favor.

—Su Majestad Imperial todavía no decide cancelar la reunión, pero delo por hecho en caso de que su presidente pronuncie otra bravuconada, sea cual sea.

—Tal vez ellos se entiendan bastante bien cuando estén juntos —dijo la embajadora—, y usted ya está tomando las cosas con demasiada pasión, algo muy propio de los mexicanos en la política.

—Embajadora, le aseguro que estoy siguiendo con absoluta precisión las órdenes de mi emperador. Él está totalmente decidido a romper incluso las relaciones si su presidente no se modera.

—Por favor, canciller, no es necesario llegar a tanto. Le repito que tan solo han sido comentarios informales, cosas de campaña. Yo tengo mucha fe en que todo quedará resuelto en cuanto el emperador Fernando Carlos vaya a la Casa Blanca.

—Ah, pero Su Majestad no irá a Washington, es el presidente Trump quien tendría que venir a Aztlán —respondió Bonaparte.

—Canciller, el acuerdo era que el emperador de México fuera a mi país.

—Esa reunión se planeó en vida del emperador Maximiliano IV, debido a que la tradición indica que el anfitrión sea el gobernante que recientemente ha ocupado sus funciones. Pero las cosas, como usted bien sabe, han cambiado.

—En ese caso, ambos tienen derecho a pedir ser el anfitrión.

—Pero el presidente Trump tiene una disculpa que ofrecer. Así que lo más adecuado es que venga a ofrecerla aquí.

—Sinceramente, no creo que se disculpe —dijo la embajadora.

—Ya veremos qué hacer en ese caso.

—Infamaré a mi gobierno sobre la modificación que el emperador solicita sobre la reunión pactada —dijo la embajadora—. Yo tenía una fecha qué proponerle, el diez de febrero, pero esto era en caso de que los planes de que la reunión se celebrara en Washington no variaran. Ahora no estoy autorizada para acordar nada con usted, canciller, tendré que esperar las instrucciones de mi gobierno.

—Si el presidente Trump quiere venir el diez de febrero —dijo Bonaparte—, estoy autorizado por mi emperador para aceptar esa fecha.

—Y en caso de que el venga, ¿será recibido en Chapultepec, en el despacho de los cuatro bustos?

—No, embajadora, no será allí. Su Majestad quiere que la reunión se celebre en el Palacio Imperial.

—¿Y por qué no en Chapultepec? Se supone que es allí donde el emperador de México recibe a sus aliados y amigos.

—Precisamente...

Fue hasta que la solitaria fragata de la comitiva imperial ya se hallaba cerca de las costas de Nueva York, cuando la emperatriz Carlota supo que por fin, gracias a la insistencia de los representantes de Bélgica y Austria, el presidente Andrew Johnson aceptaba recibirla, pero sólo como princesa de Bélgica, en calidad de hermana del rey, y como archiduquesa de Austria, por ser cuñada del emperador, nunca como la emperatriz de México. Carlota, sin embargo, se sintió satisfecha, ya que no le importaba en calidad de qué la recibiera Johnson, sino que tuviera la posibilidad de hablar cara a cara con él.

Ya en Washington, al llegar a las afueras de aquel edificio blanco que imitaba el estilo de los antiguos romanos, una formación militar le rindió honores y ella pasó revista, por tratarse, a fin de cuentas, de un importante miembro de la realeza europea. Johnson la recibió cordialmente a las afueras del edificio y la llevó del brazo hasta su despacho. Al verla pasear su mirada arrogante de un muro a otro, evitó hacerle comentarios sobre las pinturas y la decoración, ya que al ser el presidente de una república y venir de un origen modesto, hablar de arte y buen gusto con una princesa con fama de ser la más culta de Europa era pisar terreno pantanoso y correr el riesgo de quedar en ridículo. Prefirió que la conversación iniciara directamente en el terreno político, donde creía que era invulnerable, porque él representaba a una república sostenida por el pueblo y ella a una forma de gobierno desprestigiada y decadente. Carlota, ante la mirada de Johnson, no se veía intimidada en absoluto. Había meditado durante dos meses muy bien lo que debía decir, al mismo tiempo que practicaba el inglés para hablarlo perfectamente bien y no dejar ninguna duda sobre sus pretensiones.

Sabía que se hallaba ante un hombre acosado por infinidad de problemas. Si bien era cierto que en ese momento Estados Unidos era ya una gran potencia, con capacidad de poner a dos millones de hombres en armas, las facultades de Johnson estaban en entredicho en amplios sectores del país. No era precisamente un mandatario surgido directamente de la democracia, sino la consecuencia del asesinato de

Lincoln, y tampoco, pese al conmovedor suceso que lo había llevado a la presidencia, recibía el apoyo de los poderes de facto de la unión. En ese momento no sólo se hallaba ante la difícil tarea de reincorporar al Sur rebelde y derrotado, sino que los senadores republicanos se traían entre manos un plan para apartarlo de la presidencia y abrir la posibilidad de romper el equilibrio de poderes para crear una especie de dictadura legislativa con una figura presidencial amordazada. La gran empresa de Washington y los demás padres fundadores corría en ese momento un serio peligro de colapsar por la pérdida de sus cimientos. Así las cosas, en algunos aspectos la situación de Johnson en los Estados Unidos era apenas un poco mejor que la de Maximiliano en México. La guerra civil había hecho, parcialmente, de los poderes de la unión un rompecabezas difícil de volver a armar.

—Perdone si cometo errores, señora —dijo Johnson—, pero aquí no son comunes las princesas.

—Las mismas disculpas le pido yo en tal caso —respondió Carlota—, ya que no tengo experiencia hablando con presidentes.

—Me dicen, señora —continuó Johnson—, que usted quiere hablar conmigo en favor del supuesto Imperio Mexicano, pero nosotros en ese país sólo reconocemos el gobierno de la República. El señor Maximiliano de Habsburgo no es, ante nuestro gobierno, otra cosa que un aventurero que pretende imponer por la fuerza de las armas una monarquía que los mexicanos no desean.

—Me complaceré entonces en corregir en usted ese error, que supongo no se debe a ninguna mala intención, tan sólo al desconocimiento de la verdad absoluta, señor presidente. El pueblo mexicano ya está harto de gobiernos militares que no han traído al país más que revoluciones, hambre y miseria. Por eso ha decidido volver a la forma de gobierno monárquica, que tuvo durante más de tres siglos bajo el Imperio Español y que incluso practicó su primer gobernante como país libre. Los mexicanos han decidido, por voluntad propia, poner su destino en manos de un príncipe europeo. Y el resultado de ello es el actual Imperio Mexicano, que yo y mi esposo encarnamos con las mejores intenciones del mundo, puesto que nuestro compromiso de crear un buen gobierno es ante los mexicanos y ante Dios mismo.

—Tengo fundamentos para creer que no estoy en error alguno, señora —dijo Johnson, esbozando una sonrisa maliciosa—. Estoy enterado de que los mexicanos se han opuesto a las tropas francesas por la vía de las armas, con tal determinación y coraje para salvar a su país republicano que han logrado que Napoleón III ordene la retirada. ¿O acaso estoy en un error?

—Lo que ocurre en México, señor presidente —dijo Carlota, recibiendo con naturalidad un argumento que ya esperaba—, es una guerra civil, como también la han tenido aquí recientemente. Algunas veces en un país surgen dos ideales tan opuestos que terminan en hechos de armas. Con certeza, y se lo digo con total sinceridad, no sabemos a qué bandera sigue la mayoría de los mexicanos, pero lo que sí le puedo asegurar es que unos pelean por un ideal corrompido y sin fundamento, que en medio siglo no ha podido hallar el camino de la paz, en tanto que otros siguen a un imperio que tiene un verdadero plan de gobierno, para hacer de México un pueblo seguro, libre y pacífico, que pueda beneficiar con su comercio a otros pueblos del mundo, incluidos los Estados Unidos.

—Aunque usted tuviera razón, señora —dijo Johnson—, y ese aventurado imperio que usted y su esposo encabezan fuera lo mejor para México, tengo conocimiento de que ustedes apoyaron al Sur, y eso nos vuelve enemigos. El señor Juárez, por el contrario, se mostró partidario de la Unión, lo que significa que nosotros tenemos una deuda de honor con él. Por lo tanto, no puedo menos que seguir dando mi apoyo a sus herederos republicanos.

—Me conmueve que sienta usted respeto por el señor Juárez, puesto que fue un gran mexicano que quiso para los suyos paz, libertad y progreso. Lamentablemente, sus herederos no pueden garantizar nada de eso para México, lo digo con total seguridad. Antes se mataran entre ellos por el poder. México ha sufrido mucho desde que es un país independiente, y en gran medida ustedes han contribuido a ello, declarando una guerra sin los más mínimos fundamentos. Usted sabe bien que los militares herederos de Juárez sólo perpetuarán el caos y la destrucción, y nunca la estabilidad que merece un pueblo que ha sufrido tanto. Si es verdad, señor presidente, que usted desea ayudar a que se consoliden los anhelos del gran Juárez, y si también, por el debido temor a Dios, sabe que Estados Unidos, en reparación del daño injustamente causado, debe de contribuir a la paz de ese pueblo tan golpeado por la ambición, entonces su deber es apoyar al Imperio, porque si continua respaldando a los que se llaman Juaristas, será también culpable del sufrimiento que espera a los mexicanos de aquí en adelante.

—Cuando murió el presidente Juárez, recibí una carta de un hombre que no es militar —dijo Johnson—, un tal señor... Lerdo. En esa carta pude ver en él una sabiduría admirable. Él sería un buen sucesor de Juárez, estoy seguro de ello.

—¿Y cuánto tiempo cree que el podrá sobrevivir a los militares, que se sienten con el mayor derecho a gobernar el país? Señor presidente, el imperio no aspira a ser un gobierno militarizado. Mi esposo es un hombre que detesta la guerra y sus planes son diametralmente opuestos a ella. Por favor, no lo quite a un pueblo que ha sufrido tanto la posibilidad de conocer la paz.

En aquel momento, Carlota sentía estar representando un papel, y por ello supuso que Johnson hacía lo mismo, así que no se creyó del todo su amarga expresión, al dar al entender que realmente sus palabras le habían calado muy hondo.

—Señora, le repito que aunque puede ser que usted tenga razón, el ejército de la Unión simpatiza totalmente con los republicanos de México. Cambiar mi apoyo de bando me es imposible.

—No tiene que hacer tal cosa —dijo Carlota, satisfecha—, tan sólo le pido que deje de ayudar con armas a bando contrario...

—Lo diré lo único que puedo hacer sin comprometerme —dijo Johnson, tras meditar bastantes segundos—, de ninguna manera voy a reconocer al Imperio Mexicano, pero ya que nuestra situación es bastante difícil en este momento, haré que mi gobierno se desentienda del tema de México por un período de un año. Si es verdad todo lo que usted me ha dicho, su esposo deberá aprovechar ese año, y quizás, si logran la paz en ese desgraciado país, con el tiempo también logren el reconocimiento de un presidente de los Estados Unidos, que seguramente no habré de ser yo.

—No le pido más que eso —dijo Carlota, feliz—, tan sólo que me haga de sus palabras un juramento que no va a olvidar. ¿Me jura usted no intervenir en los asuntos de México durante un año?

—Señora —dijo Johnson, algo contrariado—, se lo juro.

"Quizás en diez años, en medio siglo, en un siglo o en un siglo y medio, tu sucesor te maldiga", pensó Carlota, mientras sonreía agradecida, "por permitir que se consolide el Imperio que habrá de cobrarles al doble todo lo que nos deben".

—Señor presidente —dijo al fin—, algún día el Imperio Mexicano tendrá el honor de corresponder a este gesto de los Estados Unidos. No tenga usted ninguna duda de ello. En México decimos algo que es muy cierto: no hay día que no se llegue, ni plazo que no se cumpla.

—Hola, sé bienvenido. Siéntate, por favor.

—Creo que se dice "A las órdenes de Vuestra Majestad", en estos casos.

—¿Así le decías a nuestro padre cuando venías a visitarlo?

—Veo que usted sabe quién soy. Mi tía no me dijo nada, tan sólo que debía venir aquí con urgencia. Pero de inmediato sospeché a qué se debía. No pienso meterme en su vida, ni reclamar absolutamente nada. No voy a molestarlo nunca, tiene mi palabra. Tengo claro lo que soy y lo que no soy.

—Cálmate —dijo el emperador—. No te hice venir para pelearnos. ¿Podrías tutearme?

—Usted es el emperador y yo sólo soy Juan Robledo.

—También soy tu hermano.

—Medio hermano, Majestad.

—Pero hermano, a fin de cuentas. ¿A qué te dedicas?

—Canto en un antro, por las noches. Pero dígame, francamente, ¿qué pretende, Majestad?

—¿Crees que tengo malas intenciones contigo?

—No, en realidad no, pero sí me extraña mucho su comportamiento.

—¿Podríamos intentar ser amigos? —dijo el emperador—. Tal vez ambos nos necesitamos.

—Sabe, el emperador...

—Nuestro padre.

–... él jamás se enojó conmigo, ni me regañó, salvo una sola vez. Recuerdo que estaba de visita en casa de mi madre, y en ese momento reíamos porque él me levantó de los pies, haciendo que mi cabeza rosara el suelo, y yo en represalia le despeiné su rubia cabellera. En ese instante apareció usted en la televisión, tendría entonces seis años, y yo tuve el atrevimiento de decir: "es mi hermano, papá". El emperador se puso furioso, me miró como si yo fuera su enemigo y me dijo con una voz tan grave que lo desconocí: "Él es el archiduque Fernando Carlos, y no tiene absolutamente nada que ver contigo. Jamás olvides eso, ¿te quedó claro, Juan?" Cuando respondí afirmativamente con la cabeza, él se fue. Entonces comprendí que yo y usted nunca podríamos ser amigos y mucho menos hermanos.

–Vaya, así que jugaba contigo.

–Siempre que nos veíamos cuando yo era niño, una vez por mes, para ser precisos, que era el día que él se tomaba de descanso. En ocasiones hasta me llevó a pescar, me enseñó a nadar en un rio y cocinábamos nuestra comida en el campo, nosotros solos. ¿Con usted no hacía eso?

Fernando Carlos se quedó pensativo por varios segundos. Parecía que su mente se había ido.

–¿Ese busto es el del emperador Rodolfo I? –preguntó Juan, para traerlo de vuelta.

–Ah, sí –dijo el emperador, reaccionando–. ¿Acaso no lo habías visto nunca?

–No, es la primera vez que entro aquí.

–Mi tía me dijo que algunas veces llegaste a venir.

–Al castillo, pero el emperador jamás me invitó a entrar a su despacho. Con el tiempo comprendí por qué. Este lugar está reservado para los Habsburgo.

–Parece que hablamos de dos hombres completamente diferentes –dijo Fernando Carlos–, a mí me sentada en esa silla, donde estás tú, y me sermoneaba por espacio de una hora sobre mis obligaciones. Pero nunca jugó conmigo. Si yo hubiera tocado su rubia cabellera quizás me habría enviado a prisión una semana.

—Será porque nos veía de forma diferente.

—No debió hacer tal cosa, los dos somos sus hijos. Supongo que tampoco conociste a Max. Él nunca mencionó haberte visto.

—No, y de hecho, cuando salían en televisión, me agradabas más tú. Él se veía muy arrogante.

—Era sólo un poco vanidoso, pero fue un gran hermano. Lo extraño mucho, más de lo que te puedes imaginar.

—Definitivamente no me lo puedo imaginar de ninguna manera — respondió Juan—. Por el lado de mi madre, soy hijo único. No tengo ninguna experiencia en cuestiones de fraternidad.

—¿Tu madre vive?

—Sí, estuvo en Aztlán hasta... hasta la muerte de nuestro padre. Pero ya no soportó vivir aquí. Es originaria de Guadalajara, y regresó a su ciudad natal hace unos días.

—¿A qué se dedica?

—A nada, comprenderás que el emperador se ocupaba de nuestros gastos, y a ella le dejó una modesta herencia. Básicamente no volvió a trabajar desde que lo conoció.

—¿Y a qué se dedicaba antes?

—Era bailarina exótica —respondió Juan—. Qué contraste con tu madre, una princesa rusa de la familia Romanov. Supongo que en ellas radica el trato tan diferente que recibimos de niños por parte de nuestro padre.

—Según tengo entendido, tu madre fue su gran amor.

—Así son los emperadores —respondió Juan—, por ley se casan con una princesa, pero la felicidad la buscan en otra parte.

—Cuando decidiste dedicarte a cantar, ¿protestó por ello nuestro padre?

—No, en absoluto. Me felicitó por mi determinación y me deseó la mejor de las suertes.

—Yo de niño quería ser pintor y… recuerdo que no me felicitó por ello. Dime una cosa, aquella ocasión, cuando al verme en la televisión dijiste que era tu hermano, ¿te emocionó verme?

—Sí, tenía deseos de conocerte y jugar contigo. Aunque nunca lo dije, siempre esperaba que en alguna de sus visitas el emperador te llevara con él.

—Gracias.

—¿Por qué?

—Porque me haces sentir que aprendiste a quererme desde que eras un niño, y también porque desde hace unos instantes me tuteas.

—No me di cuenta… Supongo que hiciste que me sintiera en confianza.

—Nunca dejes de tutearme, ¿de acuerdo?

—¿Me vas a dar órdenes? —preguntó Juan, sonriendo.

—Es un favor que te pido, hermano.

—Sabes, Fer, veo que eres a toda madre.

—Jamás me habían dicho eso.

—Ni te lo dirán. Y no porque no lo seas, sino porque eres el emperador. A hablarte de esa forma nadie se atrevería.

—Cuando Max murió, creí que jamás volvería a disfrutar el abrazo de un hermano. ¿Me darías un abrazo?

El emperador dio la vuelta a su escritorio y su hermano fue a su encuentro. Se abrazaron con fuerza y sus rostros reflejaban alegría sincera.

—Te pareces mucho a nuestro padre —dijo Fernando Carlos—, y jamás imaginé su rostro sonriendo, así como lo haces en este momento.

—Ahora que te veo de cerca, noto que tú te pareces un poco a la antigua emperatriz Carlota.

—Ojalá también haya heredado su determinación y sobre todo su inteligencia.

—¿Es verdad eso de que ella hizo todas las grandes proezas y Maximiliano *el Grande* tan sólo se dedicó a fomentar las artes?

—Maximiliano sí hizo una gran proeza, que benefició a los mexicanos de varias generaciones —dijo el emperador.

—¿Cuál?

—Casarse con ella.

—¿Lo dices en serio?

—Si él se hubiera casado con otra princesa de menor talento y coraje, quizás no hubiera aceptado venir aquí, o la habría traído a México como su consorte y tal vez ella no hubiera ayudado tanto al imperio. Así las cosas, Porfirio Díaz habría sido presidente y ahora México estaría gobernando por Morador o por alguien con menos inteligencia que él, si es que ese alguien puede existir. Ya me lo imagino: robando como pirata, rodeado por un gabinete de analfabetos corruptos, y también gastando los impuestos de los mexicanos sólo en estupideces o dándoselos a los que no quieren trabajar.

—Veo que estás muy convencido de la importancia del Imperio, Fer.

—Sí, ahora lo estoy.

—Harás las cosas bien. Yo confío en ti.

—Quizás necesite a mi hermano conmigo, para ayudarme —dijo el emperador.

—¿A qué te refieres?

—Quería pedirte un favor.

—Dime.

—¿Por qué no vienes aquí todos los días? Le pediré al príncipe Bonaparte que te vuelva su asistente, aprenderás mucho de él y en uno o dos años estarás listo para un ministerio.

—No, hermano, lo lamento. No me sentiría cómodo aquí.

—Bueno —dijo el emperador—, entonces, ¿qué te parece ser gobernador interino de Veracruz? Te enviaré asesores para que no te equivoques. Serán sólo unos meses y adquirirás experiencia...

—Fer, me gusta disfrutar las noches y despertarme después del mediodía. No tengo ambiciones de político. Pero si realmente crees necesitarme, quizás pueda hacer el intento.

—No —dijo el emperador, tras reflexionar—. No tengo derecho a quitarte tu amada libertad. Sé lo que se siente cuando te hacen eso. Pero, si en algún momento las cosas se me complican, ¿puedo contar con mi hermano?

—Fer, si te llega el agua al cuello, seré tu canciller o tu ministro de guerra en plena guerra si hace falta. Pero si no me necesitas tanto, déjame seguir en lo mío.

—Está bien. Pero no quiero que perdamos contacto, ¿de acuerdo? Es más, ven a cenar conmigo uno de estos días.

—¿Y tú irás a oírme cantar? —preguntó Juan—. Mi antro no es precisamente para un emperador. Pero te puedes poner una barba postiza y una peluca...

—Claro, será un placer oír cantar a mi hermano. Incluso tengo una idea...

Esa noche, centro histórico de Aztlán

Carlota sintió una extraña sensación al no ver a Fernando Carlos y a su motocicleta en la misma esquina de las otras veces, una en el suelo y la otra de pie. Esperaba verlo y eso la entristeció un poco, pero al mismo tiempo se sintió aliviada. Llevar una amistad con el emperador era incómodo para ella. Así que creyó tener que sentirse agradecida porque Su Majestad ya hubiera perdido el interés.

A punto estaba de empezar a caminar nuevamente cuando escuchó el ruido de un motor de motocicleta a sus espaldas. Volteó, muy a su pesar, deseando que fuera él.

—Hoy llegaste primero que yo —dijo Fernando Carlos, antes de que ella estuviera totalmente girada—. Gracias por esperarme.

—¿Quién te dijo que te esperé?

—Estabas aquí.

—Pude detenerme por cualquier otra cosa, mientras caminaba.

—Ahora eres tú la necia. Pero no quiero discutir contigo, así que acepto que no me esperabas.

—Ah, pues gracias —respondió Carlota.

—Dime, ¿a qué hora entras mañana a tu trabajo matutino?

—A las nueve, ¿por qué?

—Entonces puedes aceptarme una invitación.

—No, Maj...Fer.

—Sí, correcto, Fer está bien.

—Te decía que no puedo.

—Yo entro a trabajar cinco horas antes que tú, y aun así deseo que me acompañes a un lugar esta noche.

—¿A dónde?

—A un antro.

—¿El emperador acude a antros? —preguntó Carlota, extrañada.

—Ésta será mi primera vez.

—¿Y dónde queda ese antro?

—No lo sé con certeza, pero aquí tengo anotada la dirección —dijo Fernando Carlos y le extendió un pequeño trozó de papel.

—Éste no es un lugar para aristócratas —dijo Carlota, al leer el contenido—. Yo he ido allí algunas veces.

—¿De verdad? Entonces serás mi guía. ¿Qué tal está?

—Para mí está muy bien. Pero no sé si tú lo veas igual. No te imagino en un lugar así.

—¿Entonces me acompañas? —dijo el emperador.

—Está bien —respondió ella—. Como mexicana, es mi deber cuidarte, no sea que en ese lugar te vayan a matar de un botellazo en la cabeza.

Cuando llegaron al antro, el emperador detuvo la motocicleta a escasos metros. Pero nadie podía imaginar de quién se trataba en esa noche oscura. Sacó un teléfono de una bolsa de su abrigo e hizo una llamada. "Ya estoy aquí", dijo y colgó. Apenas un par de segundos después, encendió nuevamente la motocicleta y le dio la vuelta al antro. En la parte de atrás alguien ya lo esperaba, con una pequeña puerta abierta, y los condujo por un pasillo a oscuras, hasta llegar a un palco también con muy escasa iluminación, que quedaba justo frente al escenario y arriba de la gran mayoría de los asistentes. Carlota pudo notar que quien les servía de guía no sabía que se trataba del emperador.

—Con su permiso —dijo el guía—. En seguida vendrán a atenderlos.

Y poco menos de un minuto después, un mesero que no pudo distinguir el rostro del emperador entre las sombras, les estaba tomando la orden.

—Pulque con hielo —pidió Carlota.

—Lo mismo —dijo Fernando Carlos.

—¿Es cierto que el pulque nunca llegó a gustarle del todo a tu antepasado, Maximiliano *el Grande* —dijo Carlota, cuando se quedaron solos—, y que aun así hizo todo lo posible por convertirlo en una bebida famosa a nivel mundial?

—Eso dicen los libros. Y a mí tampoco me gusta —respondió el emperador—, porque nunca bebo alcohol.

—Entonces, ¿por qué lo pediste?

—Para tomar lo mismo que tú.

—A ver si no te emborrachas por imitarme. Oye, esta es la hora en que empieza a cantar Juan Robledo. Llegamos justo a tiempo. Me encanta su voz.

—¿Lo conoces?

—No en persona, pero ya es algo famoso en Aztlán. Su música es muy emotiva, romántica…

—¿Y te gustaría conocerlo en persona y saludarlo?

—¡Claro!

—Pues considéralo hecho.

—Supongo que ahora le enviarás una nota que diga más o menos así: "Es mi voluntad que se presente usted inmediatamente en mi palco. Firmado, Fernando Carlos I de México, mariscal de campo del ejército imperial, gran duque y príncipe de Aztlán, conde de Habsburgo, rey de Jerusalén, archiduque de México y etcétera, etcétera".

—No hace falta —dijo Fernando Carlos, sin dejar de verla a los ojos, que le brillaban entre la escasa luz—, él vendrá en cualquier momento.

—¿Entonces ya habías enviado la nota?

—No fue necesario.

—¿Acaso él adivinó que el emperador ordena tenerlo ante su presencia?

—Buenas noches —dijo la voz de alguien que abrió la puerta del palco, y Carlota reconoció en ella a Juan Robledo—. ¿Cómo están? Aquí hay un interruptor —añadió encendiendo la luz—, por si no lo habían encontrado, aunque si quieren estar a oscuras, lo apagan en cuanto me vaya. Me encontré al mesero en el camino: pulque con hielo para la señorita, y también pulque con hielo para Su Majestad Imperial por la gracia de Dios y del pueblo. No se exceda, señor. Quizás se ponga ebrio y al amanecer nombre a Morador canciller del imperio.

—Carlota, te presentó a mi hermano, Juan.

—¿Tu hermano? —dijo ella, impresionada—. ¿En verdad son hermanos?

—A la mitad, pero sí —dijo Juan.

—Ahora que los veo bien, se parecen un poco. Vaya, pues qué sorpresa.

—Es más guapa de lo que me dijiste, Fer —dijo Juan, mientras la saludaba—. Bueno, yo tengo que cantar. Los dejo. Y supongo que aparte de que me marche también quieren que vuelva a apagar la luz.

—¡No! Así está bien —dijo Carlota—, desde afuera nadie puede ver al emperador, así que no hay necesidad de estar aquí a oscuras.

—Como usted ordene.

—En verdad que me he llevado una gran sorpresa —dijo Carlota, cuando Juan cerró la puerta—. Nunca me imaginé que él fuera... Es tu medio hermano por parte de tu padre, ¿cierto?

—Sí, los dos somos hijos del emperador.

—¿Y siempre se han llevado bien?

—Siempre, desde que nos conocemos...

—Ah, qué bueno. ¿Y desde cuándo se conocen?, ¿desde niños?

—No, desde hoy al medio día.

—¿Lo dices en serio?

—Por mi honor que no miento. Salud.

—Salud. Por esa expresión veo que es verdad que el alcohol no es lo tuyo. Pide otra cosa.

—Tengo que acostumbrarme, el pulque es la bebida nacional y sería un crimen imperdonable que el emperador no la disfrute. Es cuestión de practicar.

—Pues a ver si no chocamos esta noche, por culpa de tus prácticas —dijo Carlota.

—Sólo tomaré éste. Ni una gota más. También sería imperdonable que el emperador conduzca ebrio.

—Los políticos comúnmente violan las reglas.

—Es verdad, pero los emperadores de México no lo hacen.

—Buenas noches a todos —los interrumpió por las bocinas la voz de Juan—. Espero que todos se encuentren bien este día, porque yo estoy de maravilla. A decir verdad, éste es uno de los días más especiales de mi vida. —añadió e hizo una pausa hasta que cesaran los gritos—. Estoy feliz, y por ello quiero empezar esta velada con una canción para enamorados, una canción que a ustedes les ha gustado mucho, y también quiero dedicarla para alguien muy especial, para mi hermano Fer, que está aquí esta noche. —la gente volvió a gritar y Juan guardó silenció nuevamente—. Les decía que esta canción, que es para los enamorados, quiero dedicarla a mi hermano Fer y a su novia, Carlota, que están aquí con nosotros, felices y disfrutando de la velada.

—¿Tu novia? —dijo Carlota.

—Creo que Juan me entendió mal —se disculpó el emperador.

—¿Tú le pediste la canción para nosotros?

—¡Sí!, pero le dejé claro que todavía no somos novios...

—¿Cómo está eso? —preguntó Carlota, nerviosa.

—Pues todavía no somos novios. Pero creo que podemos corregir el error de mi hermano en este preciso momento.

—¡Fer, espera...!

—¿Aceptarías ser mi novia?

—Yo no soy una princesa, no hablo varios idiomas, no sé comer con cubiertos, jamás he ido a un evento importante ni he usado un vestido de gala. Tampoco soy rubia, sino morena de ascendencia negra, y mis ojos no son azules ni verdes, son cafés. No tengo nada que ver con la aristocracia.

—Ésa no es la respuesta a mi pregunta —dijo el emperador.

—Pero es la verdad. Yo no quiero ser la amante oculta que estará llorando el día que te cases con una princesa, quizás con Ana María de Iturbide.

—Carlota, no te estoy pidiendo que seas mi amante, te estoy pidiendo que seas mi novia.

—Fer, los noviazgos suelen ser con miras a un matrimonio.

—Eso lo tengo claro. Te lo aseguro.

—¿Qué van a decir los aristócratas que integran tu gabinete y tu tía, cuando sepan que soy tu novia?

—No vas a ser la novia de ninguno de ellos —respondió Fernando Carlos—, ni mucho menos de mi tía. A ella no le atraen las mujeres.

Carlota aprovechó aquella broma para reír unos segundos y liberarse un poco de los nervios.

—Fer, esto...

—Carlota —dijo el emperador, y tomó sus manos—, creo que ya dijiste muchas cosas y no has respondido lo que te pregunté, cuando es la respuesta más práctica del mundo. Tan sólo es sí o es no.

—¿Sabes lo que estás haciendo?

—Jamás he pedido algo en mi vida con tantas esperanzas puestas en ello. ¿Cuál es la respuesta a mi pregunta?

—Sí, Fer —dijo Carlota, y sintió que una briza cálida entraba al interior de su cuerpo—. Sí acepto ser tu novia.

—Júrame que mañana no vas a decirme que fue una mala decisión y que lo mejor es olvidarnos de esto.

—Te lo juro —dijo Carlota—, si tú me juras lo mismo.

—Te lo juro.

Carlota sonrió, y apretó las manos del emperador con fuerza.

—Vaya, mi hermano nos dedicó una canción, y ya ha acabado y no recuerdo una palabra de lo que cantó. Si se entera no le va a gustar.

—Yo tampoco le puse atención —reconoció Carlota.

—Creo que si le pedimos que la repita y le explicamos a qué se debió que no lo escucháramos, nos va a entender.

—Buena idea. Sabes, Fer, hace un par de horas, antes de que llegaras al lugar donde nos conocimos, creí que ya no te vería otra vez, y por un momento, aunque quise negarme a reconocerlo, me sentí la persona más infeliz del mundo. Si te digo esto es para que sepas que aun sin que fuéramos nada habría sido un golpe muy duro que te alejaras repentinamente, así que siendo novios, si se te ocurre dejarme… si sólo me has pedido que sea tu novia porque no sabes bien lo que sientes.

—Carlota, tengo absolutamente claros mis sentimientos, puedes estar segura de ello. Y si hoy llegué un poco más tarde que ayer y el día que me accidenté frente a ti, fue porque desde la mañana tuve un departamento sin gobernador. No podía salir de mi despacho sin designar a un gobernar interino confiable.

—Te entiendo, Fer —dijo Carlota—. No te estaba reclamando que llegaras unos minutos tarde, cuando ayer yo te hice esperar mucho más tiempo. ¿Y ya solucionaste ese problema?

—Sí, esta misma noche nombré gobernador al conde Adán de Neipperg. Tiene ya ochenta años, pero también tiene mucha experiencia, y es famoso por su honradez y su escrupulosidad con los fondos públicos. Él es exactamente lo que necesito.

—Vaya, no tengo idea de lo complejas que son todas tus responsabilidades –dijo Carlota.

—Pues ve imaginándolas, el tiempo pasa muy rápido.

—¿A qué te refieres?

El emperador no respondió, tan sólo la miró a los ojos y sonrió como un niño. Minutos después, volvió Juan a disculparse por "haberse equivocado" al decir que eran novios, pero su hermano le dijo que ya no hacía falta disculparse. Las dos horas siguientes, se hablaron de su infancia, Fernando Carlos tocó el tema de su tristeza por no haber conocido a su madre, y por el autoritarismo y la exigencia con que su padre se había conducido siempre al educarlo. Carlota, por el contrario, tenía tras de ella una infancia feliz, con carencias pero nunca sobre lo más elemental, y dentro de una familia unida que se apoyaba en todo, antes y después de la muerte de su padre.

Al salir del antro, se fueron tomados de la mano hasta donde habían dejado la motocicleta. El emperador le colocó su abrigo con mucho cuidado a Carlota, al notar que sentía un poco de frio. Nuevamente, como el día anterior, mientras ella iba a brazada a él, deseó que el camino a su casa fuera eterno.

—Creo que ya sabes muy bien cómo llegar a mi casa –dijo Carlota, cuando se bajó de la motocicleta.

—Desde el día que te conocí, habría sabido regresar con las luces de todo Aztlán apagadas.

—Ese día me sentí un poco extraña por cómo te comportaste –reconoció Carlota–, no podía creer que yo te gustaba, aunque parecía obvio.

—¿Y yo te gusté ese día?

—Es extraño, Fer, porque me gustaste desde un principio, aunque la oscuridad no me dejaba verte bien. Después me asusté al saber quién eras, pero cuando te pusiste tan necio, extrañamente me gustaste todavía más.

—Carlota —dijo el emperador, acercándose—, aunque vengo de una familia arraigada en el pasado, tengo entendido que los novios ya se besan en esta época.

—Pero creo que ignoras que quien debe de tomar la iniciativa es el hombre, sobre todo la primera vez.

—Creo que tienes razón —dijo el emperador, acercándose todavía más, y luchando porque no volviera su antigua timidez.

—Llegué a pensar que no querías hacerlo.

Fernando Carlos la rodeó con sus manos, y poco a poco la fue apretando contra su pecho, sintiendo a cada instante una sensación desconocida para él hasta entonces. Cuando empezó a besarla tímidamente, ella lo tomó de la nuca y lo acercó con fuerza. Quizás había tomado la determinación de enseñarlo a besar.

—Tú pensaste que yo no quería hacerlo —dijo él, cuando por fin se separó—, y sin embargo era lo que yo más deseaba en la vida.

—Falta de comunicación —dijo Carlota, sonriendo—. No quisiera, pero ya tengo que irme a dormir, y tú también. Los dos tenemos que trabajar en unas horas, tú dentro de dos, para ser precisos.

—Sobre el hecho de que tengas que trabajar...

—Ni lo digas, Fer, soy tu novia, no tu amante.

El emperador la volvió a besar, y está vez ella se amoldó a sus movimientos. Visto estaba que él ya había aprendido un poco, o que ya sabía cómo quería Carlota que la besara.

—Me voy, pero no dormiré, tan sólo voy a recostarme, mientras llega mi ayuda de cámara a prepararme el baño.

—Deberías de dormir aunque sea un poco —le recomendó ella.

—Si duermo, corro el riesgo de no soñar contigo, pero si permanezco despierto soy totalmente libre de pensar en ti. Por eso no me pienso dormir.

—Eso es lo más lindo que me han dicho en la vida. Pero si tu día resulta muy pesado, lo lamentarás.

—Nunca lamentaría pensar en ti.

—Gracias, Fer.

Él la volvió a besar.

—Y bueno —dijo ella, cuando separó sus labios—, ya tienes mi número.

—¿Por qué no vienes mañana a cenar conmigo? —dijo el emperador.

—¿A dónde? —preguntó Carlota, nerviosa.

—A Chapultepec, para presentarte a mi tía.

—Fer, aunque curiosamente mañana es mi día de descanso en mi empleo nocturno, no sé qué me intimida más, si ir a cenar contigo al castillo o traerte a cenar a mi casa.

—Ninguna de las dos cosas debería intimidarte. Soy tu novio...

—¿Y qué sugieres que le diga a mi mamá?, ¿algo así como: mami, te presentó a Fernando Carlos José de Habsburgo, emperador de México, etcétera, etcétera, y también mi novio?

—En ningún momento estarías mintiendo.

—Lo sé, aunque... para empezar, ¿qué cena un emperador?

—Lo mismo que ustedes. También soy mexicano. Se me ocurre que puedo venir con mi tía, o que tú puedes ir con tu mamá y tus hermanos a Chapultepec.

—No lo sé. ¿No te parece que es muy pronto? Mañana apenas llevaremos un día de novios.

—Cierto, será nuestro aniversario. Mañana cumpliremos un día de novios, y los aniversarios se festejan con una cena.

Ella trató de sonreír, pero no lo logró.

Fer, ¿acaso no ves que tengo miedo?

—Pues no deberías tenerlo —dijo el emperador, abrazándola—. Yo te cuidaré siempre, de quien sea.

—¿Me lo juras?

—Te lo juro. Y entonces, ¿mando por ustedes a las nueve?

—Aún no sé cómo decirle a mi mamá que soy novia del emperador, así que sólo iré yo a Chapultepec. Quiero sondear el terreno, no deseo llevar a mi familia y que sean víctimas de algún cometario hiriente... ¿Me entiendes?

—A quien diga algo que te ofenda a ti o a alguien de tu familia, mandaré a la guardia imperial a que lo echen por una ventana, pero no tengas miedo, no pasará nunca. Llévalos.

—Por favor, Fer, ya no me presiones. Iré yo sola, y no es necesario que envíes por mí. Me las arreglaré para llegar. Te llamo cuando esté cerca.

—Está bien, como tú digas —dijo el emperador, resignado.

—Trataré de vestirme para la ocasión con lo que tengo. Espero que no te importe que me vea más alta que tú con los tacones.

—Mi tía María Luisa también era más alta que Napoleón, y eso creo que concretamente no desató ninguna guerra. Así que tampoco tiene porque ocurrir aquí. Pero no es obligación que te vistas para una boda de la realeza, no lo es... todavía. Ve informal, yo así estaré vestido.

—Fer, tu abrigo informal cuesta mil pesos, si te lo trajeron Francia cuesta dos mil euros, y si es de Estados Unidos cuesta poco menos de dos mil quinientos dólares.

—Bueno, entonces lo arreglaremos de otra manera. Te enviaré...

—Ni lo digas, me vestiré con lo que tengo. Ya te dije que no soy tu amante.

—Me gusta que tengas bastante claro que eres mi novia —dijo el emperador, luego la abrazó y la volvió a besar—. Ya te dejaré dormir. Hasta mañana a las nueve.

—Tu abrigo...

—Quédatelo, y si es posible, cúbrete con él en tu cama. Así sentirás que te abrazo mientas duermes.

Castillo de Chapultepec, agosto de 1945

Otón de Habsburgo fue recibido por las autoridades mexicanas como un verdadero emperador. El canciller del imperio, el archiduque Francisco José, lo recibió en el recientemente construido Aeropuerto Agustín II. Desde allí fueron juntos en helicóptero hasta los jardines de Chapultepec, donde el ejército imperial mexicano le hizo honores de emperador junto a la bandera de extinto Imperio Austrohúngaro, honores tales que jamás había recibido un jefe de Estado autentico de visita en México. Concluidos éstos, el emperador Maximiliano II recibió a su primo en el despacho de los cuatro bustos.

—A tu gobierno sin duda le enviarán alguna queja por el recibimiento que me diste, Max —dijo Otón, cuando estuvo junto al emperador—. Aunque te lo agradezco de todo corazón.

—Los que se pueden quejar son esos comunistas descerebrados y criminales que tienen en sus manos a Austria —dijo el emperador—, y me importa un bledo lo que ellos piensen.

—¿Por qué no hablamos en alemán? —dijo Otón, cambiando del español a este idioma—, me consta que lo dominas a la perfección y es el idioma de nuestra familia.

—Eso es imposible —respondió Maximiliano II—. Yo soy mexicano, Otón, mi idioma es el español. Y aunque no niego el origen alemán de mi familia, en mi país sólo hablo mi idioma. Es una suerte que hayas vivido en España y también hables el español, porque así podemos comunicarnos sin ayuda de traductores.

—Está bien, calmante, tal pareciera que te he ofendido con lo que te propuse. Hablemos pues sólo en español.

—Te prometo que si el Imperio Austrohúngaro vuelve a existir, contigo como su emperador, cuando vaya a visitarte, hablaremos en alemán.

—Quizás lo dices porque sabes bien que eso nunca va a pasar —dijo Otón—, los comunistas nunca lo permitirían.

—¿Por qué te refugiaste con los yanquis, pese a que te pedí repetidas veces que vivieras en México durante la guerra? —preguntó Maximiliano II—, ¿acaso querías hacerme enfurecer? Por si no lo sabes, me molesta que un miembro de mi familia les deba favores a ellos.

—Si mi padre no aceptó la oferta que le hizo el tuyo de venir a vivir a México, y sus circunstancias eran peores que las mías, ¿por qué yo sí lo habría hecho? Los Habsburgo austriacos tenemos que demostrarnos a nosotros mismos que somos capaces de sobrevivir en cualquier gobierno.

—No digas tonterías, si vuelves a Europa, en cuanto estés al alcance de los comunistas, van a matarte. Te lo pediré otra vez, Otón, ven a vivir a México, ahora en tiempos de paz. Si te casas y tus hijos nacen aquí, serán Habsburgo y serán mexicanos por nacimiento, lo necesario para que puedan entrar al relevo si surge algún problema sucesorio. Sabes bien que mi hermano Francisco José se casó morganáticamente, y que yo sólo tengo un hijo. Como nunca sabemos los designios de Dios, me ayudaría el hecho de que aceptaras mi oferta.

—Gracias, Max, pero quiero demostrarme que puedo hacer cosas importantes yo sólo, ya ni siquiera con el respaldo del nombre de mi familia, que es tan odiada en algunos sectores de Europa y en la propia Austria, sino simplemente con mi inteligencia. Tú mismo hace unos instantes, al negarte a hablar en alemán, me dejaste claro que aun cuando somos Hamburgo los dos, somos de pueblos y culturas diferentes. Aunque algunos no lo ven así. Hitler creía que eras austriaco e insistió en verme muchas veces porque quería pedirme que te convenciera de declararles la guerra a los yanquis.

—Sí, a mí también me mandó varias cartas recordándome mi origen, para que me uniera a él. Como si el emperador de México estuviera a las órdenes de cualquier loco aprendiz de mesías.

—Hitler será una vergüenza eterna para nosotros los austriacos —dijo Otón—. Todavía me resulta difícil creer que un hombre así naciera y se formara en nuestro amado imperio.

—¿Y qué te propones hacer ahora? —dijo el emperador.

—Volveré a Austria. Quiero ayudarla a reconstruirse institucionalmente.

—¿Entonces tú aún...?

—No, Max, como están las cosas, una restauración del Imperio es imposible. Pero sigo siendo austriaco, y tengo responsabilidades como tal. No sólo Austria, sino toda Europa necesita reconciliarse consigo misma, restablecer los espacios para la paz y la convivencia mutua, de manera que ya no nos dé miedo a los europeos vivir en nuestra propia casa.

—Hitler probablemente está muerto, pero Stalin no. En Europa abundan los criminales que no buscan la reconciliación y la paz, sino instaurar gobiernos represivos y radicales, peores, si es posible, que el que tenían los nazis. No se puede hablar de reconstruir nada cuando media Europa quiere continuar con el período de la destrucción, Otón. Reflexiona.

—Max, después de un tornado, cada quien es responsable de reconstruir su casa, pese a lo difícil que eso pueda ser —respondió Otón—, y los europeos tenemos que intentar reconstruir la nuestra. Nunca dije que fuera algo fácil, pero no puedo dejar de intentarlo, siendo quien soy. Es probable que los Habsburgo tengamos un poco de culpa por todo lo malo que ha pasado. A fin de cuentas, fue el emperador Francisco José quien, aquel verano tan triste de 1914, hizo la declaración de guerra que rompió todo el equilibrio existente en Europa.

—Admiro tu determinación, Otón, y me enorgullece que seas un miembro de mi familia —confesó el emperador—. Sabes que cuentas conmigo, ¿verdad? Puedes acudir a cualquiera de nuestras embajadas en Europa, tal como si fueran tu propia casa. Allí nunca se te negará el asilo, proteste quien proteste. Se te tratará, por ser primo del emperador, incluso como si fueras mexicano.

—Gracias, Max. Es bueno saber que nunca me abandonarías.

—Ni lo pienses, Otón. Un mexicano no abandona a su familia.

—Sí, eso me han dicho.

—Otón, supongo que en Europa, debido a tu importancia, quienes simpatizan contigo te harán llegar información privilegiada sobre infinidad de asuntos políticos.

—Supongo lo mismo. ¿Por qué, Max?

—¿Tendrías inconveniente en hacérmela llegar? Nunca se sabe cuándo podría ser útil. Aunque el volcán ya no está en erupción, todavía están calientes sus cenizas.

—Claro, Max. Cuenta con ello.

Castillo de Chapultepec, enero de 2017

—A las órdenes de Vuestra Majestad —dijo el príncipe Iturbide, mientras veía fijamente a Fernando Carlos.

—Bienvenido, príncipe. Siéntese, por favor.

—Gracias, Majestad —respondió Iturbide—. No hace mucho, en el funeral de su hermano Max, todavía lo llamaba Fer, y así lo llamé siempre desde niño, como todos. Me resulta un poco extraño apegarme al protocolo con usted, dado que lo conozco desde que nació. ¿Sería posible que pudiera llamarlo como antes? A fin de cuentas, somos amigos, y también nuestras familias son amigas desde hace siglo y medio.

—Dígame, príncipe, ¿mi padre le permitió que lo llamara Max? Se lo preguntó porque también eran amigos.

—No —dijo Iturbide—. Usted sabe mejor que nadie el carácter que tenía su padre.

—¿Y acaso piensa que yo soy débil?

—No quise decir eso, Majestad.

—Príncipe, no lo tome como arrogancia o como un complejo de mi parte, pero creo que en este gobierno hay una forma ya muy definida de dirigirse al emperador. Es parte de nuestra institución. El pueblo valora el hecho de que los ministros traten al emperador con respeto, puesto que el emperador es la persona que cuida de la seguridad del pueblo. Así que no creo conveniente que me llame como antes. Espero que me entienda, ya que una falta de respeto a mi persona es también una falta de respeto a todos los mexicanos. No obstante, lo que ha dicho es cierto, somos amigos y también nuestras familias lo han sido por siglo y medio. El tratamiento que nos demos no afecta eso en lo más mínimo.

—De acuerdo, Majestad, será como usted lo considere más pertinente —dijo Iturbide, quizás ocultando con una sonrisa no muy bien lograda sus deseos de abofetear al emperador—. Y permítame agradecerle que me haya recibido, por fin.

—Lamento haberlo hecho esperar, pero tenía que conocer a fondo mi gobierno para poder aprovechar estas reuniones.

—Eso me hace imaginar que ya leyó mi informe sobre la situación financiera del imperio y las necesarias reformas tributarias.

—Ya lo leí, príncipe, y les agradezco haberlo elaborado a usted y a su equipo de colaboradores. Pero de momento no vamos a hablar de eso.

—¿Ah, no? Entonces, ¿de qué quiere hablar Su Majestad?

—Como supongo ya sabe, ayer por la mañana destituí al gobernador Quirarte.

—Sí, y me habría gustado que me recibiera ayer mismo para ofrecerme como gobernador interino mientras se organizan las elecciones. Le aseguro que podría con ese cargo junto con mis demás funciones. Soy senador, ministro de Hacienda y me ocupo de mis empresas. Pero también habría podido ser gobernador, incluso sin moverme de Aztlán.

—Francamente, no lo creo —dijo el emperador.

—¿Cómo dice?

—Príncipe, no dudo que sus empresas funcionen de manera impecable, pero quizás le quitan mucho tiempo y no puede hacer bien su trabajo como ministro de Hacienda.

—¡Majestad, no entiendo a qué se refiere! Le pido que por favor se explique.

—Príncipe, Quirarte se llevó a su casa hasta las vajillas de plata del Palacio de Gobierno, y después todo cuanto tenía valor que se atravesó en su camino. Al parecer el saqueo empezó desde el inicio de su administración. ¿Cómo es posible que el ministerio de Hacienda no haya detectado nada en casi seis años de descarados robos?, ¿acaso piensa usted que un buen ministro es el que permite una conducta tan alarmante? No me he enterado que convoque usted a los medios, para disculparse con los mexicanos públicamente por no detectar un suceso que ya a todos nos causa vergüenza. Así que le ordenó que lo haga mañana, cuando más tarde.

—¡Majestad, le exijo una disculpa! —Se levantó Iturbide, furioso— ¡No es justo que me culpe a mí de la conducta de Quirarte!

—No lo culpo de su conducta, sino de permitirla. ¿O a quién quiere que responsabilice de ello?, ¿acaso al ministro de Fomento, al de Agricultura o al de Educación? Puedo llevar pocos días siendo lo que soy, pero tengo bastante claro que de supervisar el correcto uso de los impuestos de los mexicanos se ocupa el ministerio de Hacienda. Así que no le permito que trate de eludir la responsabilidad que le corresponde, príncipe, y que sea ésta la última vez que monta de cólera delante de mí. Puedo ser joven, pero soy el emperador.

—Permítame recordarle algo, Majestad —dijo Iturbide, serenándose—, llevo quince años como ministro de Hacienda, y durante ese tiempo las finanzas del imperio han ido de forma impecable, gracias a las reformas que yo en su momento he sugerido como ministro y apoyado como senador. Su padre, el emperador, me llegó a agradecer infinidad de veces mis servicios al imperio.

—Y yo también se los agradezco, príncipe, pero igual que celebro sus aciertos, repruebo tajantemente este descuido. Si surge otro gobernador igual de delincuente que Quirarte, y que también haya pasado inadvertido para usted por años, tendré que pedirle que entregue su ministerio. ¿De acuerdo?

—Majestad —dijo Iturbide, apretando los dientes porque jamás pensó que ése fuera el peor día de su vida—. Le aseguro que Quirarte fue una desafortunada excepción, y si se nos escapó se debió a que los departamentos de vigilancia se enfocan en las empresas, y lo hacen de forma bastante eficiente gracias a mis exigencias. En México la evasión de impuestos es casi inexistente, lo que sin duda se debe a mis aciertos.

—Lo sé y créame que lo felicito por ello. Pero ahora quiero que haga una estrecha vigilancia sobre el uso del dinero público en cualquier institución y nivel del gobierno, aunque descuide al sector privado. Prefiero mil veces enviar a la cárcel a quien se roba el dinero del pueblo que a quien se roba el propio. Si un mexicano no paga impuestos, al menos se niega a entregar lo que su trabajo le costó ganar, pero si un funcionario público se roba esos impuestos, que no ha ganado y de ninguna manera le pertenecen, nunca lo voy a perdonar, y haré que caiga sobre él todo el peso de la ley.

—Descuidar el cumplimiento de las empresas podría ser perjudicial para las arcas del imperio, Majestad.

—Quizás no —dijo el emperador—. Desde mi punto de vista, se recauda más de la cuenta.

—¿Está hablando en serio? —preguntó Iturbide.

—Creo, príncipe, que ahora sí podemos hablar sobre el informe que me envío —dijo el emperador—. Sugiere usted en él aumentar los impuestos, sin embargo, yo pienso reducirlos poco a poco, de manera que en diez años los mexicanos paguen sólo la mitad de lo que contribuyen ahora.

—Con el debido respeto, Majestad, creo que usted no comprende aún las funciones de nuestro gobierno...

—Las comprendo perfectamente —interrumpió el emperador—. Somos una dictadura tributaria. Actualmente los mexicanos trabajan la mitad del año para el Estado, porque les exigimos, en diferentes impuestos, casi la mitad de sus ingresos. Se supone que esta monarquía se estableció prometiendo paz, justicia, seguridad y libertad, pero si continuamos aumentando los impuestos, no podremos seguir cumpliendo con nuestra promesa de libertad, puesto que los mexicanos ya casi serian esclavos del Estado. En cien años ha habido quince aumentos de impuestos en México, jamás se ha desaparecido uno ni reducido su taza siquiera. Por el contrario, en sus quince años a cargo del ministerio de Hacienda, ya creó usted tres nuevos.

—Majestad, son muchas las personas, a nivel internacional incluso, las que aplauden en mí el afán de aumentar los impuestos, aun siendo un empresario exitoso que sale perjudicado con ello.

—Será acaso que desconocen que la mayoría de sus empresas están establecidas en países pobres y pequeños con impuestos reducidos, y que usted no trae sus ganancias a México, sino que las guarda en paraísos fiscales —dijo el emperador—. Escúcheme bien príncipe, no quiero que vuelva a intentar tratarme como un niño o un inexperto. Es cierto que soy joven, pero haré todo cuando pueda para evitar ser lo que los mexicanos no merecen: un emperador idiota. Puede usted seguir haciendo sus negocios en el extranjero, es su derecho, pero no se haga una víctima de la hacienda mexicana. Me enfurece que me quieran ver la cara de pendejo.

Iturbide había pensado que trascurrido el tiempo que llevaba frente al emperador, ya lo habría convencido de abdicar y ya se estaría midiendo la corona, para avisar al mundo que México sería gobernado en adelante por Agustín III, y sin embargo estaba siendo regañado como un niño que no hizo la tarea, por su profesor.

—Majestad, entiendo y respeto sus ideas —dijo tratando de mantenerse firme—. Pero México es un enorme imperio con doscientos sesenta millones de habitantes, no se trata de un pequeño país escasamente poblado que se puede dar el lujo de practicar el minarquismo. La palabra imperio significa poder, y tratándose de un país significa que ese poder está en manos del gobierno. Tan sólo nuestro ejército en activo para tiempos de paz es de un millón de elementos y año con año se revoluciona su armamento. ¿Tiene idea de lo que eso cuesta? El Estado tiene que ser necesariamente rico en un país como el nuestro. A estas alturas de la historia, la filosofía de Ayn Rand y las teorías de Hayek son sólo estupideces. Si bien es cierto que es necesario el libre comercio, el Estado tiene que intervenir económica y legalmente en él para mantener el equilibrio. De lo contrario el capitalismo establecerá su dictadura donde los ricos devoran a los pobres sin ninguna consideración. Tan sólo limite totalmente un año la injerencia del gobierno en las relaciones comerciales, y verá cómo irremediablemente los ricos se habrán hecho más ricos y los pobres se habrán hecho más pobres.

—Para ser lo que es, un príncipe muy rico, tiene usted alma de comunista y mente de capitalista. Lo felicito, así la conciencia vive en armonía con las comodidades.

—¿Cómo quiere que tome eso, Majestad? —dijo Iturbide, sintiendo que le hervía la sangre.

—¿Qué puedo decirle yo? La administración de su mente no es asunto mío. Pero quiero dejarle algo bien claro: mis intenciones no son hacer una revolución relámpago en las finanzas públicas. Todo proceso apresurado suele llevar a resultados catastróficos. Sin embargo, no pienso seguir permitiendo que los mexicanos vean al Estado como un cocodrilo que va detrás de ellos para morderles los bolsillos. Eso sólo mermará su patriotismo. Me enferma que los impuestos sean tan altos y eso que somos unos de los países menos corruptos del mundo, así que no me quiero imaginar si México fuera un país asquerosamente corrupto. Significaría que casi todo el dinero que los mexicanos pagaran en calidad de impuestos iría a pasar a manos de delincuentes vestidos de burócratas. Afortunadamente, y con excepciones tan lamentables como el caso Quirarte, el dinero del pueblo recibe un buen uso. Sin embargo, mi deseo es que los mexicanos se sientan menos comprometidos y menos esclavos del gobierno, que su sueldo sea más alto y puedan satisfacer más de sus necesidades.

—Entiendo, Majestad, pero si bajamos los impuestos, tendremos que sacrificar instituciones. ¿Con cuál empezamos?, ¿con el ejército acaso?

—No soy idiota, el ejército significa la seguridad de mi pueblo —dijo el emperador—. Con el terrorismo en su primavera y con locos como Putin y Trump sueltos no voy a desmembrarlo sino a procurar fortalecerlo todavía más. Pero otras instituciones no tienen por qué ser subsidiadas por el Estado.

—¿Por ejemplo?

—Empezaré por la iglesia. Los sueldos de los ministros católicos de ninguna manera seguirán corriendo a cargo del pueblo. Ésa fue una medida que adoptó Maximiliano *el Grande* para ganarse su colaboración. Pero tras siglo y medio ya fue suficiente, pienso ponerle fin en los próximos días.

—¿Y usted cree que tal medida será del agrado del cardenal Fischer? —dijo Iturbide—. Es senador y cuenta con una enorme fracción que lo apoya. A casi todos los hombres importantes de México les ha bautizado sus hijos. Enemistarse con él sería correr el riesgo de perder parte del senado, la institución que siempre ha apoyado incondicionalmente al emperador desde su creación.

—Apenas puedo creer —dijo el emperador—, que ese cardenal sea descendiente directo del legendario cura que logró que Pio Nono lo nombrara como el primer cardenal de México y de toda América.

—Y, curiosamente, éste también tiene hijos —añadió Iturbide—. No será un enemigo débil. Además, tomando en cuenta que él se enemistó con el Papa por la... famosa carta que le envió a usted, se sentirá traicionado por su actitud. Es, como tantos otros, un hombre leal al imperio, siempre y cuando no sean tocados sus privilegios.

—¿Y acaso usted piensa que prefiero darle gusto a un solo mexicano y renunciar a la posibilidad de bajarles los impuestos a otros doscientos sesenta millones? —preguntó Fernando Carlos—. Si es cierto que cayó de la gracia del Papa, Fischer tendrá que caminar de mi lado, o no respondo de mis actos.

—Majestad, su política es diametralmente opuesta al neutralismo paternalista de su padre, en muchos aspectos. Creí que usted sería un continuador, pero ahora veo que no. Dígame exactamente qué espera de mi ministerio.

—Ya nos estamos entendiendo —dijo el emperador—. Si cree que puede seguir siendo ministro en mi gobierno, quiero que me ayude a localizar, en cualquier nivel del Estado, los funcionarios y las instituciones mismas que podemos desaparecer poco a poco, sin alterar en absoluto las cosas. Sólo así será posible iniciar un proceso seguro en la reducción de impuestos. ¿Comprende?

—A la perfección —dijo Iturbide, quizás entendiendo que tenía que cambiar radicalmente su actitud.

—Príncipe, estoy enterado de sus planes sobre Agustín III —dijo el emperador—. No se lo reprocho, celebro que tenga ambiciones y me gustaría que todo mexicano las tuviera. Pero le recomiendo que no trate de desestabilizar mi gobierno, porque quizás pierda en lugar de ganar.

—No se preocupe al respecto, Majestad. No soy un adolescente impulsivo —respondió Iturbide.

—Es todo por hoy, príncipe —dijo el emperador—, poniéndose de pie. Aunque me gustaría seguir charlando con usted, tengo muchas cosas que hacer todavía. Pero quiero a la brevedad un nuevo informe sobre lo que le he pedido. Quiero un proyecto de trabajo que habrá de seguir su ministerio, y de verdad se lo digo, lo quiero pronto. En una semana deseo revisar el primer borrador. Y no se olvide de dar la conferencia de prensa sobre Quirarte.

—Hace unos minutos, Majestad, me dijo usted que tengo alma de comunista y mente de capitalista. Pues bien, si me permite decírselo, usted tiene alma de santo y la mente de diablo.

—De todos los elogios que me han dicho desde que soy emperador —dijo Fernando Carlos—, éste suyo es el único que me ha gustado. Venga a cenar conmigo uno de estos días. ¿Le parece?

—Será un honor.

—Bien —dijo el emperador, acercándose a él y extendiendo la mano—, le deseo un buen día, príncipe.

—A las órdenes de Vuestra Majestad.

Oficina del príncipe Bonaparte

Terminada su reunión con el emperador, el príncipe Iturbide no salió del castillo de Chapultepec para irse a sus oficinas de Palacio Imperial, sino que pidió ser recibido por el canciller Bonaparte, quien no dudo ni tardó un instante en hacerlo entrar a su oficina.

—Traes la boca seca, Agustín, ¿quieres un pulque helado?

—No, gracias. Es muy temprano todavía para eso. Sólo café.

—Yo mismo te lo sirvo, permíteme. ¿Y cómo te fue con el emperador? —preguntó Bonaparte, muy interesado.

—Salvé el cuello de milagro. Es el Diablo en persona, tiene el mismo carácter que tenía su padre cuando se trataba de defender los intereses de los mexicanos.

—Eso nos debería alegrar a ti y a mí, ya que somos mexicanos.

—Luis, ¿de qué brujería se valieron Carlota y tú para prepararlo tan bien en tan poco tiempo?

—No creo que hayamos contribuido tanto, Agustín —respondió Bonaparte—. Él ya lo traía en la sangre. Tan sólo le hacía falta despertar y entender cuál era su ineludible deber.

—Debiste advertirme lo que me esperaba. Yo creí que llegaba aquí a tratar con un niño y me encuentro con un Julio César que ya tenía la espada en la mano para degollarme.

—Si te lo decía, no me lo ibas a creer —dijo el canciller, sonriendo—. Y también llegué a pensar que te hacía falta una pequeña lección. Estabas perdiendo el piso. Los Iturbide son una importante familia mexicana, ni duda cabe, tu antepasado está con plena justicia reconocido como el padre de la patria, pero todos sabemos quién manda, Agustín. La colaboración de ustedes dentro de la monarquía es importante, pero no debe llegar más allá de lo que siempre ha sido. Además, ¿tú crees que al león con el que acabas de hablar le queda grande la corona? Yo, aunque lo creí, sinceramente ya no lo creo. Y por nuestra tradición dentro de este imperio, creo que lo mejor que podemos hacer es colaborar de la mejor manera con él, sin envidias, ambiciones locas o rencores. Somos hijos de un gran país y tenemos el privilegio de contribuir diariamente a su grandeza. No eches a perder eso que es tan valioso.

—Ya no tienes que sermonearme, Luis. Es cierto que me hizo sentir como un imbécil y hasta ganas me dieron de ahorcarlo, pero logré controlarme y comprender qué es realmente lo que me corresponde hacer. El emperador estaba furioso pero entendí que se debió a que no hice nada para frenar los robos descarados de ese miserable de Quirarte.

—¿Y en qué terminó todo?

—Creo que al final hasta le caí bien a Su Majestad. Cierto que me regañó como nunca lo hicieron ni cuando era niño, pero reconoce mi talento y mis esfuerzos por el imperio, y tal cosa me complace. Aunque aun así necesito pedirte un favor.

—Tú dirías —respondió el canciller.

—Si sale a la luz otro escándalo como el de Quirarte, que también se haya escapado a la vigilancia de mi ministerio, el emperador me pondrá de patitas en la calle. Ya me lo advirtió y no parecía estar bromeando. Tampoco es que me urja el empleo, es sólo una cuestión de honor. Ninguno de mis antepasados que ha sido ministro o diplomático con los otros seis emperadores ha sido despedido nunca. ¿Me entiendes, Luis?

—¿Y qué propones?

—Que si sale otro escándalo de corrupción, lo arreglemos entre tú y yo, sin tener que recurrir a Su Majestad Imperial.

—Agustín —dijo Bonaparte, tocándose la barba—, si el escandalo es tan gran como el de Quirarte, será imposible que no se entere. Se pasa las madrugadas leyendo informes y a las ocho de la mañana ya me deja sorprendido con sus conocimientos sobre los problemas de los rincones más escondidos del imperio. Creo que lo mejor que puedo hacer por ti es hablar con él, le explicaré que si descuidaste a los funcionarios públicos fue porque las órdenes de su padre eran las de vigilar al sector privado. No fue del todo culpa tuya. Estoy seguro que entenderá, créeme. Le explicaré que debe de tenerte un poco de paciencia, mientras te adaptas a su política.

—Y supongo que ya sabes cuál es su política. Se trae entre manos una austeridad y una reducción de impuestos que en un país con varios millones de personas en la nómina del Estado no va a gustar mucho. Tal vez el emperador no tiene idea de dónde se está metiendo.

—No lo creas tan insensato —dijo Bonaparte—. Su Majestad ve cómo el mundo se llena de Estados cada vez más gigantescos, deseosos de acapararlo todo y tener año con año más control sobre la población. Ya sólo falta poner impuestos al aire, al sol y a la lluvia, y un chip a las personas para saber cuándo mienten y a dónde van cada día, como si los funcionarios públicos fueran en todas partes del mundo dignos de confianza. Su Majestad sólo quiere que el gran Imperio Mexicano sea un ejemplo sobre libertad y autonomía de los ciudadanos, volviendo a la injerencia que tenía el Estado en la sociedad a principios del siglo XX.

—No niego sus buenas intenciones —respondió Iturbide—, pero lo que más pronto va a conseguir será hacerse de enemigos aquí en México, y en el mundo tacharán a nuestro país de paraíso fiscal. Los funcionarios públicos no querrán desprenderse nunca de su empleo seguro y con ciertas comodidades y beneficios, en tanto que los políticos poderosos jamás renunciarán a la vida de magnates que llevan a costillas de los contribuyentes. Inventarán cualquier cosa para no tomar a México como un ejemplo y descartar cualquier posibilidad de reducir los impuestos. Eso te lo puedo jurar, Luis.

—El emperador no quiere hacer todos esos grandes cambios que se propone en un solo día —dijo Bonaparte—. Y de cualquier forma, por riesgosos que puedan ser los proyectos que se trae entre manos, nuestro deber es apoyarlo. Un emperador liberal, enemigo de esa elefantiasis de la que están enfermos los Estados en todas partes, puede hacerle mucho bien al mundo, pasados algunos años. Tengamos fe en él.

—Pero te recomiendo que hagas acompañar tu fe de objetividad, Luis —dijo Iturbide—. México sigue siendo una monarquía donde el Jefe de Estado, que tiene tanto poder como los sultanes del antiguo imperio otomano, no pasa por el filtro de las elecciones. Durante el siglo pasado las monarquías europeas prefirieron pasar a ser solo símbolos, con tal de evitar desaparecer. México, gracias a su neutralidad en las guerras, no tuvo que someterse a ese proceso de degradación de poderes. Y no tiene un rey, sino un emperador, goza de las mismas facultades que hace siglo y medio. Es una gran excepción en occidente que, aunque funciona bastante bien, al mundo no le gusta por ser lo que es, y usará ese pretexto para desprestigiarnos, así que dudo mucho que se empiece a decir en Europa que México está dando buenos ejemplos en algo, por más que sea cierto. Quizás lo que más fácilmente puede pasarnos es que nos tachen de incongruentes, porque será una rareza que un imperio —imperio del siglo XXI pero imperio a fin de cuentas- cobre impuestos muy bajos. ¿Dónde se ha visto tal cosa en toda la historia?

—probablemente tengas razón, Agustín, pero el emperador ya ha marcado el rumbo de su gobierno y yo estaré con él pase lo que pase.

—¿Y estás con él incondicionalmente por patriota, por tu fidelidad a la monarquía o por la duquesa, su tía, que aún sigue siendo una mujer muy hermosa, a pesar de los años han transcurrido desde que se negó a ser tu esposa?

—Creo que debería ofenderme por la estupidez de tu curiosidad —dijo Bonaparte—, pero no tiene caso. Supongo que la respuesta es que estoy totalmente a las órdenes del emperador por las tres cosas que dijiste. ¿Contento?

Al mismo tiempo que Iturbide y Bonaparte charlaban, la duquesa Carlota entró al despacho de su sobrino, principalmente debido a que la inquietaba un poco el resultado de la reunión entre el emperador y su ministro de Hacienda. Sabía perfectamente que domesticar al ambicioso príncipe era uno de los retos fundamentales que tendría Fernando Carlos al inicio de su gobierno.

—Le traje un poco de fruta con yogurt, Majestad. Ya se parece a mi hermano más de la cuenta: omite el desayuno, duerme poco y toma durante el día litros de café. Como ya lo sabe, ninguno de los emperadores de México ha llegado a anciano.

—Gracias, tía, y perdón por no desayunar contigo, pero tenía algunas cosas que revisar antes de recibir a Iturbide.

—¿Y cómo se desarrolló el encuentro? –preguntó la duquesa.

—Tenso al principio, pero bastante bien al final.

—¿Lo dice de verdad?

—Absolutamente, hasta lo invité a cenar uno de estos días.

—Eso me alegra, Majestad. Y a propósito de cenas, para esta noche había invitado al canciller Bonaparte a cenar con nosotros, y hace media hora me llamó la princesa Ana María. Insinuó que le gustaría venir a cenar, y no tuve más remedio que invitarla. Espero que no le moleste.

—No, creo que no –dijo Fernando Caros, tras meditar unos segundos–, pero te informo que seremos cinco en la mesa esta noche.

—¿Y quién es el otro invitado?

—Mi novia –dijo el emperador, ojeando unos documentos.

—¿Cómo dice?

—Tía, no me gusta que me pregunten como si yo susurrara las cosas o hablara desde muy lejos.

—Perdón, Majestad –dijo la duquesa–, pero le confieso que me he sorprendido mucho con sus palabras. ¿Quién es esa novia de la que habla?

—Imposible que la conozcas a ella o a su familia. Pero se llama igual que tú.

—Si es imposible que yo sepa de quien se trata, eso significa que...

—Que efectivamente no es una aristócrata en lo más mínimo. Tía, si no te agrada, no te voy a pedir que simpatices con ella, pero te pido que seas educada y respetuosa. Hazlo por mí. Siendo el príncipe Luis todo un caballero no temo que haga ningún cometario estúpido. Pero no confío Ana Iturbide. Puede decir cualquier estupidez, con tal de hacerla sentir inferior. Así que te pido que hables con ella antes de la cena. Adviértele que cualquier comentario malicioso, incluso una frase en apariencia inocente, me va a hacer enfurecer y sólo va a conseguir que le prohíba volver a entrar a Chapultepec por el resto de su vida.

—Majestad, me queda claro que la princesa Iturbide quiere venir a cenar para convivir con usted. Imagínese la impresión que le voy a causar cuando le diga lo que usted me está pidiendo.

—No creo que le dé un infarto —dijo el emperador—, a lo mucho hará un berrinche. En fin, por favor, déjame trabajar. Y, tía, Carlota es muy importante para mí, y a ti te quiero como si fueras mi madre. Espero entiendas lo que te quiero decir con ello.

—Majestad, yo daría mi vida por usted, también lo quiero como si fuera mi hijo, y deseo por ello que sea el hombre más feliz del mundo, pero usted es el emperador. Cuando la prensa se entere, el impacto en el todo el país será enorme. ¿Está seguro de que esa joven merece ser su novia? Recuerde que no siendo ella una princesa, si se casan, sus hijos estarán imposibilitados constitucionalmente para acceder al trono de México. Usted sabe lo que dice muy claramente el artículo referente a la sucesión: "el heredero al trono será el primer hijo varón del emperador, concebido dentro de su matrimonio con una mujer *no inferior*". ¿Se da cuenta de lo que eso significa?

—Carlota no es inferior puesto que es mexicana, y ninguna mexicana es inferior a nadie. Por si eso fuera poco, trabaja todos los días en tareas bastante agotadoras, por ella y por su familia. Eso la vuelve una persona excepcional. En verdad, tengo mucho trabajo, tía, y deja de preocuparte por mi novia. Preocúpate cuando no cumpla mi deber para con los mexicanos, porque de mi vida privada sólo me ocupo yo, y no acepto que nadie se meta en ello, ni la propia Constitución.

—Majestad, usted no es un presidente, casarse con una princesa y dar herederos al imperio, es parte de su deber —replicó la duquesa—. Si no lo hace, y siendo usted el último Habsburgo mexicano, estaría poniendo fin al imperio de nuestra familia. Lo dejo trabajar, pero le pido que pienso en ello.

Cuando la duquesa cerró la puerta, el emperador hizo una llamaba desde su teléfono particular. Escuchó música en cuanto contestaron la llamada, Carlota sin duda estaba dando su clase de baile.

—Hola, Fer. No creí que fueras a llamarme.

—¿Por qué no? Eres mi novia, que te llame debe de ser la cosa más normal del mundo.

—Es cierto, Fer, pero tus ocupaciones no son ordinarias, y no deberías de interrumpirlas por mí.

—Ya no podía aguantar un minuto más sin oír tu voz.

—Yo también quería escucharte, pero no tuve el valor de hacer la llamada. Te imaginaba hablando con Vladimir Putin o con Felipe VI de España, qué sé yo.

—Quizás les habría colgado la llamada para responderte —dijo el emperador.

—No digas tonterías.

—Tan sólo quería decirte que si me fuera posible ocultaría el sol para que llegara de una vez la noche y verte por fin.

—Fer, esa cena me tiene muy nerviosa.

—No tienes por qué estarlo —dijo el emperador—. Yo te voy a cuidar en todo momento.

—Lo sé, pero aun así estoy nerviosa.

—Te comento que mi tía invitó al canciller Luis Bonaparte y a la princesa Ana de Iturbide. La idea en un principio no me agradó, porque tenía planeado algo más en familia, pero a fin de cuentas tenían que conocerte tarde o temprano.

—Vaya, Fer, no sabes cómo me ayuda eso a controlar mis nervios. ¿De qué quieres que hable yo con la princesa Iturbide, de la moda italiana y francesa, o de los cruceros por el Mediterráneo?

—Por favor, Carlota, confía en mí. El príncipe va a agradarte, es todo un caballero. Y a la princesa ya mandé ponerle un bozal. Te aseguro que el protocolo aquí es muy estricto, nadie se atreve a hacer ninguna broma estúpida delante del emperador, y tú estarás sentada a mi lado.

—Está bien, Fer, confío en ti.

—Sabes, ayer olvidé decirte algo muy importante, pero te lo diré esta noche.

—Ayer me dijiste muchas cosas importantes —dijo Carlota—. No creí que hubiera faltado algo.

—Faltó lo más importante.

—¿Y no me vas a dar una pista?

—No, hasta esta noche te lo diré en persona. Y de verdad, no estoy exagerando, te extraño como no te imaginas.

—Yo también a ti, Fer. Hasta la noche.

Diario El Republicano, 31 de enero de 2017

¿Y si Juárez hubiera ganado la guerra?

Por Ángel Miguel Morador

Este año se cumplen ciento cincuenta y un años de la muerte del presídete Benito Juárez, el último gobernante elegido democráticamente por los mexicanos, y también se cumplen ciento cincuenta años del cobarde fusilamiento del general Porfirio Díaz, el más valiente militar mexicano del siglo diecinueve y un héroe verdadero que luchó y murió por su patria, sin someterse un solo instante a los invasores. Era un mexicano tan ejemplar, tan íntegro, tan fiel a sus convicciones republicanas y a su patriotismo, que el invasor Maximiliano supo que no podía de ninguna manera dejar vivo a un hombre como él, que una figura tan grande, tan impoluta en cada uno de sus actos, tenía que desaparecer para que se consumara la infamia de arrebatar a los mexicanos su patria y su identidad. Y fue ejecutado para satisfacción del usurpador, con el traidor Mejía presenciando el acto, riéndose de cómo moría un valiente y cerciorándose personalmente del hecho, para poder ir a decirle a su jefe que ya no tenía nada que temer, que el Gran Hombre estaba totalmente muerto.

Tengo la plena seguridad de que la consumación de la dictadura se debió a un acontecimiento en el cual el destino fue traidor a los mexicanos por decisión propia: la prematura muerte del presidente Juárez. Si él no hubiera muerto -como consecuencia de descuidar su salud al dedicarse de forma incansable a salvar a la República-, y al tener a su lado a un general de la talla y figura de Díaz, que le profesaba ciega lealtad, indudablemente, la suerte de los mexicanos habría sido otra. Hoy gozaríamos de democracia, de un gobierno republicano, como todos los pueblos libres del mundo. Juárez era un gran intelectual, hasta la propia Carlota lo reconoció y por ello secuestró su nombre, se lo dio a escuelas, plazas y avenidas, como si él hubiera colaborado verdaderamente con el imperio. Se le compara, por parte de la dictadura, injustamente con auténticos traidores de la talla de Alamán y Gutiérrez de Estrada, cuando Juárez nunca fue tal cosa.

Pero en lo que coincido con Carlota es en su gran inteligencia. Era un hombre ilustrado, adelantado a su tiempo, y junto a los grandes hombres que lo seguían —a algunos de ellos les faltó valor y se unieron al imperio—, tenía un verdadero proyecto de gobierno, con el cual hacer de México un país institucionalizado y justo para todos, un país de libertades, y sobre todo de democracia. La herencia de Juárez que gozaríamos sería un país igual de poderoso, igual de ajeno a la corrupción y con sus mismas riquezas, pero mucho mejor porque los mexicanos seriamos libres de elegir sensatamente a quien nos gobierne.

Me dan lástima esos retrasados mentales que circulan como académicos y catedráticos en las universidades y que aseguran que si no se hubiera establecido la dictadura seriamos un país igual de corrupto y atrasado que otros tantos de la región, que la República juarista triunfante hubiera derivado a los pacos años en un caos que habría reinstaurado el régimen de inestabilidad y revoluciones anterior a la llegada de los franceses. Quienes hacen tales aseveraciones, indudablemente quieren igualar a patriotas auténticos como Juárez y Díaz a traidores de la talla de Santa Anna, y eso indudablemente es mentir. En Juárez había una idea para gobernar, y en Santa Anna había una idea para robar. Eran hombres diametralmente diferentes en ideas y convicciones. Mas quieren convencernos a los mexicanos de que la República habría sido un fracaso, que habría llenado al país de caos, corrupción, inestabilidad y hambre, para que pensemos que esta dictadura mal llamada imperio fue lo mejor que nos pudo pasar. No es una teoría de académicos, sino un proyecto desarrollado por el propio canciller Bonaparte y sus antecesores, para seguir manteniendo los privilegios de una aristocracia extranjera, que al recibir un salario producto del dinero público indudablemente nos roba a los verdaderos mexicanos.

Seguir tolerando esta situación es traicionar a Juárez y a Díaz, pero también es traicionarnos a nosotros mismos como pueblo, al permitir que nos sigan ocultando nuestra verdadera identidad. Estoy totalmente convencido de que los mexicanos ya no podemos seguir tolerando esta situación, y también sé que el cambio no va a venir de la dictadura. Ese débil emperador seguirá en su sitio, leyendo los discursos que le escriba su tía mientras ella le sostiene la corona. Es una historia ya vieja en México que se vuelve a repetir, igual pasó con Moctezuma III y su madre. Pero si ellos quieren seguir representando esa farsa, que se vayan a Austria, a ver si allá también les pagan la actuación. Aquí ya nos cansamos de mantenerlos con las riquezas que son nuestras, de los verdaderos mexicanos.

Repito que el cambio no va a venir de la dictadura, nos toca a nosotros, a los mexicanos, hacerlo. Será nuestra tercera revolución de independencia, pero por vías pacíficas. El próximo veintiuno de marzo se cumplen doscientos once años del natalicio del presidente Juárez, y qué mejor fecha ésa para que también sea la de nuestra verdadera y tan deseada independencia. Ese día, desde las seis de la mañana, miembros de mi movimiento en todas las ciudades de México, desde el norte de California hasta el sur de Panamá, recibirán en cajas selladas, en una plaza pública, a la vista de todos, un trozo de papel minúsculo con una palabra escrita de puño y letra de los mexicanos, y esa palabra deberá de ser sencillamente imperio o república. Los mexicanos habrán de presentarse con un documento de identidad, y se les entregará el papel con un folio y se les hará una marca con tinta en un dedo, para que no sea posible alterar de ninguna forma los resultados. Esa misma noche se hará un conteo, y se invita a ser testigos de su legitimidad a medios de comunicación, periodistas y por supuestos a las autoridades de cada ciudad, para que todo sea transparente y claro, para que se decida ese día la auténtica voluntad del pueblo.

Este movimiento es pacífico, es un derecho natural que debemos de tener los ciudadanos de expresar lo que queremos. No se trata de un golpe de Estado, ni de nada parecido. Mas estoy seguro que la dictadura no va a verlo así. Mandarán arrestarme en cuanto este artículo sea publicado. Pero no hace falta que vengan por mí los miembros de la represiva guardia imperial. Yo mismo iré a pararme afuera de la oficina de policía más cercana. Ciertamente, no por encerrarme a mí ese acto ya tan deseado por todo el pueblo va a evitarse. Los miembros de mi movimiento ya saben lo que tienen que hacer, y lo harán, aunque yo esté tras las rejas y sometido a las peores torturas.

Tampoco creo que les funcione la misma estrategia que usaron con don Francisco I. Madero, ésa de cambiar leyes a última hora para ganarse las simpatías de los mexicanos. Ya no somos idiotas, idiota es el que cree que lo seguimos siendo. Ya no caeremos en las estrategias viles de la dictadura. Los mexicanos, la gran mayoría, habremos de decidir nuestro destino, le guste a quien le guste. Y le aviso a ese señor, Fernando Carlos, que quizás yo mañana duerma en una prisión, pero que en menos de dos meses con gusto voy a cedérsela. Todavía, señor, es tiempo de parar esta dictadura voluntariamente e irse a Austria. De lo contrario lo lamentará.

De vuelta en Chapultepec

Fernando Carlos llegó al comedor vestido como había anunciado, con un atuendo informal, pero muy elegante, con un abrigo negro, fiel a su luto, que hacía resaltar bastante su piel blanca. La princesa Iturbide, la duquesa Carlota y el canciller Bonaparte se pusieron de pie para hacerle una reverencia. Pero el emperador apenas notaba que estaban allí, ya que se mantenía pendiente de su teléfono. Eran ya las nueve con quince y Carlota aún no lo llamaba para anunciar que estaba llegando al Castillo. Atribuía su retraso al tráfico de Aztlán, pero al mismo tiempo se convencía de que debió haber insistido más para que permitiera que enviara por ella.

—Te vez más guapo vestido así que con los trajes tan impecables que usas en tu despacho, Fer —dijo la princesa Iturbide. Ella, al saber que una supuesta novia del emperador estaría en la cena, había ido vestida como para formalizar su compromiso.

El príncipe Bonaparte se sintió algo incómodo al escuchar que tuteara al emperador. El protocolo era tan estricto, sobre todo en Chapultepec, que no recordaba que alguna vez alguien en su presencia hubiera tuteado a Maximiliano IV.

Fernando Carlos, por su parte, apenas agradeció con un discreto movimiento de cabeza el comentario de Ana Iturbide.

—¿Le preocupa, algo Majestad? —preguntó la duquesa.

—No.

—¿Acaso tu novia te dejará plantado, Fer? —dijo la princesa—. Eso no sería correcto, en México se puede plantar a cualquier hombre, menos al emperador.

—¿Podrían permitirme un momento? —dijo el emperador, con su teléfono en la mano. Hizo una llamada y se llevó el aparato al oído.

—¿No contesta? –dijo la princesa, pasados varios segundos.

El emperador la vio con los mismos ojos que el día anterior al ex gobernador Quirarte. No estaba para comentarios idiotas desde que se hacía cargo de sus funciones, y menos en ese momento en que el teléfono de Carlota lo enviaba directo al buzón. Su teléfono estaba apagado. Aquello era muy raro, Carlota no podía hacerle eso a menos que... que le hubiera pasado algo o que alguien hubiera hablado con ella para tratar de alejarla de él. Pero, ¿quién? A excepción de su hermano Juan, nadie sabía que Carlota era su novia.

—¿Está el conde Andrássy en el castillo? –le preguntó a Bonaparte.

—Creo que sí, Majestad.

—Que venga en seguida a mi despacho –dijo el emperador, poniéndose de pie.

—Majestad –dijo la duquesa–, ¿no estará con nosotros en la cena?

—No lo creo, cenen ustedes.

—¡Fer! –dijo la princesa Iturbide, pero el emperador ya se estaba alejando.

—A las órdenes de Vuestra Majestad.

—Conde Andrássy, buenas noches. Me dicen que estaba a punto de retirarse a su casa, así que me disculpo por entretenerlo unos minutos más.

—Yo estoy a las órdenes de mi emperador cualquier día del año a cualquier hora –dijo el conde.

—Trataré de ser breve, pero necesito que sea totalmente sincero conmigo –dijo el emperador–. ¿Usted está enterado de lo que hago en mis salidas nocturnas?

—Sólo la primera noche se nos escapó, Majestad. Después pusimos un pequeño chip en su motocicleta. Puede despedirme si lo cree conveniente, pero yo cumplí con mi deber. Anoche en el antro donde estaba usted había treinta de mis subordinados dispersos entre la gente.

—¿Y con quién ha hablado de ello?

—Con nadie, Majestad.

—¿Está seguro?

—Majestad, si usted llegará a correr peligro, inmediatamente llamaría al príncipe Bonaparte y al ministro Peña-Bazaine, si es que la situación fuera muy riesgosa, pero no se ha dado el caso.

—Conde, no me molesta que me cuide, incluso a mis espaldas, pero si usted ha dicho algo…

—Le juro por mi honor que con nadie he hablado de adónde va usted y qué hace. Y los hombres que lo cuidan son totalmente leales a mí y sólo me desobedecerían por una orden expresa de Vuestra Majestad, de nadie más. Todos han hecho un juramento de fidelidad al emperador y jamás andarían de chismosos.

—¿Entonces es imposible que alguien de mi entorno sepa a donde he ido estas noches?

—A menos que sean adivinos.

—De acuerdo, conde, confío en usted. Que tengan listo un auto, necesito salir.

—¿Va a dónde siempre?

—Así es.

—Daré las órdenes precisas —dijo Andrássy—. Y créame que me alegra que hoy haya decidido dejar descansar la motocicleta. Me es más fácil cuidarlo de esta manera.

Media hora más tarde, una limosina negra se detenía al inicio de la calle donde vivía Carlota. El emperador descendió y fue caminando hasta su casa. Tocó el timbre y escuchó una voz de mujer decir "van".

La puerta se abrió y apareció una mujer de cuarenta y tantos, más morena que Carlota, que casi se cae de espaldas tras observar dos segundos el rostro del visitante.

—¡En el nombre de Dios!

—Usted debe de ser la señora Alma.

—¿Su Majestad sabe quién soy?

—A los pies de usted, señora —dijo Fernando Carlos, dándole la mano—. ¿Está Carlota?

—¿Mi hija?

—Ella está bien, ¿verdad?

—¿Cómo es que Su Majestad conoce a mi hija? —dijo la mujer, sorprendida y asustada.

—Soy su novio —dijo el emperador.

—Te presento a Fer, mami, mi novio —dijo Carlota, bajando de unas pequeñas escaleras. No estaba maquillada y su cabello estaba algo revuelto. Llevaba un pantalón ajustado y una playera un poco grande que aun así se amoldaba muy bien a su figura.

—¿Su Majestad es novio de mi hija? —dijo la mujer, al borde del colapso. El emperador, sonriendo, la detuvo antes de que se fuera directo al suelo.

—¿Quién vino, mamá? —dijo una voz de niño.

En eso aparecieron dos niños morenos, que veían con mucha curiosidad al recién llegado.

—Tú sin duda eres David —dijo el emperador—, y tú, el más pequeño, eres Maximiliano, ¿cierto?

—Vaya, recuerdas el nombre de mis hermanos.

—¿Tú eres el emperador? —dijo el pequeño Maximiliano.

—Así es, y también soy el novio de tu hermana.

—¡Max, no tutes a Su Majestad! —dijo la madre.

—No hay problema —dijo el emperador—, puedes tutearme y llamarme Fer.

—Mami, llévatelos a acostar —dijo Carlota—. Necesito hablar con Fer a solas.

—Vamos, niños. Buenas noches, Majestad, a vuestras órdenes. Niños, despídanse de Su Majestad.

—Adiós, Fer.

—Hasta pronto.

—¿Te importa si charlamos afuera? Mi casa, como puedes ver, es pequeña, y mis hermanos van a escucharlo todo desde su cuarto.

—Está bien —dijo el emperador, tomándola de la mano y guiándola a la calle.

—Creí que estarías enojado —dijo Carlota.

—Estaba preocupado. ¿Qué pasó? —preguntó el emperador, mirándola a los ojos.

—Fer...

—Carlota, sea cual sea tu respuesta, ¿me juras que no romperás nuestro noviazgo?

—Te lo juro —dijo ella, sin tratar de evadir su mirada.

—En ese caso, puedes hablar.

—He estado pensando lo que significa ser tu novia —comenzó ella—, en cuanto se sepa, habrá periodistas en mis dos trabajos, tomándome fotos, y vendrán a mi casa a fastidiar a mi mamá y a mis hermanos. Y en tu caso, no creo que te enorgullezca que los diarios de todo el mundo publiquen que tu novia es una mesera y maestra de baile que ha dejado parcialmente la universidad. Todo eso me dio vueltas en la cabeza durante el día, y cuando llegó la noche sentí pánico de pararme en Chapultepec. Fer, no quiero que lo que yo soy te haga daño.

—Precisamente —dijo el emperador—, yo tampoco quiero que lo que yo soy te haga daño. Carlota, somos lo que somos, eso no podemos cambiarlo, pero tampoco podemos separarnos por algo que a la vez no deja de ser trivial. Yo por mi parte me sentiré orgulloso de que se haga público que mi novia tiene dos trabajos y no descansa en todo el día con tal de ayudar a su familia. Cualquier hombre con los pies en la tierra se sentiría orgulloso de tener una novia así.

—A veces no sé si todas las cosas tan extraordinarias que dices están anotadas en un libro de tu familia y todos los emperadores de México las repiten. Porque de lo contrario me resultaría casi mágica tu capacidad de improvisación.

—No existe tal libro —dijo el emperador—, porque ninguno de mis antepasados ha tenido que conquistar a su esposa, los de ellos fueron matrimonios pactados por intereses aristocráticos.

—¿De qué hablas?

—Carlota, ¿recuerdas que te dije que te diría algo importante esta noche?

—Sí...

—No sé si pasó en el momento que te vi, al estar mareado el día que me accidenté, o si pasó al besarte y ser ésa la primera vez que besaba en los labios a una mujer, pero lo que olvidé decirte anoche que es que te amo. ¡Te amo, Carlota!

Carlota iba a decir algo, pero el emperador la acercó hacia él con sus brazos y la besó, la apretó contra él fuerzas, como si la hubiera perdido por mucho tiempo y la acabara de recuperar.

—De un día para otro has mejorado mucho —dijo Carlota, algo sofocada.

—Lo mismo me dijo el canciller Bonaparte sobre mi forma de gobernar.

—También te amo, Fer, y pase lo que pase, quiero que me pase junto a ti.

Y ahora fue Carlota quien lo tomó de la nuca y lo acercó a sus labios.

—¿Me perdonas por dejarte plantado?

—Todavía no ocurre tal cosa —dijo el emperador.

—¿Mmmm?

—Quedaste de cenar conmigo esta noche, y he decidido salvarte. En el Palacio de Cortés ahora están arreglando una mesa, con velas y champagne, sólo para nosotros dos.

—Fer, Cuernavaca no está en la calle de al lado.

—No, pero lo que sí está en una plaza cerca de aquí es un helicóptero con el motor encendido. Te espero mientras vas a avisarle a tu mamá que volverás en unas horas.

—Y mientras me cambio…

—No, así estás perfecta.

—Considerando que tengo el novio más necio de México, volveré en cinco minutos. Pero, ¿no crees que estás dando un mal uso a los impuestos de los mexicanos? Lo digo porque una sorpresa así no la da cualquier novio.

—Estás terriblemente equivocada —dijo el emperador—. Yo, al igual que mi padre, no tomo de los mexicanos un sólo peso en calidad de sueldo. Mi antepasada, la emperatriz Carlota, recibió de su familia una herencia descomunal para su época, y esa herencia sigue existiendo y está distribuida en bancos de varios países de Europa. Tan sólo con los intereses de los últimos diez años yo podría vivir toda mi vida como si fuera dueño de la mitad del petróleo del Golfo Pérsico. Y te quedan cuatro minutos para ir a avisar a tu madre que irás a cenar conmigo.

Dentro del Palacio del conquistador el clima era agradable aquel día del poco perceptible invierno mexicano para una ciudad como

Cuernavaca. En cuanto se sentaron a la mesa, el emperador despachó a la servidumbre y él y Carlota se quedaron totalmente solos.

—Vaya, enchiladas y arrachera asada —dijo Carlota—. Creí que me servirían algún platillo extranjero con el que no sabría cómo comportarme.

—Tengo gustos totalmente mexicano —respondió el emperador—, por más que Ángel Miguel me acuse de austriaco. Cuando estuve en Miramar, fueron cocineros mexicanos los que me alimentaron todos los días. Puedo comer el chile más picante de México sin empezar a llorar a los treinta segundos.

—Es bueno saberlo. Francamente tenía miedo de invitarte a cenar a mi casa. Pero ahora ya me estás dando ideas.

—¿Más champagne?

—¿Me quieres emborrachar?

—En realidad sí. Ya no me has vuelto a decir que me amas, desde que estábamos afuera de tu casa, por ello quiero emborracharte, a ver si así confiesas.

—No es necesario que me emborraches —dijo ella, mirándolo a los ojos—. Te amo, Fer. Eres el sueño más hermoso que jamás pude imaginar.

—Creo que esa confesión merece un beso —dijo el emperador, poniéndose de pie para acercarse a ella.

Carlota también se levantó de su silla, y permitió que el emperador la abrazara. Fue ella quien empezó a besarlo desesperadamente. Fernando Carlos correspondió con la misma intensidad a sus besos, mientras movía sus manos en el cuerpo de ella con cierta timidez, como dudando.

—Fer —dijo Carlota, separando sus labios por un instante apenas un centímetro—, no puedo creer que el hombre que manda a un millón de militares dude en tomarme de las nalgas.

Al escuchar esas palabras, el emperador la tomó con fuerza del trasero y la apretó contra él. Carlota se dejó llevar por aquellos movimientos.

–¿Será que aparte de la cena tenías también condones listos?

–No es posible que se le pida al emperador de México por la gracia de Dios y del pueblo que use un condón en su primera vez.

–De acuerdo –dijo Carlota–, supongo que es poco probable que me embarace con una sola vez.

El emperador le tapó la boca con sus labios, mientras le recorría el cuerpo con sus manos. Luego se dejó caer poco a poco de espaldas, y ella quedó encima de él. Carlota se quitó la playera y la aventó lejos.

–Déjame a mí –le dijo–, la siguiente vez tú me guías. Ya sé que todo lo aprendes muy rápido.

Ahora fue él quien la tomó de la nuca y la acercó a sus labios. Carlota lo besó mientras empezaba a explotarle el cuerpo, haciéndolo vibrar por donde pasaban sus manos. Aunque le había dado a entender que se mantuviera quieto, Fernando Carlos no dejó de colaborar ni un instante. Ella muy adentro de sus pensamientos, mientras él movía sus manos y la besaba, reconoció que era bastante bueno improvisando.

Mientras tanto, en Chapultepec

—Pues me retiro —dijo la princesa Iturbide—. Carlota, la cena ha estado deliciosa, y tu compañía, como siempre, impagable. Y usted, príncipe, retomando las palabras de su tío frente a Talleyrand, le aseguro que tiene la conversación más agradable de todo México. Me ha ayudado muy bien a olvidar que el emperador se fue repentinamente, importándole muy poco que estábamos aquí como invitados. Si no fuera usted casado y un caballero tan integro, créame, le coquetearía. Siempre me han atraído los hombres mayores que yo.

—Princesa —dijo Bonaparte, inclinándose—, a los pies de usted. Y le aseguro que si Su Majestad se retiró de forma un tanto brusca fue por una importante cuestión de Estado.

—Pronto veremos, querido príncipe, que esa importante cuestión de Estado ha de tener un trasero envidiable. Hasta pronto.

—Me desconcierta el comportamiento del emperador, Luis —dijo la duquesa, cuando se quedaron solos—. Creí que ya tenía clara su misión en la vida, que ya lo habíamos pulido más que al mejor de los diamantes, y véalo. N sé qué pensar.

—Señora, creo que a Su Majestad Imperial ya no hay nada que decirle respecto a sus funciones. Ya tiene la mirada de León de su padre y una visión bastante coherente de la política nacional e internacional. En cuanto a su comportamiento de esta noche, no se me ocurre nada de su agrado qué decirle, tan sólo que sospecho que está enamorado. Algo normal en un joven, aunque sea el emperador.

—¿Y acaso no ve que ese extraño noviazgo puede ser terrible para el imperio, Luis? Tenemos que hacer algo.

—Con el debido respeto, Señora, en la vida sentimental de mi emperador no voy a meterme. Por el contrario, le deseo que tenga la dicha que yo no pude experimentar: casarse con la mujer que ama. —Al concluir estas palabras, Bonaparte buscó insistentemente la mirada de la duquesa.

—Por favor, Luis —dijo ella, con cierta dulzura—, tú sabes bien que en el corazón no se manda. Yo me enamoré de otro hombre, y seguí las órdenes de mi corazón.

—Tal vez lo mismo está haciendo el emperador —respondió Bonaparte.

—Pero él, siendo quien es, sabe que está negado a esos privilegios si lo instan a no buscarse una esposa adecuada. El príncipe imperial tiene que nacer del vientre de una princesa, aunque sea de la víbora que se acaba de ir. De lo contrario las cosas se podrían complicar, y Morador y sus grillos tendrías más pretextos para fastidiarnos la vida.

—El emperador es su sobrino, señora, ¿acaso quiere que toda la vida sienta el mismo frío dentro del alma que siento yo? Créame, no se lo deseo a él por nada del mundo.

—Por un lado te doy la razón, Luis. Me gustaría que mi amado sobrino fuera feliz, y que por fin, desde que llegó Maximiliano *el Grande* a estas tierras, el heredero al trono fuera engendrado por amor y no por protocolo. Pero mi amado Fer es el último Habsburgo mexicano, la situación no es sencilla, tú lo sabes bien.

—Yo creo, señora, que en ese aspecto debemos de permitir que el emperador actúe como lo crea conveniente. No es ningún idiota, hará las cosas bien.

—El amor nunca ha sido buen consejero de los grandes gobernantes, Luis —respondió la duquesa.

—Pero siempre hay una excepción.

—Parece que esta vez no cuento contigo.

—No, Carlota, esta vez no estoy de tu lado.

—No te lo reprocho, créeme. Tu fidelidad, a fin de cuentas, le pertenece al emperador.

—Carlota, si en otra vida nos volvemos a ver, ¿me prometes que en esa ocasión me darás un poco más de tiempo para conquistarte?

La duquesa por fin decidió hallar la mirada del canciller, y respondió con una calidez y ternura poco frecuentes en su carácter.

—Querido Luis, te lo juro.

De vuelta en el Palacio de Cortés

—¡Carlota! —dijo Fernando Carlos, con su teléfono en la mano—, nos quedamos dormidos. Son las cuatro y media.

—¡De verdad! —dijo ella, despertándose repentinamente—. Mi madre nunca va a creerme que cenamos durante tantas horas, y de hecho ni cenamos.

—No tengo perdón de mi pueblo —dijo el emperador—, mi tiempo les pertenece a los mexicanos desde hace una hora. Mateo, mi ayuda de cámara, ya fue a despertarme y halló mi cama vacía.

—Amor, según lo que me has dicho, por la madrugada sólo lees despachos, hasta a las ocho recibes al canciller. Nadie además de Mateo va a saber que no dormiste en Chapultepec, en cambio a mí, si me madre no me mata, va a correrme de la casa.

—Pues vente a vivir conmigo a Chapultepec —dijo el emperador.

—Muy gracioso.

—No estaba bromeando. Pero en verdad me siento muy mal. Carlota, hace bastante poco que soy emperador, como para que me tome la libertad de faltar a mis deberes. Si el pueblo lo supiera, se pensaría que a México lo gobierna un farsante caudillo comunista y no un emperador de la dinastía Habsburgo.

—Fer, ya nos quedamos dormidos, ya deja de lamentarte. Te repito que a tu canciller lo recibirás hasta las ocho. Me harás pensar que no estás feliz de haber estado conmigo.

—Carlota, ésta fue la noche más extraordinaria de mi vida, y si muero a los noventa años, la recordaré como si sólo hubiera pasado un día. Jamás lo dudes.

—Pues entonces relájate, amor. A ti nadie va a regañarte, y a mí con mi madre me espera la inquisición.

—Yo hablaré con la señora... ¿Cuál es tu apellido?

—¿Me quieres llevar a vivir a Chapultepec y ni siquiera lo sabes?

—Olvidé preguntártelo.

—Te vas a sorprender, mi apellido es Lorena. Pero no es una traducción o reinterpretación de Lothringen, ni tengo nada que ver con la aristocracia. Mi bisabuela era huérfana, y se llamaba María Lorena. Así que Lorena pasó a ser su apellido, que le dio a mi abuelo por ser madre soltera. Con esa explicación comprenderás que no somos parientes, no te hagas ilusiones.

—Eso se puede resolver —dijo el emperador, besándola—. Y en serio, yo hablaré con tu madre.

—¿Y qué le vas a decir? Se supone que el emperador no le miente a su pueblo, pero si le dices la verdad me estarías mandando a la hoguera. Mejor relájate y quedémonos aquí otra media hora. Tengo una buena idea sobre lo que podríamos hacer en ese tiempo.

—¿Y si me cuentas tus planes?

—No, prefiero dejar que los adivines. Oye, anoche, cuando arrancaste el mantel para colocarlo en el suelo, tiraste todo lo que había en la mesa. Quien entre aquí va a pensar que traté de matar al emperador.

—Te firmaré cien indultos imperiales sin fecha para que los uses cada que te haga falta —dijo Fernando Carlos, apretándola contra su cuerpo—, pero antes dime qué tienes en mente para la próxima media hora. Soy un hombre curioso.

—Amor, lo que anoche pensé que pasaría sólo una vez, se convirtió en tres, y eso francamente me sorprendió de forma muy positiva. Por ello me consta que ahora ya tienes experiencia, así que la siguiente media hora la dejo totalmente a tu criterio. Y apresúrate, porque ya sólo te quedan veinticinco minutos.

Antes de que la capital se llamara Aztlán, 19 de junio de 1867

La emperatriz Carlota armó tan enredada fuga del Palacio Imperial, subiendo de un carruaje a otro en cada calle y dándoles mensajes diferentes a sus damas para que todas pensaran que se hallaba dentro del Palacio, que pasada la media noche ni ella misma tenía una idea clara de en qué parte de la capital del imperio se hallaba.

Ataviada con un rebozo que le cubría media cara y con las demás prendas propias de una mujer pública, recorría a pie una callejuela donde era más probable que la asesinaran en lugar de que le hicieran un hijo. Si de algo estaba segura era de que se hallaba en una zona atestada de pulquerías, y de que algunos soldados belgas, austriacos o franceses, de los que se habían quedado tras la retirada, se habían vuelto muy aficionados al pulque y pasaban algunas noches emborrachándose, perdidos en alguna calle de mala muerte de la capital. Tan sólo le pedía a Dios encontrarse con un hombre apenas medio ebrio de rasgos europeos que no la reconociera y en cambio la confundiera por una mujer pública. No era mucho dados los ilimitados poderes de Dios.

De pronto, mientras caminaba, notó que se abría una puerta tras de ella.

—Ven aquí, mujercita —le dijo alguien en español y con acento bastante familiar. Sin duda era un mexicano y de ser así no era lo que andaba buscando.

Sin poder explicárselo siquiera, Carlota no sintió ningún miedo. Su misión era muy grande como para intimidarse con la voz de un borracho. Trataba de retomar su caminata, cuando apenas a los dos pasos el hombre la alcanzó y le dio una nalgada, a ella, a la nieta del rey Luis Felipe, descendiente directa de los borbones.

—Te voy a pagar —añadió el hombre.

Dispuesta a enfrentar al atrevido, Carlota se giró. Cuál fue su sorpresa al ver, ayudada por la escasa luz de un farol, que ese mexicano ya de cierta edad era un hombre de rostro colorado, cuyos cabellos, ya escasos, eran delgados y de un tono café. Los ojos, brillantes y grandes, indudablemente eran azules. El hombre olía a alcohol, era justo lo que andaba buscando, y el hecho de que se mostrara tan descaradamente lúcido afirmaba que no estaba tan borracho y podía servirle perfectamente para lo que ella necesitaba. Al verle apenas la mitad de su rostro dentro de aquella semioscuridad, el tipo sonrió complacido. Sospechó que la mujer era joven y guapa. La puerta de donde había salido era una barbería. Carlota la señaló con la mirada y él respondió con otra señal afirmativa. Cuando ella entró, le dio la espalda. El hombre la siguió y cerró la puerta. Allí sólo había una linterna que ofrecía una luz tan débil como la de afuera. Carlota escuchaba las risas del hombre sin intimidarse siquiera un poco. Pero tenía en mente no prolongar las cosas en lo más mínimo, nada de preámbulos. Vio una silla delante de ella y fue a recargar allí sus rodillas. No pasaron ni diez segundos cuando el hombre ya estaba levantando su vestido y quitando lo que pudiera estorbarle. Carlota mantuvo sus labios apretados ante la embestida, y vaya que ese mexicano era mucho más grande que Max. Pero no estaba allí para quejarse de nada, había ido por algo que necesitaba con urgencia y lo estaba obteniendo a fin de cuentas. En ese instante no se sintió agredida o usada en lo más mínimo, se sintió esperanzada. Para su satisfacción, el hombre resultó ser bastante rápido. Apenas dos minutos después gritó como si lo estuvieran golpeando y se recargo en ella. Cuando por fin guardó silencio, la emperatriz se quitó de la misma forma que si le hubiera echado encima una serpiente y se acomodó el vestido.

Mientras el hombre aún se hallaba debilitado, Carlota corrió hacia la puerta.

—Tú también querías —dijo el mexicano cuando la estaba abriendo—, así que no te voy a pagar nada.

—Ya me pagaste —dijo la emperatriz, haciendo lo posible porque su español tuviera un auténtico acento mexicano. Ese hombre jamás podrías imaginar de quien se trataba realmente, a quien había tomado con fuerza de las nalgas y estrujado a su antojo. Era posible que al día siguiente, debido a su estado actual, ni siquiera recordara el acto.

Su regreso al Palacio Imperial fue una odisea peor que el escape. Y al hallarse en sus aposentos, dos largas horas después, gracias a su astucia y a un plan meditado durante un mes tenía la seguridad de que su salida no sería conocida plenamente por nadie. Tan sólo alguna de sus damas podría decir que "Su Majestad pasó mala noche". Se bañó sola y después se sentó en su cama sin ningún sueño, mientras se tocaba el vientre experimentando cierta felicidad. No pensaba ni por un instante en la posibilidad de no haber quedado embarazada, al contrario, tenía la completa seguridad de estarlo. Ya había olvidado por completo la calle y sabía que al salir el sol nuevamente tampoco recordaría al tipo ebrio, a quien no volvió a ver el rostro después de cerciorarse de que sus rasgos eran los de un hombre blanco. Se prometió convencerse de que tal cosa no había ocurrido, y si pasado el tiempo en algún momento las dudas asaltaban su mente, pensaría entonces que el hombre en verdad había estado con una mujer pública y que a ella la había preñado un ángel.

Pero si ni siquiera esa estrategia daba resultado, al fin de cuentas le quedaba la posibilidad de recordar que la gran mayoría de soberanos de la historia habían sido engendrados sin amor, en actos tan fríos como el de esa noche. No importaba cómo fuera, sino sembrar la semilla para que México llegara a ser un poderoso imperio, con sus descendientes a la cabeza, descendientes de ella exclusivamente, no de Max, que no sería el padre de su hijo, ni tampoco del barbero ebrio, un desconocido a quien el tiempo borraría para siempre tras su muerte. Los emperadores mexicanos que nacieran durante siglos serian solo de ella. Y una vez hecha la historia, concluida su misión, era posible que dentro de muchos años un emperador descendiente suyo fuera engendrado con verdadero amor, lo que en su tumba o donde se hallara su espíritu la haría muy feliz. El día en el que dentro de unas horas saldría el sol sería el 19 de junio de 1867. Para ella significaría en adelante, y en el más absoluto secreto, la verdadera fecha del nacimiento del Imperio Mexicano.

Castillo de Chapultepec, febrero de 2017

Fernando Carlos dejó en su escritorio la tableta en que acababa de leer el artículo en el que Morador invitaba a los mexicanos a votar en contra de la monarquía. Echó su espalda hacia atrás, sin tocas apenas el respaldo de la legendaria silla que Francisco José I había regalado a su sobrino Moctezuma, y fijó toda su atención en lo que iba a decirle el príncipe Bonaparte al respecto.

—Tenemos dos opciones con este agitador, Majestad —comenzó el príncipe—, pero ninguna de las dos está exenta de riesgos graves. Si lo encerramos por tratar de desestabilizar la institucionalidad del imperio, lo haremos mártir, y si lo dejamos libre el gobierno se verá débil, y al realizar esa absurda consulta ciudadana podría traernos serios problemas. Es totalmente seguro que una abrumadora mayoría de los mexicanos se siente segura y a gusto con el imperio, pero nunca se sabe lo que puede pasar en estos tiempos con una cosa así. Después de que fue elegido Trump en los Estados Unidos, ya cualquier aborto indeseable puede salir de la democracia. Además, no confío en Morador y sus seguidores, que se traen bien oculto un ridículo romanticismo postsoviético. Sean cuales sean los resultados, sin duda los van a alterar a su favor, con la intención de hacer el mayor daño posible.

—¿Y usted qué sugiere, príncipe?

—Ir por él y por los suyos, hacer un escarmiento como el que hizo su abuelo, el emperador Maximiliano III, con los comunistas que intentaron derribar la monarquía e imponer una dictadura apadrinada por Rusia. Habrá muchas críticas hacia usted, Majestad, pero creo que es la única solución viable. Porque una opción también sería que el imperio respalde esa consulta, para garantizar que los resultados sean limpios con una estrecha vigilancia. El problema de esa posibilidad, por el cual no la aconsejo, es que aun cuando seguramente el pueblo se inclinaría por la continuidad de la monarquía, daríamos entender que dudamos de la legitimidad de su gobierno, y eso sería un suicidio. De tal suerte que la única opción por la que yo en su lugar me inclinaría, es la de ir por Morador y meterlo en una prisión. Pero ésa es mi opinión. Decidir le corresponde exclusivamente a Vuestra Majestad. Sus órdenes serán obedecidas al instante.

—Bien —dijo Fernando Carlos—, vamos a dejar a ese Morador que haga su consulta ciudadana.

—¿Habla usted en serio, Majestad?

—Absolutamente.

—¿Y si ese loco semianalfabeto altera los resultados y da un golpe mortal al imperio?

—Pues me iré a Austria —dijo el emperador—. Hablo bastante bien el alemán. Y usted me imagino que a Francia. Me consta que su francés es perfecto, príncipe. Ambos países no quedan muy lejos uno del otro. Podremos vernos con frecuencia, para tomar un café juntos.

—Majestad, francamente, no lo entiendo.

—Escúcheme bien, príncipe, honestamente yo no me quiero ir a Austria, y supongo que usted tampoco a Francia. Ambos somos mexicanos y amamos la tierra donde hemos nacido. Pero eso sería en el peor de los casos, si es que podemos evitar que Morador nos encierre antes de cruzar la frontera. Mas en el mejor de los casos, quizás ese loco, sin proponérselo, nos está dando una oportunidad para legitimar el imperio ante nuestros detractores. Si es verdad que los mexicanos están tan contentos con nuestra forma de gobierno, lo harán saber en esa consulta. Lo que tenemos que garantizar es que Morador no haga ninguna trampa al estilo comunista. Pero tampoco podemos involucrar a las autoridades del primer orden, precisamente para evitar lo que usted ha dicho. Serán los prefectos de las provincias, quienes pretextando cuidar que no haya actos de violencia, colocarán agentes encargados de verificar que todos los conteos sean precisos.

—Quizás ésa sea una buena opción —dijo Bonaparte—. Pero si le permitimos a Morador hacer esa consulta y los resultados no le gustan, al vernos blandos en adelante la hará cada quince días, hasta que los resultados sean de su agrado.

—De ninguna manera —respondió Fernando Carlos—. El imperio no moverá un dedo para impedirla esta vez. Pero Morador tendrá que aceptar lo que diga el pueblo, incluso que la abstención seria a favor nuestro porque los mexicanos estarían considerando su consulta absurda. Si persiste se habrá acabado mi magnanimidad y le enviaré a prisión. Soy un emperador dispuesto a tolerar las diferencias, pero no precisamente un santo. Dé las instrucciones precisas para que ningún ministro ni funcionario cercano al gabinete imperial comente nada sobre esa consulta. Mi gobierno se tiene que mostrar ajeno totalmente a ella. Pero también encárguese de que sean reforzadas las autoridades de las provincias, incluso con militares, si es preciso. La consulta va a celebrarse pero los resultados tendrán que ser absolutamente reales. ¿Está claro, príncipe?

—Sinceramente, Majestad, me parece que su estrategia es buena. Pero le confieso que me habría encantado mandar encerrar a Morador.

—Príncipe, si metemos a ese hombre a prisión, vivirá de los impuestos de los demás mexicanos, y eso no sería de mi agrado.

—Majestad, tengo informes de que esa sanguijuela se ha alimentado del dinero de otros desde que gobernaba su abuelo. Hay imbéciles que lo ven como una especie de mesías iluminado y no tienen ningún reparo en apoyarlo económicamente. Morador es una criatura insignificante para los mexicanos educados que sabes valorar los verdaderos méritos. Pero también hay varios millones de mexicanos que todavía viven en la ignorancia y el fanatismo. Algunos están así por decisión propia, y otros porque ningún país es perfecto e incluso en el Imperio Mexicano germinan las plagas más antiguas de la humanidad en ciertos sectores de la población. Y esas personas francamente no ven diferencia entre Morador y Dios.

—Eso indica que si México fuera un país con una población mayoritariamente sumida en la ignorancia, Morador ya sería presidente desde hace muchos años.

—Y también le faltarían muchos para irse de la presidencia, con total seguridad —respondió Bonaparte—. Majestad lo veo cansado, ojeroso, como si no hubiera podido reponer sus fuerzas anoche. Son todavía varios los temas importantes que tenemos que tratar este día, y no sé si usted prefiera que los dejemos para la tarde.

—De ninguna manera —dijo el emperador, un poco sonrojado—. Sólo se trata de que mi cuerpo aún no termina de adaptarse a estas rutinas, pero la que manda es mi mente, no mi cuerpo. Lo escucho, príncipe, y le suplico que no vuelva a distraerse por mi aspecto cansado. Insisto en que no soy un niño.

—De acuerdo, Majestad. El siguiente tema es Venezuela. El gobierno populista está llegando a extremos alarmantes. Tienen a los ciudadanos viviendo en la más absoluta miseria y se enfurecen ante cualquier crítica hacia ellos alegando que las demás naciones no deben de meterse en sus asuntos internos.

—Es verdad, ya leí varios informes del embajador al respecto —dijo Fernando Carlos—. La situación es bastante grave en ese país tan desdichado, y no es justo que los demás gobernantes del mundo nos mostremos apáticos pretextando el respeto que debe de haber entre las naciones. Los venezolanos no se lo merecen. Quiero, príncipe, que hoy mismos se retire el embajador, mantenerlo allí sería seguir reconociendo a un gobierno que ya perdió todo derecho de gobernar.

—Su decisión es exactamente lo que yo haría —dijo Bonaparte—. Pero le advierto que nos gritarán de todo. Ya casi escucho a los políticos venezolanos diciendo que cómo puede ser posible que una dictadura de siglo y medio critique a un gobierno elegido democráticamente por el pueblo.

—Príncipe, si usted pudiera hablar con las serpientes y les preguntara por qué se comen a las lagartijas, éstas dirían que se las comen porque las lagartijas son malas y se las quieren comer a ellas. Las tiranías siempre bramarán los pretextos más absurdos para legitimar sus actos. Pero sencillamente yo no puedo mantenerme apático al sufrimiento de un pueblo tan sólo por ahorrarme algunas críticas.

—Totalmente de acuerdo, Majestad, hoy mismo retiraremos al embajador y nos mantendremos atentos a la respuesta del gobierno venezolano. En otro asunto, aunque sin salirnos de la política exterior, ya he analizado con profundidad su informe respecto a sus pretensiones con Israel. Veo que realmente piensa revolucionar nuestras relaciones diplomáticas con ellos.

—Príncipe —dijo el emperador, juntando los dedos de sus dos manos—, aunque aquí viven varios millones de judíos, en tiempos pasados el Imperio Mexicano se ha mantenido distante del Estado judío, y eso tan sólo se debió a que si los yanquis tenían impecables relaciones con determinado país, el nuestro por naturaleza adoptaba hacia éste una política hostil. Y debido a que Israel ha dependido mucho de los yanquis, mi padre, mi abuelo y mi bisabuelo evitaron todo cuanto les fue posible brindar el menor apoyo incluso diplomático, por justo que fuera. Yo creo, príncipe, que ha llegado el momento de pasar página a esa política sin el menor fundamento. Usted y yo somos hijos de una civilización católica, y por tal razón si llegáramos a radicar en un país musulmán vecino de Israel, podrían cortarnos la cabeza sin tener que hacer nada para merecer tal cosa, tan sólo por ser lo que somos. En cambio en Israel no pasaría igual, allí hay tolerancia a la diversidad cultural, es un país civilizado que cree que en el esfuerzo, en el trabajo y en los merecidos frutos de éstos. Al igual que no tolero el desgobierno y el autoritarismo de Venezuela, admiro profundamente el gran logro de los judíos, al poder construir un país tan prospero en un entorno tan hostil. No me importa que Trump vaya a ser amigo y aliado de Netanyahu, yo también quiero serlo. En las causas justas, príncipe, estoy dispuesto a caminar del lado de los yanquis. Durante mi gobierno, el Imperio Mexicano habrá de ser aliado de los países que sean capaces de propiciar para sus ciudadanos un entorno seguro, donde proliferen las libertades, la justicia y el respeto a los derechos humanos, y a la vez nos alejaremos por completo de las tiranías, para que el mundo sepa que México no las aprueba. Y si tal medida implica revolucionar nuestras relaciones comerciales, estoy dispuesto a ello. Me propongo que en un plazo de seis años no le vendamos ni le compremos un solo plato de lentejas a una dictadura, y ruego a Dios que otros pueblos sigan ese ejemplo. Es el mejor camino hacia la libertad, por más que no esté exento de tragedias.

—Con el debido respeto para Vuestra Majestad, desentendernos de las tiranías y arruinar su comercio conlleva complicar más la vida de los infelices que viven dentro de sus fronteras.

—Y mantener relaciones con ellos significa aprobar su existencia –dijo el emperador–, en tanto que hacemos ricos a los dictadores, lo que es un terrible error, porque los dictadores cuando tienen dinero de sobra es cuando más fácilmente consolidan sus regímenes represores.

—Ciertamente, cabe añadir que no todos los regímenes dictatoriales son catastróficos para la humanidad. Algunos países no están preparados para otra cosa, y el orden sólo llega de esa manera. Oriente Medio y sus alrededores son una gran prueba de ello. A la civilización y a los derechos que vienen con ella se llega por un largo camino que la mayoría de los pueblos del mundo se han negado a recorrer. No se gobierna con cultura a un pueblo que la desconoce, sino con mano dura. Los países de Europa que se hicieron extraordinariamente prósperos tras sacudirse sus respectivas dictaduras comunistas, no llegaron a tales proezas por arte de magia o de algún milagro, ya eran pueblos cultos que jamás merecieron esas dictaduras y al no tenerlas corrieron hacia el progreso. Pero eso no va a pasar en los pueblos que se han negado a absorber la cultura universal. Desearles democracia es burlarse de ellos, así que lo mejor que se les puede desear es un dictador que pueda mantener el orden.

—¿Algo así como México en tiempos de la emperatriz Carlota?

—Precisamente –dijo Bonaparte–. Y vea usted lo bien que nos fue al cabo de siglo y medio. México es un país rico, seguro y civilizado. Los que opinan que Juárez habría logrado tal cosa sin duda leen demasiada literatura fantástica.

—¿Y qué me está tratando de decir con todo esto?

—Que no se puede tratar a todas las dictaduras de la misma forma, algunas, quizás dentro de muchos años, deriven en algo bueno. Nunca se sabe. Estoy seguro que la civilizada Europa, si pudiera, volvería el tiempo atrás y colocaría nuevamente en su sitio anterior a los mismos dictadores árabes que fueron defenestrados, para poder evitar ese terrorismo sin precedentes en la historia. Quizás incluso empezarían por revivir a Husein.

—Ciertamente, ni Europa ni Estados Unidos tuvieron el menor acierto al intervenir en esa zona llena de volcanes en erupción.

—Yo me atrevería a decir, Majestad, que lo que pasa realmente allí solo lo entiende Putin.

—Quizás —dijo Fernando Carlos— sea cierto que para entender bien a las dictaduras hay que ser dictador.

—Y a propósito de él, ¿ya leyó su carta?

—Sí, aquí la tiene —dijo el emperador, extendiéndole una carpeta a Bonaparte—. Léala en voz alta.

—Majestad —respondió Bonaparte, con la carpeta en las manos y los ojos muy abiertos—, ¡está en ruso! No sé ni jota de ese idioma, si es que en él existe la jota, cosa que dudo. Es tan hispana como la envidia.

—Perdón, príncipe, no sé en qué estaba pensando. Permítamela, la traduciré al español.

Querido emperador Fernando Carlos

Deseo fervorosamente felicitarse por el inicio de tu gobierno, que espero sea muy largo y próspero. Sé que no te extraña la familiaridad de mi trato, porque debido a tu madre eres un Romanov, lo que te hace ruso, y los rusos, aún sin conocernos, nos tratamos todos con familiaridad. Tengo entendido que hace poco enviaste un grupo de rescate a Egipto, a realizar una delicada misión. No te lo reprocho, al contrario, te felicito por el éxito obtenido. Y si me hubieras pedido ayuda para evitar riesgos, te la habría dado con mucho gusto. Deseo, sinceramente, que me consideres tu amigo, y tener yo la posibilidad de considerarte también amigo mío. Como bien debes saber, los occidentales de nosotros los rusos solo pregonan lo malos que podemos llegar a ser, pero nunca hablan de que jamás está solo quien tiene por amigo a un ruso, porque Rusia no abandona a sus amigos.

Espero pronto concretemos una reunión entre nosotros, y mientras tanto, me sentiría alagado de que me respondieras mi carta en ruso, nuestro idioma. Estoy enterado de que como un homenaje a tu madre lo has aprendido bastante bien, y que lo hablas y lo escribes sin ningún problema. Sé que en tu país la tradición manda que no hables otro idioma más que el español con los líderes extranjeros, pero creo que esa misma tradición no dice nada sobre escribir cartas en un idioma diferente.

Me interesa mucho saber cuál es tu posición frente a Rusia, y también si aceptas la amistad y el apoyo que te estoy ofreciendo, si podemos realmente considerarnos amigos y aliados.

Afectuosamente

Vladímir Vladímirovich Putin

—Aunque la traducción fue rápida —dijo el emperador—, creo que fui lo más preciso posible. Putin quiere ser mi amigo, o al menos tratarme como un niño para que sea su títere. Y para ello quiere empezar con hacerme sentir ruso. Hasta me extraña que no me llamara Fernando Carlos Maximilianovich.

—Así que los rusos sí detectaron a nuestros helicópteros en Egipto —dijo Bonaparte—. Era de esperarse.

—No sé qué se me hace más cómico, si cuando Hitler quiso convencer a mi bisabuelo Maximiliano II de que era austriaco para que lo apoyara en la guerra, o ahora que Putin sugiere que soy ruso. Por otro lado, él es el heredero de un régimen que a los antepasados de mi madre los asesinó con escalofriante brutalidad. De allí no podemos partir para ser amigos.

—Tal vez dentro de todo sea un poco sincero. Putin tiene su propio concepto sobre qué es luchar por la estabilidad del mundo, y cree que en esa lucha sólo Rusia se esfuerza. Es normal que quiera un poderoso aliado en Occidente, y que vea en usted la oportunidad para conseguirlo. Al ser un miembro de los Romanov por el lado de su madre, quizás piensa que usted y él son iguales, que tienen la misma visión como gobernantes.

—Mis iguales, como ser humano, son todos los mexicanos, y mis iguales como gobernante están sepultados en la Cripta Imperial de Guadalupe, y son sólo seis. Perdón, son siete, se me olvidaba la emperatriz Carlota, lo que es imperdonable. Pero no tengo más iguales en ninguna otra parte del mundo. Putin se equivoca.

—De cualquier forma, es innegable que ha visto en usted una valiosa oportunidad. Un ejército de un millón de hombres, con armamento sofisticado, listos para entrar en combate y junto a la frontera yanqui debe de ser para él como si hubiera ido Dios a verlo al Kremlin.

—Por la fama que tiene Putin, pienso que cree que lo admiro y sueña con que yo tome el papel de Pedro III mientras él se viste de Federico *el Grande*. No deja de ser un dictador que se ha enamorado del poder y se niega a soltarlo, mientras se atribuye el derecho de intervenir militarmente a los países que se separaron de la Unión Soviética para buscar un mejor destino. Putin sólo entiende la ley de la fuerza, y muestra la peor cara de Rusia e impide que el país se reivindique ante el mundo civilizado por el régimen soviético y por sus actos en Berlín al finalizar la segunda guerra mundial.

—¿Eso quiere decir, Majestad, que no va a responderle su carta en ruso?

—Naturalmente que no, príncipe, yo soy mexicano, y mi idioma es el español. Si quiere leer en ruso, allí tiene a Pushkin y a Dostoyevski.

—Majestad, ¿por qué no espera a ver cómo se desenvuelven las relaciones con Trump, antes despreciar la amistad de Putin?

—Porque ya le he dicho —respondió el emperador— que mi gobierno no será nunca amigo de dictadores. A Putin podría perdonársele su régimen, que de alguna manera conserva la estabilidad en Rusia, pero no sus intervenciones militares en pueblos desprotegidos. Así que en respuesta a su intento de acercamiento, que nuestro embajador en Moscú se limite a agradecerle por los buenos deseos que tiene hacia mi gobierno, y con eso que se dé por bien servido. Si acaso llega a preguntar por su carta, que se le informe que la he leído, pero que ordené que me la tradujeran al español antes de leerla, ¿de acuerdo, príncipe?

—Como Vuestra Majestad lo ordene. Hoy mismo daré la instrucción.

—Gracias, príncipe. Y ya que ha mencionado el nombre de Trump, ¿ha tenido noticias del embajador Iturbide?

—Está mañana, precisamente, llegó un informe suyo. La reunión del próximo día diez queda totalmente descartada. Parece que Trump se ha ofendido porque usted no le ha querido contestar el teléfono y se empeña en tratarlo con cierto desdén.

—Él fue el primero que dijo que los mexicanos no éramos sus amigos —respondió el emperador—. Además, se nota que ese tipo apenas está aprendiendo a gobernar, de nada sirve verlo ahora cuando las circunstancias lo harán cambiar su actitud en un mes.

—Trump es sólo una víctima de la realidad, eso cada vez está más claro. Pero es cierto que tenemos que llegar a un acuerdo con él, para que de alguna manera quede claro cuál será nuestra política comercial con los yanquis durante los próximos cuatro años, así los empresarios podrán tranquilizarse. La incertidumbre sólo destruirá empleos y subirá los precios, en ambos lados de la frontera.

—Creo que lo peor que podía hacer Trump ya lo hizo, príncipe. Con sus estúpidos comentarios ha reavivado el odio entre mexicanos y estadounidenses, el mismo que ya había bajado sus niveles un poco desde el conflicto de mediados del siglo antepasado. Y eso me tiene intranquilo, albergo un mal presentimiento. Decirles a sus compatriotas que si ellos están mal es por culpa de nosotros, electoralmente quizás fue un acierto, pero políticamente no sólo fue una cobardía, también fue una pendejada.

Hoy es un buen día para escribir una larga entrada en mi diario, puesto que hoy infinidad de dudas que acosaban mi mente y me distraían de mis deberes se han disipado, y tengo la plena seguridad de que no van a volver. El milagro en mi espíritu ocurrió con un acto rutinario hasta hace algunos meses, al que sin embargo acudí con una determinación bajo el brazo: mi renuncia. Fui citado a este medio día por Su Majestad Imperial Fernando Carlos I de México, y pretendía aprovechar la reunión con él para hacerle entrega de mi ministerio, del que llevo ocupándome diecinueve años, y en caso de que el emperador requiriera mi consejo para nombrar a un nuevo ministro, tenía planeado sugerir al duque de Miramón, un hombre con una amplia tradición militar en su familia y que actualmente no desempeña ministerio alguno, sino simplemente el cargo de senador al que tiene derecho por herencia.

Mi determinación de alejarme del ejército imperial, al que he dedicado mi vida entera, no se debió a que ya tengo sesenta y cinco años y por ello desee jubilarme. Pensaba seguir ejerciendo mi puesto de senador y votar en un evento que veía por momentos cercano e ineludible, y de competencia absoluta del senado: la disolución del imperio. A esta conjetura tan catastrófica llegue días después de la muerte del emperador Maximiliano IV. Aquella madrugada, cuando fui al aeropuerto a recibir a mi nuevo emperador, vi frente a mí a un jovencito tímido que apenas pudo saludarme, mientras su tía casi trataba de cubrirlo con sus faltas para que nadie notara que tenía miedo. Al ver a ese hombre como soberano de doscientos sesenta millones de seres humanos y como comandante absoluto de un millón de soldados, sentí que el imperio había llegado a su fin. Y realmente yo no era el único que lo pensaba: tanto aquí en México como en el extranjero se hablaba mucho de que la monarquía Habsburgo, tras siete siglos agotadores, tenía que apegarse por fin al beneficio de la jubilación.

Muy dentro de mi ser no me sentía extrañado de que el final estuviera llegando, más bien, si algo me desconcertaba, era el hecho de que el Imperio Mexicano hubiera durado tanto. Somos la última monarquía en la cual llamar a personas con títulos como duque, príncipe o conde, aún se hace y se hace con respeto. Ya ni en el Reino Unido se lo toman con la misma seriedad que nosotros. En nuestra monarquía el emperador tiene poderes absolutos, y aunque el canciller hace las funciones de una especie de presidente o de primer ministro, en realidad no deja de ser un secretario o asistente privado de Su Majestad, puesto que aun cuando puede tomar iniciativas y buscar la aprobación de leyes, todas sus facultades están limitadas a la autoridad de éste. México jamás se ha sometido a las reformas de degradación de la monarquía que han adoptado los países de Europa que aún conservan esta forma de gobierno, y ello sin duda se debe a que no hemos tenido ni guerras ni revoluciones durante siglo y medio, lo que ha evitado cualquier proceso de desestabilización del gobierno que exija hacer reformas drásticas para calmar los ánimos. La paz del Imperio Mexicano lo ha llevado a ser, como forma de gobierno, un anacronismo funcional, y a la vez una rareza. Es también indudable que la paz de que ha gozado México se ha derivado de su preparación constante para la guerra. Desde que apenas pudo consolidarse el imperio, dio inicio la conformación de un ejército nutrido de una muy seleccionada oficialidad y dueño de un armamento siempre en constante modernización, como si a México pronto le esperaba una guerra, mas esa guerra nunca llegó y me atrevo a jurar que si no llegó fue precisamente porque el imperio estaba preparado para ella. Los tiranos rara vez en la historia han elegido a una víctima que sí se sabe defender y tiene cómo hacerlo.

Al haber decidido entregar mi ministerio al emperador, deseaba conservar mi puesto en el senado para, en caso de que naciera una república, poder hacer algo para que ésta al menos fuera a caer en manos de gente sensata. No quiero imaginarme, ni siquiera en mis peores pesadillas, que todo el poderío militar del Imperio Mexicano de un día para otro fuera a ser propiedad absoluta de ese loco insufrible de Ángel Miguel Morador. Quizás habrá quien piense que como ministro de la guerra se tienen más posibilidades de salvar al país que como senador. Ciertamente yo también lo creería si mi país fuera el pueblo más fanático e ignorante del mundo, pero los mexicanos somos un pueblo civilizado. Aquí las cosas se deben de hacer en la tribuna de oradores, con argumentos sólidos, apoyados en nuestra estabilidad, en nuestra paz y en nuestra historia, y no haciendo desfilar a los carros militares entre las calles de Aztlán, intimidando a los ciudadanos.

De haber entregado mi ministerio y si continuara creyendo en la disolución pronta del imperio, es cierto que como senador tendría poco que hacer, pero como mexicano y patriota me acorrala una gran responsabilidad. Mi familia, y permítaseme la arrogancia, no ha sido anodina en la historia de México. Ya pasaron muchos años desde que mi tatarabuela, la mariscala Josefa de la Peña y Azcárate, volvió a México después de la fuga de prisión de su esposo, caído en desgracia tras la debacle de la guerra franco-prusiana, con lo puesto y sintiéndose una verdadera patriota francesa, a pesar de ser más mexicana que el pulque. En aquel entonces, la emperatriz Carlota le recomendó dos cosas que la hirieron mucho y de las que dejó constancia en su diario: "aquí olvídese de hablar francés, y que sus hijos sólo lleven el apellido Peña, o al menos que lo antepongan al de Bazaine. Ese nombre no nos resulta grato a los mexicanos". Mi tatarabuela se echó a llorar a los pies de la emperatriz, y continuó llorando durante varios días, pero, tras reflexionar, siguió sus consejos. Así fue como pasamos a formar parte del imperio, a ocupar cargos importantes y a contribuir a su grandeza. Por ello creía que al entregarle mi puesto al emperador no debía alejarme por completo de las instituciones, porque como mexicano, como patriota y como senador, no pensaba dejar morir el imperio sin que antes me escucharan. Incluso llegué a considerar pertinente defender con mi oratoria el entronamiento del príncipe Iturbide como Agustín III, quizás una opción arriesgada e incluso poco popular, pero todo me parecía factible antes que ver a ese fanático inculto de Morador convertido en presidente de mi país y sentado en el despacho de los cuatro bustos, tras tirar éstos a la basura.

En tal incertidumbre navegó mi mente durante los días pasados, que me fue realmente difícil mantenerme lúcido ante la responsabilidad de tener a mi mando a un ejército tan grande. Cuando solicitaba ver a Su Majestad, la respuesta del príncipe Bonaparte era siempre la misma: "el emperador de momento no recibe a los ministros, todos los asuntos serán tratados directamente conmigo". Para mí tales respuestas trataban de ocultar sin éxito algo bastante claro: Su Majestad se negaba a gobernar y entretanto el canciller y la duquesa de Cuernavaca maniobraban para posponer el fin de algo inevitable, lo que me parecía en el fondo bastante reprobable, puesto que como militar obedezco sólo a mi emperador y a nadie más, de ninguna manera a otro hombre, por más poderoso que sea dentro del imperio, e incluso sobrino del más extraordinario estratega militar de todos los tiempos. Quería entregar mi espada de ministro de la guerra a Su Majestad Fernando Carlos con el más absoluto respeto, sin verlo un solo instante como un a hombre inferior por no aceptar sus responsabilidades. Como miembro convencido de la monarquía, tengo claro a fin de cuentas lo que significa la figura del emperador, y tanto es así que había buscado las palabras adecuadas para no ofenderlo ni siquiera mínimamente con mi renuncia.

No obstante, después de dudar durante días, como ya he dicho antes, mi espíritu ha recobrado completamente la calma, y ésta no va a desaparecer ni con una amenaza de guerra. Todas mis dudas, absolutamente todas, se aclararon hoy gracias a la reunión que tuve con el emperador. Cuando me recibió en el despacho de los cuatro bustos, francamente no reconocí en él al jovencito tímido que días atrás había llegado de Trieste. Allí, sentado en medio de las cabezas de piedra de sus antepasados, me miró como un león líder que ve venir a un miembro de su manada, con respeto, hasta con cierto afecto, pero con una seriedad que me transportó a una escena de misticismo absoluto. Inmediatamente comprendí que yo no estaba allí para renunciar, sino simplemente para recibir las órdenes de mi emperador. Con los mismos ademanes de Maximiliano IV, y con cierta elegancia quizás derivada de su voz —es ésta más grave incluso que la de su padre-, se interesó primero por cómo me sentía al mando del ministerio de guerra; quiso saber qué necesitaba, qué consideraba obsoleto y cuál es la opinión de los soldados sobre la institución a la que pertenecen, si están de acuerdo con su sueldo, sus funciones, etc. Ante algunas faltas menores que consideró inapropiadas, me reprendió sin dudarlo siquiera y mirándome directamente a los ojos, y ante lo que consideró mis mejores aciertos, me felicitó y me dio las gracias por mi apoyo. Cada que hablaba, yo sentía realmente estar frente a la poderosísima figura que él representa en el imperio, un hombre superior a mí y a quien, siendo yo un soldado, le debo mi total lealtad.

Como por arte de magia, mis dudas y mis temores se alejaron de mi cabeza. De pronto yo no vi a la monarquía con pesimismo: anacrónica y con un pie en la tumba, sino poderosa y joven durante todo el tiempo que nosotros, los propios mexicanos y nadie más, así lo deseemos.

Aunque la primera vez que lo vi ya como emperador me pareció, en el mejor de los casos, que tenía aspecto de un santo, creo, por lo que me ha dicho, que es un hombre resulto y que considera al ejército imperial como una extremidad más de su cuerpo. No está dispuesto ni remotamente a permitir que la dignidad y el honor de su pueblo sean ofendidos o cuestionados. Si en algún otro país son violados los derechos de un sólo mexicano y el gobierno de allí no da una satisfacción adecuada, creo que este joven del que tanto llegué a dudar no tardaría en tomar una determinación que a los gobernantes de aquel desdichado pueblo los llevaría a padecer diabetes de un día para otro. Por mi parte, en los dos o tres años que pienso seguir al mando de mi ministerio, pienso apoyarlo en absolutamente todo, como soldado y como patriota. Al salir del despacho de los cuatro bustos este medio día, no pude evitar que desde lo más profundo de mi corazón de soldado salieran estas palabras: "!Dios salve a mi emperador!".

Castillo de Chapultepec, diciembre del 2006

—Y por fin la última prueba, Maximiliano —dijo el emperador Maximiliano IV a su hijo favorito—. Dime, si repentinamente despertaras como rey de un país pobre, pequeño e insignificante, dominado por el analfabetismo y las costumbres irracionales dentro tus súbditos, ¿qué harías para mejorar su situación?

El joven archiduque de diecisiete años, sin el menor nerviosismo en su rostro, se apresuró a responder.

—En esa situación, Majestad, no tendría más remedio que conducirme con mano de hierro para propiciar un orden capaz de sostener una dinámica de trabajo estable. Invitaría a empresas extranjeras y les daría todas las facilidades posibles, desde reducidos impuestos hasta los terrenos donde habrían de levantar sus instalaciones. Eliminaría el salario mínimo y todas las leyes laborales los primeros años. Desgraciadamente en muchos casos las empresas abusarían hasta rayar en la esclavitud, pero estoy seguro que después de diez años el pequeño reino sería otro, con los impuestos que las empresas pagaran ya habríamos construido infraestructura y equipamiento en la medida de nuestras necesidades, y la riqueza que hubieran derramado entre el pueblo ya habrían generado el surgimiento de una clase media robusta y capaz de educar a sus hijos. Ésta Majestad, a grandes rasgos, sería la mejor opción a seguir, y ciertamente lleva sus riesgos, pero igual actuaria así ahora que dentro de treinta años. Nunca sería mi intención que mis súbditos trabajaran como esclavos por diez años, pero si no tomo esa medida, lo harían toda su vida, ellos, sus hijos y sus nietos, y se formaría un siclo de miseria sin fin. En cambio, Majestad, con ese procedimiento que le he señalado, en una década se habría formado un tejido empresarial sólido y diversificado, y una sociedad capaz de aprovecharlo.

—Me satisface tu respuesta, Maximiliano —dijo el emperador—. Para terminar, repítemela en griego, en alemán, en inglés, en francés y en náhuatl.

El emperador se reclinó sobre la legendaria silla que había llegado desde Austria, cruzó sus dedos satisfecho y escuchó a su hijo predilecto pasar de un idioma a otro sin trabarse o torcer la mirada en busca de alguna palabra escurridiza.

—Perfecto, estoy orgulloso de ti —dijo cuando el archiduque concluyó—. Puedes retirarte, y que pase tu hermano.

—Majestad, si me permite decirle algo al respecto...

—Claro, habla.

—Veo que está muy ocupado, y según tengo entendido ya casi es hora de que reciba al príncipe Khevenhüller. Permítame que yo le haga el examen al archiduque Fernando Carlos, así usted podrá dedicarse a su trabajo. Estos exámenes le quitan mucho de su valioso tiempo. No se preocupe por mi hermano, le prometo que seré exigente con él.

—Ah, pues, debo decirte que tu intento ha sido muy bueno para salvar a Fernando Carlos. Pero no te permito que trates de aligerar las obligaciones de ese perezoso. Tengo que ser muy estricto con él, y aprovechar su inteligencia que, contrario al carácter, sí tiene mucha. Además, tú mismo deberías de preocuparte porque él también se prepare, tan sólo imagínate —¡Dios no lo quiera!— que el destino lo convierta en emperador algún día, debe de estar listo para ello. Los mexicanos no pueden tener a un inculto e idiota por gobernante, que no sepa nada de las funciones de un Jefe de Estado y que sólo hable el español. La sabiduría autentica se esconde entre muchas lenguas. Sin cultura se pondría a hacer experimentos estúpidos que el pueblo pagaría con hambre e injusticias. Y eso no me lo discutas, porque es una gran verdad. Que entre en el acto tu hermano.

—A las órdenes de Vuestra Majestad.

El archiduque Maximiliano se puso de pie y fue hacia la puerta, al abrirla, Fernando Carlos casi se cae de espaldas. Estaba temblando.

—Lo siento, hermanito. No pude salvarte. Pero de verdad te juro que lo intenté.

—¡Fernando Carlos, no te quedes allí! ¡Entra ahora mismo, que no tengo tu tiempo! —exclamó el emperador.

—¿Entonces, hija, Su Majestad se sintió un poco mal anoche, debido al cansancio, y te quedaste a su lado hasta que ya casi amanecía?

Carlota había llegado a su casa a la hora de la comida, tras concluir su empleo matutino, y había ayudado a su madre a servir la mesa. Cuando estuvo lista, llamaron a los niños, que volvieron corriendo de la calle, el más pequeño detrás del más grande.

—¡Siéntense de una vez, ustedes dos! —les ordenó su hermana—. Corren como caballos, y si alguno se rompe una pierna estaremos en serios problemas. Y sí, mami —añadió volteando la cara—, las cosas fueron tal como dices.

—Es preocupante que Su Majestad se pueda enfermar, hija. ¿Qué haríamos los mexicanos sin nuestro emperador?

—No te preocupes, aguanta más de lo que yo misma me imaginaba.

—Hija, ningún de los emperadores anteriores llegó a morir viejo. Eso de trabajar desde la madrugada hasta la noche agota incluso al más fuerte.

—¿Cuándo va a volver a venir Fer a la casa? —preguntó el pequeño Maximiliano, sacándose la cuchara de la boca.

—Su Majestad, Max. No seas irrespetuoso.

—Él dijo que podíamos llamarlo Fer —argumentó el niño.

—Lo dijo porque es muy amable, pero nadie puede tutear al emperador, nadie. Grábatelo bien en tu cabezota.

—¿Ni Carlota puede? Ella es su novia.

—Hija —dijo la madre, reflexionando un momento—, en verdad que no puedo creer todavía que tú seas la novia del emperador. Es como si no estuviéramos dentro de la realidad.

—Te confieso que yo también a veces todavía lo dudo, mami.

—¿Y cómo pasó?

—Tan rápido que necesito que alguien más me lo cuente para creerlo. Yo sólo me acerqué a ayudar a un pobre infeliz que se había caído junto con su motocicleta, y menos de una semana después resulta que sin ser princesa soy la novia del heredero y descendiente directo de Maximiliano *el Grande*.

—Debería de sentirme feliz, hija, y considerarme la mamá más dichosa del mundo. Sin embargo no es así, y no se debe a que dude de él y piense que nuestro amado emperador puede hacerte algo malo. En la televisión inspira mucha confianza y en persona la impresión es todavía más positiva, pero siendo nosotros como familia tan diferentes a él, tengo miedo de lo que puede pasar en un futuro incluso muy cercano.

—No soy tonta, mami —respondió Carlota—. También he pensado en ello, y francamente no sé qué decirte al respecto. Fer es un sueño, pero no lo digo en el sentido más romántico de la expresión, sino que quiero decir que Fer es realmente un sueño de ésos de los cuales se despierta, aunque una no quiera.

—¿Y él sabe que piensas así?

—Supongo que lo sospecha. Sabe que estoy llena de temores.

—Carlota —interrumpió David—, ¿y cuándo vas a casarte con Fer?

—¡Sí!, ¿cuándo? —añadió Maximiliano.

—¡Coman y dejen de escuchar lo que no les importa! —les gritó Carlota.

Dos horas más tarde, Carlota salió de su casa para dirigirse a su trabajo como mesera. Durante todo el trayecto, la idea de que Fernando Carlos se iría pronto de su vida no dejó de atormentarla ni un instante. Era absurdo que se quedara con ella por mucho tiempo. Sí la trataba como a un diosa se debía únicamente a que ella era su primera novia, la primera en besarlo y la primera con quien había hecho el amor. Pero sabía que a los hombres les duraba poco ese agradecimiento. El emperador pronto se sentiría atraído por más mujeres, se acostaría con ellas y su forma de pensar cambiaria. Era un hombre que aprendía pronto, y no tardaría en aprender que ningún hombre se casa con la primera mujer con quien se acuesta. En el siglo XXI, tal cosa ya no era propia ni de las mujeres. Carlota se sentía totalmente segura de que Fernando Carlos, más temprano que tarde, le ofrecería el papel de amante, mientras planeaba su boda con la princesa Iturbide o con alguna europea que supiera levantar su copa con elegancia, supiera el nombre de sus antepasados en la Edad Media y hablara, cuando menos, siete idiomas. La realidad era triste pero también generosa por mostrársele en su cabeza antes de hacerse presente en su realidad. El saber que Fernando Carlos no era realmente suyo, allí, caminado sola entre las calles de Aztlán, la hacía llorar.

Palacio de Iturbide, esa misma noche

—Así que cenaste con la víbora de Carlota y Luis Bonaparte —le dijo el príncipe Iturbide a su hermana.

—No me molestes, estoy platicando con Ángel por WhatsApp.

—Ustedes dos siguen charlando como si fueran adolescentes. Tan sólo les advierto que no digan nada que tenga ver con los asuntos de Estado. Ángel es nuestro embajador en Washington, y seguramente sus teléfonos están intervenidos. Si dicen alguna imprudencia y eso causa un conflicto diplomático, Su Majestad Imperial va a colgarlos.

—Demasiado tarde, nos estábamos burlando del cabello de Trump. Es imposible no hacerlo. Pero me causa gracia que ahora llames a Fer Su Majestad Imperial, cuando hace una semana te referías a él como "el idiota", y me consta que no lo hacías pensando en el libro de Dostoyevski, algo que de todas formas no sería un alago, ya que Myshkin tampoco es dueño de una personalidad deslumbrante.

—Supongo que tengo que aceptar la primera derrota de mi vida —dijo el príncipe—. La sensatez me obliga a hacerlo, y culpo de mi decisión al hecho de que soy un hombre demasiado inteligente. Unirme al emperador y no estar en contra de él me garantiza seguir siendo uno de los hombres más poderosos de México y del mundo. El orgullo a veces es sólo un estorbo y yo soy un especialista en quitar los estorbos de mi camino.

—No te preocupes, hermano —dijo la princesa Ana, sonriendo—, tú no serás emperador, eso está muy claro, pero nuestra familia no se quedará fuera de Chapultepec, porque yo voy a sustituirte en esa proeza a la que has renunciado tan pronto.

—¿Me quieres decir con ello que te casarás con Fernando Carlos y serás emperatriz?

—Ni duda cabe, hermano, que eres inteligente. Has comprendido todo bastante rápido.

—Por si no lo sabes, pequeña víbora, ya sé que anoche el emperador te abandonó en la cena para irse con su... novia. Eres bonita, pero quizás le gustan las mujeres inteligentes.

—¡Pendejo! Es cierto que Fer tiene novia. Pero ella no pertenece a la aristocracia mexicana. Quizás hasta tengan algún bastardito, o dos, lo que me tiene sin cuidado. Fer va a casarse con una princesa, para que le dé un heredero al trono, y ésa voy a ser yo. Así que me vale madre que llegue a tener veinte bastardos con las mujeres que quiera. Yo tampoco pienso portarme como una monja cuando sea su esposa.

—¿Así que estás decidida a casarte con el emperador?

—Realmente no es que sueñe con ser emperatriz —dijo la princesa—, pero desde que aún no sabía maquillarme correctamente tenía claro que a Fer le gustaba, que podía manipularlo a mi antojo o tan sólo acobardarlo con mi mirada. Y ahora que es emperador he notado que se me revela, que ya no lo tengo en mis manos, lo que me da directo en el orgullo. Así que comprenderás, hermano, que tengo que recuperar mi terreno perdido. Estoy en la mejor etapa de mi vida, y justo ahora ningún hombre se me resiste. Tampoco lo hará el mismísimo emperador. Que me deje por otra cuanto mi edad sea de cincuenta años, pero de momento no se lo voy a permitir. ¿Comprendes?

—Estás loca. Y deja de llamarlo Fer...

—Ah, te informo, Agustín, que a mí sí me permitió llamarlo Fer. Anoche Carlota y el apuesto Bonaparte se rieron de que a ti no. Qué lástima. Procura no volver a hacerlo, o de lo contrario te formaran consejo de guerra. Ya me imagino al ministro Peña-Bazaine, tan tradicionalista con el protocolo, diciendo: "se acusa al facineroso Iturbide de tutear a Su Majestad Imperial, y se le condena a perder sus títulos y a ser pasado por las armas".

—¡Ya cállate, víbora!

—No te enojes, hermano. Imagina que Fer va a morir cuando mi hijo aún no sea mayor de dieciocho años. Eso me haría emperatriz regente, y en caso de que así sean las cosas, te prometo que te prestaré la corona de vez en cuando para que te tomes algunas autofotos, para tu perfil en las redes sociales.

—¡Deja de decir pendejadas! —gritó el príncipe, mientras su hermana daba vueltas en un sofá a causa de la risa.

—¡Cálmate! Yo creí que la idea te agradaría.

—Tan sólo te voy a recomendar una cosa —dijo el príncipe—, que tú y Ángel no hablen de más. Si los están interviniendo, el emperador va a destituir a tu hermano consentido de su puesto antes de lo que te imaginas.

—No te preocupes, él no es ningún idiota, sabe cuidarse. Desde que es embajador, tenemos un alfabeto bastante bien alterado y muy confuso que sólo nosotros dos sabemos, de memoria, no está escrito en ninguna parte. No importa cuánto los yanquis se rompan la cabeza, no van a sacar nada de nuestros jeroglíficos.

—Vaya, eso me tranquiliza. ¿Y te ha dicho algo importante hoy, aparte de burlarse del cabello de Trump?

—Pues, al parecer, las relaciones se están calentando más de la cuenta. Ángel considera que no habían estado tan mal desde que Roosevelt le pidió en una carta a Maximiliano II que se bajara el rango y se proclamara rey.

—¿Tanto así? —dijo el príncipe.

—Al parecer a Trump no le gustó que el emperador lo quiera recibir en Palacio Imperial como a cualquier presidentillo que igual da si viene o no viene o que bien puede recibirlo el ministro de correos en una bodega sin techo. Ángel estaba invitado a cenar mañana en la Casa Blanca, y esta tarde le informaron que el presidente canceló la invitación. ¿No crees que eso dice mucho?

—Con lo orgulloso que es Bonaparte, va a considerar ese desplante como una mentada de madre. Después irá con el chisme al emperador, y según vi en su carácter cuando me recibió, se calienta más rápido que el agua para café, lo que no augura nada bueno en nuestras relaciones con los yanquis.

—¿Y qué puede pasar? —dijo la princesa—, ¿ya voy buscando un refugio anti bombas nucleares?

—Deja de bromear, niña tonta. Muchas catástrofes han empezado por simples desplantes y reacciones por orgullo. Trump está cometiendo el mismo error que yo, piensa que el emperador es un niño sin carácter. En lugar de buscar la forma de corregir las pendejadas que se le salieron por la boca, busca cualquier pretexto para hacerse el ofendido. Eso lo va a empeorar todo. Yo creo que una llamada entre Fernando Carlos y Trump, donde hagan una broma cada uno y se adulen mutuamente un par de minutos, quitaría el hielo que ahora lo nubla todo. Pero la política exterior del Imperio Mexicano está muy definida por la ideología de Bonaparte, un orgulloso que no tolera que nos falten al respeto siquiera mínimamente, y Trump se saltó la barda. Bonaparte aconsejará al emperador, y va a impedir por todos los medios posibles que le tome una llamada a Trump hasta que éste no se disculpe.

—¿Acaso Fer se deja aconsejar? —preguntó la princesa—. Lo digo porque ya parece tener todo bajo control.

—A Bonaparte le tolera cualquier consejo. Su tía se lo vendió como el hombre más confiable dentro del imperio y el emperador le cree a ella ciegamente. Pero Luis le está jugando al Bismarck más de la cuenta. Él no quiere una armonía entre dos potencias vecinas, nunca la ha querido. Considera que el poderío de México radica en causar miedo y respeto a los yanquis, y hará cuanto pueda para que las relaciones se enfríen hasta rozar los límites.

—Yo considero a Bonaparte, además de un cuarentón muy atractivo, un hombre bastante inteligente —dijo la princesa—. No creo que sean tan imprudente como para causarle graves problemas al país que tanto ama. Pero te prometo que cuando sea emperatriz, haré que Fer te nombre canciller, hermano, ¿te gusta la idea?

Mientras Ana María soltaba estruendosamente su hermosa risa de ángel malvado, el príncipe Iturbide la veía con ganas de ahorcarla, o al menos de darle un par de bofetadas. Era la primera vez que hablaba seriamente de política con ella, lo que quería decir que ya la consideraba adulta, y en cambio su hermano no hacía más que reírse. Le resultaba intolerable.

Mientras tanto, en Chapultepec

—Sé, por el conde Andrássy, que Su Majestad se disponía a salir por una cuestión personal justo ahora —dijo el canciller Bonaparte—, comprenderá que no deseaba interrumpir sus planes. Pero la situación me obliga.

—Hable pues, Bonaparte —dijo el emperador, que ya se había quitado el ajustado traje con que solía trabajar y se había vestido con una informal mezclilla—. ¿Qué es lo que está pasando que lo tiene tan irritado?

—Pues casi nada. Los yanquis no sólo le han cerrado las puertas de la Casa Blanca en la cara al príncipe Iturbide, como si fuera el embajador de una dictadura perdida en algún rincón del mundo, lo que a estas alturas es lo de menos, sino que el vicepresidente acaba de decir en una entrevista televisada en vivo, y riéndose, que el famoso muro del que Trump habló en su campaña será una realidad, y que como el Imperio Mexicano siempre ha recibido generosamente a los emigrantes y la mitad de ellos se van a probar suerte a los Estados Unidos, a nosotros nos toca pagar desde los cimientos hasta el remeta del muro. Y añadió que eso ya lo decidieron ellos, sin consultarlo siquiera con nosotros.

—¿Eso ha dicho el muy hijo de la chingada? ¡De quien cree que está hablando ese pendejo!

—Majestad, con el debido respeto, así no habla un emperador.

—Pero así habla un mexicano cuando se enoja. Esta mamada no se las pienso tolerar, Bonaparte. Dígale a Iturbide que pida ahora mismo sus credenciales, y despierte a la embajadora. Exíjale que haga sus maletas inmediatamente. No quiero que un solo miembro de esa embajada vea un nuevo amanecer dentro del Imperio Mexicano.

—De hecho, acabo de colgar con ella —respondió el canciller—, pero fue ella quien me llamó. Quería enfriar un poco la reacción que tendríamos a causa de las declaraciones de Pence. Majestad, incluso la embajadora ha reconocido que Trump y sus más allegados dicen una cosa hoy y cambian de opinión mañana. Son más pendejos que los comunistas que gobiernan a Venezuela en cuestiones de diplomacia. Si retiramos al embajador, estaríamos demostrando que somos igual de improvisadores que ellos. Entre el Imperio Mexicano y los Estados Unidos hay relaciones comerciales con una importancia enorme para los dos países, tan extensamente poblados. Infinidad de mexicanos y yanquis están pagando su casa, su auto y sus futuras vacaciones gracias a esas relaciones comerciales. Si le pedimos a Iturbide que les miente la madre y se regrese a México, demostraríamos que no sabemos gobernar. Y lo que debemos hacer es demostrarles que somos aristócratas entrenados toda la vida para esto, no improvisadores como ellos. Créame, Majestad, yo me he encabronado más que usted, pero una reacción pasional y apresurada nos haría ver como niños. Usted lleva la sangre de hombres que han tomado decisiones de Estado y de vital importancia durante siete siglos, hágale honor a ello y cálmese un poco. Después deme una orden, ya más sereno, la acataré al instante.

—Reconozco, Bonaparte, que tiene usted toda la razón —dijo Fernando Carlos—. Pero no creo que me calme pronto. Estoy que me lleva la chingada de coraje. ¿Cómo creen esos cabrones que nosotros pagaríamos ese pinche muro?, ¿qué van a pedir después?, ¿casa de campo para todos a costillas de los impuestos de los mexicanos?

—Si nos dejamos…, júrelo.

—Creo que una buena reacción a esto podré darla hasta mañana, príncipe, cuando ya esté con la cabeza un poco más fría. Pero de momento le doy carta abierta para que publique cualquier comunicado en el que afirma que mi gobierno rechaza tajantemente las pendejadas que dijo Pence. Expláyese a gusto y ofenda en la misma medida que lo hicieron ellos. Si transcurren los minutos y los mexicanos ven que dejamos pasar como si nada esas declaraciones, van a pensar que su emperador es un pendejo que no los defiende, y tendrán razón si piden que Morador me sustituya.

—Lo haré enseguida, Majestad —respondió el canciller—, pero antes permítame decirle que hace apenas unos minutos me llamó el presidente de Cuba. Él comprendió que esas declaraciones nos harían enfurecer y se ofreció muy amablemente a ayudarnos como mediador. Cuba es una gran democracia y un país próspero y libre, y su pujante economía depende mucho de hallarse en el mar, justo en medio de dos potencias tan apegadas al libre comercio. Por ello el presidente aboga por que nuestras relaciones con los yanquis sean armoniosas.

—No sólo es su ubicación geográfica —dijo el emperador—. Cuba es un país tan rico y lleno de libertades gracias a que el presidente Carlos Montaner es un hombre sensato, que jamás permite con los prejuicios estúpidos tan ligados al nacionalismo más primitivo interfieran en sus planes como gobernante. Aquél que sabe alejar de su cabeza toda clase de fanatismos sin un fundamento práctico, y que tiene el necesario carácter, será siempre un buen gobernante.

—Yo pienso exactamente igual que usted, Majestad, buena parte de la grandeza de Cuba existe gracias a la inteligencia y sensatez del presidente Montaner. En esta llamada, aprovechamos para acordar que su visita a México sea, tentativamente, dentro de tres semanas. ¿Le parece bien?

—Estoy totalmente de acuerdo. Y quiero que se le rindan los honores debidos como presidente de un país que ha demostrado ser un gran ejemplo para el mundo, gracias a su respeto a las libertades más indispensables para que cualquier persona luche por sus sueños. Yo mismo acompañaré al presidente Montaner a pasar revista al ejército imperial mexicano, honor que no pienso concederle a Trump por nada del mundo.

—Mañana mismo, Majestad —respondió Bonaparte—, le diré a Montaner que a usted le parece ideal la fecha que él y yo sugerimos. Y en cuanto a su intervención en el asunto con los yanquis, ¿qué ordena usted que le diga?

—Dele las gracias al honorable presidente Montaner por su ofrecimiento, pero no necesito su ayuda en esto, ni que se meta en lo más mínimo. Este asunto lo arreglo yo, y si no consigo que esos pendejos empiecen a respetarnos, renuncio a mi cargo y después me corto los huevos. Ya no me harían falta.

—¡Majestad!

—Es todo, príncipe. Dispóngase a hacer lo que le he ordenado, y nos vemos aquí mañana a las ocho.

—A las órdenes de Vuestra Majestad.

Cuando el emperador se quedó sólo en el despacho de los cuatro bustos, pidió que le llevaran un litro de pulque bien frio, y antes de servirse por primera vez, hizo una llamada desde su teléfono particular.

—Carlota...

—Fer, llevo media hora esperándote aquí, en el mismo lugar donde te caíste.

—Estoy en Chapultepec. No podré ir. Lo siento.

—Todo el día supe que esto pasaría, no te preocupes, Fer.

—¿Por qué dices eso? Carlota, tengo un asunto muy importante de qué ocuparme.

—Supongo que es la princesa Iturbide tu asunto tan importante. Hoy dos diarios publicaron que es muy probable que ella sea tu futura esposa

—¿De verdad? No leí esos diarios. No tengo nada en contra de la libertad de expresión, pero sí contra la publicación de mentiras tan estúpidas. Mañana me ocuparé de ello. Te lo juro.

—No te preocupes, quizás debes dejar que las cosas transcurran con normalidad.

—No sé de qué hablas. Lo que me impide verte hoy es un importante asunto de Estado. Necesito concentrarme en ello, por más que me duela no verte.

—Está bien, Fer. No te preocupes.

—Carlota, te amo, te amaré más todavía mañana, y no sé dónde estará mi alma en mil años, pero sí sé que lo que entonces quede aún de mí te estará amando. No lo dudes, por favor.

Carlota colgó sin responder   y Fernando Carlos dejó caer su teléfono en el escritorio.

—¡Yanquis hijos del a chingada! ¡Hasta en esto me causan problemas!

A la mañana siguiente

Fernando Carlos estaba vestido con su habitual traje negro, propio de su luto. Su camisa blanca hacía resaltar la corbata color café claro, a la vez que también hacía resaltar su tez blanca y el conjunto generaba un especial brillo en sus ojos verdes. Las tres cámaras que tenía enfrente y a ambos lados, enfocaban tan sólo su figura, el cuadro de Maximiliano *el Grande* a sus espaldas, parte de su escritorio y del librero que también tenía detrás, decorado con dos pequeñas esculturas aztecas de la mejor factura, en tanto que las lentes se quedaban a tan sólo un metro de enfocar dos de los cuatro bustos que hacían famoso el despacho del emperador.

—A las tres estaremos al aire en todo el imperio, Majestad: uno, dos..., tres.

—Pueblo de México —comenzó Fernando Carlos—, el día de ayer, como todos ustedes ya sabrán en estos momentos, el vicepresidente de los Estados Unidos tuvo el atrevimiento de decir que su gobierno construirá un muro en la frontera que nos une y que nosotros, los mexicanos, vamos a pagarlo, tan sólo porque ellos así lo han decidido. Comparto la misma indignación que sienten todos ustedes ante una ofensa tan grande, y, como su emperador, les juro que este terrible agravio a nuestro honor no va a quedar impune. Cuentan que el gran Juárez, uno de nuestros mejores estadistas a lo largo de la historia, dijo en su lecho de muerte que entre los individuos como entre las naciones, el respeto al derecho ajeno es la paz. Son tan solo algunas pocas palabras las que dijo ese extraordinario mexicano, pero encierran tal sabiduría que muy probablemente incluso en su tumba la envidian los más importantes filósofos de la historia de la humanidad. Es en este momento cuando las palabras de Juárez retumban como cañonazos en mi cabeza, puesto que México, como un pueblo libre y soberano, que enfoca todo el poder de sus instituciones en hacer cada día de éste un mejor país para vivir, no permitirá bajo ninguna circunstancia que se nos trate de esta manera. No voy a implantar aranceles irracionales ni a interrumpir de ninguna forma el comercio entre ambos países. Ningún gobernante tiene derecho de bloquear por ningún motivo, en tiempos de paz, el comercio entre los individuos, sea cual sea su nacionalidad. Pero quiero dejar totalmente claro que si la primera piedra de ese muro en nuestra frontera norte invade tan sólo un milímetro del territorio mexicano, la fuerza área imperial la hará volar en mil pedazos, sean cuales sean las reacciones del gobierno de los Estados Unidos. Si ellos toman decisiones arbitrarias, nosotros también lo haremos. Desde este momento, no compartiremos ninguna información sobre el terrorismo islamista o sobre el narcotráfico en Latinoamérica con el gobierno de los Estados Unidos, y no es que México abandone esa lucha, tan necesaria para la paz del mundo, sino que no podemos ser aliados de un gobierno que no nos respeta. Sé que este asunto preocupa a la gran mayoría de los mexicanos, y que aparte tienen que solucionar problemas en su trabajo, pagar sus deudas personales, resolver dilemas de su matrimonio, de los comportamientos de sus hijos, e incluso del funcionamiento de sus automóviles. Así que les pido a todos que se ocupen de resolver esos problemas, algo muy necesario para que prolifere la armonía dentro de nuestro imperio. Ustedes resuelvan sus problemas diarios, es su responsabilidad, yo entretanto he de ocuparme de Trump y de los Estados Unidos…, ésa es mi responsabilidad absoluta. Y les juro que no voy a decepcionarlos. Que tengan un excelente día.

—¡Corte!

Esa misma tarde

Cuando Ángel Miguel Morador entró al despacho de los cuatro bustos, lo recorrió de arriba abajo y de izquierda a derecha con la mirada de una ave de rapiña. A diferencia del Despacho Oval en los Estados Unidos, en México no eran comunes las fotografías del interior del lugar donde trabajaba el emperador. Las fotografías y grabaciones difundidas apenas y mostraban una pequeña parte del despacho, razón por la cual aquellos que acudían allí por primera vez, como era el caso de Morador, no podían resistir la tentación de voltear para todos lados. Cuando el popular caudillo terminó de verlo todo, fijó su mirada en el hombre que tenía frente a sí, sentado, con la espalda recta y mirándolo a él fijamente.

–Sea usted bienvenido, señor Morador. Siéntese –dijo el emperador.

–Gracias, señor, eh…, Fernando Carlos de Austria.

–Ni siquiera Maximiliano *el Grande* cuando llegó a México se llamaba de Austria. Él ya había renunciado a ese derecho ante su hermano, precisamente para poder venir aquí. Si quiere llamarme por el patronímico derivado del lugar a donde pertenezco, algo que es totalmente legal en mi nombre, llámeme Fernando Carlos de México. Ése es mi verdadero nombre como emperador, y me siento orgulloso de él.

–Todos sabemos –respondió Morador–, que ustedes no se sienten verdaderamente mexicanos, que ven a México como una mina de oro a la cual están vaciando, pero su origen es austriaco, como lo ha sido, eh, siempre, a lo largo de los siglos. Y allá van a volver, más temprano que tarde, usted y su tía.

–Escúcheme bien, Morador, habíamos fijado su audiencia para hoy y no la cancelé incluso cuando han ocurrido sucesos que me exigen completa atención. Y si no decidí pedirle que viniera otro día, fue tan sólo porque ingenuamente creí que usted tendría algo importante que decirme. Pero si va a repetir las mismas estupideces de siempre, tendré que pedirle que marche ahora mismo.

—¿Mencionó algo importante que decirle, señor Fernando Carlos de Austria? Por supuesto que tengo algo importante que decirle, y eso es que los mexicanos ya estamos hartos de que se nos niegue la democracia, de ser el país más atrasado del mundo en cuanto al ejercicio que debe de hacer el pueblo, eligiendo a su gobernante. La democracia es la forma de gobierno más justa, más igualitaria y más noble que existe sobre la tierra, y usted nos la está negando.

—Según entiendo yo la democracia, Morador, puedo afirmar que es una forma de gobierno en la que decide la gran mayoría, pero nunca la mejor mayoría. La democracia es un salto al vacío, y si bien es cierto que algunos pueblos caen entre cojines, la gran mayoría se rompen en pedazos. Existen imbéciles que no tienen la más remota idea de cómo gobernar, pero aun así se empeñan en que se les permita hacerlo. Y cuando la democracia por fin se los permite, ensayan con las vidas de millones de infelices. Primero les quitan sus instituciones, después su trabajo, el valor de su dinero, su seguridad y al final la vida. Pero lo que estoy diciéndole es solo mi opinión sobre la democracia, no argumento una excusa para seguir en mi puesto. Soy emperador porque mi país legalmente está constituido como una monarquía, sobre la que descansan infinidad de instituciones que velan por la seguridad de los mexicanos. Y no voy a quitarme sólo porque a un retrasado metal y ambicioso se le antoja ser presidente de un país que él no hizo grande. Eso sería absurdo.

—¡Está hablando de mí! —gritó Morador, poniéndose de pie.

—Por favor, ¿todavía cree que sea necesario que se lo confirme? —dijo el emperador—. Cuando Francisco I. Madero acudió a una audiencia con mi tatarabuelo, Agustín II, está claro que llevaba consigo argumentos sólidos, a los que el emperador tuvo que hacer frente no sin dificultades. Nadie duda que Madero era un hombre listo e ilustrado, y le confieso que llegué a pesar, todavía esta mañana, que yo tendría un adversario igual de preparado. Pero me he encontrado con un tipejillo vulgar y ambicioso, que tan sólo repite la parte más insustancial de los argumentos de Madero, como si eso fuera a convencerme de algo importante. Francamente, Morador, no me cabe en la cabeza cómo es que usted cree que puede gobernar a México. ¿Acaso lo ciega tanto su ambición al grado de no permitirle ver que usted no da la talla ni para ser funcionario de correos?

—¡No le pienso permitir que me ofenda de esa manera! —gritó Morador, aún más irritado.

—Pues si no quiere que le siga diciendo sus verdades, ya se puede ir. Francamente, tengo mucho trabajo que hacer, y estoy convencido de esta reunión no dará el menor provecho a los mexicanos.

—¿Y usted cree, dictador, que descalificándome, negando mi liderazgo y la importancia del movimiento que yo represento, va a lograr que decline de mi misión como patriota? Yo, señor Habsburgo, soy capaz de dar mi vida, con tal de que México sea libre.

—México es un país tan libre, Morador, tan libre que incluso hasta los vagos perezosos que nada producen viven pacíficamente, no se mueren de hambre, se expresan cómo quieren y a veces hasta logran que los reciba el emperador, y que él se esmere en un principio por tratarlos con respeto. ¿Qué más quiere?, ¿no le parece que tenemos un gran país? Hace apenas unos minutos —añadió Fernando Carlos—, vi cómo recorrió con la mirada este despacho. Me consta que le ha gustado, incluso me atrevería a jurar que se imaginó sentado en mi ligar. A usted, Morador, no le molesta el gobierno de México, sino simplemente el hecho de que usted no gobierna.

—Es verdad, no lo niego, yo quiero ser presidente —dijo Morador, bajando un poco su tono—. Pero mi gobierno saldrá de la democracia, de la voz del pueblo, y cuando al pueblo no le parezcan mis actos de gobierno, me iré del poder.

—Qué curioso. Lo mismo exactamente dijeron sus amigos venezolanos y ya llevan casi veinte años gobernando a gritos. Los habitantes de ese infeliz pueblo ya deben de tener algún problema de sordera.

—¡Yo no tengo ninguna relación con ese gobierno!

—Usted mismo, Morador, ha dicho algunas veces que la guardia secreta imperial es muy eficiente. Así que no venga a subestimarla delante de mí. Pero créame que yo no cuestiono sus amistades. Cada quien sabe con qué clase personas se relaciona. Incluso si algún gobierno decide usar los ingresos derivados de la venta de petróleo para ayudar a sus amigos, mientras su pueblo se muere de hambre, yo no puedo legalmente hacer nada, por más que me parezca una práctica infame e inhumana.

—Ya decía yo —respondió Morador, tratando de reír—, ya decía yo, he, que se estaba armando un complot para desprestigiarme y a la vez desaparecer al movimiento que yo represento. Para nadie es un secreto que esta dictadura es experta en crear y difundir mentiras. Estoy totalmente convencido, eh, no tengo ninguna duda, de que ese conflicto con Trump que ustedes se traen, es realmente una artimaña que —ayudados por él, porque el capitalismo se protege entre sí—, repito, es una artimaña para que usted se dé importancia, se venda al pueblo como un gobernante indispensable, que no se puede ir de su puesto. Está muy claro, esta mentira es una más de esas ideas que Bonaparte pone en práctica para darle un poco más de vida a esta dictadura moribunda. Pero el pueblo no es tonto, el pueblo no va a creer este engaño. Vamos a desbaratar su red de mentiras, vamos a crear un gobierno del pueblo, conformado por mexicanos, por mexicanos honestos, comprometidos con la verdad.

—Vaya —dijo el emperador—, pues no sé de dónde va a sacarlos. Sus más allegados no son precisamente sinceros en cuanto a lo que tienen y respecto a lo que realmente son. Tampoco usted, Morador —le dijo mirándolo a los ojos—. Tengo datos precisos de que todos los miembros fundadores de su partido cooperaron con mil pesos, sin embargo, su partido, como una entidad legamente reconocida, está obligado a reportar al ministerio de Hacienda tanto sus ingresos, por más que éstos vengan de donaciones, como sus gastos. Eso usted lo sabe muy bien, por ello me he extrañado mucho cuando el ministro Iturbide me ha informado que su partido no ha enterado qué uso le dio a ese dinero. Y si tomamos en cuenta que se estima en cien mil a los mexicanos que dieron su cooperación, es una verdadera fortuna de lo que estamos hablando.

Dígame, Morador, ya que tanto alardea de honestidad, ¿qué uso le dio a ese dinero?

Morador se aflojó la corbata un poco, mientras daba la impresión de desear un vaso de pulque helado.

—Ya sé por dónde va usted. Eh, era de esperarse esta artimañita. Pero voy a responderle, porque yo soy un hombre honesto, no me interesa robar. No soy como usted y Bonaparte. Los recursos que nos han donado se utilizan para las giras de mi movimiento. Hemos recorrido todo el imperio, hemos pasado por todos los pueblos, hemos estrechado todas las manos que salen a nuestro encuentro, hemos escuchado todos los problemas que usted no ha querido resolver, porque sólo se interesa por la aristocracia del imperio. Los demás no le importan.

—De acuerdo —interrumpió el emperador—, no tengo porque dudar que ese dinero se ha usado para los viajes que usted menciona. Pero su partido, al gozar de personalidad jurídica, está obligado a llevar una contabilidad, y en ella un desglose minucioso de sus gastos efectivamente comprobados. Usted no va a decir que cada viaje le ha costado un millón de pesos y va a esperar a que el ministerio de Hacienda crea en su palabra ciegamente, sin demostrar absolutamente nada.

—¡Usted está tratando de enlodar mi nombre! —dijo Morador—. Su plan es manchar la integridad con que siempre he actuado, para que el pueblo deje de confiar en mí. Pero no le va a funcionar, eh, porque yo soy un hombre honesto, y el pueblo sabe quién soy.

—Dichoso aquel que puede recurrir a una estrategia como la suya cuando no cuadran las cuentas que le hacen, pero más dichoso todavía es al que le funciona —dijo Fernando Carlos—. Le aviso de una vez, Morador, el ministerio de Hacienda ya recibió la instrucción de averiguar qué ha pasado con todo ese dinero, porque es demasiado y no pienso tolerar que hipnotizadores profesionales que se meten en política se hagan millonarios a costillas de la buena fe de algunos mexicanos. Si miembros de su partido, usted entre ellos, se han apropiado de ese dinero, no me tentaré el corazón y haré que pasen toda su vida encerrados en una jaula.

—¡Le repito que ese dinero se ha gastado en las giras de mi movimiento! Y eso es muy lógico, ya que el gobierno se niega a financiarnos.

—Y nos seguiremos negando a cometer semejante crimen —dijo el emperador—, los impuestos de los mexicanos no son para mantener hue... perezosos.

—Sólo voy a decirle una cosa más —respondió Morador, sudando igual que Quirarte cuando estuvo frente a Fernando Carlos—. Usted hace todo esto para mantener viva una dictadura que ya no debe de existir, que es demasiado antigua para ajustarse a los anhelos de libertad de los mexicanos. Usted miente sobre el uso que le he dado a esos recursos porque no desea perder sus privilegios de aristócrata. Pero también sé que lo hace adoctrinado por su tía y por Bonaparte, los dos dictadores detrás del muñeco de ventrílocuo que es usted. Porque yo estoy enterado de que usted no quería gobernar, y que ellos le pusieron a fuerzas la corona por una sola razón: que esa mafia que tiene al país en sus manos nos siga saqueando. Pero no se los pienso permitir, de ninguna manera. Su hora ha llegado, señor Habsburgo. Tendrán que irse, y tendrán que desenterrar y llevarse también los cadáveres que están en la Cripta Imperial de Guadalupe, porque son una ofensa para los mexicanos, para los verdaderos mexicanos, y no los queremos aquí. Con gusto le regalaré una pala para que usted mismo los desentierre.

—Quizás, señor Morador, el Diablo ya se cansó de ser diablo y Dios ya se cansó de ser dios —dijo Fernando Carlos, sin verse alterado siquiera mínimamente—; es probable que ningún de los tres estemos contentos en nuestro puesto. Pero los tres tenemos la completa seguridad de que nuestro puesto no es canjeable y de que debemos hacer las cosas lo mejor que podemos, nos guste o no nos guste lo que hacemos. A fin de cuentas, el de diablo, el de dios y el de emperador, son los cargos vigentes más antiguos de que tiene memoria la humanidad, y si ellos no renuncian, yo tampoco pienso hacerlo. Nosotros tres no sabemos de democracia, estamos arraigados en algo más antiguo que eso, cuya legitimidad radica exclusivamente en hacer las cosas bien. Usted tiene razón en señalar que yo no quería ser emperador. Pero eso no debería preocuparlo. Nuestro país está lleno de grandes mujeres y hombres que hubieran querido ser otra cosa, pero sus circunstancias no lo permitieron. Hay obreros que habrían querido ser médicos, escritores, músicos o un sinfín de etcéteras, mas sin embargo, pese a no estar donde quisieran estar, hacen en el trabajo que la vida les dio lo mejor que pueden, y gracias a su ejemplo yo estoy aquí, firme, sin dudar un solo instante sobre cuáles son mis obligaciones. Sé que mi puesto tiene privilegios, pero si algo está más que claro es que yo no lo elegí. Mas ahora le doy las gracias a Dios por haberme lanzado a esta silla, ya que con ello evitó que un fanático lleno de odio como usted, que no anhela más que enemistar a los mexicanos con ellos mismos y cumplir su sueño de ser presidente, pueda gobernar un solo día a mi país. Esto todo, Morador, le ordeno que se retire de aquí inmediatamente.

—Visto está que usted, dictador despreciable, subestima mi movimiento porque es la voz de los más pobres. Pero hoy mismo le daremos una pequeña muestra de lo que somos capaces de hacer. Hoy mismo lamentará haberme ofendido con sus calumnias sin fundamentos.

—Sólo le advierto una cosa, Morador, cien mil personas manifestándose no son la voz de doscientos sesenta millones que sí valoran las instituciones del país donde viven. Si sus seguidores se ponen a bloquear calles en todas partes, provocando con ello que los mexicanos que sí son productivos lleguen a sus destinos, van a hacerme enfurecer y tomaré las medias que sean necesarias para restaurar el orden.

Cuando Morador salió del despacho, Fernando Carlos se puso de pie y fue hacia una ventana. Quería distraerse con algo antes de que le entrara la idea de ir tras él y ahorcarlo con sus propias manos. De pie, junto a la ventana, el aire empezó a golpearlo en la cara y le provocó una sensación agradable. Su mirada se perdió entre los enormes rascacielos que se veían a lo lejos, a varios kilómetros del castillo, y que databan algunos de la primera mitad del siglo XX, cuando Aztlán había competido con Nueva York por demostrar qué ciudad podía construir el edificio más alto del mundo. Una ligera niebla que inundaba la ciudad hacía parecer a aquellos gigantes como una especie de seres siniestros salidos de entre las penumbras. Al emperador le gustaba más verlos durante la noche, cuando la iluminación de las moles lo hacía pensar que navegaba en el espacio. Transcurridos varios minutos, se sintió más tranquilo. Tomó su teléfono y dio la orden de que tuvieran un vehículo listo para salir.

Después de que se fue la última de sus alumnas, Carlota cerró la puerta del local donde impartía clases de baile, y luego fue a mirarse unos segundos al espejo. Estaba sudada de la cabeza a los pies, el sudor mojaba su ropa e incluso tenía cabellos pegados a sus mejillas. Ahora que había dejado de hacer ejercicio, en su cabeza volvían los pensamientos que tanto quería evitar, así que decidió ir a darse un baño para después irse a su casa a comer. Quizás regañando a sus hermanos para que dejaran de hacer travesuras, el emperador se iría por algunos minutos de su cabeza. La primera vez que tocaron la puerta, ni siquiera supo definir si era en su local. Pero un nuevo golpe varios segundos después le confirmó que tenía que ir a abrir. Vio a su alrededor para ver si alguna de sus alumnas había dejado olvidada una de sus pertenencias, lo que solía ocurrir a menudo. Pero no vio nada. Así que probablemente no era una alumna quien llamaba. Cuando por fin fue a abrir, dio dos pasos hacia atrás. Fernando Carlos estaba vestido como nunca lo había visto en persona, con un elegante traje que le quedaba a la perfección, el mismo con el que había aparecido por la mañana en las noticias, dando un discurso que en las redes sociales el pueblo había aplaudido con sobrada satisfacción.

—¡Fer!, ¿qué haces aquí?

—Te llamé varias veces…

—Estaba ocupada, no sólo tú trabajas todo el día.

—Lo sé, sólo quería escuchar tu voz un par de segundos —se disculpó el emperador—. ¿Puedo pasar?

—Sí, Fer, pero no sé si me gusta que me interrumpas en mi trabajo.

—Me habías dicho que a esta hora ya no hay nadie, y como prometiste enseñarme a bailar.

—En este momento no, estoy cansada.

—No te preocupes, tan sólo si me dejas abrazarte, me sentiré feliz —dijo Fernando Carlos, y con sus brazos la acercó a su cuerpo. Aunque Carlota en un principio quiso resistirse, terminó besándola.

—Fer, estoy empapada en sudor –dijo ella, tratando de alejarse.

Al ver que el emperador no la soltaba por nada del mundo, intentó cambiar de tema.

—¿Qué te parece el local?

—Está bien –dijo Fernando Carlos, soltándola por fin–. Parece un lugar agradable. ¿Así que tú lo rentas exclusivamente para impartir tus clases?

—Y lo seguiré haciendo mientras lo que cobro a mis alumnas siga siendo suficiente para pagar la renta, la electricidad, el agua y me sobre un poco para mí. Como ves no es muy grande, pero funciona bastante bien.

—Me enorgullece que mi novia sea una mujer tan independiente, te lo juro –dijo el emperador–, pero sabes que en cualquier momento puedes acudir a mí...

—Ya hablamos de eso, Fer. No repitas las cosas como si no te las hubiera dejado bastante claras.

—Entonces, si eres tan escrupulosa, ¿también me vas a cobrar a mí las clases de baile?

—No, Fer... A ti no. Oye, no te quiero correr, pero debo darme un baño para ir a mi casa. Ya casi es hora de la comida.

—¿Un baño? Qué buena idea. Hace apenas una hora, un idiota me estresó mucho, y creo que un baño me caería de maravilla.

—Fer, me bañaré yo. Tú no puedes bañarte aquí.

—¿Por qué no? Estamos solos, y la puerta está cerrada. Apuesto a que el baño es aquella otra puerta.

El emperador empezó a caminar, mientras se quitaba la corbata. Carlota fue detrás de él, bastante molesta, el hecho de que su novio fuera tan necio empezaba a desagradarle un poco. Él abrió la regadera y se alejó un poco, para seguirse desvistiendo.

—¡Fer, esto no es gracioso! No me gusta que hagas tu voluntad —dijo cuando lo vio totalmente desnudo.

—Para estar tan molesta, no dejas de verme. Una mujer indignada voltearía para otro lado.

—¡Eres un idiota!

—¿Te ayudo a desvestirte?

—No, gracias, yo puedo sola.

—El hecho de que puedas sola, no quiere decir que no te sea útil mi ayuda —dijo el emperador y le levantó la playera para sacársela.

Carlota aún estaba seria cuando la abrazó totalmente desnuda y la llevó hacia la regadera. Pronto el agua ya había empapado sus cuerpos, el empezó a besarla y ella por fin lo abrazó con fuerza y correspondió con decisión a sus besos. Segundos después, lo abrazaba y lo besaba con tal fuerza, que era obvio que quería asegurarse de que Fernando Carlos le pertenecía a ella y a nadie más. Durante la siguiente media hora no le permitió que dejara de tocarla un solo instante, y para su satisfacción, él dejó claro que tampoco tenía pensado dejar de sentir el calor de su cuerpo ni siquiera un segundo.

Cuando el emperador se recostó en el suelo mojado, mientras la lluvia de la regadera seguía cayendo en sus cuerpos, Carlota se subió arriba de él, lo besó y le acarició el cabello.

—Tus ojos son todavía más hermosos con la cara mojada —le dijo.

—A mí me gustan más los tuyos. De hecho no hay nada de ti que no me guste, Carlota.

—Creo que ya con eso te perdono por haberme dejado plantada anoche.

—Lo siento, mi amor, ansiaba verte más que nada en el mundo, pero...

—Ya lo sé, Fer. Créeme que te entiendo. Te vi en las noticias por la mañana, me gustó tu discurso. Pero sinceramente creo que estoy afectando los intereses de todos los mexicanos. El otro día, cuando nos quedamos dormidos, casi te das un tiro por faltar a tus responsabilidades, y ahora te escapas a medio día del despacho de los cuatro bustos y vienes a buscarme. ¿Qué sigue?

—No es que no esté consiente de mi deber, pero tal vez no actuaria con la suficiente cordura si sigo pensando en ti cada segundo. Vine a recobrar la calma, y estoy seguro que al volver a Chapultepec podré concentrarme mejor. Además, el emperador de México se toma un día libre al mes, y yo casi llevo un mes en mis funciones. Así que estas horas se las voy a descontar a mi día de descanso.

—¿Y con quién vas a pasar ese día, cuando llegue? —preguntó Carlota, sonriendo.

—Pensaba invitar a Morador a Chapultepec, para que hablemos de filosofía en griego y en latín. Supongo que domina esos idiomas perfectamente, ya que siempre alega ser un hombre sabio e ilustrado, que conoce todos los problemas de México y sabe cómo resolverlos. ¿Qué opinas?

—Vete a la chingada.

Fernando Carlos se soltó a reír, y trato se besarla, pero Carlota le retiró sus labios.

—Sabes perfectamente con quién quiero estar ese día, y todos los días libres de mi vida. No tenías que preguntarlo, por eso te hice una pequeña broma.

—Fer —dijo ella, en tono serio—, la próxima vez que quieras hacerlo, trae condones. Nos estamos arriesgando mucho.

—No venía precisamente a hacerlo, sólo quería verte, abrazarte. Pero cuando mencionaste el baño me diste una gran idea.

—Ahora que te conozco, amor, sé que tú no vas a dejar pasar una sola oportunidad cuando estemos solos. Así que tendré que ser yo quien compre los condones. Tú siempre encontrarás un pretexto para no usarlos.

—Mi pretexto es que te amo.

—El hecho de amarnos no resta ningún riesgo al hecho de que yo pueda quedar embarazada. Nuestro noviazgo acaba de iniciar y tenemos veinte años, Fer, eso no podemos ignorarlo. Y deja de mirarme así, porque harás que no quiera irme y tengo que llegar a mi casa, ya tan sólo a saludar. Si me siento a comer con mi familia, llegaré tarde a mi otro empleo.

—Carlota, quiero casarme contigo.

—¿Qué parte de que nuestro noviazgo apenas acaba de iniciar no entendiste?, ¿acaso hablas tantos idiomas que ya se te olvidó el español?

—No me ignores…

—Te daré una toalla —dijo Carlota, levantándose—. Tendrás que ponerte la misma ropa.

—No tengo más opción. La tuya no se me vería muy bien que digamos.

—Gracioso.

—¿Qué te parece si vamos esta noche al bar donde canta mi hermano, para retomar ese tema del que no quisiste hablar?

—Fer, te he dicho varias veces que aún tengo miedo por nuestro noviazgo, para mí no es tan fácil asimilar las cosas, y tú no dejas que pase un día sin darme otro motivo de preocupación.

—¿Vamos?

—Sí, amor, vamos. Si te digo que no, con lo necio que eres, hasta mañana me dejarías llegar a mi casa.

Cuando estuvieron vestidos, Carlota peinó a Fernando Carlos cuidadosamente, de tal manera que pudiera regresar presentable a Chapultepec. Después lo tomó de la mano y lo llevó hasta la puerta del local.

—No quiero separarme de ti —le dijo él—. No me gusta, quisiera llevarte conmigo a Chapultepec, y tener la completa seguridad de que eres mía.

—Soy tuya, Fer, eso no lo dudes. Pero no me iré contigo a Chapultepec.

El emperador le detuvo la mano cuando ella se disponía a abrir la puerta. La jaló hacia él y la besó. Después la recargó contra un muro y siguió besándola más intensamente.

—Fer, tengo que ir a mi casa, y tú tienes que ir a trabajar —le dijo cuando él le desabrochaba el pantalón.

—Sencillamente, no puedo apartarme de ti —dijo Fernando Carlos, separando sus labios de los de Carlota sólo un instante.

Ella correspondió a sus besos, y con sus manos le aflojó el cinturón.

—Supongo que estando como estás —le dijo mientras lo sujetaba con una mano—, es imposible que me dejes ir, así que mejor colaboro contigo. Pero ésta es la última vez que lo hacemos sin condón. ¿Está claro?

—Definitivamente, no, no está claro —dijo el emperador, y la volteó hacia la pared.

—Tres pulques helados —dijo el príncipe Iturbide a la joven camarera que entró a su oficina, justo detrás del canciller Bonaparte y el general Peña-Bazaine, sin voltear a verla siquiera, pero con delicadeza, acentuando su refinamiento aristocrático.

—Enseguida, Alteza.

—Luis, general, siéntense, por favor. Espero que no les incomode al adelantarme a sus gustos, pero, supongo que, como cualquier mexicano, ustedes también disfrutan de un buen pulque todas las tardes.

—No te preocupes, Agustín, de hecho, me leíste la mente.

—¿Y usted, general, desea otra cosa?

—Pulque está bien —dijo Peña-Bazaine, con una inconfundible seriedad castrense.

—Bien, caballeros, supongo que ya saben por qué les pedí que vinieran. La situación del imperio es un poco delicada y quiero cambiar impresiones con ustedes. Así podremos ver cuál es la mejor forma de solucionar los problemas del emperador. Para eso nos tiene en nuestros puestos.

—Creo, Agustín —respondió Bonaparte—, que la situación a la que te refieres tiene que ver, exclusivamente, con Morador y Trump.

—Son sólo dos hombres —dijo Iturbide—, pero si no manejamos bien las cosas, nos pueden dar momentos muy desagradables. Además, es posible que el emperador no esté en las mejores condiciones para domesticar a esos dos animales salvajes. He sabido que anda un poco caliente —añadió riendo.

En ese instante, la camarera entró llevando una bandeja en las manos. A cada uno ofreció un vaso y se retiró. No obstante, ella misma notó que al general le temblaba una mano y dos venas se habían inflamado en su frente.

—Príncipe —dijo el ministro Peña-Bazaine—, que ésta sea la última vez que vuelve a hacer una broma estúpida sobre el emperador en mi presencia. La próxima ocasión, no se la voy a tolerar.

—Opino lo mismo, Agustín —dijo el canciller Bonaparte—, Su Majestad Imperial es intocable, su persona no puede ser objeto de bromas estúpidas. Me extraña tu atrevimiento.

—Cálmese, caballeros, y discúlpenme. No era mi intención ofenderlos. Sólo quise hacer notar que Su Majestad anda un poco enamorado, y un estadista enamorado suele bajar la guardia.

—Aun así estás cometiendo una falta, Agustín —dijo Bonaparte—, ya que el emperador no es cualquier estadista, sino un vástago legítimo de la casa de Habsburgo. Y, por lo tanto, él está exento de todos los males que afectan a tantos presidentillos mediocres que abundan en todas partes. Desde los cinco años se le educó como un archiduque de México, su mente y su espíritu fueron nutridos con las experiencias de sus antepasados durante siete siglos y los conocimientos de los más grandes filósofos de la historia de la humanidad. Puede, ciertamente, estar enamorado, como le pasa a cualquier hombre, pero eso no lo hará distraerse de sus responsabilidades. Debes estar seguro de ello.

—Por favor, Luis, general, no se alteren, créanme que mi intención no fue herirlos. Soy sólo un hombre que recurre al sarcasmo de vez en cuando para hacer algo amenas las reuniones, pero también estoy tan apegado a nuestra monarquía como ustedes. Les pido que dejemos atrás este penoso incidente y hablemos de lo que realmente importa. ¿Les parece?

—Está bien, Agustín —dijo Bonaparte—, pasemos pues al grano.

—De acuerdo, caballeros. Les aseguro que es lo más sensato, porque las cosas se pueden complicar para el imperio si no tomamos pronto las medidas necesarias para que aminore la incertidumbre que, como ministro de Hacienda, tantos problemas me está causando. Luis, las relaciones exteriores y la seguridad política interior dependen de ti, pero la salud de las finanzas es un asunto completamente mío, y si tú no le mandas poner un alto a Morador y arreglas una entrevista entre el emperador Trump para que lleguen a un pinche acuerdo, los empresarios empezarán a desconfiar de la estabilidad de México, guardarán o se llevarán su dinero y eso va a volver locas nuestras finanzas. Entonces el emperador va a destituirme por algo que tú estás haciendo mal, lo que no considero justo. Sencillamente, si no puedes, Luis, con todo respeto, renuncia a tu cargo, yo le pediré al emperador que me haga canciller, y verás cómo en dos semanas pongo remedio a esto.

—Agustín, si en tus funciones no puedes sostener estable el barco en un mes de turbulencia, ¿cómo se te ocurre que podrías ser canciller? —se defendió Bonaparte—. México no es un país inestable que cambie de gobierno cada quince días, estadísticamente cambia cada cuarto de siglo, y eso debería de ser una columna bastante gruesa para que aleje los rumores de inestabilidad. Tus reproches los habría aceptado hace un mes, cuando no sabíamos, honestamente, si teníamos un emperador. Pero ahora todo está claro, Su Majestad Imperial está sentado en el despacho de los cuatro bustos justo en este momento, y ese simple hecho al imperio le da una solidez enorme. Problemas con los yanquis, a excepción de los tres años que Maximiliano III y Kennedy fueron grandes amigos, los hemos tenido siempre, y comunistas locos que quieren implantar aquí el régimen de Lenin, acusando a la monarquía de obsoleta, tampoco son una rareza. ¿De qué te extrañas? Los anteriores ministros de Hacienda han sabido hacer las cosas bien en situaciones similares, así que no me hagas pensar, Agustín, que el cargo te queda grande.

El general Peña-Bazaine observó fijamente a Iturbide para ver salir las chispas de sus ojos, pero se sorprendió al comprobar que el príncipe mantenía magistralmente bien la calma. Era, innegablemente, un vástago destacado de una familia de estadistas. Si días atrás se había salido de sus casillas en presencia del mismísimo emperador, sin duda había sido un error que no pensaba volver a cometer.

—Te recuerdo, Luis —respondió Iturbide—, que Trump es el primer loco impredecible que llega a mandar al Despacho Oval, y que Morador es el primer fanático comunista al que en México se le permite hacer una consulta para que el pueblo decida si continúa o no la monarquía.

Además, un emperador de casi veintiún años con fama de débil mental no ayuda mucho. Ustedes y yo sabemos que no lo es, que el hombre tiene huevos de mexicano y que su inteligencia sobrepasa los estándares normales por mucho. De niño era un llorón escurridizo, pero su cerebro absorbía todo como una aspiradora, su preparación es extraordinaria, su capacidad para defenderse en un prolongado alegato pondría en aprietos al propio Cicerón, y sus argumentos en economía hasta a mí me acorralan, además, es el primer emperador desde Agustín II que habla más de diez idiomas con una fluidez sorprendente, pero, pese a tantos méritos, Morador se ha encargado de difundir el rumor de que al primer disparo se irá a esconder en las faldas de su tía, y de que no está preparado y tampoco quiere desempeñar su cargo, como si el maldito hablara bien siquiera el español. No obstante, los rumores difundidos por comunistas locos son las armas más peligrosas de la historia. En parte, el emperador tiene la culpa, si no se hubiera encerrado en Miramar como producto de una crisis nerviosa, nadie cuestionaría su fortaleza. Pero ahora no duden que Trump piensa que le tiene miedo, y que por eso ni siquiera el teléfono quiere contestarle.

—Príncipe —respondió el general Peña-Bazaine—, tomando en cuenta el discurso que apenas esta mañana pronunció en vivo Su Majestad Imperial, en el que amenazó con hacer volar la primera piedra del muro de Trump, ¿usted cree que aún exista quien lo pueda considerar débil?

—En el mejor de los casos —dijo Iturbide—, van a considerarlo un niño bravucón, comparable al dictador norcoreano.

—Te estás equivocando, Agustín —dijo Bonaparte—, Su Majestad no es homologable a dictadores tan vulgares y despreciables, inflados de poder...

—Los dos gobiernan una monarquía, Luis. Aunque allá no la llaman como tal.

—Eso es absurdo —replicó el canciller—, las monarquías son formas de gobierno antiguas, dirigidas por miembros de dinastías ancestrales, educados en un protocolo revestido de disciplina y elegancia en todos los aspectos. Y la única que sobrevive impoluta es la nuestra. Los dictadores que se adueñan del poder por la fuerza y que luego se lo heredan a sus hijos, no son más que hombrecillos vulgares que ven los derechos del pueblo como un patrimonio propio, en tanto que nuestro emperador los ve como un deber que lo tiene atado a su trabajo. La comparación que haces en grotesca e incompatible, digna de Morador.

—Entiendo lo que dices, querido Luis, pero te estoy invitando a que veas las cosas con una perspectiva imparcial, como su fueras un extranjero. Su Majestad, al igual que el lidercito norcoreano, también amenazó con las armas.

—Y en eso también hay una gran diferencia —interrumpió el general—, los dictadores amenazan con las armas a las democracias todos los días antes del desayuno, en tanto que el emperador de México no lo había hecho desde la Segunda Guerra Mundial. Si a Trump un dictador tercermundista lo amenaza con usar la fuerza, el tipo va a reírse como un niño, pero, ¿acaso le causaron gracia las palabras de nuestro emperador? Estoy seguro que no. Una amenaza del emperador de México es algo bastante serio, ningún jefe de Estado la consideraría trivial y rutinaria.

—Debo de reconocer que fue algo arriesgado, no obstante, enorgullecedor para el patriotismo mexicano. Se te pasó la mano al escribirle ese discurso al muchacho, Luis, pero funcionó. Todas las reacciones tardías delatan el miedo. La Casa Blanca no ha emitido aún un comunicado, y eso quiere decir que ya tiraron a la basura más de cincuenta borradores.

—Te estás equivocando, Agustín, yo no le escribí nada al emperador, de hecho, le recomendé no mencionar la fuerza en ningún momento, pero él actuó como lo creyó conveniente, y me consta que ni siquiera escribió un borrador, les habló en vivo a los mexicanos guiándose tan sólo por la seguridad que tiene en sí mismo.

—Vaya, pues yo creí que sus últimas palabras —dijo Iturbide—, en las que pidió al pueblo ocuparse de sus propios problemas mientras él se ocupa de Trump, habían sido lentamente planeadas por los mejores diplomáticos salidos de la Universidad Imperial de Aztlán. Nunca me imaginé que al emperador se le fueran a ocurrir mientras hablaba. A todos los mexicanos, sin duda, nos hizo sentir que nos gobierna un hombre de pies a cabeza, que sabe lo que tiene que hacer y que no dudará en hacerlo. Pero, caballeros, yo insisto en que estamos inmersos en una nube de inestabilidad, y que debemos movernos para aclarar las cosas, o al menos para propiciar un escenario que nos sea favorable. Y así las cosas, ¿qué les parece si empezamos por Morador? El cabrón no ha sacado una cuenta bancaria en veinte años, pero su entorno está lleno de personas a las que les podemos enviar un citatorio por acumulación de riqueza de procedencia desconocida. Aquéllos que comúnmente suelen ser los depositarios de grandes fortunas, son personas sin inteligencia ni educación, que poseen cuentas con cantidades exorbitantes, y que incluso desconocen poseerlas, porque toda la documentación y las tarjetas están en manos de los operadores más leales a Morador, verdaderos reptiles. Estoy seguro que al muy cabrón le importa poco que metamos en prisión a esa gente, pero al neutralizarlos a ellos, al mismo tiempo estaríamos naturalizando las riquezas con las que se financia su famoso Movimiento.

—Yo pienso —dijo el general—, que el dinero de Morador en su gran mayoría es en efectivo. Es bastante cuidadoso en ese aspecto. Su liderazgo lo ha construido promocionándose a sí mismo como un hombre sin ambiciones, así que no va a permitir muy fácilmente que salga a la luz el hecho de que sus allegados mueven fortunas por órdenes absolutamente suyas.

—También pienso lo mismo —respondió Iturbide—, pero una vez que penetremos en su estructura financiera, fincada completamente afuera de las leyes tributarias, podremos tener facultades legales para ingresar a las propiedades de los más leales a Morador y sus parientes. Les aseguro que encontraremos infinidad de casas de pobres cuyo subsuelo estará lleno de millones de pesos. ¿Qué te parece la idea, Luis? La libertad y la abundancia son compatibles con la lealtad, pero la prisión suele tomar posiciones diferentes. Los hombres de Morador tras las rejas seguramente van a decirnos muchos de sus más celosos secretos.

—Las órdenes del emperador —dijo Bonaparte—, son las de permitir que Morador haga su consulta. Y contra eso no podemos hacer nada. Pero, ciertamente, si le quitamos su dinero, le dejaremos menos posibilidades de hacer las trampas que sin duda se trae entre manos. El problema es que si metemos a uno de sus allegados a prisión, el tipo se echará a gritar por las calles que se trata de una conspiración en su contra por parte de la mafia que gobierna el imperio. Eso nos restaría credibilidad.

—Lo que podemos hacer —dijo el general— es, mientras pasa la famosa consulta, sólo neutralizarles el dinero, no a los hombres, los mismos que sin recursos serán inútiles. Morador puede clamar por sus allegados, pero no es tan pendejo como para reclamar el dinero que le incautemos como suyo.

—El problema, general —respondió Bonaparte—, es que no podemos incautar dinero si no procesamos a su presunto dueño por algún delito por medio del cual se lo adueñó. A menos que… lo hagamos como un proceso de una investigación, una mera medida cautelar. Gracia le va a hacer a Morador el hecho de que lo dejemos sin su fortuna, pero que al mismo tiempo no metamos a nadie de los suyos a la cárcel. Mientras pasa la famosa consulta, claro está.

—Bien —dijo Iturbide—, si manejamos adecuadamente esa tontería, es probable que le saquemos provecho. Morador nos está dando la soga con la quiere que lo colguemos. Pero sigue siendo irritante que un hombrecillo vulgar ponga en aprietos a nuestras instituciones. Quizás Su Majestad debió proceder como en los viejos tiempos y alojarlo en la celda donde murió Castro, el agitador cubano.

—De ser así, sus seguidores lo harían mártir y Francisco lo canonizaría —respondió Bonaparte—. Su tonalidad rojiza es casi la misma, y a cierta distancia resulta exactamente igual. Así que haremos las cosas tal como las quiere Su Majestad, que es lo más propicio en esta época donde la mayor parte de la información corre a cargo de las redes sociales, sin control alguno. Mejor dime, Agustín, ¿en cuánto tiempo me podrás tener una lista confiable con los nombres de quienes resguardan el dinero de Morador, la ubicación de sus cuentas, si las hay, propiedades y demás detalles?

—Dame una semana, y te diré hasta debajo de qué busto de su amado San Stalin guarda Morador sus más preciados secretos. Mis colaboradores ya están trabajando, y son bastante eficientes. Morador estaba gozando de muchos privilegios gracias a que Maximiliano IV prefería una política fiscal orientada a vigilar a las empresas, dejando a las dependencias públicas y partidos políticos ciertas libertades. Pero su hijo piensa de forma totalmente distinta, así que aun si no nos estuviera fastidiando la existencia, ese idiota tendría sus días de gloria contados. Pero, caballeros, ya hemos definido cómo neutralizar a un loco, ¿y el otro?, ¿qué haremos con el otro?

—Es un tipo orgulloso que quiere imponer su forma de pensar –dijo el general–, y un cabrón así nunca le va a caer bien al Imperio Mexicano.

—El emperador también es un hombre necio –dijo Iturbide–, y creo que tanto los más allegados a Trump como nosotros mismos tenemos claro que hay que propiciar un acercamiento entre ellos. El comercio entre dos países tan densamente poblados lo necesita. Luis, si hubieras tenido la sensata idea de programar una llamada amistosa el veinte de enero, ahora las cosas serían menos tensas.

—Eso es imposible, ese cabrón se la ha pasado insultando a los mexicanos, y si no le dejamos claro que tiene que respetarnos, nos tratará como peleles el resto de su gobierno. Es verdad que el comercio entre ambos países es importante, lo tengo bastante claro, pero nadie, ni siquiera Trump, tiene derecho a insultarnos. En tiempos de la emperatriz Carlota, cuando México ya era considerado una gran potencia, esa palabrería estúpida habría propiciado una guerra.

—Sí, Luis, pero en ese tiempo no había bombas nucleares, ni allá ni acá. Ambos países se podían partir la madre sin que peligrara la especie humana. En esta época en lo menos que podemos pensar es en la guerra. Trump ya nos insultó, el emperador ya lo amenazó y fue descortés con él, creo que ha llegado el momento de pasar página, arregla cuanto antes un encuentro. Tan sólo órdenaselo a mi hermano, con su don de gentes y sus influencias en Washington, conseguirá que el loco del nido de pájaros en la cabeza se exprese elogiosamente del emperador en público. Después, una entrevista aquí en Aztlán será un asunto de agenda ineludible. Sé bien, Luis, que una gran república y un gran imperio son, por antonomasia, como agua y aceite, nosotros somos aristócratas y ellos nuevos ricos que decoran sus casas con el mismo buen gusto que los capos de la droga colombianos, pero en honor al comercio y a los negocios lucrativos, tenemos que hacer el esfuerzo de llevarnos bien. Así que déjate de orgullos estúpidos, sé bien que estás aconsejando al emperador para que siga con una actitud a la defensiva, y con eso sólo consigues sembrar incertidumbre en los mercados, lo que perjudica a muchos mexicanos.

—Un momento, Agustín, yo sólo estoy procediendo de acuerdo a mi rango y a mis obligaciones como canciller. Propiciar un acercamiento después de esa estupidez de que nosotros pagaremos el pinche muro nos haría ver como pendejos. Es necesaria una disculpa por parte de Trump, para que yo contemple la idea de bajar la temperatura.

—Pues entonces informa a mi hermano qué es exactamente lo que quieres, él buscará la forma de conseguirlo con esos aprendices de estadistas que ahora ocupan la Casa Blanca. Es un Iturbide, descendiente directo del padre de la patria, no le quedará mal a su país. Pero ponlo a trabajar, lo tienes encerrado en la maldita embajada, sin la autorización de que ejercite sus grandes capacidades. No la chingues. Eso es lo mismo que esperar a que las cosas empeoren. ¿Usted qué opina, general? —dijo Iturbide volteando a ver al ministro Peña-Bazaine.

—Yo estoy convencido de que Su Majestad Imperial ha actuado sensatamente, pero también creo que la diplomacia secreta a cargo de la cancillería tiene la responsabilidad de buscar un acuerdo antes de que el agua llegue al río. Bonaparte, la responsabilidad está en sus manos. ¿O acaso espera, príncipe, que Su Majestad transfiera esa responsabilidad a mi ministerio? Señores, rueguen a Dios que no lo haga. Porque yo sólo soy un soldado y sólo sé obedecer.

—General, por favor —dijo Iturbide—, yo amo a la especie humana, tengo hijos pequeños y deseo que ellos tengan hijos, y usted habla como si nos contara un cuento de terror. Luis, eres, según se dice, el mejor diplomático de México. Has lo que tienes que hacer, y olvídate de un conflicto para engrandecer nuestro orgullo. Ya no estamos en los tiempos de tu admirado tío. Ahora las bombas llegan a todas partes y hacen unos desmadres que no se olvidan ni en un siglo. Ten eso bien presente.

Esa tarde, restaurante Los tres chiles, centro histórico de Aztlán

Ana María de Iturbide entró al lugar vestida casualmente, pero caminando con la elegancia de una reina. El primer mesero en reconocerla casi pega un salto, y corrió a avisarle al gerente del lugar, quien se presentó ante la princesa, nervioso, segundos después.

—Es un honor para mí recibir a Su Alteza en mi establecimiento — dijo el hombre—, todo aquí, incluida mi persona, está a sus órdenes. Elija la mesa que más le agrade, no importa que esté ocupada. En breve resolveremos el pequeño inconveniente.

Ana sonrió amablemente, sin una gota de hipocresía en su expresión.

—Gracias, caballero, pero no he venido a comer. En realidad estoy buscando a una persona que, según me han dicho, trabaja aquí.

—Si Su Alteza me dijera el nombre...

—Se llama Carlota Lorena —dijo la princesa.

—¿Usted conoce a Carlota?

—No tengo el gusto, pero confío en que eso se resuelva por intermediación de usted. Me gustaría hablar con ella en un lugar privado, a no ser que ello le cause molestia.

—Para nada, la presencia de Su Alteza tan sólo nos causa honor. ¿Le complace acompañarme a mi oficina? Es un lugar bastante privado. En seguida le enviaré a Carlota.

—Claro, y permítame darle las gracias por la amabilidad que tiene la delicadeza de profesarme —dijo la princesa.

—Por aquí —dijo el hombre, feliz de la vida.

Segundos después entraron en una pequeña oficina, escasamente amueblada y decorada. El hombre le indicó a la princesa que se sentara donde ella quisiera –no había mucho de dónde escoger–, y en seguida dijo retirarse para pedirle a Carlota que acudiera allí.

–Por favor –pidió la princesa–, no le diga que soy yo quien la busca.

El hombre asintió amablemente y salió de la oficina. La princesa Ana no tuvo que esperar mucho, apenas acababa de sentarse en un pequeño sofá, cuando abrió la puerta Carlota, vestida con su uniforme de trabajo. Reconoció inmediatamente a la famosa modelo, considerada por la prensa como la mujer más hermosa de México.

–Pasa –dijo la princesa–, y siéntate. Necesito hablar contigo.

–Sospecho a qué vienes –dijo Carlota–, y también sospecho que la conversación que vamos a tener la he leído en infinidad de novelas baratas.

–Celebro tu gusto por la lectura, querida, pero yo me inclino por los rusos del siglo diecinueve. Las novelas románticas y mediocres las dejo para las personas de inteligencia reducida.

–Vaya, pues –dijo Carlota–, aunque ya sé a qué vienes, me haré pendeja y voy a preguntar. ¿Qué se te ofrece?

–Aun vestida así, eres muy hermosa –dijo Ana María–, y me imagino que vestida para una recepción harías que los hombres se fracturaran el cuello. Algunas veces pienso que hubiera querido un color de piel como el tuyo, el mío resulta muy sensible al sol.

–Pues hazle como Michael Jackson, pero a la inversa. O qué sé yo. Cada quien arregla sus problemas de la forma que quiere o puede. Sabes, en agradecimiento a tu comentario, tú también eres muy guapa. Ahora, si me disculpas, tengo trabajo…

–Espera, todavía ni tocamos el tema por el que vine –dijo la princesa.

–Oh, ya vas a empezar a chingar.

—¿Así de maleducada quieres ser emperatriz? —dijo Ana María, sonriendo.

—¿Quién te dijo que quiero ser tal cosa?

—Pues según sé, te consideras la novia del emperador.

—No me considero, lo soy.

—Aquí entre nosotros, Carlota, ¿reamente crees que eso es cierto?

—Pregúntaselo al emperador.

—Realmente él es tan joven, y está tan triste por la muerte de su hermano, sus sobrinos y su padre, que quizás en estos momentos de debilidad confunde a una novia por una mujer que le baje la calentura.

—Ya sabía que una pendejada así te traías entre manos —dijo Carlota, tratando de sonreír—. Sabes, yo no le pedí a Fer que fuera mi novio, ni que se enamorara de mí. La decisión fue de él, y ahora, princesita, pues te chingas, porque así son las cosas, y te comes tu veneno sola. ¡Provechito!

—Espera, Carlota, no te vayas. Apenas estamos empezando a hablar. Sabes, querida, sólo hay dos familias en México que podrían darle una esposa al emperador, los Bonaparte y los Iturbide. Pero la hija del atractivo canciller Luis tiene diez años, y la hermana soltera tiene ya cincuenta y se rumora que es lesbiana. Así las cosas, sólo quedo yo. Por otro lado, la aristocracia del imperio considera que con estas agitaciones nacionalistas que se han suscitado en los últimos tiempos, el emperador debe de casarse con una mujer mexicana. Pero la ley le exige que se case con una princesa, para que los hijos de ese matrimonio puedan ser Habsburgo y puedan heredar el imperio. Y otra vez, querida, sólo quedo yo como una única opción. Así que la que te chingas eres tú. ¿Cómo ves?

—Anita, ¿te han partido la madre alguna vez? Porque ya me estás colmando la paciencia, ¡querida! Y si quieres que Fer se case contigo, pues ve y díselo a él. Conmigo no tienes que venir a chingar.

—Vamos a hacer un trato, Carlota —respondió la princesa—. Sigue siendo su novia a oscuras, entrénalo, hazlo un buen amante. Te lo voy a agradecer, créeme, y si tienes un bastardito, yo consentiré que le pague una impecable educación y que lo vea una vez al mes, como manda la tradición. Es más, si es niño, que se llame Juan. ¿Te parece?

—Vamos a hacer otro trato —dijo Carlota—, si sales corriendo en este preciso momento, no te voy a partir la madre. Pero si dices otra pendejada, vas a necesitar más que un buen maquillista, ¡querida!

—Carlota, entiende, Fer es el último Habsburgo mexicano, y si se casa contigo, sus hijos ya no lo serán y el imperio podría desaparecer. Pero eso no va a pasar, porque a un hombre con su educación lo dominará pronto la razón de Estado. Quizás te diga como Napoleón a Josefina: "todavía te quiero, pero en política el amor no cuenta". Y terminará alejándose de ti, ¡querida!

—Sabes, ¡querida! —respondió Carlota, dando dos pasos para acercarse más a la princesa—, lo que dices tiene lógica, de verdad, pero te advertí que te fueras o te partiría la madre. Y yo soy una mujer de palabra.

Acto seguido, Carlota le propinó un golpe en el rostro con el puño cerrado, y la princesa fue a caer de espadas en el sofá donde se había sentado al principio.

—¡Las mujeres no pegan con el puño cerrado, estúpida! —gritó Ana María.

—Mala suerte, ¡querida!, no sé pelear como mujer. Y en serio, si quieres que Fer se case contigo, pues ve y pídeselo a él. Es ridículo que vengas a molestarme a mí. Eres una princesa mexicana, desciendes del padre de la patria, no te comportes así, hasta a mí me da vergüenza lo ridícula que te vez.

Para que no la volviera a golpear, la princesa mejor se quedó tirada en el sofá.

—Carlota, no importa lo bien que te le subas encima al emperador, él no se va a casar contigo.

—No lo conoces, es algo dominante. Además, si con la que se va a casar eres tú, ¿de qué te preocupas? Déjame seguir disfrutando mi momento, y si después me deja para casarse contigo, lo bailado nadie me lo va a quitar. Oye, y qué rápido se te hincha la piel. Ustedes los aristócratas sí que son frágiles. Adiós, ¡querida!, ponte hielo –dijo Carlota, y salió de la habitación.

Esa noche, Castillo de Chapultepec

—Y así es en varios puntos de Aztlán, Majestad —dijo Bonaparte, al apagar una televisión que se había instalado en el despacho de los cuatro bustos, para ver en vivo las manifestaciones contra la dictadura que en unas horas se habían extendido por toda la capital, que invadían comercios, bloqueaban vialidades y destruían todo a su paso.

—Morador me dijo que hoy mismo me daría una prueba de su poder —dijo Fernando Carlos—, y yo no le creí. Pensé que eras las bravuconadas de un loco.

—Majestad, la guardia imperial está dispersa entre esas multitudes, pero no le recomiendo ordenar que actúe. Su algún moradorista muere, se harán las víctimas, nos acusarán de represores y de asesinos.

—Y si los dejamos continuar —dijo el emperador—, van a seguir rompiendo cosas como si no valieran y no pertenecieran a nadie. ¿Dónde está el conde Andrássy?

—También allí, en el centro de la capital. Esperando las órdenes de Vuestra Majestad.

—Bien, ordénele que sus hombres entren en acción inmediatamente. No voy a permitir que se piense que en México no hay seguridad, ni que esos locos sigan desmadrándolo todo. Seguro que Morador se está muriendo de la risa.

—Majestad, con el debido respeto, no es lo más conveniente usar la fuerza. Algunos sectores de la prensa los ven con simpatías.

—Hay cámaras en todo Aztlán, ya sean de negocios o instaladas por los departamentos de seguridad, ¿cierto?

—Efectivamente, Majestad.

—Bien, entonces seguramente están grabados todos aquellos que se han encargado de romper o incendiar todo a su paso, incluyendo vehículos y negocios.

—Por supuesto, Majestad. Incluso los miembros de la guardia imperial que están dispersos allí los tienen ya identificados.

—Perfecto, príncipe. Ordénele al conde Andrássy que entre en acción, y quiero en una celda a los más violentos, aquéllos que con sus manos han causados destrozos en los bienes públicos y privados. Estoy seguro que todos ellos poseen algo, una casa, un auto o una cuenta bancaria, o las tres cosas. Les incautaremos sus bienes, y éstos serán subastados para pagar sus destrozos. ¿Está claro?

—Pero, Majestad, una medida así lo haría terriblemente impopular —dijo Bonaparte—. Morador va a exhibir a sus locos en una cruz sangrando, y lo responsabilizará a usted. Sé que la situación es indignante, que ese demente lo planeó todo con el propósito de hacer daño. La mayoría de los manifestantes ni siquiera son de Aztlán, Morador los trajo de otros departamentos, de algunos tan lejanos como California, Panamá o Belice, pero no podemos caer en su juego, eso es exactamente lo que Morador quiere. Reúna a todos los ministros y verá que todos van a recomendarle lo mismo que yo, Majestad.

—Príncipe, vivimos en un régimen de legalidad. El respeto al derecho ajeno, como dijo al gran Juárez, se consigue gracias a que todos los mexicanos tenemos claro que si algo rompemos lo mismo que pagamos. Si dejo libres a esos locos, le demostraré a todo el imperio que aquí los daños que se hacen en grupo, por terribles que sean, no tendrán consecuencias, que los dueños de los negocios y autos quemados tendrán que pedirle justicia a Dios, porque su emperador es incapaz de dárselas. Y tal cosa no la pienso permitir, que esos locos paguen por todo lo que han destrozado, y si sus bienes no alcanzan, entonces completarán la deuda con años de prisión. Para mí es mil veces más importante un mexicano que tiene un negocio y hace con ello un bien al imperio que un loco que ha perdido la virtud del respeto. Y si no actúo con mano dura en esta situación, estaría demostrando lo contraria.

—Majestad…

—Príncipe, si usted no puede llamar al conde Andrássy y ordenarle que entre en acción, no se preocupe, yo puedo hacerlo —dijo el emperador—. Retírese y mañana a las ocho quiero su renuncia en mi escritorio.

—No, Majestad, perdóneme, sólo insistía en lo que consideraba más prudente. Pero las órdenes de mi emperador son como si me las diera el mismo Dios. Me retiro a mi oficina, para coordinarme con el conde Andrássy, y tiene mi palabra de que en una hora ninguno de esos dementes estará corriendo en las calles.

—Gracias, príncipe, y disculpe por favor mi actitud. Por un momento olvidé todo lo que debo. Le prometo que no volverá a pasar.

—Ni lo diga, Majestad. Por el contrario, perdone mi impertinencia, fui yo quien por un momento olvidé que las órdenes del emperador no se discuten, sino que se llevan a cabo en el acto.

—Príncipe, quiero que alguien vaya a hablar con Morador esta misma noche. De preferencia que no sea un ministro, estaría bien el duque de Miramón. Y quiero que le quede bien claro a ese loco que le vamos a permitir hacer su consulta, pero que si vuelve a convocar a otra manifestación como ésta, habrá perdido ante mí incluso el derecho de ser mexicano. Que le quede bien claro que es muy probable que de los siete emperadores que han gobernado México desde Maximiliano *el Grande*, yo soy el que menos paciencia tiene.

—Majestad, el duque de Miramón sería el hombre indicado, pero como creí que usted no lo requeriría, lo envié a Washington en una misión extraoficial, para entrevistarse con senadores y miembros del gabinete de Trump. Si quiere voy yo a ver a ese pendejo, o enviamos al mismísimo general Peña-Bazaine, lo hará que se orine en los pantalones.

—No, se me ocurre otra persona —dijo el emperador—. Hay un oficial en el departamento de conducta vial de Aztlán, se llama Benito Rueda. Es un hombre de todas mis confianzas. Quiero que lo envíe a él a darle mi mensaje a Morador.

—¿Un oficial del departamento de conducta vial?

—Príncipe, no se lo dije en ruso. Dígale al oficial Benito Rueda que se lo pido como un gran favor, y que después iré a agradecérselo en persona.

—A las órdenes de Vuestra Majestad —dijo Bonaparte—. Me retiro a mi oficina, para darle las órdenes precisas al conde Andrássy.

Cuando el canciller cerró la puerta, el emperador hizo una llamada desde su teléfono particular.

—Carlota…

—¡Fer! No vas a creérmelo, justo estaba deseando que me llamaras. Ya quiero verte, tengo algo importante que contarte, algo que me pasó justo esta tarde.

—¿Ya viste las noticias?

—Me imagino que te refieres a los manifestantes. Aquí donde trabajo pasaron muchos corriendo y rompieron los cristales.

—¿Estás bien?

—Sí, no entraron. Solo gritaban que Morador será el presidente, que eres un dictador y cosas por el estilo.

—Entenderás que no puedo salir de Chapultepec, mientras las cosas se calmen… ¿Comprendes?

—Sí, Fer, pero… Bueno, no te preocupes.

—¿Qué ibas a decirme?

—Que en verdad quería verte. Y quizás sea egoísta con mi actitud, porque eres el emperador, le perteneces al pueblo.

—Te pertenezco a ti.

—No se nota, mi amor. La realidad dice lo contrario. Hablamos después, ¿de acuerdo?

—Carlota, no te enojes conmigo, por favor.

El emperador supo que ella ya no lo escuchaba, había cortado la llamada. Lanzó el teléfono contra un muro, y deseó que fuera la cara de Morador.

Tres horas más tarde, el canciller le dio "el parte de guerra", ya no había manifestantes en las calles, había sido arrestados más de mil y los daños en la ciudad eran cuantiosos.

—La guardia imperial tiene ya todo bajo control –dijo Bonaparte–, y el general Peña-Bazaine tiene dispuestos a veinte mil hombres, para que patrullen las calles de Aztlán y así poder evitar que la ciudad amanezca como estaba hace apenas unas horas.

—No, los soldados asustarían a la población –dijo Fernando Carlos–. De momento quiero que el conde Andrássy se siga ocupando de todo. Creo que ha hecho bien las cosas.

—Como Vuestra Majestad lo ordene. Se ve cansado, debería irse a dormir. Esta noche parece que no nos dará más sorpresas.

—Sí, lo haré, príncipe. Gracias. Usted también debería irse a dormir. Mañana quizás nos espere otro día complicado.

En otro punto de Aztlán

El departamento donde vivía Ángel Miguel Morador era bastante espacioso y antiguo, mas se hallaba en una zona poco glamurosa de Aztlán. En el interior no había lujos en lo más mínimo, y las paredes estaban totalmente desnudas, exhibiendo la antigüedad de su adobe. La oficina del líder de las masas estaba repleta de libros, algunos sin ningún orden, esparcidos sobre el suelo, y otros tantos en su escritorio, donde convivían con un busto del general Porfirio Díaz, el único objeto de ornato que podía verse en la habitación. Los libros, el viejo escritorio, las vigas de madera y los polvorientos adobes, aunados a las canas de Morador, daban la impresión de ser la cloaca de un viejo hechicero. O al menos ésa fue la impresión del oficial Benito Rueda, cuando estuvo frente al caudillo.

–Siéntate –dijo Morador–. No te he visto nunca, ni en las noticias. Yo francamente esperaba que viniera Miramón, Iturbide o el propio Bonaparte.

–No te gustan los aristócratas, Ángel Miguel, y sin embargo te ofendes cuando el emperador no te envía a uno. Eres un tipo raro.

–¿Quién eres?

–Me llamo Benito Rueda.

–¿Y cuál es tu puesto en el gabinete imperial…, perdón, dictatorial?

–Te sorprenderías si te lo dijera. Pero eso no viene al caso, estoy aquí para darte un mensaje del emperador, y eso lo que único que importa.

–Me tuteas sin ningún respeto. Y yo represento un movimiento muy grande, que se extiende por todo el imperio. No cualquiera tiene derecho a tutearme.

—¡A la chingada con eso! Considerando tu comportamiento de hoy, Ángel Miguel, tutearte ya es dirigirme a ti con demasiada deferencia. Eres un hombrecillo vulgar y ambicioso, que lleva años sin trabajar e instando a otros a que no trabajen y exijan que el gobierno los mantenga. ¿Cómo se te ocurre pedir respeto? Cualquier mexicano que paga impuestos tiene todo el derecho de mentarte la madre.

—¡Pero cómo te atreves!

—Ya deja de ponerte digno, te digo que he venido a traerte un mensaje de Su Majestad, no a tratarte como si fueras Jesucristo.

—¡Habla pues! —dijo Ángel Miguel—, que yo también quiero enviarle un mensaje al dictador.

—Se te va a permitir que hagas tu famosa consulta ciudadana, y considéralo un derecho simplemente porque eres mexicano. Pero no habrá trucos. Los resultados que conocerán los mexicanos serán los reales, que eso te quede bien claro.

—No hace falta hacer trampa alguna, el pueblo está decidido a expulsar al austriaco.

—Yo pienso muy diferente, pero eso ya no vamos a discutirlo. Te decía que podrás hacer tu consulta, pero si ordenas otro desmadre como el de hoy, te lo vamos a cobrar completito. El emperador no va a tolerar otra de tus pendejadas.

—¡Esto es intolerable!, ni el emperador ni Bonaparte me han tratado como tú, y ya me he entrevistado con los dos resptiloides. Por si no lo sabes, yo soy un representante del pueblo.

—Eso no está claro —dijo Benito Rueda—, en cambio, yo sí soy un representante de Su Majestad, y de eso, cabrón parasito, que no te quepa ninguna duda.

—Tú tienes un nombre mexicano, eres un mexicano tal cual soy yo. ¿Por qué aceptas una dictadura de extranjeros?

—No compares, yo sí trabajo. Y eso nos hace dos hombres diametralmente opuestos. Por otro lado, el emperador es mexicano de pies a cabeza, y si tú no lo quieres aceptar, es muy tu problema. Yo amo la monarquía porque de ella se deriva un país próspero y regulado por leyes que sí se aplican, donde todos podemos vivir en paz. Así cualquiera es patriota.

—A ti te han comido el cerebro los reptiles. Ya no sirves como ser humano, no piensas por ti mismo.

—¿Lo dices porque no opino como tú, Ángel Miguel? Vaya que eres cabrón. En fin, te lo repito una vez más, porque ya veo que estás medio pendejo: una manifestación más, por modesta que sea, y vamos a venir por ti, digan lo que digan los medios nacionales y extranjeros. Es preferible soportar las críticas que tolerar a un loco que desea implantar el desgobierno absoluto, que es lo que sería tu jodida república.

—Pues ahora te voy a dar yo un mensaje para el dictadorcillo, o más bien para su tía, la mama de todos los reptiles: mañana mismo quiero que liberen a todos los manifestantes que ilegal y arbitrariamente hoy fueron privados de su libertad. De lo contrario, aténganse a las consecuencias. Ya les di una pequeña probadita —dijo Morador riendo— de lo que puedo ser capaz. Los quiero a todos libres y sanos. Ve y diles eso a tus jefes, esclavo.

—No vamos a liberar a nadie, hasta que se vendan sus bienes y se paguen sus destrozos. Y aquellos que llegaron a herir a miembros de la guardia imperial, les esperan de uno a dos años en la cárcel.

—¿Les van a robar sus bienes a los mexicanos que se manifestaron libremente?

—No se manifestaron, no te hagas pendejo, los mandaste a romper lo que se les atravesara. Y con lo que tienen van a pagar lo que destruyeron, lo que es muy justo. Si el emperador no toma esa medida, mañana cualquier cabrón va a querer cometer fechorías, pensando que en México eso no se castiga. Tal medida no está a discusión, Su Majestad no va a dar marcha atrás. Y te aseguro que es un hombre de poca paciencia, Ángel Miguel, y ya le estás llegando al límite. Así que cálmate, sólo con ello seguirás libre y podrás hacer la consulta que tanto añoras. Pero si mañana haces otra pendejada, yo mismo vendré a ponerte las esposas. Te lo juro, cabrón. Ni la paz ni los bienes de los mexicanos son materia de tus caprichos.

—A mí no...

—¡Y ya cállate, deja de decir pendejadas! Cómo no vas a agotar la paciencia del emperador, si ya me la agotaste a mí.

El oficial Rueda se puso de pie y caminó hacia la puerta, en su camino tomó un libro de los que estaban en el suelo, dio la vuelta y lo lanzó a Morador. Éste lo detuvo con sus manos.

—Ponte a leerlos, cabrón —le dijo—. De nada sirve que sólo los amontones.

—¡Yo he pasado mi vida leyendo libros! —gritó Morador.

—Vaya, pues qué equivocado estaba. Yo creí toda mi vida que los libros quitaban lo pendejo. Pero tú me estás demostrando hasta con la forma de reírte que no es así —dijo el oficial y continuó su marcha, sin detenerse ante otra cascada de palabras inentendibles que soltó Morador, furioso, a sus espaldas.

De vuelta a Chapultepec

Fernando Carlos, cubierto de negro con un grueso abrigo, entró lentamente a la Cripta Imperial de Guadalupe. Pese a su indumentaria, sentía frío, y tenía la certeza de que de ninguna forma podría quitárselo. La cripta estaba en penumbras, como siempre, pero aun así podía ver las tumbas delante de él. Repentinamente, su cuerpo sintió calor y una gota de sudor helado corrió por su frente. Los seis emperadores, desde Maximiliano *el Grande* hasta su padre, estaban de pie en sus respetivas tumbas.

—Te estábamos esperando —le dijo su abuelo, Maximiliano III.

—¿Por qué ustedes...?

—Porque somos tus jueces —le respondió Agustín II—. Por eso estamos de pie. Nos verás toda tu vida.

—¿Y qué es lo que he hecho mal?

—Nada —dijo Maximiliano *el Grande*—. Te has comportado tal como lo esperábamos de ti.

—¿Entonces?

—Solo queríamos decirte —respondió Maximiliano II—, que siempre te estaremos vigilando, y que si algún día haces algo que no sea por el bienestar de los mexicanos, no te lo vamos a perdonar.

—Fer, hijo —habló Maximiliano IV—, perdóname. Fui muy injusto contigo, no confiaba en ti, no creí que fueras capaz de enorgullecerme. Pero ahora te digo que ningún padre mexicano jamás ha estado tan orgulloso como yo lo estoy de ti. Te amo, hijo, perdóname por no habértelo dicho nunca.

—¡Papa!

Fernando Carlos dejó de sentir sudor en su rostro, pero algo humedecía sus labios, algo cálido, agradable y desconcertante. De pronto los seis emperadores empezaron a desdibujarse, y sus ojos ya no vieron nada más entre la oscuridad, que se cerró encima de él. Pero sus labios seguían húmedos, pese a que todo lo demás había desaparecido, junto con la piedra gris de la cripta. Desconcertado, manoteo para hallar un punto de donde sujetarse, y un grito de mujer lo despertó.

Cuando abrió los ojos, la luz de su habitación estaba encendida, él ya no tenía puesto el abrigo negro, sino una pijama, y en su cama, casi junto a él, se hallaba la princesa Ana de Iturbide, desnuda de la cintura para arriba, y más abajo tan sólo tenía una prenda tan provocativa que lo terminó de despertar.

—¿Qué haces aquí, Ana?, ¿cómo entraste?

—¿Qué hago aquí? Es obvio, Fer, ¿y cómo entré? Eso no importa ahora —dijo y se incorporó, asegurándose de que el emperador la viera en cada uno de sus movimientos.

Él no pudo evitar que su mente reaccionara. La contempló por varios segundos, mientras su frente volvía a sudar. Pero ahora no se trataba de un sueño.

—¿Te gusto?

—Me resultas muy atractiva. No te lo voy a negar.

—Sabía que no lo negarías —dijo Ana, tratando de subirse encima de él.

—Vístete, por favor, y vete. Tengo que dormir.

—¿Qué dijiste?

—Que te vayas, Ana, no estás autorizada para entrar en mi habitación.

—Pero aceptaste que te gusto, Fer.

—Demasiado, soy hombre y no estoy ciego. Pero también dije que te fueras.

—¿Por qué?

—Porque amo a otra mujer.

—Ella no está aquí. No le diremos nada.

—No se trata de eso. Ana, tal vez no me entiendas, pero soy feliz a su lado porque no le guardo secretos, y porque sólo le pertenezco a ella. Si tuviera relaciones contigo, ya no podría estar con Carlota, porque a cada instante estaría pensando que traicioné a la mujer que me ama, y eso me impediría hacerla feliz. Y yo quiero ser feliz, y verla feliz a mi lado. No voy a renunciar a un maravilloso futuro que me espera junto a Carlota por una noche contigo, por placentera que pueda ser. Nunca, ni en mis peores pesadillas, la haría sufrir intencionalmente. La amo.

—Fer, no te prohíbas hacer lo que evidentemente deseas. Eres el emperador, tú no puedes ser infiel o fiel.

—Ana, vístete, y vete, antes de que pierda la paciencia. No soy un niño al que se le pueda manipular. Mis decisiones no contemplan la marcha atrás, nunca. Oye, espera, te maquillaste de más esa mejilla, ¿qué te pasó allí? Parece un golpe.

—Me caí, pero me duelen más tus palabras.

—Ana, yo no te pedí que vinieras. Vístete, pronto, ya me cansé de repetírtelo, o voy a ordenar que vengan por ti, y te sacarán de Chapultepec así como estás.

—¡No te atreverías!

—Yo no hago bromas, pero si lo dudas, podemos hacer la prueba.

—¡Eres un imbécil! —dijo la princesa, y entonces sí empezó a buscar su ropa.

El emperador se puso de pie, y como ya era su costumbre caminó hacia una ventana, disfrutaba ver Aztlán de noche. Aunque su intención también era darle la espalda a la princesa mientras terminaba de vestirse. Cuando sintió que ella ya caminaba hacia la puerta de la habitación, le dijo:

—Buenas noches, Ana.

—Vete a la chingada, pendejo —fue la respuesta de la princesa.

Dos minutos después ya estaba de regreso en la cama, y pensaba no en Ana de Iturbide, sino en su sueño. Había sido muy real, había visto a Maximiliano *el Grande* de carne y hueso. Si la Dama Blanca merodeaba por Chapultepec y eso ningún Habsburgo lo dudaba, era probable que también deambularan por Aztlán los seis emperadores. Mas era cierto que su sueño había sido una satisfacción que le daban los laberintos ocultos de su mente. En él su padre le había dicho lo que tantas veces le hubiera gustado oír, y era probable que a fin de cuentas sólo se tratara de un sueño, y que su padre, dondequiera que se hallara, no se sintiera orgulloso de sus acciones, ni de lo mucho que había cambiado desde su muerte.

Recordó, justo antes de quedarse dormido nuevamente, que él no era el único emperador que creía que sus antecesores se le habían aparecido. Su tía le había contado que incluso a su padre, en un momento de terribles dudas, se le había aparecido Maximiliano *el Grande*, una noche que se quedó a trabajar hasta tarde en el despacho de los cuatro bustos.

Por la mañana

Como todos los días, la duquesa Carlota y su sobrino se sentaron a desayunar. Ella incluso le sirvió el café, costumbre que había tenido también con su hermano, y ambos le habían dicho ya repetidas veces que no tenía que hacerlo.

—Quería hablar contigo de algo importante —dijo el emperador.

—Lo escucho, Majestad.

—Hoy mismo voy a firmar el decreto por el cual te devuelvo tu rango de archiduquesa, anulando el castigo que te impuso mi padre por haberte casado morganáticamente.

—Majestad, no hace falta. Yo me siento bien tal como me llamo ahora.

—Por supuesto que sí hace falta. Es lo justo. Volverás a ser archiduquesa de México, y también conservarás tu título de duquesa de Cuernavaca.

—No es que no me agrade volver a mi familia, por decirlo de alguna manera, porque yo sé que nunca me he marchado, pero lo que mi hermano hizo conmigo es lo que han hecho siempre los emperadores cuando un miembro de la familia viola las reglas. Es una tradición muy nuestra, es parte de lo que somos como dinastía.

—Eso es cierto, pero considero necesario que recuperes tu rango porque si en algún momento llego a estar indispuesto, tú legalmente, como archiduquesa, podrás intervenir en el gobierno. Cuando estuve en Miramar mandaste soldados mexicanos a Egipto, sin que nada te autorizara a ello. Eras sólo una duquesa mexicana, sin poder real. También tu cargo en el senado lo perdiste al casarte. No te reprocho lo que hiciste, te lo agradezco, pero ciertamente te extralimitaste en tus funciones. Y no es que quiera estar enfermo o morirme, pero es bueno ser precavido, así que hoy mismo vas a volver a ser, legalmente, miembro de la casa de Habsburgo.

—Gracias, Majestad.

—¿Cómo está tu esposo?

—Bien, muy bien. Gracias por interesarse por él.

—¿Lo amas?

—Me extraña su pregunta, Majestad, pero sí, lo amo. Alberto es el hombre más extraordinario que he conocido. Cómo no habrá de serlo, desprecié mi matrimonio con un archiduque austriaco por él, y también le dije que no al príncipe Luis, un hombre arrebatadoramente guapo, que se conserva como los buenos vinos.

—Deberías de volver a tu casa, yo me las arreglaré sólo, o tráelo a vivir aquí. No es justo que estén separados.

—Lo veo todos los días —dijo la duquesa—. Él entiende mi situación, y sabe que por nada del mundo voy a dejarlo a usted solo. Y de traerlo a vivir aquí, ni hablar. Alberto no quiere y yo también me sentiría incomoda. No se siente a gusto entre aristócratas, jamás ha usado legalmente el título de duque de Cuernavaca, y jura que nunca lo hará. Así que las cosas se quedarán como están en ese aspecto, Majestad. Ya cuando usted se case y tenga a sus hijos, entonces podré retirarme. Aunque pienso venir de vez en cuando a poner orden.

—¿Vendrán tus hijos de Europa en Semana Santa?

—Sí, ya me lo confirmaron. Pasarán sus vacaciones en Aztlán.

—Supongo que quieren estar con su padre, pero me gustaría pasar uno o dos días con ellos, aquí en Chapultepec.

—Ellos también. Lo quieren tanto como yo, no lo dude.

—Y yo los quiero a ellos. Así debe de ser. Somos una familia. ¿Recuerdas cuando mi padre me regañaba y tú me sentabas en tus rodillas y me abrazabas por horas, hasta que me veías más tranquilo?

—Claro que lo recuerdo. Algunas veces llegué a llorar con usted. Majestad, no quisiera que le guardara rencor a mi hermano, él sólo...

—No te preocupes, tía. No le guardo ningún rencor a mi padre. Él se preocupó por hacer de mí un hombre de bien, y un buen mexicano. Si hablo tantos idiomas y puedo desempeñarme sin problemas en mi cargo fue por la educación que me dio el emperador, a veces a la fuerza. Algunos hijos buscan cualquier pretexto, un mal recuerdo comúnmente, para no sentirse agradecidos con sus padres. Pero ése no será nunca mi caso, los padres, pese a sus errores, se preocupan diariamente por sus hijos, y ese sacrificio muchos hijos no lo reconocen. Pero yo sí tengo claro que mi padre, si bien nunca me demostró que me amaba, sí se preocupaba diariamente por mí, a su manera. Y eso siempre se lo voy a agradecer.

—No sabe lo feliz que me hace escucharlo hablar así de mi hermano —dijo la duquesa.

—Va venir de Italia un escultor amigo mío, Venosta. Su talento es admirable, y quiero que haga una estatua de mi padre. Pero no la colocaremos en la ciudad, sino aquí, en los jardines del castillo, para tenerlo cerca de mí y verlo todos los días.

—Es innegable, Majestad, lo mucho que usted añora el amor de su familia. Desde niño ha sido así, le gusta que lo mimen, que lo abracen y lo besen.

—¿Cuándo fue la última vez que me besaste la frente y las mejillas?

—Creo que... fue cuando usted volvió de Miramar, cuando murió Max. Meses después, cuando murió mi hermano, bajó usted del avión convertido en el emperador de México, ya no me atreví a besarlo.

—Lo hubieras hecho, era lo que yo más deseaba —dijo Fernando Carlos, se puso de pie y fue hasta la silla de su tía—. ¿Me podrías besar, otra vez?

La duquesa se puso de pie, conmovida, tomó a su sobrino de la cabeza y le dio tres besos.

—Perdóneme si no lo trato con frecuencia como mi sobrino al que tanto amo, pero no puedo instarlo a las emociones que son tan propicias a hacer a los hombres débiles, usted es el emperador.

—Un emperador también necesita que lo quieran —dijo Fernando Carlos, volviendo a su silla.

—Eso lo sé, Majestad, y por eso quizás sería bueno que se casara…

—Tía, que yo sepa, la princesa Ana no fue entrenada por la guardia imperial, ¿o sí?

—Claro que no, ella es modelo.

—Precisamente por eso me extraña que si no fue entrenada como espía o algo parecido, ¿Cómo es que pudo llegar hasta mi habitación anoche, burlando todos los filtros de seguridad? Una persona con mucho poder en el castillo tuvo que permitirle la entrada, y no creo que el príncipe Bonaparte o el conde Andrássy sean capaces de meterse en mi vida privada.

—Su conclusión, Majestad, es correcta. Yo lo hice, yo fui quien la dejó entrar y le recomendé seducirlo en su cama. Pero no crea que me agrada esa joven tan vanidosa y arrogante, o que yo pienso que es la esposa que usted merece. Los Habsburgo somos una familia milenaria, en tanto que los Iturbide son apenas unos advenedizos, y tan sólo un miembro de su familia ha sido emperador de México. No obstante, eso a ella la vuelve princesa, y una princesa es lo que necesitamos para que usted tenga hijos legítimos. Ésa es la solución que veo más práctica, dadas las circunstancias actuales, para que nuestra familia no desaparezca de México.

—Tía, ya te había dicho que tengo novia.

—Y eso es lo que más me preocupa, Majestad.

—De mi vida sentimental me ocupo yo —dijo Fernando Carlos—. No quiero que esto se vuelva a repetir, y tampoco deseo ser grosero con la princesa, más de lo que ya fui anoche, pero sería conveniente que no volviera a Chapultepec. Si es que ella quiere volver alguna vez.

—Me dijo hace apenas una hora que no piensa darse por vencida, aunque anoche cuando se marchó iba que echaba lumbre por la boca, y juró que jamás volvería a rogarle.

—No vuelvas a ayudarla a que se acerque a mí, y menos desnuda. Es una orden del emperador y quiero que la obedezcas. —Fernando Carlos se acercó a su tía y la besó en ambas mejillas—. Me voy al despacho, a las nueve tengo que recibir al cardenal Fischer.

El mencionado cardenal era un gigante rubio y robusto, de casi dos metros. Iba ataviado de forma ostentosa y elegante, tradición de vestir que ya sólo conservaban los ministros católicos de alto rango en el Imperio Mexicano.

—Bienvenido, Eminencia —dijo el emperador.

—A las órdenes de Vuestra Majestad —respondió el cardenal, luego fue junto a Fernando Carlos, éste extendió su mano y Fischer se agachó para besarla.

—Siéntese, por favor, Eminencia. ¿Cómo está usted?

—Preocupado, Majestad.

—Si en mí está la posibilidad de aminorar sus preocupaciones, créame, Eminencia, que con gusto voy a ayudarlo.

—Precisamente, mis más grandes preocupaciones dependen de Vuestra Majestad —dijo Fischer, sonriendo.

—Usted dirá…

—Por principio de cuentas, Majestad, ningún domingo, desde que usted volvió de Miramar, ha acudido a la celebración de la Santa Misa en la catedral. Y Vuestro padre, por el contrario, jamás faltaba. ¿Acaso los mexicanos tenemos a un emperador ateo?

—No, no soy ateo, pero les doy prioridad a mis obligaciones al mando del Estado. No he tenido tiempo de acudir a misa, Eminencia. Eso es todo.

—¿Vuestra Majestad acaso no se preocupa por la salvación de su alma?

—No tengo tiempo de salvarla, al menos no de la manera que usted quiere. Para mí primero está el pueblo, luego está Dios.

—¡Majestad, eso es terrible! ¡Blasfema usted! Dios puede tomar su vida en el momento que lo desee, y si eso pasa, usted ya no podrá hacer nada por el pueblo.

—No tengo manera de evitar que eso pase, Eminencia —dijo el emperador.

—Claro que sí, tan sólo basta con que sea un buen católico, y le dedique una hora a Dios todos los domingos. ¡Es tan poco el tiempo que Dios nos pide!

—Dudo mucho que pueda salvar mi alma y mi vida con ir a misa, y Dios no sería tan grande si pudiéramos complacerlo tan sólo con ello. Eminencia, no dispongo de mucho tiempo, si le parece, pasemos a otros tema de los tantos que le preocupan.

—Pues bien, Majestad —dijo Fischer, no muy complacido—, le confieso que también me preocupa mucho el hecho de que usted pretenda recortar el subsidio del Estado a los ministros de la iglesia. Muchos curas se morirán de hambre.

—Eminencia, los gastos del Estado son muchos, y por consecuencia los impuestos que cobramos a los mexicanos son muy altos. Analicé todas las instituciones y creo que la única de la que podemos prescindir, de momento, es la iglesia.

—Majestad, la iglesia es parte de la monarquía, y es también su soporte más simbólico...

—Usted lo ha dicho, simbólico. Y los impuestos de los mexicanos no se pueden gastar en simbolismos, sino en necesidades reales.

—¡Salvar el alma es una necesidad real, Majestad!

—Pero es un servicio tan piadoso que no tiene precio.

—Le repito que está usted condenando a miles de curas a morirse de hambre.

—No me viene a la memoria otro país donde tengan un sueldo por parte del Estado, y creo que no son muchos los que se mueren de hambre. Eminencia, entiendo que usted quiera defender los intereses de su gremio, es algo muy lógico, pero yo estoy defendiendo los intereses de todos los mexicanos, y no voy a dar marcha atrás.

—En eso caso, Majestad, le pido que sea un proceso lento, un pequeño porcentaje anual durante diez años...

—A partir del próximo mes ya no habrá pagos, Eminencia.

—¡Majestad, eso es terrible!

—Eminencia, sé que se ha enemistado con el Papa, por defenderme exclusivamente a mí —dijo el emperador, dando vuelta a la página—. Se lo agradezco encarecidamente. Sus servicios y su fidelidad a la monarquía no se me van a olvidar.

—Y si está tan agradecido, Majestad, ¿por qué nos retira el apoyo económico?

—Pídame cualquier otra cosa, menos que dé marcha a atrás en eso.

—Majestad, comprenda que con esta determinación tan radical nos pone en un grave predicamento a todos los miembros del clero. La lealtad a la monarquía podría verse afectada, con este golpe tan terrible.

—Entiendo —dijo el emperador, adoptando la mirada de león que caracterizaba a su padre— que entonces me venden su lealtad.

—¡No, Majestad, de ninguna manera!

—Eminencia, sé que el Papa no está muy contento con el clero mexicano, pero eso no debería de preocuparlos mucho a ustedes, porque aún tienen al emperador. Yo seguiré respetándolos, considerándolos una institución importante dentro del imperio, y dándoles ciertas preferencias, por encima de las demás religiones. Vamos, Eminencia —dijo Fernando Carlos, tras una breve pausa—, estoy seguro que lo que recaudan en calidad de limosnas, que es libre de impuestos, supera con mucho a lo que reciben del Estado. No quiera figurarme un lago como si fuera el mar, Eminencia, soy joven, pero no idiota.

—Entonces, ¿no va a dar marcha atrás, y no tenemos otra opción más que acatar sus designios, Majestad?

—Ya entendió usted perfectamente bien las cosas, Eminencia. ¿Cuento con su comprensión?

—Majestad, trata usted de resolver muy fácilmente una cuestión bastante grave.

—Si quiere nos enfrascaremos en una guerra sin cuartel, declararé al Estado laico y daré el mismo trato a todas las religiones en México. ¿Le parece buena la idea?

—¿Me está amenazando, Majestad?

—Eminencia, el tiempo corre muy rápido, y yo tengo otros asuntos que atender. Comprenderá que no alardeo, gobierno a un país de doscientos sesenta millones de habitantes. Pero le ruego que piense las cosas, ya que no quiero perjudicarlo, mas por encima de la iglesia siempre está el pueblo. Como cristiano, entiéndame, y deme su apoyo, se lo agradeceré toda la vida.

—Está bien, Majestad, lo pensaré. Se lo aseguro. Ahora, tal como usted me lo ha pedido, lo dejo para que resuelva asuntos más importantes que la Santa Iglesia —dijo el cardenal, y se puso de pie.

—Olvida algo, Eminencia —dijo el emperador, al ver que Fischer se daba la vuelta.

Cuando el cardenal volvió la cabeza, Fernando Carlos extendió su mano.

—Oh, sí, lo olvidaba —dijo Fischer, acercándose—. A las órdenes de Vuestra Majestad —añadió después de besar la mano del emperador.

—Eminencia, por encima de nuestros desacuerdos, quiero pedirle un favor muy importante para mí.

—Usted dirá, Majestad...

—Quiero que dedique sus oraciones al descanso del alma de mi padre.

—Así lo hago todos los días, Majestad —dijo Fischer, con una sonrisa amable.

—Gracias, Eminencia, tampoco esta amable cortesía de su parte voy a olvidarla. Y ya no le quito más tiempo.

—Siempre a las órdenes de Vuestra Católica Majestad —dijo el cardenal como despedida.

Al irse Fischer, entró al despacho del emperador el canciller Bonaparte, visiblemente interesando en el resultado de la entrevista.

—¿Cómo le fue con Su Eminencia, Majestad?

—Parece que bien, traté de calmarlo todo cuanto pude, y de hacerle ver lo que perdería si me da un trato hostil. No nos conviene enemistarnos con la Iglesia, príncipe. Nos provee de excelentes diplomáticos que trabajan bastante bien en las sombras.

—Ciertamente, Majestad. Hasta me parece un desperdicio que en otros países ya no les saquen provecho a los curas. Siempre es un buen diplomático quien lleva a Dios a su lado.

Cuando el emperador se quedó solo en el despacho de los cuatro bustos, tomó su teléfono particular para llamar a Carlota, ya no soportaba estar sin verla, incluso tenía que hacer un gran esfuerzo para no pensar en ella cuando atendía un asunto importante. Carlota respondió cuando el teléfono ya había sonado cinco veces.

—¿Estás ocupada?

—Sí, Fer, estoy trabajando.

—No te voy a quitar mucho tiempo. Solo quería decirte que este día parece que va a estar tranquilo, podremos vernos en la noche.

—Lo siento, Fer, yo no puedo.

—¿Por qué?

—Porque no puedo.

—¿Ni siquiera un momento?

—No, Fer, ni siquiera un momento.

—¿Y mañana?

—Mañana tampoco. Fer, quiero aclarar mis ideas, saber a dónde voy, y para ello necesito no verte durante algunos días, o semanas. Desde que soy tu novia, he tenido pocos minutos de tranquilidad, y eso no me gusta. Así que no voy a verte ni hoy, ni mañana, y no sé durante cuántos días más.

—¡Carlota, eso es imposible!

—Tendrá que ser posible, Fer, y te dejo, debo trabajar.

—¡Carlota…!

La primera idea de Fernando Carlos fue ir a buscarla en seguida, pero ya para cuando le informaron que su vehículo estaba esperándolo, cambió de idea. Si ella no quería verlo, si su presencia la haría sentir mal o incomoda, lo mejor era no molestarla. Pero, ciertamente, no estaba seguro de poder soportar siquiera dos días sin verla.

Residencia del príncipe Bonaparte en Aztlán

El despacho particular del canciller Bonaparte era una habitación amplia, de estilo neoclásico, al que él llamaba *Imperio*, decorada con colores claros y con muebles antiguos de exquisita factura, que la emperatriz Eugenia había logrado subir al barco que la llevó de Europa a México, tras el desastre de la guerra franco-prusiana. Una de las particularidades de la habitación era que los libros allí ordenados, aproximadamente seis mil, estaban todos escritos en francés y no había uno siquiera en otra lengua. La única escultura que decoraba el recinto era un busto, como podría suponerse, de Napoleón I. Ésta se hallaba en un costado de la habitación, y justo arriba, sujeta al muro, lucía su brillo una magnifica espada que había pertenecido al Gran Hombre.

El canciller saboreaba un exquisito pulque de Tula cuando entro su mayordomo a infórmale que tenía visitas. Aunque era casi la media noche, Bonaparte no se sorprendió, ya que estaba esperando a una persona.

—Condúcelo hasta aquí, François —dijo en francés, reclinado en un sofá, sin voltear a ver al mayordomo.

Apenas un minuto después entraba en el despacho el duque de Miramón.

—Miguel, pasa —dijo Bonaparte—. Prueba este pulque, está delicioso.

—Buenas noches, Luis.

—¿Te sirvo?

—Sí, gracias. Creo que me caerá bien.

—Aquí tienes, supongo que tu avión aterrizó hace apenas unos minutos.

—Gracias, Luis, y sí, en cuanto bajé del avión me vine directamente para acá.

—Muy bien, ¿y qué noticias me tienes?

—Washington es un campo de batalla —dijo Miramón—. En todas las instituciones y en todas las oficinas, me atrevería a decir que incluso en la Casa Blanca, se pelean por y contra Trump. Y respecto al príncipe Iturbide no podemos negar que es un genio. Ha logrado ser el consejero de personajes muy importantes. Es el embajador más estimado en Washington, tanto que su presencia, su elegancia y su buen gusto son indispensables en las cenas de los hombres poderosos.

—Bueno, para eso lo enviamos. Es el embajador del Imperio Mexicano, no de la república de Zamabumba. Su obligación es desquitar el sueldo. Y vaya que cobra caro.

—De acuerdo a lo que vi, no podría decirte nada que haga peligrar su cargo. Incluso en estos días de zozobra ha logrado que lo vean como un moderador imparcial.

—¿Y qué se piensa allí de nosotros?

—Luis, si un conflicto con una pequeña dictadura comunista siembra la incertidumbre en Washington. Incluso en la era de Trump, imaginarse de enemigo al Imperio Mexicano los preocupa más de lo que te imaginas. Los yanquis no son cobardes, pero vistos con paciencia se ve al instante que se han vuelto más pacíficos de lo que te imaginas. Anoche cené con el senador McCain, una de las mentes más brillantes en la política yanqui, y uno de los hombres fuertes del partido republicano. Su opinión del emperador es muy favorable. Él sabe diferenciar perfectamente al heredero de una antigua familia educada para gobernar del heredero de un una familia de comunistas criminales y ambiciosos. Me aseguró que su partido no está dispuesto a permitir que Trump genere un conflicto impredecible con el Imperio Mexicano, al que considera un país fundamental para el equilibrio y la paz del mundo.

—¿Y qué concluyes de tu visita a Washington?

—Creo, sinceramente, Luis, que es hora de que le recomiendes a Su Majestad que programe una reunión sería y respetuosa con el hombre del nido pajados en la cabeza.

—Miguel, si fuiste a Washington, fue a averiguar qué disposición tienen hacia nosotros, no a preparar el terreno para en un encuentro entre los dos mandatarios. Aún no es tiempo, las ofensas de Trump han sido muy graves, como para decirle a los mexicanos de buenas a primeras que Su Majestad va a darle la mano. Pero celebro el éxito en tu misión.

—Luis, francamente, yo no creo que sea una buena idea seguir manteniendo tensas las relaciones. A algunos sectores en Washington no les agradó que el emperador dijera que nuestra fuerza área les haría polvo su muro, y si no se llega pronto a un acuerdo, esas voces, reducidas ahora, pueden cobrar más fuerza y forjar una hostilidad que duraría cuatro años, o que puede propiciar un suceso bastante desagradable. ¿Ya pensante en eso? Si buscas un enemigo para inflar el patriotismo mexicano, procura que ese enemigo no sea una hiperpotencia, ni mucho menos nuestro mayor socio comercial. No nos conviene.

—Yo pienso en todo. Créeme, Miguel. ¿Te sirvo más pulque?

—Sí, gracias. Está exquisito. Pero medita, por favor, lo que te he dicho, Luis. El imperio no necesita enemistades para ser tan grande.

—Lo sé, pero el honor, mi querido Miguel, es una vieja reliquia que ya sólo atesoramos unos cuantos.

En Chapultepec

Cuatro horas después de que su ayuda de cámara se retiró de su habitación, Fernando Carlos aún no lograba dormir. Carlota estaba en su mente y no parecía dispuesta a irse. Fueron varias las veces que se levantó decidido a ir a buscarla a su casa, pese a lo tarde que pudiera ser. Pero en el momento en que más grande fue desesperación, una dosis de raciocinio llegó a su mente. Estaba perdiendo la cabeza por Carlota y eso perjudicaba sus funciones al mando del imperio. De seguir así, poco a poco la disciplina que con tanto esfuerzo le había inculcado su padre, se estaría marchando de su conciencia, y en el transcurso de los días podía llegar al límite de abandonar una visita de Estado para ir corriendo a buscarla. Los emperadores de México siempre se habían mofado de la debilidad de otros mandatarios, de su falta de disciplina y compromiso para gobernar, y él estaba a punto de dejar la prestigiada institución en ridículo. Quizás, después de todo, no era tan mala la idea de Carlota de separarse unos días. La amaba, no tenía la menor duda de ello, pero le parecía ridículo que diariamente, mientras tenía a Bonaparte frente a él desglosándole los problemas del imperio, estuviera añorando que llegara la noche para ir a buscarla. Esa actitud no era digna del emperador de México. Si había soñado a sus antepasados diciéndole que estaban complacidos con su despeño en el cargo que le habían heredado, tenía que comportarse a la altura, domesticar su mente, su espíritu, y también el amor que sentía. Convencido de ello, se obligó a dormir. Al día siguiente, si bien pensó en Carlota varias veces, en ningún momento pensó en llamarla y en salir corriendo para verla siquiera unos minutos. Trabajó todo el día y por la noche se quedó dormido en cuanto cayó a la cama.

Varios días transcurrieron de la misma manera, y tan sólo de cuando en cuando, sobre todo por las noches, de pie en la ventana de su habitación con Aztlán frente a sus ojos, se preguntaba por qué Carlota no lo buscaba, si acaso había decidido romper su noviazgo y ni siquiera decírselo. Pero eso no podía ser así, Carlota no era una persona cobarde que se ocultara para tomar una decisión tan importante. En el transcurso de dos semanas, Fernando Carlos la llamó sólo dos veces. Cuando en la primera el teléfono de Carlota lo envió directo al buzón, no pensó que hubiera pasado algo fuera de lo común. La segunda vez, cuando ocurrió lo mismo, empezó a preocuparse. Quizás Carlota había cambiado de número para que él no la buscara. Pero eso de ninguna manera podía significar que ella no lo amaba. De su amor estaba totalmente seguro, lo había notado cuando la tocaba, cuando la miraba a los ojos y cuando la besaba. Si Carlota se estaba alejando se debía únicamente a que tenía miedo de ser la novia del emperador, y ese miedo tenían que solucionarlo juntos. Si no la ayudaba a supéralo, podía perderla, y tan solo pensar en esa posibilidad lo hacía sentir que se le escapaba el alma del pecho. La tarde que llegó a esa conclusión, decidió que en la noche iría a buscarla.

Consciente de que Carlota llegaba a su casa, tras salir de su segundo trabajo, después de las once de la noche, se presentó a las once y media. Si bien se sentía apenado por hacerlo tan tarde, también sentía que si se iba a Chapultepec sin verla, su noche sería un infierno. A la tercera vez que tocó el timbre, apareció la madre de Carlota, ya en pijama, y con una expresión de malhumor que cambió hasta que pudo ver que se trataba de él.

—¡Majestad!..., pase, por favor. Está en su casa.

—Gracias, señora —dijo Fernando Carlos, tomándola de la mano y entrando junto a ella.

—¿Le ofrezco algo de tomar, Majestad?

—En realidad, señora, lo que más deseo es ver a Carlota.

—¿Ver a Carlota?

—Por favor...

—Mi hija no está, Majestad.

—¿Aún no llega?

—Se fue hace cuatro días.

—¿A dónde? —dijo el emperador, sintiendo que le daba un infarto.

La mujer se quedó muda.

—¡Por favor, dígamelo!

—Majestad, usted es quien es, pero no puedo traicionar a mi hija. Ella estaba segura de que usted vendría a buscarla, y me hizo jurarle que no le diría a dónde se fue.

—¿Por qué? Al menos dígame —pidió el emperador al ver que la mujer no respondía—, ¿sigue en México?

—Sí, Majestad, pero algo lejos de Aztlán. Una hermana mía le consiguió un buen trabajo. Mi hija nunca para de trabajar.

—¿Eso quiere decir que no piensa volver pronto?

—No lo sé, Majestad, ni ella mismo lo sabe. Pero lo más seguro es que no.

—Señora, esto es… el infierno para mí. ¿Por qué se fue?

—Porque tiene miedo, Majestad. Por eso.

—Sé que es difícil para ella nuestra relación, que la incómoda mi entorno. Pero estoy dispuesto a hacer todo lo posible para se sienta cómoda siendo mi novia. Le juro que si alguien le faltara al respeto, no le alcanzaría la vida para pedirme perdón.

—Majestad, ella no duda que usted la quiere. Se le nota en la mirada, yo misma lo veo ahora. Pero no sabe qué va a pasar, usted es el emperador y quizás más adelante desee relacionarse con una mujer más adecuada para ser su esposa.

—Señora, eso es como si yo temiera que ella más adelante busque relacionarse con un moreno de uno noventa y lleno de músculos. Nos amamos, y siendo así las cosas, ella es la única mujer que puede haber en mi vida. Nadie más. Y estoy seguro que Carlota tampoco podría amar a otro hombre. Dígaselo, por favor. Al alejarse de mí me está mandando al infierno, o a un lugar todavía más profundo y triste.

—Ella lo sabe, Majestad, pero le repito que tiene miedo.

—No debería, nada puede impedirnos estar juntos. Cuando hable con ella, por favor, dígale que la amo, y que la estaré esperando.

—Majestad —dijo la mujer, dudando—, hay…, hay algo que mi hija no me pidió que no se lo dijera a usted, y eso fue porque ella ignora que lo sé.

—¿De qué se trata?

—Carlota se ha echado a su espalda a la familia siempre, incluso cuando aún vivía mi esposo. Desde niña compraba dulces y los vendía a sus compañeros en la escuela, y después empezó a hacer cualquier tipo de actividades para que nunca faltara el dinero en esta casa. Por ello, cuando descubrí algo muy importante, no me hice la madre digna y monté en cólera. Carlota ha sido el jefe de esta familia y, no es que mi esposo haya sido un irresponsable perezoso, sino que siempre estuvo enfermo. Ya lo estaba cuando nos casamos, y aunque supe que nuestra vida sería difícil, acepté ser su esposa porque era un hombre bueno, que me cuidaba y me respetaba, haciéndome sentir la mujer más especial del mundo. Fue un gran padre para Carlota y los niños. En cuanto a amor y atención, les dio sobradamente aunque eso nunca está de más, y en cuanto a sus necesidades, pues hizo lo que pudo en contra de los designios de su debilitado y enfermizo cuerpo. Afortunadamente, mi hija creció sana y fuerte como un roble, y ella buscó la manera de que aquí siempre hubiera lo que no alcanzaba a comprar su padre. Por eso, Majestad, cuando descubrí el secreto de Carlota, no le dije nada, sino que decidí esperar a que ella me lo contara. Es una mujer hecha y derecha, el sustento de esta familia, yo no puedo reprocharle nada, no tengo derecho a ello, por el contrario, tengo la obligación de agradecerle mucho.

—Señora, me satisface saber por sus propias palabras la gran mujer que es Carlota, pero si no me dice de qué secreto habla, voy a volverme loco.

—Majestad —dijo la mujer, tomándolo de la cabeza y acercándole su boca al oído—, mi hija está embarazada.

Juan Robledo vivía en un no muy grande pero sí agradable departamento en un barrio bohemio de Aztlán. Sus vecinos eran pintores, poetas, literatos, escultores y arquitectos que sufrían mucho más que él para pagar la renta. Allí Juan se sentía cómodo, el entorno olía a libertad y a sueños, las dos cosas, a su juicio, más importantes en la vida. Aquella noche, cuando llegó su hermano Fernando Carlos a visitarlo, justo a las doce, aún faltaban varias horas para que se decidiera a irse a dormir.

—Bienvenido, Fer. ¿Qué te parece mi departamento?

—Se ve cómodo. ¿Y quién es aquel hombre que está en la fotografía contigo?

—Fue un poeta y activista de izquierda argentino, muerto hace dos años. De joven estuvo en México, entrenando con unos guerrilleros cubanos. Pero tu abuelo lo metió a prisión veinte años, para que se le quitara esa idea de andar haciendo travesuras. Cuando salió se dedicó a escribir poesía y a dar conferencias en todas partes, las cuales resultaban didácticas para mucha gente. El tipo era agradable, y en su juventud las mujeres lo veían exageradamente guapo. Lástima que la pasó en la cárcel. Medio año antes de su muerte estuvo dando una conferencia aquí, en Aztlán, y accedió a tomarse esa fotografía conmigo. No fui a su conferencia porque comulgara con sus ideas, pero su poesía me relaja. La que escribió antes de ir a prisión es infumable, pero la que escribió al salir es brillante. La cárcel hace buenos artistas. Aunque creo que si hubiera sabido de quién soy nieto, aun siendo por línea bastarda, no habría aceptado fotografiarse conmigo. Oye, Fer, ¿me estás escuchando? Cuando llegaste creí que tu aspecto era sólo por tu tez tan blanca, pero ahora veo que estás pálido. ¿Te pasa algo, hermano?, ¿acaso Trump envió tropas a la frontera?

—¿Tienes algo de tomar?

—Claro, ¿pulque está bien?

—Algo más fuerte, hermano.

—También tengo mezcal...

—Sí, ése sí está bien.

—¿Y ya vas a decirme qué te pasa? —preguntó Juan, cuando puso la copa en manos del emperador.

—Carlota está embarazada.

—Bueno, no te asustes, lo pondremos Juan al niño y yo procuraré ser un buen tío. Lo aconsejaré para que no almacene rencores cuando sepa que un hermano suyo más joven, pero hijo de la modelo y princesa Ana de Iturbide, será el emperador de México. No te preocupes, hermano, todo saldrá bien.

—Juan, no estoy preocupado, estoy feliz. Sólo que aún no asimilo la noticia. Pero no vine a hablarte de un problema, vine a celebrar con mi hermano que voy a ser padre.

—Pues, felicidades, hermano. Y salud por mi sobrino.

—Salud, hermano.

—¿Y Carlota qué piensa?

—No sé, se ha ido.

—¿Por qué?, ¿acaso rompieron?

—No, eso jamás. Pero creo que está asustada.

—¿Supones que no quiere para su hijo el rango de bastardo del emperador?

—Necesito hablar con ella. No pienso perder ni a Carlota ni a mi hijo, hermano.

—Yo te apoyo. Cuentas conmigo para lo que sea.

—Gracias, Juan. ¿Ya te dije hoy que te quiero?

—En la mañana, cuando me despertó tu llamada a las siete, me lo dijiste. Hermano, ¿no podrías decírmelo un poco más tarde?

—¡Cabrón! Yo a esa hora ya llevo mucho tiempo despierto.

—Sí, pero tú eres el emperador. Tienes mucho trabajo. Eso te pasa por nacer como hijo legítimo. Y a apropósito de tus funciones, Fer, mañana es la famosa consulta de Morador. ¿Ya estás listo?

—Claro.

—No te vaya a dar un susto ese cabrón, hermano. Nunca se sabe qué va a pasar cuando opina la gente.

—Estoy preparado, Juan, no te preocupes. El susto se lo va a llevar él.

Cuando el emperador iba de regreso a Chapultepec, tras despedirse de su hermano, llamó al canciller Bonaparte por teléfono. Pese a la hora, el príncipe respondió en seguida.

—Perdone que lo despierte tan tarde, príncipe.

—No se preocupe, Majestad. Estaba despierto. Leía a Aristóteles. ¿En qué le puedo servir?

—Mañana, o mejor dicho, hoy a las ocho quiero las cámaras listas. Voy a dar un mensaje en vivo a todo el imperio.

—¿Será sobre Morador?

—No, príncipe. Es algo todavía más importante para mí.

—Majestad, ¿pasa algo grave que aún no sé?

—Nada, príncipe. No se preocupe. Mañana nos vemos. Buenas noches.

—Buenas noches, Majestad. A vuestras órdenes.

Al día siguiente, por la mañana, castillo de Chapultepec

—A las tres estaremos al aire, Majestad: uno, dos, tres...

—Pueblo de México —comenzó el emperador—, tengo un mensaje que dar a mis compatriotas, y que a la vez se trata de la noticia que más felicidad me ha causado en toda mi vida: voy a ser padre. Las leyes mexicanas indican que si no estoy casado, y que si la madre de mi hijo es una mujer *inferior*, no podré reconocerlo a él legalmente como tal, no llevará el nombre de mi familia y no podrá ser el heredero del Imperio Mexicano. Pero definitivamente, yo no pienso tener a mi hijo relegado a un segundo plano y alejado de mí. Hacer tal cosa, que no niego que ha ocurrido anteriormente en la historia del imperio, seria traicionar a mi hijo, y abandonarlo. Pero tengo la total seguridad de que nunca lograré ser un buen emperador si no puedo ser un buen padre. Sería capaz de abandonar muchas cosas que forman parte de mi identidad como emperador y de la tradición de mi familia, incluso algunas veces estaré dispuesto a abandonar la clemencia, mi capacidad cristiana de perdonar, mis ambiciones y mis proyectos como soberano, pero nunca abandonaré a mi hijo.

Esta misma mañana enviaré a las cámaras una propuesta de reforma constitucional, concerniente a la sucesión en el imperio. La frase *mujer inferior* habrá de desaparecer del texto, puesto que es indigna en un país de libertades e igualdad, y porque ninguna mexicana lo es ante nada ni ante nadie. También la constitución dejará de reconocer como heredero del imperio al primer varón. Sea cual sea el sexo de mi hijo, la constitución y todas nuestras instituciones, desde su nacimiento, habrán de reconocerle como la persona destinada a sucederme al mando del imperio cuando muera. En México todos, mujeres y hombres, tenemos los mismos derechos y las mismas obligaciones ante la ley, por lo tanto, la constitución no puede albergar un artículo discriminatorio, que exclusivamente se aplique a la hija del emperador. Si soy padre de una niña, cuando yo muera la jefatura del Estado mexicano caerá en la cabeza de una emperatriz.

Sé que los legisladores están en su derecho de no aprobar las reformas que les he propuesto, y si así fuera, yo estaría renunciando a mi cargo, puesto que no permitiré que nuestras propias leyes, las que tanto idolatro, me impidan ser un buen padre y reconocer a mi hijo como tal. Quizás mi decisión les parezca muy drástica, pero mis deberes para con mi hijo, mi deseo de educarlo, amarlo, cuidar de él, y tenerlo a mi lado todos días mientras crece, no los pienso poner a consideración de nadie, ya que darle a mi hijo el tratamiento de bastardo, significaría también abandonarlo, y nadie jamás, ni yo mismo, va a creerme que ni en las peores circunstancias abandonaría a mi pueblo, si caigo en la cobardía de abandonar a mi hijo. Gracias a todos por escucharme, que tengan un excelente día.

Por la noche

El canciller entró al despacho del emperador con una muy notoria sonrisa en el rostro y una carpeta en la mano.

—Listo, Majestad —dijo—, tenemos ya los resultados de la consulta de Morador.

—Por su expresión, príncipe, parece que nos fue bien.

—Majestad, las encuestadoras habían previsto una participación de veinte millones de mexicano, las nuestras, y las de Morador aseguraban que cuando menos cien millones irían a las urnas.

—¿Y...?

—Sólo fueron tres.

—Eso quiere decir que al resto de la población ni siquiera le atrae debatir sobre el tema.

—Exactamente.

—¿Y cuál fue el resultado de esos tres millones?

—Dos millones de mexicanos quieren una república, novecientos mil de los que votaron se inclinan por la continuidad del imperio, y cien mil que —desconozco si se pusieron de acuerdo por medio de las redes sociales—, le escribieron a Morador un mensaje que decía: "Ponte a trabajar, huevón".

—Vaya, ¿así que dos millones de mexicanos no están de acuerdo con nuestra forma de gobierno?

—Majestad, yo pensaba que serían muchos más. Llegué a temer que fueran cincuenta millones de mexicanos, no los necesarios para derrumbar el imperio, pero bastantes como para que ese loco siguiera dando guerra.

–¿Y qué fue lo que le falló a Morador?

–Estoy seguro, Majestad –respondió Bonaparte–, que fue su discurso de hoy en la mañana. Francamente, en ese momento yo no supe si fue una buena o una mala idea. Pero conforme transcurría el día me di cuenta que había sido una determinación brillante. La gente recibió bien su mensaje, bastante bien, se acercó al pueblo más de los límites establecidos. Sus seguidores en Twitter ya se habían duplicado para la hora de la comida, y la frase "Dios salve al emperador" fue la tendencia de todo el día. La sociedad de madres solteras de Aztlán le cambió el nombre a su sede, ahora se llama Fernando Carlos I, y ha propuesto que el día del padre sea cambiado por el día de su cumpleaños, iniciativa que por medio de las redes sociales ya respaldan la mitad de los mexicanos. Uno de sus más grandes críticos, y amigo personal de Morador, escribió en su artículo de hoy: "Nos gobierna un buen hombre, y eso es bueno para todos". Sobra decir que Morador ya le retiró su amistad y aseguró que lo sobornamos.

–¿Así que tengo una cuenta en Twitter?

–Ah, pues cuando usted estaba en Miramar, tan indispuesto para ocuparse de sus funciones, le creamos una, desde donde diariamente enviaba mensajes a su pueblo. Cuando quiera le puedo dar la contraseña…

–Y si al pueblo le agradaron las reformas que propuse a la Constitución, ¿eso querrá decir –dijo el emperador–, que tengo grandes posibilidades de que se aprueben?

–Majestad, ningún senador va a votar en contra. Y en la cámara de diputados, los moradoristas, que no son mayoría, se verán obligaos a apoyar la reforma porque todo el tiempo se la pasan hablando en favor de los derechos de las mujeres y de los niños. Ir en contra de su propuesta sería traicionar sus convicciones, lo que los haría muy impopulares. Yo mismo iré a hablar al senado, confíe en que voy a sacarle esa reforma integra en, cuando mucho, una semana.

–Gracias, príncipe. No sé qué haría sin usted.

—¿Su Majestad me permite responder esta llamada? —dijo Bonaparte cuando sonó su teléfono—. Es el conde Andrássy.

—Adelante.

—¿Qué pasa, Julio? —respondió Bonaparte—. Estoy con el emperador. No, no estamos viendo las noticias, ¿qué dice ese loco?...¿Cómo?... ¿Fraude? ¿Que alteramos los resultados? ¡Pero si la consulta fue de él!... ¿Ciento cincuenta millones fueron los mexicanos que pretendían votar y no se los permitimos? ¿Que piensa bloquear el Paseo de Juárez hasta que se respete la voz del pueblo? ¡Hijo de la chingada! Ten listos a tus hombres, Julio. En seguida hablo con el emperador al respecto y te devuelvo la llamada. Majestad... —dijo Bonaparte cuando colgó.

—Ya escuché, príncipe. Le doy mi autorización para que la guardia imperial haga todo lo que tenga que hacer y que no se altere el orden. Si Morador hace otra consulta y sólo votan treinta mexicanos, él va a seguir chingando, y mi paciencia ya se acabó.

—¿Y con Morador qué hacemos? El príncipe de Iturbide ya encontró algunos gastos muy irregulares ante los que él, como presidente de su partido, tiene que responder.

—Como le dije, príncipe, mi paciencia ya llegó al límite. Creo que le voy a pedir otro favor al oficial Benito Rueda.

Dos horas más tarde, el conde Andrássy informó que la manifestación ya había sido controlada, con un saldo de cuarenta vehículos incendiados, más de ochenta negocios destruidos y alrededor de mil quinientos detenidos. Fernando Carlos dio las órdenes pertinentes para garantizar la reparación de los daños, y que quienes pagaran fueran los mismos que los causaron, no los demás mexicanos con sus impuestos. Después se retiró a dormir. Llevaría apenas media hora en su cama cuando sonó su teléfono. El corazón casi se le sale del pecho cundo vio que se trataba de Carlota.

—¡Mi amor!

—Justo esas palabras quería oír, Fer.

—¿Dónde estás?

—Voy llegando a Aztlán. ¿Te gustaría que nos viéramos?

—¡Por supuesto!

—¿Puedes pasar por mí?

—En diez minutos un helicóptero me llevará al aeropuerto.

—No vengo en avión, Fer, no me puedo permitir esos gastos. Y si así fuera, habría llegado a Aztlán a las once de la mañana. Pero el hecho de que mencionaras la palabra helicóptero me hizo recordar el Palacio de Cortés.

—Daré instrucciones para que todo esté listo cuando lleguemos.

—Está bien, pero quizás deberías de dejar de despilfarrar la herencia de la emperatriz Carlota, de lo contrario a mi hijo no le va a tocar nada.

—Procuraré que algo sobre para él.

—Ni cómo dudar de tu palabra, ya todo México te ve como el mejor padre del mundo. Oye, pero no pidas una cena, no tengo hambre.

—¿Entonces?

—Con una habitación para nosotros dos es suficiente.

Palacio de Cortés

Durante el vuelo en helicóptero apenas hablaron, Carlota se había limitado a abrazarse a él y recargarle su cabeza en el pecho. El emperador también la había abrazado, mientras se preguntaba cómo había sido posible que soportara estar tantos días sin ella.

—Vaya, en esa cama cabemos tú, yo y siete hijos —dijo Carlota, cuando entraron a la habitación que les habían preparado.

El emperador la abrazó por la espalda y se aferró a ella.

—¡Te extrañé! —le dijo al oído.

—Sí, ya sentí entre las pompas que me extrañaste.

Él la giró para verla a los ojos.

—¿Qué te hizo volver?

—Tu discurso, obviamente. Como nuestro hijo todavía no nace, supe enseguida que lo pronunciaste para que yo te escuchara. Estaba llorando cuando terminaste de hablar. Te amor, Fer, te amo.

—¡Pues ya no te vuelvas a ir nunca de mi vida! —dijo él, y la besó.

—Sabes —dijo Carlota, separando sus labios, dos minutos después—, si de un día para otro me resultó difícil mermar tus energías, no sé cómo me va a ir ahora que llevas varias semanas de abstinencia.

—Justo en este momento saldremos de dudas —dijo el emperador—, y la volvió a besar.

De vuelta en Aztlán

Y si el gran general Porfirio Díaz, el más grande de nuestros mártires de la patria, dio su vida por esta causa tan justa, yo con gusto seguiré el caminó que él nos dejó señalado, si es que la dictadura ha decidido ya la fecha de mi muerte. Que me maten, que me llenen de calumnias. No me importa. ¡La historia me absolverá!

Cuando Ángel Miguel Morador terminó de escribir el último párrafo del artículo que tan concentrado lo había tenido por horas, volteó a ver a su asistente, que llevaba allí varios minutos para informarle que alguien estaba llamando a la puerta.

—Toma, escóndelo —dijo Morador, entregándole las hojas con el artículo escrito a mano—. Quizás este sea mi testamento, y mi humilde herencia a los mexicanos. Abre pues la puerta. Seguro se trata de esbirros de la dictadura que vienen por mí. Déjalos pasar, no opongas resistencia, no arriesgues tu vida. Pero antes esconde bien el artículo, no dejes que te lo quiten. En ti confío. La dictadura tratará por todos los medios de evitar que se publique.

El asistente escondió las hojas debajo de su camisa, y luego fue abrir la puerta. Un minuto después entraba en el despacho de Morador el oficial Benito Rueda.

—Así que tú eres mi verdugo —le dijo Morador—. Pues bien, dispara al corazón, para que mis hijos puedan ver el rostro de su padre impoluto. Sólo ese favor te pido.

—Estás loco, cabrón.

—Eso dirán ustedes de mí. Siempre de los hombres íntegros se busca manchar su nombre con calumnias.

—Sí, pues. Lo que tú digas. Pero te lo advertí, te dejé bastante claro que si volvías a alterar el orden público vendría por ti. Era una advertencia del emperador y no hiciste caso.

—¿Y tú crees que esas amenazas me habrían intimidado al grado de dejar de luchar por la libertad de mi país? ¡Nunca! Ni siquiera lo sueñen.

—¿Sabes cuál es tu problema, Ángel Miguel? —preguntó el oficial Rueda—. Hay muchas cosas que funcionan en México. No digo que sea el país perfecto, pero millones de mexicanos son felices aquí, pueden trabajar, vivir en paz y educar a sus hijos gracias a las instituciones que tenemos. Pero tú todo, absolutamente todo, lo ves mal, simplemente porque lo que existe no te gusta. Jamás vas a elogiar algo que esté bien hecho, porque quisieras hacerlo tú. Si todos los mexicanos se estuvieran muriendo de hambre, tú serías el hombre más feliz del mundo, porque tendrías la razón. Pero te chingas, porque millones de mexicanos que sí quieren trabajar, llevan una vida digna gracias a su esfuerzo y a que nuestro país no está tan mal. Y si tú quieres negar que esos triunfadores que no atesoran la pereza existen porque simplemente no te gusta que existan, pues sencillamente eres un gran hijo de la chingada, Ángel Miguel.

—¿Qué puedo decirte? Soy un hombre libre. Desconozco por completo el idioma de los esclavos que ya olvidaron que la libertad existe, y tú eres uno de ellos. Ni duda cabe.

—Bueno pues, para ahorrar saliva: afuera están los agentes de la guardia imperial. Vienen por ti. Te tratarán con el respeto debido si sigues sus instrucciones, así que no te resistas.

—Toda mi vida he luchado porque México recupere su independencia, y mi pago, a fin de cuentas, será la prisión. ¿Cuál es mi delito?, ¿convocar a una manifestación?

—¿Manifestación? ¡No seas cínico, cabrón! Ordenaste a tus grillos que sembraran el caos en Aztlán, que fastidiaran la vida de los ciudadanos que sólo quieren vivir en paz, ¿y a eso lo llamas una manifestación? Vaya pues, sí que estás loco. ¿Qué querías que el emperador te diera a cambio?, ¿un pastel?

—¿Sabes cuál es mi peor castigo? Que a un caudillo de la libertad como yo lo trate de esta forma un esclavo ciego como tú. Eso es peor que la prisión.

—Lo que tú digas. Ahora sígueme, porque de lo contrario ordenaré que vengan por ti, Ángel Miguel, y mis hombres te darán unos buenos chingadazos si te resistes al arresto, que bien ganados te los tienes.

—Antes, dime por fin, ¿cuál es tu puesto en la dictadura?

—Claro, soy oficial del departamento de conducta vial. Benito Rueda, a las órdenes del emperador.

—¿Un oficial de departamento de conducta vial viene a arrestarme?

—¿Qué tiene de malo mi puesto? Es un trabajo honrado que he desempeñado toda mi vida con la mayor honestidad. Bueno, ahora que lo pienso, tú de trabajar sí que no sabes nada, cabrón. Y sígueme, con una chingada, porque ya me estoy fastidiando de que digas pendejadas.

Nuevamente en el palacio de Cortés

Carlota estaba recostada encima del emperador, con sus cabellos cubriéndole parte del rostro, mientras con su dedo le dibujaba círculos en el pecho.

–¿Y dónde estabas?

–En el departamento de Tabasco, junto a la playa –respondió Carlota–. Allí se estableció mi abuelo, cuando llegó de Haití buscando una mejor vida, y allí viven muchos miembros de mi familia, incluyendo una hermana de mi mami.

–¿Y pensabas quedarte allí?

–Toda mi vida, hasta que tu discurso me hizo cambiar de opinión al instante. Realmente pensaba que con el paso del tiempo me verías como una amante, como una mujer indigna de ser tu esposa, y que mi bebé lo obligarías a ver a sus hermanos legítimos hacia arriba. Por eso había pensado ocultarte su existencia.

–Nunca debiste pensar esas tonterías –dijo el emperador–. Si no te amara más que a mi vida, estaría enojado contigo por ello.

–Para que me perdones, te daré información importante, que seguro te interesa.

–¿Ah sí?, ¿cuál es ésa información?

–No le dije a mi mami que llegaría esta noche. Piensa que estaré en Aztlán hasta mañana temprano. Dime, ¿te sirve esa información?

–Es buena. Sabré hacer un adecuado uso de ella.

–Juraría que nadie que te ve esa cara de santo en la televisión sospecha que eres tan caliente, Fer.

–Que sea nuestro secreto, por favor.

—Mmmm, créeme que no tengo ningún interés de divulgarlo. Oye, el día que cancelaste nuestra cita, quería contarte algo importante que me había ocurrido.

—Cierto. ¿De qué se trata? —dijo el emperador.

—Recibí una visita muy desagradable en mi trabajo, la princesa Ana María de Iturbide y Green fue a reclamarme su derecho a ser tu esposa.

—¿Y qué hiciste?

—Para no abundar tanto, la golpee.

—¡Es verdad! Ella tenía una mejilla inflamada.

—¿Fue a contártelo?

—No, evitó decírmelo esa noche, cuando apareció desnuda en mi habitación.

—¡Qué!

—No había tenido oportunidad de contártelo.

—¿Y qué fue lo que ocurrió? ¡Dime la verdad!

—Le ordené que se vistiera y la eché de mi habitación.

—Fer —dijo Carlota, sujetándolo con una sola mano de las mejillas con fuerza—, ¿me juras que eso hiciste?

—Te lo juro por el descanso del alma de mi padre. No podría, de ninguna manera, verte a los ojos si hubiera seguido su juego.

—¿Y qué hizo ella?

—¿Qué te digo? Supongo que todavía me está mentando la madre.

—Gracias.

—¿Por...?

—No soy lesbiana, pero es indudable que la princesa es una mujer extraordinariamente atractiva. Su porte y su elegancia al caminar y al sonreír no los voy a tener más que volviendo a nacer. Y a su cuerpo no se le ve un solo defecto. Cualquier otro hombre, ni duda cabe, no la habría echado de su cama.

—Quería ser feliz al tenerte en mis brazos —dijo el emperador—, estar seguro de que tenía derecho a ello, y si no la echaba de mi habitación, estaba seguro que jamás volvería a experimentar la felicidad que siento en este momento.

—Mi mami me dijo que tenías miedo de que me gustara un moreno de metro noventa y fornido.

—Vaya, sí que tienen comunicación ustedes dos.

—Adonde fui hay muchos, y son bastante coquetos.

—No me hagas despertar a toda mi guardia imperial, están cansados, tuvieron un día difícil.

—El hecho de que sean coquetos no quiere decir que yo me haya interesado por alguien. Te amo, tonto, y no tienes ningún motivo para sentir celos. Te lo juro. Hace un momento tú juraste por el descanso del alma de tu padre, y al decir esas palabras se iluminó tu mirada. Anteriormente notaba que te dolía mencionarlo.

—Lo soñé.

—¿De verdad?, ¿y te dijo algo?

—Sí, que está orgulloso de mí y que me ama. Quizás me lo habría repetido, pero la princesa Ana me despertó besándome, por eso tuve dos motivos para echarla de mi habitación. No me gustó que me privara del gusto de ver a mi padre orgulloso de mí.

—¡Hija de la chingada! Eso no me lo habías contado, Fer.

—Oye, yo no podía evitar que me besara dormido. No soy culpable de ello.

—¿Y crees que con eso me voy a quedar satisfecha?

—Bueno, cuando seas emperatriz podrás desquitarte. Te va a sobrar el poder para hacerlo.

—¿Yo emperatriz?

—Claro, voy a reformar la constitución del imperio para que mi heredero al trono no tenga que ser hijo de una princesa, pero la ley seguirá ordenando que la madre tiene que ser mi esposa. Sé que el motivo para que te cases conmigo tiene que ser el amor que sientes por mí. Pero me gusta tomar precauciones, así que si no aceptas ser mi esposa, tu hijo no podrá ser emperador.

—Vaya, tendré que sacrificarme por mi hijo, sólo por él —dijo Carlota, sonriendo.

—La boda religiosa —dijo el emperador, en tono serio— no podrá ser este año. Max y mi padre llevan muy poco tiempo en sus tumbas. No me sentiría feliz celebrando mi boda. ¿Comprendes?

—Claro, amor.

—Pero la boda civil tendrá que ser pronto. Ya quiero que seas mi esposa, y que duermas conmigo en Chapultepec. Además, mi hijo tiene que nacer como un Habsburgo y Lorena.

—¿Ya pensaste que sus apellidos van a ser Habsburgo y Lorena y Lorena?

—Sí, pero no te preocupes. Va a ser un aristócrata, y en la aristocracia siempre hay repeticiones de ese tipo.

—¿Y cómo te gustaría que se llamara, si es niño?

—Marco —dijo el emperador.

—¿Cómo mi papá? —preguntó Carlota, emocionada.

—Sí, fue un buen padre que se ganó el respeto de su esposa y de sus hijos, y un hombre así merece que un emperador de México lo honre llevando su nombre.

—Marco I de México —dijo Carlota—. Vaya, y supongo que después de Marco llevaría los nombres de Maximiliano José Carlos Leopoldo Fernando Rodolfo Francisco…

—No, Marco será suficiente.

—¿Y si es niña?

—Me gustaría llamarla Carlota.

—¿En honor a tu tía o a mí?

—A las dos, pero así cuando sea emperatriz podrá llevar el nombre de Carlota II, en honor a la madre del Imperio Mexicano, que aunque sólo fue emperatriz consorte, en realidad gobernó con mano de hierro durante seis décadas. Estoy convencido de que México siempre será un país seguro y próspero mientras tenga a una Carlota moviendo los hilos del Estado.

—Cuando mencionaste que ya deseas que duerma contigo en Chapultepec —dijo Carlota—, me quedé pensando en algo. ¿Tendré que despertarme yo a las tres, para vestirme antes de que llegue tu ayuda de cámara a las tres y media a despertarte?

—Pondré un despertador, y mi fiel Mateo podrá vestirme en la habitación de al lado. ¿Contenta? Tampoco voy a despedirlo.

—¿Eso hacían tus padres?

—Ellos no dormían juntos, ni mis abuelos ni mis bisabuelos. De hecho, serás la primera emperatriz de México que pasa toda la noche con su esposo.

—¿De verdad?

—Sí —dijo Fernando Carlos—. La emperatriz y el emperador nunca duermen juntos, tan sólo él la visita durante media hora cuando tiene ganas…, o cuando hace falta un heredero. Pero nosotros vamos a romper el protocolo.

—¿Y nos iremos de aquí a las tres, para que puedas estar en Chapultepec a tiempo?

—No, las últimas semanas me he levantado a la hora que acostumbran los emperadores, así que creo que ya me gané el derecho de tomarme una madrugada y una mañana de vacaciones. Nos iremos a las ocho, a fin de cuentas, tu madre te espera hasta bien entrada la mañana.

—Te estás portando muy bien, amor.

—No quiero que me regañes, incluso traigo unos condones en mi abrigo, recordando las condiciones que me habías puesto la última vez.

—¡Tonto, ya para qué!

Al día siguiente, por la noche

—Lástima que no puedas tomar alcohol, cuñada querida —dijo Juan Robledo—, así que tendrás que brindar con una deliciosa limonada. ¡Salud, por mi sobrino!

—Salud, hermano —dijo el emperador.

—Es una pena que tengamos que tener el palco cerrado, para que nadie del bar vea dónde anda metido Su Majestad Imperial —añadió Juan—. Pero así no puedo fumar, por mi pequeño sobrino, a quien seguramente no le agrada el humo. Ni hablar, dejemos que los mexicanos sigan imaginando que a estas horas hablas por teléfono de heráldica y antigüedades con la reina de Inglaterra, hermano.

—Pues que tu sobrino sepa que al menos haces un pequeño sacrificio por él, Juan —dijo Carlota.

—No es lo único que pienso hacer por él, seré su maestro de guitarra, lo único útil que creo que puedo enseñarle. Aunque previendo que estará inmerso en una aristocracia llena de restricciones, también seré yo quien, a sus quince años, lo lleve a un centro nocturno. Dudo mucho que lo haga el canciller Bonaparte.

—Quizás la idea no es tan mala —dijo el emperador-. A mí me llevó Max, pero mi hijo no tendrá un hermano mayor.

—Todo arreglado —dijo Juan—. Cuenta con que yo le enseñaré a mi sobrino lo hermosas que son las noches en Aztlán.

—¡Gracias, hermano! Sabía que podía contar contigo.

—Sospecho —dijo Carlota—, que ustedes ya están seguros de que mi hijo será varón. Indudablemente hay tintes de machismo en este palco.

—Será lo mejor, cuñada, así yo podré educarlo. Si nace una niña, la va educar la duquesa Carlota de Cuernavaca, recientemente rebautizada, por segunda vez, como Carlos de Habsburgo y Lorena. Ah, me consta que mi querida tía es un ángel, pero mi experiencia es en calidad de bastardo. Tratándose de la futura emperatriz, no le dará tregua hasta que domine quince idiomas y camine diez centímetros despegada del suelo.

Los tres rompieron a reír, el emperador aún con más intensidad que Carlota y su hermano. Indudablemente, estaba feliz, y quizás nunca lo había sido tanto en su vida. Repentinamente, se abrió la puerta con un poco de violencia. El emperador recompuso su porte de aristócrata y volteó a ver quién interrumpía de esa manera. Era ni más ni menos que el conde Andrássy.

-Su Majestad perdonará mi atrevimiento –dijo–, pero... –volteó a ver los acompañantes del emperador.

–Hable, conde, ¿qué ocurre?

–Una verdadera emergencia, Majestad.

–¿Los hombres de Morador?

–Ojalá fuera eso. El canciller Bonaparte ya lo espera en Chapultepec, y urge por la presencia de Vuestra Majestad. También van en camino el príncipe Iturbide, el general Peña-Bazaine y el duque de Miramón.

Ante las palabras y la inquietud de Andrássy, la actitud feliz del emperador se trasformó en la de un león en guardia.

–Juan, por favor, lleva a Carlota a su casa. Una escolta los va a acompañar. Después te espero en Chapultepec. Vamos, conde. Iremos en mi auto, debe usted venir conmigo para que me adelante algo.

–El helicóptero ya está en el techo del antro, Majestad –dijo Andrássy.

–¿Tan graves son las cosas?

–Fer –dijo Carlota–, si necesitas a Juan, yo iré a mi casa con la escolta. Llévalo de una vez contigo.

–Pero...

—Majestad —dijo Andrássy—, hay cincuenta hombres entrenados para cuidar a nuestro príncipe imperial..., o princesa. No se preocupe en lo más mínimo por ello.

—Está bien —dijo el emperador, mirando a Carlota a los ojos—. Vamos, Juan.

En Chapultepec

Cuando el helicóptero aterrizó junto al antiguo castillo, el emperador vio que había un inusual movimiento de oficiales del ejército imperial por todas partes. Una formación con espada en mano flanqueó su entrada al edificio, y justo a las puertas de su despacho había dos oficiales que en el acto le presentaron armas. Las puertas se abrieron y entró seguido de su hermano. Dentro del despacho de los cuatro bustos ya estaban su tía, el canciller Bonaparte, el ministro de la guerra Peña-Bazaine, el príncipe Iturbide y el ministro de la marina de guerra imperial, el almirante Tomás Mejía.

–¿Qué está pasando, príncipe? –dijo dirigiéndose a Bonaparte–, el conde Andrássy sólo mencionó un tiroteo en la frontera.

–Majestad –comenzó Bonaparte–, tenía usted razón en sentir un mal presentimiento con esa pendejada del muro fronterizo que se traía Trump. Resulta que un grupo de oficiales yanquis estaban justo en la frontera, revisando el terreno donde iniciará el muro, pero en el acto llegó una patrulla de infantería del ejército imperial. Ellos tenían conocimiento de que los yanquis estaban cuando menos cinco metros de este lado. Les ordenaron entregar sus armas, ya que estaban en territorio mexicano. Los yanquis lo negaron, los nuestros contaron hasta tres para que se sometieran, ellos no hicieron caso.

–¿Y qué pasó?

–Pues, Majestad, en tiempos de Obama los nuestros habrían tenido la cortesía de buscar un acuerdo amistoso, pero Trump ha calentado mucho el terreno con las pendejadas que dice, tanto que los nuestros abrieron fuego a las tres. Hasta utilizaron una bazuca y una patrulla de la *Border Patrol* salió volando por los aires. Cuatro de nuestros soldados murieron en la refriega, pero de ellos se calcula que cuando menos fueron doce.

—¿A qué horas fue eso, príncipe? —preguntó el emperador.

—Ya casi pasó media hora, Majestad.

—Esos cabrones tienen la culpa por no fijarse dónde empieza México.

—Majestad, lo peor es que al parecer sí estaban donde deberían estar. No habían cruzado un centímetro al territorio mexicano. Los que se equivocaron, muy probablemente, fueron los nuestros.

—¡En la madre! ¿Ha habido alguna comunicación con los yanquis?

—Ninguna. La embajadora aquí se atrincheró, y el embajador Iturbide nos ha dicho por clave que nuestra embajada allá está rodeada por el ejército.

—Para empezar, hagan lo mismo aquí —dijo el emperador.

—Ya está hecho, Majestad, por soldados sin uniforme para no alarmar a la población. Tenemos francotiradores en todas las azoteas vecinas.

—Bueno, señores —comenzó el emperador—, la situación es crítica. Dentro de los siguientes minutos puede empezar la guerra más terrible que ha conocido este mundo, y quiera Dios que podamos evitarla. Pero si no es posible, los alcances incluso del primer día del conflicto pueden marcar para siempre a la humanidad, o sellar definitivamente su historia. La firma para la primera guerra mundial la puso mi antepasado, Francisco José I de Austria, y ahora, apenas un conflicto igual y un siglo después, parece que me va a tocar a mí. No puedo creer que dos responsabilidades tan grandes recaigan en la misma familia.

—Majestad —dijo su tía, la archiduquesa—, como usted lo ha dicho, una guerra sería la más terrible de todos los tiempos. Por favor, trate de evitarla.

—Es mi mayor deseo —dijo el emperador—. No quiero que mi hijo nazca en un desierto del tamaño de todo el planeta, si es que queda algo. Pero quizás ya no la podré evitar. General Peña-Bazaine, ¿cuál es nuestra situación, en caso de que se dispare otra bala?

—Majestad —respondió el general—, desde hace más de un siglo todo nuestro arsenal y nuestras bases militares están en dirección a los yanquis. Nuestros misiles con cabeza nuclear apuntan desde siempre a Nueva York, a Chicago, a Washington, a las ciudades más pobladas. Los más veloces y de menor tamaño están dirigidos a la Casa Blanca y al Capitolio. Para está guerra, Majestad, nos hemos preparado desde hace mucho tiempo. El general Tegetthoff está en las cercanías de Paso del Norte, con doscientos mil hombres listos para entrar a Texas barriendo todo a su paso. Nuestros hombres en acción en este momento serian de un millón, pero dentro de pocos días tendríamos listas nuestras reservas para entrar en combate, que suman doce millones. Nuestros vehículos y reservas de combustible alcanzan para dos años de conflicto. No estamos, como puede ver Su Majestad, indefensos.

—Bien, almirante Mejía —dijo el emperador—, supongo que usted también tiene todo su potencial dirigido hacia los yanquis.

—Desde el primer día que ocupé mi cargo, Majestad —dijo el almirante—, hace veinticuatro años.

—¿Qué más tenemos?

—El cardenal Fischer —dijo Bonaparte—, informó hace poco que está de rodillas en la catedral, rezando, para que todos los yanquis ardan en el infierno y para que Dios perdone a Su Majestad por todos los pecados que pueda cometer si se desata una guerra.

—¡Vaya! Bueno, algo es algo.

—Siendo la nuestra una monarquía católica, eso también cuenta, Majestad. Si me tomé el atrevimiento de informar a Fischer sobre la situación, es porque considero que necesitamos mucho a Dios en estos momentos. La guerra franco-prusiana, que echó a mi familia de Francia, empezó por un suceso de poca importancia y se transformó una carnicería inenarrable. Y si acaso Dios no nos ayuda a pactar la paz, al menos, si desata la guerra, que esté de nuestro lado.

—Está bien, príncipe —dijo el emperador—, cuando los humanos nos volvemos irracionales, es posible que el único que pueda imponer orden sea Dios.

—Esperemos, Majestad, que Dios no se vea en la necesidad de intervenir y que usted pueda solucionarlo todo con su sabiduría –dijo la duquesa.

—¿Nuestros radares han detectado algún movimiento extraño en dirección a nosotros? –preguntó el emperador.

—Todavía nada, Majestad –dijo el ministro de la guerra–. Todo indica que los yanquis están en el mismo dilema que nosotros.

—Siendo así, quiero escuchar la opinión de cada uno de ustedes. Empieza tú, tía. Me consta que llevas contigo la inteligencia de la emperatriz Carlota, y definitivamente, ella nos hace mucha falta en este momento.

—Majestad, una guerra en estos tiempos ya está muy alejada de aquellos en que los soldados se batían cuerpo a cuerpo y festejaban con alegría el valor de sus adversarios. Una vez que el primer misil atraviese los cielos, habrá tantos que seguramente los soldados jamás se van a ver frente a frente, sino que morirán en segundos. Será un infierno. Lo mejor que puede pasarnos es un acuerdo pacífico, aunque México tenga que pedir disculpas y se vea humillado por ello. Aquí no se trata de salvar una frontera, sino a toda la humanidad. Los tiempos de las guerras con honor se han ido para siempre por culpa de la tecnología.

—Gracias, tía. Tu opinión, sin duda, es de una sensatez extraordinaria. General…, lo escucho.

—Majestad –comenzó Peña-Bazaine–, si ordenamos el avance de las tropas de Tegetthoff, daremos a entender que no queremos una hecatombe, sino un duelo entre soldados donde habrán de ganar los más valientes, ya que nuestro armamento es similar. Es probable que por medio de la ONU podamos lograr la firma de un acuerdo en el que se nos prohíba a ambos países usar bombas nucleares. Pero si usted decide que tenemos que pelear, le sugiero que sea de inmediato. Esperar más sería dar a entender que tenemos miedo. Y, si se inclina usted por movilizar a las tropas, le pido que me permita ir a ponerme al mando de un cuerpo del ejército. No pienso ser un general de oficina en tiempos de guerra, ésa no sería una actitud digna de mi familia.

—Gracias, general. Su opinión es muy valiosa. Almirante Mejía, es su turno.

—Majestad, primero que nada, le aseguro que estoy dispuesto a ir a morir por usted en este mismo momento, puesto que no soy un cobarde. Le profeso la misma lealtad que le demostró mi trastatarabuelo a Maximiliano *el Grande*. Pero no estoy de acuerdo con el general Peña-Bazaine, puesto que aun logrando un acuerdo en el que no se usen las bombas nucleares, cualquiera de los dos países que vaya perdiendo va a recurrir a ellas para equilibrar la balanza. De eso estoy seguro. Yo, al igual que su tía, la archiduquesa, le sugiero buscar la manera de pactar la paz, antes de que eso nos resulte posible.

—Me parece muy acertada su forma de pensar, almirante. Gracias por su consejo. Príncipe Iturbide, lo escucho.

—Es innegable, Majestad, dado el arsenal nuclear de los dos países, que yo también le recomiendo encarecidamente buscar la paz. Ningún imbécil en este mundo, a menos que esté completamente loco, le recomendaría lo contrario. Si imaginamos la guerra, habrá que imaginar que el mundo será una nube humo imposible de respirar para mañana al amanecer. Por el amor de Dios, Majestad, olvídese de la palabra guerra y concéntrese en buscar un buen acuerdo.

—Gracias, príncipe. Tiene usted mucha razón en lo que dice. Y usted, duque —le dijo a Miramón—, ¿qué opina?

Extraña o intencionalmente, los duques de Miramón, cuando estaban dentro del despacho de los cuatro bustos, siempre se colocaban junto al busto de su antepasado. El duque dio un paso al frente y se alistó para hablar.

—Majestad —dijo—, es, ciertamente, muy importante y muy humano que se hable de la paz, pero no podemos olvidar que los yanquis son una raza de asesinos, los únicos que han usado bombas nucleares contra ciudades indefensas. Quizás, mientras estamos pensando en hallar un acuerdo pacífico, ellos ya decidieron atacarnos. Si uno de los dos países habrá de desaparecer de este mundo, Majestad, que sean ellos. Si nuestros radares detectan cualquier movimiento, lo más sensato es atacar con todo, porque es probable que ésa sea la única forma que tenemos de salvar a México.

—Gracias, duque —dijo el emperador—, aunque el problema de usar las bombas nucleares es que somos vecinos. Ciertamente, si atacamos sus ciudades del norte del país, es probable que usarlas no sea un suicidio. Pero no crea que subestimo o valoro poco su opinión, muy en el fondo de mí ser, me queda claro que tiene usted razón, por terrible que sea reconocerlo. Príncipe Bonaparte, dígame por favor qué piensa.

—Majestad, usted no es un niño, y no le gusta que lo traten como tal. Es un hombre inteligente que ya ha aprendido a desempeñar sus funciones. Los demás ya le dijeron todo cuanto habría que decir. Usted sabe bien lo que puede pasar si se inclina por la guerra, pero en caso de ser así, de seguir el consejo del general Peña-Bazaine, le pido que me dé un cuerpo de ejército y me permita ir al campo de batalla, donde quiera que sea. También alcancé el rango de general de división en el ejército imperial, y en tiempos de guerra juro que le he de servir más como general que como canciller.

—No podía esperar menos del vástago de una familia de valientes —dijo el emperador—. Gracias, príncipe. Tendré muy en cuenta su petición. Y tú, Juan, ¿qué consejo puedes darme? Señores, para quienes no lo conoce, les presento a mi hermano, el duque Juan de... Austria.

—Majestad, yo también quiero un acuerdo pacífico, pero al mismo tiempo quisiera sugerirle cómo conseguirlo.

—Vaya, eso estaba esperando, habla...

—Si los yanquis no se han movilizado, significa que una guerra los preocupa tanto como a nosotros. Vamos a poner a nuestra fuerza aérea en el aire, sus radares y satélites van a detectarnos y llevaremos sus nervios al límite.

—Perdón que interrumpa, Majestad —dijo el almirante Mejía—, pero hacer tal cosa los hará pensar que nos disponemos a atacarlos, y podrían reaccionar de la peor forma.

—Eso es cierto —dijo el hermano del emperador—, pero estamos en un momento muy crítico, y todas las posibles soluciones llevan a un riesgo. Dejemos que los yanquis vean que ya empezó la guerra, y de esa forma, si es que quieren la paz, van a respondernos una llamada, y si acaso quieren la guerra, con nuestros aviones en el aire ya llevaríamos algo de ventaja.

—Tú idea es buena, hermano, y, como la decisión final me toca a mí: general Peña-Bazaine, que nuestros aviones despeguen y se dirijan a la frontera norte.

—¡A las órdenes de Vuestra Majestad! —dijo el general, con su teléfono en la mano—. Pasen a la fase tres inmediatamente —añadió—. El emperador lo ordena.

—Bien, señores —dijo el emperador—, que Dios interceda para que de aquí salga un buen acuerdo, sino nos va a llevar la chingada a todos, pero los yanquis se irán por delante.

—General —dijo Iturbide—, ¿cuánto tiempo puede pasar para que los yanquis se percaten de que nuestros aviones se disponen para el combate?

—Se supone —dijo Peña-Bazaine—, que en este momento ya despegaron, y se supone que los yanquis ya detectaron el movimiento.

—¿Y ahora qué haremos, Majestad? —dijo la archiduquesa.

—Desde mi oficina tengo línea directa con el secretario de Estado —interrumpió Bonaparte—. Quizás sea un buen momento para intentar una llamada con los yanquis. Que piensen que es un último intento de acordar la paz antes de que nuestros aviones crucen la frontera.

—¿Ellos aún no reaccionan, general? —dijo el emperador.

—Me informarían en el acto si eso hicieran —respondió Peña-Bazaine.

—Bien, príncipe, vaya a hablar con el secretario de Estado. Dígale que justo en este momento se decide el futuro del mundo, que nosotros queremos la paz, pero que estamos dispuestos a ir a la guerra.

—¿Vuestra Majestad me autoriza a hablarle en inglés? Agilizaría más el dialogo si lo hago.

—¡No! Nada de concesiones ni de muestras de respeto. Eso los haría suponer que tenemos miedo. Use un traductor a su lado, y que ellos se den cuenta desde el principio. Que les quede claro que no estamos de buen humor, y que tenemos los huevos —perdón tía— donde tienen que estar.

—Como Vuestra Majestad lo ordene. Con su permiso.

Cuando Bonaparte salió del despacho, Fernando Carlos fue hacia su ventana favorita, a mirar a Aztlán de noche, quizás por última vez. ¿Quién podría saberlo? Indudablemente, los misiles yanquis estaban dirigidos a la capital del Imperio Mexicano, y la idea de que una ciudad con tanta historia, con treinta millones de seres humanos, pudiera desaparecer en un instante de la faz de la tierra lo hacía temblar desde lo más profundo de su corazón. Era algo impensable, ajeno a toda filosofía de la humanidad, pero podía ocurrir, eso estaba claro.

—Majestad —lo interrumpió Peña-Bazaine, mirando su teléfono—, los aviones yanquis ya están en el aire, y vienen hacia la frontera con México.

—¡Maldición! —dijo Iturbide.

—La fase tres, como usted lo sabe, Majestad —dijo el ministro de la guerra—, indica que los aviones se pongan en el aire, la dos que crucen la frontera, y la uno… que lancen los misiles. ¿Cuál quiere que ordene?

—¡Calma, señores! —gritó Juan—. No se alarmen, eso era de esperarse. Los yanquis están haciendo lo mismo que hicimos nosotros. No se quieren ver cobardes. Pero tal acción no indica que la guerra haya empezado. Esperemos saber qué ocurre con la llamada del canciller. Si no ha vuelto, eso quiere decir que le respondieron. Mantengan la calma y no pongan nervioso al emperador.

—Tienes razón, hermano, pero aquí el tiempo es crucial. Si en un minuto, general, no pasa nada…

—¡Majestad! —abrió la puerta de golpe el canciller Bonaparte—, ¡la paz se ha hecho! Por favor, ordene que los aviones vuelvan a sus bases y aterricen, ellos harán lo mismo justo ahora.

—¿Qué ocurrió?

—Los yanquis, Majestad, piensan que efectivamente fueron ellos quienes erróneamente cruzaron la frontera.

—¿Y en realidad qué fue lo que pasó?

—Majestad, lo ignoro. Pero si fueron ellos o nosotros, poco importa en este momento, lo crucial es bajar la temperatura.

—¿Qué actitud tenía el secretario?

—Conciliadora, Majestad. Al final casi lloramos los dos por poder llegar a un acuerdo que no cueste ni una vida más.

—Bien, demos una muestra de buena fe, a ver si no es una trampa y nos matan por pendejos. General, ordene que los aviones vuelvan.

—¡A vuestras órdenes!

—¿Y qué acordaron finalmente, príncipe?

—Quizás me adelanté, Majestad, pero he acordado que usted va a recibir aquí mismo al tipo del nido de pájaros en la cabeza, dentro de una semana, para sentar las bases de un acuerdo pacífico en toda regla. ¿Hice mal?

—No, para nada, el futuro del mundo merece que le dé la mano a ese cabrón.

—¿Y qué hacemos ahora? —dijo el almirante Mejía.

—¡Pulque para todos! —respondió el emperador—. Este pinche susto no es para menos.

—Majestad —interrumpió el general Peña-Bazaine—, los aviones yanquis también están volviendo. Están haciendo honor a su palabra.

—Con más razón traigan el pulque. Y que alguien le vaya a decir al cardenal Fischer que el próximo domingo sí iré a misa.

Dos horas duró la celebración de la paz. El emperador hasta se quitó el saco y se aflojó la corbata, cosa nunca antes vista en el despacho de los cuatro bustos. Poco a poco cada uno de los presentes se fueron marchando. La última fue la archiduquesa, quien besó a cada uno de sus sobrinos antes de cruzar la puerta. Con un vaso de pulque en una mano, Juan tomó con la otra el busto de Rodolfo I, lo que alarmó a Fernando Carlos.

—Deja ese busto en su lugar. No vayas a romperlo. Se supone que nadie lo mueve, con excepción de cuando lo restauran cada cincuenta años.

—Estaba viendo que aun cuando es un busto idealizado, en muchos rasgos se parece a ti —dijo Juan, devolviéndolo a su lugar.

—Quizás el escultor se inspiró en rostros de algunos Habsburgo, por fotografías a las que tuvo acceso, y eso justifica que se parezca a mí —dijo el emperador—. O se trata de una mera coincidencia.

—O quizás se le apareció el fantasma del emperador para que pudiera copiarlo, y luego reencarnó en ti.

—Soy el heredero de un imperio que surgió hace muchos siglos en Europa y que cuando se sintió desahuciado allá emigró a México. Tal cosa me hace sentirme, algunas veces, un poco ajeno a la especie humana. Durante varias noches he llegado a creer que soy un viejo fantasma, y eso que cuando era niño llegué a pensar que los fantasmas nunca envejecían. Quizás lo que dices es cierto, hermano. Ya nada me extraña.

—¿Y qué fue eso de duque Juan de Austria? —preguntó Juan.

—Es el título que desde mañana pienso darte, para luego enviarte cuando sea indispensable a misiones diplomáticas a defender los intereses del Imperio Mexicano. Hoy demostraste que no me decepcionarías, y que estás a la altura de esas responsabilidades. Me importa muy poco lo que piensen o digan en el gobierno austriaco, después de gobernar allí por seis siglos, los Habsburgo tenemos derecho a traernos algún recuerdo.

—Insisto en que te pareces a Rodolfo I, Fer, y tal vez también en el carácter, porque francamente yo no habría podido comportarme como tú lo hiciste hoy. Dios no se equivocó en ponerte al mando del Imperio Mexicano.

—No creas que no estuve a punto de flaquear —dijo el emperador—, la presión fue tanta que justo ahora necesito un fuerte abrazo de mi hermano.

—Vaya, a veces me das miedo con la mirada, y luego recuerdo que sólo eres mi hermanito menor, al que tanto le gustan los abrazos de sus seres queridos. Te daré el abrazo que quieres con una condición.

—Vaya, te hago duque e inmediatamente se te sube el poder a la cabeza. ¡Ahora quieres sobornar al emperador!

—Sí, y mi condición es que ya le marques a Carlota. Se quedó preocupada, y aunque apenas lleva unas semanas de embarazo, no sea que la preocupación le cause algún daño a mi sobrino.

—¿Sabes por qué te quiero más de lo que te quería hace unas horas, Juan?

—Porque di buenos consejos, supongo, cuando tus ministros se limitaban a citar las memorias de sus antepasados.

—No, porque me queda claro que vas a ser un buen tío para mi hijo.

—El helicóptero con Trump llegará en diez minutos, Majestad —dijo el canciller Bonaparte.

Fernando Carlos despegó su espalda de la histórica silla y al moverse la iluminación del despacho de los cuatro bustos hizo contrastar más su piel blanca con su traje impecablemente negro.

—Ya estoy listo —dijo.

—A fin de cuentas, fueron nuestros soldados lo que se confundieron acerca de dónde estaba la frontera. Pero los yanquis, contrario a lo que pensábamos, han sugerido que se trató de una confusión en ambos lados. Eso indica que realmente quieren unas relaciones armoniosas con México, como debe de ser entre dos pueblos que defienden la libertad individual y los derechos humanos. Supongo que al pasar por alto que fuimos nosotros los que nos equivocamos en la frontera, se han ganado el derecho de que ya no le exijamos una disculpa pública a Trump. El incidente de la frontera ni siquiera será tocado el día de hoy, seguirá siendo asunto exclusivo del secretario de Estado y mío, y fue él quien lo quiso así, pero ambos creemos que es lo mejor. Si lo comentan, en algún momento de la reunión usted y Trump podrían terminar tomados del cuello. Es obvio que los yanquis ya comprendieron que entre Rusia, China y el Imperio Mexicano, nosotros somos la potencia con la que más les conviene aliarse. Después del susto que nos llevamos, lo más recomendable es aceptar la mano si es que nos la tienden. Los Estados Unidos, mal que nos pese, son el país que mejor defiende las libertades, y el único en el mundo donde funciona el equilibrio de poderes. Y a un pueblo así hay que admirarlo, Majestad.

—El problema no es ese gran país de libertades, que ni duda cabe que lo es, el problema es que a Trump le queda grande el poder que el pueblo le dio. Pero bueno, trataré de educar a ese pendejo en la siguiente hora.

Tendrá el honor de que un vástago de la casa de Habsburgo le dé lecciones.

—Pero le recomiendo, Majestad —dijo Bonaparte—, que no se le vaya a pasar la mano. De cualquier forma, lo pendejo no sequita, y menos a esa edad.

—Príncipe, a estas alturas sólo se me pasa la mano cuando yo quiero. No se preocupe.

—Por cierto, estaba olvidando decirle que hace media hora me informaron de que Morador tuvo que ser trasladado a un hospital psiquiátrico.

—¿Por qué?

—Porque se hizo una corona de papel y jura y perjura que es el emperador Ángel Miguel I de México. Ya había repartido títulos nobiliarios a sus carceleros y a sus compañeros en la prisión.

—Me alegro por él —dijo Fernando Carlos.

—¿De verdad?

—Claro, ahora es lo que tanto soñaba ser, y nadie paga las consecuencias de ello. Eso es perfecto, príncipe. Si él anterior presidente de Venezuela hubiera podido hacerse su corona de papel y disfrutar de esa gloria en un manicomio, jure usted que ese desdichado país estaría mucho mejor de lo que está. Millones de seres humanos no estarían viendo cómo sus vidas se arruinan. Pero no fue así, lamentablemente. En comparación con él, Ángel Miguel es un héroe.

—Creo, Majestad, que tiene usted toda la razón. Ese ruido es…, Trump está llegando, vamos.

—Vaya usted.

—¿Cómo dice?

—No voy a fotografiarme con él. Ya le había dicho que no pienso dar la mano en público ni a dictadores ni a gobernantes pendejos. Recíbalo usted, deje que los periodistas los fotografíen y después enséñele cómo llegar hasta aquí. Esperemos que no se pierda.

—¡Majestad, si usted no lo recibe, se va a ofender!

—Me vale madre. Haga lo que le he dicho, por favor, príncipe.

—A las órdenes de Vuestra Majestad.

El emperador, fiel a su costumbre de cuando esperaba algo importante en el despacho, costumbre que también tenían su padre y su abuelo, fue a mirar por la ventana. El panorama le gustaba más de noche, cuando Aztlán se veía iluminado, pero ese día reconoció que los jardines de Chapultepec eran hermosos, se trataba, a fin de cuentas, de otras de las herencias de Maximiliano *el Grande*, y quizás era la más deslumbrante de todas.

De pronto se escuchó un ruido en la puerta, y tras ello las dos hojas se abrieron, a los costados se hallaban dos miembros de la marina imperial con sus uniformes impecables, y en medio Donald Trump.

Mientras los traductores ocupaban sus sitios, el emperador fue a darle la mano. Cada uno saludó cordialmente en su idioma, el emperador de México entendió todo, mientras que Trump no entendió una sola palabra de lo que el emperador le dijo. De cualquier forma se limitó a sonreír con amabilidad. Fernando Carlos pensó que igual hubiera podido llamarlo "pendejo" y habría sonreído.

Cuando cada uno tuvo a un traductor a su lado, Trump, como los anteriores presidente de los Estados Unidos al reunirse con un emperador de México, vio una discreta sonrisa en los labios de Fernando Carlos, al quedar claro que sólo esperaba a que el traductor pasara las palabras al español por protocolo, más era evidente que entendía todo en cuanto él lo pronunciaba. Obama, tres años atrás, había intentado hablar en español con Maximiliano IV, pero se quedó en el camino y ya no supo qué decir. El emperador se sintió tan halagado que estuvo a punto de pedirle que hablaran en inglés y sacaran a los traductores, pero se arrepintió en el último momento.

—Tengo entendido —comenzó Trump—, que usted habla bastante bien el inglés. Así que no veo por qué la necesidad de los traductores.

—Tengo entendido —dijo Fernando Carlos, tras esperar al traductor—, que cuarenta millones de estadounidenses hablan el español, razón por la cual sería necesario que el presidente lo hablara. Aquí viven cuatro millones de angloparlantes, y por respeto a ellos hablo inglés, también hablo hebreo porque tenemos tres millones de judíos, y árabe porque tenemos otra cantidad similar de musulmanes procedentes de la península arábiga. Francamente, desde mi concepción de lo que es un buen gobernante, no entiendo por qué usted no ha aprendido español en el mes que lleva en la presidencia. Estudiarlo tres horas todas las noches le habría ayudado a que pudiéramos hablarlo en este momento. Se lo aseguro, tengo experiencia en ello. Además, podría leer *El Quijote* en la lengua que corresponde. Hacerlo en otro idioma, considero que es un desperdicio de tiempo.

Trump abrió los ojos, y vaya que le costó trabajo, al ver que el niño del que le habían hablado no era tan niño, después de todo.

—Considero, emperador —dijo—, que ser un buen presidente no radica en hablar el español, sino en lograr que un país que produce tanta riqueza la destine a sus ciudadanos, y no la vaya a tirar a otros, donde ni siquiera darán las gracias por ello.

—Es cierto —dijo el emperador—, le doy la razón en ello. Aunque yo considero imperdonable que un gobernante no hable el idioma de una abundante minoría en su país, reconozco que su principal deber es cuidar que la riqueza que su pueblo produce lo beneficie más que a otros.

—¿De verdad? —dijo Trump, extrañado.

—Claro, yo primero me metería un tiro antes que regalar las riquezas que son de los mexicanos. Pero también me metería un tiro si no respeto a los emigrantes que viven en México las riquezas que ellos con su esfuerzo han producido. México, al igual que los Estados Unidos, está lleno de infelices que escapan de otras naciones, donde les resulta imposible que su esfuerzo tenga éxito, que el Estado lo reconozca y que sean respetados sus bienes. Venir yo a acosarlos porque han tenido el valor de renunciar a su patria y regalar su inteligencia y su esfuerzo a otra me haría peor que un criminal de guerra.

—Emperador —dijo Trump, cuando el traductor hizo su mejor esfuerzo para que entendiera lo que Fernando Carlos había dicho—, yo creo que América no puede seguir haciéndose cargo de la negligencia de otros gobiernos. No nos corresponde, no es nuestra responsabilidad. Si nosotros seguimos siendo un refugio seguro para los emigrantes, muchos gobiernos del mundo continuarán sin ocuparse de sus responsabilidades.

—Requerir de emigrantes ilegales como mano de obra —dijo el emperador en español, antes siquiera de que el traductor de Trump empezara a hablar— por un largo período de tiempo, durante el cual ellos han forjado una estabilidad economía para sus familias, y después, apoyándose en el hecho de que no poseen derechos, echarlos sin consideraciones, es una actitud de cobardes, y reduce considerablemente el prestigio que un país tan grande ha ganado durante dos siglos. Si en realidad ya no se requiere de los emigrantes ilegales en su país, lo justo sería que se les notificara que tienen para irse el mismo tiempo que ellos han desafiado al calor y al cansancio dentro de los Estados Unidos, trabajando diariamente, mientras las autoridades han cerrado los ojos para que el país lucre con el esfuerzo de aquellos, que vengan de donde vengan, no conocen la pereza.

—¿Y me puede decir, emperador, cómo vamos a corroborar la antigüedad de cada emigrante dentro de los Estados Unidos?

—Quizás en muchos casos sea difícil. Pero en otros sin duda es bastante fácil de corroborar esa antigüedad. Mas si usted, señor presidente, argumenta que en todos los casos es imposible, le creeré más al lobo que asegura que no sabe cuáles son los corderos malos y cuáles son los corderos buenos, y que por ello se los come a todos. La historia nos demuestra que la justicia siempre tiene obstáculos, pero que la injusticia suele disfrutar de caminos muy amplios.

—Habla usted, emperador, con una seguridad tan grande que me da la impresión de que pretende presumir que lo sabe todo.

—Me llamo Fernando Carlos I de México, señor presidente, y soy un miembro de la familia Habsburgo. No lo sé todo, es cierto, mi cerebro no alberga todos los conocimientos que ha acumulado la humanidad en su larga historia, pero en cuestiones de política, el oficio de mi familia, sí lo sé todo. Y si tiene alguna duda, pregúnteme, con confianza, lo que quiera saber. Siendo nuestros pueblos vecinos, estoy dispuesto a instruirlo.

—¿Y usted cree que yo necesito que me enseñe algo sobre política?

—La respuesta, señor presidente, usted la sabe —dijo el emperador—, y decirla yo sería ofender al pueblo de los Estados Unidos, lo que no considero prudente justo ahora, cuando nos reunimos para tratar de hallar un camino armonioso y mutuo durante los próximos cuatro años. Pero le daré un buen consejo, y espero que su traductor se lo exprese de la mejor manera: un buen gobernante no trabaja sólo en hacer las cosas como a él le gustaría que fueran, sino viendo realmente qué es lo que necesitan todos los grupos sociales, económicos y religiosos a su cargo, y tratando de averiguar la forma de hacer de su pueblo un hogar para todos, quizás mejor para unos que para otros, pero en general donde todos tengan derechos, oportunidades y obligaciones casi por igual. Cuando un gobernante trabaja sólo para los que le caen bien, para los que se le asemejan cultural o racialmente, para quienes lo idolatran y lo ven como un semidiós, comete errores terribles y ni siquiera por ellos logra hacer algo bueno. Créame lo que le digo, porque creer lo contrario sería suponer que cualquier imbécil puede ser un buen gobernante.

El traductor, como el emperador había supuesto, batalló un poco para explicarle su argumentación al presidente. En algunas frases probó hasta tres opciones, hasta que Trump movía la cabeza afirmativamente. Fernando Carlos, sino hubiera sentido al fantasma de la emperatriz Carlota pellizcándolo, se habría ofrecido a hacer él la traducción de sus propias palabras.

—Correcto —dijo Trump—, pero..., emperador, dígame usted, con sus enormes conocimientos, cuál sería su respuesta ante grupos raciales a quienes su país ha dado en abundancia, les ha dado trabajo, seguridad, incluso lo ha hecho ciudadanos, y ellos en cambio no agradecen, no se atreven siquiera a mirar la grandeza de ese país que los ha adoptado, sino que siguen empecinados en rendirle homenaje a su anterior país, y en negar las obligaciones que América les exige, a cambio de haberlos ayudado tanto. Dígame, ¿cómo procedería usted?

—Señor presidente —respondió el emperador—, el México actual fue fundado con la unión de dos culturas. De entre ellas, algunos grupos se apegaron lo más que les fue posible a la suya, sin abrazar por complete la nueva cultura mestiza. Y habiendo ocurrido tal cosa hace medio milenio, a los mexicanos de hoy nos resulta muy difícil separar grupos étnicos. Es cierto que tenemos a católicos, protestantes, judíos y musulmanes en cuanto a las religiones mayoritarias, a caucásicos, mestizos, indios y orientales en cuanto a razas, pero todos ellos son mexicanos, no los diferenciamos por grupos al momento de atribuirles delitos o logros. Usted como presidente habla de un grupo racial malagradecido con América, y yo como emperador veo a muchas personas de manera individual, a algunas con mayor amor a su pueblo que otras, con mayor disposición al esfuerzo, con mayor respeto a las instituciones, pero tales virtudes y defectos sólo puedo atribuirlos a personas de manera individual, ensañarme con un grupo étnico sólo porque no comparten el color de mi piel sería un crimen imperdonable. Usted bien sabe que en su país hay blancos asesinos, drogadictos, violadores y perezosos, que buscan que otros los mantengan, como también hay negros y latinos, pero ellos no definen a la mayoría, sus actos deberían de afectarlos únicamente de forma individual. Es cierto que algunas veces hay grupos sociales que se aferran a los errores de una sola persona para definir a todos aquellos que comparten con ésta afinidades culturales. Pero si el propio gobernante sigue el mismo camino, estaría   demostrando que no merece estar donde está, porque sus conocimientos y el control que tiene sobre sus pasiones no están a la altura de su responsabilidad.

—Insinúa usted —dijo Trump, ceñudo—, que América debe de seguir recibiendo a todos los emigrantes del mundo, tan sólo porque eso, a su juicio, hace del presidente de los Estados Unidos un buen presidente, y que yo estoy obligado a seguir esa línea.

—Señor Trump, usted puede proponerse impedir que entre un sólo emigrante ilegal más a los Estados Unidos. Aunque no sé si lo logre. Con ellos, con los que apenas quieren llegar, usted no tiene ninguna responsabilidad, pero con las que ya están allí, con los que han regado con su sudor los campos de trabajo de su patria, sí que la tiene, por más ilegales que sean. Echarlos sin consideraciones sólo porque puede, sería el acto de un cobarde, y demostraría que el presidente de los Estados Unidos no tiene honor.

—Señor emperador, habla usted de esa forma porque estará en su puesto quizás cincuenta años, pero yo sólo tengo asegurados cuatro en el mío, mis acciones tienen que ser drásticas para poder dar a mi pueblo la seguridad que ha perdido. Si me enfrascara en una política de largas negociaciones y de reformas tibias, mi legado sería inexistente. La emigración ilegal a América ha sido, durante muchos años, perjudicial para el pueblo, para los verdaderos americanos. Y eso no seguirá ocurriendo de ninguna manera, se lo aseguro, y no importa lo que usted opine al respecto. Los emigrantes que ahora viven en América violando la ley, deben de tener un presidente en alguna parte del mundo, y es justo, tanto para ellos como para nosotros, que regresen a buscarlo y le exijan que haga su trabajo.

—Si eso fuera tan sencillo como usted lo piensa, créame, señor presidente, muchos lo harían. Pero si usted, el líder de la mayor democracia que hay en el mundo, se irrita cuando algunos sectores de entre sus propios compatriotas no comparten su opinión, ¿cómo cree que van a reaccionar los dictadores, cuando vuelan miles de emigrantes a exigir una vida arropada por seguridad y libertades? Señor presidente, el patriotismo no puede ser una obligación, sino una reacción justa. Yo considero que aquellos infelices a los que su propia patria no les da más que injusticias y hambre, no están obligados a amarla ni a permanecer en ella, sino que como seres humanos tienen el derecho de ir a buscar un lugar donde, gracias a su esfuerzo, puedan vivir felices y en paz. Entiendo lo que usted pretende, no soy idiota. Hay en su país una población blanca con una cultura definida, que desciende de los fundadores y que ha forjado al pueblo de los Estados Unidos tal cual es, con toda su grandeza institucional, su amor a la democracia y sus envidiables libertades, pero también con todas sus injusticias y crímenes a lo largo de la historia, como consecuencia de su hambre de poder, y usted la defiende porque se siente parte de ella. No quiere que los emigrantes, que en su mayoría no son blancos, contaminen esa cultura con su presencia.

—Y si así fuera, señor emperador, ¿qué pensaría hacer usted al respecto?

—Nada, no puedo hacer nada ni pretendo hacer nada —dijo Fernando Carlos—. Soy emperador, no Dios. No seré yo quien les cambie la mentalidad a los pueblos, y menos a usted, porque muchas de las cosas que ha dicho, y algunas de las causas con las que se ha comprometido, son justas. Si bien considero que se equivoca pensando que en unos meses puede cambiar todo cuanto quiere, no tengo la más remota intención de persuadirlo de que no lleve a cabo sus proyectos.

—¿Entonces?, ¿por qué ha criticado tan fervorosamente mi postura?

—No era ésa mi intención, tan sólo quise que le quedara bastante clara la mía. Contrario a lo que usted quiere hacer, señor presidente, yo no pienso utilizar mis enormes poderes para ir a acosar a aquellos infelices que vienen entre la selva, muertos de hambre y de cansancio, preocupados por su esposa y sus hijos, que a veces los acompañaban y sufren sus penalidades y otras se han quedado en su país padeciendo los límites inimaginables del miedo porque no saben qué les aguarda el impredecible futuro. Mi guerra no será contra ellos, sino contra los dictadores y contra los presidentes corruptos y mediocres que los han obligado abandonar la patria donde nacieron para no morirse de hambre o de pena ante las injusticias. Contra esos miserables que se enamoran del poder a la vez que se olvidan de sus responsabilidades ante sus pueblos, pienso ser implacable. Jamás me verán saludándolos en ninguna cumbre, ni mucho menos recibiéndolos aquí en Aztlán. Yo pienso que cada que un jefe de Estado de un pueblo respetable da la mano a un líder corrupto o que se ha apropiado del poder por medio de la fuerza, les envía un mensaje muy claro a los infelices que viven bajo su régimen: ellos no valen nada. Pero como México les da el justo valor a todos los seres humanos, empezaremos a romper relaciones diplomáticas y comerciales con todos aquellos gobiernos que no respeten los derechos humanos, sin importar que se trate de grandes potencias.

—Señor emperador, la política exige guardar las apariencias...

—Pero cuando esas apariencias toleran a dictaduras hasta por medio siglo, dejan mucho que desear. Señor presidente, usted y yo somos personas con formas de pensar muy distintas en algunos aspectos y muy similares en otros. Y creo que ninguno de los dos, ni yo por joven ni usted por… su edad, cambiará la suya. Eso tenemos que aceptarlo y tratar de convivir al margen de nuestras diferencias. Si usted realmente considera iniciar una guerra sin precedentes contra el terrorismo, cuente con mi ayuda, y si Corea del Norte o Irán, o cualquier otro régimen enemigo de la libertad ataca a los Estados Unidos, un pueblo que tanto bien ha hecho a la humanidad, cuente usted con que nosotros habremos de declararles la guerra a ellos en el acto, porque la libertad y la justicia se defienden en cualquier lugar del mundo.

—¡Emperador!... ¿me está diciendo la verdad?

—¿Cree usted que un hombre como yo alardea? ¡Soy el emperador de México!

—No lo creo, pero…, dadas nuestras diferencias… sus palabras me extrañan. Aunque si es verdad lo que usted me dice, considéreme su mejor amigo.

—Señor Trump, yo, como la gran mayoría de los mexicanos, comería cianuro antes de ser su amigo, pero si la necesidad del mundo nos obliga, seré su aliado. Tiene mi palabra.

—Entonces…, no le entiendo.

—Está muy claro, en su larga historia, los habitantes de los Estados Unidos, no sólo los presidentes sino también los gobernadores, alcaldes, jueces, empresarios y civiles que han luchado por la libertad y por lo que es justo, han creado un gran país y ni yo mismo, siendo quien soy, me atrevería a negar esa gran verdad, ni siquiera por que se aprovecharon de nosotros en nuestros primeros años como país independiente y nos causaron daños irreparables. La grandeza de los Estados Unidos es imposible negarla, y más aún es imposible no agradecerla. Porque así todos los hombres libres de otros países con menor suerte pueden señalarla como ejemplo o huir a ella como su último recurso. Mi determinación, señor Trump, no es en honor a usted, si no en honor a las grandes mujeres y a los grandes hombres que en el pasado y en la actualidad han sido mejores que usted. Es probable que usted se marche pronto, pero la grandeza que ellos han logrado habrá de perdurar para siempre.

—Emperador, ¿cómo es que me critica tanto, si ni quiera me ha dejado hablar?

—No acepté recibirlo para que hablara, sino para que escuchara lo que quería decirle. Señor Trump, es probable que no nos volvamos a ver. Yo tengo ministros muy capaces, igual que usted secretarios, para que negocien nuestras relaciones diplomáticas y comerciales. Si usted y yo aparecemos en una fotografía dándonos la mano, algunos de mis compatriotas pesarán que nuestro comercio mutuo está seguro, pero la gran mayoría habrán de creer que tolero o que incluso comulgo que las ofensas que su forma de pensar representa para un pueblo mestizo como el mío. Y eso no lo puedo permitir. Quisiera tener la certeza de que al volver a su país hiciera público que no sólo hemos acordado la paz, sino que nos hemos comprometido a luchar juntos por la libertad, yo haré lo mismo, y le aseguro que no serán sólo palabras, le reitero mi compromiso de acompañar a los Estados Unidos en todas sus acciones que en verdad sean justas y necesarias para la paz del mundo. Pero no pienso ofender a mi pueblo permitiendo que se haga pública una fotografía donde le doy la mano. Usted jamás será fotografiado en compañía del emperador de México. Incluso si usted fuera a vivir hasta los cien o más años, después de mi muerte, le juro que ni hijo nunca le daría la mano. Con su actitud hacia mi cultura ha perdido tal privilegio.

—¿Qué es lo que me quiere decir? —dijo Trump, más ceñudo que nunca.

—Tal vez no le tradujeron mi discurso del día de mi coronación, así que voy a repetir una de mis últimas frases: cualquier ofensa a mi pueblo la cobraré diez veces, venga de donde venga.

—¿Ésa es una amenaza?

—Me alegra que lo comprenda. Señor presidente, no le quito más su tiempo…

—Pero…

—El canciller Bonaparte lo espera en el salón contiguo para despedirlo con toda la amabilidad que el protocolo exige. Si no le molesta, tengo que recibir a un juez de la supresa corte imperial en dos minutos, y media hora despúes al embajador de Israel. Jamás hago esperar a nadie.

–Comprendo –dijo Trump–, levantándose mientras echaba fuego por sus ojillos.

–Celebro que así sea. Por cierto, lleve al pueblo de los Estados Unidos un mensaje del emperador de México: los admiro, los respeto y les tengo un gran afecto, los gobierne quien los gobierne.

–Gracias...

Cuando el emperador se quedó solo en el despacho de los cuatro bustos, sacó de un cajón la maqueta que su amigo, el escultor Venosta, había hecho para que aprobara la estatua de su padre, Maximiliano IV. Cuando Venosta se lo presentó lo había visto con un rostro severo e implacable, fiel a su famosa personalidad. Pero extrañamente ahora lo veía con una ligera sonrisa en sus facciones, tan discreta o más que la de *Mona Losa*, pero era innegable que el rígido emperador sonreía, sonreía como un padre orgulloso de su hijo.

–Te amo, papá –dijo el emperador.

Ocho meses después, Castillo de Chapultepec

—Eso de que el médico de palacio —dijo el Canciller Bonaparte, caminando de un lado a otro—, no informe el sexo del bebé nunca, siendo que él lo sabe desde el principio, debería de ser abolido por Su Majestad.

—¿Para qué? —dijo el emperador—, sea niña o niño, ya soy el padre más feliz de mundo.

—Aunque al principio me habría encantado un sobrino varón, ahora en calidad de preceptor asignado por Su Majestad—dijo Juan Robledo—, ya tampoco me interesa mucho si es niña o niño.

—Por cierto, Majestad —dijo el canciller—, si es niño serán ciento un cañonazos, pero... ¿y si es niña?

—Los mismos, ¿por qué?

—No es ésa la tradición...

—¿No va a celebrar el ejército imperial mexicano, uno de los más poderosos del mundo, el nacimiento de su emperatriz? Príncipe, por favor, lo que nos sobran son cañones.

—Es que... nunca antes hemos tenido una emperatriz gobernante.

—Eso no es cierto, ya tuvimos una y usted lo sabe muy bien. No seríamos lo que somos sin ella.

—Bueno, Majestad, la archiduquesa, su tía, que sabe de embarazos por los propios y porque estuvo siempre junto a vuestra madre, me ha dicho que todo indica que será niño.

—Pues que ¡dios salve al emperador, Marco I de México! Príncipe, eso no es lo que me preocupa, sino que se están tardando mucho...

—Majestad —dijo Bonaparte—, el embarazo fue bastante normal, gracias a la fortaleza de la emperatriz Carlota. Así que no se preocupe y tenga paciencia. Los bebés no nacen en un segundo.

—Creo que debo de entrar a esa habitación.

—Y yo a la vanguardia de Vuestra Majestad, pero, señor, nosotros sabemos gobernar, el experto en partos es el médico de palacio. Junto a él no seríamos más que dos aprendices sin la menor experiencia.

—El príncipe tiene razón, Fer —dijo el hermano del emperador—, hay que esperar un poco más. Roma no se hizo en un día, y los emperadores de México no nacen corriendo. Ten calma.

—Gracias, duque —dijo Bonaparte—, en muchas cosas sólo a usted le hace caso. ¡La puerta, Majestad, la están abriendo!

—No ha llorado ningún niño...

—Majestad, estas habitaciones tan grandes de Chapultepec y los muros tan gruesos impiden que salga el ruido. Yo estuve parado justo aquí cuando usted nació, y no lo escuchamos llorar.

Cuando la puerta terminó de abrirse, apareció la archiduquesa Carlota. En cuanto vio al emperador, descolorido como nunca antes, se apresuró para ir a decirle:

—Majestad, todo ha estado bien, el parto no tuvo complicaciones.

—¿¡Y...!?

—¡Fue una niña!

El emperador fue a tomar un vaso de pulque que tenía a dos metros de distancia en una pequeña mesa.

—Salud —dijo—, Dios conceda un gobierno lleno de satisfacciones a Su Majestad Imperial, la emperatriz Carlota II de México.

Apenas dio un pequeño trago a su vaso y salió corriendo a la habitación donde se hallaba su hija. En el camino su hermano lo detuvo para abrazarlo y después también abrazó al canciller y a su tía. Cuando cruzó las puertas, se encontró al médico de palacio y se dio el tiempo de darle las gracias con una palmada en el hombro. El aludido hizo una señal a las enfermeras de que salieran junto con él, para dejar a la familia imperial a solas. Cuando Fernando Carlos llegó por fin junto a la cama, Carlota le sonrió de la mejor forma que pudo, mientras abrazaba a la bebé que estaba a su lado.

—Es morena —dijo la emperatriz—, se parece a mí en eso. Y sí hereda tus ojos verdes y tu exquisita elegancia, cuando tenga dieciocho años tendremos que poner a un centenar de miembros de la guardia imperial para contener a los príncipes que se van a formar a las afueras de Chapultepec.

—No llegarán siquiera a cruzar la frontera. Como marido, te consta que soy celoso, y como padre no pienso cambiar.

—Ya lo sé, eres el emperador de los necios.

—Los mexicanos no somos necios, sólo insistimos mucho cuando de verdad queremos algo.

—Dime, Fer, ¿qué te hace más feliz?, ¿qué te haya dado una hija, o que te haya dado una heredera?

—Me hace feliz que me amas, y que me hayas dado una familia, lo que toda mi vida he tenido sólo a medias. En este momento soy el hombre más feliz del mundo, todo gracias a ustedes dos.

—¿Y eso justifica tanto cañonazo?, ¿a qué hora van a terminar?

—Mmmm, ten paciencia. Son más de cien.

—Ese escándalo sólo te lo perdono porque eres el emperador.

—Supongo que mi bebé entiende lo que le dices con tus murmullos. Has hablado tanto con ella todas las noches, despertándome dos veces por hora, que seguramente puede comprender todos tus sonidos. Es una Habsburgo y nosotros aprendemos con mucha facilidad cualquier idioma. Quiero que le des justo ahora un mensaje de mi parte: la amo, y también te amo a ti. Las amo a las dos.

—No necesito decírselo, Fer, ya lo sabe —dijo Carlota, sin apartar la mirada de la bebé.

Made in United States
Orlando, FL
23 May 2024

47147036R00238